Acrobat® PDF Bible

Acrobat® PDF Bible

Ted Padova

IDG Books Worldwide, Inc.
An International Data Group Company

Foster City, CA ◆ Chicago, IL ◆ Indianapolis, IN ◆ New York, NY

Acrobat® PDF Bible

Published by
IDG Books Worldwide, Inc.
An International Data Group Company
919 E. Hillsdale Blvd., Suite 400
Foster City, CA 94404
www.idgbooks.com (IDG Books Worldwide Web site)

ISBN: 0-7645-3242-1

Printed in the United States of America

10 9 8 7 6 5 4

1B/SZ/QU/ZZ/FC

Distributed in the United States
by IDG Books Worldwide, Inc.

Distributed by CDG Books Canada Inc. for Canada; by Transworld Publishers Limited in the United Kingdom; by IDG Norge Books for Norway; by IDG Sweden Books for Sweden; by IDG Books Australia Publishing Corporation Pty. Ltd. for Australia; and New Zealand; by TransQuest Publishers Pte Ltd. for Singapore, Malaysia, Thailand, Indonesia, and Hong Kong; by Gotop Information Inc. for Taiwan; by ICG Muse, Inc. for Japan; by Norma Comunicaciones S.A. for Colombia; by Intersoft for South Africa; by Le Monde en Tique for France; by International Thomson Publishing for Germany, Austria and Switzerland; by Distribuidora Cuspide for Argentina; by Livraria Cultura for Brazil; by Ediciones ZETA S.C.R. Ltda. for Peru; by WS Computer Publishing Corporation, Inc., for the Philippines; by Contemporanea de Ediciones for Venezuela; by Express Computer Distributors for the Caribbean and West Indies; by Micronesia Media Distributor, Inc. for Micronesia; by Grupo Editorial Norma S.A. for Guatemala; by Chips Computadoras S.A. de C.V. for Mexico; by Editorial Norma de Panama S.A. for Panama; by American Bookshops for Finland. Authorized Sales Agent: Anthony Rudkin Associates for the Middle East and North Africa.

For general information on IDG Books Worldwide's books in the U.S., please call our Consumer Customer Service department at 800-762-2974. For reseller information, including discounts and premium sales, please call our Reseller Customer Service department at 800-434-3422.

For information on where to purchase IDG Books Worldwide's books outside the U.S., please contact our International Sales department at 317-596-5530 or fax 317-596-5692.

For consumer information on foreign language translations, please contact our Customer Service department at 800-434-3422, fax 317-596-5692, or e-mail rights@idgbooks.com.

For information on licensing foreign or domestic rights, please phone +1-650-655-3109.

For sales inquiries and special prices for bulk quantities, please contact our Sales department at 650-655-3200 or write to the address above.

For information on using IDG Books Worldwide's books in the classroom or for ordering examination copies, please contact our Educational Sales department at 800-434-2086 or fax 317-596-5499.

For press review copies, author interviews, or other publicity information, please contact our Public Relations department at 650-655-3000 or fax 650-655-3299.

For authorization to photocopy items for corporate, personal, or educational use, please contact Copyright Clearance Center, 222 Rosewood Drive, Danvers, MA 01923, or fax 978-750-4470.

Library of Congress Cataloging-in-Publication Data
Padova, Ted.
  Acrobat PDF Bible / Ted Padova.
    p. cm.
  ISBN 0-7645-3242-1 (alk. paper)
  1. Adobe Acrobat. 2. Portable document software.
I. Title.
  Z286.E43P32 1999
  005.7'–dc21   99-14030
                                                   CIP

is a registered trademark or trademark under exclusive license to IDG Books Worldwide, Inc. from International Data Group, Inc. in the United States and/or other countries.

ABOUT IDG BOOKS WORLDWIDE

Welcome to the world of IDG Books Worldwide.

IDG Books Worldwide, Inc., is a subsidiary of International Data Group, the world's largest publisher of computer-related information and the leading global provider of information services on information technology. IDG was founded more than 30 years ago by Patrick J. McGovern and now employs more than 9,000 people worldwide. IDG publishes more than 290 computer publications in over 75 countries. More than 90 million people read one or more IDG publications each month.

Launched in 1990, IDG Books Worldwide is today the #1 publisher of best-selling computer books in the United States. We are proud to have received eight awards from the Computer Press Association in recognition of editorial excellence and three from Computer Currents' First Annual Readers' Choice Awards. Our best-selling ...For Dummies® series has more than 50 million copies in print with translations in 31 languages. IDG Books Worldwide, through a joint venture with IDG's Hi-Tech Beijing, became the first U.S. publisher to publish a computer book in the People's Republic of China. In record time, IDG Books Worldwide has become the first choice for millions of readers around the world who want to learn how to better manage their businesses.

Our mission is simple: Every one of our books is designed to bring extra value and skill-building instructions to the reader. Our books are written by experts who understand and care about our readers. The knowledge base of our editorial staff comes from years of experience in publishing, education, and journalism — experience we use to produce books to carry us into the new millennium. In short, we care about books, so we attract the best people. We devote special attention to details such as audience, interior design, use of icons, and illustrations. And because we use an efficient process of authoring, editing, and desktop publishing our books electronically, we can spend more time ensuring superior content and less time on the technicalities of making books.

You can count on our commitment to deliver high-quality books at competitive prices on topics you want to read about. At IDG Books Worldwide, we continue in the IDG tradition of delivering quality for more than 30 years. You'll find no better book on a subject than one from IDG Books Worldwide.

John Kilcullen
Chairman and CEO
IDG Books Worldwide, Inc.

Steven Berkowitz
President and Publisher
IDG Books Worldwide, Inc.

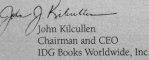

Eighth Annual Computer Press Awards ≥1992

Ninth Annual Computer Press Awards ≥1993

Tenth Annual Computer Press Awards ≥1994

Eleventh Annual Computer Press Awards ≥1995

Credits

Acquisitions Editor
Michael Roney

Development Editor
Katharine Dvorak

Technical Editor
Dennis Cohen

Copy Editor
Ami Knox

Production
Foster City Production Department

Proofreading and Indexing
York Production Services

Cover Design
Murder By Design

About the Author

Ted Padova is the chief executive officer of The Image Source, a digital imaging and photofinishing center in Ventura, California. As a speaker, Ted has delivered presentations on digital prepress, halftones, and Photoshop methods on behalf of Thunder Lizard Productions at both the Adobe Photoshop and Adobe Illustrator conferences. Ted writes a feature column for the *Los Angeles Macintosh User Group Magazine* and has published over 40 journal articles on digital prepress and application software methods.

Foreword

Adobe software is used worldwide by individuals, small businesses, and large organizations that want to turn ideas into reality. Adobe Acrobat was created to provide a means of communicating rich information of any type to others regardless of their platform or application or media.

Portable Document Format (PDF) is the de facto standard for electronic document distribution worldwide. PDF is a universal file format that preserves all the fonts, formatting, colors, and graphics of any source document, regardless of the application and platform used to create it. PDF files are compact and can be shared, viewed, navigated, and printed exactly as intended by anyone with the free Acrobat Reader. Acrobat 4.0 puts information created in any application into PDF. The information stored in a PDF is ready to be viewed on the computer platforms used by most corporations or on the Internet, or processed by large-scale print systems. PDF is the ideal format for electronic document distribution because it transcends the problems commonly encountered in electronic file sharing. Adobe solutions are the foundation for an efficient digital workflow.

PDF files can be published and distributed anywhere: attached to e-mail, located on corporate servers, posted on Web sites, or made available on CD-ROM. The free Acrobat Reader is easy to download from www.adobe.com and can be freely distributed by anyone. More than 55 million people already have it.

The Acrobat PDF Bible is a comprehensive digest of information about Acrobat 4.0 and PDF, demonstrating Ted Padova's experience in using Acrobat on the front lines — in time-sensitive real-world situations and under the scrutiny of demanding clients. This book provides complete coverage of the rich Acrobat feature set. It also provides detailed descriptions of using Acrobat in real business situations. Additionally, the chapters are full of tips and tricks that allow you to get the most out of Acrobat 4.0. Everyone, from those new to Acrobat to publishing community veterans, will find the Acrobat PDF Bible to be a complete resource for Acrobat and PDF use.

— Sheri Schurter
Group Product Manager
Adobe Systems Incorporated

Preface

When I first proposed to people at the University of California, Santa Barbara, that the university offer classes on Adobe Acrobat, those in the UCSB computer lab immediately dismissed the idea. They said that Adobe Acrobat was a simplistic program not worthy of even a short, one-day course! Despite this response, I persevered until the administration granted my wish and put a class on Adobe Acrobat on the course list.

When the class began to fill a few months prior to the scheduled date, a sudden change in attitude prevailed. Today, UCSB is planning no less than four separate classes on Adobe Acrobat to complement its programs in visual communication, Web design, and multimedia certificate programs.

Later I proposed the same idea to the University of California, Los Angeles. After all, I was certain they would share my enthusiasm. Once again, the folks in the computer lab told the administration that Acrobat was such a simple program that it could not sustain more than a few hours of instruction. Again, I persevered, and Acrobat is now a regular offering within the UCLA certificate program.

After the success of my classes at UCSB and UCLA, I thought, "Why not expose more people to Acrobat? A new book on the subject might be worthwhile." Compared to the number of available books on Web design, Microsoft Office applications, and graphic design programs, very few publications about Acrobat grace the bookshelves. When I proposed the idea to my publisher, the response I received was first inquisitive. "Isn't Acrobat a rather simple program? How can we publish a whole book on it?" If you thumb through the remaining pages, you can see why I once again persevered.

Although this book was demanding, it has been a project of great personal reward. It's not so much the amazing capabilities of Acrobat that excite me as it is the widespread use of the program throughout the world. During my research, I contacted developers in several countries who support the Portable Document Format (PDF) and offer programs or solutions to work in concert with Acrobat. Wherever you find computer systems on this planet, you will find users of Acrobat—more than 50 million of them. The generosity of developers from countries and territories such as the United Kingdom, Germany, France, Belgium, Taiwan, Japan, North America, Australia, and many others was overwhelming. People graciously contributed time and demonstration products that appear on the accompanying CD-ROM. What's more, their enthusiasm for promoting Acrobat and their individual solutions were a pleasure to experience.

If you happen to be one of those who wonders how a book on Acrobat can deserve a spot on the bookshelf next to *Photoshop 5 Bible* or *Windows 98 Bible*, then look over this volume. There's more to Acrobat than most people suspect. Regardless of what you do with a computer, you can benefit from using this product. In the *Acrobat PDF Bible*, I cover the many ways to use Acrobat and offer some solutions for different markets and purposes.

What Is Adobe Acrobat?

Many people first dismiss the thought of spending any energy on Acrobat because they lack an understanding of what Acrobat is and what it does. This, in part, is due to the ready availability of the free Adobe Acrobat Reader software on the Adobe Web site. Many folks think the viewing of PDF documents with Reader is the extent of Acrobat.

As I explain in Chapter 1, Reader is only one small component of Acrobat. Other programs are included in the suite of Acrobat software, providing you with tools for creating, editing, viewing, navigating, and searching Portable Document Format information. In Chapter 1, I offer an explanation of the Acrobat components and provide a little background on the product's evolution. If you are not certain what Acrobat is, look over the first chapter to gain an understanding of why it takes a book of this length to cover Adobe Acrobat.

About This Book

This book is written for a cross-platform audience. Users of Windows 95, Windows 98, Windows NT, and Macintosh will find references to each of these operating systems. Acrobat works almost identically on each of these platforms. However, there are some differences in a few features related to working with Acrobat on either Windows or the Macintosh. Such differences are addressed in the text. If a screen illustration is provided without reference to a particular operating system, you can expect the same options to appear on your system.

What's inside

Almost everything you can do with Acrobat is contained within the chapters that follow, with particular effort made to address the needs of different users. This book covers Acrobat features and how to work with the Acrobat suite of software in such environments as business offices, digital prepress companies, multimedia concerns, and Web publishers. Whether you are an accounting clerk, a real estate sales person, a digital prepress technician, a Web designer, or a hobbyist who likes to archive information from Web sites, Acrobat will provide a solution to your specific requirements.

This book is divided into four parts, as detailed here, that address the features of and various uses for this software suite:

Part I: Welcome to Adobe Acrobat. To start off, I offer a brief history of Acrobat and toss in a few of my own opinions about the computer industry and evolution of companies and products. I then go on to explain Acrobat and what you get when you buy the software — yes, the complete Acrobat suite of applications does require purchase. If you haven't yet purchased Acrobat, here you can find a detailed description of the free Adobe Acrobat Reader software and Acrobat Search, which is also distributed free from Adobe Systems. You can then browse the rest of the book to see if aspects of the other Acrobat software programs interest you before you purchase the suite. Part I covers viewing and navigation in Acrobat and Portable Document Format basics. By the time you finish Part I, you should be able to quickly find information in Acrobat, as well as understand how Acrobat is being embraced by many organizations, governments, and institutions throughout the world.

Part II: Creating PDF Documents. Viewing and navigation limits you to examining documents created by others. There are different ways to create a PDF document, and all of them are thoroughly covered in Part II. I start by discussing easy ways to create simple PDF files that may be used by office workers, and then move on to much more sophisticated methods of PDF file creation for more demanding environments. In addition, I describe how to export files to Portable Document Format in various applications that support this action. The advantages and disadvantages of using all these methods are discussed.

Part III: Enhancing PDF Documents. This section covers the tools, menu commands, and features, old and new, of Adobe Acrobat 4.0, known in earlier versions as Acrobat Exchange. In this section, I cover modifying and enhancing PDF files for different purposes, as well as how to add links, movies, and sounds, and create forms, bookmarks, and thumbnails. Acrobat 4.0 is the heart of the suite of applications and works in conjunction with the other modules. In addition to Acrobat, I discuss Acrobat Catalog, Acrobat Scan, and Acrobat Capture to show you how these components all work together.

Part IV: Advanced Acrobat Applications. I saved the discussion of using Acrobat with the Web for this section, in which all the new Web enhancement tools are covered. Of all the new features of Acrobat, the new Web tools, such as WebLink and Web Capture, will amaze you. If you just can't wait, jump to this section and take a peek. I haven't forgotten the world of digital prepress — Chapter 16 covers prepress printing, PDF workflows, and output of PDF documents for all purposes. In addition, you may find interesting the chapter on CD-ROM replication, which covers the distribution of PDF files on CD-ROM. The last chapter covers plug-ins.

Although all the third-party manufacturers mentioned do not have a demonstration product on the accompanying CD-ROM, I've provided the manufacturers' Web addresses, where you can find software, products, and solutions. If you have even the slightest doubt about Acrobat's role in the digital community, look over this lengthy chapter. You'll be amazed at how many people and industries are making PDF a standard, especially if you keep in mind that this chapter provides only a small sampling of all the Acrobat plug-ins out there!

Appendix. The appendix describes the contents of the CD-ROM that accompanies this book and some issues related to how the products are installed, as well as references to more information about the products.

PDF workflows

One of the nice features of working with Acrobat is it provides a means of developing a workflow environment. A workflow can be different things to different people, but quite simply, workflow solutions are intended to enable you to get the most out of a computer—increasing productivity through automation. Editing page by page and performing tasks manually to change or modify documents can hardly be called a workflow solution. Workflows help office or production workers automate common tasks for maximum efficiency. Batch-processing documents, running them through automated steps, and routing files through computer-assisted delivery systems are considered workflow solutions.

To help delineate a production workflow from manual methods, the following icon alerts you to a potential workflow implementation.

 When you see the PDF workflow icon, expect to learn about features that help you add automation to your environment.

CD-ROM

In the back of the book you'll find a CD-ROM. This is a hybrid CD-ROM in that it can be viewed on Windows or Macintosh systems. The CD-ROM contains demonstration products that are either stand-alone applications or Acrobat plug-ins. Many developers have contributed their products and offer you a chance to try out their software. In several instances, the products are fully functional for a limited time. In other cases, a single feature such as saving or printing a file has been disabled, or images will be replaced by icons on screen or in printouts. Regardless of any limitations, the products can be thoroughly tested. Third-party manufacturers are an important asset to working with Adobe Acrobat. If you have specialized needs, often you can find a developer who provides a solution. Try out these products and visit the developers' Web sites to learn more of what Acrobat can do with add-on software.

Contacting the Author

After reviewing this publication, you can contact me and let me know your views, opinions, and hoorahs, or provide information that may be covered in the next revision. By all means e-mail me at ted@west.net.

If you happen to have some problems with Acrobat, keep in mind I didn't engineer the program. Technical support inquiries should be directed to the software manufacturers of any products you use. This is one more good reason to complete your registration form.

There you have it — a short description of what follows. Don't wait. Turn the page and learn how Acrobat can help you gain more productivity with its amazing features.

Acknowledgments

Much appreciation and gratitude are extended to the following individuals and companies for their assistance in providing the information and products I needed to complete this book:

Jim Straus and Todd Donahue of Acquired Knowledge, Inc.; Ted Alspach, Jennifer Hart, Jeff Moran, Jennifer Morillo, and Shirley Sellers of Adobe Systems; Mike Agahee, Michael Jahn, Rick Kasel, Brian Miller, and Susan Wittner of Agfa Division, Bayer, Inc.; Woody Hume at Ambia Software; Ruta Medina of Autologic Information International; Hanyen Widjaja of BCL Computers; Olaf Druemmer of Callas Software GMBH; Peter Mathews of ComputerStream, Ltd.; Virginia Gavin, President of Digital Applications, Inc.; Daniel-Ari Feinberg of Dionis Software; Peter Soderlund of Enfocus Software, Inc.; Joe Schorr and Samantha Soma of Extensis Software; Diana Holm of FileOpen Systems, Inc.; Rick Hustead of Hustead Studio Productions; Ian Haywood of Iceni Technology; Mark Hartsell, President of INFOCON AMERICA CORP.; Ben Smith and Woody Hume of InfoData Systems, Inc.; Fred Bauries and April Pennacchio of the International Digital Imaging Association (IDIA); Gary Armstrong of Lantana Research; Harry Rabin, Neal Rabin, and Greg Goodman of Miramar Systems; April Parker of NetFormation, Inc.; Kurt Foss at PDFzone.COM; Gregg Elste, Tom Horan, and Johan Laurent of Prime Source and Xeikon; James G. Oliver and Ted Walker of PubSTec Corporation; Kimberly Enis and Brad Zucroff of purePDF.com; Aandi Inston of Quite Software; Robert Radtke of Radtke Consulting; Karl De Abrew and Richard Crocker of A RoundTable Solution; Mike Sinigaglia and Howard White of Scitex America; Tracey Ades of Silanis Technology, Inc.; Joanne David of Ultimate Technographics; Steve Roth and Steve Brobach at ThunderLizard Productions; Lynn Heinz of the University of California, Los Angeles; Denise Judd, Anna Lafferty, and Rich Ayling of the University of California, Santa Barbara; Chris Zsarnay and Cathi Nye of the Ventura County Ad Club; Catherine Norts and Noreen Dalton of xman Software; Pete Dyson of Ziff Davis and Seybold Seminars.

The IDG Books Worldwide Crew

I'd like to thank these folks at IDG Books Worldwide: development editor Katharine Dvorak, especially for all her fast turnarounds; technical editor Dennis Cohen, for all his great work; copy editor Ami Knox; and production coordinator Susan Parini. Above all, a special thanks to my acquisition editor, Mike Roney, who offered much support, kept me on track, and convinced me to rewrite the whole thing based on Acrobat 4.0 instead of Acrobat 3.01.

Some Special People

A special thank you to Deke McClelland, who offered words of encouragement to *hang in there*; to Barbara Obermeier, for accepting phone calls from me every Sunday afternoon for three months; to Sherry Schafer and Jim Bass, for their contributions to the CD-ROM; and to Ron Chan, for his artwork contributions. Finally, thanks to Bruce Butterbredt, Austin Ferdinand, Kris Sweaney, Al Rose, Steve Nasi, and Fred Holmes of my Bakersfield staff, who picked up the slack during my intense moments with this book.

Best of all, thanks to you, the reader. You make it all worthwhile.

Contents at a Glance

Foreword vii
Preface ix
Acknowledgments xv

Part I: Welcome to Adobe Acrobat 1
Chapter 1: Getting to Know Adobe Acrobat 3
Chapter 2: Viewing and Searching PDF Files 27
Chapter 3: Using Acrobat Reader 77

Part II: Creating PDF Documents 113
Chapter 4: Creating PDFs with PDFWriter 115
Chapter 5: Using Acrobat Distiller 143
Chapter 6: PDF Exports and Imports 201
Chapter 7: Using Acrobat Exchange 265

Part III: Enhancing PDF Documents 287
Chapter 8: Annotations, Text, and Graphics 289
Chapter 9: Articles, Bookmarks, and Thumbnails 335
Chapter 10: Creating Hypertext Links 359
Chapter 11: Working with Forms 385
Chapter 12: Creating Search Indexes with Acrobat Catalog 425
Chapter 13: Scanning in Acrobat 449
Chapter 14: Converting Scans to Text 467

Part IV: Advanced Acrobat Applications 477
Chapter 15: PDF and the Web 479
Chapter 16: Printing and Digital Prepress 539
Chapter 17: PDFs and CD-ROMs 577
Chapter 18: Using Plug-ins 591

About the CD-ROM 669
Index 667
End-User License Agreement 703
CD-ROM Installation Instructions 718

Contents

Foreword vii

Preface ix

Acknowledgments...xv

Part: Welcome to Adobe Acrobat   1

Chapter 1: Getting to Know Adobe Acrobat 3

History of Adobe Acrobat 3
What's PDF? 5
    Document repurposing...6
    PDF and PostScript 8
Adobe Acrobat Components 9
    Plug-ins 10
    Acrobat viewers...11
    Acrobat Search 11
    PDFWriter 12
    Acrobat Distiller 12
    Acrobat Catalog 13
    Acrobat Capture 13
    Acrobat Scan 14
PDF Workflow 14
    Automating digital workflows..14
    PDF as a standard..19
    PDF workflow solutions 21

Chapter 2: Viewing and Searching PDF Files.........................27

Viewing and Navigation...27
    Viewing tools...27
    Zooming..30
    Page views 31
    Full-screen views 33
    More page views 35
Navigating PDF Documents..40
    Navigation tools...40
    HyperText links..45

World Wide Web links 53
Using the Find Tool 54
Find Tool dialog box 55
Find Again 55
Using Acrobat Search 55
All about index files 56
Using the Acrobat Search dialog box 59
Understanding search results 63
Viewing search results 64
Search preferences 66
Operators 69
Boolean expressions 72
Word Assistant 74

Chapter 3: Using Acrobat Reader **77**

Understanding the Reader Environment 77
Document information 77
Modifying preferences 84
Opening and Printing PDFs 94
Making Text and Graphics Selections 94
Text Select tool 95
Column Select tool 96
Copying and pasting text 98
Copying and pasting graphics 100
Context-sensitive menus 102
Using the Online Help Commands 104
Help guides 105
Accessing Adobe's Web Link 106
Register Acrobat Reader 107
Get help from Adobe on the Web 108

Part II: Creating PDF Documents   **113**

Chapter 4: Creating PDFs with PDFWriter **115**

The PDFWriter Print Driver 116
Accessing the PDFWriter 117
PDFWriter on the Macintosh 117
PDFWriter in Windows 120
Page setup 122
Font Handling 124
Font compression 124
Font embedding 124
Font subsetting 127
Image Resampling 127

File-format compatibility 127

Compression 130

Encoding 132

Downsampling 132

Printing from PDFWriter 133

Viewing PDF files 134

Prompting for document information 135

Short (DOS) File Names 137

Creating a PDF File 137

Chapter 5: Using Acrobat Distiller **143**

Why Use Distiller 143

Understanding PostScript 145

Creating PostScript files 146

Acrobat Distiller Environment 156

Distiller preferences 156

Job Options 157

Watched folders 174

Security 182

Printing to Distiller 184

One Step Distillation 185

Combining files by name 191

Combining files in folders 193

Combining PostScript files on networks 196

Chapter 6: PDF Exports and Imports **201**

Applications Software Support for PDF 201

Acrobat and Adobe Photoshop 202

Exporting to PDF from Photoshop 203

Acrobat and Illustration Programs 212

Macromedia FreeHand 213

CorelDraw 214

Adobe Illustrator 214

Acrobat and Layout Programs 223

Exporting to PDF from PageMaker 224

pdfmark 249

Annotating PostScript Code 250

Chapter 7: Using Acrobat Exchange **265**

The Acrobat Environment 265

General preferences 266

Annotation preferences 267

Full Screen, Search, and Weblink preferences 268

Forms Grid preferences 269

Paper Capture preferences 271

TouchUp 272
PDF Document Control...273
    General Info...273
    Open Info...275
    Fonts and Security 277
    Prepress...277
    Index 278
    Base URL..279
Saving PDF Files...279
Security 281

Part III: Enhancing PDF Documents   287

Chapter 8: Annotations, Text, and Graphics 289

Acrobat Tools 289
Working with Annotations 291
    Using the Annotation tools 291
    Working with Graphic Markup tools.....................308
    Working with Text Markup tools...........................311
    Using the Annotations palette 313
    Summarizing annotations......................................319
    Using the Filter Manager 321
    Printing annotations 322
Editing Text 323
    Using the TouchUp Text tool 324
Working with Graphics 328
    Using the TouchUp Object tool 329
    Editing objects 329

Chapter 9: Articles, Bookmarks, and Thumbnails 335

Working with Articles 335
    Article viewing and navigation 336
Working with Bookmarks 343
    Adding and deleting bookmarks 344
    Ordering bookmarks...345
Working with Thumbnails..349
    Creating and deleting thumbnails 349
    Editing PDFs with thumbnails...............................351
Editing Pages 352
    Cropping pages..353
    Rotating pages...355
Understanding Destinations 355
    Creating destinations 356
    Sorting destinations...356

Chapter 10: Creating Hypertext Links..**359**

About Hypertext Links 359
        Link actions...360
        Link properties 360
        Removing links 360
        Link environment 361
Creating Links 361
        Link properties 362
        Creating Links 370
Creating Page Actions...373
        Editing page actions..373
        Using transitions with page actions.............................374
        Nesting page actions 377
Importing Sound and Video..377
        Importing sound files..378
        Importing movies 379

Chapter 11: Working with Forms **385**

What Are Acrobat Forms?..385
Understanding Form Fields...385
        Form contents...386
Creating Forms 388
        Field properties 389
Importing and Exporting Form Data...................................418
        Exporting data 418
        Importing data 420

Chapter 12: Creating Search Indexes with Acrobat Catalog **425**

Structure of Catalog files..425
Hierarchy of indexed files 426
Relocating indexes 426
Using Catalog Preferences 426
        Macintosh Catalog preferences 427
        Windows Catalog preferences 434
Creating an Index 436
        Index title..436
        Index description 437
        Include directories 439
        Exclude directories 439
        Removing directories...440
        Building the index 440
Creating Dynamic Indexes 442
        Identifying indexes 442
        Building indexes 443
        Stopping the scheduled build.......................................443

Purging data 444
Setting Up Network Catalogs 445

Chapter 13: Scanning in Acrobat 449

Accessing a Scanner 449
    ISIS software 450
    TWAIN software 451
    HP AccuPage software 452
Scanning Basics 452
    Understanding Acrobat scan types 453
    Preparing a document 456
Memory Configurations 457
    Macintosh memory requirements 457
    Windows memory requirements 459
Using Acrobat Scan 463
    Scanning images 463

Chapter 14: Converting Scans to Text 467

Using Acrobat Paper Capture 467
    Paper Capture preferences 468
    Custom dictionaries (Windows) 470
Capturing a Page 471
    Capture Suspects 472
    Capture performance 474
Capturing Imported Images 474

Part IV: Advanced Acrobat Applications   477

Chapter 15: PDF and the Web 479

HTML Programming 479
    Macintosh text editors 480
    Windows and NT editors 480
    Coding in HTML 480
PDF Versus HTML 483
    PDF advantages 483
    HTML advantages 484
    Combining PDF and HTML 484
Configuring Your Web Browser 485
    Viewing configurations 485
    Viewing PDFs in a browser 488
    Viewing preferences in the browser 491
    Viewing PDF links in the Web browser 495
Capturing Web Sites (Windows Only) 497
    Web site structure 497

Converting Web pages 498
Preferences for converting PDFs..................................509
Web Capture menu commands......................................516
Capturing a Web site 521
Working with Captured Web Sites...528
Appending Web pages 528
Editing with bookmarks...534

Chapter 16: Printing and Digital Prepress **539**

Preparing Files for Printing...539
Distilling PostScript Files 542
Customizing Job Options 542
Printing PDF Documents 549
Printing to desktop printers 549
Printing to high-end devices 554
Printing Color Separations..557
Printing process color separations...............................558
Using Transfer Functions 565
Embedding transfer functions 565
Variable Data Printing...568
Variable data and PDF...569
Creating the PDF file 571
Printing to Large Format Inkjet Printers 574

Chapter 17: PDFs and CD-ROMs **577**

CD-ROM Publishing...577
CD-ROM replication 577
Planning the content design 578
Distribution of the Acrobat Reader Software 583
Adobe License Agreement 584
Reader and Search 584
Artwork Preparation for CDs...587
Printable area of a CD 587
Continuous tone images 587

Chapter 18: Using Plug-ins **591**

Understanding Plug-ins 591
Installing plug-ins 592
Plug-in conflicts 593
Plug-in documentation...595
Disabling plug-ins 595
Adobe Acrobat Plug-ins..595
Standard plug-ins..596
Windows-only plug-ins...599
Optional plug-ins...600

Using Third-Party Plug-ins and Applications...600
Contacting Suppliers 654
Staying Connected 660
    Registering the product..660
    Web sites to contact..660

About the CD-ROM 663

Index 667

End-User License Agreement 703

CD-ROM Installation Instructions..718

Welcome to Adobe Acrobat

P A R T

◆ ◆ ◆ ◆

Chapter 1
Getting to Know
Adobe Acrobat

Chapter 2
Viewing and
Searching PDF Files

Chapter 3
Using Acrobat
Reader

Getting to Know Adobe Acrobat

✦ ✦ ✦ ✦

In This Chapter

What is Adobe Acrobat

What is PDF

Adobe Acrobat components

Understanding PDF workflows

✦ ✦ ✦ ✦

I f, after perusing your local bookstore, you decided to lay down your money at the counter, carry away this ten-pound volume, and take it to bed with you tonight, you probably already know something about Adobe Acrobat. Heck, why else would you buy this book? If you're at the bookstore shelf and you haven't bought it yet, then you're probably wondering how in the world anyone could write so many pages for such a simple application. After all, isn't Acrobat that little thingy you download from Adobe's Web site?

Assuming you know little about Acrobat, I'll start with a brief description of what Acrobat is and what it is not. As I explain to people who ask about the product, I usually define it as the most misunderstood application available today. Most of us are familiar with the Adobe Acrobat Reader software. It's a product from Adobe Systems Incorporated that you can download free of charge from Adobe's Web site (www.adobe.com). You can also acquire the Adobe Acrobat Reader from most of the installation CD-ROMs for other Adobe software. You can even acquire Acrobat Reader from other users, as long as the Adobe licensing requirements are distributed with the installer program. The Acrobat Reader, however, is *not* Adobe Acrobat. Acrobat Reader is a component of a much larger product that has evolved through several iterations.

History of Adobe Acrobat

When Acrobat was first released (as version 1.0), users could obtain the Acrobat Reader software for viewing and printing documents saved in Portable Document Format (PDF). Adobe released this product to help the growing user base view documents created on different platforms. The PC user, for example, could view a PDF file that was created on a Macintosh or UNIX workstation, and vice versa. The Acrobat Reader was free and enabled the viewing and printing of a document while maintaining that document's integrity. Fonts, graphics, design, and layout were all preserved in a PDF file, so the end user could view and print a document without needing any of the fonts, links, or applications from which the document was created.

The other two applications released in version 1.0, Acrobat Distiller and Acrobat Exchange, were software items that had to be purchased from Adobe Systems. Acrobat Distiller enabled users to create a PDF document from a PostScript file printed to disk. Virtually any file created by an application with the capability to print to disk was able to be converted to PDF. Once a PDF was created, it could be edited in Acrobat Exchange.

As the product evolved, release 2.1 was referred to as Acrobat Pro. The Acrobat Reader was still a free application distributed by Adobe Systems, but Acrobat Pro was a bundle of several applications that had to be purchased from Adobe. Acrobat Pro included Acrobat Distiller and Acrobat Exchange, and introduced a new application known as Acrobat Catalog, which enabled the end user to create searches from multiple PDF files and provided an organized index of all the words used in documents.

Note   Adobe also released Acrobat Distiller with Adobe PageMaker 6.0. PageMaker included an export menu item to create PDF files on command. When the user invoked the Create PDF command, PageMaker created a PostScript file transparent to the user and then distilled the file, which converted it to PDF. Acrobat Exchange, however, was not included with other Adobe software, so to edit and modify PDF files, users had to purchase this application from Adobe.

With the release of 2.1, Acrobat Exchange, among other enhancements, enabled the end user to add security to PDF files, which prevented other users with Exchange from modifying the documents.

With the release of version 3.0, Adobe dropped the reference to Acrobat Pro, and simply called the Acrobat suite of software *Adobe Acrobat*. This may appear somewhat confusing if you haven't followed the product closely during its evolution, as many users refer to Acrobat Reader as Adobe Acrobat. Keep in mind, the Reader is not Adobe Acrobat. The Reader software is still distributed for free by Adobe Systems, but it is limited to only viewing and printing PDF files. For performing all the editing tasks and adding bells and whistles to PDF documents, you need Adobe Acrobat, which consists of the complete complement of Acrobat products. The Adobe Acrobat release included all the previous modules that were part of the 2.1 release, with new additions Acrobat Capture and Acrobat Scan added to the bundle.

Note   Currently in version 4.0, the editing application Acrobat Exchange is now simply called *Acrobat 4.0*. This again may appear somewhat confusing, as the suite of software is called *Adobe Acrobat*. As you read through this book, keep in mind that when I use the term *Acrobat*, I'm referring to the application formerly called *Acrobat Exchange*. When I use the term *Adobe Acrobat*, I'm referring to the suite of applications.

Regardless of what you call it, Adobe Acrobat has grown into a sophisticated bundle of applications that provides the end user with many capabilities for organizing, displaying, and printing documents. It remains multiplatform and has achieved a high level of respect and performance in office, Web integration, and publishing environments.

Each of the Adobe Acrobat applications in version 4.0 are designed to work in tandem to create and modify documents for on-screen viewing, Web publishing, and printing to suit most end user desires. This book covers all the features of all the components of Adobe Acrobat. To perform the exercises contained herein, you need to purchase Adobe Acrobat, which has a street price of $180 as of this writing. If you work through all the chapters and develop a strong command of Adobe Acrobat, I think you'll agree that the suite is one of the best buys available in the computer software market.

What's PDF?

PDF, or Portable Document Format, was developed by Adobe Systems as a unique format to be viewed through Acrobat viewers. As the name implies, it is portable, which means the file you create on one computer can be viewed with an Acrobat viewer on other computers and on other platforms. For instance, you can create a page layout on a Macintosh computer and convert it to a PDF file. Once converted, this PDF document can be viewed on a UNIX, DOS, or Windows machine. Multiplatform compliance (to enable the exchange of files across different computers, for example) is one of the great values of PDF files.

The Portable Document Format itself has evolved with several revisions. The release of PDF version 1.0 corresponded to the introduction of Adobe Acrobat. With version 3.0 and the more recent 3.0.1 version of Adobe Acrobat, PDF was upgraded to version 1.2. The latest PDF version, included in Adobe Acrobat 4.0, is version 1.3, which provides benefits not available in earlier versions, such as improved printing output and device controls for specific hardware and compliance with PostScript 3. Chapters 4 through 6 describe how the most recent PDF version can be used to take advantage of these attributes.

So what's special about PDF and its multiplatform compliance? It's not so much an issue of viewing a page on one computer that was created on another computer that is impressive about PDF. After all, such popular programs as Microsoft Excel, Microsoft Word, Adobe PageMaker, and Illustrator all have counterparts for multiplatform usage. You can create a layout on one computer system and view the file on another system with the same software installed. For instance, if you have Adobe PageMaker installed on a Macintosh computer and you create a PageMaker file, that same file can be viewed on a PC with PageMaker running under Windows.

In a perfect world, you might think the capability to view documents across platforms is not so special. Viewing capability, however, is secondary to document integrity. It's the preservation of the contents of a page that makes the PDF format so extraordinary. To illustrate, let's say you have a PageMaker document created in Windows using fonts generic to Windows applications. Once converted to PDF format, the document, complete with graphics and fonts intact, can be displayed and printed on other computer platforms.

This can come in handy in business environments, where software purchases often reach quantum heights. PDF documents eliminate the need to install all applications used within a particular company on all the computers in that company. For example, art department employees can use a layout application to create display ads and then convert them to PDF so that other departments can use the free Reader software to view and print those ads for approval.

Document repurposing

The evolution of the computer world has left extraordinary volumes of data, designed to be printed on paper, on computer systems. Going all the way back to UNIVAC, the number crunching was handled by the computer and the expression was the printed piece. Today, forms of expression have evolved to many different media. No longer do people wish to confine themselves to printed material. Now, in addition to publishing information on paper, we use CD-ROMs, the Internet, and file exchanges between computers. Sometimes we use motion video, television, and satellite broadcasts. As cable TV evolves, we'll see much larger bandwidths, so real-time communication will eventually become commonplace. And the world of tomorrow will introduce more communication media. Think of outputting to plasma, crystal, and holograms, and then think about having a font display or link problem with one of those babies!

True Visionaries

The 8086 IBM PC and the first Macintosh, though products of fairly recent history, are jokes compared to the computer systems of today. Alan Kay, one of the true visionaries of the Xerox Palo Alto Research Center (PARC), once stated, "[The] Macintosh was the first computer worthy of criticism," for which he was heavily attacked. People totally misunderstood Kay's meaning. Kay was looking at what computers should be and what he envisioned for the future of computing, which we still have yet to accomplish. I would not presume to compare myself with Alan Kay, but at the risk of being criticized, I would say our present day Internet is a total joke. After all, how many times are you going to wait two, five, or ten minutes for a twenty-second VRML file to download? In a few years, people are going to talk about how in the nineties it used to take five minutes to download something that they will be able to see in real time on the Web.

Technology will advance, bringing many improvements to bandwidth, performance, and speed. To enable the public to access the mountains of digital data held on computer systems in a true information superhighway world, files will need to be converted to a common format. A common file format would also enable new documents created now to be more easily *repurposed*, to use a buzzword of the moment, to exploit the many forms of communication we use today and expect to use tomorrow. Figure 1-1 illustrates the process of repurposing a QuarkXPress file into a document suitable for viewing on the Web.

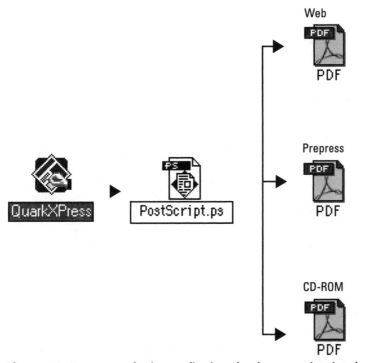

Figure 1-1: From an authoring application, the document is printed to disk as a PostScript file. With the new Distiller Job Options settings, the PostScript file designed for prepress is repurposed for screen and Web displays.

Where does Adobe see PDF heading? Adobe Systems and many software and hardware manufacturers expect most of our document exchanges by the end of 1999 to be in PDF format. Adobe is using PDF as core technology for new versions of all its software. PostScript 3, new layout applications, and the flagship programs offered by the company all support PDF compliance. AGFA, a division of the Bayer group, has built a complete PDF workflow solution with its Apogee system. Scitex is corroborating with Adobe Systems in offering seminars throughout the country on how their imaging systems will work with PDF and PostScript 3. And the list goes on. As all these companies expand their existing equipment and software to take advantage of PDF, new documents will be hosted in PDF format, and old data will be converted to PDF.

Adobe Acrobat is in its infancy now, but it will evolve, as will other technologies. Currently, the best program for both document exchange and document repurposing is Acrobat, for it excels at creating a document, with or without multimedia elements, that can be printed, viewed on a computer screen, seen on the Web, and replicated on CD-ROM. What's more, all those records created years ago can be converted to PDF format. Document repurposing is one of the true values of using Adobe Acrobat. Throughout this book, I show you how to create PDF files with an eye toward document repurposing.

PDF and PostScript

On January 24, 1984, Apple Computer released the Macintosh computer. Not an impulsive buyer, I waited until January 26 to purchase my first Mac. I remember one of my earlier uses of the Mac involved submitting documents that contained about thirty fonts and several graphics to California government offices in Sacramento. I frequently received calls from people wanting to know how I put the little choo-choo trains on my memos. Although crude, the emphasis on the visual gained the response I needed for attention to my message.

If all the Macintosh computer could do was print on an ImageWriter I dot-matrix printer, it would have died alongside the Osborne portable, and Mr. Gates would own much more of the world than he does now. The credibility of the Macintosh was not realized with the hardware (certainly not at 128K RAM and a single 400K floppy drive), nor was it with MacPaint and Habadex. In 1985, Apple Computer introduced the Macintosh-LaserWriter connection. With 13 built-in fonts and a hefty $6,500 price tag, the LaserWriter, based on true Adobe PostScript, was one of the great products of the era. The world of desktop publishing was born.

Today, the de facto standard of almost all printing in the graphics industry is PostScript. Ninety-nine percent of the computer users in North America and about seventy-five percent of the rest of the computing world use PostScript for all high-end output. Adobe developed this page description language to accurately display on your computer screen what the final printed output would look like. If graphics and fonts are included in your files, then PostScript is the only show in town. Adobe's PostScript language was responsible for the rise of so many software and hardware manufacturers. If you stop and think about it, PostScript ranks up there with MS-DOS and Windows in terms of its installed base.

One feature of successful software programs is that they run on a wide variety of hardware. The most successful software published today is MS-DOS and Windows. It's successful because it permits a lot of flexibility. Windows is not restricted to a single manufacturer's hardware. Scads of companies are producing Intel-, AMD-, and Cyrix-based machines, and they all include Windows with the purchase of the hardware. Apple's Mac OS, until recently, was only able to run on Apple-produced hardware. This limitation might have been one of the reasons that prevented Apple from enjoying the same success as companies like Microsoft.

PostScript also allows for flexibility in what hardware it works with. With its device-independent structure, PostScript can accommodate many different printers, all with different resolution capabilities. For example, you can print to a 300-dpi PostScript laser printer or to a 3600-dpi imagesetter with the same flavor of PostScript. PostScript printing requires a raster image processor (RIP), which can be either a hardware device or software. The RIP converts the image on screen to a bitmap page that can be printed on a PostScript printer. In other words, what you draw on your computer screen is defined in a language different from that used by your printer, and PostScript is like a language conversion utility in that it "translates" the screen image for printing.

Integrity of data is critical when printing files. A glitch or hiccup can blow out a font or graphic on the printed page. Software applications compliant with PostScript experience much fewer problems because data integrity is adhered to strictly. This, in fact, is another advantage of using Adobe Acrobat. One of the applications used to convert your screen files to PDF is Adobe Acrobat Distiller, which is a truly magnificent program. Distiller is like a PostScript engine in that it adheres strictly to PostScript conventions. In almost all cases, if you can distill a file with Acrobat Distiller, you can print the file on a PostScript device. As you read through this book, you'll learn how and when to use Acrobat Distiller.

Adobe Acrobat Components

When you purchase a software product, you probably already understand something about the product, what it does, and how you intend use it. If you pick Adobe Photoshop or Microsoft Excel off the shelf, you already know you want to work on image editing or number crunching. Some add-ons may be available for the product, but you're well aware that you have a single application, sophisticated as it may be, to tackle your digital needs.

With Adobe Acrobat, it's very different. Adobe Acrobat is not a single application, but rather a number of different applications performing different functions, all housed under the name Adobe Acrobat (see Figure 1-2). Think of Adobe Acrobat as a suite of programs rather than a single application. All the independent programs work together to permit you to create, view, and edit PDF files. These programs include the following:

✦ Acrobat Reader

✦ Acrobat 4.0*

✦ Acrobat Search

✦ PDFWriter

✦ Acrobat Distiller

✦ Acrobat Catalog

✦ Acrobat Capture

✦ Acrobat Scan

*All previous versions of Adobe Acrobat referred to the authoring application as Acrobat Exchange. In version 4.0, Adobe refers to the application as Acrobat 4.0. For simplicity and convenience, I use Acrobat or Acrobat 4.0 for what was once called Acrobat Exchange.

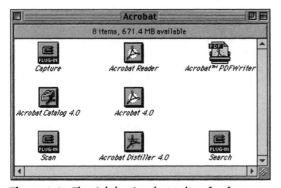

Figure 1-2: The Adobe Acrobat suite of software includes application programs, plug-ins, and a printer driver.

Plug-ins

In addition to the distinct applications available with Adobe Acrobat, included are some plug-ins developed by Adobe Systems and many third-party manufacturers. (*Plug-ins* are software components often created by third-party vendors to add more functionality to software applications.) Adobe includes several plug-ins on the installation CD-ROM that you can use with Acrobat and Acrobat Reader. When you install Adobe Acrobat, the Acrobat Capture, Scan, and Search plug-ins are also installed.

Acrobat viewers

Two Acrobat viewer applications may be used to view PDF documents: Acrobat Reader and Acrobat 4.0. As I mentioned earlier, Acrobat Reader is the free application you can acquire from the Adobe Systems Web site. You can also find the Acrobat Reader software on many application installation CD-ROMs. Adobe Systems and many other software manufacturers include documentation, updates, and the latest news about a product in PDF format. To view the PDF files, you need to install an Acrobat viewer, therefore the Reader software is often included on CD-ROMs.

Note

The Acrobat Reader software can also be distributed by end users. Adobe Systems permits you distribution rights as long as you comply with their distribution policy, which requires the licensing documents and information to be included with the installation utility.

Acrobat Reader, because it is a free application, is limited in use. You cannot edit or save PDF files with Acrobat Reader. It is designed to enable you to view a PDF document on screen or print a PDF file.

If you want to edit PDF files, you need to purchase Adobe Acrobat, which includes the Acrobat 4.0 software. Acrobat 4.0 takes off where Reader ends. Acrobat performs all the tasks of viewing files with the same tools as Acrobat Reader, but it goes a step further in enabling you to change, edit, secure, and customize PDF files. Acrobat is not just a viewer — it's the heart of the Adobe Acrobat suite of applications.

Acrobat Search

When you open a PDF document in an Acrobat viewer, you can invoke a Find command to search for a keyword, as shown in Figure 1-3. The viewer then searches through the pages and stops at the first occurrence of the searched word it finds (see Figure 1-4). This is fine if you have a single document open and need to search for the content desired. If you have several PDF files and wish to search all documents for a keyword or words, you need Acrobat Search. Like Acrobat Reader, Acrobat Search is a free plug-in, and it can be used with both Acrobat viewers.

Acrobat Search is a powerful search engine that goes beyond searching for keywords. You can search with operators or Boolean expressions and narrow searches to specific requirements, as illustrated in later chapters.

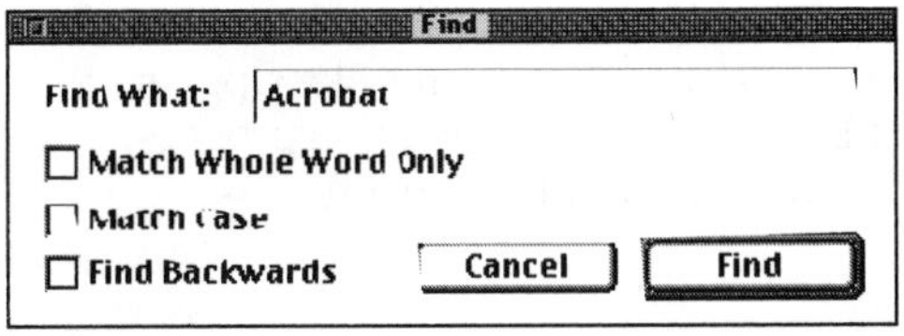

Figure 1-3: When the Find command is invoked, the search is limited to the open PDF document.

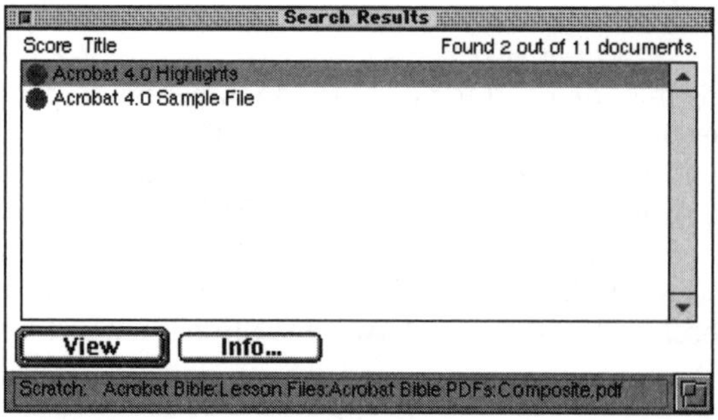

Figure 1-4: When Acrobat Search is used, it searches multiple PDF documents and reports in a result window a list of the PDF documents where the searched word(s) was found.

Note

When you acquire Acrobat Reader from the Adobe Web site, pull off the Reader from a CD-ROM, or acquire it from another user, you will find an installer for Reader and an installer for Reader + Search. If you elect to use the latter, both Acrobat Reader and Acrobat Search will be installed. If you cannot invoke a search of several PDF files at one time, you need to acquire Acrobat Search and install it.

PDFWriter

Creating PDF files is the task of two applications also included with Adobe Acrobat. Among these two applications is the PDFWriter software. PDFWriter is a simple utility that enables you to "print" a page from any application installed on your computer. The destination for this page, however, is not your printer but your hard drive. The file saved to the hard drive is a PDF document.

PDFWriter has its limitations; there are a host of reasons why you would not want to use PDFWriter to create a PDF document, and these are detailed later in the book. However, in its simplest form, PDFWriter can be used with many applications to create documents for screen viewing and printing to office printers. For example, if you work in an office and spend your time using accounting applications, you could create a PDF file of a financial statement for management review simply by printing to the PDFWriter. The resulting document could then be placed on an office server or intranet and accessed by company personnel for review before a management meeting. Creating a PDF document from PDFWriter is as easy as sending the file to print, which makes it an attractive utility for those with more limited computer experience.

Acrobat Distiller

Adobe Acrobat Distiller is the more sophisticated conversion application. Distiller creates PDF documents from PostScript files. To use Distiller, you need to first print a file from your application document to disk as a PostScript file. Opening the printed PostScript file in Acrobat Distiller begins the conversion process. Distiller appears to be a simple utility when you first use it, but in reality, it is a sophisticated PostScript engine that behaves more like a software RIP than a software program. Theoretically, if you can distill a file, the file can be printed on a PostScript device.

Many users will opt to use the PDFWriter because of its simplicity and the capability to create a PDF in a single step. However, you should be aware that Acrobat Distiller provides many more features that are preferred for many file types. I cover creating PDF files and when to use Distiller over PDFWriter in Chapters 4 and 5.

Acrobat Catalog

Earlier I mentioned Acrobat Search and the powerful search capabilities you have available to you with Adobe Acrobat. The internal search available when you open a PDF document is executed with a Find command in an Acrobat viewer. This type of search, which can only be performed on the single, open file, is further restricted by a limited set of search attributes. When you invoke a search using Acrobat Search, your Acrobat viewer searches through an index file containing key words extracted from a PDF document or several PDF documents. Index files are created with Acrobat Catalog.

In addition to developing search indexes from single or multiple PDF documents, Acrobat Catalog enables you to add more PDF files to the index and purge old data. Catalog can be designed to automatically build search indexes from PDF documents and keep them updated on a local workstation or remote server.

Acrobat Capture

Acrobat Capture is optical character recognition (OCR) software that converts scanned images to rich text. Although not as powerful as some OCR applications, Capture does a good job of converting scanned documents to text. Acrobat Capture is accessed through a command you select within Acrobat. When you invoke the command, the Capture Server is loaded into memory, and the current open PDF document is scanned for images to be converted to text. When you invoke the Capture command, you have a choice of converting all the image data to text or preserving the integrity of the scan while having the text appear in the background. This is particularly helpful for such things as legal documents, which can be preserved as they were scanned and text corrections made on an invisible layer. All the converted images can be searched and cataloged.

Note   Capture was released with Adobe Acrobat version 3.0 for Windows. For the Macintosh, you need Adobe Acrobat version 3.01 or higher to gain access to Acrobat Capture. In version 4.0, Capture has been released for both the Mac and Windows.

Acrobat Scan

Acrobat Scan is a plug-in that must be present in the Acrobat plug-in folder when you install Adobe Acrobat, otherwise you won't have access to Acrobat Scan. When you launch Acrobat, the Scan plug-in becomes accessible through a menu command. Scan uses TWAIN (technology without an important name) to access your scanner software, permitting you to scan a document from within Acrobat. Once scanned, the document will appear in the Acrobat window as a PDF. You can invoke the Capture command to convert the scan to text, or simply scan images and save them as PDF documents.

Each of the preceding individual components comprise the collection of applications Adobe Systems refers to as Adobe Acrobat. It is this collection of applications, plug-ins, and add-ons that collectively harness Adobe's vision of document development and processing for virtually all data manipulation on microcomputers. Now that you have an overview of all the capabilities of Adobe Acrobat, you can see why I refer to it as one of the best buys in the software market. Regardless of the type of work you do, Acrobat will benefit your workflow.

PDF Workflow

In what seems a very long time ago on the computer technology timeline, the advent of single-user workstations gave rise to the buzzwords *paperless office*. What we have come to learn over the past two decades is computer systems are generating more paper than ever before. Somehow, the world population has not yet learned to work in a digital environment without paper. (I suspect it will be a long time before people can get away from the need to have something in their hands to carry around and to pile up on their desks.) In the office world, it's not the absence of paper that is important to us, but the ability to find information and then generate output to printing devices in a form and style that is easily legible. Organization of files and rapid retrieval is the first step to take before we can start saving more trees.

Automating digital workflows

In complex office environments, data is assembled and regurgitated in partial digital workflows; intraoffice departments share data through multiuser systems or individual applications capable of sharing files. Users have been working with these partial digital workflows for some time. Advances with storage devices and network systems have helped move automation along. Even so, we computer users remain islands, so to speak, isolated because we haven't been able to bridge all systems and data structures. What has been needed for some time is a tool that ignores application software variances and hardware differences to communicate information among workers, whether they be in a local office, remote facility, or across the globe. In an office that uses PDF, all these components can come together, for Adobe Acrobat ignores cross-platform problems and becomes the common denominator for data flow originating from almost any application.

If you work in a large office and have a network administrator, the technical issues related to your network are likely handled by someone else. You probably don't have to worry about keeping the network alive, configuring systems, and handling all the problems that come with these complex hardware systems. If you are a small office worker, the idea of setting up a network may be frightening and intimidating. If you want to have more of a digital workflow in your office, you may be puzzled as to where to begin. Here I try to dispel some of this confusion by taking you through various fundamentals of network configuration, which will help you in implementing Adobe Acrobat.

Local area networks

If you have two computers and a printer attached to both, you have a *local area network* (LAN). Networks have two components that enable printing and/or file sharing: hardware for creating connections and software for controlling the data flow. Network hardware involves a connection interface referred to as a *transceiver* (the most common of which is Ethernet) and cabling to connect the transceivers. To connect two computers and a printer, you need a transceiver on each device. Some devices such as printers, as well as all newer Macintoshes, have Ethernet transceivers built in. PCs require the installation of an Ethernet board. With respect to the Macintosh, LocalTalk provides a transceiver alternative, but it is about 43 times slower than Ethernet.

Network cabling is needed to connect the Ethernet transceivers. The type of cabling you need depends on the type of connectors you have on the Ethernet boards and whether you use other hardware devices. In a simple network environment, you can use coaxial cable (which resembles cable TV cabling) with a BNC connector and daisy chain the connectors on the boards. In this type of environment, you need to terminate each end of your network using a device, called a *terminator*, that clips on the open end of the BNC connector. Coaxial cable has one significant problem in network architecture. If one cable is damaged or the connection is not correctly made, all computers and devices attached to the network lose access to all other network devices.

A better solution is to use a *hub*, a hardware device to which each unit on a network is connected via cabling with RJ-45 (telephone) clips. These clips plug into ports on the hub, and hubs can be purchased with 4, 8, 16, or more ports. You can also connect several hubs by bridging them. When you purchase Ethernet cards, you can find many that have BNC connectors for coaxial connections and RJ-45 receptacles.

Ethernet is also available in different speeds or capacities. 10Base-T Ethernet permits data transmissions of 10,000,000 bits per second (bps). This may seem fast, but it all depends on the amount of data you exchange with other devices or the size of the files you send off to a printer. If all you do is traffic PDF documents,

10Base-T works well, because PDF files are compressed and the file sizes generally small. If your PDF documents are large, or you perform remote processing for distilling PDF files or cataloging them, this speed may not be fast enough for you. However, 10Base-T networks are inexpensive: You can purchase hubs for $50 or less on the low end.

Ethernet also comes in 100Base-T, which transmits data at 100,000,000 bits per second, or ten times faster than 10Base-T. As of this writing, the price of 100Base-T Ethernet is still expensive: The hubs begin at around $800 to $1,000. However, if trafficking large amounts of data is a common practice in your environment, 100Base-T Ethernet might be worth your money.

Cabling for Ethernet is an important consideration. 10Base-T networks can operate on two-pair wiring (four individual strands), whereas 100Base-T requires four-pair wiring (eight individual strands) called *Category 5* or *CAT5* wiring. The difference in the price of the wiring is incidental to the amount of labor required to rewire a network if you decide to upgrade from 10Base-T to 100Base-T Ethernet. If you go about installing a network in your office, my suggestion is to wire it with CAT5 and be done with it. When the receptacles are properly connected to the wiring, you can run either 10Base-T or 100Base-T on the same wiring.

Servers

On a network, a *server* is a computer that typically contains large amounts of storage space and software installed to permit network traffic to flow to and from it. Servers can be one of many types of computers, and it doesn't matter which platform it runs on; you can access a server of another flavor if you have the proper software installed. For example, if you operate on a Macintosh network, your server can be a Macintosh computer, a PC, a UNIX workstation, or a DEC Alpha. All the Mac files you save to the server will be accessible to all Macintoshes on your network regardless of the type of server you elect to purchase. Speed and cost will dictate which system you ultimately decide to use. Perhaps one of the cheapest solutions is an Intel-based PC running Microsoft Windows NT. Windows NT has network software built into the operating system. On Macintosh-based networks, I prefer to use Miramar Systems' MacLan Connect running under Windows NT. It's easy to install and supports all of the file and print sharing you need.

Servers can play a variety of roles in a network environment. Among the possible uses for a server include the following:

✦ Store files shared in the environment

✦ Contain the host network software

✦ Link to output devices (printers, film recorders, imaging equipment)

✦ Link to media storage devices (Jaz drives, fixed and removable drives, tape drives, optical media)

✦ Link to multiple CD-ROM or DVD drives

✦ Link to modems or Internet routers

✦ Link to RIPs in imaging service centers

The fundamentals of a network can be as basic as a single workstation and a single server. More complex networks can contain multiple servers, each performing special tasks. For example, you can have a single server behave as a print server and another server dedicated to file sharing. You can break up your office environment with dedicated servers for sharing departmental data. You can password protect server access, so the office administration may access all servers and all files, whereas department personnel may only access individual servers or specific directories within a given server. Figure 1-5 shows an example of a local area network connecting client workstations, a server, and a printer.

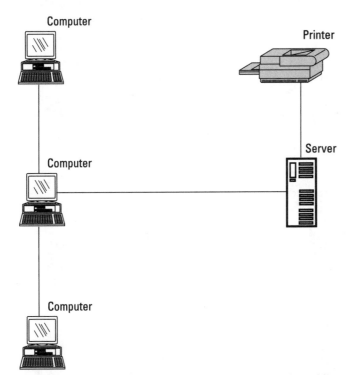

Figure 1-5: Local area networks are commonly connected by Ethernet cabling and may include client workstations, a server, and one or more printers or other output devices.

Servers are intended to be shared by people or devices. All computers connected to a network are known as *clients,* which have access to the network through the sharing software of the server(s). *Devices* are the noncomputer peripherals on the network either directly connected to the server or connected through the cabling mentioned earlier.

Wide area networks

Local area networks are contained in a single office and connected with network cables. A *wide area network* (WAN) enables network clients in one office location to connect to a server at another office location. (Figure 1-6 shows an example of a wide area network.) The location may be across town, across the country, or across the world. These systems are connected by dedicated telephone lines through which data is transmitted like a telephone call. The dedicated phone lines can't be accessed by remote terminals not connected to the network. Multiple servers can be connected in each office or a single server in one office may connect to a single server or multiple servers in another office. Wide area networks allow for centralization. A good example would be a centralized accounting system. All accounting receivables and payables as well as all other accounting operations can be performed at the home office, whereas transactions are conducted online from the remote offices. As each transaction is performed, the data immediately updates the central accounting files.

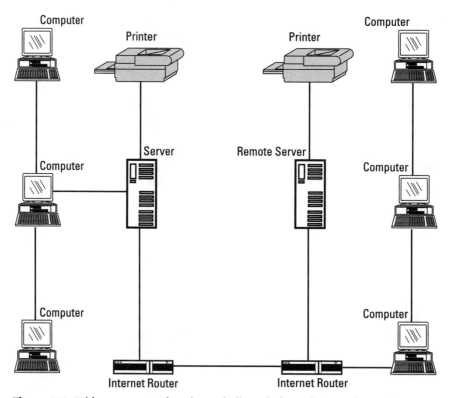

Figure 1-6: Wide area networks rely on dedicated phone lines or the Internet to connect remote workstations.

Intranets

Intranets are a more recent addition to network topology. Intranets feature a server and modem or Internet router. These systems are usually password protected to prevent unauthorized access. Remote users dial into the modem or an Internet IP address and gain access to the intranet from other offices or from computers in the home. Depending on the number of users expected to access the system at any given time, an office may have a single modem, to permit single-user access, or a router, which controls access traffic via several modems.

An intranet can work the same way as a local area network. If you decide to access a drive on a server, output a file to a printer, or view the contents of a CD-ROM, you can do so via an intranet. Once you're in with the proper password, you can have all the same privileges as anyone physically connected to the network at the office.

PDF as a standard

Stop for a moment and think about the mountains of software applications and different environments out there designed to help people exchange information. If you have just prepared a budget in Microsoft Excel and wish to post the spreadsheet on a server either through direct or remote access, anyone wanting to see your spreadsheet will need Excel. The same holds true for other documents created in word processing software, illustration software, page layout software, and dedicated vertical market applications. Imagine the software requirements for the personnel who approve budgets, display ads, corporate memos, building site improvements, legal documents, publications and so on! The cost of licensing software to many different individuals in a company can quickly become prohibitive. As mentioned before, what is needed is a common denominator that enables all documents to be exchanged and viewed by all people involved in corporate decision making.

Cost-effective uses of Adobe Acrobat

PDF has many advantages in regard to developing a common viewing platform. For those who need to make notes and edit PDF files, the site licensing of Adobe Acrobat is integral. Because all files can be reduced to PDF, only a single application site license is needed. This alone will make many office software purchases more cost effective. Compare a multiuser license of a single product to three, five, or ten different site licenses. Moreover, purchasing Adobe Acrobat may not be necessary for all personnel in an office. If viewing a file prior to board and staff meetings or retrieval for later use is the main goal of certain employees, having them use the Acrobat Reader for such thereby increases cost effectiveness.

Developing a standard

To obtain wide usage of a product such as Adobe Acrobat, we need to have a new standard. We have witnessed computers and software become standards in many cases over the past two decades. PostScript, Adobe Photoshop, and Microsoft Windows are good examples of standards. We also see other products by different manufacturers, such as Microsoft Internet Explorer and Netscape Navigator, battling to become the standard. So why hasn't Adobe Acrobat yet become a standard for document exchange?

Adobe Acrobat is not battling for the standard as much as it is for critical mass. It doesn't really have much competition, but it does have a bit of a mystique. Adobe is faced not with the challenge of marketing Adobe Acrobat as the best of its kind, but with making more users aware of Acrobat and PDF capabilities. No standard is developed overnight. It takes time and nurturing for the computer public to catch on. After all, AOL was out there long before Netscape Navigator, and both were preceded many years by CompuServe. DOS users balked at Microsoft Windows versions 1 and 2, and even Photoshop had its challenges with PixelPaint and Aldus PhotoStyler. With Adobe Acrobat, the development of version 1.0 and Acrobat Pro were more confining than the vast opportunities available in version 4. Now with advanced plug-in architecture, the capability to output to high-resolution devices and create color separations, and Web integration, the future of Adobe Acrobat looks bright for all markets, including publishing.

The challenge of Adobe Acrobat is due to the vast number of solutions it provides. If you use a word processor, your task is to create and edit text. If you use Photoshop, your world is concentrated on image editing. If you surf the Net, a browser is your solution. With Acrobat, the appeal is not only to a document developer, artist, or Web surfer, but to the whole computing population on this planet! Almost everything you do on a computer can benefit from PDF development. As a result, Adobe has focused its marketing efforts on campaigns for solutions to vertical markets, and several of them at that. Because Adobe Systems is a company that has its primary concentration in publishing, it's no surprise that some of the focus for marketing PDF workflows has been in that industry.

Adobe Acrobat in the publishing market

Associated Press, as well as many newspaper chains and affiliates around the world, has adopted PDF as a standard. If you submit a display ad to AP, you better know how to create a proper PDF file. PDF was a logical choice for publishing giants. Anyone who serves the digital imaging industry will tell you fonts and image links are major problems. With a kazillion fonts and images once not transmittable with layout documents, newspapers and magazines have longed for a standard. In these environments, PDF rules. With font and image embedding as well as file compression, one nightmare of the publishing world has almost vanished.

End users aren't the only factions of the communications industry who have embraced PDF. In 1997, AGFA introduced PDF as the standard in their advanced RIP and server architecture. AGFA has built a multimillion dollar system around PDF and sees it as the new standard for imaging. Solutions for color separations, OPI comments, and impositions have all been added to PDF workflow. In addition to

AGFA, other high-end device manufacturers such as Scitex, Harlequinn, and Linotype-Hell have all provided integrated PDF workflow in their systems.

In the publishing industry, PDF is becoming a standard, and it won't be long before all graphic designers and advertising artists will be required to submit PDF-only files to commercial printers and imaging centers. Other industries also seem to be moving in the direction of a PDF standard. Government offices are embracing PDF as a format for distributing documents. For example, the IRS posts all its tax forms in PDF format, so that now you need not run down to the post office to find forms for tax preparation. (However, you may still want to have Adobe Reader on hand well in advance of tax time. On April 14, 1998, over 190,000 people pounded Adobe's Web site to download Acrobat Reader.) In addition to the government's adoption of the PDF standard, Web integration is rapidly growing for display of PDF and file downloads where document integrity is important. Many software manufacturers are choosing PDF as the format to use for online guides, help files, and technical documents on CD-ROMs containing new software releases.

If you're wondering whether to choose PDF as a standard in your office, be assured others *are* adopting it as their standard. Reaching critical mass may take more time, but the PDF model should continue to grow as a standard for many different markets.

PDF workflow solutions

To fully take advantage of Adobe Acrobat, one needs to think in terms of solutions to digital file problems. I don't know about you, but I always tend to spend a significant part of my day searching through mountains of paper on my desk, file cabinets, and around the office at key locations where more paper piles exist. If all the telemarketers and senders of junk mail could simply send out PDF files, I could easily find what I want when I decide to make a purchase. Unfortunately, I don't have much control over the junk mail, but I do where digital files are concerned.

Office solutions

Office administration is an easy target for PDF workflow solutions. Think about the management meeting where people are discussing an employee policy that was delivered via memo to staff. If you have a well-organized system in place, the memo is probably located in a logical spot in the personnel policies manual. If not, you begin searching. The same holds true for the display ad for that charity event last year, the memo from the president, the consumer satisfaction survey conducted two years ago, the last CAD drawing of a new widget, or almost any form of data or correspondence that originated on someone's computer.

Take Widget Company as an example. The company consists of four departments, administration, accounting, marketing, and production, as illustrated in Figure 1-7. All the departments use computers and specific software. In some cases, off-the-shelf software is used, and in other cases, vertical market applications are used. All the computers are networked to a single server.

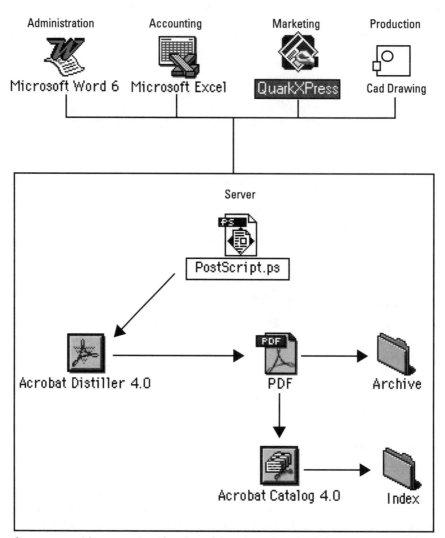

Figure 1-7: Widget Company has four departments networked to a single server. The departments print PostScript files to a server running Acrobat Distiller and Acrobat Catalog. Distiller creates PDF documents, which are then added to the search index.

The administration usually posts memos on the employee bulletin board, but in some cases, a memo may be printed and delivered to all employee mailboxes. A particular memo needs to be retrieved by an employee in production. Because the memo appeared three months prior, it has vanished from the bulletin board and cannot be found among the mountains of paper on the employee's desk.

Fortunately for Widget Company, they have adopted a PDF workflow that requires all employees to archive memos, policies, and procedures to the server in PDF form. The files are printed in PostScript to a hot folder known in Acrobat Distiller terms as a *watched folder* on the server. The server keeps both Acrobat Distiller and Acrobat Catalog operating in the background. When a PostScript file hits a watched folder, it is automatically distilled and placed in an out folder. The out folder files are monitored by the network administration and placed in the archive data folder. Once a file hits the archive data folder, Acrobat Catalog updates the search index to include the new PDF keywords. The production worker invokes a search and finds the memo in question. That employee may review the document online or print the PDF file. In either case, the amount of time to retrieve the information is a fraction of the time it takes to shuffle through those piles of paper.

Office environments can manage documents easily by creating similar workflows. Regardless of the size of your office, a PDF workflow enables you to store and retrieve information in an efficient and cost-effective way.

Publishing solutions

Publishing solutions can begin with office environments and be applied to high-end service centers, publication houses, and all forms of commercial media. In a publishing environment, the art department, design firm, or ad agency creates a document for advertising or a campaign. The material can be a display ad, brochure, catalog, or any communication piece that will eventually be printed on press. The final document will ultimately be created in a layout application such as Adobe PageMaker or QuarkXPress. Once the document is created and approved, the file can be printed to disk as a PostScript file, ready to be distilled in Acrobat Distiller for PDF file creation. Distiller affords you many choices for font embedding, compression, and sampling methods for graphic images. For prepress purposes, the sampling and compression will be different from requirements for Web, screen, and various composite color output. Because all the sampling can be controlled in Distiller, PDF files suitable for different purposes can be created from the same PostScript file.

In a traditional prepress workshop, the native files are delivered either to a RIP or OPI server. In a PDF workflow environment, application documents are printed to disk as PostScript files and distilled in Acrobat Distiller, where all OPI comments, job tickets, and prepress instructions are preserved. Figures 1-8 and 1-9 show examples from AGFA and Scitex on prepress workflows designed around PDF.

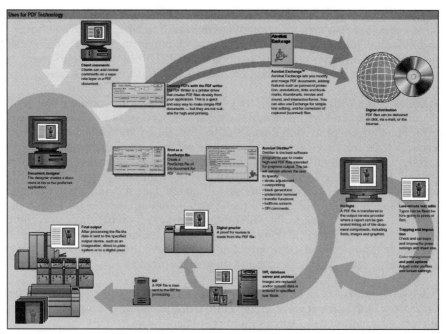

Figure 1-8: The AGFA prepress workflow.

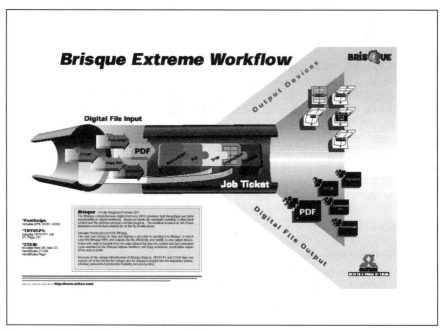

Figure 1-9: The Scitex prepress workflow.

Internet solutions

Document distribution is a major concern for many companies hosting Web sites. Product catalogs, consumer information, new product announcements, company information, and more all need distribution. Almost all these examples are typically produced for print or other viewing. Press releases go to the media, catalogs are distributed to the public, and announcements often occur at trade shows. Original designs for these items are performed in application layout programs. The requirements for the documents that ultimately wind up at a commercial print shop are much larger than would be efficiently used for distribution on the Internet. All those CMYK color files should be in RGB, and the image resolution needs to be reduced from 300 to 72 pixels per inch (ppi). The fonts need to be embedded in the files so other users don't need the same font sets. In a PDF workflow environment, the repurposing of the file for Web content can be automated with Adobe Acrobat. The alternative to repurposing the file in Adobe Acrobat is to go back and manually recreate the files. As you can see, PDF workflows reduce costs and save time.

Summary

✦ Adobe Acrobat is not a single program but rather a suite of programs, including Acrobat Reader, Acrobat 4.0, Acrobat Distiller, Acrobat Catalog, Acrobat Search, Acrobat Scan, and Acrobat Capture.

✦ PDF, short for Portable Document Format, was developed by Adobe Systems and is designed to exchange documents between computers and across computer platforms while maintaining file integrity.

✦ Document repurposing is a term used to describe the process of changing documents created for one purpose to make them suitable for other uses.

✦ PostScript is a page description language used for output to various types of imaging devices — from desktop laser printers to high-end professional devices — and it serves as a standard for the digital imaging industry.

✦ PDF workflows are automated processes used to create PDF documents and traffic jobs commonly found on networks and intranets.

✦ Networks most often include at least one server and one or more clients. Networks enable the exchange, imaging, or transfer of digital data files.

✦ PDF has become a standard document format used in many different industries and is expected to become more of a standard for all document exchange by the end of the century.

✦   ✦   ✦

Viewing and Searching PDF Files

✦ ✦ ✦ ✦

In This Chapter

Viewing PDF files in an Acrobat viewer

Navigating through PDF files

How to use the Find command

The many ways to search PDF documents

✦ ✦ ✦ ✦

If you are one of the many hundreds of thousands of people who have downloaded the Acrobat Reader software from Adobe's Web site (www.adobe.com), then moving around a PDF file might already be familiar to you. If you haven't yet used an Acrobat viewer, you'll want to carefully look over the pages in this chapter to learn how you can navigate a PDF document. If you're a seasoned user, maybe browse a bit to see how to handle preferences, full-screen viewing, and some of the new features introduced in Acrobat 4.0. Regardless of where you are in Acrobat skill, navigating a document is a fundamental task, and the more you know, the faster you can view PDF files.

Viewing and Navigation

Acrobat Reader and Acrobat are both Acrobat viewers. The viewing and navigation tools and commands in both programs are very similar. The Acrobat 4.0 viewer does have a few differences from the Reader viewer, which are examined in this chapter. Like other Adobe applications, Reader and Acrobat offer the user different means to accomplish the same ends. Something as simple as navigating through an open file can be handled through several tools, commands, and methods that achieve the same result.

Viewing tools

When you open a PDF document, you have an opportunity to customize the viewing environment through the use of several tools. These tools are located in the viewer's Command Bar at the top of your monitor or the status bar at the bottom of the Acrobat viewer window.

Note The top of your screen is referred to as the menu bar. In Acrobat Reader and Acrobat, the area containing the tools below the menu names is referred to as the Command Bar. In Acrobat, a vertical Tool Bar also appears, and this is referred to as the Floating Tool Bar. Throughout the remaining chapters, Command Bar and Tool Bar will be used to distinguish the two. Note that Acrobat Reader does not contain a Tool Bar.

The first of many viewing options is available when you open the *Navigation Pane*. To open the Navigation Pane, position the cursor over the third icon (if in Reader) or fourth icon (if in Acrobat) on the top left of the Command Bar, or press F5. Depending on which viewer you use, two or three tabs will appear in the Navigation Pane:

✦ **Page Only:** The document, usually by default, will be viewed without the Navigation Pane opened, as shown in Figure 2-1.

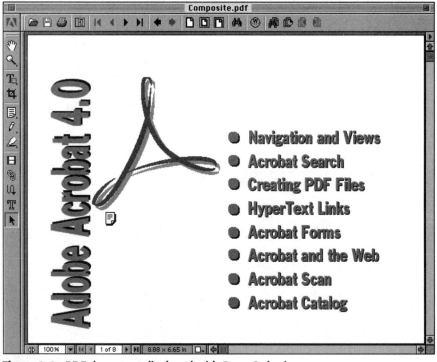

Figure 2-1: PDF document displayed with Page Only view

✦ **Bookmarks and Thumbnails:** In Reader, Bookmarks and Thumbnails tabs appear in the Navigation Pane (see Figure 2-2). The Bookmarks tab will be the front view, and any bookmarks created in the PDF file will be displayed in a list under the tab. A bookmark may take you to another page, another view, or invoke an action when selected.

If thumbnails, which are mini-views of document pages, were created during the development of the PDF file or in Acrobat, they will be displayed on the Thumbnails tab. For both bookmarks and thumbnails, a palette menu can be opened by selecting the small right arrow at the top-right corner of the pane. From the palette menu, a choice for viewing small or large thumbnails is available.

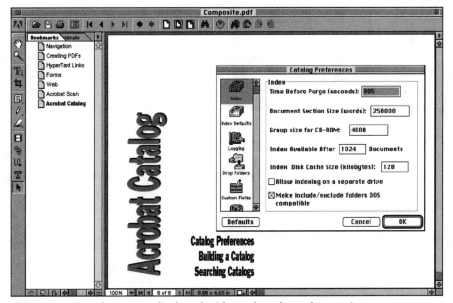

Figure 2-2: PDF document displayed with Bookmarks and Page view

✦ **Bookmarks, Thumbnails, and Annotations:** In Acrobat, the Navigation Pane appears with three tabs: Bookmarks, Thumbnails, and Annotations (see Figure 2-3). By clicking the respective tab name, the contents for the item selected will appear in the foreground. For example, selecting the Annotations tab will display a list of any annotations in the PDF document in the foreground.

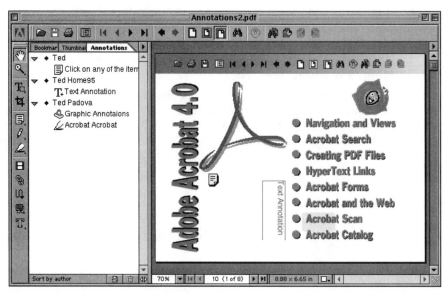

Figure 2-3: PDF document in Acrobat with Bookmarks, Thumbnails, and Annotations tabs appearing in the Navigation Pane. The Annotations tab appears in the foreground.

Tear-away palettes have been introduced in Acrobat 4.0. Depending on how you viewed palettes in your last Acrobat session, the Annotation palette may be detached from the Navigation Pane and viewed separately. Acrobat saves the palette grouping and order as they were last configured when you quit Acrobat. To move a palette away from the pane, you can select the tab and drag it away. Conversely, dragging a palette tab to the pane will place the window within the pane. Click any tab to bring the window forward.

Closing the Navigation Pane can be accomplished with the same actions used to open the pane. Click the Show/Hide Navigation Pane icon in the Command Bar or press F5 to close the pane.

Zooming

As you view an open document, you will often have a need to zoom in and out of the page. Like many other applications, Acrobat viewers provide you with the ability to zoom by use of the Zoom tool. The Zoom tool permits views from 8.33 percent to 1,600 percent of a document. The Zoom tool is selected from the viewer Command Bar in Reader or from the Tool Bar in Acrobat and placed in the document window. Click, and you zoom in on the page. Hold the Option/Alt key down when you click, and the page zooms out.

Zooms can also occur by selecting the magnification button in the status bar. The magnification button is represented by a down arrow. When you select the down arrow and keep the mouse button pressed, a pop-up menu enables you to select from several viewing magnifications. In addition, the zoom percentage readout is editable, as it is in many other Adobe applications. You can edit the zoom percentage by typing in a value within the acceptable range of 8.33 to 1,600 percent.

Like many commands and features in Acrobat, you may choose from several alternatives for viewing at different zoom magnifications. A menu command also provides zooming in and out of your PDF document. When you select View ➪ Zoom To, the Zoom To dialog box will appear, enabling you to enter a zoom value or make any of the same choices available in the status bar pop-up menu (see Figure 2-4). You can press Cmd/Ctrl+M to open the dialog box and bypass the menu selection. It may seem redundant and unnecessary, but Adobe has afforded you the opportunity to use any of the commands or menus to achieve the same results.

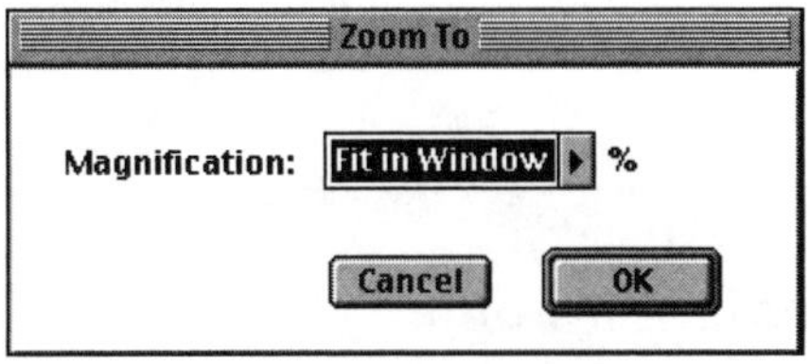

Figure 2-4: The Zoom To dialog box enables the user to specify magnification levels between 9 and 1,600 percent in 1 percent increments.

Note   As of this writing, the Zoom To dialog box will accept values between 9 and 1,600 percent. If you enter a value lower than 9 percent or higher than 1,600 percent, an error dialog box will appear. The warning informs you the zoom needs to be between 12 percent and 1,600 percent. As you can see, the warning message is inconsistent with the acceptable ranges.

Page views

The page views for Actual Size, Fit in Window, and Fit Width are static views you'll want to access frequently when navigating through a PDF document. Acrobat viewers provide several ways to change a page view. As with the Zoom tool, Acrobat viewers include three tools in the Command Bar, as shown in Figure 2-5, for the selection of these views:

✦ **Actual Size:** Displays the PDF page at actual size (that is, a 100 percent view).

✦ **Fit in Window:** Displays the page at maximum size to fit within the viewer window. If the Acrobat viewer window is sized up or down, the Fit in Window view will conform to the viewer window size.

✦ **Fit Width:** The data on a PDF page is displayed horizontally without clipping. If the page is large and data only appears in the center of the page, the page will be zoomed to fit the data and the white space at the page edges will be ignored.

Figure 2-5: Page view icons for Actual Size, Fit in Window, and Fit Width.

Other choices for zoom magnification are also available from the View menu. The View menu enables you to zoom in and zoom out at preset zoom values, or you may use the modifier keys Cmd/Ctrl+– (minus) or Cmd/Ctrl++ (plus) for zooming out or in on the PDF window. These modifier keys have all been changed from earlier versions of Acrobat to be consistent with many other Adobe applications.

As you become familiar with moving around PDF documents, you'll no doubt want to access different views in a much faster manner than moving the mouse cursor and clicking a page tool, selecting a menu item, or clicking the magnification button. Use of modifier keys will let you fly through the page views. For the Acrobat viewers, the first key modifiers you'll want to commit to memory are the page view modifiers, which are listed in Table 2-1.

Table 2-1 Page View Keyboard Modifiers		
View	**Mac**	**Windows**
Fit in Window	Cmd+0 (zero)	Ctrl+0 (zero)
Actual Size	Cmd+1	Ctrl+1
Fit Width	Cmd+2	Ctrl+2
Fit Visible	Cmd+3	Ctrl+3
Full Screen Mode	Cmd+L	Ctrl+L
Zoom in	Cmd++(plus)	Ctrl++ (plus)
Zoom out	Cmd+– (minus)	Ctrl+– (minus)
Zoom To	Cmd+M	Ctrl+M
Show/Hide Navigation Pane	F5	F5
Show/Hide Menu Bar	F7	F7
Show/Hide Command Bar	F8	F8
Show/Hide Tool Bar	F9	F9

The last item in Table 2-1 will toggle displays of the Tool Bar (Acrobat). If you inadvertently hide one of the menu bar items, you'll need to remember how to regain it with the keyboard equivalent. The equivalents for the keystrokes are found in the Window menu. However, when the menu bar is hidden, the only way to bring it back is by using the F7 keystroke.

Note   If you run an application concurrently with Acrobat that also uses the F7 keystroke to enable an action, you may wish to reassign the F7 key in your other application. For example: if you use Corel Capture in Windows, reassign the Capture keystroke to another function key. Acrobat will not always supersede another application's modifier key.

The views you choose will conform to the monitor attached to your computer. If you have a 13-inch monitor, the Fit in Window view for a file will be displayed much smaller than it would be on a 19-inch monitor. Therefore, any PDF file saved with a fixed view of its actual size will appear zoomed in on a small monitor. If you open several PDF files successively, you may want to change views immediately to find the information you want. Using the keystrokes on your keyboard will help you quickly establish the view you desire.

Full-screen views

Among other uses, Adobe Acrobat can serve as a slide or presentation program. On-screen presentations have typically been the work of programs such as Microsoft PowerPoint and Adobe Persuasion. Persuasion, which was inherited by Adobe from Aldus Corporation when the companies merged, was updated once by Adobe Systems and then discontinued. Adobe apparently saw no need to manufacture two programs that closely resemble each other. Although Acrobat lacks many features of a dedicated presentation application such as templates, an outliner, full-featured text editing, and page size defaults for film recorders, it can be effective in creating presentations and output to film recorders. As a screen presentation application, Acrobat can be used in Full Screen mode with automated slide navigation and displays that hide tools and menu bars.

To enter Full Screen mode to display a PDF document at full-screen size, select View ➪ Full Screen or press Cmd/Ctrl+L. When Full Screen is selected, the menu bar, Acrobat viewer Command Bar, and Acrobat Tool Bar will be hidden. Acrobat's different viewing choices can be changed in preferences dialog boxes. If you select File ➪ Preferences ➪ Full Screen, the Full Screen Preferences dialog box shown in Figure 2-6 will open, enabling you to control the behavior of the Full Screen view.

Full Screen Preferences

Navigation
☐ Advance every: [5] Seconds
☐ Advance On Any Click
☐ Loop After Last Page
☑ Escape Key Exits

Appearance
Background Color: [Black ▲▼]
Default Transition: [Replace ▲▼]
Mouse Cursor: [Hidden After Delay ▲▼]
Zoom To: [Largest Intersection ▲▼]
Center To: [Main ▲▼]

[Cancel] [OK]

Figure 2-6: The Full Screen Preferences dialog box enables you to control the behavior of the Full Screen view.

Controls in this dialog box include the following:

✦ **Advance Every *N* Seconds:** For auto-advancing of PDF pages, you can enter a value between 1 and 60 seconds. The Acrobat viewer will advance to the next page after the specified delay time passes.

✦ **Advance On Any Click:** When enabled by clicking the check box, the viewer will advance to the next page when the mouse button is clicked.

✦ **Loop After Last Page:** When the check box is disabled, the Acrobat viewer will stop at the last page. If enabled, the first page will appear upon advancing after the last page, and the viewer will continue to loop through the document for another cycle.

✦ **Escape Key Exits:** You should plan on keeping this check box enabled at all times. Pressing the Esc key will return you to a page view and exit the Full Screen mode. If the check box is disabled, you need to remember other key equivalents to exit Full Screen view. On the Macintosh, you can press Cmd+. (period) or Cmd+L. In Windows, you need to press Ctrl+L.

✦ **Background Color:** You can choose from several preset color values or select the Custom option from the pop-up menu to gain access to your system color palette. When the system color palette is opened, you can choose any available color for the background. The background will appear at the edges of the PDF page when in Full Screen view. Typically, the background color appears on the left and right sides of the PDF page.

✦ **Default Transition:** As you navigate through PDF pages in Full Screen view, the pages can be viewed with transition effects such as dissolves, wipes, venetian blinds, and so on. A number of transition choices appear on the pop-up menu, shown in Figure 2-7. If you select No Transition from the menu choices, the pages will advance without transition effects.

```
  Blinds Horizontal
  Blinds Vertical
  Box In
  Box Out
  Dissolve
  Glitter Down
  Glitter Right
  Glitter Right-Down
  No Transition
✓ Random Transition
  Replace
  Split Horizontal In
  Split Horizontal Out
  Split Vertical In
  Split Vertical Out
  Wipe Down
  Wipe Left
  Wipe Right
  Wipe Up
```

Figure 2-7: The Default Transition pop-up menu enables you to choose from many preset page transition effects that can be viewed in Full Screen mode.

✦ **Mouse Cursor:** The Mouse Cursor pop-up menu provides three choices for altering cursor behavior. You can select Always Visible, which will keep the mouse cursor in view as the pages are advanced; Always Hidden, which hides the mouse cursor upon entering Full Screen view and keeps it hidden when pages are advanced; or Hidden After Delay, which hides the mouse cursor during the transition and will reappear when you move the cursor across the screen.

Note

Full Screen view preferences are the same for both Acrobat viewers.

Full Screen mode is obviously designed for presentations and automated viewing of PDF files. You can display a PDF on an overhead projection screen to facilitate the delivery of a presentation. Or, you can save PDF files from Acrobat complete with automatic delivery of the Full Screen mode — together with transitions and automatic advances. You can also save the PDF document to an external media cartridge or CD-ROM and distribute it to other users to view the document in Acrobat Reader.

More page views

The default display in an Acrobat viewer is restricted to viewing one page at a time. You can fit the whole page in the viewing window, zoom in, or change to the Fit Width or Actual Size views, which continues to display a single page. In addition to single-page views, Acrobat viewers enable you to see your PDF pages in a continuous page display or side by side, much like you would see pages displayed in a layout program. To access these views, use the display choices in the status bar or choose the appropriate menu commands. The choices include the following:

✦ **Single Page:** The Single Page command can be selected from the status bar pop-up menu or by selecting View ➪ Single Page. This is the default view when you open a PDF file. The Single Page has hard breaks and will only display the selected page in the viewer window. If you scroll pages, the next page snaps to view within the Reader or Acrobat window (see Figure 2-8).

✦ **Continuous:** The Continuous command can be selected from the status bar pop-up menu or by choosing View ➪ Continuous. This display will show the current PDF page and any partial pages preceding or following the current page, with no hard breaks between pages (see Figure 2-9).

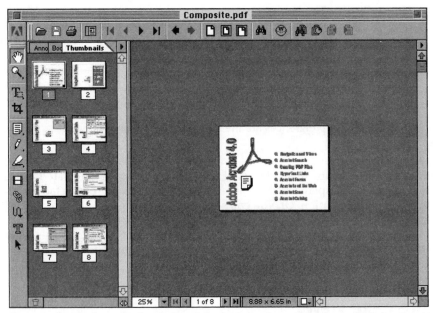

Figure 2-8: Single Page view is the default view when you open a PDF document.

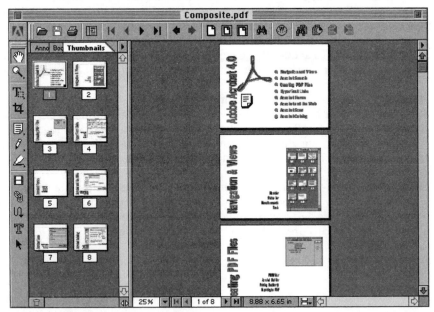

Figure 2-9: Continuous view displays the current PDF page and any partial pages before or after it.

✦ **Continuous—Facing Pages:** The Continuous—Facing Pages command can be selected from the status bar pop-up menu or by choosing View ⇨ Continuous. There is no keyboard modifier to enable this view. The display will show continuous facing pages, similar to what you might see in programs such as QuarkXPress, Adobe PageMaker, Microsoft Word, Claris Works, and so on (see Figure 2-10).

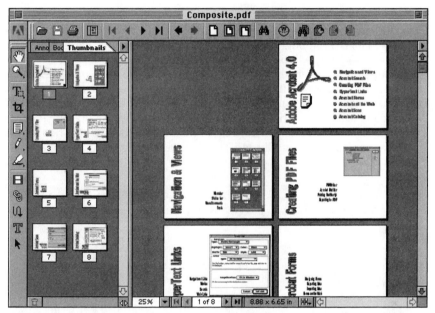

Figure 2-10: Continuous—Facing Pages view displays continuous facing pages.

At times the Continuous view can be helpful when searching through PDF files to find graphic images. However, you can find text in much easier ways as shall be demonstrated a little later in this chapter. The Continuous—Facing Pages view provides a much larger display than does the Thumbnail view, even on smaller monitors. At times, this view can be quite helpful. Changing the page display only affects your monitor view. If you decide to print the PDF file, the printed pages will consist of single-page printouts, just as you see in the Single Page view.

Multiple document viewing

More views are possible when you have several documents open in an Acrobat viewer. By default, the maximum number of PDFs that can be open are twenty. I talk about changing the maximum number of open documents when preferences are discussed, but for now, let's look at how you can view multiple PDFs on your monitor screen.

When you open a PDF file and then open a second PDF, the second file hides the first document you opened. If several more PDFs are opened, the last opened document will hide all the others. Fortunately, the Acrobat viewers have made it easy for you to select a given document from a nest of open files. If you select the Window menu, all open documents will appear by name in a list at the bottom of the menu. The Acrobat viewer will place a check mark beside the current active document. As you close files, they will disappear from the menu.

The Window menu affords you some other viewing options, which include Cascade, Tile Vertically, and Tile Horizontally. Cascading windows will display the open documents overlapping so you can see the right edges of each of the open files (see Figure 2-11). They will be offset from each other on your screen . You can easily click any of the document windows to make that file the active document. When you select Window ➪ Tile ➪ Horizontally, the PDF files will appear in individual windows stacked on top of each other, as shown in Figure 2-12. Window ➪ Tile ➪ Vertically will display the PDF files in individual windows placed side by side, as shown in Figure 2-13. If you have more than three documents open at one time, the display for Tile Horizontally and Tile Vertically will appear identical.

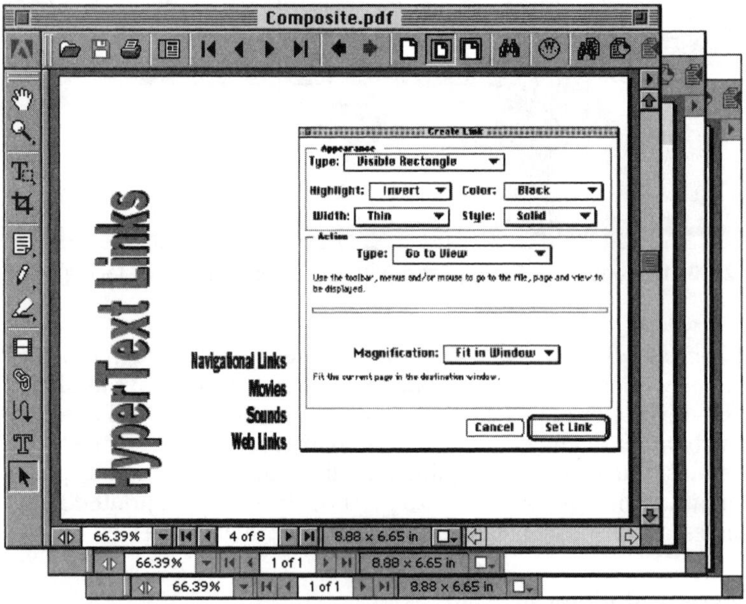

Figure 2-11: Three open documents in Cascade view

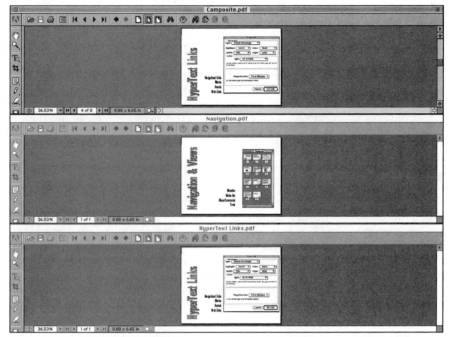

Figure 2-12: The same three documents tiled horizontally

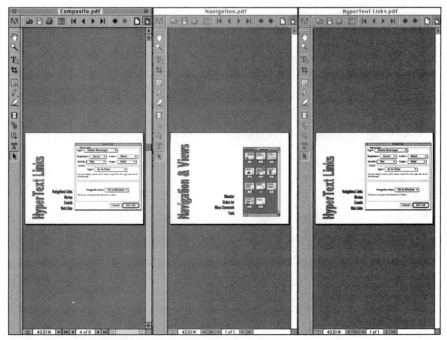

Figure 2-13: The three files tiled vertically

Navigating PDF Documents

Page navigation in an Acrobat viewer is handled by several means. You can scroll pages with tools and keystrokes, click hypertext links, and use dialog boxes to move through a web of documents and individual pages. Depending on how a PDF file is created and edited, you can also follow Web links and articles through different sections of a document. Acrobat viewers have many navigation controls. In this chapter, you first take a look at some of the navigation tools and then explore hypertext links and Web links.

Navigation tools

Navigation tools are located in the Acrobat viewer Command Bar and in the viewer status bar. As in many other applications, icons for these navigation tools resemble the buttons on VCRs, CD players, and tape recorders, which when pressed move you through the media (see Figures 2-14 and 2-15). For the most part, the icons will be familiar if you've ever dealt with video frames in applications on your computer or worked a VCR. There are a few subtle differences in the Acrobat viewer navigation tools, however, so let's take a look at each of the navigation items.

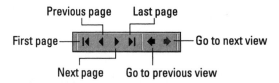

Figure 2-14: The Acrobat viewer Command Bar navigation tools

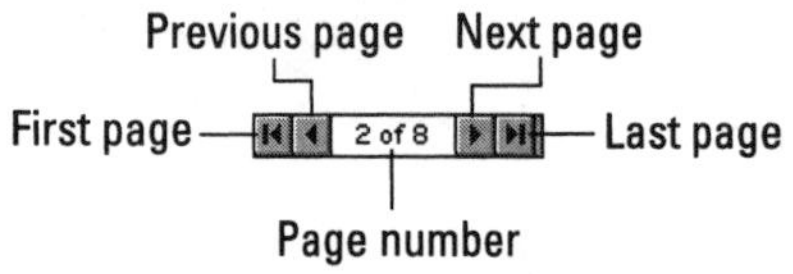

Figure 2-15: The Acrobat viewer status bar navigation tools

The tools for navigation in an Acrobat viewer include the following:

✦ **First Page:** In the current active document window, this tool returns you to the first page in the file.

✦ **Previous Page:** Used to move back one page at a time.

✦ **Next Page:** Used to scroll forward through pages one page at a time.

✦ **Last Page:** Moves you to the last page in the document.

✦ **Go to Previous View:** Returns you to the last view displayed on your screen. Whereas the four preceding tools are limited to navigation through a single open document, the Go to Previous View tool will return you to the previous view even if the last view was another file. Go to Previous View is only found in the viewer Command Bar.

✦ **Go to Next View:** Behaves like the Go to Previous View Tool, except it moves in a forward direction. Use of the Go to Previous View and Go to Next View tools can be especially helpful when navigating links that open and close documents. The Next and Last Page tools will confine you to the active document, whereas these last two tools will retrace your navigation steps regardless of how many files you have viewed. Go to Next View is only found in the viewer Command Bar.

✦ **Page *n* of *n*:** The display only appears in the viewer status bar. It is editable, so you can delete the current page number and enter a new value. When you press the Return or Enter key, the Acrobat viewer will jump to the page number you entered in the field box.

If you select the View menu, the same navigation choices are available as menu commands, as shown in Figure 2-16.

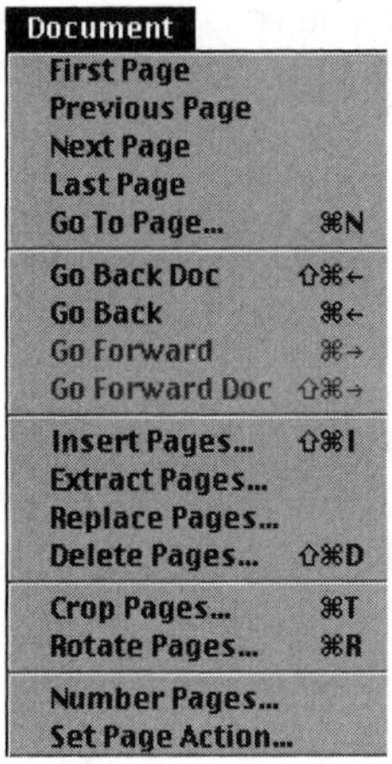

Figure 2-16: The Document menu in Acrobat

Notice in Figure 2-16 the same six navigation items are listed among the menu commands. Also notice each of these navigation items have corresponding keystroke equivalents that will produce the same action. Keystroke modifiers for page navigation are listed in Table 2-2.

Table 2-2
Page Navigation Keyboard Modifiers

Navigation	Mac	Windows
First Page	Home	Ctrl+Shift+PgUp or Home
Previous Page	PgUp or up arrow*	Ctrl+PgUp or up arrow*
Next Page	PgDn or down arrow*	Ctrl+PgDn or down arrow*
Last Page	End	Ctrl+Shift+PgDn or End
Go To Page	Cmd+N	Ctrl+N
Go Back to Doc	Cmd+Shift+left arrow	Ctrl+Shift+left arrow
Go Back	Cmd+left arrow	Ctrl+left arrow
Go Forward	Cmd+right arrow	Ctrl+right arrow
Go Forward to Doc	Cmd+Shift+right arrow	Ctrl+Shift+right arrow

* When the view is set to Fit in Window, the keystrokes will move you to the next or previous page. When partial page views appear, the keystrokes will scroll the page.

The Go to Page (Cmd/Ctrl+N) command opens a dialog box and enables you to edit the page number to visit, just as you would in the status bar field box. If you select Document ➪ Go To Page, a dialog box appears that enables you to enter the value of the specific page. If you want to move to page 199 in a 299 page document, press Cmd/Ctrl+N or select Document ➪ Go To Page, and enter 199 in the dialog box.

Context-sensitive menus

Context-sensitive menus provide another means of navigation. You bring up context-sensitive menus by pressing the Control key and clicking the mouse button on a Macintosh or by clicking the right mouse button in Windows (see Figure 2-17). Context-sensitive menus are specific to a tool. If you have the Hand tool selected and you Control+click (Mac) or right-click (Windows), a pop-up menu appears that enables you to navigate through the PDF document. Additionally, you can use this menu to change page views or invoke the Find command to perform a search. The latter is discussed later in this chapter.

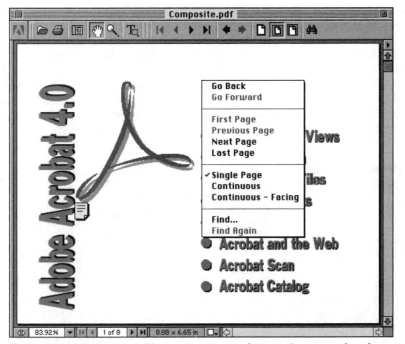

Figure 2-17: Context-sensitive menus appear by pressing Control and clicking (Mac) or by clicking the right mouse button (Windows). Menu options change according to the tool used.

Scrolling

Anyone familiar with window environments is no stranger to scrolling. Fortunately, this is a standard for how scrollbars should behave among computer platforms and among various computer software manufacturers. Page scrolling works the same in an Acrobat viewer as it does in Microsoft Word (or any other Microsoft product for that matter), or any illustration, layout, or host of other applications you may be familiar with. Drag the elevator bar up and down or left to right to move the document within the active window. Click between the elevator bar and the top or bottom of the scrolling column to jump a page segment. The arrow icons at the top, bottom, left, and right sides allow you to move in smaller segments in the respective directions.

Note   When dragging the elevator bar up or down in a multiple-page PDF file, a small pop-up window will display a page number associated with the elevator bar position as well as the total number of pages in the document. The readout will be in the form of "*n* of *n* pages." The first number will dynamically change as the elevator bar is moved.

Windows users will find an Acrobat viewer opens in the same manner they would expect any other application on their computers to open. By default, the open application occupies the entire monitor view. When you size the application window, the PDF document will be sized within the application window. The application window will appear on top of a background that prevents your view of the desktop or concurrent running applications. This behavior is similar to many other Windows applications. Some programs, such as Adobe Photoshop, enable you to size the application window, which enables you to see your desktop view or a concurrently running application (see Figure 2-18).

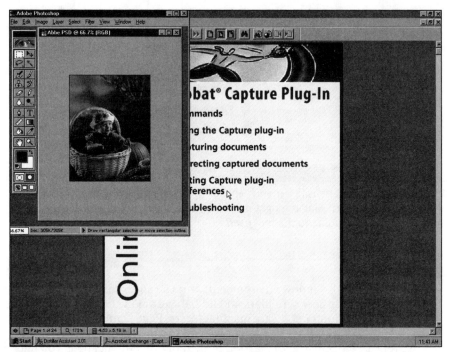

Figure 2-18: Some programs, such as Adobe Photoshop, enable you to size the application window to reveal other application windows.

Macintosh users will find the appearance of the Acrobat viewers similar to layout applications with pasteboards. You can size the pasteboard down and reveal other application windows or the desktop.

Regardless of which platform you work with, some views in an Acrobat viewer maintain the same relative position within the application window as you size them. For example, if you select View ➪ Fit in Window and size the application window down, the page will be sized within the new window dimensions. The same holds true for Fit Width and Fit Visible. As an application window is sized, you'll find the keystroke navigation and scrolling to work the same as it does in a full-size window.

HyperText links

It seems like eons ago since Apple Fellow Bill Atkinson developed a great application called HyperCard. HyperCard introduced navigation buttons, referred to as hypertext references, you could place on a card in a document. These buttons provided dynamic navigation through a series of cards or files and also provided actions executable for all kinds of commands. HyperCard was a Mac product, and even though there were some attempts at reproducing the application for Windows in the early days, it never quite made it in the Windows camp.

I suppose it's easy for us armchair software critics to talk about the past and criticize companies for mistakes made in marketing, production, and technology. We could really bash IBM and Xerox for blowing it in the computer world. Imagine if Xerox PARC got all those wonderful new developments to market or IBM burned in a little more proprietary code in ROM when they manufactured the PC? We would have an IBM and Xerox world, and Microsoft would be a small development company catering to both. Heck, even PostScript would be part of Xerox and Chuck Geschke and John Warnock might still be working there.

One of the big mistakes Apple made was not advancing HyperCard to real-world publishing. Bill Atkinson, with great ingenuity, paved the way with MacPaint and subsequently HyperCard. Unfortunately, Bill was a pixel guy and never got beyond those early developments to what publishers really needed. In the early HyperCard days, I remember begging Bill and the gang to just let me use a few PostScript fonts with the product. If Apple had continued with some foresight and pushed the development of HyperCard in the direction of publishing along with multimedia, Danny Goodman would be your author instead of me, and this book would be the *HyperCard Bible*. HyperCard could have been developed to do all the things Acrobat does, and it could have been the basis for all Web browsers.

I won't dwell anymore on the mistakes, for Apple did indeed bring the technology of hypertext to the masses. It began with HyperCard and subsequently became part of many other applications, particularly in the multimedia market. The introduction of hypertext was a vision by many to explore new methods for searching for knowledge. In a traditional learning world, we explore knowledge in a linear fashion. Reading a novel is linear. We start at the first page and read through each page sequentially. In a hypertext world, we click buttons to go wherever we desire — exploring the facts according to our interests. The Internet is probably the greatest manifestation of hypertext usage we have today. Imagine what it would be like if hypertext wasn't around, and we had to navigate the Net in a linear fashion. Let's face it — Zuma would never have gotten a single hit!

In an Acrobat viewer, hypertext references enable you to move around the PDF or many PDFs much like surfing the Net. You've probably become so accustomed to clicking buttons on your desktop computer that the navigation is almost commonplace and needs little instruction.

Buttons

Hypertext references, or *buttons,* are easily identified in a PDF document. As you move the mouse cursor around the document window, a hand icon with the forefinger pointing upward will be displayed as the cursor is positioned over a button. You click, and presto!—the action associated with the link is executed. Links can be made for a number of different actions in a PDF file, some of which include the following:

✦ **Views:** A link can be made to any of the views discussed in the preceding pages. You can click a button and zoom in or out of a page.

✦ **Pages:** Links can be made to another page in a PDF file or another PDF document.

✦ **Bookmarks:** A bookmark is a hypertext reference taking you to a page, a view, or another PDF document, or invoking a page action.

✦ **Destinations:** You can set destinations within a PDF document or between PDF documents and have them listed in a palette. Click a destination, and it will take you to the page associated with the link. Unlike bookmarks, destinations can be sorted in the Destinations palette by name or page numbers.

✦ **Thumbnails:** Thumbnails are also hypertext references and can navigate your view to the thumbnail selected within a PDF file.

✦ **Annotations:** Annotations are also links. When you create annotations in a document, they will be listed in the Annotations palette in Acrobat. Double-clicking the annotation name in the palette will take you to the page where the annotation exists.

✦ **Execute a menu item:** A link can be made to execute almost all the commands on menus.

✦ **Import data:** A link can be made to import data in an Acrobat form. This type of link would be limited to Acrobat, as you cannot import data into Acrobat Reader.

✦ **Play a movie:** Links can exist to movie files. When you click a movie frame, the movie will play.

✦ **Sounds:** A link can be made to a sound file. When executed, the sound will play.

✦ **Read an article:** A link can be made within an article. You can navigate through an article and follow the article easily through a PDF file. This type of link corresponds to a common feature in newsletters and magazines, where a story begins on page 1 and continues on page 4, and the reader is given a reference to the page on which the story continues.

✦ **Reset a form:** Acrobat provides great opportunity with forms development, as discussed in Chapter 11. You can click a link in a form document to reset the form, which clears all previous data.

✦ **Show and hide fields:** Once again in forms, you can use a link to display or hide a data field.

✦ **Submit a form:** Also with forms, you can use a button to submit form data to a Web server for posting on a Web site.

✦ **World Wide Web link:** A link can be made to a Uniform Resource Locator (URL), which will open your browser window and connect you to the specified URL.

✦ **JavaScript actions:** A link can invoke a JavaScript routine from within a form field, a link, a bookmark, or a page action.

Cross-document links

A button linking one PDF document to another is a known as a *cross-document link*. When you click a button that opens a second document, by default your original document will close and the second document will open. This was a great new feature when Acrobat 3 was introduced. In earlier versions of Acrobat, when additional documents opened, you had all these open documents to deal with. Whether a document closes when a link to another document is executed is determined in the Acrobat viewer preferences. When you select File ⇨ Preferences ⇨ General, the General Preferences dialog box opens, enabling you to determine how cross-document linking will be handled (see Figure 2-19).

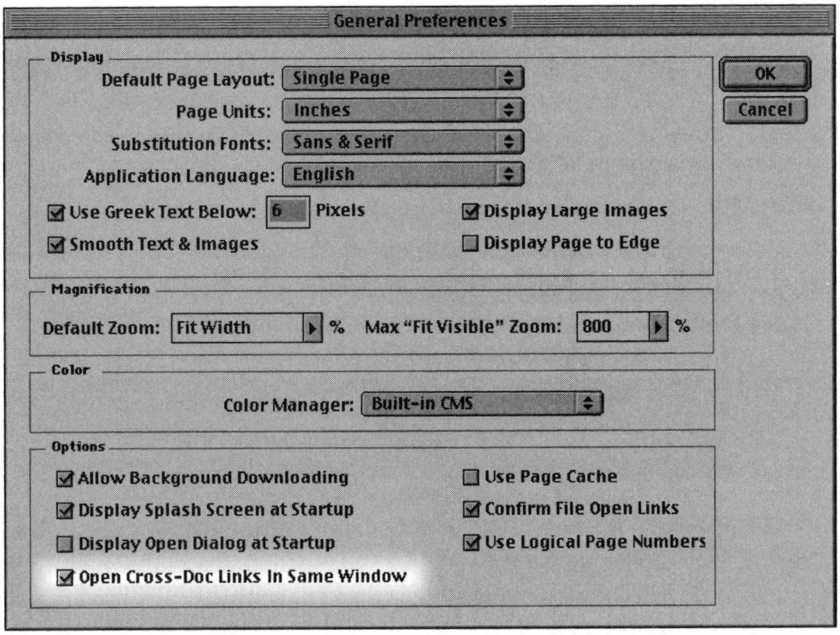

Figure 2-19: The General Preferences dialog box enables you to control the behavior of cross-document linking.

In Figure 2-19, the Open Cross-Doc Links In Same Window item is enabled. When the item is enabled, every time you click a button that opens another PDF file, the document containing the button will close. Disabling this button will keep all documents open. You can explore the differences in viewing PDFs with cross-document links by following a few sequential steps:

STEPS: Cross-document Linking

1. **Select File ➪ Preferences ➪ General** in an Acrobat viewer. Verify the Open Cross-Doc Links In Same Window option in the General Preferences dialog box has a check mark beside it. If it does not, click the check box.

2. **Select File ➪ Open.** For this exercise, you need a PDF document with a button or buttons that are used to open a second PDF file. If you do not have such a document, use the CD accompanying this book. Open the Samples folder and then the MoviePitch folder. Open the file entitled START.PDF.

3. **Click the right arrow appearing in the lower-right corner of the document window.** The START.PDF document will close and a file titled Menu.pdf will open.

4. **Select Window on the menu bar to reveal its pull-down menu.** At the bottom of the menu will be a list of all open files. You'll notice only the Menu.pdf file is listed among the menu items.

5. **Click the close button in the top-left corner (Mac) or the top-right corner (Windows) of the document window.**

6. **Select File ➪ Preferences ➪ General.** The General Preferences dialog box will appear.

7. **Disable the Open Cross-Doc Links In Same Window option.** Click the check box to disable the item. You'll notice the check mark disappear.

8. **Select File ➪ Open.** Open the START.PDF document.

9. **Click the arrow in the lower-right corner.** The Menu.pdf file will open.

10. **Select Window on the menu bar to reveal its pull-down menu.** You will notice the original file is open as well as the second file.

In this example the preference setting was immediately changed without the need for quitting the application. Many of the Acrobat viewer preferences can be changed without needing to quit the program and relaunch it for the new preferences to take effect.

The preference setting for cross-document links will be important to you when creating PDF files. By having files close upon the opening of additional files, the end user will become less confused about following a navigation sequence. Keep in mind the cross-document preference is only effective when using hypertext links. If you elect to select File ➪ Open and open another document while a PDF is in view, opening the second document will not close the original file.

Bookmark links

Earlier in this chapter, I showed you a list of bookmarks in the Navigation Pane (refer back to Figure 2-2). Each of these bookmark items are also hypertext links. Bookmark links are similar to button links in that they are created and can assume the same attributes. Most often bookmarks will be navigational items for finding sections or headings in a given PDF file.

To select a bookmark, move the cursor to the bookmark in question and click. Notice the bookmark text becomes underlined when the cursor is placed over that bookmark in the Navigation Pane. Acrobat informs you which bookmark will be used by displaying a line under the text. The action associated with the bookmark will be applied when the mouse button is clicked.

Bookmarks have an associated palette menu that is displayed when you click the right pointing arrow located in the top-right corner of the Navigation Pane, as shown in Figures 2-20 (Acrobat) and 2-21 (Reader). From the palette menu, you can make selections for viewing bookmarks. Depending on whether you use Reader or Acrobat, the number of options will differ.

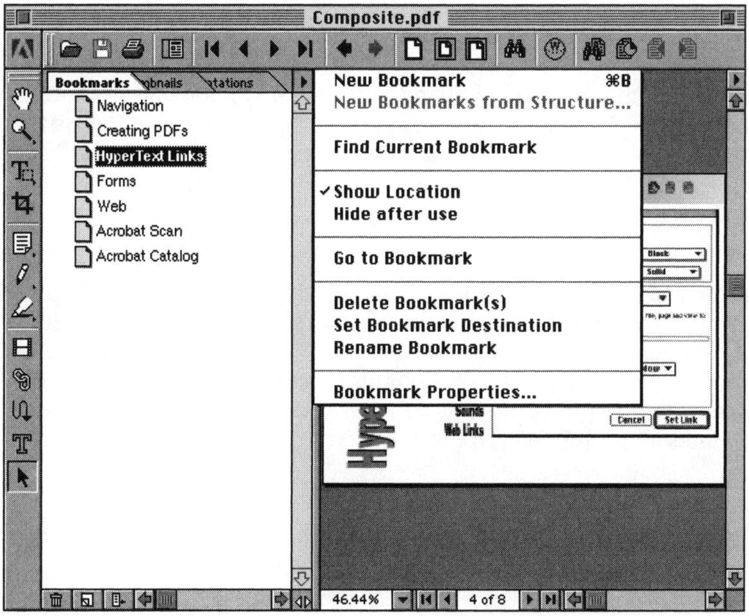

Figure 2-20: Bookmarks palette menu options viewed from Acrobat

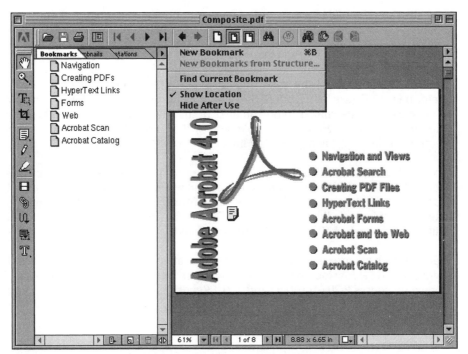

Figure 2-21: Bookmarks palette menu options viewed from Acrobat Reader

I cover bookmarks in much more detail in Chapter 9. It is important to note now, however, that many of the floating palettes in Acrobat have palette menus that make additional options available to you. If you've upgraded from an earlier version of Acrobat to version 4.0, the palette menus will be new to you.

Thumbnails

Thumbnails can also be viewed in the left column of the open PDF file. Typically thumbnails, which are mini-representations of pages, enable you to quickly see page content. Thumbnails are also hypertext links. When you click a thumbnail, the page view will change to the page corresponding to that thumbnail. Unlike buttons and bookmarks, you don't need to create the link items. The Acrobat viewer automatically links all thumbnails to their respective pages.

Like bookmarks, thumbnails also use a palette menu to provide more options. And, like bookmarks, there are many more options available to you in Acrobat than in Reader.

Annotations

Annotations have been greatly expanded in Acrobat 4.0. In addition to Notes, you can have many other kinds of annotations within a PDF file. In Acrobat, you can see all the types of annotations used in a given PDF document by viewing the Annotations palette (see Figure 2-22). If your Navigation Pane does not display a list of annotation types, select Window ⇨ Show Annotations.

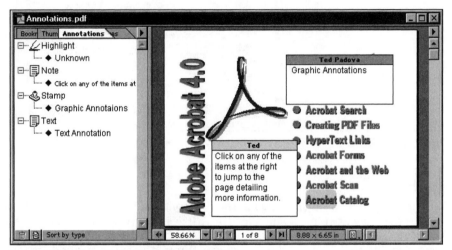

Figure 2-22: Annotations viewed in Acrobat

Don't forget the palette menu. Like other palettes, the Annotations palette also uses a palette menu for other options. A more complete discussion on annotations is covered in Chapter 8.

Signatures

Signatures are a new feature available only in Acrobat 4.0 for Windows. Digital signature fields can be created for a PDF document or a form field with a signature and printable appearance of the field data. In Windows, you have available a palette for signatures. Any signature created in the document will be listed in the palette, as shown in Figure 2-23. More about signatures and how they are created and used is covered later in Chapter 8.

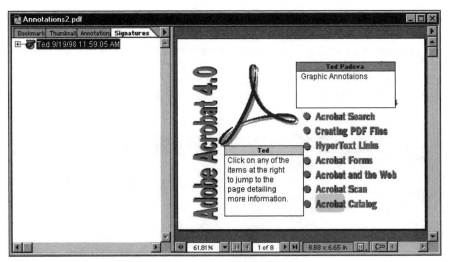

Figure 2-23: Signatures viewed in Acrobat in Windows

Articles

Yet another palette for displaying information contained in a PDF file lists all the articles that may exist in a document. The Articles palette is accessed by selecting Window ⇨ Show Articles in both Reader and Acrobat. Article threads can be created in files to help the end user navigate through a contiguous body of text or through connections to noncontiguous text (similar to what you may see reading a newspaper or magazine, where a reference indicates an article is continued on another page).

In Acrobat or Reader, following an article is much easier than in printed copy, as you can click the last column on a given page and jump to the next page where the article continues. When you open the Articles palette, a list of articles contained in the PDF will be displayed. If you wish to have the Articles palette included as a tab in the Navigation Pane, click and drag the tab to the open pane. When you release the mouse button, the Article palette will become another tab in the pane. Selecting the tab will bring the palette forward to display any listed articles.

Destinations

At first it may seem that destinations have little difference from bookmarks. Though they are similar, the destinations feature enables you to specify any destination and give it a name. A destination name can then be identified within a document or paragraph where specified. The advantage over bookmarks comes with the capability to sort destinations by name or page number, as shown in Figure 2-24. Once identified with a destination name, a paragraph or page can be moved to any location and still be found by invoking the link action.

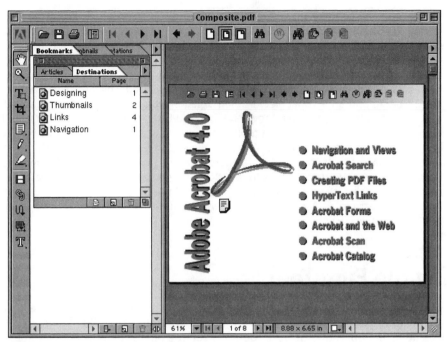

Figure 2-24: Destinations viewed in Acrobat.

World Wide Web links

If you're not a Web enthusiast, and you're sick and tired of the mere mention of Web issues with every application you purchase, hold on — Acrobat's interaction with the Web is entirely different from that of other applications that try to appeal to all people. Personally, I think it's pretty ridiculous to put HTML hooks in layout and illustrations programs, as there are so many better applications out there for Web publishing than such programs. But with Acrobat, we have another animal. It's the one solution that indeed serves you well by being all things for all purposes — well, at least for document viewing and exchanges.

It's hard to talk about any kind of link without talking about the Web. After all, the Web *is* link mania. Therefore, it's no surprise that Acrobat has the additional capability to connect you to a Web site by the simple click of a button. When you encounter a Web link, Acrobat provides you some immediate feedback that a Web link will be executed before you click the mouse button. As the cursor is positioned over a Web link, a small *w* appears inside the hand icon. Additionally, the Tool Tip display will indicate the URL you are about to launch when you click the mouse button. When you click the mouse button on a Web link, Acrobat will launch your Web browser and find the URL associated with the link. Acrobat will remain open in the background as the Web browser appears and the Web page in question is loaded. If you have limited memory, be certain to not select a Web link without sufficient memory to keep your Acrobat viewer and your Web browser open at the same time.

Tip If you don't have sufficient memory to select a Web link and keep both the Browser and an Acrobat viewer open together, you can copy and paste the URL from Acrobat to your Web browser. When the URL is identified in text in the PDF window, select the Text Select tool in the Acrobat Tool Bar in Acrobat or Text Select tool in the Command Bar in Acrobat Reader. Drag across the text. Select Edit ⇨ Copy and copy the text to the clipboard. Quit the Acrobat viewer and launch your Web browser. Paste the text into the URL Location field. Users of earlier versions of Acrobat will note no modifier key is required to select the text. When you use the Text Select tool in Acrobat 4.0, the viewer assumes you wish to edit text and not invoke a link action.

Using the Find Tool

Before getting into the specifics of the Find tool, let's look at the difference between finding information versus searching for information in a PDF file. When you execute a find operation in an Acrobat viewer, the operation is performed on an open document. You can look through the open file to find keywords you enter in a dialog box. A search, on the other hand, does not require a file to be open in the Acrobat viewer. Searches can be performed on multiple PDF files by invoking the Search Query.

The Find and Search tools appear in the Acrobat viewer. You need to think of these tasks as the responsibility of tools rather than commands. If you look at the Edit menu, you'll notice the Find and Search items listed in the menu. As tools, both are also included in the viewer Command Bar (see Figure 2-25).

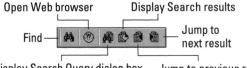

Figure 2-25: Find and Search are tools available in the Acrobat viewer Command Bar.

The responsibility of the Find tool is to locate keywords in the active PDF document. If you use the Search tool to conduct a search and locate a keyword in an open file, you subsequently will want to use the Find tool to look for additional occurrences of a found word or words.

Find Tool dialog box

Executing a find can occur by either clicking the Find tool or by selecting Edit ⇨ Find. When you select either, the Find dialog box will open in which you can establish attributes of the word or words to be found. The Find dialog box enables you to select from the following options:

✦ **Match Whole Word Only:** If the check box is disabled and you search for a word such as *on*, then *on*, *one*, *online*, and so on will be found. When the check box is enabled, only the word *on* will be found.

✦ **Match Case:** When enabled, the found words will be case sensitive. For example, searching for *WWW* will return only *WWW* and not *www*. When disabled, the Acrobat viewer disregards letter case and will find both *WWW* and *www*.

✦ **Find Backwards:** If your current view is page 28 and the check box is enabled, the Find tool will search backward from page 28. Disabling the check box will cause Find to search from the current page forward. When the Acrobat viewer reaches the end of the document, you will be prompted to either stop or continue searching the remaining pages.

Find Again

Once you find a word in a PDF file, the Acrobat viewer will stop at the first found occurrence. The word will be highlighted on the page where it was found. You can continue searching with the same attributes identified in the Find dialog box by selecting the Find Again command. The Find Again command is accessed by selecting Edit ⇨ Find Again.

If you wish to quickly navigate through found words, you'll want to use the modifier keys for Find and Find Again. The Cmd/Ctrl+F keys open the Find dialog box. Pressing Cmd/Ctrl+G invokes the Find Again command. If you attempt to find a word not found in the open PDF document, the Acrobat viewer will open a dialog box and inform you the word cannot be found.

Using Acrobat Search

Whereas the Find tool is limited to the open document and operates similarly to find commands found in word processors and layout applications, the Acrobat Search tool is a much different animal. To use Acrobat Search, you need to have Search installed on your computer. If you only have Acrobat Reader installed, you won't be able to use Acrobat Search. When installing Reader on computers in an office, be certain to acquire the Reader + Search installer. If you have Adobe Acrobat, Acrobat Search will be installed by default.

Note As of the last beta version of Acrobat Reader, Adobe has yet to ship the Acrobat Search plug-in. If you do not find Acrobat Search available for free on Adobe's Web site, you'll need to purchase Adobe Acrobat. If you own Adobe Acrobat, the Search plug-in can also be used with Reader.

Acrobat Search enables you to search multiple PDF files with a host of attributes available to enable you to narrow your search more specifically than with the attributes of the Find tool. To use Acrobat Search, you need to have a search index available on your hard drive or a server, or on an external media cartridge or CD-ROM. The search index file must be identified in the Available Indexes dialog box. By default, when you install Adobe Acrobat or Reader + Search, the Acrobat help index file is identified for you.

All about index files

Index files need to be loaded and active in order for Acrobat Search to find keywords. Indexes are created with Acrobat Catalog, which I cover in Chapter 15. However, there are some index files you can already use. You'll find an index file loaded when you install Adobe Acrobat, and you can find some index files on the CD-ROM accompanying this book. To use an index file, you'll need to add it to an Available Index list.

Adding index files

To add an index file to the search engine, you'll need to load the Acrobat Search application. When you open an Acrobat viewer, the viewer is loaded into memory. If you select the Search tool from the viewer Command Bar, you'll notice your computer will hesitate a moment. This hesitation is due to the Search application loading in additional memory. Depending on the speed of your computer and the available RAM, it may take a few moments for the Search application to load.

Index identification is accessed by selecting Edit ⇨ Search ⇨ Select Indexes (Cmd/Ctrl+X). When you select this command, you will experience the same delay as when selecting the Search tool in the Acrobat viewer Command Bar. Anything associated with the Search commands will require Acrobat Search to load into memory. When the Indexes command is selected, the Index Selection window will open, as shown in Figure 2-26.

Dialog Boxes Versus Windows

The terms *dialog box* and *window* have different meanings in regards to Acrobat. Windows are used with application programs and plug-ins. The area displayed within the Acrobat viewer, Acrobat Distiller, Acrobat Catalog, and so forth are termed windows. Dialog boxes can be of two types: those that require you to exit the dialog box before accessing any commands and those that permit menu command selections while the dialog box is open. In either case, with regard to Acrobat, these two items are termed dialog boxes.

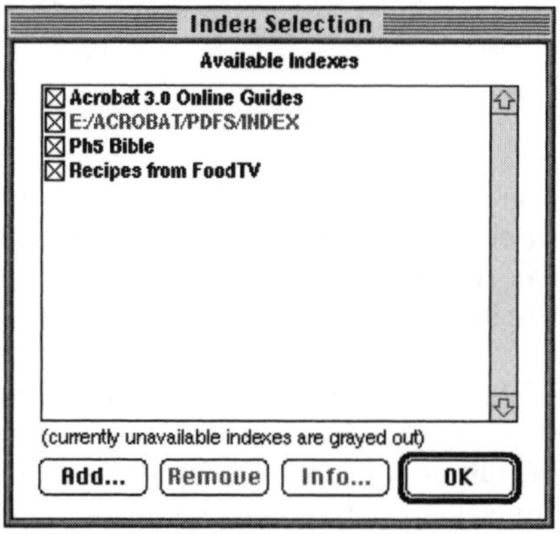

```
╔══════════════════════════════════════╗
║          Index Selection             ║
╟──────────────────────────────────────╢
║           Available Indexes          ║
║  ┌─────────────────────────────┬──┐  ║
║  │☒ Acrobat 3.0 Online Guides  │⬆ │  ║
║  │☒ E:/ACROBAT/PDFS/INDEX      │  │  ║
║  │☒ Ph5 Bible                  │  │  ║
║  │☒ Recipes from FoodTV        │  │  ║
║  │                             │  │  ║
║  │                             │  │  ║
║  │                             │  │  ║
║  │                             │⬇ │  ║
║  └─────────────────────────────┴──┘  ║
║  (currently unavailable indexes are grayed out) ║
║  [ Add... ] [Remove] [Info...]  [  OK  ] ║
╚══════════════════════════════════════╝
```

Figure 2-26: The Index Selection window opens when you select Edit ⇨ Search ⇨ Select Indexes. From this window you can add or remove different index files.

The Index Selection dialog box provides options for loading and removing index files as well as activating an index. Notice in Figure 2-26 the four index files listed in the Available Indexes list. In order for the index to be active and available to Acrobat Search, the check box for the index must be enabled. If you disable the check box of a particular index, Acrobat Search will not search through that index. If no indexes are enabled, Acrobat Search will return no results because it won't search any file.

You can add indexes to the Index Selection dialog box by clicking the Add button at the bottom of the window. When you click Add, a navigation dialog box will open and you can navigate your hard drive, CD-ROM, or server to find an index to be loaded. If an index is trashed or relocated on the drive, Acrobat Search won't be able to find the index. The index name will appear grayed out in the Index Selection dialog box, indicating Search cannot locate the file. In this case, you'll need to delete the item and click the Add button. Navigate to the new location of the index file, and add it to the Available Indexes list.

Removing indexes

If an index is to be eliminated from searches, you can deactivate the index by disabling its check box. In a later Acrobat session, you can go back and enable indexes listed in the Index Selection dialog box. You should always use this method rather than deleting an index if you intend to use it again. At times, however, you may wish to delete an index file. If the index will no longer be used, or you relocate your index to another drive or server, you may wish to completely remove the old index. If this is the case, select the index file to be deleted and click the Remove button. Indexes may be enabled or disabled when you select Remove. In either case, the index file is removed without warning.

If you inadvertently delete an index, the index can always be reloaded by selecting the Add button. It's a good idea to place index files in a directory where you can easily access them. To avoid confusion, try to keep indexes in a common directory. Acrobat doesn't care where the index file is located on your hard drive or server — it just needs to know where the file is located. If you move the index file to a different directory, be certain to reestablish the connection in the Index Selection dialog box.

Index information

When a number of index files are installed on a computer or server, the names for the files may not be descriptive enough to determine which you wish to search. If more detailed information is desired, the information provided by the Index Information dialog box may help identify the index needed for a given search.

Index information may be particularly helpful in office environments where several people in different departments create PDFs and indexes are all placed on a common server. What may be intuitive to the author of an index file in terms of index name may not be as intuitive to other users. Index information offers the capability for adding more descriptive information that can be understood by many users.

Fortunately, you can explore more descriptive information about an index file by clicking the Info button in the Index Selection dialog box. When the Info button is clicked, the Index Info dialog box opens, displaying information about the index file as shown in Figure 2-27. Some of the information displayed will require user entry at the time the index is built. Other information in the dialog box will automatically be created by Acrobat Catalog when the index is built. The Index Information dialog box provides a description of the following:

✦ **Title:** Title information is supplied by the user at the time the index is created. Titles usually consist of several words describing the index contents. Titles can be searched, as detailed later in this chapter, so the title keywords should reflect the index content.

✦ **Description:** Description can be a few words or several sentences containing information about the index created. In Figure 2-27, the description was supplied in Acrobat Catalog when the index was created.

✦ **Path:** The directory path where the index file is located on a drive or server is displayed with the last item appearing as the index filename.

✦ **Last Built:** If the index file is updated, the date of the last build is supplied here. If no updates have occurred, the date will be the same as the created date.

✦ **Created:** This date reflects the time and date the index file was originally created, and is therefore a fixed date.

✦ **Documents:** Indexes are created from one or more PDF documents. The total number of files from which the index file was created appears here.

✦ **Status:** If the index file has been identified and added to the list in the Index Selection dialog box, it will be available. Unavailable indexes will appear grayed out in the list and be described as unavailable.

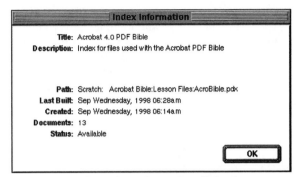

Figure 2-27: The Index Information dialog box appears when you select the Info button in the Index Selection dialog box.

If you launch an Acrobat viewer and open the Index Selection dialog box with no active index, invoking a search will open a warning dialog box indicating no documents were found that match the search query. Acrobat does not inform you that it doesn't have an active index to search. If you attempt a search and get this warning dialog box, be certain to click the Indexes button in the Adobe Acrobat Search dialog box to verify the index or indexes you intend to search have been enabled.

Using the Acrobat Search dialog box

Once you have an index file loaded and enabled, you can go about the business of creating a search. Searches are handled in Acrobat viewers by either accessing the Search tool through the viewer Command Bar or by selecting Edit ⇨ Search ⇨ Query (Cmd/Ctrl+Shift+F). Notice the Search command in the Edit menu has a submenu with several choices for conducting searches, as shown in Figure 2-28. The lower half of the submenu will be grayed out until you perform at least one search.

Query...	⇧⌘F
Select Indexes...	⇧⌘X
Results...	⇧⌘G
Word Assistant...	⇧⌘W
Previous Document	⇧⌘[
Previous	⌘[
Next	⌘]
Next Document	⇧⌘]

Figure 2-28: The Search commands are listed in a submenu available by selecting Edit ⇨ Search.

When you first start using Acrobat Search, it may be a bit confusing as to which submenu command to select to perform the search. The easiest way to go is to select the Search tool in the viewer Command Bar. When you click the tool, the Query dialog box will appear after the Search application is loaded. As you start using the submenu commands, keep in mind that *Query* is synonymous with *Search*.

When you either select the Acrobat Search tool from the viewer Command Bar or choose Edit ➪ Search ➪ Query, the same dialog box will open. Like the dialog box discussed with the Index Selection, this dialog box affords you the opportunity to select other commands while it is open. When you open the Adobe Acrobat Search dialog box, you'll immediately notice the many different data fields available for user input. As you can see in Figure 2-29, the number of search fields is much greater than that provided with the Find command.

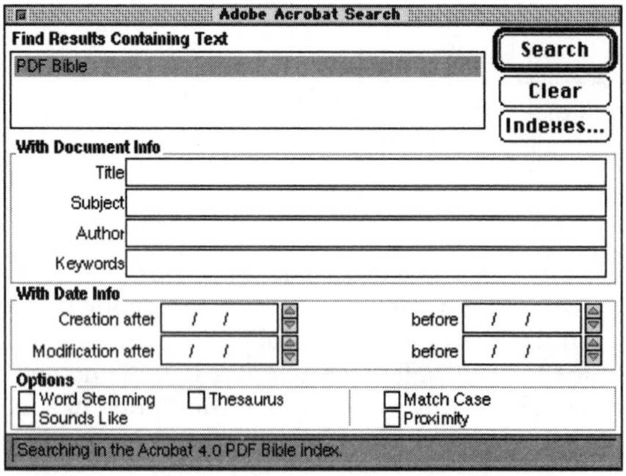

Figure 2-29: The Adobe Acrobat Search dialog box provides opportunity to search on many different data fields.

This dialog box looks like a maze and thus deserves some detailed explanation. All those fields are probably intimidating if this is your first pass through Adobe Acrobat. Let's take a moment to look at each field:

✦ **Find Results Containing Text:** The box below Find Results Containing Text is for user entry of keywords for which to search. The words you enter here are not limited to single words, but can also include operators or Boolean expressions, discussed a little later in this chapter.

✦ **With Document Info:** The four items listed below the With Document Info heading apply to information supplied when the PDF document was created. When you create a PDF file, you'll have the opportunity to supply this information. When you view PDF files created by someone else, you can observe the document information supplied by the PDF author. To view document information, select File ➪ Document Info ➪ General. The General Info dialog box will open and display document information, including information specific to the four fields listed in the Query dialog box, as shown in Figure 2-30. In Acrobat Reader, no changes are permitted, and you can't proceed in Reader until the dialog box is closed. In Acrobat, some of the fields in the General Info dialog box can be edited, thus behaving more like a window than a dialog box.

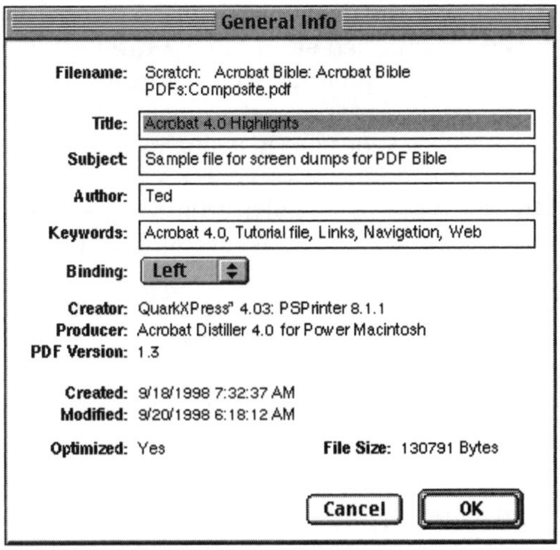

Figure 2-30: The General Info dialog box displays document information, including fields for document title, subject, author, and keyword. The field contents can be searched with Acrobat Search and edited in Acrobat.

- **Title:** The content for this field is supplied by the user, who at the time the PDF is created identifies a title for the PDF. This title name is irrespective of the filename. In Figure 2-30, the title is *Acrobat 4.0 Highlights*, yet the PDF filename is *Composite.pdf*.

- **Subject:** The Subject field, which is user supplied, generally contains keywords to identify a common subject. For example, if you had a number of PDF files for the human resources department in a company, you might indicate in the Subject field keywords associated with human resources.

- **Author:** Typically, this field will be supplied by the author of the PDF at the time the document is created. The contents of this field may be the name of a person or a department. If a company changes personnel frequently, a better choice would be to have a department or facility name appear in the Author field.

- **Keywords:** You can add any number of words for the keyword field up to a maximum of 255 characters. Keywords are usually additional descriptors, not included in the Title or Subject fields, that relate to the PDF contents and make it easy for users to search on words they expect to find in a given document. If a PDF file for an employee handbook were created, for example, the subject field might include "employee handbook." The keywords might include "benefits," "salary," "vacation," "grievances," and so on.

✦ **With Date Info:** These fields show the dates for file creation and last modification for a PDF, as was mentioned earlier in the discussion on index document information. You can search on the date fields, and narrow the date by using the after and before fields. Entering date data in any of the date fields is easy. You can supply a month, day, or year in a single field, and Acrobat will supply the remaining fields. For example, if you enter 4 in the first available field, Acrobat will enter the current day and year from your system clock (date fields follow a mm/dd/yy syntax). Enter a year, and Acrobat will enter the current month and day, and so on. All the date fields are Y2K compliant, so don't worry about the century date change. Just make certain your operating system is also Y2K compliant. The up and down arrows in the date field boxes will increase or decrease the respective selection. Select the year and click the down arrow, and the year will decrease. The same holds true for the day and month fields.

- **Creation after:** If a date is supplied in this field, Search will find all PDFs in the index file created after that date.

- **Creation before:** To the right of the Creation after date field, the word *before* appears beside a date field. If you enter a date field in the Creation after field box and another date in the before field box, Acrobat Search will find all PDFs created within the specified date range.

- **Modification after:** This field works similar to the Creation after date field. Enter a value, and Acrobat Search finds PDFs with modification dates after the field entry. If you have several similar files, all created on the same date, and you modified one of those documents a few months ago, searching on this field will help you narrow down your search.

- **Modification before:** If you enter a date in this field, which appears to the right of the Modification after field, Search will look for all PDFs modified before your specified date.

✦ **Options:** The five option items listed in the Options box frame also help you narrow down a search. These items are enabled by clicking the check boxes beside each respective option.

- **Word Stemming:** If you wish to search for all words stemming from a given word, enable this option. Words such as *header* and *heading* stem from the word *head*. If you type in *head* in the Find Results Containing Text box and select the Word Stemming option, all PDFs containing the search criteria from the word stem will be listed.

- **Sounds Like:** This option is a crude attempt at finding words that sound like other words. It's really not dependent on a rhyming scheme; for example, Acrobat Search will find words like *fix, fx, fox,* and so on for the search entry *fog*. Words like *dog, log,* and *hog* won't be found.

- **Thesaurus:** When the Thesaurus option is used, Acrobat Search will find synonyms for the searched word. If you search for *lower* with Thesaurus enabled, the returned results will include words such as *down, lower, below, beneath,* and so on.

- • **Match Case:** Case-sensitive searches are the same with Acrobat Search as with the Find command. When Match Case is enabled, only identical case-matched words will be returned in the results.

- • **Proximity:** Proximity is a powerful tool when performing searches. If you wish to search for two independent words that may appear together in a given context — for example, *Acrobat* and *PostScript* — the proximity option will find the two words if they appear within three pages of each other in a PDF.

✦ **Indexes Searched:** At the bottom of the Query dialog box a display will appear that provides feedback on the index file currently being searched. If a single index file is loaded, the name of the index file will appear in the dialog box. If more than one index file is loaded, the readout in the dialog box will appear as "Searching x out of y indexes" — where x equals the number of indexes searched and y is equal to the total number of index files loaded.

After you establish the search criteria, click the Search button. Acrobat Search will list all the occurrences of files that fit the criteria specified in the Query dialog box. This list will appear in another dialog box — the Search Results dialog box.

Understanding search results

The Search Results dialog box lists all the PDFs where at least one occurrence of the searched word(s) appears. The order displayed in the Search Results dialog box is according to a relative reference scheme based on the percentage of occurrences of the found word(s) to the number of words in the document. When you click Search in the Query dialog box, the Search Results dialog box appears (see Figure 2-31).

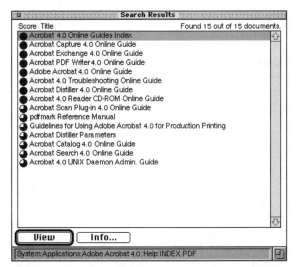

Figure 2-31: The Search Results dialog box is displayed after searching for *PDF*.

Notice in Figure 2-31 the first eight items appear with a solid circle to the left side of the title of the PDF file. Note the name is not the filename, but the name the PDF author supplied for the Title field in the Document Info dialog box when the PDF was created or modified.

The next seven names in the Search Results dialog box appear next to circles with a $3/4$ fill. In this example, the first eight items have a higher order of relative ranking than the last seven items. This is to say that the percentage of occurrence of the word *PDF* to the total number of words in the first set of files is higher than the last seven files. Keep in mind the relative ranking is based on percentages; for example, a file with 10 found occurrences out of 100 words will have a higher order of ranking than 1,000 found occurrences out of 100,000 words. The former is 10 percent, whereas the latter is 1 percent.

Relative ranking is displayed with five different icons. Ranking goes from the highest order (circle with a solid fill) to the lowest order (circle without a fill), as shown in Figure 2-32.

Figure 2-32: Beginning from left to right, the highest order of ranking is indicated by the solid circle, whereas the lowest ranking is indicated by an empty circle.

Acrobat Search enables you to use Boolean expressions and operators for conditional statements — something such as *word1* OR *word2*, where OR is a Boolean expression. When using such conditions, the relative ranking of these expressions is always higher than ordinary searches based on a single word.

When you conduct a search with the Proximity option, the closer the two words are, the higher the ranking. For example, if the two words in question appear on the same page in a PDF file, that file would have a higher order of ranking than one in which the words appear three pages apart from each other.

Viewing search results

When the Search Results dialog box displays the list of PDFs in which your word or words have been found, you can open the PDF or display its document information. Sometimes it may be handy to view document information, especially if the title, subject, author, or keywords fields can help you narrow your search. To display the document information, click the Info button in the Search Results dialog and the Document Info dialog will appear, as shown in Figure 2-33.

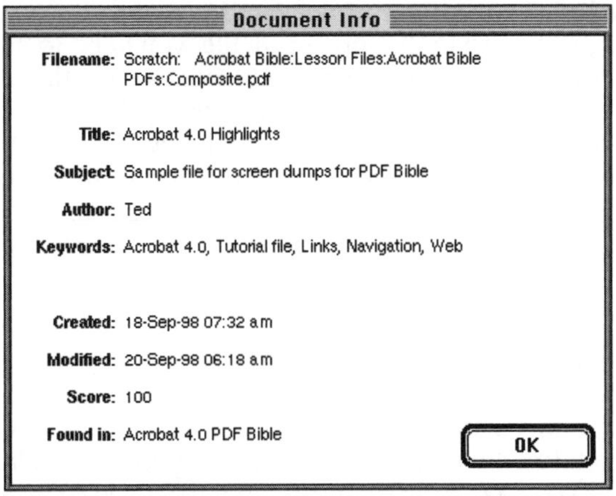

```
┌─────────────────────────────────────────────────┐
│                  Document Info                     │
├─────────────────────────────────────────────────┤
│  Filename:  Scratch:   Acrobat Bible:Lesson Files:Acrobat Bible
│             PDFs:Composite.pdf
│
│     Title:  Acrobat 4.0 Highlights
│
│   Subject:  Sample file for screen dumps for PDF Bible
│
│    Author:  Ted
│
│  Keywords:  Acrobat 4.0, Tutorial file, Links, Navigation, Web
│
│
│   Created:  18-Sep-98 07:32 am
│
│  Modified:  20-Sep-98 06:18 am
│
│     Score:  100
│                                           ┌──────────┐
│  Found in:  Acrobat 4.0 PDF Bible         │    OK    │
│                                           └──────────┘
└─────────────────────────────────────────────────┘
```

Figure 2-33: Document Info is displayed when you select the Info button in the Search Results dialog

If you wish to open a PDF file from the Search Results dialog box, select the file from the list and either click the View button or double-click the title. In this example, I searched for the word *PDF*. From the list of titles, I opened the Acrobat 4.0 Online Guide. The actual filename for the PDF is EXCHANGE.PDF. When the file is opened, the found word will be highlighted, as you can see in Figure 2-34.

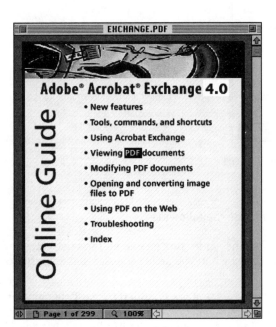

Figure 2-34: When you open a file from the Search Results dialog, the found word in the Acrobat viewer will be highlighted.

Once you've opened a PDF file from the Search Results list, if you wish to continue finding more occurrences of a given word in that open PDF file, you need to use the Find tool. Acrobat Search won't help you to find more occurrences once the document is opened. Returning to the Adobe Acrobat Search dialog box will again bring up the list of PDFs from the index file. With the Find tool, you can find the first occurrence of the word and then use the Find Again command for all subsequent occurrences.

Search preferences

Earlier, when you got your first look at the Adobe Acrobat Search dialog box (refer back to Figure 2-29), all the provisions for search criteria were displayed. The appearance of this dialog box can be customized according to preference settings you enable in the Acrobat Search Preferences dialog box. Even if you have a large monitor, the Search dialog can become overbearing, and you may need to move it around your monitor screen in order to examine the results of a search. The customization of the Search dialog box as well as the dialog behavior is handled by selecting File ➪ Preferences ➪ Search. See Figures 2-35 and 2-36.

Figure 2-35: Macintosh Search Preferences dialog box

The Search Preferences options include the following:

✦ **Query:** The items described in the Query box enable you to customize the Adobe Acrobat Search dialog box when you select the Acrobat Search tool or choose Edit ➪ Search ➪ Query.

• **Show Fields:** The fields in question are confined to the Title, Subject, Author, and Keywords fields. When you disable Show Fields, all the fields just mentioned will be hidden from view in the Adobe Acrobat Search dialog box.

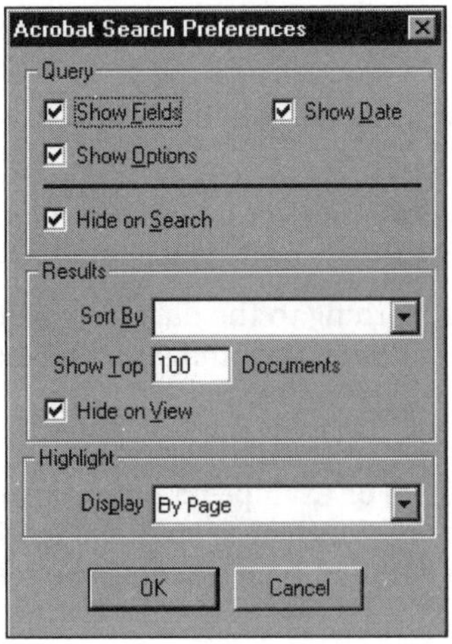

Figure 2-36: Windows Search
Preferences dialog box

- **Show Options:** The Options fields appear at the bottom of the Adobe Acrobat Search dialog box. When this preference is disabled, all these fields will be hidden in the Search dialog box.

- **Show Date:** When this option is disabled, the Created and Modified fields will be hidden in the Search dialog box.

- **Hide on Search:** The Hide on Search button will eliminate the Search dialog box after you click the Search button. It's handy for getting the Search dialog box out of the way, if you're struggling for viewing room on your monitor. The downside is the next time you search, you'll need to click the Search tool, press Cmd/Ctrl+Shift+F, or select Edit ⇨ Search ⇨ Query. Using the keyboard equivalents will be your best bet for getting the Search dialog box back quickly.

✦ **Results:** The next category of preference settings falls within the Results box. These items are reflected in the Search Results dialog box.

- **Sort By:** This pop-up menu has a number of choices you select to specify the order for the display of the PDFs in the Search Results dialog box. The pop-up menu items include those listed here:

- **Score:** The default is Score, which lists the occurrences in the relative ranking for the total number of found words.

- **Title:** The same relative ranking will be indicated by the respective icon adjacent to titles listed in the Search Results dialog box, only the files will be listed in alphabetical order by title rather than in ranking order. Essentially, those files with the same titles will be nested together.

- **Subject:** The same applies for subject as it does for title. The order of display will be in alphabetical order according to the subject specified in the document information. Like subjects will be grouped together.

- **Author:** The sort results will appear as an alphabetical list according to the first word in the Author field.

- **Keywords:** The sort results will appear as an alphabetical list according to the first word in the Keywords field.

- **Created:** The PDF files will be listed according to creation date, going from the most recent date at the top of the list to the least current.

- **Modified:** The PDF files will be listed according to the date they were last modified, going from the most recent date of modification to the least current.

- **Creator:** "Creator" refers to the program that created the original document before the PDF was generated. For example, a program such as PageMaker, which can export files to PDF format, would be identified as the Creator. The sort will result in a list of PDF files in alphabetical order according to Creator.

- **Producer:** The Producer is the application or driver that created the PDF file. Producers might be applications such as Acrobat PDFWriter or Acrobat Distiller along with the version number and platform used. The sort will result in a list of PDF files in alphabetical order according to the Producer; however, you won't see the Producer identified in the Search Results window. Producer information is available in the Document Info dialog box when you open the PDF in an Acrobat viewer.

✦ **Show Top:** This field identifies the maximum number of files that will be displayed in the Search Results window. The default is 100. You can supply a different value to display more or fewer files listed in the window. The field data box will accept values ranging from 1 to 1,000.

✦ **Hide on View:** When enabled, the Search Results dialog box will disappear when you view one of the listed documents. If you select File ➪ Open and open a PDF file, the Search Results dialog box will remain open. Only when you view one of the listed items by clicking the View button or double-clicking a listed file will the dialog box close.

✦ **Highlight:** In this category is the **Display** pop-up menu, which provides the three choices listed here:

- **By Page:** The searched word(s) will be displayed on the first page of the viewed file. If only one occurrence of a found word exists, the single word will be highlighted. If several words are found with the first occurrence on the same page, all words will be highlighted. All subsequent pages with the same word will not be highlighted.

- **By Word:** The first found word will be highlighted when a file from the Search Results list is viewed. Any other occurrences on the same page will not be highlighted.

- **No Highlighting:** No words will be highlighted when a file is viewed from the Search Results window.

✦ **Automount Servers (Mac only):** Despite the fact that Adobe Acrobat is one of the best cross-platform applications (or suite of applications), it holds some advantages specifically for Mac users and others specifically for Windows users, depending on the task to be performed. As you view all that Acrobat has to offer, I'll make some distinctions when one system offers an advantage over another. These distinctions are not based on bias, but empirically there are advantages of using one system over another for various duties. With regard to the automounting of servers, this advantage goes to the Mac. There is no opportunity to automount servers on Windows, as you can see back in Figure 2-35. When Automount Servers is enabled, all indices identified on a server or servers on your network will be mounted by Acrobat Search. This can be handy if you forget to mount a server and need to search an index located on a remote server. If a server is not mounted, Acrobat Search will display the index file grayed out in the Index Selection dialog box. In a true PDF workflow environment, you may have one or more servers containing PDF documents for your company.

As you can see, the preference settings for Acrobat Search help you customize and narrow your searches. If you elect to eliminate from view the many options available in the Adobe Acrobat Search dialog box, you can use keystrokes in the Find Results Containing Text box. You can eliminate all options from view and still enter keystrokes to create searches with all the options. I explain these keystroke equivalents in the following sections, where I show you how to use operators and Boolean expressions with Acrobat Search to make searches truly powerful.

Operators

Operators are conditions that require matching the field type to the found word or field contents. If a word is contained in the document title, the condition is <word *contained* in title>. If the word searched is not contained in the title, the condition does not exist and no results will be returned. If the word is contained in the title, the condition does exist, and you will find those documents meeting the condition listed in the Search Results dialog box.

There are a number of operators you can use with Acrobat Search to aid you in finding precisely the information you want. By using operators, you begin to tap the power of Acrobat Search. Operators, and Boolean expressions, as you see a little later in this chapter, make Acrobat Search a powerful search engine. Look over Table 2-3 and mark this page. You'll want to use these operators regularly for plowing through your stack of PDF files.

Table 2-3
Using Operators with Adobe Acrobat Search

Operator	Meaning
= (equal sign)	**Equals:** The word or words match exactly the field for text, numerics, and date. The field type will appear first, followed by the equal sign (=) and then the word(s). *Example:* Title = Adobe Acrobat
~ (tilde)	**Contains:** The word or words are contained in the field. *Example:* Subject ~ Help
!=	**Does not equal:** The word or words are not contained in the field. *Example:* Subject != Help
!~	**Does not contain:** The word or words are not contained in the field. *Example:* Title !~ Acrobat
<	**Less than:** The value is less than the field contents. This operator applies to date and numeric fields only. *Example:* Created < 9/24/96
<=	**Less than or equal to:** The value is less than or equal to the field contents. This operator applies to date and numeric fields only. *Example:* Created <= 9/25/96
>	**Greater than:** The value is greater than the field contents. This operator applies to date and numeric fields only. *Example:* Modified > 10/30/96
>=	**Greater than or equal to:** The value is greater than or equal to the field contents. This operator applies to date and numeric fields only. *Example:* Modified >= 10/25/96
*	**Wildcard character:** Matches zero, one, or more characters. *Example:* w*d returns *wood, wild, world.*
?	**Wildcard character:** Matches only a single character. *Example:* t*n returns words like *ton, tan, ten.* Words like *took, town,* and *then* will not be returned.

When you use operators, they will be entered in the Query dialog box in the Find Results Containing Text box. If you want to find all PDFs from the Acrobat online files that are designed as help guides, you might search the Subject field for the word *help*. If you have all the options disabled and your search dialog box is minimized, you can supply the attributes of your search without the aid of the options in view. In this example, you would enter *Subject ~ help*, as shown in Figure 2-37.

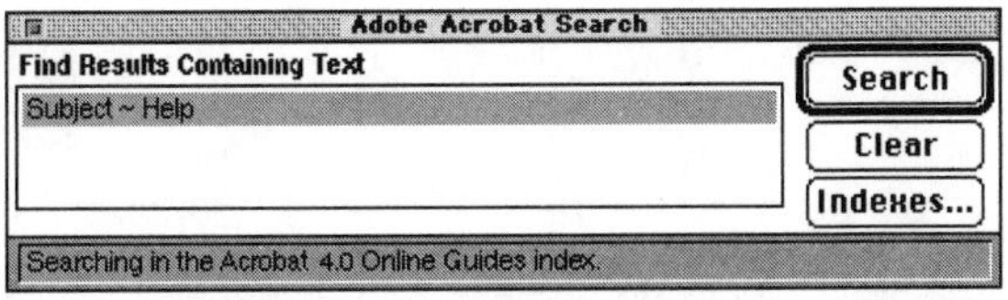

Figure 2-37: When the Search dialog box is minimized, you can enter text to search on all the field criteria. In this example, the Subject field will be searched for the word *help*.

The returned list will display all the PDFs where occurrences of the word exist. Each of the fields you hide in the Search Preferences dialog box has a keyword associated with its field name. You can minimize the Adobe Acrobat Search dialog box and use the keywords if you wish. The Adobe Acrobat Search dialog box size will be reduced to provide more viewing space on your monitor. The syntax for supplying the keywords in the Find Results Containing box include the following:

Title	Title field
Subject	Subject field
Author	Author field
Keywords	Keywords field
Created	Document Creation date
Modified	Document Modified date

Entering any of the preceding items by using keywords will enable you to search the respective field contents. The syntax must be precise. If an error or warning dialog box is opened when you invoke the search, be certain to carefully review the syntax. In addition to field and date items, you can also use identifiers to specify which of the five options you want to use to modify your search. The five option items and their corresponding identifiers are listed in Table 2-4.

Table 2-4
Search Options Identifiers

Identifier	Meaning
/st	**Word Stemming:** All found words will stem from the searched word. *Example:* go /st returns words like *going, gone*.
/so	**Sounds Like:** All found words will sound like the searched word. *Example:* fog /so returns words like *fix, fx, fog* (remember, this option doesn't necessarily return words that rhyme with the searched word).

Continued

Table 2-4 (continued)	
Identifier	**Meaning**
/th	**Thesaurus:** All found words will be synonyms to the searched word. *Example:* publish /th returns words like *author, write, issue.*
/ca	**Match Case:** All found words will exactly match the case of the searched word. Example: www /ca returns *www*, not *WWW*.
/pr	**Proximity:** Proximity is used with Boolean expressions and requires two words to be in close proximity of each other. *Example:* WWW AND PDF /pr returns files containing both the words *WWW* and *PDF* within three pages of each other.

More power in Acrobat Search is available when you use operators with Boolean expressions. Boolean expressions offer more opportunities to create searches with conditional requirements.

Boolean expressions

The Boolean operators AND, OR, and NOT allow you to specify conditions existing between words or fields for narrowing your search. For example, if you want to search the Title field for the word *Adobe* and you want all PDFs except those created by Adobe Developer Relations, you might enter (Title ~ Adobe) AND (Author !~ Developer). The search will seek all files with the word *Adobe* contained in the Title field and all files where the word *Developer* is not contained in the Author field (see Figure 2-38).

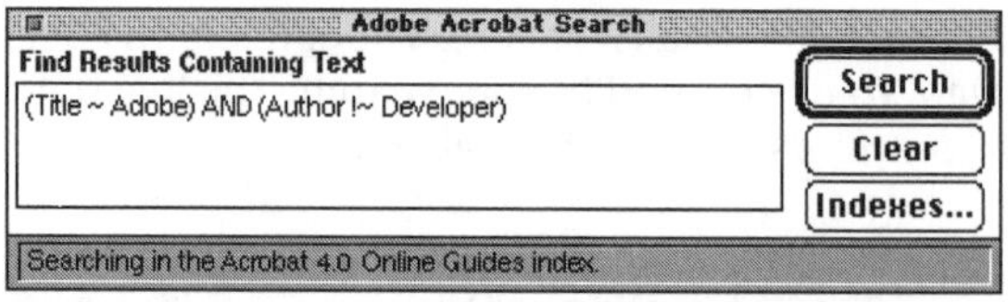

Figure 2-38: Search criteria is entered in the Adobe Acrobat Search dialog box using a Boolean expression.

In Figure 2-38, notice the parentheses used in the syntax for the statement to create the search. These characters are optional. The search could easily be accomplished without the parentheses, and the same results will occur. They are used in the preceding example to help illustrate the point. If you find using parenthetical statements simplifies the task, by all means use them. Any syntax error you may create in the Search dialog box will be immediately reported by the Acrobat viewer when you select the Search button.

You should try to get some practice creating different searches. The more you practice, the more effective you'll become in using them. To help you get started, you can follow along with this example for creating a search with Boolean expressions:

STEPS: Using Acrobat Search with Operators and Boolean Expressions

1. **Launch an Acrobat viewer.** You can use either Adobe Acrobat Reader or Acrobat.

2. **Select the Indexes button in the Adobe Acrobat Search dialog box.** You should verify the Acrobat 4.0 online guides or help files are available in the Available Indexes list and the index is active (an X should be placed in the check box).

3. **Click OK.** The Index Selection dialog box will disappear.

4. **Select File ➪ Preferences ➪ Search.** In the Search Preferences dialog box, disable all the options (Show Fields, Show Options, and Show Date should be disabled). Disabling the options reduces the size of the Adobe Acrobat Search dialog box so you can see more of the document behind the dialog box. As the dialog box is reduced and hides all the options, you need to use operators for searching in place of the options not currently in view.

5. **Click OK.** The Search Preferences dialog box will disappear.

6. **Enter the search criteria in the Find Results Containing Text box in the Adobe Acrobat Search dialog box.** Enter **Title ~ Adobe AND Title !~ Help AND Created >= 10/1/97.** This search asks for all files that show the word *Adobe* in the Title field, exclude the word *Help* in the Title field, and were created on or after October 1, 1997.

7. **Click the Search button.** Acrobat Search will return the Search Results window.

8. **Click the View button.** The PDF file will be opened in the Acrobat viewer and the first page of the document will be displayed.

You'll notice multiple expressions can be used when creating your searches. If you find a dialog box opens indicating Acrobat Search cannot understand your search criteria, you have made an error with the syntax. Be certain you carefully review the entry in the Find Results Containing Text box. The Boolean expressions are not case sensitive. I prefer to use capital letters to easily distinguish the expression from the other text. What is important though is being certain you have a space between the operators and the text (in other words, Title ~ Adobe and not Title~Adobe).

Try using several other searches. You have some wonderful opportunities to learn about Acrobat's search capabilities with the Adobe online help guides. Try to become familiar with these. The online help guides will aid you in finding information that can help you learn more about Adobe Acrobat.

Word Assistant

The last menu item in the Search submenu not yet discussed is Word Assistant. When you select Edit ➪ Search ➪ Word Assistant, the Word Assistant dialog box will appear, as shown in Figure 2-39. Assistant enables you to search through your selected index files to find matches to the word you enter in the field box. A button on the right labelled Indexes will open the Index Selection dialog box. You must have an index active for Assistant to return results as a list appearing below the pop-up menu.

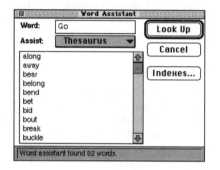

Figure 2-39: The Word Assistant dialog box has a field box for a word entry and a pop-up menu with the options Stemming, Sounds Like, and Thesaurus to refine your search.

The pop-up menu contains three items: Stemming, Sounds Like, and Thesaurus. You enter a word in the field box and select one of the three choices from the pop-up menu. The dialog box is used to aid you in finding words matching one of the three conditions available in the pop-up menu. When you search with Assistant, a list of matches will appear in the dialog box list. Double-click a word in the list, and it will be copied to the field box. Once in the field box, the word can be copied to the clipboard by selecting Edit ➪ Copy and subsequently pasted in the Query dialog box. In the example shown in Figure 2-39, I entered the word *Go* in the field box and chose Thesaurus as my Assist criteria. After clicking Look Up, the Word Assistant displayed 82 found words in the word list. (The number of found words is supplied in the status bar at the bottom of the Word Assistant dialog box.)

Summary

✦ Viewing PDF documents is handled with a number of tools, menu commands, and keyboard modifiers. When you view PDF files in the Full Screen mode, you can create an online presentation and automate page navigation.

✦ The navigation tools enable page navigation through an open document and between documents. You can return to previously viewed pages by going forward and back to retrace your steps.

✦ Hypertext links enable navigation to views, other documents, and a variety of menu commands. Dynamic linking enables you to view documents in a nonlinear manner. Bookmarks, thumbnails, and destinations add additional navigation opportunities.

✦ Links can be made to the World Wide Web whereby a button can open a Web browser and connect you to a specific URL.

✦ The Find tool works with open documents to create searches within a PDF file. The Find Again command will find additional occurrences of a searched word or words.

✦ Acrobat Search can search on index files created with Acrobat Catalog. Search indexes must be loaded in the Index Selection dialog box. The searches can be complex, including various options, keywords, operators, and Boolean expressions. Word Assistant provides options for searching word criteria related to word stems or similarity in sound, and for thesaurus lookups.

✦ ✦ ✦

Using Acrobat Reader

♦   ♦   ♦   ♦

In This Chapter

Understanding the
Reader environment

Modifying
preferences

Creating text and
graphic selections

Using the online help
commands

Adobe's Web link

♦   ♦   ♦   ♦

Because Adobe Acrobat has so many components with distinct features, it might be a good idea to tackle them one at a time, starting with Acrobat Reader. If you purchased Acrobat, all of what you do here in the Reader application will be the same in Acrobat 4.0. Acrobat has more bells and whistles than Reader does, and I discuss these in Chapter 7. If you haven't purchased Acrobat, then this chapter will introduce you to all of what Acrobat Reader has to offer (and you can go about loading it from the CD-ROM accompanying this book).

Understanding the Reader Environment

Like any other windowing application, Acrobat Reader makes use of tools, menu commands, and a set of preferences that help you customize the application environment. With Reader, the environment controls are handled by two menu commands, Document Info and Preferences, that help users customize the application for personal working conditions. This chapter first takes a look at the Document Info command and then moves on to the Preferences command.

Document information

The Document Info command gives you access to information regarding the contents and attributes of a PDF file. You can quickly access such document information to learn some particulars of a PDF file, which may help you when searching for a file that fits a certain profile. There are three categories of document information.

General document information

When a PDF file is created from many applications, either by using the PDF Writer or distilling a PostScript file with the Acrobat Distiller, you'll have an opportunity to add document information. Chapter 2 took a brief look at document information when searches were performed on the Title, Author, Subject, and Keywords fields. The field data for these items is user definable. You can elect to supply the information at the time the PDF is created, or you can modify it when the PDF is viewed in Acrobat.

Because Reader doesn't have support for saving a file, you can't alter the document information with the Reader software. If you look at the File menu, you won't see a Save command. As such, there's no provision for altering anything in the file, including document information. In Windows, it may first appear that you can edit a field, since the cursor can be placed in any of the four title fields. However, you can't change the information. Windows users can copy the data to the clipboard and paste it into other files running under different applications.

What you can do in Reader is view document information. Of course, it must be supplied by the author of the PDF or by an amendment with Acrobat, but once it's there, you can see it. To access general document information, select File ⇨ Document Info ⇨ General. The General Info dialog box opens and displays the document information for the data fields discussed previously (see Figures 3-1 and 3-2).

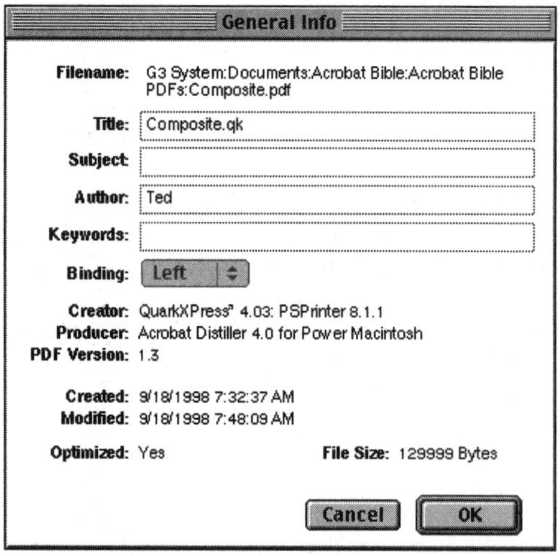

Figure 3-1: The general document information for a PDF file on a Macintosh

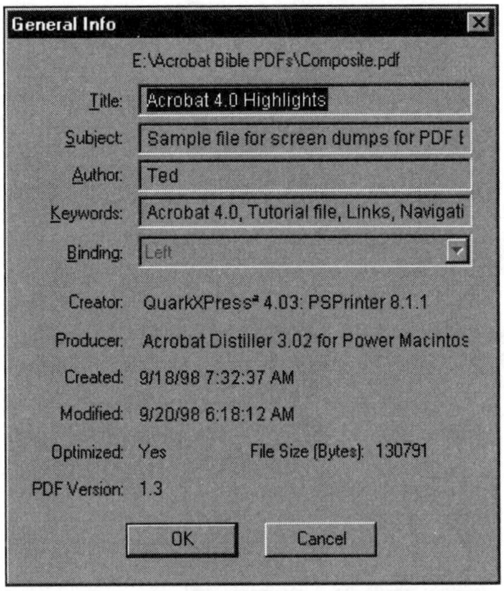

General Info ⊠

E:\Acrobat Bible PDFs\Composite.pdf

Title:	Acrobat 4.0 Highlights
Subject:	Sample file for screen dumps for PDF I
Author:	Ted
Keywords:	Acrobat 4.0, Tutorial file, Links, Navigati
Binding:	Left ▼

Creator: QuarkXPress³ 4.03: PSPrinter 8.1.1

Producer: Acrobat Distiller 3.02 for Power Macintos

Created: 9/18/98 7:32:37 AM

Modified: 9/20/98 6:18:12 AM

Optimized: Yes   File Size (Bytes): 130791

PDF Version: 1.3

[OK]   [Cancel]

Figure 3-2: The general document information for a PDF file on Windows. In Windows, the data fields can be selected.

When you examine the General Info dialog box on a Macintosh, notice the border of dashes appearing around several of the text fields. The dashed borders indicate user supplied information. The remaining fields, such as the creation and modification dates, are those that the Acrobat creator supplied from the operating system. In Windows, they appear as editable fields; however, as noted previously, you cannot change any data in Reader.

If PDF files are created without the user supplying information in the appropriate data fields, the Acrobat creator supplies two of the four fields automatically. The Title field defaults to the filename of the authoring application, and the Author field is supplied from the name you provided to your computer when you initially set up your operating system.

If you open the General Info dialog box in Acrobat, you can replace the data for the Title and Author fields. Although Acrobat offers this capability, you'll most often want to supply data at the time the PDF is created. In a true PDF Workflow environment, proper identification of the files will prevent you from spending much time appending information to the Document Info dialog box. Because these fields can be searched, you'll want to ensure all fields are completed with identifying information.

Fonts

The next item you can choose to view for document information is the font data. Reader permits you to examine the fonts contained in the PDF file by selecting File ➪ Document Info ➪ Fonts. When you select the command, the Font Info dialog box, shown in Figure 3-3, appears.

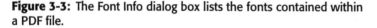

```
┌─────────────────────────── Font Info ───────────────────────────┐
│                                                                  │
│  Fonts in:  design.pdf                                           │
│                                                                  │
│  Original Font        Type      Encoding    Used Font       Type │
│  Garamond-Bold        Type 1    MacRoman     AdobeSerifMM    Type 1  ⇧ │
│                                                                  │
│                                                                  │
│                                                                  │
│                                                                  │
│                                                                  │
│                                                                  ⇩ │
│                                                                  │
│  ┌──────────────────┐                          ┌──────────────┐ │
│  │  List All Fonts...│                          │      OK      │ │
│  └──────────────────┘                          └──────────────┘ │
└──────────────────────────────────────────────────────────────────┘
```

Figure 3-3: The Font Info dialog box lists the fonts contained within a PDF file.

Font information is specific to the page being viewed and not the entire document. If you open a PDF with Times Roman appearing on page 1 and Helvetica on page 2, the first font listed in the Fonts Info dialog box will be Times Roman. Until Reader views another page with another font, you'll see only the fonts that appear on page 1 listed. If Times and Helvetica appear on page 1, both will be listed in the Font Info dialog box.

You can't navigate the pages while the Font Info dialog box is open. To view another page, click OK in the Font Info dialog box and then use the navigation tools to see another page. Selecting Font Info again retains the name of the font or fonts viewed on page 1 and adds the additional fonts found on the next page to the list in the Font Info dialog box.

As you can see in Figure 3-4, the original font from page 1 (Garamond-Bold) appears in the font list. When I scrolled to page 2 and viewed the Font Info, the additional fonts were supplied in the font list. As you move through the pages and view the font information, any additional font names will be appended to the list.

Reader handles this method of display for you so there won't be a burdensome generation of a font list for the whole document every time you open the Font Info dialog box. If there are an inordinate number of fonts in a PDF file, it may take a few moments to display all the fonts. Rather than defaulting to a display of all fonts, Reader provides those fonts encountered as pages are read. You do have an opportunity to view all fonts in a PDF by selecting the List All Fonts button in the Font Info dialog box. When you click this button, all fonts from the open document will be displayed, as shown in Figure 3-5.

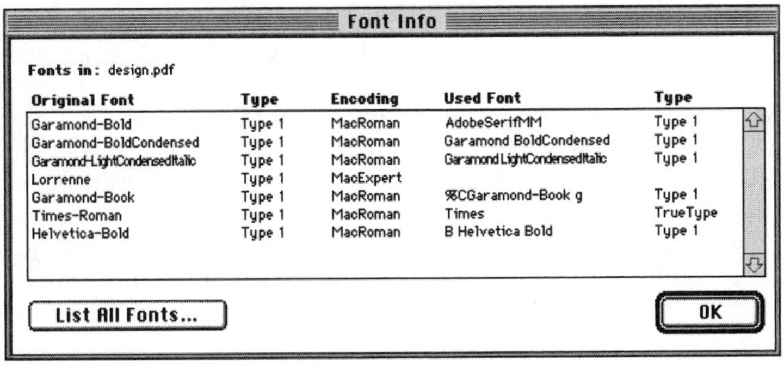

		Font Info		
Fonts in : design.pdf				
Original Font	**Type**	**Encoding**	**Used Font**	**Type**
Garamond-Bold	Type 1	MacRoman	AdobeSerifMM	Type 1
Garamond-BoldCondensed	Type 1	MacRoman	Garamond BoldCondensed	Type 1
Garamond-LightCondensedItalic	Type 1	MacRoman	Garamond LightCondensedItalic	Type 1
Lorrenne	Type 1	MacExpert		
Garamond-Book	Type 1	MacRoman	%CGaramond-Book g	Type 1
Times-Roman	Type 1	MacRoman	Times	TrueType
Helvetica-Bold	Type 1	MacRoman	B Helvetica Bold	Type 1

List All Fonts...   **OK**

Figure 3-4: I scrolled the pages, viewed another page in a PDF file, and then opened the Fonts Info dialog box to get this list.

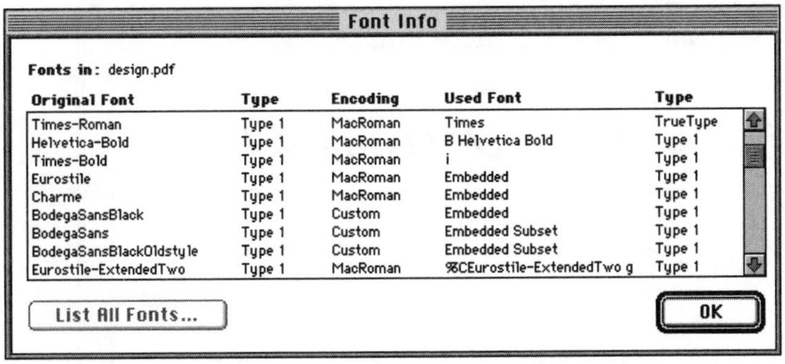

		Font Info		
Fonts in : design.pdf				
Original Font	**Type**	**Encoding**	**Used Font**	**Type**
Times-Roman	Type 1	MacRoman	Times	TrueType
Helvetica-Bold	Type 1	MacRoman	B Helvetica Bold	Type 1
Times-Bold	Type 1	MacRoman	i	Type 1
Eurostile	Type 1	MacRoman	Embedded	Type 1
Charme	Type 1	MacRoman	Embedded	Type 1
BodegaSansBlack	Type 1	Custom	Embedded	Type 1
BodegaSans	Type 1	Custom	Embedded Subset	Type 1
BodegaSansBlackOldstyle	Type 1	Custom	Embedded Subset	Type 1
Eurostile-ExtendedTwo	Type 1	MacRoman	%CEurostile-ExtendedTwo g	Type 1

List All Fonts...   **OK**

Figure 3-5: Font list in the Font Info dialog box after selecting the List All Fonts button

Note

Once the fonts are all listed, the List All Fonts button becomes grayed out. If you close the PDF file and start over, Reader won't remember the font list. If you wish to again view all the fonts in the Font Info dialog box, click List All Fonts again.

At the top of the font list appear several categories, as listed here:

✦ **Original Font:** The font(s) used in the original document.

✦ **Type** (second-column heading): The font type of the described font. If it is a Type 1 font, that will be indicated here. True Type will be specified, if used, as well as multiple master fonts.

✦ **Encoding:** The method of encoding used. Most often you'll see either MacRoman or Custom for the encoding method.

✦ **Used Font:** The reference to the font used in Reader. If you have the font installed in your system, the used font will be the same as the font employed when the PDF was created. If you do not have a font installed, a substitute font will be used.

✦ **Type** (fifth-column heading): The font type for the substitute font used.

Font Info is helpful if you want complete integrity of your PDF file output. When a PDF is created, the fonts may be substituted for similar fonts, as illustrated in Figures 3-6 and 3-7. Depending on the font and the font size, the substitution may not display the font as designed in the original document. If you have the same fonts installed on your computer as those listed in the Font Info document, you'll know which fonts to load when such data integrity is paramount to printing the file without font substitution. The only way to determine which fonts are contained in the PDF file is via the Font Info dialog box.

Figure 3-6: When the font(s) are installed or embedded in the PDF file, the display and printed file will include the original fonts.

Figure 3-7: If the font is not installed nor embedded, font substitution will be used. With script fonts, the substitution will be less accurate than with serif and sans serif fonts.

Security information

PDF authors can secure documents in Acrobat or at the time of distillation. Security can be handled at two levels: A document can be secured from viewing and secured against changes by another Acrobat user. The first level of security can be determined when you try to open a PDF file. If the document is secure, you'll need a password to open it. The second level of security can disable the following four items:

✦ **Printing:** Printing can be disabled to permit only screen viewing. A good example of the usefulness of this level of security concerns works published on the Internet by PDF authors who want to allow you to view their documents on screen, yet prevent you from easily duplicating copyrighted works.

✦ **Changing the Document:** Changes to documents involve all the authoring capabilities of Adobe Acrobat. If users are to view and/or print a PDF file, but not change it, disabling this item ensures no alterations to that PDF file can be made.

✦ **Selecting Text and Graphics:** Users can be prevented from selecting text and graphics that might ultimately be copied and pasted into other applications. Copying and subsequently pasting data cannot occur when this item is disabled.

✦ **Adding or Changing Notes and Form Fields:** If all the preceding security levels are disabled, an Acrobat user still has the opportunity to add notes or edit form fields. Disabling this item prevents users from changing note contents and data fields used in forms.

You can disable/enable one or more of these security options in the Security dialog box. If all are enabled, the end user is limited to viewing the PDF file on screen.

When you open a PDF and attempt to edit, change, or print it, and you find the task to be unavailable, it's a good idea to select File ➪ Document Info ➪ Security. When you select the command, the Security Info dialog box opens, providing you with feedback about any security that may have been included in the document when it was authored, as shown in Figure 3-8.

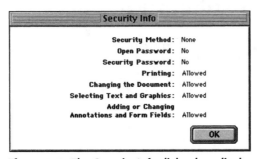

Figure 3-8: The Security Info dialog box displays all secure operations in the open PDF file.

This dialog box provides a starting point for troubleshooting printing or editing problems. As a first step, check the Security Info dialog box to see if the PDF is secure. If it is not, your inability to perform a task is related to something going on with the Acrobat viewer or printer.

Modifying preferences

Chapter 2 took a look at preference settings for Full Screen view. The preferences help users customize the Acrobat viewer environment for viewing, editing, and navigating through PDF files. Like any other application on your computer, it's always a good idea to examine preference settings when you first start using a program. All the preferences discussed in this chapter in reference to Acrobat Reader are identical to those available in Acrobat. (Additional preference settings unique to Acrobat are introduced when I cover more about the program in Chapter 7.)

General preferences

The general preference settings establish the viewing environment for the Acrobat viewer, enabling you to take control over how the documents you see on screen will be displayed. These settings have little to do with any PDF authoring you do. There are controls you can embed in a PDF document to control viewing, but these are handled through commands in Acrobat (as discussed in Part II of this book, which focuses on authoring PDF files). For the moment, take a look at the General Preferences dialog box, accessed by selecting File ➪ Preferences ➪ General (see Figure 3-9).

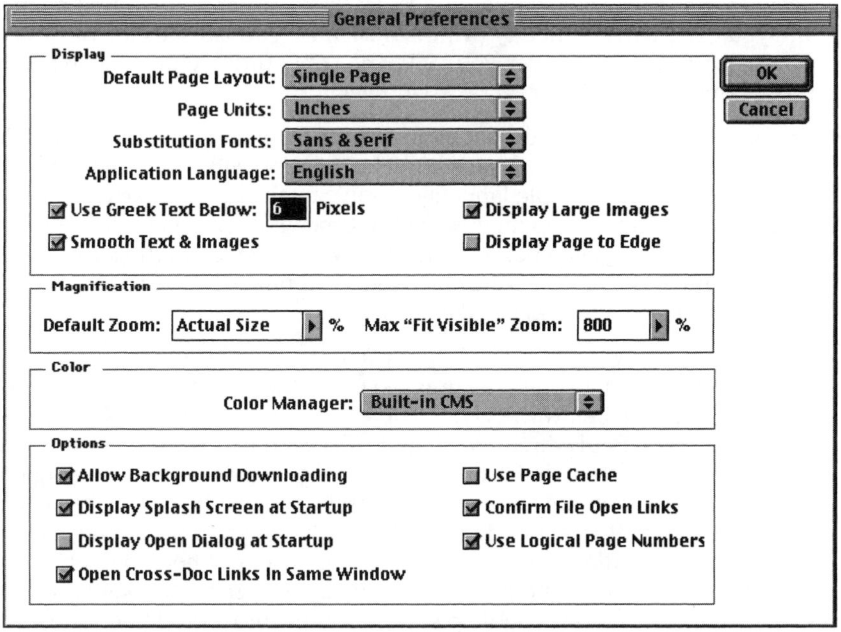

Figure 3-9: The General Preferences dialog box as viewed from Acrobat Reader 4.0

The General Preferences dialog box enables you to adjust the following settings:

✦ **Default Page Layout:** The default is Single Page. You can change to a new default by selecting either the Continuous or Continuous Facing Pages options from the pop-up menu. Either of these two options displays PDF files in the layout shown in Chapter 2. Once you change the viewing default, all subsequent documents will be displayed accordingly until you reset the preferences to another view. This preference setting is not dynamic. You need to make a choice from the pop-up menu appearing in the General Preferences dialog box and close any open PDF files. When you open a document after a new Default Page Layout change has been made, that document will be displayed according to your choice. If the change occurs when a document is open, the view of that document will not correspond to the change until you close and reopen that PDF file.

✦ **Page Units:** You can view the page dimensions in one of the three choices available: points, inches, or millimeters. The dimensions are indicated in the status bar in both Reader and Acrobat and also in the Crop dialog box in Acrobat only.

✦ **Substitution Fonts:** This setting enables you to determine which multiple master fonts Reader will use for substituting Type 1 and TrueType fonts. The default is Sans & Serif. If you have a Postscript Printer with limited memory, and you experience difficulty printing PDF files, choose Sans for the substitution font. Whenever you make the substitution change, you need to restart the Mac system or restart Windows.

✦ **Application Language:** Acrobat ships with multiple language support. The application language you choose upon installation will be the default language used. If you install multiple languages, you can elect to choose another language from the pop-up menu choices. Changing options in this menu causes all menus, dialog boxes, and windows to display in the language chosen. You must quit the Acrobat viewer and relaunch the application for the new language changes to take place.

✦ **Greek Text: Below [__] Pixels:** When you have a value entered in the Below__Pixels field, text will be greeked when the page view is reduced to display a font size below the given field entry. *Greeked text* displays as a gray bar, the characters of which are illegible. Greeked text is used to improve screen refreshes and help you navigate through pages faster. Greeking text has no effect on printing a file — regardless of the display, the pages will print with complete font integrity. Entries for the data field range between 0 and 99, with many applications using 6 points as the default. When you enter 0, no greeking of text occurs, no matter how small you size the viewer window. A good candidate for this would be screen dumps for tutorial handouts or Web graphics. If you desire no greeking, set the value to 2 or less or disable the check box. When you enter 99 in the data field, the font display in your viewer window will need to be larger than 99 pixels for the characters to be displayed without greeking. Greeking text is also dynamic. You can make any change in the field box and have the view reflected when you return to the viewer window.

✦ **Smooth Text and Images:** Produces an anti-aliased effect that smoothly renders the edges of text and monochrome images, minimizing the contrast between foreground and background elements. The result is usually a more improved appearance. When you disable the check box, fonts and monochrome images will be displayed with jagged edges (see Figure 3-10). This preference is dynamic; that is, you can change the view while a PDF is open, and when you return to the document window, the new view will take effect.

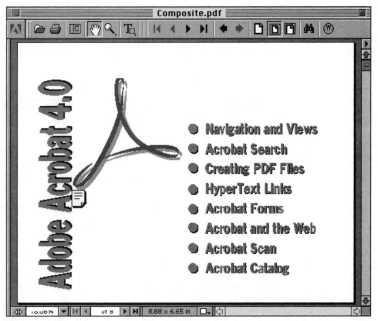

Figure 3-10: The PDF file is viewed while the preference setting for Smooth Text & Images is disabled. Notice the jagged display of the text.

✦ **Display Large Images:** When this option is enabled, all image data is viewed in Reader. When disabled, all images larger than 128K are displayed as a gray box. This toggle is available in the event image display slows your viewing; toggle the option off if you wish to move through pages faster. The Display Large Images option is also dynamic. If you elect to change the preferences while viewing an open PDF file, the changes will take effect immediately when you return to the document window.

✦ **Display Page to Edge:** This preference setting was introduced with Acrobat 3.01 and was only available in Acrobat Exchange 3.01. When Acrobat 3.0 was introduced, distilled PDFs were not clipped according to the printer driver's page dimension. This was actually a bug in the program. However, when Acrobat was upgraded, Adobe reinstituted the bug based on requests from users. When Display Page to Edge is enabled, the Acrobat viewer honors the page clipping provided by the driver. In many cases, when PDFs are properly created, you won't see any difference regardless of whether the preference is enabled or not.

✦ **Default Zoom:** The default is Actual Size, which translates to a 100 percent view. If your monitor is either small or large, and you wish to view all documents at another size, the pop-up menu offers many different choices. Sizes ranging from 25 to 1,600 percent are available as well as the options Fit in Window, Actual Size, Fit Width, and Fit Visible. The Fit in Window, Fit Width, and Fit Visible options are the same ones discussed in Chapter 2. Changes you make to the default magnification are not dynamic. Any change will require you to close an open PDF file and reopen it for the new view to take effect.

✦ **Max "Fit Visible" Zoom:** If you specify Fit Visible as the default zoom, this option enables you to describe the maximum amount of magnification for this view. For example, if you wish to fit only the visible data in a PDF file on screen but want the magnification to be no greater than 400 percent, you would select 400% from the Max "Fit Visible" Zoom pop-up menu. In such a case, the page view would never exceed 400 percent. The default for Acrobat viewers is 200 percent, which zooms in on the window. At times, you may navigate through articles or pages in a PDF file and find the zoom to be too high for comfortable viewing. In such cases, return to the General Preferences dialog box and select a new Max "Fit Visible" Zoom default. Changes made to this option are dynamic. If you find the magnification of an open PDF file to be too high, you can make a change in the General Preferences dialog box and return to the open window. The next time you view a page where this option is used, the new change will take effect.

✦ **Color Manager:** Earlier versions of Acrobat viewers provided the option to either use calibrated color or not. In Acrobat 4.0, you can choose from a color management system you have installed on your computer. If you have no other systems installed, the built-in color management system, displayed as Built-in CMS on the pop-up menu, will be the default.

✦ **Allow Background Downloading:** When viewing PDF files on the Web, you can have a requested page download to your computer, and the remainder of the PDF document will also be downloaded. If this preference setting is disabled, only the requested page will be downloaded. However, you may experience some complications when navigating via a Web browser if you do disable this option.

✦ **Display Splash Screen at Startup:** When enabled, the Acrobat splash screen comes into view while Reader is loading. Disabling this option will eliminate the screen from view when Reader is launched.

✦ **Display Open Dialog at Startup:** When enabled, the Open dialog box will appear each time Reader is launched. If you launch a PDF file by double-clicking a document, the document will load in the viewer window and bypass the Open dialog box.

✦ **Open Cross-Doc Links In Same Window:** When this option is enabled, document links are opened in a single window to minimize the number of windows open at any given time. When disabled, a new window opens whenever a link is accessed. When you have the Open Cross-Doc Links In Same Window preference enabled, you can temporarily disable it by holding down the Option/Ctrl key when clicking the link. When viewing PDF files from other authors, check that this setting is enabled. Many authors will assume you have the Cross-Doc Links In Same Window preference enabled, as this will help you navigate through their PDF files with much less confusion. (Cross-document links were reviewed in Chapter 2 in the discussion on navigating PDFs via hypertext links.)

✦ **Use Page Cache:** When enabled, the Page Cache will require more system memory, but the viewing of PDF pages will move faster as pages are loaded to the cache. Disabling the option will conserve RAM on your computer.

✦ **Confirm File Open Links** Provides a warning dialog box when attempting to open a secure file from another application via a link in the PDF document. The warning dialog box enables you to cancel the operation.

✦ **Use Logical Page Numbers**: In Acrobat, you have the ability to renumber pages and create sections. If, for example, you have a 20-page document, and you specify the first page to be designated page 10, the document pages will be numbered 10 to 29. When you open the PDF file in Reader and disable Use Logical Page Numbers, the pages will appear in their original numbered form (that is, pages 1 to 20). If you enable the preference setting, the status bar will show something like 10 (1 to 20), indicating the new first page number has been changed to 10, but you are viewing the first page out of a total of 20 pages.

If you encounter any problems related to the speed of navigating through PDF files, you may wish to return to the General Preferences dialog box and set preferences that will affect the speed of your display. The display of large images, text greeking, smoothing of text and graphics, and page caching each affect the overall performance of your page viewing.

Annotation preferences

The second item in the Preferences submenu is Annotations. When you select File ➪ Preferences ➪ Annotations, the Annotations Preferences dialog box opens. In Acrobat Reader, you're limited to the display of annotations in the PDF file you view. With Acrobat, because you can author annotations, more options are available to you. One of the nice new features of Acrobat 4.0 is it enables you to create many different types of annotations (which I cover in Chapter 8).

When annotations are created in a PDF file, the annotation view and position is saved with the authoring application. Annotations can be collapsed, with the annotation appearing as an icon and the text within the annotation hidden from view, as shown in Figure 3-11.

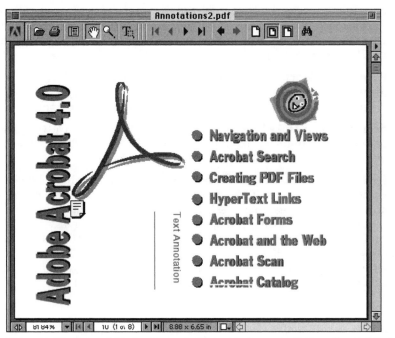

Figure 3-11: Several kinds of annotations are shown in their collapsed form.

While in an Acrobat viewer, if you encounter a collapsed annotation, double-click the icon to open it. The document shown in Figure 3-12 contains annotations that have been expanded. If you wish to collapse an annotation while viewing a PDF, click the small box in the top-left corner of the note title bar. While in Reader, you can move an annotation by clicking the title bar and dragging it to a new location. If you close the document window and reopen the file, the icon will return to its original position. If you perform the same steps in Acrobat and save a file after an annotation is moved, the new location of the icon will be retained in the saved file.

You are limited to two choices for annotation preferences in Reader. You can view annotations with any of the installed fonts in your system, or you can view the contents at custom or preset font point sizes. The Font pop-up menu in the Note Preferences dialog box displays all available fonts. You can choose any of the listed fonts for viewing notes in Reader, as shown in Figure 3-13.

The font point size can be selected from preset values in the Point Size pop-up menu made available when you click the down arrow icon in the Note Preferences dialog box.

Note   You have only five preset font size choices in the pop-up menu. If you wish to use another size, enter a value in the Point Size field box. Changes you make in the Note Preferences dialog box are dynamic — they will be displayed when you return to the viewer window.

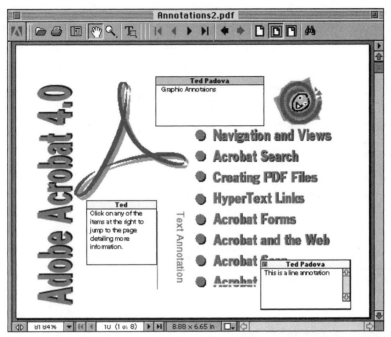

Figure 3-12: All the annotations from Figure 3-11 are expanded to reveal their text.

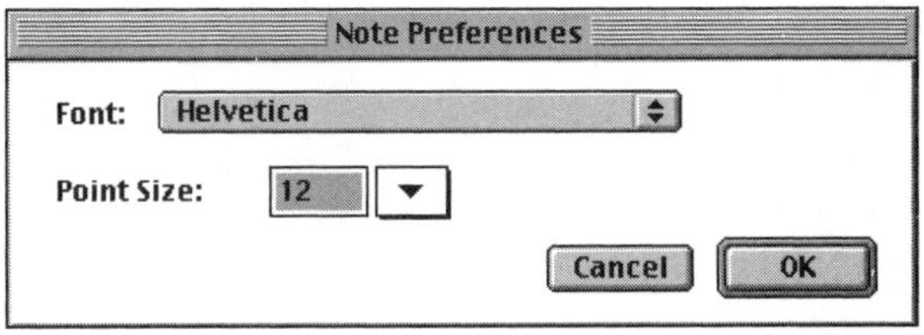

Figure 3-13: Annotation preferences in Acrobat Reader offer two choices: the font and font size for viewing annotation notes.

Acceptable values for the Point Size field box fall in the range of 8 and 24 points. Ideally, you'll want to adjust the settings for comfortable viewing. A sans serif font usually displays better for on-screen reading, especially at smaller point sizes.

WebLink preferences

Chapter 2 discussed all the preference settings for Full Screen and Search. If you have read that chapter, you also learned that hypertext links can be made to Uniform Resource Locators (URLs) on the World Wide Web. Clicking a hypertext button with such a link in a PDF document will launch a Web browser and connect you to the site specified in the URL. Determining a browser and changing browsers can all be accomplished in the WebLink Preferences dialog box, shown in Figures 3-14 (Mac) and 3-15 (Windows). When you select File ⇨ Preferences ⇨ Weblink, the dialog box appears.

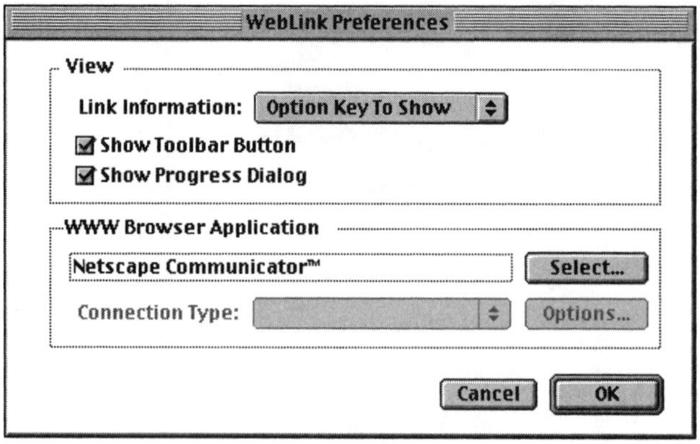

Figure 3-14: WebLink Preferences dialog box on the Macintosh

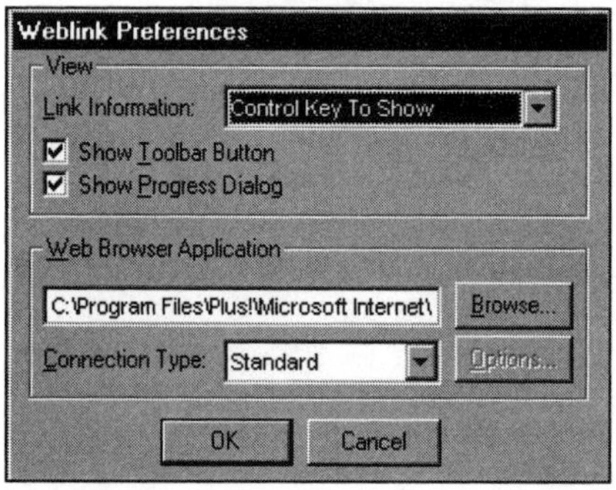

Figure 3-15: WebLink Preferences dialog box in Windows

The WebLink Preferences dialog box enables you to navigate to your hard drive and locate the Web browser you wish to use in the Acrobat viewer. This dialog box has a few selections for specifying Web link views and addressing the browser as listed here:

✦ **Link Information:** On the Macintosh you have three choices for Link Information: Always Show, Option Key to Show, and Never Show. In Windows, you have two choices: Control Key to Show or Never Show. When you elect to show link information, the URL specified by the hypertext link will be displayed as a Tool Tip (see Figure 3-16).

When Option Key to Show (Mac) or Control Key to Show (Windows) is selected from the Link Information pop-up menu, you need to press Option/Ctrl and move the cursor over the URL link to show the URL you are about to launch. The Never Show option specifies that no Web Link information will be displayed, regardless of which key is depressed.

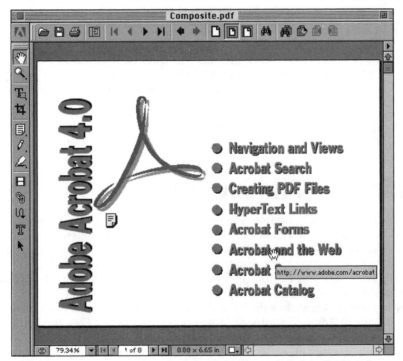

Figure 3-16: On the Macintosh, the URL for the Web link is displayed as a Tool Tip when you select the modifier key identified in the WebLink Preferences dialog box. In Windows, the default modifier is the Ctrl key.

✦ **Show Toolbar Button:** When enabled, an icon representing the browser you specify in the WebLink dialog box is displayed in the viewer's Command Bar. If you select the button in the Command Bar, this browser will be launched. The Web Page viewed will be the one you defined for your home view. This action is just like launching the browser from the desktop or Windows status bar.

✦ **Show Progress Dialog:** If this option is enabled, a progress bar will be displayed as your Web browser is launched. If you have a fast computer and fast connection to the Internet, no display may be visible. Disabling the item will eliminate the appearance of a progress bar during connection to a Web site.

✦ **WWW Browser Application** (Mac) or **Web Browser Application** (Windows): In the Macintosh version of the WebLink Preferences dialog box, you'll notice a button denoted Select. In the Windows version, the button is Browse. On either platform, selecting this button will open a navigation dialog box, which enables you to search your hard drive and locate the browser of choice. If you use both Microsoft Internet Explorer and Netscape Navigator, you can return to the WebLink Preferences dialog box to toggle back and forth between browsers during your Acrobat viewer sessions.

✦ **Connection Type:** On the Macintosh, you won't have an option for Connection Type, as it is supplied automatically for you. In Windows, you have a choice of connection standards from various browser manufacturers. Typically, you won't need to select from the Connection Type pop-up menu in Windows, because a default choice is made for you when identifying the browser.

✦ **Options:** The Options button will often be disabled. With either Microsoft Internet Explorer or Netscape Navigator specified, this button is unavailable.

Opening and Printing PDFs

To add a little more consistency across computer applications, Adobe has added tools in the Command Bar in both Reader and Acrobat for opening and printing files. The Open tool, whose button is adjacent to the Adobe Online button (see the end of the chapter for an explanation of the Adobe Online button), is used for opening files. Clicking this button produces the same navigation dialog box that appears when you select File ➪ Open. Next to the Open tool is the Print tool. Clicking this tool launches the Print dialog box, the same as if you had selected File ➪ Print. In Acrobat, another button appears for saving files and behaves just like selecting File ➪ Save. Although a bit redundant, the icons for these tool buttons are familiar to computer users of many applications, including most of the Microsoft products (see Figure 3-17).

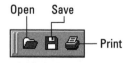

Figure 3-17: The Open, Save, and Print tools as they appear in Acrobat

Making Text and Graphics Selections

Up to this point we've looked at tools in Reader for views and displays, navigation, finding and searching text, and Web links. As you examine the Reader Command Bar, notice that only one tool is available. Reader, as a viewer, cannot create or modify text. You can, however, select both text and graphics in Reader. By default, the Text Select tool is visible in the Reader Command Bar. Pressing the mouse button over this tool expands the toolbar to reveal two additional tools. These tools include the Text Select tool, the Column Select tool, and the Graphics Select tool, shown in Figure 3-18.

Text Select tool
Column Select tool

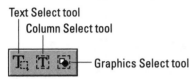 — Graphics Select tool

Figure 3-18: Pressing the mouse button over the Text Select tool reveals two additional tool options.

Text Select tool

The Text Select tool appears in the Reader Command Bar to the right of the Zoom tool. To select the tool, move the cursor to the tool and click or press the V key on your keyboard. Press Shift+V to toggle all the Select tools.

Use of this tool behaves a little differently than similar text tools in other applications. When you click a word with the cursor in a PDF document, the entire word is selected. You can't select individual characters. Multiple words can be selected by dragging through a line of text or down several lines of text to select the text in a paragraph. All the text on a page can be selected by choosing Edit ➪ Select All. Select All is available regardless of the tool you have selected from the Reader Command Bar. When using the Text Select tool, it doesn't matter if the text is contained in a contiguous block. Reader will select all the text on the page when you drag from top to bottom or vice versa. You needn't be concerned about selecting the first word when you drag across the page either. All text is selected even if you drag from an area where no text appears and move the cursor up or down.

To select a horizontal line of text, drag the Text Select tool across the line of text to be selected. You can start the cursor position from outside the first characters to be selected and drag across the line. All text in the line will be selected as you drag the mouse cursor, as shown in Figure 3-19.

Figure 3-19: When the Text Select tool is dragged across a line of text, all the text in a horizontal line will be selected. Acrobat viewers make no distinction between single and multiple columns.

Column Select tool

Acrobat viewers don't interpret text the way word processors or text editing applications do. The viewers handle text more like clumps spattered across the page. If you wish to select a column of text, the Text Select tool is not the ideal choice; dragging this tool down the column will select not only the text in the column but also the text in adjacent columns, as shown in Figure 3-20. The Column Select tool behaves more like a selection marquee, which restricts text selection to the area confined within the marquee. If you wish to select a column of text, use the Column Select tool and draw a marquee around the text column (see Figures 3-21 and 3-22).

When using either the Text Select tool or the Column Select tool, you can temporarily toggle to one or the other by pressing the Option/Alt key. If, for example, your current tool is the Text Select tool, pressing Option/Alt enables the Column Select tool. Using the modifier keys eliminates the need to return to the Command Bar or to swap tools by pressing Shift+V.

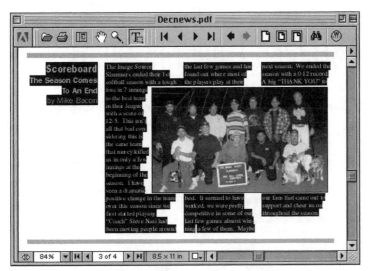

Figure 3-20: When the Text Select tool is dragged down the page, multiple columns are selected.

Figure 3-21: By using the Column Select tool, you place a marquee around the text to be selected.

Figure 3-22: When the mouse button is released, all the text within a marquee drawn by the Column Select tool will be selected.

Copying and pasting text

If you want to move text from a Reader page to a word processor, you can select the text and copy it to your system clipboard. Once copied to the clipboard, the text can be pasted into any document that supports text. Pasted text will not retain formatting with complete integrity. Even though text does not convert to ASCII text, in which all formatting attributes are lost, you may lose some tabs and paragraph formatting. Depending on the application you use, more or less of the formatting will be retained when pasted into a new document. If colors have not been identified in the resultant document, an application supporting text colors different from those in the Reader file may use a close proximity of a particular color identified in the pasted text.

To see how this works, let's perform a simple copy and paste operation so you can examine the results. If you have Microsoft Word or another word processor, use it for the example. If you do not have a word processor, you can use a layout application or text editor.

STEPS: Copying Text in Reader and Pasting in a Word Processor

1. **Launch Reader and Microsoft Word:** If you do not have enough memory to keep both Reader and your word processor open concurrently, launch Reader.

2. **Select File ⇨ Open:** Open a PDF file of your choice. If you have no file available, use one of the Help files in your Acrobat folder.

3. **Navigate to a page with a large body of text:** Use the navigation tools to move to a page that has a large body of text. (In this example, the results of which are shown in Figure 3-23, I used a PDF created from a newsletter.)

4. **Select the Select All command:** Select Edit ⇨ Select All or strike Cmd/Ctrl+A. All the text on the page should be highlighted, as shown in Figure 3-23.

Figure 3-23: All the text on a single PDF page is selected when you choose Edit ⇨ Select All.

5. **Select Edit ⇨ Copy:** The text will be copied to the clipboard.

6. **Select Window ⇨ Show Clipboard:** Examine the clipboard. You should see the text from the selection appear in the clipboard window. Observe the text and note the different font sizes and colors have been retained.

7. **Open your word processor:** If you have Microsoft Word launched, select Word from the application selections in the top-right corner of your screen (Mac) or from the status bar (Windows). If you don't have a word processor loaded in memory, quit Reader and launch your word processor.

8. **Select Edit ⇨ Paste:** If your word processor opens with a new document window, you can paste the clipboard contents immediately (see Figure 3-24). If you need to create a new window, select File ⇨ New. After a new document is displayed, select Edit ⇨ Paste.

Continued

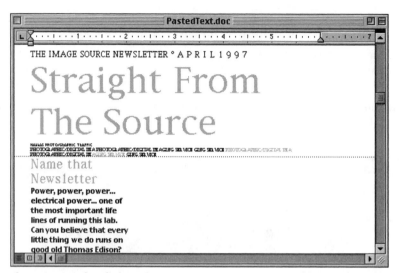

Figure 3-24: The clipboard contents appear in the new document window.

In Microsoft Word, some of the text formatting is retained. Fonts displayed in the Word toolbar will show substituted font names from Adobe multiple master fonts. The text appears with colors either identical to the values in the Reader file or with a color range similar to the colors in the original Reader file.

Copying and pasting graphics

Graphics selections in an Acrobat viewer are handled similarly to the text selections made through the Column Select tool. The Graphics Select tool behaves like some of the available utilities for screen dumps. Mainstay Capture for the Macintosh or Corel Capture for Windows enable you to define the area of the screen to be captured by dragging open a marquee. Whereas capture utilities save the defined region to disk, the Graphics Select tool in the Acrobat viewer merely selects the marquee contents. From there, you need to copy the selection and paste it into an image editing application. Regardless of whichever method you use, you can't raise the resolution of the captured area above 72 pixels per inch (ppi). At best, this tool enables you to use graphic selections for screen views. Printing the selections on almost any kind of output device requires a higher resolution image.

When you select the Graphics Select tool and place the cursor in the Acrobat document window, the cursor will change to a plus (+) symbol, indicating the Acrobat viewer expects you to create a marquee. Click and drag to open a marquee around the image you want to select. When you release the mouse button, a marquee will be displayed, but the contents will not appear to be selected (see Figure 3-25). The traditional "marching ants" do not appear, and the selection is not highlighted. Though this behavior is different from almost any other type of selection you may create in any application, the image you want actually has been selected.

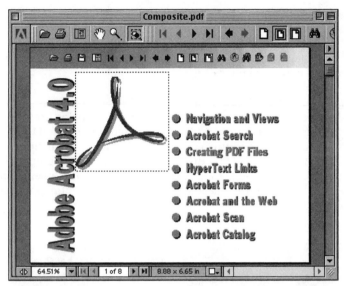

Figure 3-25: When you create a selection with the Graphics
Select tool, a marquee rectangle delineates the selected area.

To copy the selection contents, use the same method described for text selections:
Select Edit ⇨ Copy to place the image contents on the clipboard. Files copied to the
clipboard will use your system native file format. On Windows, the file format for
clipboard information will be Windows Metafile (WMF); on the Macintosh, the
format is PICT. After copying the data, you can display the clipboard contents and
view your copied file data by selecting Window ⇨ Show Clipboard in your Acrobat
viewer (see Figure 3-26).

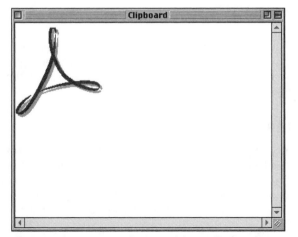

Figure 3-26: You can view graphics copied to the
clipboard by selecting Window ⇨ Show Clipboard.

Copied graphics can be edited in image editing programs such as Adobe Photoshop. Photoshop enables you to create a new document with the default size determined from the clipboard contents. If you copy a graphic in an Acrobat viewer, launch Photoshop, and then select File ⇨ New, the dimensions for width and height will be supplied from the clipboard image's width and height.

As illustrated in Figure 3-27, the physical dimensions of the new Photoshop window will conform to the data on the clipboard. As you view the New dialog box in Photoshop, notice the default resolution is 72 ppi. You might be tempted to pump up the resolution in an attempt to capture a high-resolution image. Unfortunately, the Metafile or PICT format won't give you the same results as an EPS graphic from a vector editing program. If you change the resolution in the new document and then paste the clipboard contents, the image will appear severely bitmapped, as shown in Figure 3-28.

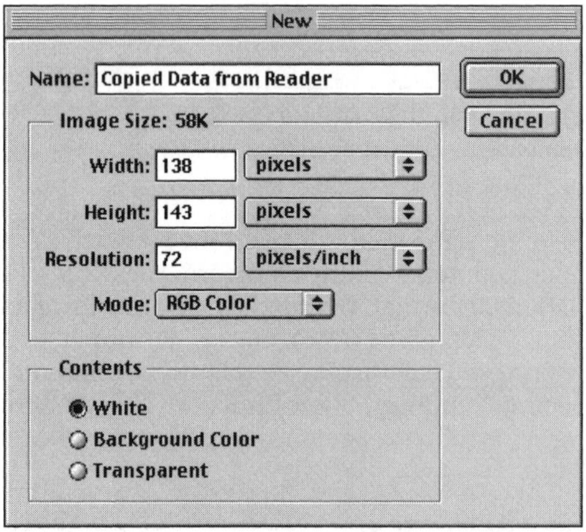

Figure 3-27: I copied a graphic from Acrobat Reader and launched Photoshop 5.0. When I selected File ⇨ New, the new document size was determined from my clipboard contents.

Copying and pasting graphics in most cases will be restricted to image editing you might perform for screen graphics. For any kind of printed documents or high-end digital prepress, you'll want to return to the original document(s) and open the original images in your editing application.

Context-sensitive menus

In Chapter 2, I discussed the use of context-sensitive menus. You can use context-sensitive menus with the Text Select tool, the Column Select tool, or the Graphics Select tool. When any of the three tools are positioned in the PDF window, hold the Control key down (Macintosh) or press the right mouse button (Windows) to open a pop-up menu. With the Graphics Select tool you have three options (see Figure 3-29):

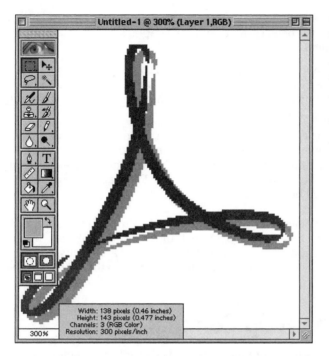

igure 3-28: When I selected File ➪ New in Photoshop, I changed the default resolution from 72 ppi to 300 ppi and then pasted my PDF graphic selection. The pasted image appears severely bitmapped.

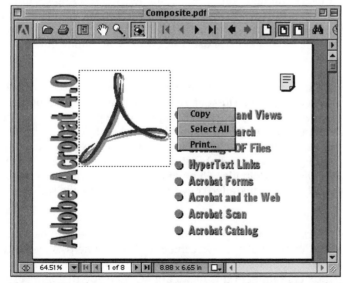

Figure 3-29: The context-sensitive menu for the Graphics Select tool offers three menu options: Copy, Select All, and Print.

✦ **Copy:** Selecting this option will copy the marquee contents to the clipboard. If a marquee has not yet been created with the Graphics Select tool, the Copy option will be grayed out.

✦ **Select All:** If you choose Select All from the pop-up menu, a marquee will be created around the PDF page. The entire page can then be copied to the clipboard by selecting Edit ➪ Copy or by bringing back the context-sensitive menu and selecting Copy.

✦ **Print:** When Print is chosen, the Acrobat viewer opens the Print dialog box. At first you might think the contents of a graphic selection will print when you select Print from the context-sensitive menu. Making this choice only brings up the Print dialog box. When printed, the entire PDF page or pages specified in the dialog box will be printed.

If you use either the Text Select tool or the Column Select tool, the options available from the context-sensitive menu are Copy, Select All, and New Bookmark. You can select text on a page and add a bookmark to it. (Bookmarks are discussed in Chapter 9.) Print is not an option when using the menu with either of these tools.

Using the Online Help Commands

Online help for all the Acrobat components is available through a menu command. Macintosh System 7.x users will find online help commands in the Apple Guide menu appearing at the top-right corner of the monitor screen. Macintosh System 8.x and Windows users will find a Help menu appearing after the Window menu in an Acrobat viewer. Whichever system you use, there will be an online guide available to you.

These help menu commands perform two different types of assistance. When you open one of the Acrobat components (Reader, Acrobat, Distiller, or Catalog), an online guide menu item will appear in the menu respective to your system software. When you select this menu item, a PDF document installed with Adobe Acrobat will open in an Acrobat viewer related to the application from which you are choosing the guide. For example, if you have Acrobat Distiller open and select Help ➪ Acrobat Distiller Guide, the PDF Distiller Help file will open in an Acrobat viewer. If you have both Acrobat Reader and Acrobat installed on your computer, the file will open in Acrobat.

Whereas any of the Acrobat components can address an online help guide from the installed help files, only the Acrobat viewers can open Web link help. A menu item denoted Adobe on the Web appears on the Help menu in Reader and in Acrobat. The submenu commands contained in this menu item enable you to connect to Adobe's Web site for online support for Acrobat, as shown in Figure 3-30.

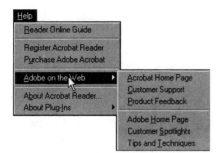

Figure 3-30: The Help menu in Acrobat Reader offers a connection to Adobe's Web site and the Acrobat home page, as well as links to the many help guides installed with your Acrobat application.

Help guides

For ease of discussion, I'll refer to the menu commands for Macintosh System 8.*x* and Windows users. If you are using a Macintosh with System 7.*x*, use the Apple Guide menu when I refer to the Acrobat viewer Help menu.

When you open Reader and view the Help menu, one of two items will access the Reader help guide. Select Help ➪ Reader Online Guide, and the READER.PDF file will open. This file is installed on your computer in the Reader folder created during the installation of Acrobat Reader. If you install Adobe Acrobat and Reader, the READER.PDF file is installed in a subfolder called Help. If you select Help ➪ Purchase Adobe Acrobat, the Acrobat.pdf file will open, and a page describing Acrobat will appear. Links from this page to another page and, subsequently, another link to Adobe's Web site will take you to information related to Acrobat.

The file that opens is your online user manual for the Adobe Acrobat Reader software. Because Reader is distributed free from Adobe Systems, there are no printed user manuals. All the support for Reader is contained in PDF documents. Even when you purchase Adobe Acrobat, many documents and references are contained in online guides, which are installed in the Help folder. Acrobat 4.0 comes with more printed documentation than earlier versions, but you'll find much more available when you explore the online guides. If you can use the many different search capabilities of Acrobat Search, as examined in Chapter 2, you'll find support for Adobe Acrobat much easier in the online guides than you could possibly find in printed publications. In addition to the searches you may use with an online guide, you'll find an elaborate set of bookmarks that further your capability to find help fast.

If you have Adobe Acrobat installed, the Help folder inside your Acrobat folder will contain many different help files. The help file respective to the application you are using will be accessible in the Help menu, or you can select File ➪ Open from an Acrobat viewer and open any of the PDF files contained among the help guides. An index file is also included in the Help folder with hypertext links to pages in all the PDF online guides respective to the information being sought.

Accessing Adobe's Web Link

Like most of the other Adobe applications, you can access Adobe's Web site while in Reader by clicking a tool in the Command Bar, selecting File ➪ Adobe Online, or selecting Help ➪ Adobe on the Web. You need an Internet connection to take advantage of the Web link, whether it be a simple dial-up connection or a faster method. The top-left icon in the Reader and Acrobat Command Bar will connect you to Adobe's Acrobat Web site. Click this icon or use one of the other choices, and you'll see a splash screen for browsing information about your Acrobat viewer, as shown in Figure 3-31. If this is your first connection to the Acrobat Web site, you may see a dialog box appear asking if you would like to download missing files. If the dialog box appears, select Yes, and a status bar will appear as the files are downloaded.

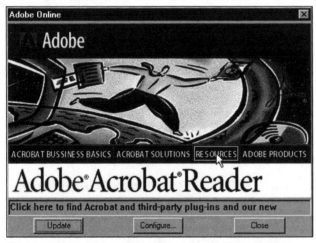

Figure 3-31: Adobe's Web site is accessed by selecting File ➪ Adobe Online or clicking the first tool in the Command Bar.

As you move the cursor across the text above the viewer name, Web link buttons will be identified. When you click a button, your Web browser will be launched and you will be taken you to the button's respective Web page.

Tip   Adobe maintains an excellent Web site, which is intuitive and easy to navigate. As you work with Acrobat or any other Adobe product, it's a good idea to revisit the Web pages related to your application. Upgrade information, new features, new releases of software, tips, technical information, and help are all available.

At the bottom of the Adobe Online dialog box appears three buttons. The Update button downloads files from Adobe's Web site that have updated links for navigating through the Acrobat Web pages. When you click the Update button, a status bar will open showing you the download progress. The Configure button enables you to configure some options for updating your connection. From the dialog box that opens on clicking the Configure button, you can elect to manually update the Adobe Web links or set automatic update intervals. The third button, Close, closes the Adobe Online splash screen and returns you to your Acrobat viewer.

As Acrobat evolves and becomes updated, you will need additional documentation for changes and upgrades. Because the Adobe Web site can offer you updates faster than printed documentation, you'll find this method a useful tool in keeping you up to date with Acrobat products. The Adobe on the Web submenu, which can only be accessed through an Acrobat viewer, affords several helpful Web links from which to choose. If you launch either Distiller or Catalog, the Adobe Web links will not be available.

Register Acrobat Reader

The menu command for Register Acrobat Reader is a Web link that takes you to a page where a form can be completed for registration of the Reader software. Because Reader requires no serial number at the time you install it, registration is often overlooked by the 50,000+ people who download it daily. Adobe Systems doesn't require you to register the software, but it is advisable to take a moment and complete the registration. Once in the Reader user data bank, you'll be updated on information related to Acrobat software, and, if you choose, you'll be added to Adobe's e-mail list, through which you can receive electronic information about the product and upgrades to it.

Note Completing the online registration requires an Internet connection. When you select Help ➪ Register Acrobat Reader, the registration page for the Reader software will appear in your browser window (see Figure 3-32).

A Web link to a page for registration is only offered with Acrobat Reader. If you view the Help menu in Acrobat, there is no provision to use this menu for online registration. When you purchase Adobe Acrobat, the registration can be performed at the time the product is installed or by launching an application saved to your Acrobat folder when Acrobat is installed. A folder called Register will be included inside the Acrobat folder at the time of installation. A file called Register Online (Mac) or Register.exe (Win) inside the Register folder can be launched to complete online registration.

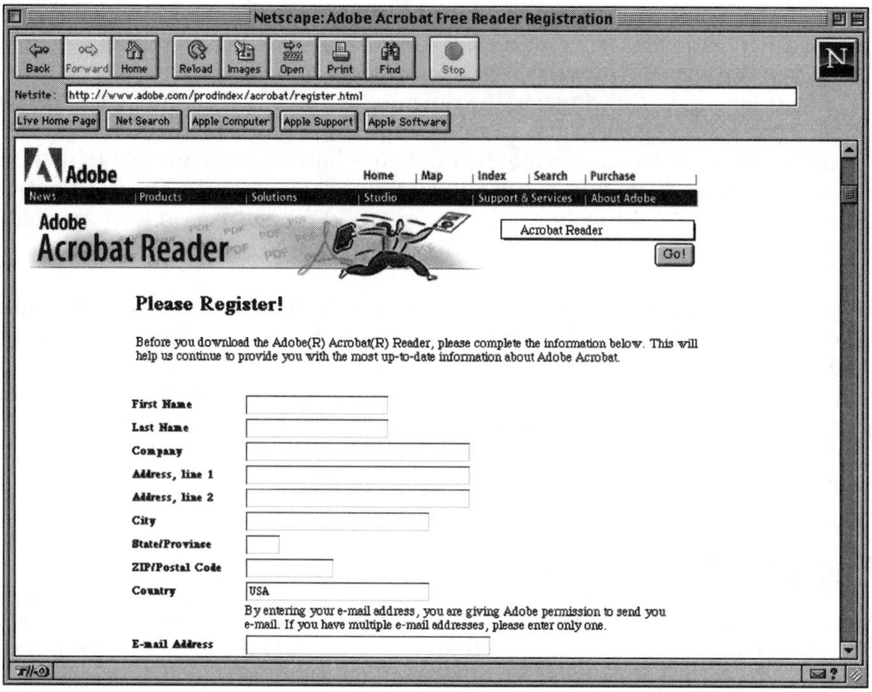

Figure 3-32: The Acrobat Reader registration Web page provides for online registration of the Reader software.

Get help from Adobe on the Web

All the menu commands in the Adobe on the Web submenu are Web links to Adobe's Web site. Regardless of which Acrobat viewer you use, the submenu commands are identical.

Acrobat home page

The first of the six menu items in the Adobe on the Web submenu will launch your browser and take you to the home page for Adobe Acrobat. The Adobe Acrobat home page (see Figure 3-33) is the central navigation point for all the information related to Adobe Acrobat. From this page you can navigate through Adobe's Web site and explore information related to the Acrobat applications and PDF workflows, and select buttons for update information and third-party software that works with Acrobat.

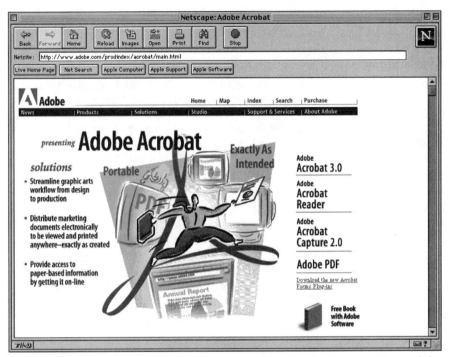

Figure 3-33: The Adobe Acrobat home page supplies information specific to Adobe Acrobat.

Customer support

The Customer Support Web page deals with support for Acrobat, technical support in particular. Here you can browse a Web page detailing the top ten problems with Acrobat performance; reach a tech support e-mail center where you can e-mail questions, which are answered by Adobe's technical support staff within 24 hours; or peruse the frequently asked questions page, where common problems and solutions are displayed. Like many other Web pages, the Customer Support site may be updated periodically, thereby offering more solutions for your Acrobat performance.

Product feedback

The Product Feedback page is a generic page dealing with all of Adobe's software. This page enables you to offer Adobe feedback on their products. If you have an idea or find an annoyance with Acrobat or any other Adobe-developed application, by all means send Adobe your comments. You may think these comments don't mean much to the developers, but I assure you they do. I have been involved with a number of Adobe application beta test programs for several years, and I know the many user comments are considered when testing new releases. Quite often software engineers alert the beta testers to review particular features because of the user feedback requests. Not all user input can be incorporated in new upgrades, but you can be certain that if your comments are shared by several other users, Adobe Systems will make an attempt to include a feature request the next time the product is upgraded.

Adobe home page

When you select Help ➪ Adobe on the Web ➪ Adobe Home Page, the home page for http://www.adobe.com will be displayed. Although the Adobe Acrobat home page is specific to the Acrobat suite of products, the Adobe home page spans all Adobe software. This page, resembling the front page of a newspaper where the headlines are displayed, is ever changing and demonstrates the hottest new features or developments of Adobe Systems. From this page, you can navigate Adobe's Web site to view information related to Acrobat or any other Adobe product.

Customer spotlights

The Customer Spotlights page lists all the Adobe links to pages that contain examples of real-world customer experiences. Some of the more impressive work performed in Adobe applications are highlighted on specific pages related to a given software product. When you view the Customer Spotlights Web page, a link to the Acrobat Case Studies page will be displayed, as shown in Figure 3-34. In the list, click Acrobat, and you'll see a page appear with case studies of actual customers who have used Acrobat for various solutions.

Figure 3-34: The Case Studies Web page for Acrobat lists several examples of how people have used Acrobat for different solutions.

Tips and techniques

The last of the Web links appearing in the Adobe on the Web submenu is a link to a Web page listing several tips and techniques in using Acrobat — particularly Acrobat 4.0. Adobe software engineers, product managers, and senior designers often supply how-to's and workarounds for using Adobe applications on the Tips and Techniques Web page, shown in Figure 3-35. You should plan on making a visit to this page periodically, especially when the product is updated. You'll find many interesting techniques that can help you use the software more effectively.

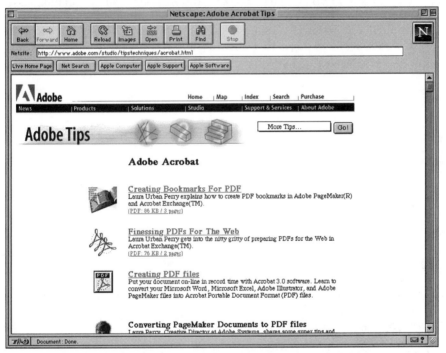

Figure 3-35: The Tips and Techniques Web page offers many helpful tips on using Acrobat more effectively.

Summary

✦ The Reader environment is controlled through menu commands for document information and preferences. You can change preferences to suit your individual needs when viewing documents in Acrobat Reader.

✦ Weblink preferences enable you to determine which Web browser you wish to use when selecting Web links in PDF documents and accessing Adobe Web pages.

✦ Text selections are made with the Text Select tool. Text can be copied from an Acrobat viewer and pasted into a text editor.

✦ Graphic image selections can be made with the Graphics Select tool, which is located on the Command Bar in an Acrobat viewer. Graphics, like text, can be copied. The copied images can be pasted into an image editor.

✦ Online help guides are installed with Acrobat Reader and Acrobat 4.0. Help can be selected from the Help menu, which will open a help guide in an Acrobat viewer.

✦ Web links to Adobe's Web site offer additional help and information about Adobe Acrobat. You can view the Adobe Acrobat home page and navigate through a site related to information about Acrobat. Among other information is a special link to pages that offer tips and techniques in using Acrobat.

✦   ✦   ✦

Creating PDF Documents

Chapter 4
Creating PDFs with PDFWriter

Chapter 5
Using Acrobat Distiller

Chapter 6
PDF Exports and Imports

Chapter 7
Using Acrobat Exchange

Creating PDFs with PDFWriter

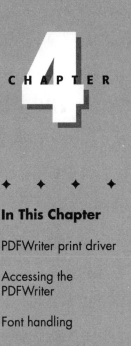
◆ ◆ ◆ ◆

In This Chapter

PDFWriter print driver

Accessing the PDFWriter

Font handling

File compression

Printing from PDFWriter

Creating a PDF file

◆ ◆ ◆ ◆

Two components of the Adobe Acrobat software enable you to create a PDF file from the documents of various applications: the Adobe Acrobat PDFWriter and Acrobat Distiller. Both of these components are part of the Adobe Acrobat Suite of software. PDF files can also be created within many applications directly via an Export command. (Many of the Adobe applications support such a feature.) Other software manufacturers such as Macromedia and Corel Corporation include PDF exports with programs such as FreeHand and CorelDraw.

Upon first view of Acrobat, you may wonder why Adobe ships two applications* to perform the same task. The answer is not entirely clear, but I suspect it's an effort by Adobe to help ease the general population of users into more widespread usage of the PDF format.

Since version 1.0 of Acrobat, users have had the Acrobat Distiller to create PDF files. However, Distiller is more complicated to use than PDFWriter and requires a two-step process versus PDFWriter's one-step process. When PDFWriter was introduced, it simplified the PDF creation. Unfortunately, simplicity in high-tech terms does not always mean better and often comes at a price. The price you pay to create files with the PDFWriter rather than with Distiller, in some cases, will be an unusable document. Therefore, it is important to know something about both products and learn when to use one instead of the other.

*The reference to two applications is used for simplicity. In actuality, PDFWriter is a printer driver and Acrobat Distiller is an application program. In referring to both items, I'll use the term *applications*.

The PDFWriter Print Driver

Version 3.0 of Adobe Acrobat introduced many new upgrades to the various components of the software. When version 3.0 was introduced for Windows and the Macintosh, Acrobat Capture and Acrobat Scan were only supported on Windows. Adobe quickly upgraded Acrobat to version 3.0.1, giving Macintosh users access to Capture and Scan. With the 3.0.1 upgrade came a PDFWriter upgrade as well.

Tip   If you're a Mac user with version 3.0.1 of Acrobat, be certain you use the PDFWriter version 3.0.1. The PDFWriter will be installed in your System: Extensions folder. Find the extension and select File ⇨ Get Info to verify the version number. If you've upgraded to the newest release of Acrobat 4.0, check the PDFWriter version number. Version 4.0 users should see the version identified as Acrobat PDFWriter 4.0 (see Figure 4-1).

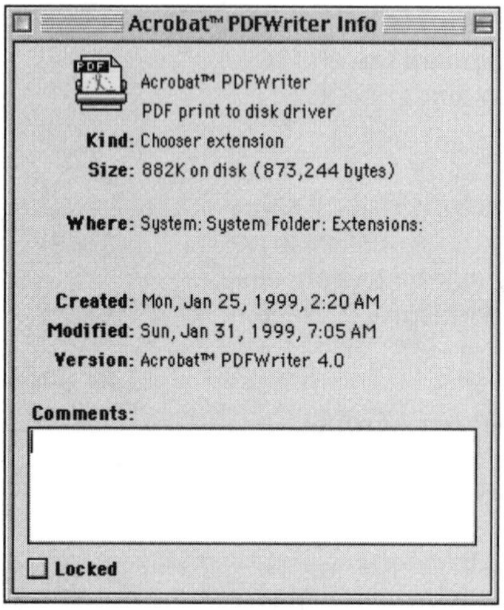

Acrobat™ PDFWriter Info
Acrobat™ PDFWriter
PDF print to disk driver
Kind: Chooser extension
Size: 882K on disk (873,244 bytes)
Where: System: System Folder: Extensions:
Created: Mon, Jan 25, 1999, 2:20 AM
Modified: Sun, Jan 31, 1999, 7:05 AM
Version: Acrobat™ PDFWriter 4.0
Comments:
☐ Locked

Figure 4-1: On the Mac, to display the PDFWriter version number, open the Extensions folder, select the Acrobat PDFWriter Chooser extension, and select File ⇨ Get Info to open the Get Info dialog box shown here.

Windows NT users were also handicapped when Acrobat 3.0 was released. The PDFWriter was not supported in NT. If you tried to use it, the system would crash. When Adobe released version 3.0.3 of PDFWriter, it added support for Windows NT.

Tip   If you are using NT and an earlier version of Acrobat, be certain to visit Adobe's Web site and download the latest version of PDFWriter for Windows NT. You can use the Help menus reviewed in Chapter 3 to access Adobe On-line or go to http://www.adobe.com/acrobat/resources.html. The resources Web page will list many of the new Acrobat upgrades available for downloading including the latest version of the PDFWriter for Windows NT. If you upgraded to version 4.0 of Acrobat, your installer CD will support the latest version of the PDFWriter for your operating system.

Regardless of what you use to create PDF files, think *print*. PDF documents are saved to disk, but this happens via the Print command. For example, you print with the PDFWriter, and the file is saved to disk. When you use Acrobat Distiller, you print a PostScript file first, then open the print file in the Acrobat Distiller application. All PDF documents originally come from a print file saved to disk. In the most elementary form, you can select the PDFWriter print driver and select File ⇨ Print. Click OK, and you've just created a PDF file. There are several ways to access the PDFWriter depending on the platform you use. Macintosh users, you have a few nifty tools for quick access to PDFWriter. Windows users, don't be concerned. You can easily create PDF files with the PDFWriter, and the result will be just as effective as that of your Mac counterparts.

Accessing the PDFWriter

PDFWriter is a printer driver. Access to the PDFWriter can be handled in much the same way as you might select a printer on your network. On a Macintosh, you can select the PDFWriter in the Chooser that appears under the Apple menu. On Windows, you can select PDFWriter as your default printer in the Control Panel or you can select the printer driver when you print from within an application. Because the procedures vary distinctively between platforms, it's probably a good idea to make special mention of each platform. Acrobat is a great cross-platform product, but there are some differences in the way it interacts with various operating systems, due to the nature of the disparity among operating systems.

PDFWriter on the Macintosh

On the Macintosh, access to the PDFWriter can be handled through a few methods. The traditional means of accessing a printer driver is through the Chooser. When you select Apple ⇨ Chooser, the Chooser dialog box will appear displaying your printer drivers.

In Figure 4-2, notice the version number of the PDFWriter appearing in the top-right corner of the graphic on the right of the dialog box. The display of the version number in this dialog box is the same as you can see in the Get Info dialog box.

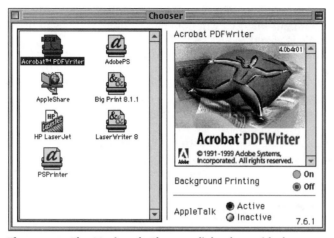

Figure 4-2: The Macintosh Chooser dialog box with the PDFWriter printer driver selected.

Using the PDFWriter on the Macintosh is simple. Bring up the Chooser dialog box and select the PDFWriter icon in the window on the left of the dialog box. Close the dialog box, and your current default printer is now the PDFWriter. Regardless of which application you use, when you select File ⇨ Print or File ⇨ Page Setup, the attributes of the printed page will be established for a PDF file, as shown in Figure 4-3.

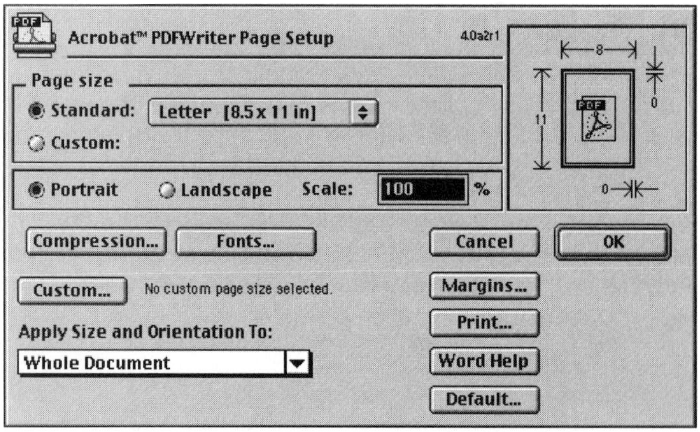

Figure 4-3: After the PDFWriter is selected in the Chooser, selecting File ⇨ Page Setup in Microsoft Word opens the PDFWriter Page Setup dialog box.

When you select the PDFWriter printer driver in the Chooser dialog box, the new default printer will be the PDFWriter. If you want to print to a network printer, you need to go back to the Chooser and select the driver for the printer you intend to use. If you go back and forth between exporting PDF files and printing to hard copy, toggling back and forth can be a hassle. Fortunately for Macintosh users, you have a shortcut that can temporarily enable the PDFWriter without changing the default printer. In order for the shortcut to work, you need to have the PDFWriter Shortcut installed in your Control Panel folder inside your System folder. To verify the inclusion of the PDFWriter Shortcut, open the Control Panel folder and search for it. If it does not appear, you can copy the Control Panel Device (cdev) from the Acrobat Installer CD and drag it on top of your System folder. The file will automatically be copied to the Control Panel folder.

When the PDFWriter Shortcut cdev is in the Control Panel folder, select Apple ➪ Control Panels ➪ PDFWriter Shortcut. A dialog box will open that enables you to define the *hot key* for temporarily accessing the PDFWriter, as shown in Figure 4-4. By default, the hot key is the Control key. This is to say that when you press the Control key and select File ➪ Page Setup or File ➪ Print, the PDFWriter page setup or print command will override your default printer. Once you print to the PDFWriter and close the page setup or print dialog box, the default printer will remain in effect.

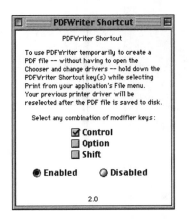

Figure 4-4: You can change the hot key for accessing the PDFWriter Shortcut when you open the cdev through the Control Panel by selecting Apple ➪ Control Panels ➪ PDFWriter Shortcut.

The PDFWriter Shortcut dialog box has an option for disabling the shortcut or changing the hot key. If you find your choice of modifier key interferes with an application program's use of the same modifier, you can change to either the Option or Shift key or you can disable the shortcut by selecting the Disabled button in the dialog box.

Tip

If at all possible, I recommend you leave the Control key modifier as the default and always use it when accessing the PDFWriter. Once you become familiar with the keys used for opening the Page Setup and Print dialog boxes for PDFWriter usage, you'll never again return to the Chooser dialog box.

PDFWriter in Windows

When you install Acrobat on Windows, the PDFWriter printer driver will be installed. If you do not see it available in Settings ➪ Control Panel ➪ Printers, you will need to add it as you would any other printer. You can set up the defaults as you would with other printers by highlighting the Adobe PDFWriter icon in the Printers folder and clicking the right mouse button. When you click with the right mouse button, a pop-up menu will appear. From the menu item choices, select Properties. The Acrobat PDFWriter Properties dialog box appears, as shown in Figure 4-5.

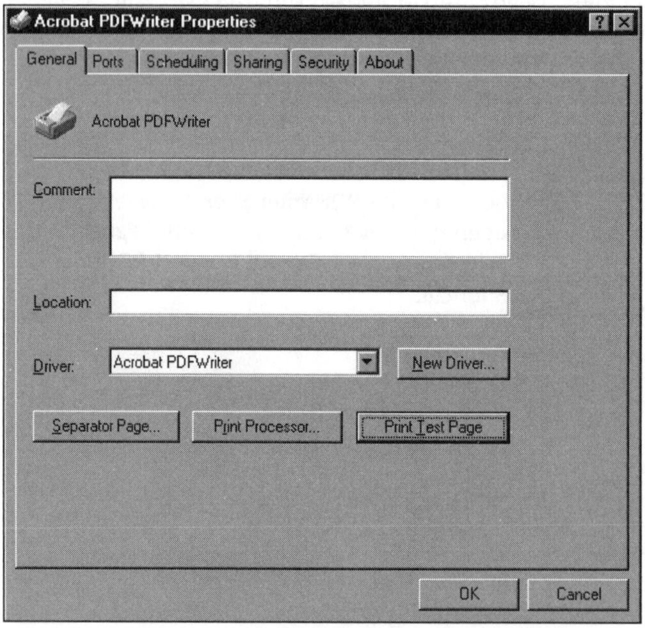

Figure 4-5: The Properties dialog box for the PDFWriter

In the Properties dialog box, click the Print Test Page button. A dialog box appears, enabling you to select the destination for the print file, as shown in Figure 4-6.

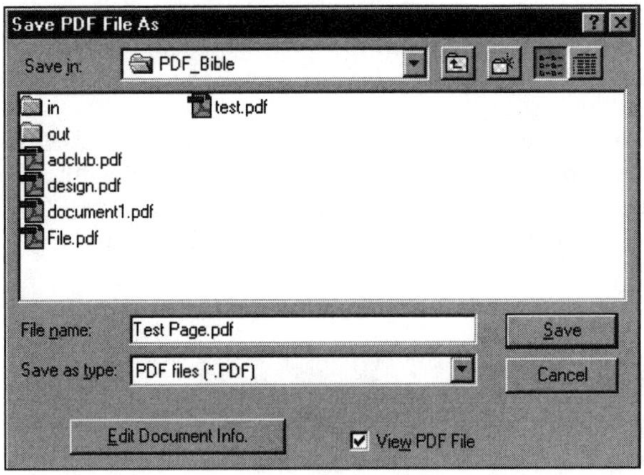

Figure 4-6: Selecting the Print Test Page button in the Properties dialog box reveals the Save PDF File As dialog box, enabling you to select the destination for the print file.

From the Properties window you can make various changes to the port destinations and the PDFWriter default settings. To be certain your printer driver is configured properly, select the General tab in the Properties dialog box. Click the Print Test Page button. A dialog box appears, enabling you to select a destination and filename. The default filename will appear as TestPage.pdf, as shown in Figure 4-7. Click OK when you have selected the destination folder desired. The file will be saved as a PDF document, which can be read in an Acrobat viewer.

Figure 4-7: The Test Print Page can be opened in an Acrobat viewer.

Launch an Acrobat viewer and open the TestPage.pdf file. If your printer driver was not installed properly or the settings are not appropriate for the application, the test print will fail before you arrive at the Save dialog box.

You needn't change your printer driver's default in Windows. Regardless of the application you use, you can choose among printer drivers from the application Print dialog box. In Windows there isn't a need for a shortcut to access PDFWriter, as the printer choice can be made every time you address the Print dialog box (see Figure 4-8).

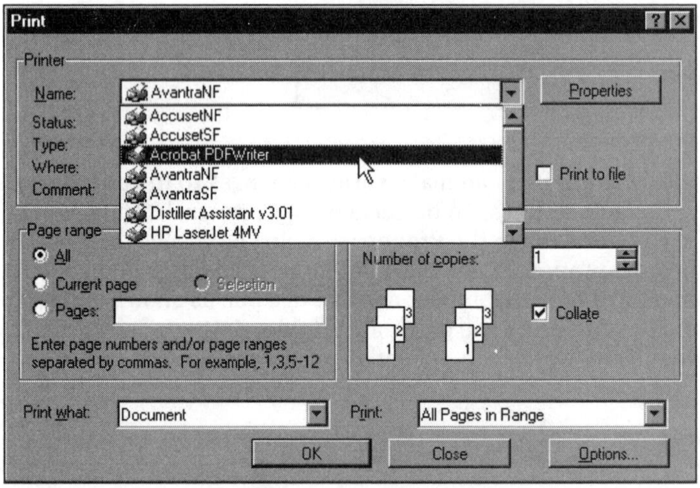

Figure 4-8: When printing from an application in Windows, you can select the destination printer from the available installed printers appearing in the dialog box. Your ability to select a printer from the Print dialog box eliminates any need for a shortcut key to access PDFWriter.

Page setup

In most applications you will find a Page Setup dialog box that enables you to define the print attributes for your output file. In the case of the PDFWriter, the output file will be to a saved disk file. In the PDFWriter Page Setup dialog box, you can choose among font handling, compression schemes, and compatibility methods, which will be saved with the print file. As you work with different programs, you will also notice there will be program-specific items contained in the PDFWriter Page Setup dialog box (compare Figures 4-9 and 4-10). Generally the top half of the Page Setup dialog box is specific to PDFWriter, whereas the bottom half of the dialog box will be program specific.

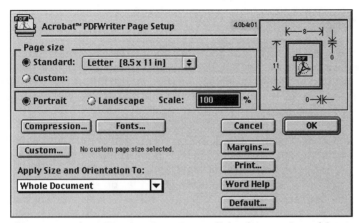

Figure 4-9: The PDFWriter Page Setup dialog box as viewed from Microsoft Word

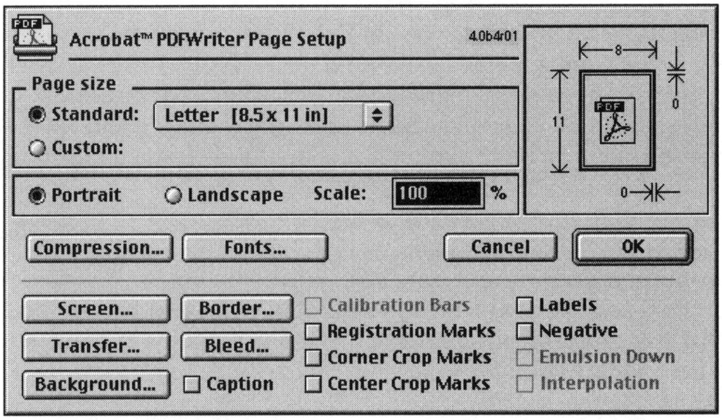

Figure 4-10: The PDFWriter Page Setup dialog box as viewed from Adobe Photoshop 5.0

Note

In Figures 4-9 and 4-10, notice the difference between the options at the bottom of the dialog boxes. Microsoft Word enables you to define page sizes, margins, and orientation. Photoshop offers screening, separation, and labeling definitions. In the top half of both dialog boxes, notice identical attributes for page size, orientation, scaling, compression, and font handling.

Font Handling

Before you go about creating a PDF file, there are some attribute issues to deal with in regard to how the PDF will be created. You can elect to include fonts in the PDF file, compress fonts, and use font subsetting. All the font attributes are identified in the Page Setup dialog box for the PDFWriter. From this dialog box, you can make several choices for font usage.

During your Acrobat experiences, most of the problems you are likely to encounter will be related to fonts. Acrobat viewers cannot be launched if the required fonts are not installed properly. Acrobat Distiller and Capture cannot be used if the required fonts are not installed properly. Viewing PDF files on screen can be problematic if font substitution is not working. Regardless of how you work with Acrobat, you need to pay some attention to font handling, which is also important when creating PDF files.

Font compression

Compression is commonly referred to as one of two types — lossy or lossless — based on various compression schemes used for data. Lossy compression schemes lose data and in some cases result in degraded images. These compression methods are used to compress image files such as scanned images and raster data. Lossless compression schemes, on the other hand, do not degrade image quality.

Images created in vector illustration programs can take advantage of these methods. Fonts are like vector objects as opposed to image files and can therefore take advantage of compression without data loss. When you create PDF files with Acrobat PDFWriter, you have an opportunity to compress the text in the document. Compression of text will typically not interfere with image quality, and you should always choose to use compression for fonts.

Font embedding

One of the great benefits of the PDF format is the capability to include fonts in a document that can be transported to another computer and printed with complete data integrity. To embed fonts, you need to have all the document fonts loaded on your computer. Once the PDF is created with font embedding, any computer without the same fonts loaded can print the PDF document without font substitution. The printed PDF file will appear identical to the original document. When you open the Page Setup dialog box and select the Fonts button, another dialog box will appear enabling you to make some choices about font embedding, as shown in Figure 4-11.

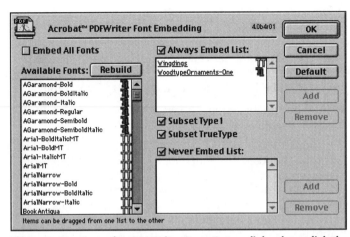

Figure 4-11: From the PDFWriter Page Setup dialog box, click the Fonts button to open the Acrobat PDFWriter Font Embedding dialog box.

In the PDFWriter Font Embedding dialog box, you can choose from many options, as listed here:

✦ **Embed All Fonts:** This option, when enabled, causes embedding of all fonts. When you deselect the check box, no font embedding will occur, unless you specify items in the Always Embed List.

✦ **Rebuild:** When you click this button, the installed font list will be rebuilt. If you load a font in your system and the font doesn't appear in the Available font list, selecting the Rebuild button will enable PDFWriter to recognize the newly loaded font.

✦ **Available Fonts:** All the fonts loaded in your system and recognized by PDFWriter will be listed in this window. You can scroll down the window and see the full font list. To the right of each font name will appear a symbol indicating the font type. T1 indicates a Type 1 font. TT signifies a TrueType font.

✦ **Always Embed List:** The Always Embed List enables you to choose specific fonts to embed in your document. To make this list active, you must deselect the Embed All Fonts check box. PDFWriter assumes if you want to embed all fonts, there is no need to specify individual fonts for embedding. To place an item in the Always Embed List, click and drag a font from the Available Font List to this window. When you release the mouse button, the font will appear in the list.

✦ **Never Embed List:** This item works whether Embed All Fonts is enabled or not. You can elect to prevent certain fonts from being embedded in a document, even if the Embed All Fonts option is enabled, by dragging them to this window.

✦ **Subset Type 1:** When font embedding is used, the entire character set is embedded in the PDF document. If only a few characters are used, the entire character set is not needed to reproduce the PDF on a printer. When you subset fonts, only the font characters used in the document will be embedded. When more than 35 percent of the characters within a font set are used, the entire set is embedded. This option applies to Type 1 fonts.

✦ **Subset TrueType:** When enabled, font subsetting, as described in the preceding entry, will be applied to TrueType fonts.

✦ **Add:** Two Add buttons appear in the PDFWriter Font Embedding dialog box. If you select a font from the Available Fonts list and click the Add button appearing at the top-right of the dialog box, the font will be added to the Always Embed List. The Add button in the lower-right corner of the dialog box will add a font to the Never Embed List. In either case, a font must first be selected in the Available Fonts list before clicking the respective Add button. As mentioned above, you can only add a font to the Always Embed List when the Embed All Fonts check box is disabled.

✦ **Remove:** The two Remove buttons will remove selected fonts from either the Always Embed List or the Never Embed List. The Remove buttons are active only when a font is selected in either list. Neither button will enable you to remove a font from the Available Fonts list, however. The only way to remove fonts from the Available Fonts list is to remove the font from your system and then rebuild the list.

When embedding fonts with PDFWriter, you will need to make a few considerations and understand some potential restrictions:

✦ **File Size:** File sizes are impacted with the format you use for the PDF file. If you use either the 3.0 or 4.0 compatibility, fonts will be compressed, thus resulting in a smaller file size. Earlier versions of the PDF format compatibility don't use font compression.

✦ **Properly Installed Fonts:** To include font embedding, you need to be certain all fonts are installed properly. With Type 1 fonts, be certain the screen and outline fonts are both installed on your computer.

✦ **Licensing:** There are many different font manufacturers, and the permissions for use of fonts from these manufacturers vary considerably. To legally include font embedding in a PDF file, you need to know whether the permission for inclusion is provided by the manufacturer. Adobe original fonts that are owned by Linotype-Hell, International Typeface Corporation, AGFA, AlphaOmega, Bigelow & Holmes, Fundicion Typografica Neufville, and Monotype Typography, Ltd., as well as those in the Adobe library, can be used for font embedding without written releases. If you have a font from a foundry not listed here, you'll need to check with the manufacturer or distributor to inquire as to whether you can legally distribute PDF files that include that font. Failure to do so may create a copyright violation.

Font subsetting

Font subsetting can be enabled in the PDFWriter Page Setup dialog box for both Type 1 and TrueType fonts. When a character set is embedded in the PDF file, all available characters in that set will be embedded. If the only appearance in your document of a particular font is in a headline of a few characters, you may elect to not embed the entire character set. Font subsetting will embed only the characters used for that headline. When using PDFWriter, you will want to use font subsetting often to help reduce file size.

Image Resampling

For almost all the work you perform with Acrobat, some form of compression will be part of your final PDF file. PDF files can be amazingly smaller in size than documents created in any other application. I once had a 150MB file that kept generating PostScript errors on an Imation Rainbow dye-sublimation printer. After distilling the PostScript file in Acrobat Distiller, the file size was reduced to 192K. The PDF file printed in two minutes without image degradation. This example may sound extraordinary, but it does happen.

File compression will be important for any use of PDF files. If design for the Web, multimedia, screen presentations, CD-ROM replication, or even output to high-end digital prepress is part of your work, Acrobat has a compression scheme suitable for your design requirements. Depending on which output need you have and the compression method you use, you'll have some choices for defining compression attributes. With the PDFWriter, these attributes are defined in the Acrobat PDFWriter Compression dialog box. Compression methods are first determined by your choice of PDF file-format compatibility.

File-format compatibility

When creating PDF files in either the PDFWriter or Acrobat Distiller, a choice for file-format compatibility must be determined. A number of compression schemes are available when creating a PDF file, but some of the methods are dependent on the format you use. For Acrobat 3.0, the format choices are Acrobat 2.1 or Acrobat 3.0. With Acrobat 4.0, you can choose between the 3.0 and 4.0 format. In more recent applications such as Adobe Illustrator 8, exporting PDF files enables you to choose between Acrobat 3.0 and Acrobat 4.0 formats. Older applications that have PDF export capabilities may offer choices between 2.1 and 3.0 formats. Until these applications are upgraded, you may not have a choice for 4.0 format.

Using Older Acrobat Formats

In some earlier documentation on Acrobat, you may see many references for using Acrobat 2.1 format to maintain compatibility for users of Acrobat viewers earlier than version 3.0. People have advised using the 2.1 format to ensure compatibility with all users. Today, I find little advantage to using the 2.1 format. The Acrobat Reader software is available free from Adobe Systems, so the few who may not have acquired it will need to visit Adobe's Web site to download a more recent version of Reader. In addition, most of the popular commercial software applications are in a continual upgrade path and support new formats with each new version of their software. Now with the advent of Acrobat 4.0, you will seldom find a need to use the 2.1 format. Because Acrobat 4.0 is new as of this writing, you may need to use 3.0 compatibility until users upgrade to Acrobat Reader 4.0.

The Acrobat file-format compatibility options are selected in the Page Setup dialog box (Mac) or Properties dialog box (Windows). When you select the Compression button in the respective dialog box, another dialog box will appear (see Figures 4-12 and 4-13).

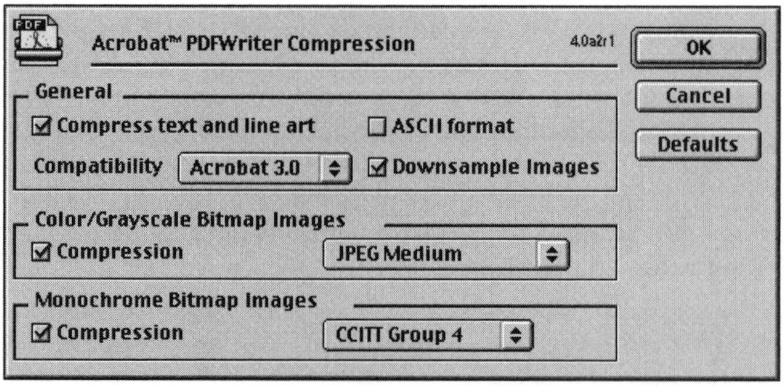

Figure 4-12: The Acrobat PDFWriter Compression dialog box is opened by selecting the Compression button in the Page Setup dialog box for the PDFWriter on the Macintosh.

In the PDFWriter Compression dialog box, the Compatibility item has a pop-up menu for choosing between the Acrobat 3.0 and Acrobat 4.0 formats. If you are using an earlier version of the PDFWriter, your choices will be between the 2.1 and 3.0 formats. Available choices for image compression are dependent on which compatibility option you select. The different choices are listed in Table 4-1.

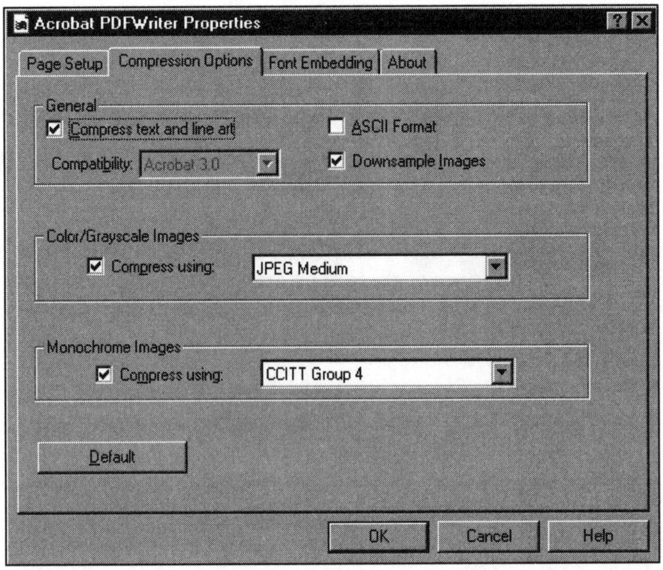

Figure 4-13: The Acrobat PDFWriter Compression options become available by selecting the Properties button in the Print dialog box for the PDFWriter in Windows.

Table 4-1
Compression and File-format Compatibility

Image Type	Acrobat 2.1	Acrobat 3.0 and 4.0
Color/Grayscale	JPEG High	JPEG High
	JPEG Medium-High	JPEG Medium-High
	JPEG Medium	JPEG Medium
	JPEG Medium-Low	JPEG Medium-Low
	JPEG Low	JPEG Low
	LZW	ZIP
Monochrome Bitmap Images	CCITT Group 3	CCITT Group 3
	CCITT Group 4	CCITT Group 4
	LZW	ZIP
	Run Length	Run Length
PDF Version	1.2	Acrobat 3.0 – version 1.2
		Acrobat 4.0 – version 1.3

Compression

Once the file-format compatibility is decided, the compression for images can be determined. As you'll note from Table 4-1, the only difference between the 2.1 and 3.0/4.0 compatibilities is LZW versus ZIP compression. JPEG, Run Length, and CCITT compression is available with either format. Font and line art compression, as you observed earlier, is also determined in the Compression dialog box. When using the PDFWriter, you need to make selections manually for compression methods by choosing from the pop-up menus for each type of compression applied to the image types in your file. Compression choices are handled a little differently with Acrobat Distiller, as discussed in Chapter 5. To make appropriate choices, you need to know a little bit about the source data and the compression schemes available:

✦ **Compress text and line art:** Text will be compressed without any options for the compression method when the check box is enabled. When you compress text, line art will also be compressed. The line art description here applies to vector objects only. This is not to be confused with line art you may use in programs such as Adobe Photoshop, in which line art consists of raster data.

✦ **Color/Grayscale Images:** Color and grayscale images are raster files most often from scanned images. Any Photoshop file defined in a color mode or grayscale will be compressed according to the compression choice you make from the pop-up menu in this section. If the check box is disabled, no compression will occur.

✦ **Monochome Bitmap Images:** These images are commonly referred to as bitmaps or line art from Photoshop files. They are raster images with two color values — black and white.

The Compression choices for both the color/grayscale and monochrome bitmap images are identical:

✦ **JPEG:** The Joint Photographic Experts Group (JPEG) format compresses files with the greatest amount of compression. It is a lossy compression scheme that will toss away or lose data. Therefore, when compressing at the maximum level, the data loss will be greatest. JPEG compression for images in the PDFWriter Compression dialog box provides for five different levels of JPEG compression:

• **JPEG High:** This provides the highest level of compression. A 2MB file will compress down to approximately 196K.

• **JPEG Medium-High:** High and medium-high levels will often compress images so that there is little distinction in the amount of file-size reduction. Much will be dependent on the image contents. If a common background color is predominant in the file, the amount of compression will be almost the same. A 2MB file will also compress down to 196K.

- **JPEG Medium:** Medium JPEG compression is a good starting point for files to be printed. Compression is strong with little degradation in image quality. Quite often you can use this selection for composite color printing. The same 2MB file will compress down to 245K.

- **JPEG Medium-Low:** This option provides slightly less compression than JPEG Medium. A 2MB file will compress down to 343K.

- **JPEG Low:** This provides the least amount of compression and data loss. JPEG Low will compress an image with little obvious data loss when output to most high-end devices. A 2MB file will compress to 441K.

✦ **ZIP:** ZIP is only available when saving PDF files in Acrobat 3.0 or 4.0 format. ZIP compression is more efficient than LZW and will achieve approximately 20 percent more compression. It should be used when large areas of a single color appear in an image. In the example of the 2MB file, the ZIP-compressed image reduces to 343K — the same size as results with the JPEG Medium-Low option.

✦ **CCITT Group 3:** The International Coordinating Committee for Telephony and Telegraphy (CCITT) Group 3 compression is used by fax machines. The images are compressed in horizontal rows, one row at a time.

✦ **CCITT Group 4:** CCITT Group 4 is a general-purpose compression method that produces good compression for most types of bitmap images. This compression method is the default when you first launch the PDFWriter Compression dialog box.

✦ **LZW:** The Lempel-Ziv-Welch (LZW) compression format has been commonly used with TIFF images from the early days of TIFF format development. LZW will not be available when you use the Acrobat 3.0 or 4.0 format as the ZIP compression method noted previously is much more efficient. This compression scheme is also used with images having large areas of a single color.

✦ **Run Length (RLE):** The Run Length format is a lossless compression scheme particularly favorable to bitmap monochrome images. You can run tests yourself for the compression method that works best for you. Typically CCITT Group 4 will handle most of your needs when compressing these images.

With all these choices, it may seem an overwhelming task to try and decide on a particular method to use. Unfortunately, there is no strict formula for handling your output requirements for every condition. With screen graphics for multimedia, Web publishing, and CD-ROM replication, you will often use the maximum compression available. It's easy to see the results because you will ultimately observe them on your monitor. If something doesn't look right, you know you need to go back and reprint your file with less compression.

When outputting to high-end devices and various printing machines, your choices become more difficult to decide. The only general rule applicable is to run tests. Test your file output to different devices and observe the prints. Take notes and develop your own formulas for achieving the results suitable for your design needs.

Generally, JPEG-Medium to JPEG-Low or ZIP compression will be the best places to start and leave the CCITT Group 4 for monochome bitmaps at the default. Note here, however, that PDFWriter will not be the best choice for creating files for high-end output. The next chapter, in its discussion of Acrobat Distiller, presents some reasons for not choosing PDFWriter.

Encoding

Another choice available to you in the PDFWriter Compression dialog box is the encoding method for the output file. The default for file encoding is binary, which you won't see as an option. In the dialog box, notice the option ASCII format (ASCII is an acronym for American Standard Code for Information Interchange). When you select this option, ASCII encoding will be used instead of binary encoding.

Tip　　As a general rule, you'll always want binary encoding for your PDF files. PostScript Level 2 and above are favorable to binary encoding, and the file sizes are smaller than those using ASCII encoding. Use ASCII only when in situations where it is required or you happen to experience problems printing PDF documents.

Downsampling

Downsampling raster images is also commonly referred to as *resampling*. When an image is resampled, the resolution is reduced through a form of interpolation. Interpolation involves mathematical recalculation of pixels by combining several original pixels of a given value to a single pixel, thereby reducing the file size. In PDFWriter, you can enable the Downsample Images check box to reduce the file size, but you have no control as to how much downsampling will occur. This is one of several options you have more control over in Acrobat Distiller than in PDFWriter. If you select Downsample Image in the PDFWriter Compression dialog box, images will automatically be resampled as indicated below:

✦ **Color images:** On Windows, color images will be downsampled to 96 pixels per inch (ppi). On the Macintosh, color images will be downsampled to 72 ppi.

✦ **Grayscale images:** On Windows, grayscale images will be downsampled to 96 ppi. On the Macintosh, grayscale images will be downsampled to 150 ppi.

✦ **Monochome images:** On both Windows and the Macintosh, monochrome bitmaps will be downsampled to 300ppi.

Downsampling should not be confused with compression. If you have a 300 ppi image and use the maximum compression, the file size will be larger than first downsampling to 96 or 72 ppi, depending on your platform, and then compressing the downsampled image with JPEG compression. For screen views particularly, you may wish to enable the Downsampling Image option in the PDFWriter Compression dialog box and then select your compression method.

Printing from PDFWriter

After you wade through the maze of all the options in the Page Setup dialog box and make your selections, you're ready to move to the PDFWriter Print dialog box.

Printing to PDFWriter is handled in the same manner as printing a file to your network printer. The Print command for PDFWriter on a Macintosh with the PDFWriter Shortcut cdev installed is accessed by holding the Control key down when selecting File ➪ Print (see Figure 4-14). If the PDFWriter Shortcut cdev is not installed, you'll need to select Apple ➪ Chooser and select the PDFWriter print driver.

In Windows, select File ➪ Print from your application and select the PDFWriter from the Printer Name pop-up menu (see Figure 4-15).

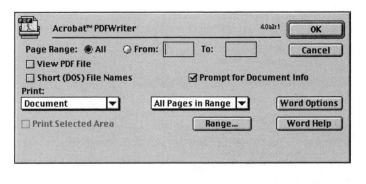

Figure 4-14: Hold the Control key down and select File ➪ Print to access the PDFWriter Print dialog box on the Macintosh. To use the modifier key, the PDFWriter Shortcut cdev must be installed on your system.

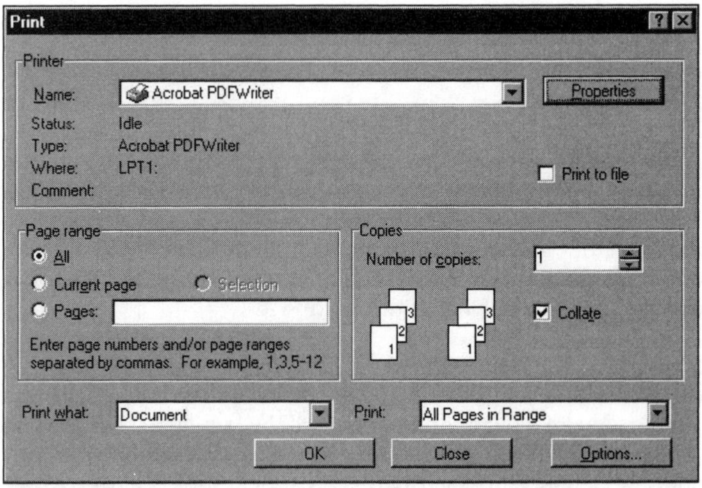

Figure 4-15: In Windows, select File ➪ Print from within an open application and select the PDFWriter print driver from the Printer Name pop-up menu.

From the Print dialog box on the Macintosh you can choose among several options for the print file, which include View PDF File, Short (DOS) File Names, and Prompt for Document Info. Options for viewing the PDF file and specifying document information are also available for Windows, but you need to access another dialog box to gain access to the options. On Windows, click the OK button in the Print dialog box. The Save PDF File As dialog box will appear, prompting you for a filename and destination, as shown in Figure 4-16. This dialog box also contains the View PDF File option and Edit Document Info button, which enables you to access the Acrobat PDFWriter Document Info dialog box.

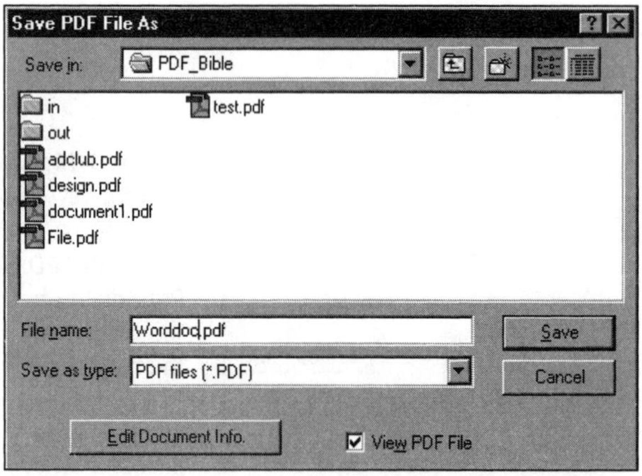

Figure 4-16: In Windows, click OK in the Print dialog box. The Save PDF File As dialog box appears in which you can access the Document Info dialog box and a choice for viewing the PDF.

Viewing PDF files

PDFWriter will create the PDF file and save it to your hard drive. After you create a PDF document, you can go about your business and work in the host application from which the PDF file was generated, print another PDF file, and so on. All the PDF files will be created, but as yet, you haven't seen them. The PDFWriter Print dialog box (Mac) or Save PDF File As (Windows) dialog box provides you with a means to immediately view the PDF file after creating it.

When you enable the View PDF File option in either of the dialog boxes just mentioned, your Acrobat viewer will automatically be launched. If you have both Acrobat Reader and Acrobat 4.0 installed, Acrobat will be launched. The PDF file you just created will open in the Acrobat viewer, which provides an opportunity to immediately double-check the file and verify that its appearance is as you expected it.

Enabling View PDF File eliminates the mouse click or keystrokes you need to select the viewer and open the PDF. If you have a number of applications installed or limited RAM, enabling this option may result in the Acrobat viewer not being able to open, or you may even experience a system crash. Ultimately, this is a personal preference item, and the choice is yours. If you work on machines with limited memory and can't keep an Acrobat viewer open when in another application, then by all means don't enable this option.

Prompting for document information

Document information is detailed in Chapter 2, when searches were discussed. You know that searches can be performed on the data fields Title, Subject, Author, and Keywords. Information for all of these fields can be supplied by the user at the time the PDF is created.

 Inasmuch as the fields can be changed in Acrobat, your workflow will be easier if you supply the data at the time the PDF is created. Ignoring document information is like ignoring a messy garage. You know you'll get around to organizing it some-day, but often that day never arrives, and the mess keeps piling up. The same holds true for document information. You may think you'll get around to it some day; but in the meantime the work will pile up and become more cumbersome. When a PDF is created, much of the information for Title, Subject, and Keywords will be fresh in your mind. If you hold off, you may have to spend some time read-ing through documents to select the right words and phrases when appending this information in Acrobat.

Clicking the Prompt for Document Info check box in the Acrobat PDFWriter dialog box and then clicking OK (on the Mac) or clicking the Edit Document Info button on the Save PDF File As dialog box (in Windows) brings up the Acrobat PDFWriter Document Information dialog box, as shown in Figures 4-17 and 4-18.

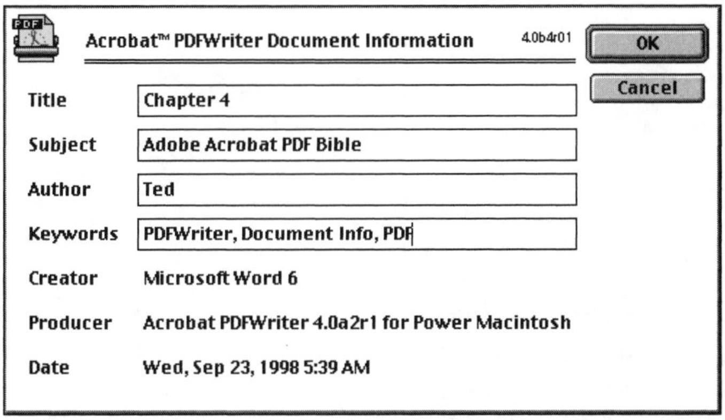

Acrobat™ PDFWriter Document Information 4.0b4r01	OK Cancel
Title	Chapter 4
Subject	Adobe Acrobat PDF Bible
Author	Ted
Keywords	PDFWriter, Document Info, PDF
Creator	Microsoft Word 6
Producer	Acrobat PDFWriter 4.0a2r1 for Power Macintosh
Date	Wed, Sep 23, 1998 5:39 AM

Figure 4-17: The Document Info dialog box from PDFWriter on the Macintosh, with the Title, Subject, and Keyword fields filled in

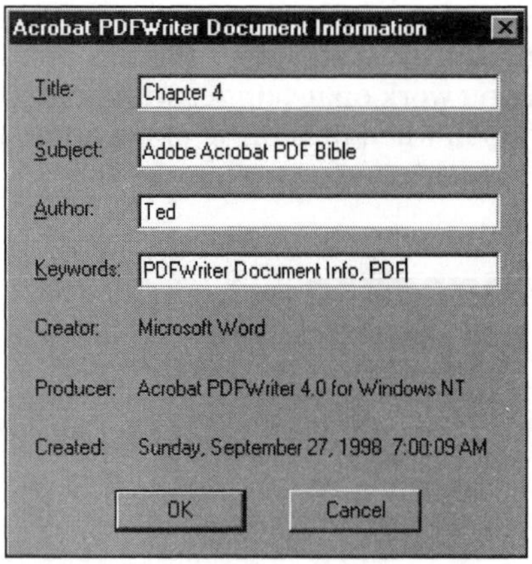

Figure 4-18: The Document Info dialog box from PDFWriter on Windows

After you create a PDF file and open it in an Acrobat viewer, select File ➪ Document Info ➪ General. The General Info dialog box will display information according to what you entered in the user-definable fields, as shown in Figure 4-19. When a search index is created, these field contents will be included in the index.

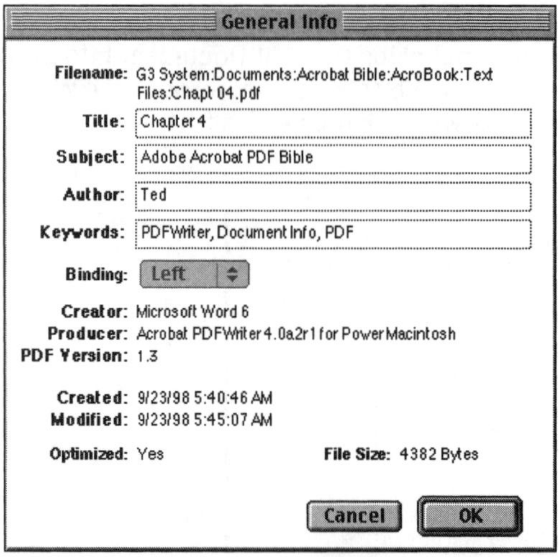

Figure 4-19: The General Info dialog box as viewed in Acrobat Reader. Notice the Keyword fields are displayed as entered when the PDF was created.

Short (DOS) File Names

Specific to Macintosh users is the check box for DOS filename compatibility. Macintosh users can save files with a maximum of 31 characters including spaces between words. DOS naming conventions restrict the maximum filename to eight characters (no spaces) and a maximum of three characters for the extension. In the example shown in Figure 4-19, the filename is *Chapt 04.pdf* (a space was placed between *Chapt* and *04*). If you enable the Short (DOS) Filenames check box, the save navigation dialog box will supply a name consistent with DOS conventions. Specifying this option in the example would result in the filename *Chapt04.pdf*. Spaces are automatically eliminated. In another example, if you use a filename such as My Document.pdf, the resultant short DOS name would be MyDocume.pdf. The extension would automatically default to *.pdf*, but the spaces would be eliminated in the name and the name would be shortened to the first eight characters.

The appearance of the Save dialog box with the supplied DOS name is a suggestion offered by PDFWriter. You can change the name in the Save dialog box before you actually record the PDF to disk. Enabling the Short (DOS) Filenames option will serve as a check when creating PDF files designed for cross-platform use. Keep in mind, you always have the opportunity to change the name before the PDF is actually saved.

Tip A more precise way of handling naming conventions is to always use the DOS standard of eight-character names with three-character extensions even if you don't expect to publish your PDF files in a cross-platform environment. Once you get in the habit of naming files with these standards, you won't ever have to go back and modify names when the unexpected DOS user needs your file(s).

Creating a PDF File

Now that all the options and basics for setting up a page for output to PDF have been covered, let's look at a potential real-world situation in which the PDFWriter can help you. Actual use of PDF files are almost limitless and only restricted by your imagination. I can think of hundreds a ways to use PDF files, and one of my favorites is archiving information. Because the best source of research and information around is the World Wide Web, it seems natural to go to the Web for source material.

Millions of sites exist on the Web, and on these sites people post helpful hints, articles, tips, and shortcuts for using computers, application software, and almost anything else you can dream up. One of my favorite places on the Web is FoodTV.com. If you've ever viewed programs like Emeril Live, Dining Around, Mediterranean Mario, or a host of other cable television cooking shows on the FoodTV network, you know that the pace of such TV shows is often too fast to record all the steps to reproduce a recipe. Fortunately, FoodTV has a Web site where all the recipes from the popular shows appear.

One could go about searching a Web site, finding the article of interest, printing it to hard copy on a laser printer, and storing it in a file cabinet. The problem I find with hard copy is I never store like papers in the same place. Even if they were stored in the same cabinet drawer or folder, I would still have to search through all those documents to find that great Cajun recipe from Emeril Live I once saw on TV. With Adobe Acrobat, I can create PDF files from all the recipes provided on http://www.foodtv.com, save them to an external media cartridge or my hard drive, and create a search catalog. When I want the recipe for a particular dish, I can easily invoke a search, and a list of all the recipes containing the type of food I want will be displayed in the Search Results window.

The following steps explain how you might go about creating PDF files from Web pages. You'll need an Internet connection to perform the steps as well as the PDFWriter.

STEPS: Creating PDF Files from Web Pages

1. **Launch your Web browser**. Use Microsoft Internet Explorer or Netscape Navigator and log on to a site where you wish to archive information. In this example I use www.foodtv.com. You can browse the Adobe Web site if you prefer and examine the Tips and Techniques Web pages for Adobe Acrobat. If you see a particular tip of interest, use it to follow along with this exercise.

2. **Navigate to the Web page containing the information you wish to archive.** On the FoodTV Web site, I navigated to the specific recipe I wanted to archive.

3. **Select File ➪ Print.** On the Macintosh, if you have the PDFWriter Shortcut cdev installed, hold the Control key down when you select File ➪ Print. If the PDFWriter Shortcut cdev is not installed, be certain to select Apple ➪ Chooser, select the PDFWriter print driver, close the Chooser dialog box, and then select File ➪ Print. On Windows, select File ➪ Print and choose PDFWriter from the Printer name list.

4. **Select the destination and filename.** Navigate to the location on your hard drive and provide a filename for the PDF, as shown in Figure 4-20.

5. **Bring up the Acrobat PDFWriter Document Info dialog box.** In the Print dialog box, be certain the Prompt for Document Info check box has a check mark in it and click OK in the Save PDF File As dialog box (Mac). Or, click the Edit Document Info button in the Save PDF File As dialog box (Windows). When using the PDFWriter with Web pages, you need not be concerned with addressing the Page Setup dialog box (Mac) or Properties dialog box (Windows) to adjust compression and fonts. Use the defaults for adjusting these items.

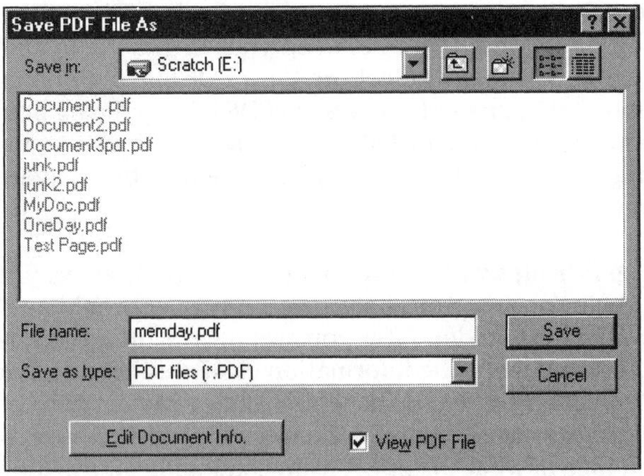

Figure 4-20: In the Save PDF File As dialog box, I decided to save my file to the root location of my E: drive and supplied the name memday.pdf for the file.

6. **Specifying the document information.** In the Acrobat PDFWriter Document Info dialog box, shown in Figure 4-21, the Title field will list the URL from the file you want to make into a PDF. This is a great benefit when archiving data from the Web, as each site you visit will automatically have its full URL listed in the Title field. The Author field will also be supplied by PDFWriter from the name used when you set up your operating system. Add data to the Subject and the Keywords fields. Click OK after supplying the field data.

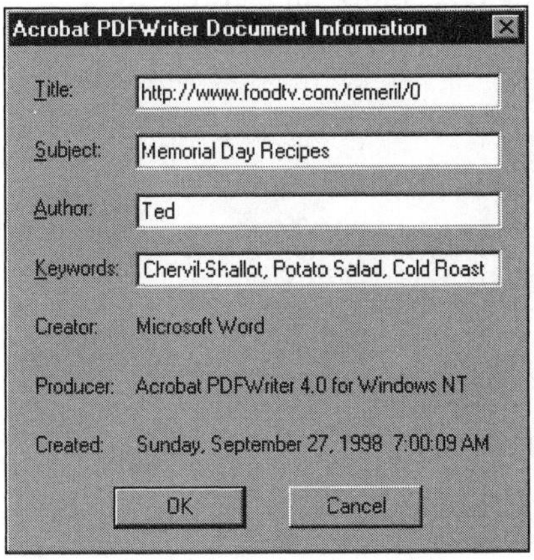

Figure 4-21: I supplied data for the Subject and the Keywords fields, which included the name for all the recipes in the PDF file.

Continued

7. View the PDF file. Open your Acrobat viewer and select File ⇨ Open to open the PDF file. If you have enough RAM to keep your browser and an Acrobat viewer open together, you could select the View PDF File option in the Acrobat PDFWriter dialog box (Mac) or Save PDF File As dialog box (Windows). When you open the PDF file, examine the status bar and observe the number of pages in the PDF file. An HTML page may be equivalent to several PDF pages.

As you can see, creating PDF files with the Acrobat PDFWriter is an easy task. Having a bunch of PDF files hanging around your hard drive, however, would not be much better than piling up papers in a folder. After you archive the files, you'll want to bring some order to them and make the information easily retrievable. Information retrieval is best handled with a search index, which allows keywords to be found easily. Creating search indexes is explained in Chapter 15, which covers Acrobat Catalog. To give you an idea of what to expect from cataloging information, let me use the preceding example to demonstrate how to search for information from the PDF files created from Web pages.

From the FoodTV Web site, I created several PDF files of recipes featured in different episodes. Because these pages are updated each month, you can't return to the URL and find a recipe you might have seen on TV a few months ago. Even if you could return to the URL, you'd have to launch your Web browser, log on to the Internet, and use a search engine, if one was provided by the Web site host. All of this I find to be a hassle. I'd rather browse through my recipes folder on my hard drive and find what I want through Acrobat.

From all the PDF files in my recipes folder I created a catalog. When I open my Acrobat viewer, I first need to load my index file created with Acrobat Catalog. This is handled in the Index Selection dialog box, shown in Figure 4-23.

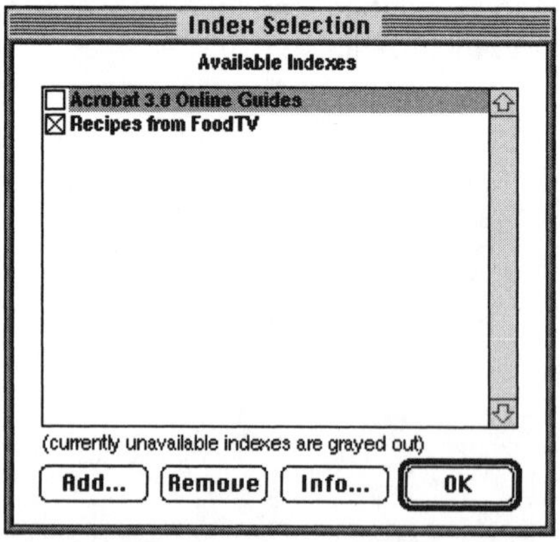

Figure 4-22: The search index to be used is added to the Index Selection dialog box.

If I want to make a chicken dish, I might search for the word *chicken* in the Adobe Acrobat Search window. Chicken is a broad subject, and when I invoked a search using this word, I found several recipes for chicken appearing in the Acrobat Search Results window, shown in Figure 4-23.

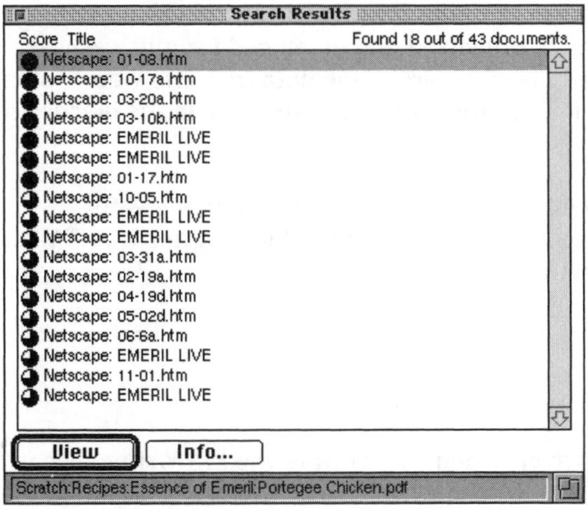

Figure 4-23: From my recipes index I searched for *chicken,* and the Results Window returned 18 different PDF files in which chicken recipes were found.

At this point I could view all the recipes and find the dish most appealing for the dinner to be prepared. But, what if I want to narrow this down a bit? Suppose something more specific — say, stir-fried chicken — sounds more appealing? Rather than reading through all 18 PDF files to find a recipe for stir-fried chicken, with Acrobat Search I can narrow the search by using operators and Boolean expressions and can also find keywords within close proximity (see Figure 4-24). To narrow my search, I go back to the Acrobat Search Window and enter search data to help me find a recipe for stir-fried chicken.

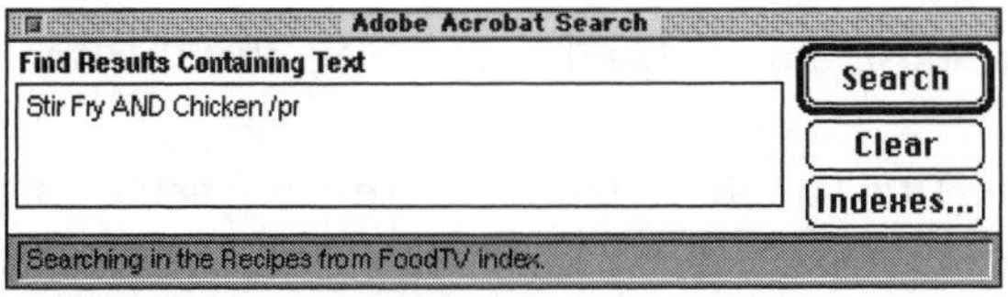

Figure 4-24: In the Adobe Acrobat Search window, the /pr operator will find the keywords within close proximity.

When I select the Search button in the Adobe Acrobat Search window, the Search Results window displays only two PDF files in which the words *stir fry* and *chicken* appear in proximity.

When I enable the View PDF File option for one of the found items in the Search Results window, the file will be displayed with the keywords highlighted. In this example, I was able to quickly retrieve the recipe I wanted.

Web page archiving is only one of many ways you might store information in PDF form. As suggested earlier, the same procedures can be employed with other Web sites or any number of digital document files around the office. Once saved in PDF form, the information can be easily organized and cataloged for quick access. PDFWriter is an excellent tool to use when archiving data from the Web or some office documents. It does have limitations, though, as detailed in the discussion of Acrobat Distiller in Chapter 5.

With regard to Web page archiving, Windows users have a much greater opportunity to do so when using Acrobat. As discussed in Chapter 15, HTML files can be automatically converted to PDF.

Summary

✦ The PDFWriter is a print driver. When you print to the PDFWriter, files will be saved in PDF form.

✦ Accessing the PDFWriter is handled in the Print dialog box. In Windows, you can select the PDFWriter from the available printer choices. On the Macintosh, you can either use the PDFWriter Shortcut by holding down the Control key while selecting File ⇨ Print or selecting the PDFWriter in the Chooser dialog box before opening the Print dialog box.

✦ In many applications, PDFWriter options are available in the PDFWriter Page Setup dialog box on the Macintosh or the Properties dialog box in Windows.

✦ Image compression schemes are dependent on the PDF compatibility between Acrobat version 2.1 and Acrobat version 3.0/4.0 formats. For most applications, version 3.0 or 4.0 format is recommended.

✦ Font embedding and font subsetting are handled in the Acrobat PDFWriter Font Embedding dialog box.

✦ Document information for Title, Author, Subject, and Keyword fields can be supplied by the user at the time the PDF file is created.

✦ Data archives can be converted to PDF files, which can be cataloged and searched through an index file created in Acrobat Catalog.

✦   ✦   ✦

Using Acrobat Distiller

In This Chapter

Why use Acrobat Distiller

Understanding PostScript

The Distiller environment

Printing to Distiller

Concatenating PDF files

If you've read Chapter 4, with its discussion of options for using the PDFWriter, and you are now experiencing brain overload, I'm going to recommend that you forget what you've read! Well, maybe not all of what was contained in the last chapter, but perhaps everything except for how to use PDFWriter in office document exchange environments and in Web page archiving. Whereas PDFWriter is a nice little tool much like a Volkswagen is a nice little car, Acrobat Distiller is the hot-ticket Ferrari. PDFWriter has limitations and is not recommended for some uses, among which is high-end digital prepress and printing. Momentarily, you will learn some of the additional feature advantages Distiller has over PDFWriter, but for now, accept the fact that most of your PDF creation needs will be resolved through Distiller.

PDFWriter provides a quick and simple means of creating a PDF file; even with all those controls and options reviewed in the last chapter, it's a simple solution. With Distiller's handling of many more controls, PDF file creation can be used for all document display and printing needs. You may remember back in Chapter 1 the discussion on document repurposing. If you think now that you will need a file for internal office use and later want to employ that document for some other purpose, you may need to go back to the original application document and reprint the file to PDF. If this is the case, you'll be involved in duplicating unnecessary steps. To develop a true PDF workflow, Distiller's options will provide a much better solution.

Why Use Distiller

Acrobat Distiller is like a PostScript engine. Theoretically, if a page can be distilled, it can be printed. Therefore, it comes as no surprise that some of the greatest value of Distiller lies in its capability to create PDF files to be printed on PostScript devices. With Distiller, you can add prepress controls and file attributes that can assist you in developing a PDF workflow for output to many different printing devices. The entire PDF workflow can be handled in many different, automated ways with Acrobat Distiller. In addition, there are some files and file types that will always be better suited for distilling rather than exporting via PDFWriter. Reasons to use Acrobat Distiller over the PDFWriter include these listed here:

✦ **Digital prepress:** For all printing output in digital prepress, approximately 90 to 95 percent of the computer-using U.S. population is married to PostScript. About 75 percent of the computer users the world over use PostScript for all digital print needs. Distiller uses PostScript while PDFWriter uses the screen image language, depending on the platform, to create the PDF file. To keep the integrity of the PDF file on par with the print file, always use Distiller.

✦ **Files containing EPS graphics:** You should always use Acrobat Distiller on files containing Encapsulated PostScript (EPS) images.

✦ **EPS file format:** If you save a file in EPS format from programs such as Adobe Illustrator, CorelDraw, or Macromedia FreeHand, the files can be distilled directly by Acrobat Distiller. In some cases, the best way to handle EPS files is to place them in a layout application and then distill printed PostScript files. Fortunately, the Acrobat 4.0 version of Distiller handles EPS files much better than previous versions.

✦ **Sophisticated publishing applications:** Some applications programs, such as Adobe PageMaker, QuarkXPress, Adobe Illustrator, Macromedia FreeHand, CorelDraw, and Adobe Framemaker, are optimized to take advantage of PostScript printing. Use Distiller with all applications where PostScript integrity is needed.

✦ **Compression controls:** Bitmap resampling is much more limited with PDFWriter than Distiller. You may recall the discussion in Chapter 4 related to downsampling. Distiller offers several choices for resampling images: Downsampling and subsampling, as well as the bicubic method of downsampling, are used by Distiller. Subsampling and bicubic downsampling are not available in PDFWriter. When you need to exercise more control over the sampling methods of images, always use Distiller.

✦ **Automated PDF development:** If you wish to have files automatically converted to PDF, you can set up a watched folder and have your PostScript files converted to PDF. If you get in the habit of creating PostScript files for printing devices, your files can serve a dual purpose: to be sent to a PostScript printer and to be distilled into a PDF file.

✦ **Automatic image color conversion:** Distiller provides you an opportunity to convert CMYK color images to RGB for screen viewing. If you want to repurpose a catalog for Web publishing, Distiller will automate all the necessary steps needed to properly create the PDF file.

✦ **Concatenating PDF Pages:** If you have different document files that need to be converted to a single PDF file, Distiller can concatenate individual PostScript files into a single PDF file with multiple pages.

✦ **OPI and prepress controls:** With Distiller, you can preserve OPI comments, overprints, halftone frequencies, and transfer functions, and preserve or remove undercolor removal (UCR) and gray color removal (GCR).

✦ **Monitor viewing color conversion:** Distiller provides the capability to convert color spaces to device-dependent or device-independent color.

The bottom line on whether to use PDFWriter or Distiller for PDF file creation is this: Always use Distiller except for simple document correspondence and information archives that will never be repurposed.

Distiller's only worth on the planet is to convert PostScript files to PDF documents. To use Distiller, you must start with either an EPS or PostScript file. Before you can examine all the controls available with Acrobat Distiller, you need to begin with an understanding of PostScript.

About Imaging Devices

Imagesetters are high-end devices ranging from $10,000 to over a $100,000 and are usually found in computer service bureaus and commercial print shops. Imagesetters use laser beams to plot the raster image on either sheet-fed or roll-fed paper or film. The paper is resin coated, and both paper and film require chemical processing through a developer, fix, and wash much like a photographic print. The material is used by a commercial printer to make plates that are wrapped around cylinders on a printing press. These prepress materials are an integral part of offset printing, and almost all printing performed today is handled from a form of digital output to material that is used to create plates for presses.

Direct-to-plate and direct-to-press systems bypass the prepress materials and expose images on either plates that are used on print cylinders or directly to the press blankets where the impression receives the ink.

On-demand printing is a term describing machines that bypass the prepress process by taking the digital file from a computer directly to the press. Depending on the engineering of the output device, the consumable materials may consist of toner (as used in copy machines) or ink (as used on printing presses).

Understanding PostScript

Adobe PostScript is a page description language—that is, it describes the text and images on your monitor screen in a language. The interpretation of this language is performed by a raster image processor (RIP). Whereas PostScript is the language, the RIP behaves like a compiler. The RIP interprets the file and converts the text and images you see on your monitor to a bitmap image in dots that are plotted on the printing device. In the office environment, you won't see a RIP independent of a PostScript laser printer you use—but it exists. It's built into the printer. With high-end devices such as imagesetters, platesetters, large format ink-jet printers, on-demand printing systems, high-end composite color devices, and film recorders, the RIP is often a separate component that may be either a hardware device or software operating on a dedicated computer.

One of the reasons PostScript has grown to its present popularity is its device independence. When you draw a bézier curve on your computer, the resolution displayed by your monitor is 72 pixels per inch (ppi). This image can be printed to a 300 dots per inch (dpi) laser printer or a 3,600 dpi imagesetter. Through the device independence of PostScript, essentially the computer "says" to the printer, "Give me all you can." The printer responds by imaging the page at the resolution it is capable of handling. When the file is ripped, the laser printer RIP creates a 300-dpi bitmap, whereas the imagesetter RIP creates a 3,600-dpi bitmap.

With all its popularity and dominance in the market, PostScript does have problems. It comes in many different dialects and is known as a *streamed* language. If you have a QuarkXPress file, for example, and import an Adobe Illustrator EPS file and a Macromedia EPS file, you'll wind up with three different flavors of PostScript—each according to the way the individual manufacturer handles their coding. If the same font is used by each of the three components, the font description will reside in three separate areas of the PostScript file when printed to disk. PostScript is notorious for redundancy, especially with fonts.

As a streamed language, PostScript requires the entire code to be processed by the interpreter before the image bitmap can be created. Ever wonder why you need to wait while the RIP is churning for an endless amount of time only to eventually end up with a PostScript error or RIP crash? PostScript can't begin plotting the bitmap image until the entire PostScript stream has been interpreted.

PDF, on the other hand, is like a database file—it has a database structure. PDF eliminates all redundancy with file resources. Fonts, for example, only appear once, no matter how many iterations are used in imported EPS files. In addition, PDF takes all the dialectical differences of PostScript and converts them to a single dialect. Whereas a PostScript file containing many pages requires the entire file to be downloaded to the RIP and ultimately printed, a PDF file is page independent in that each individual page can be imaged. In short, PDF is much more efficient than PostScript.

Creating PostScript files

In some ways a PostScript file is very similar to a PDF file. If, for example, you create a layout in Adobe PageMaker or QuarkXPress with images and type fonts, the document page can be printed to disk as a PostScript file. In doing so, you can embed all graphic images and fonts in the file. If you take your file to a service center, the file can be downloaded to a printing device. To ensure proper printing, though, you need to be certain the PostScript Printer Description (PPD) file was properly selected for the output device. Assuming you created the PostScript file properly, the file will print with complete integrity.

On desktop printers, printing to a PostScript file is just like printing to a device. On printers in commercial imaging centers, many different requirements need to be considered that are not typically found on a desktop printer. Some of the considerations that need to be understood when printing files for high-end devices include the following:

✦ **PPD device selection:** Whenever printing a PostScript file for direct download, always be certain to choose the proper PPD file. PPD files for imaging equipment can be obtained from imaging centers or from Web addresses. You first need to know the device name; for example, an AGFA SelectSet Avantra25 is a specific printing machine. You need the PPD for an Avantra25 to properly prepare the PostScript file, which will include specific parameters for the printer such as page dimensions, screening, and media length (see Figure 5-1).

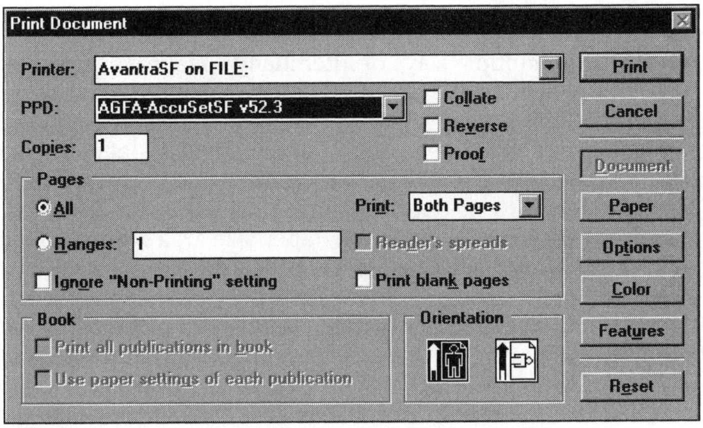

Figure 5-1: From the Print Document dialog box in Adobe PageMaker 6.5, the destination printer is identified as AvantraSF, which indicates it is an AGFA SelectSet Avantra25.

Note The PPD selection you make for a specific output device will only be used when a file is to be imaged on the device in question, and no other repurposing of your document will be needed. The PPD selection in the preceding example is used only to send a PDF file to an imaging center for output on a particular device.

Tip PPD files are ASCII text files. In cross-platform environments where a PPD file is installed on one platform and you do not have access to the same PPD file for another platform, the file can be copied across platforms. Be certain to copy the PPD file to the required directory when adding new PPD files for printing devices.

✦ **Acrobat Distiller PPD:** When document repurposing and PDF workflows are important, and your file may be used for output to several devices or for many purposes, always use the Acrobat Distiller PPD. If, for example, you wish to image a file to a laser printer and use a PPD specific to your device, and then you want to image the same file on a color printer, the PPD you may have used for the laser printer will exclude all color information. You would need to reprint the job's PostScript file to disk, and then distill it again for the color output. If you use the Acrobat Distiller PPD, you can print the PDF file to both the laser printer and the color device. When Distiller is installed, the Acrobat Distiller PPD will be installed in the System:Extensions:Printer:Descriptions folder on the Macintosh and in the Distiller application folder in Windows.

Note The Acrobat Distiller PPD may not always work with every device, and you may need to run some tests to ensure complete integrity in your printed files. Be certain to perform tests, and use the Acrobat Distiller PPD whenever possible. What you may think is a single-application PDF file might later need to be repurposed for other uses.

✦ **Page size:** With desktop printers, you often have only one page size. With printers that have multiple trays or interchangeable trays, you select the appropriate page size for the tray used. With imaging equipment, you need to be sure the page size is properly selected to include all image data and printer's marks. Say that a document is created in the standard page size for a letter (8.5 x 11 inches). However, when printer's marks (registration and color bars) are included, it turns out the page area needs to be defined larger than a letter page for everything to fit. In the Paper Size area of the dialog box shown in Figure 5-2, the word Custom appears, indicating the page size is a custom size. The thumbnail on the right in Figure 5-2 shows how the page will fit within the defined size. In this example, all data and printer's marks will print within the defined page. If your page size is too small, some clipping of the data will occur when printed or when a PDF file is generated.

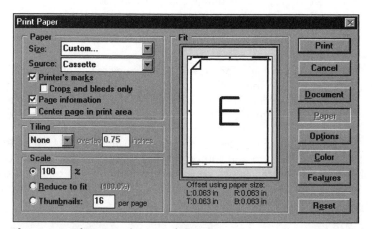

Figure 5-2: The page size was defined as a Custom Size to include the printer's marks and page information.

✦ **Font inclusion:** You may need to specifically tell the host application to include fonts in the PostScript file. If the file is printed at a service center, you definitely need to include the fonts in the file you submit for output. If you distill the file in Acrobat Distiller, the fonts need to be loaded on your system in order to embed the fonts in the PDF file.

An item specific to PageMaker is the Write PostScript to File field. With PageMaker, this item exists to eliminate the need to identify a port for a file in Windows. With many other Windows applications, you can specify you want to print to file in the Print dialog box. On the Macintosh, the Destination pull-down menu in the Print dialog box provides choices for Printer or File.

✦ **Screening:** Halftone frequencies, or *line screens,* can be printed at different settings. With desktop printers the maximum line screen available for the device is typically used. Six-hundred-dpi laser printers, for example, most commonly use a maximum line screen of 85 lines per inch (lpi). With imaging equipment, you need to first know the requirements of the commercial printer and take his/her advice depending on the paper, press, and prepress material. Therefore, if your file will ultimately be printed at 133 lpi, this value must be entered in the Print dialog box for the application creating the PostScript file (see Figure 5-3).

Screening can also be a particular type relative to the printing device and RIP. Stochastic screening, Crystal Raster, AGFA Balanced Screens, and others will be available from a PPD selection for a particular device. In this example, the SelectSet Avantra25 enables you to choose between using a screen filter for balanced screens or no filter (in which case balanced screens are turned off). When the PPD denoted AvantraSF is selected, the screen filter will be used. These kinds of nuances require you to direct inquiries to the imaging center to determine if a PPD with a screen filter should be used. If the Acrobat Distiller PPD was used to create the PDF file, the imaging center will typically make choices for screening alternatives according to the requirements of their RIPs and imaging devices.

✦ **Color:** Will the file be color separated or composite? If separations are to be printed, you must make certain all identified colors are properly named in the host document. There will often be an option in a Print dialog box to specify whether the file will be separated. In Figure 5-3, the radio button for separations is enabled. As you view the color list, it is imperative to verify all colors appearing are those you specified in the document. Even if a spot color is in the current document, the color won't print unless it is an identified color in the Print Ink list. Inasmuch as you may view colors to determine if they will be printed properly, you can always send a composite color PDF file to an imaging center and let them do the separations. If you really want to be certain of proper printing, you can print separations as PostScript files to disk, distill the files, and view them in an Acrobat viewer. Each of the separated pages will be included in one PDF file so you can check knockouts, overprints and colors.

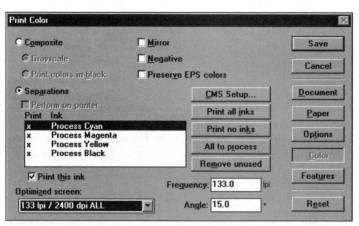

Figure 5-3: In PageMaker 6.5, the screening is determined from the Print Color dialog box. With the AGFA Avantra25 imagesetter, the screen filter will have preset screening choices, which are selectable from the pop-up menu for Optimized screen.

Tip   After toggling through all the file attributes for the PostScript file, clicking OK or Print will begin the save to disk. What's important to know is that all your PDF files to be delivered to the imaging center should be created from PostScript files in which the proper PPD selection is made. You have some latitude with screening and color separation because the imaging center can use Acrobat plug-ins or workarounds for overriding screening and separations. However, page size is determined by the PPD, and you should try to use the right PPD for the right device.

Encoding

As discussed in the last chapter, encoding comes in two flavors: binary and ASCII. Binary encoding will result in smaller files and print faster on PostScript Level 2 and PostScript 3 devices. In most cases, you'll want to use binary encoding when the option is available in the Print dialog box from the host application. In some cases, you may need to have ASCII as a choice. This will be rare, and you should be informed by an imaging center if ASCII is required.

PostScript levels

PostScript originated sometime in 1976, and later it was updated to a version called Interpress at the Xerox Palo Alto Research Center (PARC). Interpress was designed for output to early laser printers. Xerox abandoned the project, and two of the staff at Xerox PARC decided to take it forth and develop it. In 1981, John Warnock and Chuck Geschke formed Adobe Systems, and PostScript was their first product.

On March 21, 1985, the digital print revolution was founded when Apple Computer, Aldus Corporation, Adobe Systems, and Linotype collaborated on an open architecture system for electronic typesetting. Later that year Apple Computer introduced the LaserWriter printer, which came with a whopping 13 fonts fried into the printer's ROM chips and a price tag of $6,500. If you were outputting to a PostScript device by 1987, when Adobe Illustrator first appeared, you may still be waiting for that 12K Illustrator file to spit out of your laser printer. PostScript Level 1 was a major technological advance, but by today's standards it was painfully slow. Many in the imaging world remember all too well those countless times at 3:00 a.m. waiting for the final file to print after ripping over eight hours.

In 1990, Adobe Systems introduced PostScript Level 2, which was a more robust version of PostScript and a screamer compared to the first release. In addition to speed, PostScript Level 2 provided these features:

✦ **Color separation:** In earlier days, color was preseparated on Level 1 devices. PostScript Level 2 enabled imaging specialists to separate a composite color file into the four process colors, Cyan, Magenta, Yellow, and Black. Also, there was support for spot color in PostScript Level 2.

✦ **Improved font handling:** In the early days of PostScript imaging, there were more font nightmares than you can imagine. Font encoding for PostScript fonts only handled a maximum of 256 characters. Other font sets such as Japanese have thousands of individual characters. PostScript Level 2 introduced a composite font technology that handled many different foreign character sets.

✦ **Compression:** Getting the large files across a 10-Base-T network was also burdensome in the Level 1 days. PostScript Level 2 introduced data compression and supported such compression schemes as JPEG, LZW, and RLE. The files are transmitted compressed, which means they get to the RIP faster, and then decompressed at the RIP. In a large imaging center, the compression greatly improved network traffic and workflows.

In 1996, Adobe introduced PostScript 3 (note *Level* has been dropped from the name). Perhaps one of the more remarkable and technologically advanced features of PostScript 3 is the inclusion of Web publishing with direct support for HTML, PDF, and Web content. PostScript 3 support has been slow to grow, but you can count on eventual conversion to PostScript 3. PostScript 3 was also built around the PDF architecture, consuming PDF files directly and bypassing the interpreter functions of PostScript Level 2.

Encoding and PostScript Levels

You may find contradictory recommendations for the encoding method and PostScript level depending on recommendations from software vendors and hardware manufacturers.. In some instances, Level 2 and binary encoding may not work with some other applications or software utilities. Level 2 PostScript will handle color much better than Level 1 and provides for separating spot colors. Most often Level 2 PostScript and binary encoding will be the preferred choice when creating PostScript files. As a matter of rule, always use binary encoding and Level 2 for creating a PostScript file. If you encounter problems, use the alternative settings.

To proceed with a review of Acrobat Distiller, you need a PostScript file to open. If your head is swimming from all the details presented thus far, follow this simple example for creating a PostScript file and bypass all the PPD and high-end output requirements for now.

STEPS: Creating a PostScript File

1. **Open a word processor or text editor.** If you have Microsoft Word installed on your computer, use Word.

2. **Create a document.** If you have some text that can be opened, use it. Import a graphic image if your text editor supports it. You can use any file that you currently have on your hard drive.

3. **Select File ⇨ Print.** For Windows users, select the destination printer in the Name pop-up menu in the Print dialog box. Macintosh users will need to select a printer from the Chooser prior to selecting File ⇨ Print. If using a Macintosh, skip the Print dialog box and open the Chooser.

4. **PPD selection.** Depending on the platform and print driver you use, PPD selection will be handled differently between systems and versions of the print driver.

   Windows: Click the Properties button in the Print dialog box after you have selected the destination printer. The Properties dialog box offers many choices for output options, image and text handling, and resolution. These settings are inherent in the print driver, and usually the default settings will be sufficient for most of your output needs, especially with PDF creation. Leave the settings at the default and click OK.

   Macintosh: In the Chooser dialog box, select the printer driver for the destination printer. In the Chooser, click the Setup button. Another dialog box will appear enabling you to select the proper PPD for the device used. Click the PPD button. Another dialog box will open and default to the Printer Descriptions folder on your hard drive (System:Extensions:Printer Descriptions) where your PPDs will be stored, as shown in Figure 5-4. Select the PPD for the device you use and click the Select button.

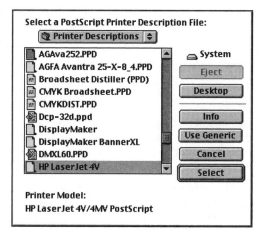

Figure 5-4: This dialog box displays all the PPDs from the Printer Descriptions folder on my computer.

5. **Print to file.** Depending on the platform and version of your print driver, there will be some differences in the choices for printing to a file:

Windows: In Windows, click the Print to file check box to enable printing to a file. Click OK in the Print dialog box, shown in Figure 5-5.

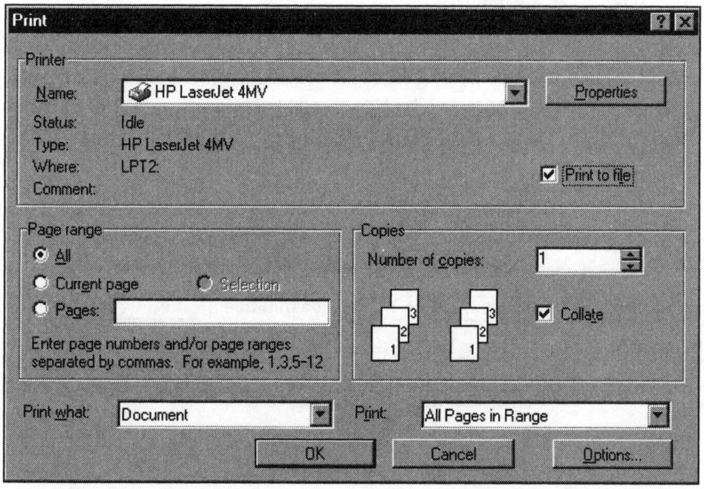

Figure 5-5: The Print dialog box in Windows includes the option Print to file. Enable this option when you want the destination to be a PostScript file.

Macintosh System 7.x: On a Macintosh with System 7.x, if the LaserWriter print driver is below version 8.5, select the File radio button. When you select the File radio button, in the dialog box the word *Print* will change to *Save,* indicating the file will be saved as a PostScript file.

Continued

Macintosh System 8.x: With the LaserWriter 8.5 and later, the Print dialog box includes these choices:

- **Printer:** The Printer pop-up menu lists the printers on your network. Choose the printer from the pop-up menu choices.

- **Save As File:** The dialog box features a pop-up menu where Save As File is listed.

- **Destination:** The Destination pop-up menu offers two choices: Printer and File. If you select the Save as File option and Printer for the destination, your file will be sent to the printer. To avoid this, be sure the Destination choice is File.

- **Format:** The output to be achieved is a PostScript job, so be certain PostScript Job is selected in this pop-up menu. If either of the EPS options is chosen, the file will be saved to disk as an EPS image file and not a PostScript print file.

- **PostScript Level:** As mentioned earlier in this chapter, your default should be PostScript Level 2 and 3. Later printer drives will have separate choices for PostScript Level 2 and PostScript 3. Make the appropriate choice for the level of PostScript on the output device to be used.

- **Data Format:** Also as mentioned earlier, the recommended default is binary. Unless there is a special need for Level 1 and ASCII, always choose the defaults noted here.

- **Font Inclusion:** With the LaserWriter 8.5.x printer driver, font inclusion is determined in this dialog box. In Figure 5-6, the choice shown is All But Standard 13. If you print to PostScript devices, typically the standard 13 fonts will be built into the printer. The Standard 13 fonts are covered a little later. For now, select the All But Standard 13 option as your choice for font inclusion.

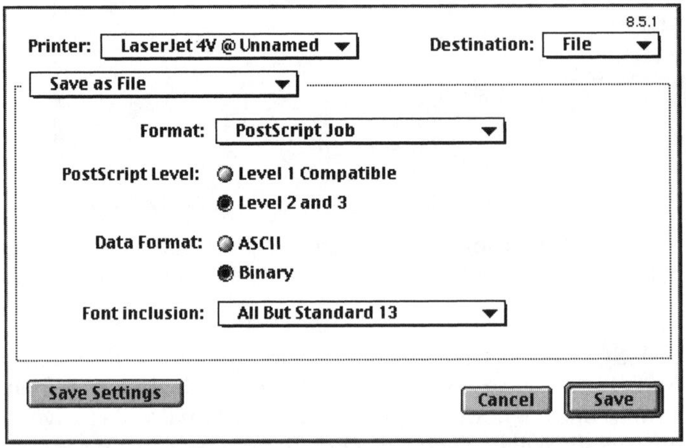

Figure 5-6: The LaserWriter 8.5.1 print driver dialog box

6. Click the Save button in the Print dialog box.

Windows: In Windows, the button to click is OK. Click OK in the Print dialog box, and another dialog box will appear. In the Print to File dialog box, you can make your selection for a filename and destination. The default extension for PostScript filenames provided by Windows is .prn. Adobe Acrobat uses a default extension of .ps. Whenever saving files for distillation, use the .ps extension. In this dialog box, supply a name and choose the destination for your PostScript file.

Macintosh System 7.x and LaserWriter 8.3 to 8.4: When using printer driver versions earlier than 8.5, another dialog box will appear providing choices for encoding and font inclusion after you click the Save button in the Print dialog box (see Figure 5-7). Make the same choices noted in Step 5 for the LaserWriter 8.5.x driver and click the Save button. The file will be written to the folder indicated in this dialog box.

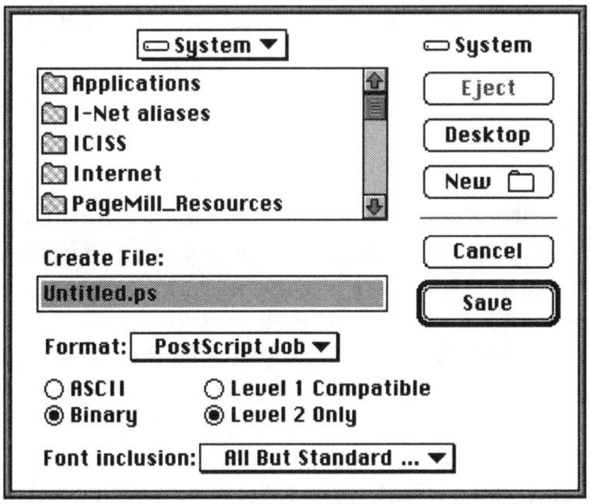

Figure 5-7: With a LaserWriter print driver earlier than version 8.5, the encoding and PostScript level is determined in this dialog box.

Macintosh System 8 and LaserWriter 8.5.x print driver. Because all the attributes of the PostScript file have been determined, the only remaining task is to identify the destination and filename. As a matter of habit, it's a good idea to use the .ps extension in the names of all the files you plan to distill in Acrobat Distiller.

Preparation of PostScript files may seem complicated and excruciating, but once you practice a few times, you'll become accustomed to it. Fortunately, you can check your PostScript output immediately when you distill the file in Acrobat Distiller. The PDF file created by Distiller enables you to view the final file in an

Acrobat viewer. If you made some mistakes, they will often be visible in the PDF document. If you followed these steps and created a PostScript file, save it as you work through the next exercise, distilling a file in Acrobat Distiller.

Acrobat Distiller Environment

When you first launch Acrobat Distiller, it looks like a fairly simple application. Examining the menus immediately tells you there's not much to do in the File and Edit menu. In the File menu, you can open a file, address preferences, and quit the program. Nothing else is offered in this menu. The Edit menu features the traditional Cut, Copy, and Paste commands; but they don't work, and you'll always see them grayed out. Distiller's power is contained in the Settings menu. The commands listed in this menu offer all the control for creating PDF files. There are four choices in the Settings menu for defining how Distiller will work in your environment and the attributes for converting PostScript code to PDF. But before examining the options on the Settings menu, let's look at the Preference settings under the File menu.

Distiller preferences

In all earlier versions of Acrobat, the Preferences option for Distiller was located in the Distiller menu. In Acrobat 4.0, Preferences now appears in the File menu and the Distiller menu has been renamed the Settings menu. When you open the Preferences dialog box by selecting File ➪ Preferences, you'll see three choices related to the general behavior of Distiller. More specific PDF attribute settings are listed in the Job Options command. The three options in the Preferences dialog box are as follows:

✦ **Restart Distiller [Windows] after PostScript fatal error:** When distilling a file, you may encounter a PostScript error. A fatal error will close Distiller. If the check box is enabled, Distiller will automatically relaunch. Relaunching Distiller is particularly important in network environments where you may have a server automatically distilling files in the background. If Distiller is closed, all your PDF workflow tasks will come to a halt. Be certain to enable this option when using Distiller on a network.

In Windows, the item will be denoted Restart Windows after PostScript fatal error. If a fatal error occurs in Windows, the operating system may crash. If Windows is restarted and the Autoexec.bat file launches Distiller, Distiller will be reopened after the fatal crash.

✦ **Notify when watched folders are unavailable:** This command enables Distiller to monitor a folder or directory on your computer or network server to automatically distill PostScript files placed in the watched folders. (Setting up watched folders is discussed later in this chapter.) In an office

environment, you can have different users create PostScript files and send
them to a server for automatic distillation.

✦ **Notify when startup volume is nearly full:** Distiller needs temporary disk
space to convert the PostScript files to PDF documents. If the available hard
disk space on your startup volume becomes less than 1 megabyte, Distiller
will prompt you with a warning dialog box. It's a good idea to always leave
this preference setting enabled.

As you can see, the preferences are limited to the general working environment for
Distiller. Nothing in the Preferences menu relates to particular attributes for a PDF
created with Distiller. More specific preferences related to PDF development are
available via a selection of settings known as *Job Options*.

Job Options

Distiller's Job Options provide controls for the resultant PDF files. This set of
options encompasses many of the same settings that were mentioned in
conjunction with the PDFWriter in Chapter 4 with respect to compression and font
handling. With Distiller, though, you have more control over these settings than
those provided with Acrobat PDFWriter. Job Options attribute control is handled in
two ways. First, you can choose various preset settings by selecting one of the
preset Job Options choices in a pop-up menu in the Distiller window. The other
choice available to you is to open the Job Options window by selecting Settings ⇨
Job Options. When you open the Job Options window, five tabs containing specific
settings for several categories will enable you to choose from among many options
to specify how the PostScript file will be distilled.

Preset Job Options

The Job Options pop-up menu in the Distiller window is a welcomed addition to
Acrobat Distiller 4.0. All earlier versions of Distiller required users to manually
move through the Job Options windows where changes for the many options were
made. If you wanted to create a PDF for screen viewing, you made the related
option changes. The next time you opened Distiller and wanted to create a PDF for
prepress, you had to revisit the Job Options window and once more change many
options for prepress conditions. Now in Acrobat 4.0, you have the opportunity to
bypass the manual toggles and choose from one of three preset conditions for the
kind of PDF to be produced, as shown in the dialog box in Figure 5-8. Choices for
these preset conditions include the following:

✦ **PressOptimized:** The preset settings associated with this option are
established for the highest-quality images to be produced for high-end digital
prepress and printing. The lowest levels of compression and downsampling
are used to preserve image quality.

✦ **PrintOptimized:** The preset settings for this option are established for output to printing devices such as desktop color printers and others where color separations will not be produced.

✦ **ScreenOptimized:** The preset settings associated with this option are established for screen views and Web graphics. ScreenOptimized will use a higher level of compression and downsampling on files than you would choose to use with printed graphics.

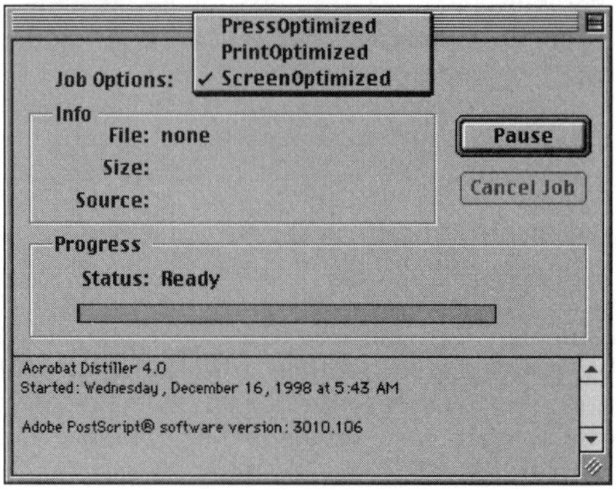

Figure 5-8: The Distiller window enables you to choose from one of three preset conditions for Job Options.

If one of these preset conditions comes close to producing the type of PDF you wish to create, but it doesn't exactly meet your needs, go ahead and select that preset option and then move to the Job Options dialog box to make changes as needed. When you finish editing the Job Options settings to your satisfaction, you have an opportunity to save your own custom preset file, which can be loaded at a later time. Custom preset files are saved in the Job Options window.

General Job Options

If you need to make any changes in the Job Options settings from one of the preset options, or you need to create a new set of Job Options settings, select Settings ⇨ Job Options to open the Job Options dialog box, which is shown in Figure 5-9. The first of five tabs will appear, labeled "General," which covers some general controls:

✦ **Compatibility:** This is the first option you encounter in the General Job Options dialog box. You have a choice between 3.0 or 4.0 compatibility. If you elect to use 3.0, the PDF version you create will be PDF version 1.2. All users of Acrobat 3.0 will be able to use PDFs with Acrobat 3.0 compatibility. If your files will be exchanged among users who have not yet upgraded to an Acrobat viewer later than version 3.01, then use this compatibility version. If you intend to have files printed to PostScript 3 devices, choose Acrobat 4.0 compatibility. Version 1.3 of PDF is designed to print directly to PostScript 3 devices. Until use of Acrobat 4.0 is widespread in the user community, you may wish to keep your PDF files designed for screen and Web use to the earlier compatibility version.

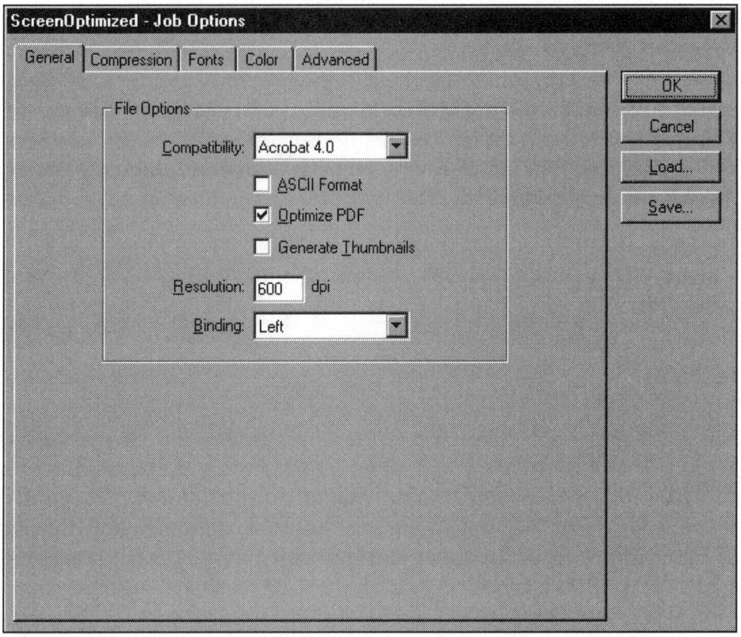

Figure 5-9: The first Job Options settings that appear when you select Settings ➪ Job Options are those under the General tab.

✦ **ASCII Format:** By default, ASCII will be toggled off, which means binary encoding will be used. Unless there is a specific reason to use ASCII encoding, keep this option disabled.

✦ **Optimize PDF:** An optimized PDF file will be smaller than one created without optimization. All files intended to be used for screen views, CD-ROM replication, and Web usage should all be optimized. Generally, almost any device will accept optimized files. As a default, keep this option on. You'll want to turn it off if instructed by an imaging center or if you experience problems when printing PDF files.

✦ **Generate Thumbnails:** Thumbnails add about 3K per page to your PDF file. Thumbnails are helpful when editing PDF files in Acrobat or when browsing PDF files on screen. However, because they create larger files, you may want to eliminate thumbnails when producing PDF files for Web use or sending your PDF files for output to printing devices.

✦ **Resolution:** Any setting you make in the Resolution field will have little to do with the final PDF file. The ranges between 72 and 4000 dpi are available. This setting will impact vector-based applications where gradients have been created from resolution output settings. In the old days of vector applications, many gradient steps were calculated from the resolution specified in the document setup or output dialog boxes. Today, most applications use algorithms independent from the document setup controls. For screen graphics, keep the setting at the default of 600 dpi. For output to press, use 2400 as your default. Changing this field from 600 to 2400 will add only 3K to the file size. Use 2400 as a safeguard with high-end imaging devices to avoid any potential problems.

✦ **Binding:** This setting relates only to viewing pages in an Acrobat viewer with Facing Page – Continuous layouts and with thumbnails. By default, the binding will be left-sided.

Compression

All the familiar compression schemes viewed in relation to PDFWriter in Chapter 4 are also available in the Distiller Job Options dialog box under the Compression tab, as shown in Figure 5-10. As you may recall, Acrobat 2.1 format compatibility will use LZW compression, whereas Acrobat 3.0 and 4.0 format compatibility will use Zip compression. Inasmuch as the compression schemes are the same between the PDFWriter and Acrobat Distiller, you have more choices for the handling of compression with Distiller:

✦ **Average Downsampling at [__]:** Image resampling by downsampling specified in PDFWriter's Compression dialog box only permits resampling to fixed values. In Distiller, you can downsample images to specifications you supply by entering values in the field box. For PostScript files to be repurposed for screen, Web, and CD-ROM replication, you can distill a file that was originally printed to disk for high-end output and downsample all the images to create a smaller file. Likewise, you can take the same PostScript file and downsample images for output to color printers where resolution requirements might be lower than press requirements but higher than screen resolutions. For all your press needs, I recommend you not use Distiller to resample images. You should leave the task of resampling to Photoshop, or better yet, scan images at target resolutions. Downsampling for press needs should be reserved for imaging centers in the case of files that have been poorly constructed and resolutions exceed the output needs for high-end output.

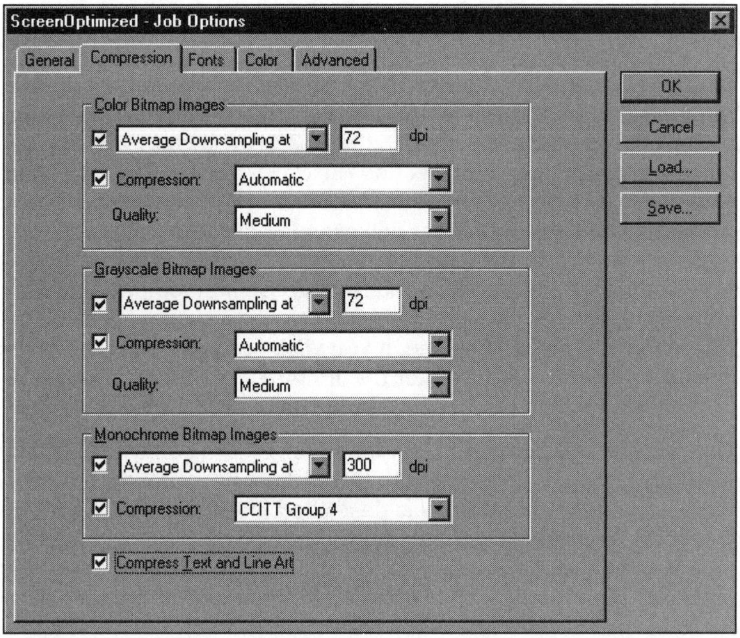

Figure 5-10: Distiller provides many more compression controls than PDFWriter.

✦ **Subsampling at [__]:** If you enable one of the Average Downsampling at check boxes and select from the pop-up menu beside that check box, Subsampling at will appear as one of two additional menu choices. When you resample an image by downsampling, the average pixel value of a sample area is replaced with a pixel of the averaged color. When Subsampling at is specified, a pixel within the center of the sample area is chosen as the value applied to the sample area. Thus, one method replaces pixels from averaged color values, whereas the other replaces pixels from a given color value. Of the two methods, subsampling significantly reduces the amount of time to resample the image. Because all that averaging is taking place with downsampling, the calculations are more extensive, thereby increasing the distillation time. Subsampling, however, may result in more problems in the printed PDF file. Unless you have a large, single-color background, most often you will be better off choosing Downsample when printing to hard copy.

✦ **Bicubic Downsampling at [__]:** The third option that shares space on the same pop-up menu as Average Downsampling at and Subsampling at is Bicubic Downsampling at. Bicubic downsampling uses a weighted average to determine the resampled pixel color. The algorithm is much more mathematically intensive, and as a result this method takes the longest time to complete distillation when files are downsampled. The upside is this method produces the best image quality for continuous tone images.

✦ **Compression:** Acrobat Distiller has a choice for automatic compression in the Compression tab of the Job Options dialog box. In Figure 5-10, note a check box for Compression. When this check box is selected, you can open the adjacent pop-up menu by selecting the down arrow. This pop-up menu enables you to select the Automatic, JPEG, or ZIP compression option. When Automatic is selected, Distiller will examine each image and automatically determine which compression to use (that is, either ZIP or JPEG). If the image to be compressed has large amounts of a common color value, ZIP compression will be used. If the image consists of many varying color values, JPEG compression will be used. If you wish to apply the same compression to all images, you can select either the JPEG or ZIP options. Doing so, eliminates any decision making by Distiller about the type of compression to be applied.

✦ **Quality:** After the compression type is selected, you have one of five choices for the amount of compression to be applied. In earlier versions of Acrobat, the amount of compression was described in terms opposite of what one would choose in Photoshop for JPEG compression. In Acrobat 4.0, the compression amounts are similar to Photoshop 5.0 and eliminates much confusion. High quality relates to less compression, whereas Minimum quality relates to high compression. For high-end prepress, use the High quality setting (that is, Maximum). For desktop color printers, use Medium quality; and for Web, screen, or CD-ROM replication, use Low quality.

✦ **Compress Text and Line Art:** Compression handling for text and line art as they appear in Distiller's Job Options dialog box are handled the same as they are in PDFWriter. Text and line art compression uses RLE (Run Length), which is a lossless compression scheme. You will see virtually no difference in files printed compressed or noncompressed with this setting. Line art definition in this window relates to vector artwork and not raster bitmaps. You may want to avoid compression of line art when line weights are less than .5 points and lines are drawn at diagonals. In some cases, you might see some fallout as a result of selecting the Compress Text and Line Art option. If this occurs, disable the option.

Font embedding

Font embedding, as it related to PDFWriter, was covered in Chapter 4. When you select the Fonts tab in the Job Options box, as shown in Figure 5-11, Distiller displays the familiar font list, Always Embed list, and Never Embed list.

✦ **Embed All Fonts:** Unless you have a specific reason to not embed fonts, this option should be enabled. As you may recall from the discussion of font embedding in Chapter 4, some fonts don't do well with font substitution. For all PDF documents to be printed, especially those that are to be sent to an imaging center, always embed the fonts.

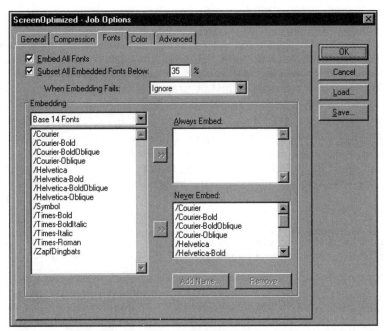

Figure 5-11: The Distiller Job Options dialog box with the Fonts tab selected

✦ **Subset All Embedded Fonts Below [__]:** PDFWriter provides you an opportunity to subset both PostScript and TrueType fonts. The difference between the subsetting in Distiller as opposed to in PDFWriter is your ability to determine when a font is subset. With PDFWriter, any time characters contain more than 35 percent of the font, subsetting will occur. With Distiller, you can specify when you want subsetting to occur. If you think your files need to be edited in Acrobat or you plan to send a file off to an imaging center, enter 100 in the % field box. With this value supplied, the entire character set will be embedded in the PDF document.

✦ **When Embedding Fails:** This pop-up menu offers three choices. Choose Ignore to ignore a failed font being embedded, in which case distillation will continue. The Warn and Continue option will display a warning and then continue distillation. Choose Cancel to cancel the distillation if a font embedding error occurs. When sending files off to service centers for imaging, you may wish to default to the Cancel option. If the PDF is not created, you won't inadvertently forget there was a problem with font embedding.

✦ **Embedding:** The left side of the dialog box lists all fonts available for embedding. Distiller can monitor font locations on your computer. If several font locations exist, the only fonts displayed in the list will be those in the currently selected folder being monitored. By default, you'll see the Base 14 fonts listed. If you wish to view the font list from a monitored folder, click the pop-up menu and select the folder. Monitored font directories can be identified in the Settings menu, as discussed a little later in this chapter. Regardless of what is listed in the Embedding list, Distiller can embed fonts that were included in the PostScript file or all the folders listed for monitoring. The font to be embedded must be present in either the PostScript file or a monitored folder.

✦ **Always Embed:** A list of fonts to always embed appears to the right of the Embedding list. You add fonts to this list by selecting them from the Embedding list and clicking the right-pointing chevron (double arrows). You can select multiple fonts by pressing the Cmd (Macintosh) or Control (Windows) key and clicking all the fonts to be included. If the fonts are listed in a contiguous display, use the Shift-Click keys. After selecting the font(s), click the right-pointing chevron. A good use for the Always Embed list might be for a font that appears in your company logo. Regardless of the type of document you may create, you may wish to always include your corporate font set in all your documents to avoid any font substitution.

✦ **Never Embed:** This list operates the same way as the Always Embed list. You can select fonts to be eliminated from the set of monitored fonts or fonts contained in a PostScript file. One use for this list might be to eliminate Courier, Times, Helvetica, and Symbol (the Base 13 fonts). Because these fonts ship with Acrobat and are usually burned into ROM chips on most PostScript devices, you will rarely have a problem either viewing them or printing documents with these fonts included. Because every user of Acrobat Reader has the Base 13 fonts installed, you can reduce some file size by eliminating them from the PDF files you create.

Note

The Base 14 fonts are sometimes referred to as the Base 13 + 1 fonts. The extra font added to the base set is Zapf Dingbats. You should plan on embedding this font — do not include it in your Never Embed list. PostScript RIPs do not include Zapf Dingbats in ROM.

✦ **Add Name:** Fonts can be added to the Always Embed list or the Never Embed list by entering the font name in a separate dialog box. To add a font name, you must type the name in the dialog box precisely as the font is identified. When you select the Add Name button in the Fonts tab in the Job Options dialog box, the dialog box for adding the name will appear, as shown in Figure 5-12.

In the Add Font name dialog box, you can type the name in the field box. Two radio buttons exist for determining where the font will be added. Select either the Always Embed list or Never Embed list as needed. Click Done, and the font will appear in the appropriate list, as shown in Figure 5-13.

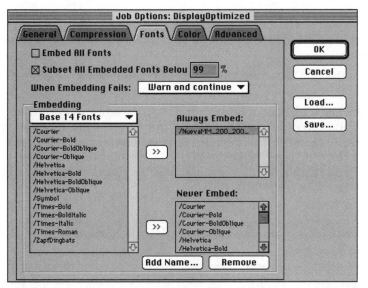

Add Font Name

Add the Font

NuevaMM_200_200_

to the   ● **Always Embed list.**
         ○ **Never Embed list.**

[Done]   [Add]

Figure 5-12: Font names are added in the Add Font Name dialog box, which appears when you select the Add Name button.

Job Options: DisplayOptimized

General \ Compression \ Fonts \ Color \ Advanced

☐ Embed All Fonts
☒ Subset All Embedded Fonts Below [99] %
When Embedding Fails: [Warn and continue ▼]

Embedding

[Base 14 Fonts ▼]

/Courier
/Courier-Bold
/Courier-BoldOblique
/Courier-Oblique
/Helvetica
/Helvetica-Bold
/Helvetica-BoldOblique
/Helvetica-Oblique
/Symbol
/Times-Bold
/Times-BoldItalic
/Times-Italic
/Times-Roman
/ZapfDingbats

Always Embed:

/NuevaMM_200_200_

[>>]

Never Embed:

/Courier
/Courier-Bold
/Courier-BoldOblique
/Courier-Oblique
/Helvetica
/Helvetica-Bold

[>>]

[Add Name...]   [Remove]

[OK]
[Cancel]
[Load...]
[Save...]

Figure 5-13: When you return to the Fonts tab in the Job Options dialog box, the new font will appear in the list selected.

Tip

Font names must be accurate. To ensure accuracy for the name you enter in the Add Font name dialog box, open a PDF file in an Acrobat viewer containing the font to be described. Select File ➪ Document Info ➪ Fonts. If the font is included in your PDF file but not displayed in the font list, click the List All Fonts button. Under the Original Font heading, you will see the font name as it should appear when you add the name in the Add Font name dialog box. Make note of the name including all case sensitivity and special characters. Return to your Add Font name dialog box and enter the name exactly as it appeared in your viewer's font list.

✦ **Remove:** If you add a font name to either the Always Embed list or the Never Embed list, and you wish to delete that name, select the font name to be deleted and click Remove. Fonts can't be removed from the Embedding list. The only time Remove is enabled is when you select a font name in either the Always Embed list or Never Embed list.

Let's look at how a font name might be added to Distiller's font lists by walking through an exercise.

STEPS: Adding Font Names to Distiller's Font Embedding List

1. **Open a document in a text editor or word processor.** Any application will serve for this example. A text editor or other application that provides the capability to use multiple fonts should be used.

2. **Use several fonts.** You can use a simple block of text, select a few words, and change the font. Then select a few other words or sentences, and define a new font. Repeat these actions a few times.

3. **Print to the PDFWriter.** Create a PDF file with PDFWriter, as discussed in Chapter 4.

4. **Open the PDF file in an Acrobat viewer.** Either Reader or Acrobat can be used.

5. **Select File ⇨ Document Info ⇨ Fonts.** A dialog box displaying the font names will appear as shown in Figure 5-14. Write the font name down on a piece of paper. Be certain to include letter case and dashes, and verify spelling. You can't copy and paste font names, but you can take a screen dump of the dialog box by using an application such as Corel Capture in Windows or by pressing Cmd+Shift+3 on the Macintosh.

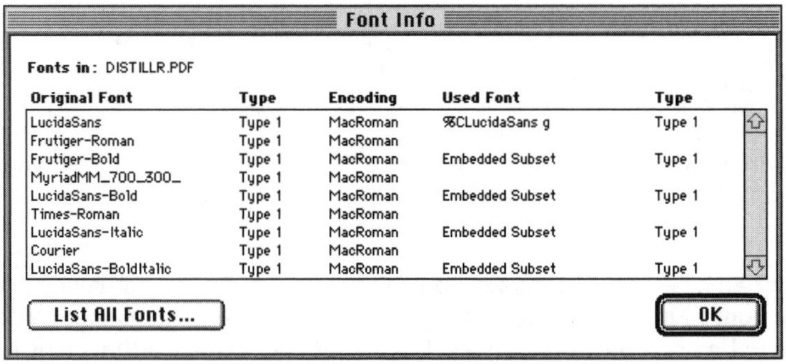

Font Info				
Fonts in : DISTILLR.PDF				
Original Font	**Type**	**Encoding**	**Used Font**	**Type**
LucidaSans	Type 1	MacRoman	%CLucidaSans g	Type 1
Frutiger-Roman	Type 1	MacRoman		
Frutiger-Bold	Type 1	MacRoman	Embedded Subset	Type 1
MyriadMM_700_300_	Type 1	MacRoman		
LucidaSans-Bold	Type 1	MacRoman	Embedded Subset	Type 1
Times-Roman	Type 1	MacRoman		
LucidaSans-Italic	Type 1	MacRoman	Embedded Subset	Type 1
Courier	Type 1	MacRoman		
LucidaSans-BoldItalic	Type 1	MacRoman	Embedded Subset	Type 1

[List All Fonts...]   [OK]

Figure 5-14: The Font Info dialog box in an Acrobat viewer lists font names under the Original Font heading.

6. **Open Acrobat Distiller.** In Distiller, select Settings ➪ Job Options. Click the Fonts tab.

7. **Select the Add Name button** in the Add Font name dialog box.

8. **Enter a font name exactly as was viewed in the Font Info dialog box.** Be certain to type the name precisely in the field box.

9. **Select the appropriate Embed list.** Two radio buttons appear in the Add Font Name dialog box. You can add the new font to the Always Embed list or Never Embed list by selecting the respective radio button.

10. **Add the new font.** Select one of the radio buttons and click the Add button. If you select Done before adding the font, you'll return to the Fonts window without the new font added. You must first enter the name and then click Done.

11. **Observe the Font Embedding lists.** When you return to the Font Embedding dialog box, verify the inclusion of the new font within the list you intended. From here you can move the font to the User List and then move it to the Never Embed list or Always Embed list by selecting the font name and clicking the respective arrows.

Color Job Options

Adobe has been working on developing standard color viewing and file tagging for color spaces for some time. Releases of the latest software products have included many new, sophisticated color-handling methods. If you examine the new features for Illustrator 8 and Photoshop 5, you'll see some examples of how Adobe products offer you some capability in identifying color spaces for your monitor views, tagging and embedding color profiles in images for consistent viewing across platforms and systems, and handling ICC profiles. With the release of Acrobat 4.0, you now have a special window in Acrobat Distiller to describe color conversions and file tagging. The first options you have available describe color conversion. Your first decision to make is whether to convert color. After your conversion choice, you move on to profile assumptions. If you tag a file for conversion, what profiles will be embedded in the document? Under the Options settings, you can choose to control many conditions for prepress operations. As you view the Color tab in the Job Options dialog box, examine each of the controls available for color handling (see Figure 5-15):

✦ **Leave Color Unchanged:** The first radio button appearing in the Color window should be enabled if you presume all color handling in the PostScript file is defined for your specific needs. No color conversion will occur, and device-dependent colors will remain unchanged. When sending files to color-calibrated devices, this option should be used. The presumption is the device will specify all color handling, and the file will not be tagged for color management.

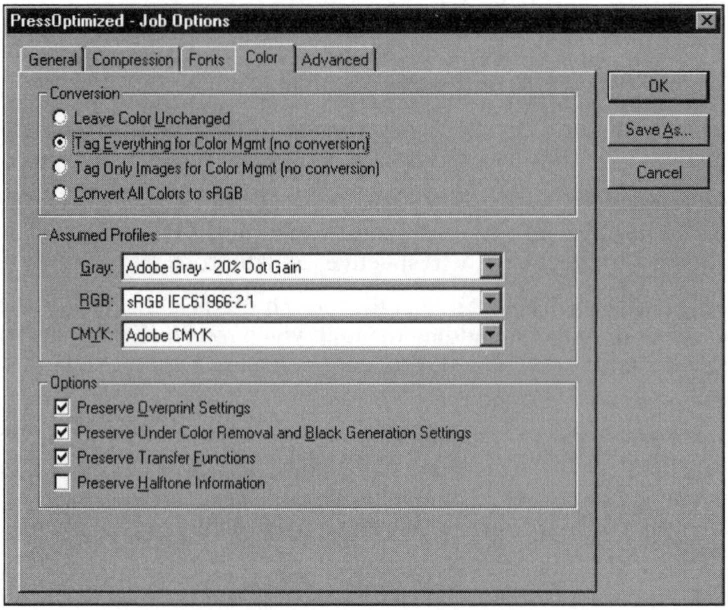

Figure 5-15: The Distiller Job Options dialog box with the Color tab selected

✦ **Tag Everything for Color Mgmt (no conversion):** The PDF is mapped with specific information related to your RGB color viewing space, the grayscale dot gain, and the CMYK profiles to be used. When you select this option, select from the Assumed Profiles section a color profile to be tagged for the color mode(s) of your images. The printed PDF file will maintain the integrity of any documents containing embedded profiles; however, the view on your monitor screen will assume the color viewing space of the assumed profile selected — thus the *no conversion* definition. All data will be subject to tagging for color management.

✦ **Tag Only Images for Color Mgmt (no conversion):** The same holds true as noted in the preceding entry except only raster images will be tagged with color management.

✦ **Convert All Colors to sRGB/CalRGB:** Selecting this option will convert all colors to either sRGB or calibrated RGB. When the Acrobat 4.0 format compatibility is selected, RGB and CMYK images are converted to sRGB. When Acrobat 3.0 format compatibility is selected, RGB and CMYK images are converted to calibrated RGB. In either case, file sizes will be smaller and screen redraws will appear faster. This option is recommended for screen viewing and Web graphics.

✦ **Gray:** If you select either the Tag for Color Management option or the Convert All Colors to sRGB/CalRGB option, the Assumed Profiles section pop-up menus, Gray, RGB, and CMYK, become available The first pop-up menu, Gray, provides two options for dealing with grayscale images. Selecting None from this menu will prevent grayscale images from being converted. If you select Adobe Gray - 20% Dot Gain, the image will use the 20 percent dot gain default.

✦ **RGB:** If you use a color calibration system or monitor profile, the respective profile can be selected from this pop-up menu. The default is sRGB IEC61966-2.1, which is increasingly becoming an industry standard. If in doubt, use the default setting. Choosing None will result in RGB images not being converted.

✦ **CMYK:** Through this pop-up menu, you can choose from ICC profiles installed on your system or color models used with CMYK color. The default is Adobe CMYK. If you select None, CMYK images will not be converted. Choosing None from all three of the pop-up menus under Assumed Profiles will leave all images unchanged — the same as if you selected Leave Color Unchanged in the Conversion section.

✦ **Preserve Overprint settings:** Overprints manually applied in applications such as illustration and layout programs will be preserved when you enable this option. Overprinting will only have an effect when your files will be color separated, unless you print composite color to proofing machines that display trapping problems from files printed as separations.

✦ **Preserve Under Color Removal and Black Generation Settings:** If you made changes to undercolor removal or black generation settings in Photoshop, these changes will be preserved when the file is distilled. Disabling the check box will eliminate any settings made in Photoshop.

✦ **Preserve Transfer Functions:** If you embed transfer functions in Adobe Photoshop, you can preserve them by enabling this option. If transfer functions have not been saved with your Photoshop file, it won't matter if the option is enabled. Choose to preserve the transfer functions when you intentionally set them up. You can eliminate transfer functions by disabling the option.

✦ **Preserve Halftone Information:** Preserving the halftone information will not disturb halftone frequencies embedded in documents, as well as custom angles, spot shapes, and functions specified. As a rule, you don't need this setting enabled when outputting to high-end devices unless you wish to intentionally control frequencies or spot color angles within the application where the artwork was created.

Advanced Job Options

The final tab in Distiller's Job Options dialog box, Advanced, enables you to make advanced settings. The controls listed in this dialog box greatly distinguish Acrobat Distiller from PDFWriter. When you select the Advanced tab in the Job Options dialog box, the settings illustrated in Figure 5-16 will appear.

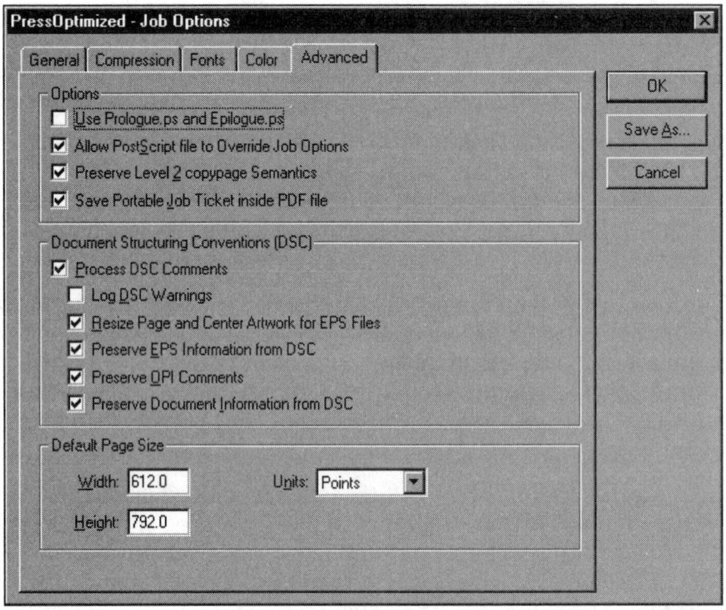

PressOptimized - Job Options   ☒

General | Compression | Fonts | Color | Advanced

┌─ Options ──────────────────────────────────────┐
│ ☐ Use Prologue.ps and Epilogue.ps   │
│ ☑ Allow PostScript file to Override Job Options │
│ ☑ Preserve Level 2 copypage Semantics   │
│ ☑ Save Portable Job Ticket inside PDF file   │
└──┘

┌─ Document Structuring Conventions (DSC) ────────┐
│ ☑ Process DSC Comments   │
│   ☐ Log DSC Warnings   │
│   ☑ Resize Page and Center Artwork for EPS Files│
│   ☑ Preserve EPS Information from DSC   │
│   ☑ Preserve OPI Comments   │
│   ☑ Preserve Document Information from DSC   │
└───┘

┌─ Default Page Size ─────────────────────────────┐
│ Width: 612.0   Units: Points ▼   │
│ Height: 792.0   │
└───┘

OK   Save As...   Cancel

Figure 5-16: The Distiller Job Options dialog box with the Advanced tab selected

Advanced contains many controls designed for prepress and high-end output:

✦ **Use Prologue.ps and Epilogue.ps:** There are two files, named *prologue.ps* and *epilogue.ps,* located in the Adobe Acrobat 4:Xtras:high_end folder (Macintosh) or Acrobat4:Distilr:Xtras:High_end folder (Windows) when you install Acrobat. In order to use either or both of these files, they must be moved to the same folder as the Acrobat Distiller application. The files contain PostScript code that is appended to a PDF file when it is created in Distiller. These files should always be used for PDF files to be delivered to imaging centers. The prologue.ps file can be used for cover pages and watermarks. The epilogue.ps file is used to resolve a series of procedures in the PostScript file.

When outputting to high-end devices, you should use both files. After moving (copying) them to the Distiller Application folder, enable the Use prologue.ps and epilogue.ps option. (More on high-end output appears in Chapter 16.)

Note   Both of these files can be edited; however, you need to be familiar with the PostScript language to effectively change the files. When relocating either file, be certain to place a copy in the Distiller folder and leave the original in the Xtras:High_end folder, especially if you decide to edit either file. You can also use the files with watched folders, as explained a little later in this chapter. When using watched folders, place the prologue.ps and epilogue.ps files at the same directory level as the In and Out folders.

✦ **Allow PostScript file to Override Job Options:** If you are certain the PostScript file you printed to disk has all the settings handled properly for output, enabling this option allows the PostScript file to supersede any changes you make in the Distiller Job Options dialog box. Disabling the check box allows all Distiller Job Options specifications to take precedence.

✦ **Preserve Level 2 copypage Semantics:** This setting has to do with semantic differences between PostScript Level 2 and PostScript 3. If you are imaging to PostScript Level 2 devices, enable this option. If printing to PostScript 3 devices, disable this option. If you are sending files to an imaging center, ask the technicians which level of PostScript is used on their devices.

✦ **Save Portable Job Ticket inside PDF File:** Job tickets contain information about the original PostScript file and not the content of the PDF file. Information related to page sizes, resolution, halftone frequencies, and so on is some of what is contained in job tickets. When printing PDF files, enable this option. If you produce PDF files for screen, Web, or CD-ROM, you can eliminate job ticket information.

✦ **Process DSC:** Document structuring comments (DSC) contain information about a PDF file. Items such as originating application, creation date, modification date, page orientation, and so on are all document structuring comments. To maintain the DSC, enable this option. Because some important information such as page orientation and beginning and ending statements for the prologue.ps file are part of the document structure, you'll want to enable this option.

✦ **Log DSC Warnings:** During distillation, if the processing of the document structuring comments encounters an error, the error is noted in a log file. When you enable this check box, the log file will be created. You can open the log file in a word processor or text editor to determine where the error occurred. Enable this option whenever document structuring comments are processed.

✦ **Resize Page and Center Artwork for EPS Files:** This is a wonderful new addition to Acrobat Distiller in version 4.0. In earlier versions of Acrobat, distillation of a single-page EPS file, created from programs such as Adobe Illustrator, Macromedia FreeHand, or CorelDraw, would use the EPS bounding box for the final page size. Many problems were experienced in distilling EPS files directly as opposed to printed PostScript files. At times, a user would experience clipping and lose part of an image. With this option you have a choice between creating a PDF with the page dimensions equal to the artwork or having the artwork appear on the size of the original page you defined in your host application. When the check box is enabled, the page size will be reduced to the size of the artwork, and the artwork will be centered on the page. When the check box is disabled, the entire page will appear as you laid it out in the host application.

✦ **Preserve EPS Information from DSC:** This item is similar to the Process DSC option. If your file is an EPS file, enabling this check box will preserve document structuring comments.

✦ **Preserve OPI Comments:** Open Press Interface (OPI) is a management tool used by many high-end imaging centers to control production. An OPI comment might include the replacement of high-resolution images for low-resolution FPO (the acronym for *for position only*) files used in a layout program. OPI comments can include many different issues related to digital prepress such as image position on a page, crop area, sampling resolution, color bit depth, colors (in other words, CMYK, spot, and so on), overprint instructions, and more. If outputting to high-end imaging devices at service centers using OPI management, enable this option.

✦ **Preserve Document Information from DSC:** Document information items, discussed earlier in this book, include such things as title, subject, author, and keywords. Enabling this option preserves document information.

✦ **Default Page Size:** Setting page sizes in the field boxes only applies to distillation of EPS files. Whatever you enter in the field boxes when distilling PostScript files will be ignored. If you wish to trim the page size or create a larger page size for the EPS file, you can establish the dimensions in the field boxes for width and height. The Units pop-up menu enables you to choose from four different units of measure.

Many of the controls available in the Advanced tab will be further amplified in Chapter 16's discussion of digital prepress. At this time, it is important to realize that Acrobat Distiller provides you with many more controls for establishing attributes with PDF document creation and permits flexibility in designing PDF files for specific purposes. With all these toggles and check boxes, it's easy to become confused and feel overwhelmed. Fortunately, Acrobat can help make this job a little easier for you. If you work in an office environment where a network administrator sets up all the controls for your PDF workflow, you can load preset custom Job Options. If you are the responsible party for establishing Job Options, you can create different custom settings and save them for loading. Either way, you won't have to go back and reread this chapter every time you wish to distill a file for another purpose.

As you view the different Job Options tabs, notice the Load and Save buttons on the right side of the Job Options window.

✦ **Load:** Acrobat ships with several Job Options settings that are installed when you install the programs. Click the Load button, and you will automatically be taken to the directory where the Job Options are stored — Acrobat\Distiller\ Settings. From the list, double-click or select the filename and click Open in the navigation dialog box to bring up the Job Options settings suited to the PDF you wish to distill (see Figure 5-17).

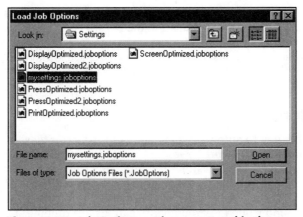

Figure 5-17: Job Options settings are stored in the Settings folder residing inside the Acrobat Distiller folder, which is created when you install Adobe Acrobat.

✦ **Save:** The Save button captures all the settings you make for all the Distiller Job Options and opens a dialog box that defaults to the Settings folder. Provide a filename and click the Save button to create a new Job Options set. In Figure 5-18, I named the new set mysettings.joboptions. As you examine Figure 5-17, notice the new settings available for loading.

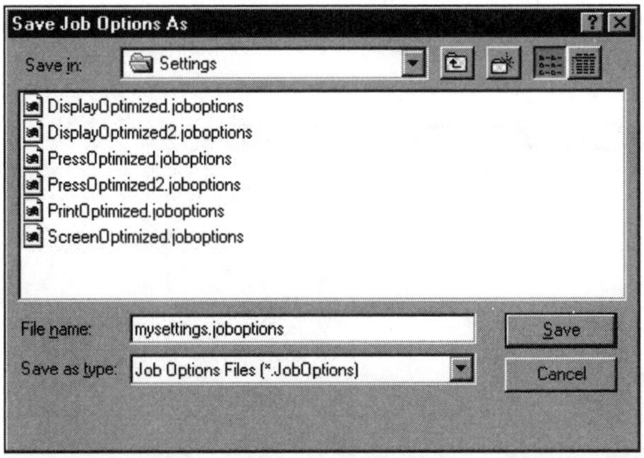

Figure 5-18: When you select the Save button, a navigation dialog box opens, enabling you to supply a name and find a location for the new settings to be saved. By default, the new file will be saved to the Job Options folder.

Tip

When saving Job Options, use the Settings folder created during Acrobat's installation. Try to keep all Job Options for loading in the Distiller Job Options window in the same location on your hard drive. Using the same folder will help you find them quickly. When naming files saved from capturing Job Options, try to use descriptive names that can easily identify their specific use for PDF documents.

Watched folders

Watched folders enable you to automate distillation of PostScript files in a business or production environment. PDF workflows can be easily developed by hosting a server on a network where Acrobat Distiller is continually running in the background and watching a folder or many folders for the introduction of new PostScript files. When Distiller encounters a new PostScript file, the file can be distilled in the background while foreground applications are running. The resulting PDF files can be automatically moved to another folder or directory, and the PostScript files can be either preserved or deleted automatically.

Watched folders can be individual folders, hard drive partitions, or dedicated hard drives. When you select Settings ➪ Watched Folders, a dialog box appears enabling you to establish preferences for the watched folders attributes.

The options available in the Watched Folders dialog box include these:

✦ **Watched folders list:** The list window displays all folders you have identified to be watched. The name of the watched folder will appear in the list as well as the directory path. In Figure 5-19, notice the directory is E:\ and the folder name is Acrobat.

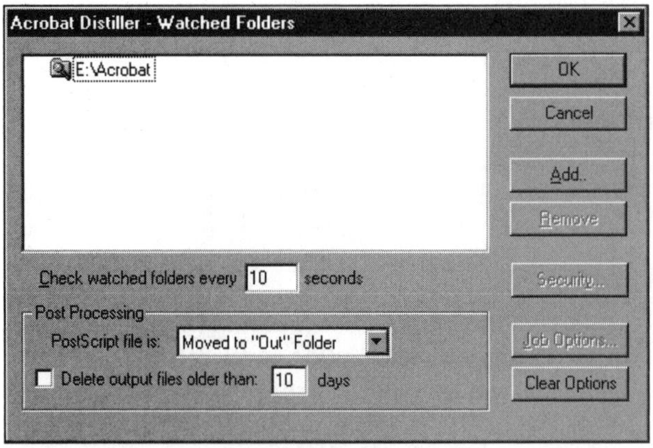

Figure 5-19: Watched folder preferences are established in the Watched Folders dialog box.

✦ **Check Watched Folders every [__] seconds:** This user-definable field will accept values between 1 and 10,000 seconds. When Distiller monitors a watched folder, the folder will be examined according to the value entered in this field box.

✦ **PostScript file is:** Distiller will automatically treat the PostScript file according to the options available in this pop-up menu. You can select the Deleted menu item, which will delete the PostScript file after distillation; or select Moved to "Out" folder, which will move the PostScript file to a folder entitled *Out*.

✦ **Delete output files older than [__] days:** If you elect to keep the PostScript files in the Out folder, they can be deleted after the time interval specified in this field box. The acceptable range is between 1 and 365 days.

✦ **Add:** To create a watched folder or add to the current list of watched folders, click the Add Folder button. When the button is selected, a navigation dialog box will appear. You can select a directory, drive partition, or entire hard drive.

To add a folder to the watched folders list, the folder must first be created before you open the Watched Folders dialog box. Folders as well as partitions and drives can be added to your list. On a network, remote folders, partitions, and drives can also be added to the list. If you wish to select a folder similar to the one displayed in Figure 5-19, select a folder and click the Select *«folder name»* button. If you wish to have the entire hard drive watched, select the drive designation (C:\, D:\, E:\, and so on in Windows or Macintosh HD, Hard Drive, and so on on a Macintosh) and click the Select *«drive name»* button.

✦ **Remove:** To delete watched folders, select the folder name in the watched folders list and click the Remove Folder button. If a folder is moved on or deleted from your hard drive, the next time you launch Distiller, you will see a warning dialog box appear notifying you that Distiller cannot find the watched folder(s). Removal of watched folders must occur in the Watched Folder Settings window. If you inadvertently deleted a watched folder, you need to delete the folder name in the watched folders list. Return to your desktop and create a new folder; then return to the Watched Folders dialog box and add the new folder to the list.

✦ **Security:** Security can be established for the PDF files distilled. Adding security during distillation is a nice new addition to Acrobat 4.0. In earlier versions of Acrobat, users had to add security to each PDF document individually in Acrobat. Now in version 4.0, users can distill many files all with the security they wish to add to the distilled files. Options for securing PDF documents are discussed a little later in this chapter when I cover the security settings.

✦ **Job Options:** The Job Options button becomes active when you select a watched folder name in the watched folders list. With a folder name selected in the list, clicking the Job Options button will open the Job Options dialog box. You can apply different Job Options to different watched folders. If, for example, you print PostScript files to disk and have them distilled for high-end output and Web page design, you might wish to have compression and color modes appropriate for the output sources. You can set up two watched folders and have the same PostScript file distilled with the different Job Options. Setting Job Options here will override Distiller's defaults and apply new options to the specific watched folder where the attributes are established.

✦ **Clear Options:** This button in the Watched Folders settings dialog box can only be used after the Job Options button is selected and the Job Options for the watched folder have been changed from Distiller's defaults. Once the Job Options have been changed from the Job Options control, the icon adjacent to the directory path and folder name in the watched folders list will change, as illustrated in Figure 5-20. The symbol indicates the Job Options have been changed from Distiller's defaults. When you select the name in the list and click the Clear Options button, the icon will change back to the view displayed in Figure 5-19.

```
┌──────────────────────────────────────────────────────────┐
│  ▤ ⊞ Scratch: Acrobat Bible:                    ⇧          │
│                                              ┌──────────┐  │
│                                              │    OK    │  │
│                                              └──────────┘  │
│                                              ┌──────────┐  │
│                                              │  Cancel  │  │
│                                              └──────────┘  │
│                                              ┌──────────┐  │
│                                              │   Add... │  │
│                                              └──────────┘  │
│                                              ┌──────────┐  │
│                                              │  Remove  │  │
│                                              └──────────┘  │
│                                      ⇩       ┌──────────┐  │
│  Check watched folders every: [10]  seconds  │ Security...│ │
│  ┌ Post Processing ──────────────────┐       └──────────┘  │
│  Postscript file is: [Moved to "Out" folder ▼] │Job Options...│ │
│  ☐ Delete output files older than: [10] days  │Clear Options│ │
└──────────────────────────────────────────────────────────┘
```

Figure 5-20: When custom Job Options settings are made for a watched folder, the display for that folder in the watched folders list changes. Notice the icon added adjacent to the folder icon.

Watched folders greatly help your PDF workflow and assist you in automating the smallest office environment to large offices with multiple networks and servers. When you install Acrobat Distiller on a server, the burden of PDF creation is dedicated to the server and relieves individual workstations — not to mention the cost savings of only having to purchase a single copy of Acrobat for the server as opposed to multiple copies running on independent workstations.

In identifying watched folders, you need only have the directory or folder created on a hard disk. Once you identify the watched folder, Distiller will automatically create the other folders needed to execute distillation from watched folder files. The In folder created by Distiller will be monitored. When a PostScript file is placed or written to the In folder, the distillation will commence according to the interval you establish in the Watched Folder settings dialog box. Files can be *dropped* into the In folder, or you can print to PostScript from within an application directly to the In folder.

Watched folders work well in cross-platform environments, too. In order to use a watched folder from one platform and have the distillation performed on another platform, you need to have the computers networked and have software installed that will enable you to communicate between two or more computers on your network. To give you an idea of how easy cross-platform networking and remote distillation is, I walk you through the steps I use in my home office in the following exercise.

STEPS: Creating Watched Folders for Network Distillation

1. **Network topology.** On my network I have a Pentium running Windows NT Workstation, a Mac 9500 with a G3 upgrade card, and a Mac G3. To communicate between the Macs and the PC, I use Miramar Systems MacLan Connect software (http://www.miramarsystems.com). MacLan Connect provides one of the best applications for cross-platform network communication (see Figure 5-21).

2. **Launch the server software.** I open MacLan Connect in Windows NT.

Figure 5-21: MacLan Connect software is opened on the PC to enable file sharing and communication between PCs and Macs.

3. **Privileges.** After launching MacLan Connect, I identify the Users and Groups, which will grant privileges to users. In this example, I create guest privileges with file sharing access. In Figure 5-22, I specify Guest in the Users section, which will enable me to log on from my Mac as a guest, which doesn't require a password.

4. **Shared volumes.** I need to let MacLan Connect know which drive(s) are to be shared. On my Pentium, I have one drive with two partitions and another fixed drive installed. The drives are identified as C:\, D:\, and E:\. I identified all my drives and partitions to be shared.

Continued

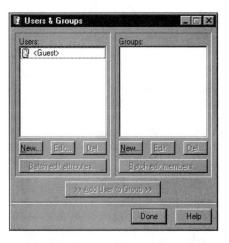

Figure 5-22: The Users and Groups dialog box enables me to establish file sharing privileges.

5. **Start the file sharing.** After I have the privileges and volumes identified, I start the server software by clicking the icon to start MacLan Connect.

6. **Create a folder to be watched.** The Folder to be watched can be created either before or after the server is running. MacLan Connect will display new documents and folders after your server connection has been established. In this example, I created the folder after the server software was running (see Figure 5-23).

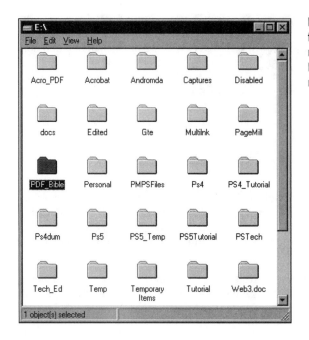

Figure 5-23: I created a folder on my Windows NT machine and named it PDF_Bible, which I'll use for my watched folder.

7. **Log on to the network.** On a Macintosh, I select Apple ➪ Chooser to open the Chooser dialog box and select AppleShare, which displays the computers that are currently being shared (see Figures 5-24 and 5-25). I select the PC MACLAN workstation and click OK in the Chooser dialog box.

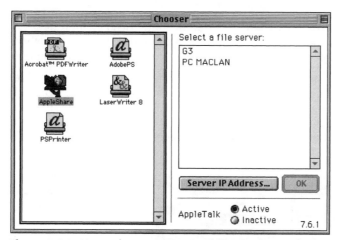

Figure 5-24: Network connections and file sharing are built into the Mac operating system. Addressing network communications is handled in the Chooser by selecting AppleShare.

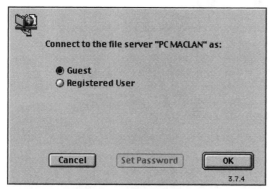

Figure 5-25: When logging onto the network with AppleShare, you can choose to log on as a guest or as a registered user. Logging on as a guest eliminates the need for name and password entries.

Continued

When the workstation has been identified, another dialog box enables me to connect as a registered user or guest. Because I established myself as a guest in the Users and Groups dialog box in MacLan, I select the Guest radio button and click OK, which opens a third dialog box. The list in the PC MACLAN dialog box displays the volumes published. Because my folder was created on the E:\ drive, I select drive E in the dialog box and click OK.

8. **Launch Acrobat Distiller.** The watched folder can be identified either before or after the network connection. In this example, I first established my network connection, and now I need to set up the watched folder.

9. **Create a watched folder.** The folder I created earlier is just a folder or directory on my hard drive. To make this folder a watched folder, I need to select Settings ⇨ Watched Folders and select the folder to be watched. When the Watched Folders dialog box appears, I click the Add button, which opens the navigation dialog box shown in Figure 5-26.

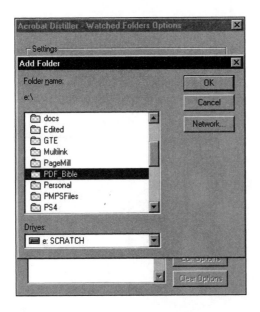

Figure 5-26: My drive E displays the folder list, among which includes my PDF_Bible folder.

If you click OK, the entire drive will be selected as the watched folder. To use the PDF_Bible folder, I need to open it.

I open the PDF_Bible folder and click OK in the dialog box. When I return to the Watched Folder dialog box, the new folder name will be displayed in the watched folder list.

10. **Examine the watched folder.** When I return to my desktop and open the PDF_Bible folder, I double-check it to be certain Distiller has created the subfolders necessary to make this a watched folder, as shown in Figure 5-27. If you find the In and Out subfolders within the watched folder, you know Distiller will monitor this folder.

Figure 5-27: When I open the watched folder, the In and Out folders, automatically created by Distiller, should appear. Verifying that the folders have been created ensures that Distiller has identified the folder as a watched folder.

11. **Printing the PostScript file.** I could drop a PostScript file into the In folder, and within 10 seconds (as determined in the watched folder settings) the file will be distilled. I can also print a PostScript file directly from my Macintosh to the In folder inside the watched folder. From an application document I select File ⇨ Print to open the Print dialog box. I select File as the destination and click the Save button.

12. **Saving the file.** When the Save button is selected, a progress display dialog box will appear indicating the printing status of the PostScript file. At this time, you need to wait a moment for the file to finish writing to disk.

13. **Distilling the PostScript file.** In order for Distiller to monitor the watched folder and distill the PostScript files added to the In folder, you need to have Distiller launched. If you use a workstation and have other programs open, Distiller can still work in the background, but it must be resident in memory.

14. **Examine the In folder.** After distillation is complete, I open the In folder to check its contents. From observing the folder, I can see the new PDF file created and the PostScript file that was written to the folder. In addition, there is a file named Messages.log, which Distiller created as a log file as it progressed through the Job Options (see Figure 5-28).

Figure 5-28: The original PostScript file, the new PDF file, and a log file created by Distiller will be visible within the In folder.

Continued

If you elect to delete the PostScript file in the Watched Folder settings dialog box, the PostScript file will be deleted by Distiller after the PDF is created. Also, the new PDF file will be moved to the Out folder according to the time interval you established in the Watched Folder settings dialog box.

15. **Review the log file.** The Messages.log file is an ASCII text file you can open in Windows Notepad, Simple Text on the Mac, or any word processor or text editor. This file contains information about distillation to create the PDF file and the Job Options it performed while distilling. You can verify attributes such as font embedding, image compression, format compatibility, and the like by reviewing the log file (see Figure 5-29).

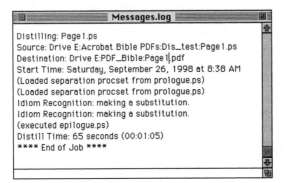

Figure 5-29: The Messages.log file was viewed in Simple Text on the Macintosh to review the distillation process.

Security

Ahh . . . the blessings of Acrobat 4.0. As I mentioned earlier, Acrobat versions prior to release 4.0 did not enable users to create any security in PDF documents during distillation. Security, being left to Acrobat, required a user to open each PDF file individually and enter the passwords and security features for the individual PDF documents. Then edits had to be saved file by file. If you created a massive amount of PDF files needing security, you were committed to many hours of computer time. If you are like me, remembering passwords is, at least, a challenge. I've been on CompuServe for almost 20 years now and have forgotten my password so many times I'm embarrassed to ask the support people for help — and I repeated the problem with AOL.

I once created a HyperCard stack and secured it. Shortly thereafter I tried to open it knowing I had used a password similar to my father's birth date. To this day I can't open that stack. Security has been downright frustrating to me. The moral of this story: If you use security, make a note of all your passwords and store them safely. And, I'd like to caution you on one more note. I have about 20 different notes with passwords around somewhere. Where, I don't know. I always figured passwords need to be somewhat secret, so I tried to think of hiding places where they could not be easily found. Well, they're secure all right — even I can't find them. Therefore, if you record your passwords, keep them in a logical place you frequent.

Enough about the pitfalls of losing security passwords — let's look at how Distiller handles security. To access the Security settings, select Settings ➪ Security in Acrobat Distiller. When you select the Security item from the pull-down menu, a window will appear where your security options are established. Figures 5-30 and 5-31 display the Security window, which enables you to change your password and security options. Options for Security include the following:

Figure 5-30: The Security window viewed from Distiller allows different passwords for opening and/or changing PDF files.

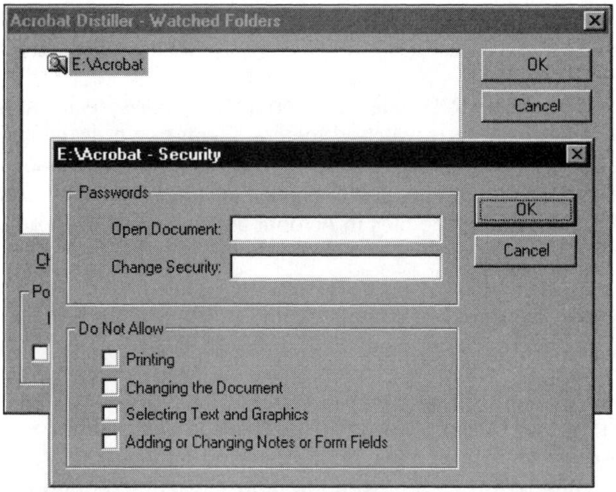

Figure 5-31: The same Security dialog box is used when adding security with watched folders, as described earlier in this chapter.

✦ **Open Document:** This is a field box where you can add a security password that controls viewing PDF documents. If a password is supplied, anyone with an Acrobat viewer will need the password in order to open the document.

✦ **Change:** Acrobat makes a distinction between viewing PDF files and editing them with regards to password protection. Whereas the first item deals with viewing, the Change field box is used to prevent users from changing the original file or using commands as listed in the four options that follow. You can supply two different passwords in the two field boxes. If you wish to have all users allowed to open a PDF file without entering a password but do not want anyone to change your document; you can eliminate a password from the first field box, and only provide a password to prevent changes.

✦ **Printing:** When the Change field box contains a password, and you enable the check box for printing, the user will need to open the PDF file with the Change password. If not, no printing will be allowed.

✦ **Changing the Document:** When enabled, this check box prevents any changing and saving updates to the file.

✦ **Selecting Text and Graphics:** This item is used to prevent any copying of data and pasting into other applications. When enabled, the TouchUp tool, Text Select tool, Column Select tool, and Graphics Select tool will all be disabled in Acrobat viewers.

✦ **Adding or Changing Notes and Form Fields:** The behavior of notes and annotations is different than text selections, thus this item is separate from the preceding option. When enabled, no note changing or form field editing can occur.

After entering the password(s) and selecting the various options, click the OK button. When you return to the Distiller window, all files will be distilled with the security settings you specify enabled.

When using security with Acrobat Distiller, be certain to always recheck your Distiller Security settings and/or your watched folders. If you begin distilling files with security, Acrobat offers no warning. You can easily inadvertently add security to files where you do not want it. If you need to change secure PDF files to nonsecure PDF files, you'll need to open the files in Acrobat and individually save them without security.

Printing to Distiller

In Chapter 6, I cover many different direct exports to PDF from within applications. Some of the exports to PDF write directly from the application document to a PDF file, much like PDFWriter does. In other cases, an application may print a PostScript file to disk, which will be transparent to the user, and automatically launch Distiller. Distiller will open, distill the file, and then return you to the application document. With all kinds of different applications and many approaches to creating PDF files, you may become confused as to which method to use. Should you manually print a file to disk and then open Distiller, or use an export feature to create the PDF? When you know a file should be distilled, then your clue is whether or not you see the Distiller window open. If the export creates the PDF, and you didn't see Distiller appear, then you're not creating the PDF file through Distiller. If Distiller does open, the job will be produced according to all the attribute changes you last made in the Job Options dialog boxes or Watched Folder dialog box. If exports include distilling a file, it really doesn't matter whether you print to PostScript and distill through Distiller or export the application document, which automatically opens Distiller.

The launching of Acrobat Distiller can be handled in several ways and different methods on individual platforms. Rather than print a PostScript file to disk, and then open the file in Distiller, you can economize your steps by accessing Distiller directly through an application command via a printer driver or a command from the Run options in the Windows status bar. In either case, when Distiller is launched, all the Job Options currently set in Distiller will be used to convert your document to PDF.

One Step Distillation

Printing a PostScript file and opening the file in Distiller is a two-step process. There are several ways to create PDF files though distillation by using a single step. Single-step conversions require you to have the appropriate printer divers, PPDs, and/or applications installed on your computer. Economizing steps to create PDF documents through Distiller is handled differently on different computer platforms. To examine these methods, let's start with Macintosh-supported examples for single-step procedures, and then move on to Windows.

AdobePS printer driver on the Macintosh

The AdobePS printer driver affords you the opportunity to print to PDF using Acrobat Distiller in the background. The printer driver is contained on the installer CD and will be installed with your Acrobat installation. To use the printer driver, open the Chooser dialog box and select AdobePS as viewed in Figure 5-32.

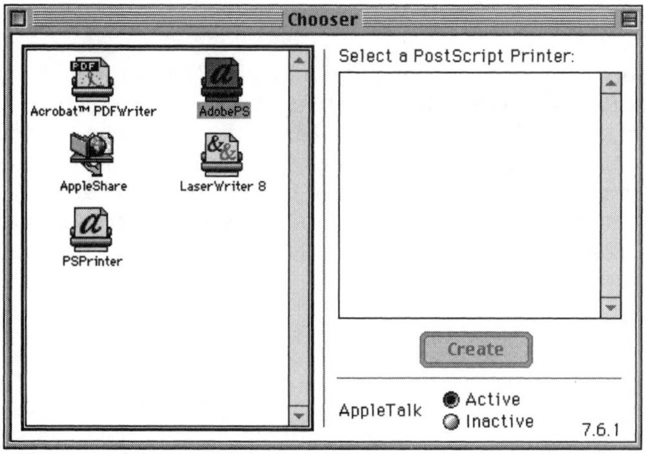

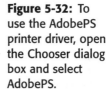

Figure 5-32: To use the AdobePS printer driver, open the Chooser dialog box and select AdobePS.

Previous versions of Acrobat made use of Acrobat Distiller Assistant, which enabled other printer drivers to produce PDF files that were then routed directly to Acrobat Distiller. With the AdobePS printer driver, the steps to produce a PDF have been economized. You can use the AdobePS driver to either print directly to a PostScript printer or prepare the file for distillation. When the printer driver is selected in the Chooser control panel, select File ↪ Page Setup in the application for which you wish to print. At the top-left side of the dialog box appears a pop-up menu. From the menu options, select PostScript Options. The default settings, as viewed in Figure 5-33 under Image & Text, will show check box options for Substitute Fonts, Smooth Text, and Smooth Graphics. Disable these three items by clicking the check boxes. Smoothing of text and graphics will anti-alias the edges for both text and graphics, creating many small pixels that won't be needed in the final document. If you leave these items enabled, the file size of the final PDF will be larger due to the smoothing effect.

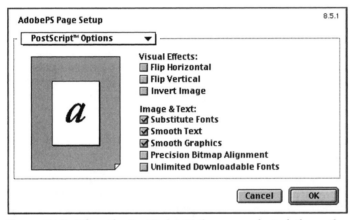

Figure 5-33: When the PostScript Options are selected, the options for Substitute Fonts, Smooth Text and Smooth Graphics will appear. Disable these three items in the dialog box.

The first item in the pop-up menu available in the AdobePS Page Setup dialog box is Page Attributes. Select Page Attributes after disabling the three options just discussed. On the right side of the dialog box the Format for: pop-up menu offers options for choosing either Acrobat PDF or Adobe Driver, as shown in Figure 5-34. When the Adobe Driver is used, the file will be sent to a printer. Acrobat PDF provides the means to route the printed file to Acrobat Distiller. Select Acrobat PDF and click OK in this dialog box.

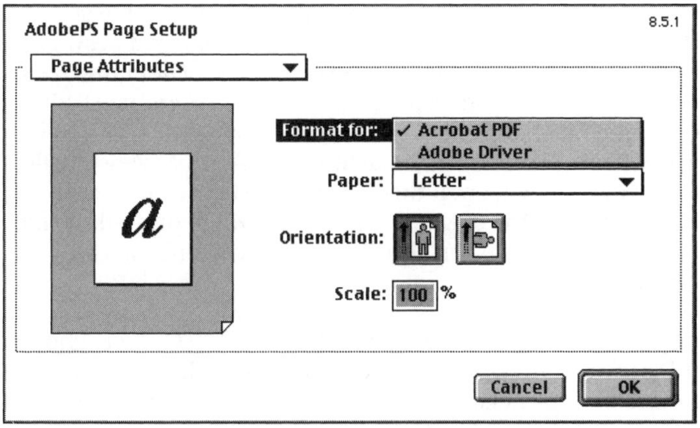

Figure 5-34: When the Page Attributes menu item is selected, you can choose either Acrobat PDF or Adobe Driver from the pop-up menu for Format.

After the Page Setup options are selected, choose the File ➪ Print command from the application menu bar. The Print dialog box will pick up the printer designation from the Page Setup dialog box. If you did not select Acrobat PDF in the Page Setup dialog box, you can still make the selection from the Printer pop-up menu. In either case, when Acrobat PDF is selected, the Print button in the lower-right corner will change to Distill, as illustrated in Figure 5-35.

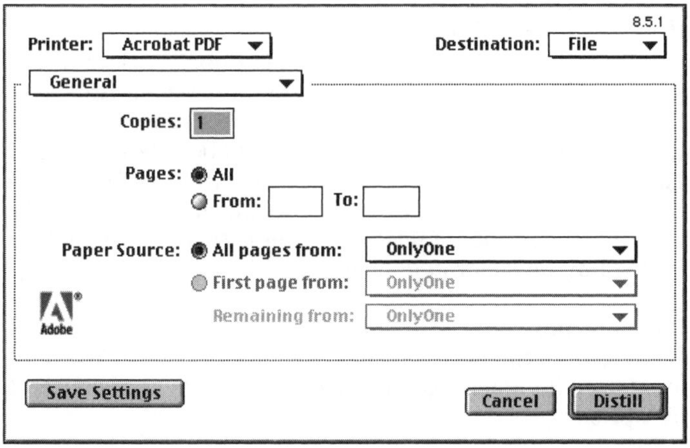

Figure 5-35: When the format for Acrobat PDF is selected, the Print button will change to Distill.

Clicking the Distill button in the Print dialog box will perform multiple steps. First, a navigation dialog box will open, enabling you to supply a name and destination for the PDF document to be produced by Distiller. After you click OK in the navigation dialog box, the file will be printed to disk as a PostScript file. Acrobat Distiller will be auto-launched, and the PostScript file will be opened by Distiller. When Distiller completes its task, the PostScript file will be deleted. An Acrobat viewer will automatically be launched and will open the PDF document. At this point, you'll have three open applications — the original application which printed the file, Acrobat Distiller, and an Acrobat viewer. Distiller will remain open in the background until you quit it.

The PDF document produced will use the current Distiller Job Options chosen when you last quit Distiller. If Job Options need to be changed, you must perform the Job Option changes before clicking the Distill button in the Print dialog box.

The Save Settings button in the Print dialog box enables you to save the settings you make. When you select Save Settings in the Print dialog box, a warning dialog box will appear informing you the new settings will be applied to the currently selected printer.

Note   The saved settings do not apply directly to the printer. Rather, they apply to the printer and the output options you select from the pop-up menu below the printer choice. If you select File ⇨ Print, the default will be General, and all the attribute settings will apply to a file that will be sent to the printer selected in the Printer pop-up menu. When Acrobat PDF is selected from the pop-up menu for the output options, the settings you last saved will appear.

AdobePS printer driver on Windows

When Acrobat is installed on a Windows computer, the AdobePS printer driver will also be installed, as it is on Macintosh systems. Also as with Macintosh systems, you can print directly to PDF from an authoring application. From the application document window, select File ⇨ Print. Acrobat Distiller will be listed among the printer drivers available on the Name pop-up menu. Select Acrobat Distiller from the pop-up menu. The default directory for the PDF document produced will appear in the Output folder inside the Acrobat folder. The complete directory path will be listed in the Print dialog box, as illustrated in Figure 5-36.

Click OK in the Print dialog box, and the document will be converted to PDF. To find the PDF document, navigate to the Acrobat 4.0\PDF Output folder on the hard drive. Like the method used for Macintosh users, the PDF produced will use the current Distiller Job Options.

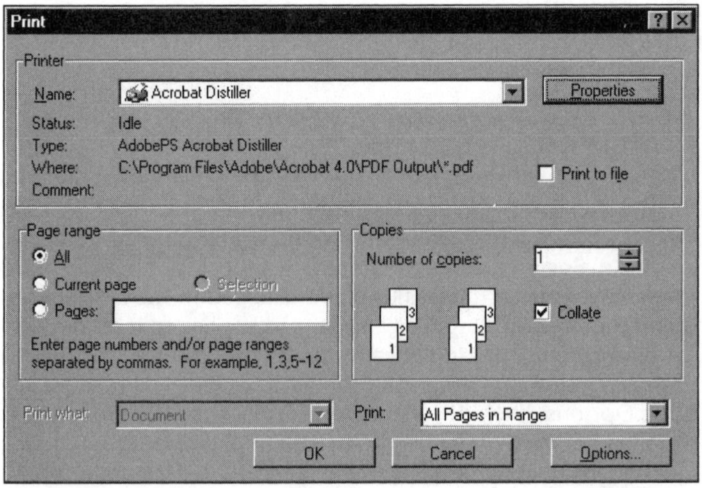

Figure 5-36: When Acrobat Distiller is selected from the Name pop-up menu in the Print dialog box, the path for the PDF file will appear.

Using the Windows Run command

Yet another means of creating PDF documents via Acrobat Distiller is available to Windows users through the Run command in the status bar. To use the command, you will want to create PostScript files and save them to a common directory. After the PostScript files have been placed in a directory, select Run from the Windows status bar. You can type the directory path for Distiller and the directory for the folder of PostScript files on the Open line in the Run dialog box. An easier way to identify the directory is to select the Browse command and find the Distiller.exe file on your hard drive. Add the drive designation and folder path of PostScript files after the AcroDist.exe listing, as shown in Figure 5-37.

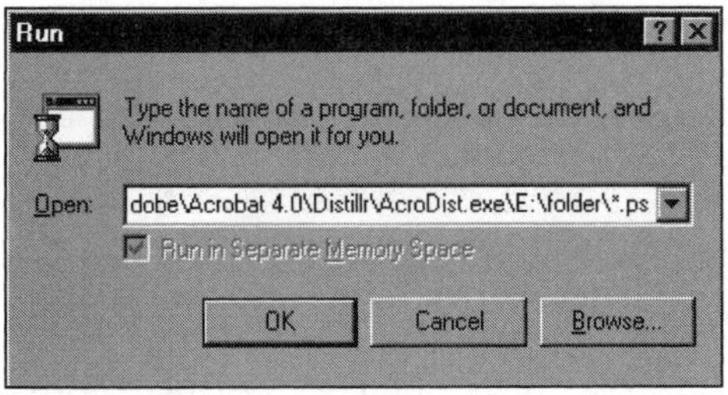

Figure 5-37: Select Run from the Windows status bar and enter both the path for distiller and the files to be converted to PDF. When you click OK, all the PostScript files will be distilled.

When OK is clicked in the dialog box, Acrobat Distiller will be launched and convert all the files identified in the directory path. If something goes awry and the PDF documents are not produced, there was an error in the syntax used to identify the path for Distiller and/or the PostScript files. If this happens, return to the Run command and reenter the path(s) designation.

Drag-and-drop distillation

In the last few examples, PostScript files were deleted after distillation. If you wish to retain the PostScript files, you can print a number of files to disk as PostScript files from the AdobePS printer driver using the Adobe Driver instead of the Acrobat PDF format in the Print dialog box. Once the PostScript files have been produced, multiple files can be selected from the Desktop and dragged to the Distiller window. The drag-and-drop method of distilling files can be accomplished in either the Distiller window or by dropping multiple files on the Distiller application icon or an alias of the icon. Regardless on the method used, multiple files will be distilled using the current Job Options. Each file will become individual PDF documents. After the files have been converted to PDF, the original PostScript files will be retained in the directory from which they were selected. The drag-and-drop method is supported on both Macintosh and Windows systems. If you wish to create a single PDF document from multiple PostScript files, then another method using Acrobat Distiller must be used.

Concatenating PostScript Files

Suppose you have several documents that you wish to convert to a single PDF file. All these documents can be of a single application type—for example, a bunch of Microsoft Excel spreadsheets. Or the documents may come from many different applications—for example, PageMaker, Microsoft Word, Microsoft Excel, QuarkXPress, and Photoshop. In either case, if we wish to create a single PDF document from all those separate files, the task of combining them in Acrobat could take a little time. With Acrobat, you need to insert each page individually. This could take some time if you have a hundred pages or more.

Another situation in which you want to combine several PostScript files into a single PDF document is when using font subsetting. If you distill several files individually, separate font subsets are used with each file. This method adds unnecessary redundancy to the PDF documents. When you concatenate several PDF files, a single font subset is used, thereby reducing file size and eliminating redundant font subsets.

Acrobat Distiller reads PostScript code and as such, you can have Distiller begin its job by looking at a PostScript file that will include instructions to concatenate, or join together, all PostScript files in a given directory. If you attempt to write this code from scratch, you'll need to be fluent in PostScript. For those of us with much more limited skills, Adobe has made it easier to perform the task.

When Acrobat is installed, a folder entitled Xtras will include two files with PostScript code that are used for concatenating distilled files into a single PDF file.

The PostScript code is generic and needs to be edited in a text editor. Edits to define the directory path for your files and the specific filenames of the PostScript files to be distilled need to be identified.

The RunFilEx.txt and RunDirEx.txt files installed in the Xtras folder inside your Acrobat folder will concatenate PostScript files — the former will concatenate files that you specify, and the latter will include all the files in a specified directory whose names include a particular extension. These two files need to be edited individually, so let's examine both here.

Combining files by name

The *Fil* in RunFilEx.txt is your first clue that this file is used for concatenating PostScript files, each of which you specify. When using this file, you must tell Distiller specifically which files (by exact name) will be distilled. To edit the file for entering user-supplied filenames, open the RunFilEx.txt document in a text editor, as shown in Figure 5-38. If using the Macintosh, you can edit this file in Simple Text. In Windows, use Windows Notepad.

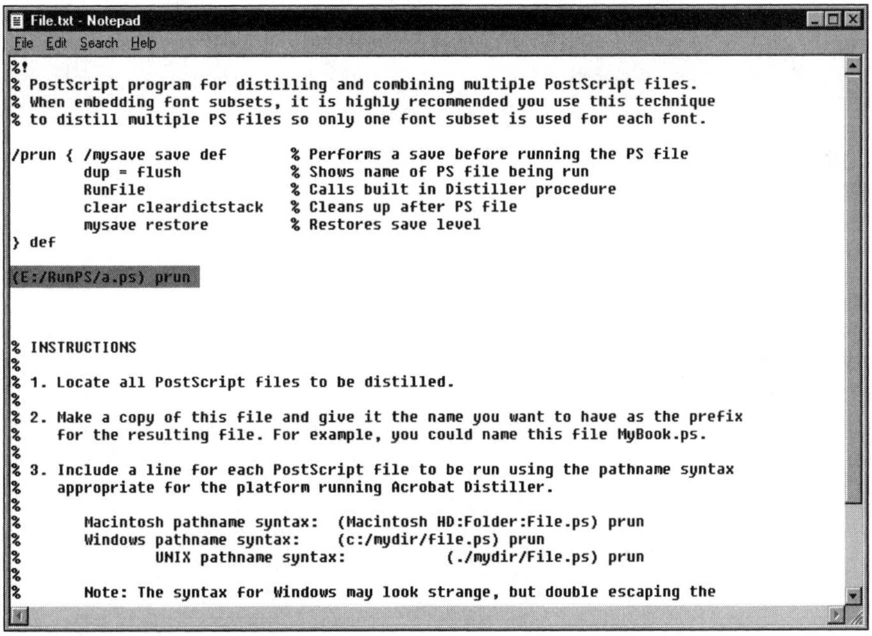

Figure 5-38: Open the file RunFilEx.txt in a text editor to supply filenames for distilling in Acrobat Distiller.

When RunFilEx.txt is opened, the PostScript code for instructions on procedures in concatenating files from user-supplied names will be displayed. All lines of code beginning with a % symbol are comment lines, which do not affect the program. These comments are provided to explain the procedures.

RunFilEx.txt on the Macintosh

When the RunFilEx.txt is opened in a text editor, there will be a few lines of code that will need to be edited. In Figure 5-39, a description of a Macintosh directory path and filenames are supplied.

```
RunFilEx.txt
%!
% PostScript program for distilling and combining multiple PostScript files.
% When embedding font subsets, it is highly recommended you use this technique
% to distill multiple PS files so only one font subset is used for each font.

/prun { /mysave save def      % Performs a save before running the PS file
      dup = flush           % Shows name of PS file being run
      RunFile               % Calls built in Distiller procedure
      clear cleardictstack   % Cleans up after PS file
      mysave restore         % Restores save level
} def

(Scratch:RunPS:a.ps) prun
(Scratch:RunPS:SubDir:0.ps) prun



% INSTRUCTIONS
%
% 1. Locate all PostScript files to be distilled.
%
% 2. Make a copy of this file and give it the name you want to have as the prefix
%    for the resulting file. For example, you could name this file MyBook.ps.
%
% 3. Include a line for each PostScript file to be run using the pathname syntax
%    appropriate for the platform running Acrobat Distiller.
%
%     Macintosh pathname syntax:  (Macintosh HD:Folder:File.ps) prun
%     Windows pathname syntax:    (c:/mydir/file.ps) prun
%  UNIX pathname syntax:     (./mydir/File.ps) prun
%
%     Note: The syntax for Windows may look strange, but double escaping the
%        backslash character is required when using filenameforall.
%
% 4. Distill the file on the machine running Acrobat Distiller.
```

Figure 5-39: The highlighted lines of code indicate the hard drive name (Scratch) and directory path followed by the filenames to be distilled.

It is critical to precisely code the directory path and filename(s) for Distiller to recognize the location and files to be distilled. The name of your volume (that is Macintosh HD, Hard Drive, and so on) would be the name you have provided for your hard disk. By default, many Macintosh hard drives are labeled Macintosh HD. If you have named your hard drive another name, enter it exactly as found on your Desktop. In Figure 5-39, you can see I have a secondary hard drive I named Scratch, which appears as the first item in the highlighted code following the open parenthesis. After the hard drive name, enter a colon (:) followed by a folder name. Folders are not necessary, but it is recommended you save the files to a folder inside your hard drive. Folders can be nested as long as you follow the proper syntax (in other words, *Hard Drive:FolderA:FolderB:FolderC*, and so on). The last entry for each line of code will be the filename. In Figure 5-39, I named two files a.ps and 0.ps.

From Simple Text or any other text editor, save your file as text-only. Save the file with a descriptive name — you needn't use the RunFilEx.txt name of the original file. Be certain the file is a copy of the original, so you can return to the Xtras folder and find this file when needed.

RunFilEx.txt in Windows

The same file and location is used in Windows as observed in the previous section with the Macintosh. The syntax for directory paths in the PostScript code, however, is different from the Mac syntax and varies somewhat from standard DOS syntax. When you open the RunFilEx.txt file in Windows Notepad or a text editor, the sample lines of code demonstrate directory paths and filenames for Macintosh users. The comments below the code provide a guideline for proper syntax when using Windows. In Figure 5-39, notice the comment line for Windows pathname syntax located toward the bottom of the figure. In Windows, identify your drive as a standard drive letter — for example, C. After the drive letter, use a forward slash instead of a backslash to separate the drive name from the directory name. Nesting occurs in Windows the way it does in the Macintosh example, but be certain to use forward slashes to separate the folder names. The filename should include the name and extension as it was written.

When describing drive, directory, and filenames, case sensitivity is not an issue. Any of these identifiers can be either upper- or lowercase. In Figure 5-38, I used my E drive and a directory labeled RunPS. Only the file a.ps will be distilled, as it is the only file identified in the code. Notice the filename was changed from RunFilEx.txt to File.txt, as can be seen in the top-left corner of Figure 5-38.

Combining files in folders

The second file in the Xtras folder used for concatenating PostScript files is RunDirEx.txt. Whereas RunFilEx.txt requires you to name all the PostScript files to be distilled, this file uses a wildcard character to distill all files with a particular extension in a specified directory. The directory path for either the Mac or Windows uses the same syntax as illustrated previously; however, instead of filename(s), a wildcard character followed by the extension for the filenames is used. The wildcard is the standard asterisk (*), which is used to indicate all files with the same extension you specify in the line of code for the pathname.

In Figure 5-40, I specified my Scratch hard drive on my Macintosh and the RunPS folder. All the files with a .ps extension will be distilled by Acrobat Distiller. In Windows, follow the same syntax as described earlier. If Figure 5-40 were on a Windows machine, the syntax would be /*PathName* (E:/RunPS/*.ps) prun.

```
                          RunDirEx.txt
%!
% PostScript program for distilling and combining an entire folder or
% directory of PostScript files.
% When embedding font subsets, it is highly recommended you use this technique
% to distill multiple PS files so only one font subset is used for each font.

/PathName (Scratch:RunPS:*.ps) def   % Edit this to point to the folder
                            %  containing the PS files.

/RunDir {             % Uses PathName variable on the operand stack
  { /mysave save def      % Performs a save before running the PS file
      dup = flush         % Shows name of PS file being run
      RunFile             % Calls built in Distiller procedure
      clear cleardictstack % Cleans up after PS file
      mysave restore      % Restores save level
  }
  255 string
  filenameforall
} def

PathName RunDir
```

Figure 5-40: Following /*PathName* in the RunDirEx.txt file, enter the path and *.extension* for all the files to be included in the distillation.

Distillation and page order

After the RunFilEx.txt or RunDirEx.txt file has been edited, it becomes the file that will be opened in Acrobat Distiller. This file tells Distiller where to go and which files to convert to PDF. The file can be located in any directory on your hard drive, because it instructs Distiller where to go to find the files for distillation. If the file is saved in the same folder where the files to be distilled are stored, it is important to provide a different extension for this filename from the extension of the files to be distilled when using RunDirEx.txt. If you name the file Run.ps and include it in a directory with a number of files also having a .ps extension, the PostScript code file for combining the other files will be included in the final PDF file. The default filenames you find in the Xtras folder have .txt extensions, and it's a good idea to leave them with the default extension to avoid confusion.

When RunDirEx.txt (or whatever name you have supplied for the file) is run, the page order will occur in the same order as an alphameric character set. To help simplify understanding how the page order will be applied, view your files in a folder as a list by order. Be certain the order is not date, type, or anything other than an alphabetical order. The order you view will display the same page order as the resulting PDF.

In Figure 5-41, the top of the list will begin the page order. The 0.ps file will be the first page in the PDF file, followed by 1.ps, and so on. All seven pages will be distilled if the RunDirEx.txt file is used and will include all files ending in .ps in the RunTemp folder.

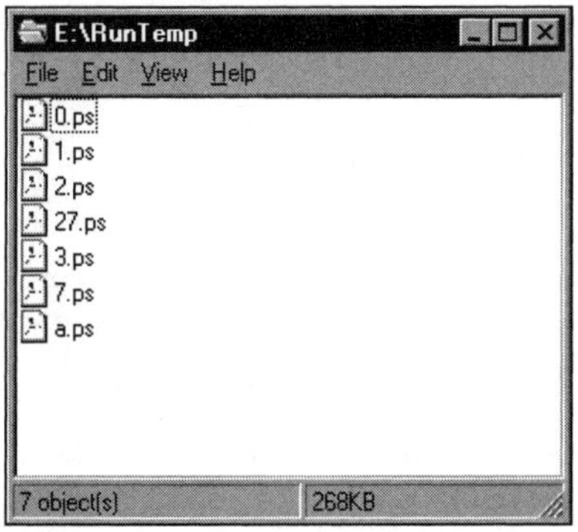

Figure 5-41: PostScript files in a Windows directory are viewed as a list with the icons arranged by name.

Note

As you examine the list in Figure 5-41, notice that 2.ps is followed by 27.ps and then 3.ps. If you want these files to be consecutively ordered, the file naming has to follow some different rules. Both Distiller and your operating system will arrange the files according to the characters in left-to-right (dictionary) order. If two files have the same first character, the second character is examined and the file placed in the list accordingly. In this example, Windows doesn't care about 27 being larger than 3. It looks at the 2 in 27 and sees it as a lower order than 3.

To rearrange your files in the order you wish to have them appear in an Acrobat viewer, rename them before distilling, taking into consideration the first character will be the highest order of priority. For this example, I renamed my files as illustrated in Figure 5-42. When the PDF file is produced, the page order will match my new order as viewed in Windows.

Figure 5-42: I renamed the files in the RunTemp directory by including a zero (0) in front of the single digit filenames so the two digit filenames would follow in numerical order.

Tip

Because Distiller and your operating system order alphameric characters the same, view your folder contents as a list before distilling the files. The list order you see will be the same order of the page numbers in the final PDF document.

Combining PostScript files on networks

If you wish to develop a PDF workflow and use a server to collect all your PDF files on a local area network, some simple guidelines need to be followed in order to produce PDF documents. Whereas files can be printed to disk on remote systems and drives that are cross platform, Distiller can't follow cross-platform directory paths. Therefore, if you use RunDirEx.txt and wish to distill files in C:\MyFolder*.ps, Distiller running on a Macintosh won't be able to execute instructions for following cross-platform directory paths. This also applies to Windows users who may wish to use a file describing directory paths on a Macintosh. Distiller can be used cross platform to distill files on remote drives, and the RunDirEx.txt file will work between two computers running the same operating system. Using Distiller and RunDirEx.txt on networks have the following capabilities and limitations:

✦ **Running Distiller across platforms:** Distiller can open PostScript files on local hard drives and across platforms. PDF files from distillation can be saved to local hard drives and across platforms. For example, using Distiller on a Macintosh, you can open a PostScript file on a PC and save it to either computer's hard drive.

✦ **RunDirEx.txt across platforms:** RunDirEx.txt cannot be run across platforms where directory paths are specified for one platform while distilling on another platform. For example, you can't open from a Mac the RunDirEx.txt file that resides on a PC with directory paths specified for the PC. The alternative solution would be to run Distiller on the platform consistent with the path identity or set up watched folders where the RunDirEx.txt file is introduced into a watched folder.

✦ **RunDirEx.txt in a common platform:** Distiller can open the RunDirEx.txt file that resides on one computer where the directory path includes files on another computer of the same platform. The RunDirEx.txt file can be located on either computer, the destination of the PDF can be saved to either computer, and the path to find the .ps files can be on either computer.

To understand how files can be concatenated across two computers on the same platform, here are some steps I used to produce a single PDF document from files located on another computer running the same operating system on my network.

STEPS: RunDirEx.txt and Networked Computers

1. **Create the PostScript files.** I created PostScript files from several application document windows and stored them on my G3 computer.

2. **Edit the RunDirEx.txt file.** I opened the RunDirEx.txt file from my Xtras folder inside the Acrobat folder (in Windows, the path is Acrobat3\Distillr\Xtras). The path directory on my G3 computer is G3 System:Documents:RunPS:*.ps. The hard drive name is G3 System, and I want to distill all files in the RunPS folder (see Figure 5-43).

```
%!
% PostScript program for distilling and combining an entire folder or
% directory of PostScript files.
% When embedding font subsets, it is highly recommended you use this technique
% to distill multiple PS files so only one font subset is used for each font.

/PathName (G3 System:Documents:RunPS:*.ps) def   % Edit this to point to the folder
                              %  containing the PS files.

/RunDir {              % Uses PathName variable on the operand stack
  { /mysave save def     % Performs a save before running the PS file
      dup = flush        % Shows name of PS file being run
      RunFile            % Calls built in Distiller procedure
      clear cleardictstack  % Cleans up after PS file
      mysave restore      % Restores save level
```

Figure 5-43: I edited the RunDirEx.txt file in Simple Text and saved it to my Mac 9500's Desktop as Run.txt.

3. **Open the RunDirEx.txt file in Acrobat Distiller.** The file is saved on my Mac 9500 computer, and I also run Acrobat Distiller from the 9500. In Distiller, I select File ⇨ Open and navigate to the Desktop level to find the file I saved as Run.txt.

4. **Name and identify the file destination.** I renamed the file Run.txt.pdf to Run.pdf and identified the RunPS folder on the G3 System computer as the destination, as shown in Figure 5-44.

Continued

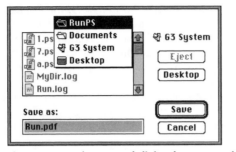

Figure 5-44: The second dialog box appearing n Distiller is used to identify the filename and destination.

5. **Distill the Run.txt file.** When you click the Save button, Distiller's progress will be displayed in the Distiller window, shown in Figure 5-45. The directory path will be displayed for each file distilled. My Run.txt file was opened in Distiller on my Mac 9500. The file asked Distiller to find the .ps files in the RunPS folder on the G3 computer and saved the concatenated PostScript files in a single PDF document on the G3.

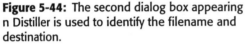

Figure 5-45: Distiller's window displays the job progress and includes the directory path for all files opened and distilled.

6. Examine the destination folder. When I opened the RunPS folder on the G3 computer, the Run.pdf was found along with the log file.

Most often it won't be necessary to run Distiller on your local computer to distill files on another computer. The option exists if you need it, but in many cases you'll find a better solution to be setting up watched folders and having Distiller run on the computer where the files are located. If you give a little thought to setting up the network for creating PDF files, the workflow can be seamless.

Summary

✦ Acrobat Distiller is preferred over PDFWriter when creating PDF files for all but simple office documents and information archiving.

✦ PostScript is a streamed language that can contain many different dialects and is often redundant in describing page elements for imaging. PDF is a much more efficient file format, as it is structured like a database that offers logical order and eliminates redundancy.

✦ When creating PostScript files, the preferred PPD to use is one of the Acrobat Distiller PPDs, unless specific output needs require use of a device PPD.

✦ Acrobat Distiller has many Job Options that behave like preferences enabling you to control font compression, image compression, color, and high-end digital output prepress attributes.

✦ Watched folders enable you to establish PDF workflows, which automate the PDF creation process. Watched folders can be contained on local or remote storage systems in network environments.

✦ Acrobat 4.0 enables you to supply security passwords at the time of distillation. PDF files can be secured from opening and viewing as well as changing documents.

✦ Acrobat Distiller can be auto launched from application documents to create PDFs (Macintosh) or printed directly to the Acrobat Distiller printer driver (Windows).

✦ PostScript files can be joined in a single PDF document by using either the RunFilEx.txt or RunDirEx.txt PostScript file supplied on the Adobe Acrobat Installer CD. RunFilEx.txt is used to concatenate files by filename, and RunDirEx.txt is used to concatenate all files within a folder that have the same extension.

✦   ✦   ✦

PDF Exports and Imports

◆ ◆ ◆ ◆

In This Chapter

Direct exports to PDF from other applications

Acrobat and Adobe Photoshop

Acrobat and illustration programs

Acrobat and layout programs

Creating pdfmark annotations

◆ ◆ ◆ ◆

The last two chapters discussed PDF file creation using Adobe Acrobat PDFWriter and Acrobat Distiller. If you've read those chapters, you've learned when to use Distiller over Writer in addition to some of the differences between the two in setting up preferences and job options. Yet another means of creating PDF files is with direct exports from applications software. Adobe Systems has been implementing PDF support for some time in many of its design applications. Early methods for creating these exports were fairly simple in that they were similar to the way PDFWriter generates PDF files; current methods rely on more sophisticated approaches that use Distiller in the background. Whatever application you use to create a PDF file through an export command, the basic assumptions made for the differences between PDFWriter and Acrobat Distiller hold true. If, for example, you export directly from within an application to PDF and Distiller is not used in the background, the file ultimately created will be the same as one created by PDFWriter. As mentioned in earlier chapters, the PDFWriter documents are not recommended for output to most printing devices and especially not recommended for digital prepress.

Applications Software Support for PDF

With all the different ways of creating PDFs, it may become somewhat overwhelming to decide which method you should choose when working in programs. The decision becomes more difficult if you work in some programs that support PDF exports and other programs that don't. Add to this the occasional need for legitimate PDFWriter documents, and the other times that you definitely need to use Distiller. What you require is a formula and maybe an understanding of the PDF "food chain" to come up with an ordered approach to PDF development. Among the considerations you should make in setting up your PDF workflows are the following:

✦ **Consistency:** Regardless of which method you use, try to be consistent when creating PDF documents. If you use a program such as Adobe Illustrator to generate files, and sometimes print those files to PDFWriter, other times distill EPS files, and occasionally use the PDF export feature of Illustrator, eventually you'll wind up with some unexpected results. Try to assess your output needs, use the guidelines discussed in Chapters 4 and 5, and be consistent when creating PDFs from your authoring applications.

✦ **Use Acrobat Distiller:** The first order of the Acrobat PDF "food chain" is Distiller. If you have some documents that require distilling and others that don't, try not to go back and forth between two or more methods of creating PDF files. Make an effort to always use Distiller for everything, and you'll become more fluent in using it as well as experienced in predicting output results. Recall that in the example I showed of creating PDF files from Web pages in Chapter 4 I used PDFWriter. In my personal work, however, I never use PDFWriter, even for archiving those Web pages. Distiller is always my first choice, regardless of the intended use of the resulting PDF files.

✦ **Export PDFs.** If PDFWriter documents satisfy all your PDF needs, always use a PDF export command from within an application before choosing PDFWriter. Documents created by such programs as Adobe Illustrator are much better suited for exporting to PDF files than printing to PDFWriter.

✦ **PDFWriter.** Last on the PDF "food chain" is PDFWriter. Use PDFWriter when none of your PDF needs require Distiller, and your authoring application doesn't have an export command.

In some instances PDF support is not limited to exports. Some applications can also import PDF files. Because Acrobat is not a full-featured editor, importing PDF files into the appropriate applications can be useful for page editing and alterations. Ideally, you would return to the application that produced the PDF file for major editing of that file, but at times you may find it helpful to import PDF files into another program where editing can be accomplished. This is particularly true in a situation where you are the recipient of a PDF file created by another person, and you do not have the producer application or the original document. In such cases, you could open the PDF file in a program such as Adobe Illustrator, make your edits, and create another PDF file.

Acrobat and Adobe Photoshop

Adobe Photoshop version 4 introduced support for exports and imports of PDF documents. You could save a Photoshop image directly in PDF format and open the file in an Acrobat viewer. Importing PDF files, however, was only limited to those files that were originally saved from Photoshop. If a PDF was created from another application through PDFWriter, Acrobat Distiller, or an export to PDF, Photoshop couldn't open it. Version 5 of Adobe Photoshop includes much better support for PDF; Photoshop now recognizes any PDF file from any producer.

Exporting to PDF from Photoshop

Creating a PDF file from Photoshop is nothing more than choosing the format from the Save dialog box. Photoshop supports many different file formats in opening and saving documents. The only catch with Photoshop is making certain you have the image flattened and not resting on a layer.

Photoshop supports multiple layers, which can be preserved when saving in a Photoshop format for editing purposes. When you prepare a file for output, the layers need to be flattened so all the data rests on the background. In Photoshop, your first clue about whether the file can be exported to PDF is when you select File ⇨ Save. If the PDF format (or any of the other alternative formats for that matter) does not appear in the format options within the Save dialog box, as shown in Figure 6-1, then your image is resting on a layer. To prepare the file for saving to PDF, you can either flatten the layers through the Layers palette or Layer menu, or you can select File ⇨ Save a Copy. With the Save a Copy command, Photoshop can automatically flatten the layers when you make the appropriate choice from available format options.

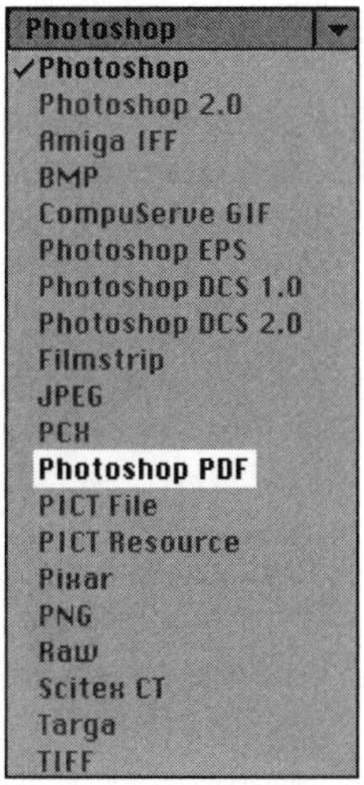

Photoshop
✓ Photoshop
Photoshop 2.0
Amiga IFF
BMP
CompuServe GIF
Photoshop EPS
Photoshop DCS 1.0
Photoshop DCS 2.0
Filmstrip
JPEG
PCH
Photoshop PDF
PICT File
PICT Resource
Pixar
PNG
Raw
Scitex CT
Targa
TIFF

Figure 6-1: Exporting directly to PDF is handled in the Save or Save As dialog box in Photoshop. If Photoshop PDF does not appear in the pull-down menu, the image is resting on a layer and must be flattened before it can be exported to PDF.

PDF and color modes

Photoshop provides a number of choices for the color mode used to define your image. You can open files from different color modes, convert color modes in Photoshop, and save among different formats available for a given color mode. File formats are dependent on color modes, and some format options are not available if the image data is defined in a mode not acceptable to the format. (See Table 6-1 later in this section for Photoshop PDF exports supported in the Photoshop color modes and relative uses for each mode.) Color mode choices in Photoshop include the following:

✦ **Bitmap:** The image will be defined in two colors: black and white. In Photoshop terms, images in the bitmap mode are referred to as line art. In Acrobat terms, this color mode is called monochrome bitmap. Bitmap images will usually be about $\frac{1}{8}$ the size of a grayscale file. The bitmap format can be used with Acrobat Capture for scanning text and recognizing the text in a scan.

✦ **Grayscale:** This is your anchor mode in Photoshop. Grayscale is like a black-and white-photo, a halftone, or a Charlie Chaplin movie. You see grayscale images everywhere, including in most of the pages in this book. I refer to this as an anchor mode because you can convert to any of the other modes from grayscale. RGB files cannot be converted directly to either bitmaps or duotones. You first need to convert to grayscale, and then to either of the other two modes. From grayscale, you can also convert back to any of the other color modes. Grayscale images significantly reduce file sizes — they're approximately $\frac{1}{3}$ the size of an RGB file, but larger than the bitmaps discussed previously.

✦ **RGB:** For screen views, multimedia, and Web graphics, RGB is the most commonly used mode. It has a color gamut much larger than CMYK and will be best suited for display on computer monitors. There are a few printing devices that take advantage of RGB — for example, film recorders, large inkjet printers, and some desktop color printers. In most cases, however, this mode will not be used when printing files to output devices, especially when color separating and using high-end digital prepress.

✦ **CMYK:** The process colors of cyan, magenta, yellow, and black are used in offset printing and most commercial output devices. The color gamut is much narrower than RGB; and when you convert an image from RGB to CMYK using Photoshop's mode conversion command, you will usually see some noticeable dilution of color appearing on your monitor. When exporting files to PDF directly from Photoshop or when opening files in other applications and then distilling them, you should always make your color conversions first in Photoshop.

✦ **Lab:** Lab color in theory encompasses all the color from both the RGB and CMYK color spaces. This color mode is based on a mathematical model to describe all perceptible color within the human universe. In practicality, its color space is limited to approximately 6 million colors, about 10+ million less than RGB color. Lab color is device-independent color, which theoretically means the color will be true regardless of the device on which your image is edited and printed. Lab mode is commonly preferred by high-end color editing professionals and will color-separate on PostScript Level 2 devices. With PDF, however, you don't want to use the Lab color mode. Photoshop can export to PDF from Lab, and you can place Lab EPS files in other applications. However, once you convert the final document to PDF, the lab images won't separate properly whether you export the document from Acrobat as EPS or use an Acrobat plug-in such as CrackerJack.

✦ **Multichannel:** If you convert any of the other color modes to Multichannel mode, all the individual channels used to define the image color will be converted to grayscale. The resultant document will be a grayscale image with multiple channels. With regard to exporting to PDF, you will likely never use this mode.

✦ **Duotone:** The Duotone mode can actually support one of four individual color modes. Monotone is selectable from the Duotone mode, which holds a single color value in the image, like a tint. Duotone defines the image in two color values, Tritone in three, and Quadtone in four. When you export to PDF from Photoshop, none of these modes are supported. You can create a duotone image, and then you will need to convert to another color mode in order to export to PDF. If you wish to color-separate a duotone image imported into another application, you need to export from Photoshop as a Photoshop EPS file, import the EPS in another application, and then prepare the file to be properly separated. Separating PDF files with duotones is covered in Chapter 16.

✦ **Indexed Color:** Whereas the other color modes such as RGB, Lab, and CMYK define an image with large color gamuts up to millions of colors, the Indexed Color mode limits the total colors to a maximum of 256. Color reduction in images are ideal for Web graphics where the fewer colors will significantly reduce the file sizes. You can export indexed color images directly to PDF format from Photoshop.

Table 6-1
Photoshop Color Modes

Color Mode	Export to PDF	Screen View	Print Composite	Print Separations
Bitmap	Yes	Yes	Yes	No
Grayscale	Yes	Yes	Yes	No
RGB	Yes	Yes	Yes*	No
CMYK	Yes	No	Yes	Yes
Lab	Yes	Yes	Yes	No
Multichannel	Yes	No	No	No
Duotone	No	Yes	No	No
Indexed	Yes	Yes	No	No
Spot Color (DCS 2.0)	No	No	No	No

* In most cases, CMYK is preferred.

Exporting to PDF

Direct exports to PDF will most often be used with screen images and presentations. Composite color printing might be an option for files exchanged with users who don't have Photoshop or maybe where output to instruments such as large format inkjets can take advantage of enlarged sizes — for example, printing at a 200 or 300 percent size directly from a PDF. If you intend to color-separate Photoshop files or output to composite film at an imaging center, your layout will often include text composed in a layout application. In these cases, your Photoshop files will be imported as a TIFF or EPS file, and the layout application will be responsible for getting the application document to PDF form.

Photoshop images are raster based, which eliminates any need for font embedding and subsetting. Once the type is rendered in Photoshop or imported into Photoshop, it will lose its object-oriented characteristics and become an image as opposed to type. Therefore, PDF exports from Photoshop don't have any of the attribute options for type as do PDF files created with PDFWriter and Acrobat Distiller. Nor are there any Job Options for controlling other attributes of the PDF file created.

Image compression, however, is one control you can exercise when exporting to PDF. When you select File ➪ Save or File ➪ Save a Copy and choose PDF as the format, a dialog box appears, enabling you to name the file and choose the directory path (see Figure 6-2). After leaving this dialog box by clicking the Save button, another dialog box will open, offering compression choices. You will have different compression choices depending on the color mode of the Photoshop image. Table 6-2 includes the compression choice Photoshop will make according to the color mode of the image to be exported.

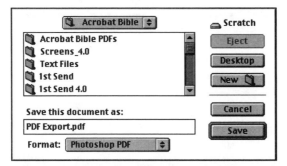

Figure 6-2: When an image is flattened or you select File ➪ Save a Copy, the Photoshop PDF format will be supported in the Save dialog box, where the filename and directory path can be determined.

Table 6-2
Compression Methods According to Color Mode

Color Mode	Export to PDF	Compression Type
Bitmap	Yes	No compression option
Grayscale	Yes	JPEG/ZIP
RGB	Yes	JPEG/ZIP
CMYK	Yes	JPEG/ZIP
Lab	Yes	JPEG/ZIP
Multichannel	No	N/A
Duotone	No	N/A
Indexed	Yes	ZIP

Note

When a Photoshop image is defined in a color mode other than Indexed Color and the PDF export is also supported, Photoshop will offer you the option of choosing ZIP or JPEG compression. ZIP or JPEG considerations are the same as discussed in Chapter 4. If the image content contains a large area of a single color, use ZIP compression. If the image contains a range of color as you may encounter with a continuous tone photo image, use JPEG. When you select ZIP, the amount of compression is determined by the ZIP method algorithm. When you use JPEG, the amount of compression can be user specified in the PDF Options dialog box, as shown in Figure 6-3.

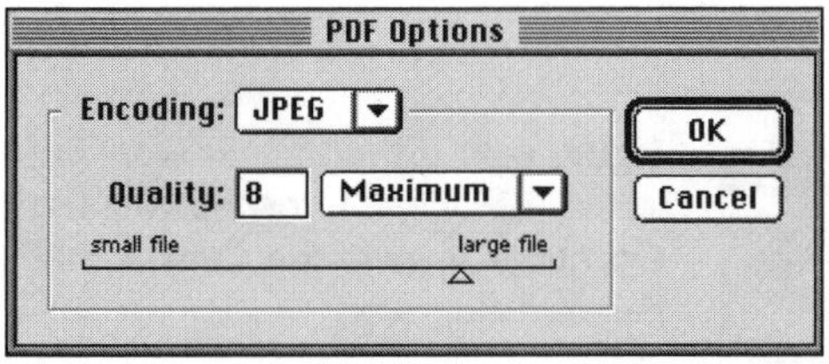

Figure 6-3: When using JPEG compression, you can select from ten levels for the amount of compression.

Note

You should be aware that the compression settings between Acrobat and Photoshop are now in parity in Acrobat 4. Earlier versions of Acrobat used JPEG Low for a maximum quality image. This was confusing to many Photoshop users, because the Low setting provided the highest amount of compression with the lowest quality. Now in Acrobat 4, the compression for the Maximum setting equals Photoshop 5's maximum quality. If you're used to handling the Acrobat and Photoshop JPEG compression as opposites, be careful. The new changes make it easier to understand, but you'll have to rethink your attribute settings.

Importing PDF files in Photoshop

PDF documents may be composed of many different elements depending on the design of the original file. If you design a page in a layout program for which you create text, import Photoshop images, and also import EPS illustrations, the different elements retain their characteristics when converted to PDF. Text, for example, remains as text, raster images such as Photoshop files remain as raster images, and EPS illustrations remain as EPS vector objects. Although the images, text, and line art may be compressed when distilled in Acrobat Distiller, all the text and line art remain as vector elements. In Photoshop, if you open an illustration or text created in any program, the document contents will be rasterized and lose their vector-based attributes. Photoshop rasterizes PDF documents much as it does any EPS file.

In Photoshop 5, you have two methods of handling PDF imports. PDF documents may be opened in Photoshop by selecting File ➪ Open and choosing the PDF to be opened, or you can batch process PDF-to-Photoshop file conversions. When you use the Open command from the File menu, Photoshop will open a dialog box enabling you to select the page to open in Photoshop. If you have a multipage PDF document, Photoshop can only open one page at a time. A dialog box will prompt you to select the page to rasterize in Photoshop. If thumbnails were included in the PDF file, a thumbnail icon will appear in the Photoshop Generic MPS PDF Parser dialog box, as shown in Figure 6-4. If no thumbnails were included in the PDF file, Photoshop will display a message indicating no thumbnail is available, as shown in Figure 6-5.

Tip   If you want to navigate to a specific page within a multipage PDF document, click the button displaying the label 1 of *n* pages. When you click the mouse button, a Go To page number dialog box will appear. In the dialog box, you can supply the page number desired. This behavior works the same for opening PDF files in both Photoshop and Illustrator 8.

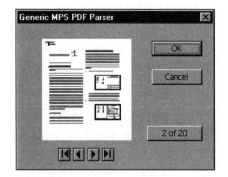

Figure 6-4: If thumbnails were included in the PDF file, Photoshop will display a thumbnail view in the Generic MPS PDF Parser dialog box.

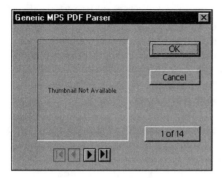

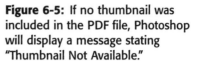

Figure 6-5: If no thumbnail was included in the PDF file, Photoshop will display a message stating "Thumbnail Not Available."

Below the thumbnail in the Generic MPS PDF Parser dialog box, you can see navigation arrows similar to those used in the Acrobat viewers. The far left arrow will navigate to the first page in the PDF file. By default, when you begin to open a PDF file in Photoshop, you will see the first page of the PDF displayed. To the bottom-right of the thumbnail icon will appear a readout displaying the current page and the total number of pages. In Figure 6-4, page 2 of 20 is displayed, indicating the current page is page 2 and there are a total of 20 pages in the document. The left navigation arrow icon is used to scroll pages to the left. The right navigation icon is used to scroll single pages to the right. The last navigation icon will take you to the last page in the document.

When you click OK in the Parser dialog box, the Rasterize Generic PDF dialog box will appear. In this dialog box, you can supply various attributes for rasterizing the PDF file.

✦ **Width/Height:** The physical size of the final Photoshop image can be determined by changing the width and/or height of the rasterized image. The default size of the original PDF document will appear in this dialog box.

✦ **Resolution:** The default resolution regardless of the size is 72 ppi. You can choose to supply a user-defined resolution in this dialog box. If the original raster images were at a resolution different than the amount supplied in this dialog box, the images will be resampled. Text and line art will be rasterized according to the amount you define in the dialog box without interpolation.

✦ **Mode:** The color mode can be selected from the pop-up menu that includes choices for Grayscale, RGB, CMYK, and Lab color. The default will be CMYK regardless of whether there is any color in the original PDF file.

✦ **Anti-Aliased:** This option is used to smooth edges of text, line art, and images that are interpolated through resampling. If you disable this option, text will appear with jagged edges. Text in PDF files rasterized in Photoshop will look best when anti-aliased, and the display will be more consistent with the original font used when the PDF was created.

✦ **Constrain Proportions:** If you change a value in either the Width or the Height field and the Constrain Proportions option is enabled, the value in the other field (Height or Width) will automatically be supplied by Photoshop to preserve proportional sizing. When the check box is disabled, both the Width and Height values will be independent — values that is, they have no effect on each other. If you elect not to preserve proportions, the PDF page appearing in Photoshop after rasterizing may be distorted.

One problem you may encounter when rasterizing PDF documents in Photoshop is maintaining font integrity. Photoshop will display a warning dialog box when it encounters a font not installed on your system, which will present problems when you attempt to rasterize the font. If such a problem exists, the font may be eliminated from the document when opened in Photoshop. In Figure 6-6, notice the space between *Apple Menu* and *Chooser*. The font used for the Zapf Dingbats symbol could not be recognized when the file was converted from PDF to PSD (Photoshop Document format), so no font substitution was supplied. The original document, viewed in an Acrobat viewer, is illustrated in Figure 6-7.

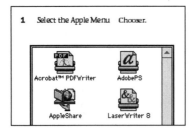

Figure 6-6: Rasterizing Photoshop images with a font missing from your system may cause that font to drop out of the final Photoshop document.

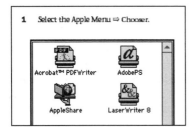

Figure 6-7: The original PDF document in Acrobat displays the font that was missed when the PDF file was converted to the Photoshop document shown in the preceding figure.

When files are password protected, users are prevented from opening a Photoshop file. If you attempt to open a secure document, a warning dialog box will appear. The warning dialog box indicates the PDF file can't be parsed. If you encounter such a dialog box, open it in an Acrobat viewer and check the security settings, as discussed in Chapter 2.

Multipage PDF to PSD

Selecting the Open command is fine if you want to convert a single-page PDF file or one page within a PDF file to a Photoshop file, but what about a multiple page PDF file that needs to be converted to Photoshop documents? Photoshop can only have a single-page document constructed, but you may wish to have all the pages in a PDF converted to individual Photoshop files. Fortunately, Photoshop 5 now supports multipage PDF to PSD conversion.

File ➪ Automate ➪ Multi-page PSD to PDF is a command similar to a Photoshop Action in that it will automatically open PDF files, rasterize them in Photoshop, and save the file to a destination directory specified by the user. When you select this command in Photoshop, a dialog box will open that enables you to determine the same rasterizing characteristics as used with the Open command.

The options available in the Convert Multi-Page PDF to PSD dialog box include the following:

✦ **Choose:** The source PDF file is selected by clicking the Choose button at the top left of the dialog box, as shown in Figure 6-8. Photoshop can't use multiple PDF files as a source. You are limited to opening a single PDF document. The document, of course, can have multiple pages.

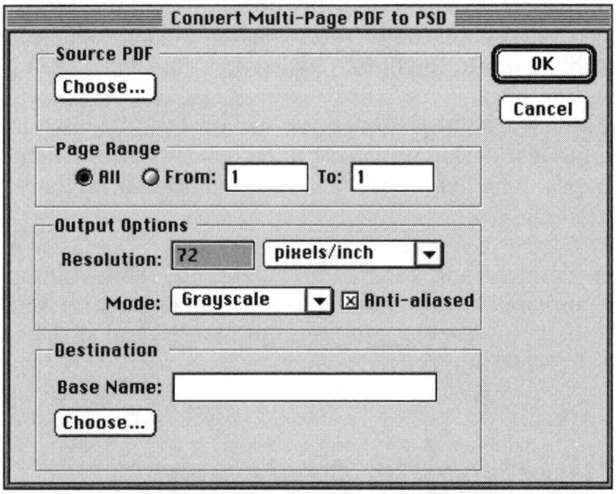

```
┌─────────────────────────────────────────────┐
│      Convert Multi-Page PDF to PSD            │
│ ┌─ Source PDF ──────────────┐   ┌────────┐  │
│ │ [ Choose... ]             │   │   OK   │  │
│ │                           │   └────────┘  │
│ │                           │   ┌────────┐  │
│ │                           │   │ Cancel │  │
│ └───────────────────────────┘   └────────┘  │
│ ┌─ Page Range ──────────────┐                │
│ │ ● All  ○ From: [1]  To: [1]│               │
│ └───────────────────────────┘                │
│ ┌─ Output Options ──────────────┐            │
│ │ Resolution: [72] [pixels/inch ▼] │         │
│ │    Mode: [Grayscale ▼] ⊠ Anti-aliased │    │
│ └───────────────────────────────┘            │
│ ┌─ Destination ─────────────┐                │
│ │ Base Name: [            ] │                │
│ │ [ Choose... ]             │                │
│ └───────────────────────────┘                │
└─────────────────────────────────────────────┘
```

Figure 6-8: Photoshop 5 enables you to convert multipage PDF files to Photoshop images. You can batch process files and set up automated Actions for file conversions.

✦ **Page Range:** You can select all pages in the PDF or a range of pages. The page range choices require you to know ahead of time the number of pages in the PDF file to be converted. If you select pages by clicking the From radio button and choosing a range outside the PDF page range, a warning dialog box will appear indicating the problem. For example, if you attempt to select pages 21 to 22 in a 20-page PDF file, pages 21 and 22 will be out of range. Photoshop will open a warning dialog box to inform you the first page it attempts to convert is out of range. If you attempt to convert pages 18 to 22 in the same example, Photoshop will convert pages 18 through 20 and then open another dialog box informing you that not all pages within the specified range exist in the PDF document.

✦ **Output Options:** These options are the same as the ones for single-page conversions. You can choose the resolution, color mode, and whether anti-aliasing will be used. One option you do not have available in the dialog box is the capability to choose sizing and proportions. If you wish to size the PSD files, you can set up a Photoshop Action to open the saved files and resize them with values used in creating the Action.

✦ **Base Name:** The base name you specify will appear in the filename for the saved PSD files. If you use a name like *MyFile*, Photoshop will save the PSD files as MyFile0001.psd, MyFile0002.psd, MyFile0003.psd, and so on. Photoshop adds the 000n and .psd extension to the filename you supply as the base name.

✦ **Destination:** The destination will typically be a folder or directory. You can highlight a directory name in the hierarchy list and click the Select button, or you can open a directory in the hierarchy list and click the Select button.

When you click OK in the dialog box, Photoshop will proceed to rasterize individual pages, save them to the destination directory, and close each document window as it processes all the pages. When you observe the destination directory, you will see all the individual PSD files.

If you want to convert catalogs and lengthy documents to HTML-supported files, the PDF to PSD conversion may become useful. You can set up Actions in Photoshop to downsample images, convert color modes, and save copies of the converted files in HTML-supported formats.

Acrobat and Illustration Programs

Illustration programs, at least the most popular ones, are vector-based applications. You can import raster data such as Photoshop images; however, all you create in an illustration program is object-oriented art. Programs such as Adobe Illustrator, Macromedia FreeHand, and CorelDraw are among the most popular, and they all have the capability to save files in EPS format and export directly to PDF.

With programs such as Adobe Photoshop and Adobe Acrobat, there exists little significant competition among manufacturers for market share. Photoshop clearly dominates the market in photo-imaging applications, and Acrobat has no worthy counterpart. Illustration programs, on the other hand, have some pretty fierce competition. CorelDraw has a tremendous share of the PC user market, and it clearly overshadows Illustrator and FreeHand. On the Mac side, most of Corel's attempts have seen failure, which leaves the major market first to Adobe, then to Macromedia. Because these three companies are battling to both keep current market share and gobble up more, the advances in feature-rich applications have been aggressive. All three products are in version 8 as of this writing, although there have been some skips in version numbers, and the total iterations of each product may not be clearly eight versions.

The competitive nature of the manufacturers of these products can present some problems for all of us end users. With each revision of illustration software, it appears as though the manufacturers are attempting to make the programs all things to all people. Each of these three illustration programs use a different dialect when exporting files in PostScript, which may impact your output for distillation in Acrobat Distiller. Add to this the difference in the way the PostScript coding is handled, and the addition of new whiz-bang features, and we wind up with some additional printing or distillation problems. Depending on which program you use, you may wish to reorganize the PDF creation "food chain" mentioned earlier in this chapter according to the strengths and weaknesses for each individual program.

Macromedia FreeHand

Whereas Adobe Illustrator has a weaker set of print controls, FreeHand has always excelled at printing files either as composites or color separations. FreeHand has great control over bleeds, too. As the first order for creating PDFs from FreeHand, print your PostScript files directly from FreeHand. Don't export to EPS and place the file in other applications just to create the PDF file. If FreeHand graphics are imported into page layout applications as EPS files, you can print the layout document to disk. Most often this will work fine, but only use it when FreeHand EPS files are contained within a larger layout.

As with Illustrator, in FreeHand don't use PDFWriter and don't distill any EPS exports directly. FreeHand also has an export to PDF feature, which can be used second to distilling PostScript files. Use of this feature would follow the same rules as when you use PDFWriter.

Overcoming problems with FreeHand illustrations may be needed if the resultant EPS export or PostScript file does not print properly. One solution to the problem is to open (not place) the file in Adobe Illustrator. Once opened in Illustrator, save the file as an EPS file, place it into a layout program, and then print it to disk as a PostScript file. Adobe Illustrator is one of the purest PostScript applications in that it adheres to PostScript conventions more than any other computer program. When all else fails, use this method to create your PDF files.

CorelDraw

Whereas Adobe illustrator is the purest of the PostScript-compliant applications, CorelDraw has commonly been the most deviant. Your first order of business with CorelDraw is to print the file to disk. As with FreeHand, CorelDraw has been stable in its print controls, but the maze of dialog boxes need attention to ensure that the printed file will be as you expect.

If problems are encountered with CorelDraw, try opening the file in Illustrator and use the method described previously for exporting to EPS. Once again, as the Illustrator file is saved, the EPS format will be rewritten following stronger PostScript conventions.

If you experience some problems, try exporting to EPS and importing directly to layout applications. Because CorelDraw is the dominant illustration program on the PC and PageMaker is the dominant layout application on the PC, try importing the file into PageMaker and exporting it to Acrobat PDF. PageMaker's export to PDF, as discussed a little later in this chapter, will print the file to disk and run Distiller in the background. CorelDraw also supports a direct export to PDF feature, and it also follows the same rules as when you use PDFWriter.

Adobe Illustrator

Printing directly from Illustrator has always been one of the weakest areas of that program. In version 8, some of the problems with printing still exist. If you attempt to print an Illustrator file to disk, you will face some challenges, including page boundaries not syncing with PPD page definitions; the controls for composite images not being the same as those for separations; separations defaulting to negative, emulsion down (E-down); and inclusion of bleeds sometimes requiring that crop marks be drawn manually.

EPS exports can be distilled in Acrobat Distiller. As this is an EPS drawing program, you should not use PDFWriter in this case. You might experience more success by first exporting the Illustrator file to EPS, placing it in a layout application, printing the application document to disk as a PostScript file, and then distilling it in Acrobat Distiller. I know this sounds like a lot of work, but I think you'll find this option more reliable than distilling EPS files.

PDF exports are best for Illustrator, as compared to the other two illustration applications mentioned here. In version 8 of Adobe Illustrator, you see your first glimpse of the Acrobat 4 format as an export option. Like all new Adobe software applications, Illustrator is progressing with expanded PDF support. Therefore, in the PDF creation food chain, with Adobe Illustrator use the export to PDF feature as your second choice.

Exporting to PDF from Adobe Illustrator

I could gobble up a few thousand pages describing all the methods of PDF export from all the illustration software programs, but I'm in a hurry to get you to

PageMaker, which is the best PDF exporter on the planet, as detailed a little later. If you follow the preceding guidelines, you should be able to poke around and figure out how to best use PDF exports with your favorite illustration application.

Adobe Illustrator does deserve some special attention, so before moving on to PageMaker, let's take a look at some of the new Illustrator 8 export features. Adobe Illustrator 8 has the best capabilities you can find for printing to PDF *without* the use of Acrobat Distiller. Illustrator 8's new PDF export controls make it almost as good as Distiller. The ideal for prepress and printing to high-end devices is still in converting a PostScript file to PDF. In Illustrator 8, though, you can go beyond what PDFWriter has to offer and use the direct export to PDF feature for all but color separation and creating a high-end digital workflow. If Web or screen graphics are what you need, you can safely use Illustrator 8 to export to PDF. If printing to composite color devices is your goal, you can also use the export to PDF feature in Illustrator. If you have bleeds and oversized pages, you'll be best off using PPD selection and printing a PostScript file to disk, which will be subsequently distilled.

Exporting PDF files from Adobe Illustrator is handled through the Save command. When you select File ➪ Save, the format options available to you include the native Illustrator format, EPS, and Acrobat PDF. In Illustrator, select File ➪ Save from a new document window. A dialog box will appear that enables you to name the file, choose the destination, and select one of the formats just noted. When you select Acrobat PDF and click the Save button, the PDF Export Options dialog box will appear to enable you to select various PDF options, as shown in Figure 6-9.

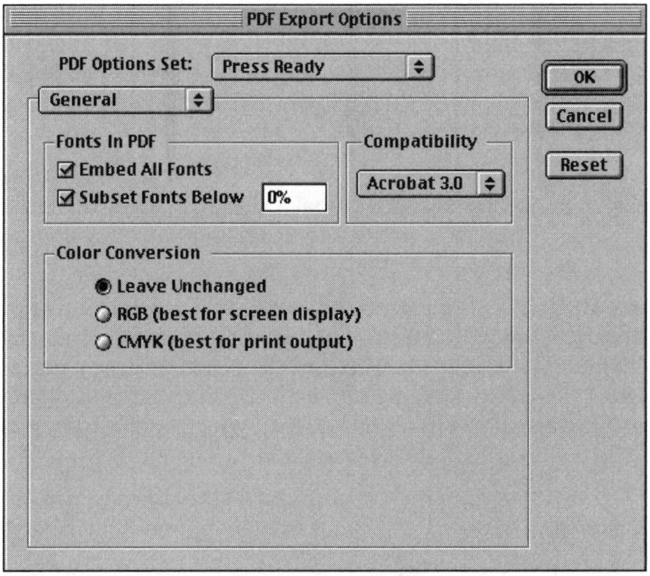

Figure 6-9: When you select the PDF format and click the Save button in the Save dialog box, a new dialog box will open enabling you to select PDF export options.

✦ **PDF Options Set:** There are three choices available for PDF options from this pop-up menu. You can choose from Press Ready, Print Quality, or Web Ready. Choices you make here will change the downsampling and compression options according to the output requirements.

- **Press Ready:** The default choice from the pop-up menu is Press Ready. When this option is selected, the font subsetting will default to 99 percent, which means the entire character set will be included in the PDF file. In addition to the font options, compression will default to that allowing the highest quality and downsampling will be reduced to 300 dpi for color and grayscale images. Monochrome bitmaps will be downsampled to 1,200 dpi.

- **Print Quality:** This option should not be confused with the Press Ready selection. If your files will be output to high-end devices, the previous option should be chosen. Print Quality is best used with composite color devices, desktop printers, and some proofing systems. When you make this choice, the font subsetting will default to 25 percent, the compression will default to medium, and downsampling will occur at 240/600 dpi for the color/grayscale and monochrome bitmaps.

- **Web Ready:** For all screen graphics intended for the Web, multimedia, or presentations, you would use this option. The defaults will include no font embedding, and the compression levels used will be the highest available. Downsampling will be to 72/300 dpi for color/grayscale and monochrome bitmaps.

✦ **Fonts in PDF:** Embedding and font subsetting percentage choices like those in Acrobat Distiller are available. When you make a choice for the PDF Options Set, the default values of that choice can be overridden in the field box where the font subsetting default percentage appears. For example, if you select Print Quality, the default font subsetting will be 25 percent, unless you change the value in the Subset Fonts Below field.

✦ **Compatibility:** Illustrator 8 has dismissed Acrobat 2.1 format compatibility and now supports both Acrobat 3 and Acrobat 4 compatibility. As more users adopt PostScript 3, you'll want to use the Acrobat 4 compatibility choice, which saves the PDF in version 1.3 format.

✦ **Color Conversion:** When the Press Ready and Print Quality options are selected, the color conversion default will be Leave Unchanged. If you select Web Ready, the default will change to RGB. CMYK is an option you can select when there may be RGB colors specified in the Illustrator file and the output is destined for a CMYK device. When you know all your color is to be output as CMYK, you should select the CMYK option.

✦ **Compression:** The default setting for the pop-up menu below PDF Options Set is General. If you choose Compression from the pop-up menu, the dialog box options will change to the those displayed in Figure 6-10.

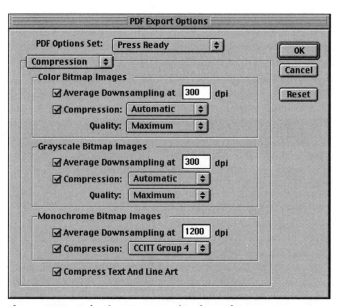

Figure 6-10: Selecting Compression from the pop-up menu where the default setting General appears brings up controls for compression.

Compression settings, like font subsetting, can be changed from the defaults associated with the choices you make for PDF Options Set. If you wish to use a different level of compression or manually set the compression type, you can make those changes here. Also, the downsampling amounts can be established in this dialog box. While the Compression options are in view, you can change the PDF Options Set and make your choices according to the attributes of the PDF file to be created.

When you click OK in the PDF Export Options dialog box from either the settings for General or Compression, the document will be saved in PDF format. From Illustrator, the file is converted to PDF directly, and Distiller won't be introduced in the background.

Note Notice there are no options for viewing the PDF and document information in the PDF Export Options dialog box within Adobe Illustrator. These options will only be available in PDFWriter.

Opening PDFs in Adobe Illustrator

Perhaps one of the best features in using Adobe Illustrator with PDF files is the capability to open a PDF in Illustrator. Other programs such as Adobe PageMaker offer you an opportunity to *place* PDF files; however, the placed PDFs are useless for anything beyond printing or impositions. Files opened in Adobe Illustrator provide you access to the elements contained within the PDF. If you need to edit these elements, Illustrator will enable you to change vector art and text attributes, just as if your document had originated in Illustrator. There are a few limitations, but for the most part, you can make many changes in a PDF document opened in Adobe Illustrator.

PDF files are opened in Illustrator via the File ➪ Open command. There are no special import commands or filters needed by Illustrator to recognize a PDF file. When you select File ➪ Open to open a single-page PDF file, the document appears in Illustrator without any translation or import conversions. Illustrator recognizes PDF files as it does .ai and EPS files. As a matter of fact, when you select the Open command and view the navigation dialog box, the PDF icons appear in Illustrator, indicating Illustrator recognizes the files.

Because Illustrator is capable of opening single-page documents only, the same scrolling features discussed earlier with Adobe Photoshop apply equally to Illustrator. Also, when no thumbnails have been created in the PDF, you will see the message "No Thumbnail Available." When thumbnails have been created, the thumbnail for the respective page will be viewed in the thumbnail preview box.

On opening the PDF file, you will have access to all the elements contained within the document. If vector objects need to be edited or type needs to be changed, you can make those edits in Illustrator.

Limitations with editing PDF files in Illustrator

File integrity is not exactly the same with PDF files opened in Illustrator as it is with native Illustrator or EPS documents. You do have some limitations. Ideally, almost anything you do with PDF editing will best be performed in the host application from which the PDF was created. Illustrator is no exception. If you have an original Illustrator document, it would be best to open the .ai or EPS file in Illustrator, make your changes, and re-create the PDF. If you do not have the original file, or the producer application was something other than Illustrator and the original file cannot be found, then this is your best opportunity for making changes short of any special plug-ins you may find for Acrobat PDF editing. If the need calls for editing PDFs in Illustrator, you should be aware of some potential problems that need to be overcome:

✦ **Text limitations:** All text — titles, headlines, body copy, and so on — will lose text block attributes. A single line of text will often be a noncontiguous grouping of characters. The text can be broken up both between words and within a given word on the same text line. These broken text blocks may be difficult to edit, especially if you make major copy changes. In some cases, it may be easier to re-create the text block (see Figures 6-11 and 6-12).

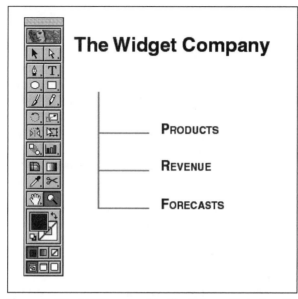

Figure 6-11: A PDF opened in Illustrator with text as it appeared in the original PDF document

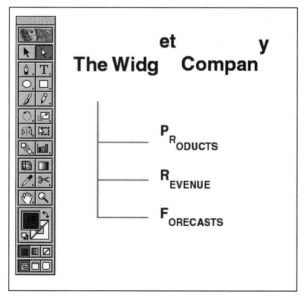

Figure 6-12: The text shown in Figure 6-11 was moved in Illustrator. Notice the broken text blocks and noncontiguous grouping of the text.

✦ **Font problems:** If fonts are not embedded in the PDF documents, font substitution will be used, and any text changes will make use of the substituted fonts. Those documents in which fonts have been embedded and subsetted will only contain the subset fonts. Edited text may appear in a font different than the nonedited text in your document. In addition, character sets across platforms vary, and font characters may not offer an accurate substitution. When you open a PDF in Illustrator, a warning dialog box will appear if there are any font problems.

✦ **Masked objects:** Some objects will appear masked when you open a PDF file in Adobe Illustrator. Although not a major problem, as you can easily unmask the objects, care should be used when relocating objects contained within a mask. If you attempt to move an object within the mask, it may disappear.

Although you have a few limitations with making changes to PDFs in Illustrator, Illustrator remains the best application for editing PDF documents without special plug-ins.

Illustrator as a problem solver

Since the introduction of Adobe Acrobat, many imaging centers have used it to develop workarounds and solve imaging problems. Most computer users, especially the non-tech types, develop a comfort zone in creating documents for utilitarian purposes. Design professionals as a group are one of the best examples of users who don't care much about the technical stuff, but just want to get a job completed without any hassle. As such, many designers use one or two applications to do almost all of their work. If one uses Adobe Illustrator as his/her primary application, the program may be used for illustration, page layout, writing memos, and almost any other purpose. People who use a program such as QuarkXPress may extend their use from layout to illustration.

Professional applications software has evolved to meet many professional needs with the inclusion of tools and commands that offer more functionality. Designers, being the creative group they are, will push these tools and commands to the limit. Sometimes they even develop some "creative" means of using tools in a program to accomplish a task. "Gimme Quark and Photoshop," cries the designer, "and I can do anything." Meanwhile, down at the imaging center, the techs are saying, "Come here and look at this. Can you believe it?!" Ultimately what happens is problems are encountered in imaging files when tools and workarounds don't quite work with PostScript and the device RIP.

To illustrate a problem and create a solution, let's look at a step-by-step approach for how to use Adobe Illustrator as a problem solver. Figure 6-13 illustrates an imaging problem.

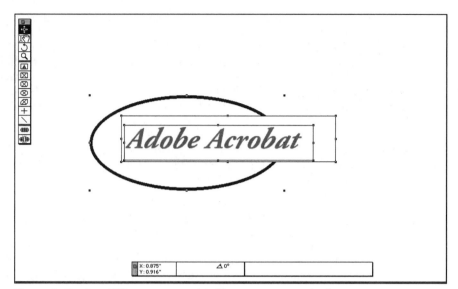

Figure 6-13: QuarkXPress was used to illustrate a two-color logo.

In Figure 6-13, the elliptical shape in the logo is clipped on the right side by a picture box filled with white. Black is used for the ellipse and a spot color for the type. When separated on an imaging device, the white picture box doesn't knock out the area of the ellipse as it does in the file. Ideally, it would have been better to create the logo in an EPS drawing program and import the drawing in QuarkXPress. To edit the file in Illustrator, the QuarkXPress document needs to be converted to PDF. You could use the Save Page as EPS command in QuarkXPress and edit the elements in Illustrator. EPS exports from all programs, but earlier versions of some software don't always enable you to access the elements. For this example, I use the QuarkXPress layout just to illustrate the point.

STEPS: Editing QuarkXPress Data in Adobe Illustrator

1. **Select the Acrobat Distiller PPD.** I selected File ➪ Page Setup in QuarkXPress. In the Page Setup dialog box, I selected the Acrobat Distiller PPD and then clicked OK to leave the Page Setup dialog box.

2. **Print to PostScript.** I selected File ➪ Print. In the Print dialog box, I selected the File option on my Macintosh (in Windows, select the Distiller Assistant printer).

3. **Distill the PostScript file.** I then opened Acrobat Distiller and distilled the PostScript file. If I had used Distiller Assistant, the PDF would have been created when the file was printed to disk, and Distiller would have been launched in the background.

Continued

Note   You can open PostScript files created from single-page documents directly in Adobe Illustrator without needing to convert them to PDF. Illustrator will display the data on a standard letter page. When you distill the PDF and open it in Illustrator, the page boundaries will remain intact. In this example, either method could be used to edit the logo. In some cases, however, you may need the page size to remain the same when editing in Illustrator for positioning data relative to page size. In this example, I edited a PDF file to illustrate a procedure when such referencing is needed.

4. **Release the masks.** The objects will appear with masks. To release the masks, select Edit ⇨ Select All, and then select Object ⇨ Masks ⇨ Release. Repeat the procedure until all masks have been released.

5. **Clip the ellipse.** I selected the ellipse with the Object Selection arrow and selected Object ⇨ Arrange ⇨ Bring to Front. The Scissors tool from the Illustrator toolbox was chosen. To reference the exact area for clipping the ellipse, I selected Edit ⇨ Select All so the masking rectangle was viewed along with the ellipse. The area where these elements intersect needed to be cut with the Scissors tool. I clipped at both intersections (see Figure 6-14).

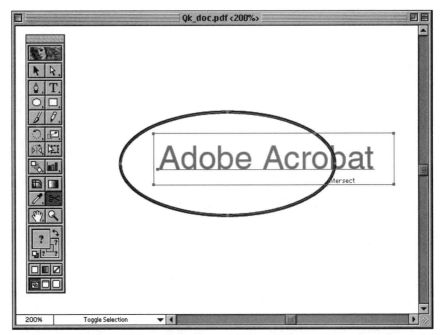

Figure 6-14: With the ellipse in the foreground and all elements selected, use the Scissors tool to clip the intersection of the masking rectangle and the ellipse.

6. **Delete the clipped data.** I selected the Direct Selection arrow from the Illustrator toolbox and clicked the clipped portion of the ellipse. I then pressed the Backspace/Delete key to eliminate the unwanted data.

7. **Save as EPS.** I saved the document as an EPS file and reimported it into QuarkXPress. The finished logo appears as illustrated in Figure 6-15.

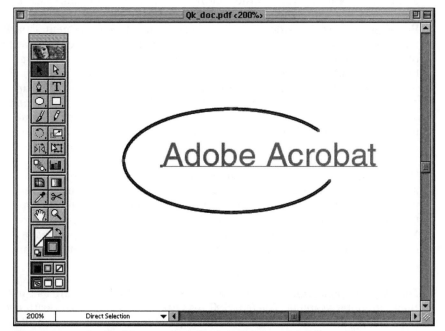

Figure 6-15: The final image after clipping data in Adobe Illustrator

Note If you have multiple pages printed to disk as a PostScript file, you will need to generate a PDF file or exported EPS file from that PostScript file to open in Adobe Illustrator. Illustrator can't recognize PostScript files containing more than one page.

Acrobat and Layout Programs

In the previous example, QuarkXPress was mentioned as a means of exporting data to PDF, which is similar to other applications discussed in earlier chapters. When using QuarkXPress, you can choose to print the document to disk as a PostScript file or use a QuarkXTension for exporting to PDF. A PDF export XTension is available for QuarkXPress version 4.02 and above.

QuarkXPress has been the premier choice of layout applications for design professionals on Macintosh computers. Quark, Inc., has paved its own road and traveled the digital highway in its own way. What has been accomplished in page layout for high-end design professionals has been magnificent, and one only needs to look at the incredible number of Quark XTensions to see the pinnacle of success accomplished by a company that has survived on a single product in a fiercely competitive world. For all intent and purposes, the company has literally maintained its dominance in page layout software without a major revision for almost a six-year period. No other off-the-shelf product can claim such success.

However, on the other side of the hoopla lies some disappointment. Quark is muddling around in its own pool of technology without much collaboration with other application software vendors. Pick up the new QuarkXPress 4 user manual, jump to the index, and you won't find a single reference to PDF, Portable Document, Adobe, or anything else to associated with Acrobat. By contrast, pick up the Adobe Acrobat manuals, search through the Acrobat CDs, or browse the online guides, and you find many references to working with QuarkXPress. Unfortunately, PDF integration with QuarkXPress has been slow — which is too bad, since much can be accomplished when a layout application can work with PDF documents.

The PDF revolution, however, is so overwhelming that no developer can deny Acrobat's importance in the digital community. Slow as it has been, Quark, Inc., has now developed an XTension for importing and exporting PDF files from QuarkXPress. As noted, you need QuarkXPress version 4.02 or above to use the XTension. In addition to Quark's XTension, third-party developers have also developed XTensions for handling many of the PDF editing features found within Adobe PageMaker.

Page layout applications aficionados are as loyal to their software as they are to their computer systems. The QuarkXPress user blasts PageMaker with every opportunity, and the PageMaker user cringes at the thought of using all those box frames. Getting a user of a particular layout application to try a new layout application is like asking a Mac user to work on a Windows machine. If you happen to be one of those QuarkXPress users, hold on — I'm going to scratch my fingernails across the chalkboard.

Absolutely the single best PDF producer on the planet, bar none, is Adobe PageMaker. This is not opinion, but a verifiable fact! PageMaker goes well beyond the controls you can exercise in PDFWriter, Acrobat Distiller, and direct exports from other applications. Over several generations of PageMaker Adobe has added much PDF integration to the product without recoding the entire program. Acrobat Distiller ships on the PageMaker installer CD and has accompanied PageMaker since version 5. If you happen to not use Adobe PageMaker and you want to convert layouts to PDF, I recommend you run out and purchase the product to streamline your PDF workflows. Unlike QuarkXPress, PageMaker already contains features for importing and exporting PDF files when you purchase the product.

Exporting to PDF from PageMaker

Adobe PageMaker has an export command, which permits export to PDF first by printing the file to PostScript, and then automatically launching Distiller in the background. Distiller will produce the PDF file and return you to the PageMaker document window when distillation has completed.

Running Distiller in the background to produce the PDF file is not unique to PageMaker, as you already know if you've read the earlier sections in this chapter. Nor are font embedding, compression, and some of the other controls also examined earlier unique to PageMaker. PageMaker goes well beyond the definition of PDF attributes you can control from other applications. PageMaker can directly override all of Distiller's Job Options. You can add notes to PDF files from within PageMaker, and you can add bookmarks developed from tables of contents and indices. All these changes are automatically handled by PageMaker through a few options in the Export dialog box. Most other layout applications will also enable you to create PDF files with automatic links to tables of contents and indices, but PageMaker offers internal controls not found in other programs.

Adobe PageMaker is a cross-platform product, and all of what you can do in the Macintosh version of the program can also be performed in a Windows-based version of the program and vice versa. However, one of essentially two different export dialog boxes will appear when you export to PDF from PageMaker. Although these boxes vary greatly in appearance, all the controls are basically the same. If you have PageMaker 6.52 and have not updated the PDF exporter plug-in, the dialog boxes and some controls will be different from those that appear when using the Export Adobe PDF 3.01 plug-in, which can also be downloaded from Adobe's Web site. Because of the obvious difference in the dialog boxes, I explain both the use of the PDF export feature prior to version 3.01 and the use of the Export Adobe PDF 3.01 export plug-in.

Export plug-ins earlier than version 3.01

When installing PageMaker on your computer, be certain to include Acrobat Distiller as part of your installation. Distiller can be installed as part of the PageMaker installation, or you can browse the PageMaker CD and find a separate Distiller installer. Additionally, if you are using a version of Acrobat prior to 4.0, browse the Adobe Web site and download the latest version of the Distiller update. If you have an earlier version of PageMaker, you may also need to download the version 6.52 or later update. Exporting to PDF from PageMaker requires the use of Acrobat Distiller. Inasmuch as you can postpone distillation, eventually you need it to convert the PostScript files to PDF with Distiller.

When you select File ➪ Export Adobe PDF from within PageMaker, the Export Adobe PDF dialog box, in which all the PDF attributes are controlled, will appear (see Figure 6-16). There's a maze of options available in this dialog box — enough to make your head swim. If you have a handle on the Job Options in Acrobat Distiller, you've reduced your learning curve by about half. The remaining half of the settings you will encounter are used for controls that aren't available from Distiller, some of which are specific to PageMaker. The first level of options you encounter deals with workflow distillation and printer styles.

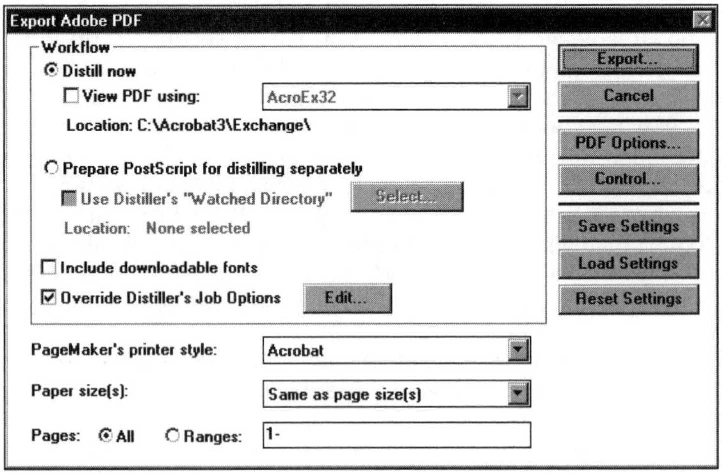

Figure 6-16: When you select File ➪ Export Adobe PDF, the Export Adobe PDF dialog box, through which all PDF attributes and workflow is determined, will appear.

✦ **Distill now:** The Distill now option will auto-launch Acrobat Distiller. When you select the Export button in the top-right corner of the dialog box, your PageMaker file will be printed to disk as a PostScript file and then distilled in Acrobat Distiller. On completion of distillation, you will be returned to the PageMaker document window.

✦ **View PDF using:** Once the file has been converted to PDF, you can view it immediately in an Acrobat viewer. If you enable this option, the viewer chosen from the pop-up menu to the right of the check box will be automatically launched and the document opened in the viewer. If View PDF is enabled, you will not be returned to the PageMaker document window, as the viewer will assume precedence.

✦ **Choosing a viewer:** One advantage PageMaker has over other means of enabling a View PDF option is you can select the viewer to be used. If you open the pop-up menu, you'll see the Add/Remove option. Selecting this menu choice opens the Add Viewer dialog box, which offers you choices for adding a new viewer to the pop-up menu list or removing a viewer from the list (see Figure 6-17). Previously added viewers will be displayed in the list. When you click the Add button, a navigation dialog box will appear, enabling you to choose the directory location and viewer you wish to add. Select the viewer to be added and click the Open button in the dialog box.

After clicking Open, you will be returned to the Add Viewer dialog box, and the new viewer will be displayed in the list. If you wish to delete a viewer, you must select it and click the Remove button.

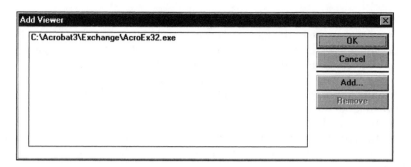

Figure 6-17: When selecting the Add/Remove item from the pop-up menu beside the View PDF using option, this dialog box will appear in which you can select the viewer to be used.

✦ **Prepare PostScript for distilling separately:** When the radio button is selected, the Distill Now option will be disabled. If the Export button is clicked with this option enabled, the file will be printed to disk as a PostScript file. You can develop PDF workflows by using watched folders and remote systems for distillation.

✦ **Use Distiller's "Watched Directory":** When the preceding option is enabled, this option for using watched directories will become available and the Select button to the right will be active. If you click Select, a dialog box will appear listing all watched directories. By default, you won't have a directory listed.

Click the Add button to navigate to the watched directory you established with Distiller's Watched Folders command. To select a directory, you must have it identified as a watched folder in Distiller. You won't be able to select a directory not established as a watched folder.

If you aren't certain where your watched folders are located, you can enable the Auto-list from Distiller option, at the bottom left of the dialog box. PageMaker will automatically list all of Distiller's watched folders.

✦ **View Options:** In the Watched Directories dialog box, you'll notice a button labeled View Options. When you select this button, the Job Options associated with the watched folder, which you established when the folder was added, will appear in a window. You can scroll the window and view all the Job Options that will be employed when distilling files in this directory. The view you have here eliminates the need to return to Distiller and examine the Job Options. This is particularly helpful when using many different watched folders and working within a PDF workflow.

✦ **Include Downloadable Fonts:** You can specify fonts for inclusion when the PostScript file is generated. If you wish to download the PostScript file to a printing device and later distill the file in Acrobat Distiller, be certain to enable this option — especially if you send the file off to an imaging center. For font embedding in the PDF file, you can choose to embed fonts here, or use Distiller's watched folders for font embedding.

Overriding Distiller's Job Options

Another nice feature in the Export Adobe PDF dialog box is the capability to control all of Distiller's Job Options. If you use a watched folder, you will typically use the Job Options associated with the watched folder. If you wish to create a PDF by exporting from PageMaker with a different set of Job Options, those changes can be made in the Export dialog box. Having this kind of control eliminates the need to open Distiller and reset Job Options from the Distiller menu. In Acrobat 4.0, you can choose to let the PostScript file override Job Options. To enable this option, you would still need to return to Distiller. With PageMaker, you can make all your choices in the Export Adobe PDF dialog box and not have to worry what Job Options you last created in Distiller.

By default, Override Distiller's Job Options is enabled. If you want to change Job Options in PageMaker, click the Edit button adjacent to the option. When Edit is clicked, the PDF Job Options dialog box will appear. (See Figure 6-18.)

PageMaker's display of Job Options consolidates the General and Compression Job Options found in two separate dialog boxes when making these changes in Distiller. All you see in this dialog box are the same options as those discussed in Chapter 5 when examining the Distiller Job Options dialog box.

Advanced Job Options include many of those I mentioned in relation to Distiller. You can't get to the Advanced settings, though, until you select the Acrobat 3 format in the Compatibility pop-up menu, as shown in Figure 6-18. The current version of PageMaker makes no provision for using Acrobat 4 format. To view the Advanced settings, select choose Acrobat 3 on the pull-down menu. The Advanced button will become active. When you click this button, a new dialog box will appear, as shown in Figure 6-19.

Notice not all the Advanced settings are available in this dialog box. PageMaker scrambles some controls and makes them available in other dialog boxes. Basically, you will be able to get to the other controls when navigating through the other dialog boxes. For example, the Convert CMYK to RGB setting, available in version 3.02 of Distiller's Advanced Job Options, appears in the PDF Control dialog box in PageMaker and not the Advanced dialog box. What you do have available in the Advanced settings dialog box are the same options as those I discussed with Distiller.

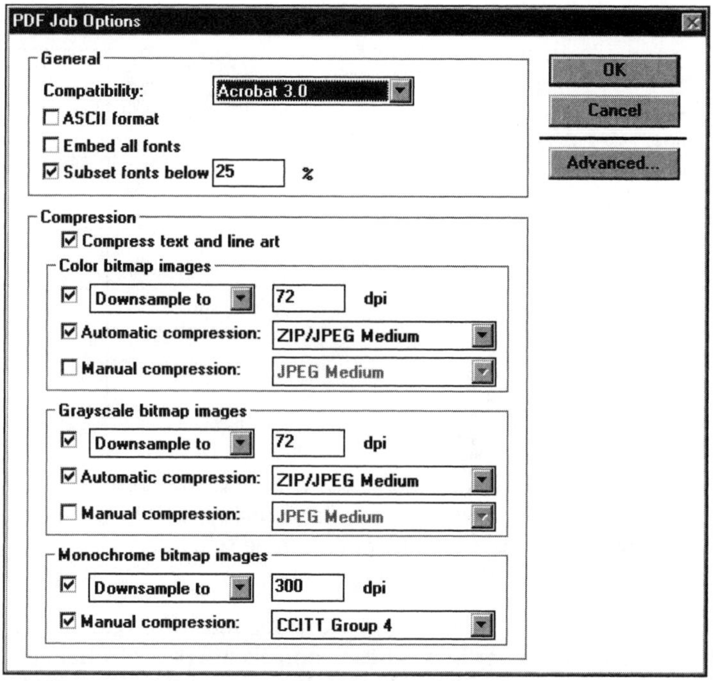

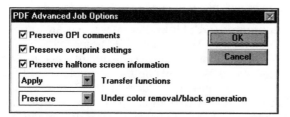

Figure 6-18: When the Acrobat 3 format is selected in the Job Options dialog box, the Advanced button will become active.

Figure 6-19: When you click Advanced, the PDF Advanced Job Options dialog box appears, in which advanced controls can be selected.

PDF options

If you open the Advanced settings dialog box, you need to click OK and then click OK again to return to the Export Adobe PDF dialog box. From here you can select the PDF Options button, which includes a few settings from Distiller's Advanced Job Options and several controls specific to PageMaker (see Figure 6-20).

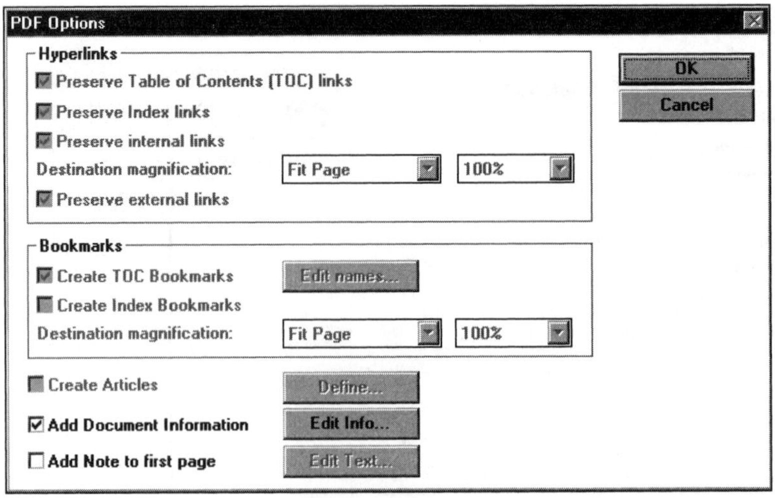

Figure 6-20: When you click PDF Options, another dialog box appears in which options controlling items specific to PageMaker can be set.

✦ **Hyperlinks:** The PDF Options dialog box is divided into three categories — the first of which deals with hyperlinks. These controls are part of what sets PageMaker apart from other PDF producers. You can create auto-links to many different document items in a file, and these links will be visible in an Acrobat viewer. When you create a PageMaker publication and use some of these auto-linking settings, you will save much time by eliminating the need to create links in Acrobat. The hyperlinks you can create are as follows:

 • **Preserve Table of Contents (TOC) Links:** PageMaker has an automatic generator for tables of contents. You identify TOC items in PageMaker's story editor, select a menu command, place the contents, and presto — your TOC has been generated. When this option is enabled for PDF exports, items in the table of contents included in the PageMaker file will serve as hyperlinks to the pages where those items appear. If you work in a publishing environment where you produce print documents and CD-ROMs, you can develop a PDF workflow where watched folders are used to convert PDF files for both purposes. The links for the CD-ROM will have no effect on the documents developed for print, therefore only a single PostScript file needs to be exported. Job Options for the watched folders can be developed to handle compression and downsampling for the respective output.

 • **Preserve Index links:** The same capability for indexes exist as they do for tables of contents. When an index has been developed, the index items will serve as hyperlinks to the pages where the words or phrases appear.

- **Preserve internal links:** PageMaker has an internal hyperlink palette, which enables you to set up links from selected words or graphics to other pages in your document, rather than linking to a table of contents or index. When Preserve internal links is enabled, you can select from a number of different views, the same as those available in Acrobat viewers. The default view is Fit Page. You can edit the view from the pop-up menu, or you can select from preset views. When you view the page magnification pop-up menu, you'll see the choices available. Only the Fit Top Left of Page and Fit Top Left choices enable you to edit the view magnification. The percentage pop-up menu will be inactive with the other three choices. If Fit Top Left of Page or Fit Top Left is selected, you can open the pop-up menu to select a preset view magnification or select Other and then enter a value between 12% and 800% in the field.

- **Preserve external links:** Links can also be made to URLs on the World Wide Web from within PageMaker. If you create a Web link, enabling this option will preserve the link.

✦ **Bookmarks:** Bookmarks were discussed in earlier chapters in the context of navigating through the Acrobat viewers. PageMaker can automatically create bookmarks from two sources.

- **Create TOC Bookmarks:** Table of contents items in PageMaker are defined in the Paragraph Specifications dialog box, shown in Figure 6-21. When you select Type ➪ Paragraph, this dialog box will open. Any words you have highlighted can be included in the table of contents by selecting the option Include in table of contents.

After you define all the TOC entries, you need to open the PageMaker Story Editor (Edit ➪ Edit Story) and select Utilities ➪ Create TOC. PageMaker will calculate all the TOC entries and load the text gun, which can be used to place the text on a page. After placing the text, the TOC items will be linked to the pages where the entries were defined. When the PDF file is created, bookmarks will be generated (see Figure 6-22), and hypertext links from the bookmarks will provide a connection to the respective pages.

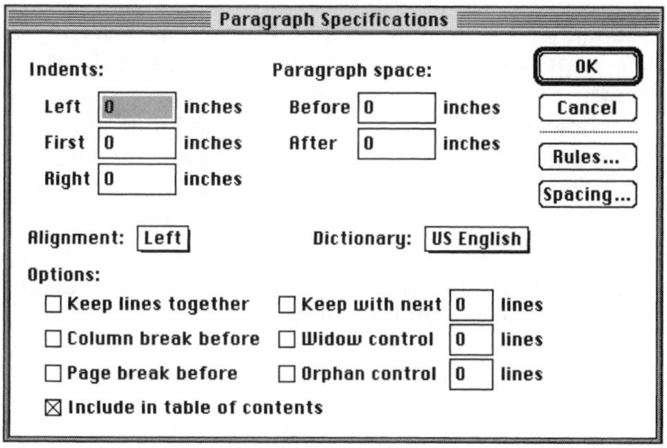

Figure 6-21: I defined TOC entries in the Paragraph Specifications dialog box in Adobe PageMaker. Subsequently, I created the table of contents by selecting Utilities ➪ Create TOC.

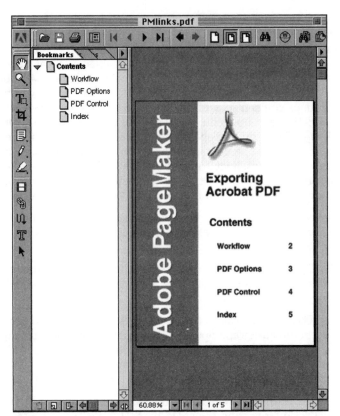

Figure 6-22: When the PDF was created, the bookmarks were nested under the title I specified for the table of contents. The bookmarks link to the pages where the TOC items were defined.

- **Create Index Bookmarks:** Bookmarks can be created from all your index definitions in much the same manner as TOC entries are created. To define index text, you open the Story Editor and select the line of text or the individual characters to be included in your index. After selecting the characters or word for the index item, select Utilities ⇨ Index Entry from within the Story Editor. A dialog box will open that enables you to make some choices about the attributes of the index entry. Among the choices in the Index Entry dialog box is a sort option. Once sorted and exported to PDF, the entries will appear as bookmarks in the same order in an Acrobat viewer. As you define index entries in the Story Editor, the editor window will display a symbol indicating which items have been added to the index. To the left of each item will be a description of the index level corresponding to the entry.

• **Edit Names:** You may at times need to create a table of contents for a publication that will be repurposed for screen display, and the content items may need to be changed. PageMaker provides you much control over the bookmarks used in a table of contents to be generated for PDF viewing without disturbing the text to be printed. When you select the Edit names button, a dialog box will appear, enabling you to redefine some of the attributes of the bookmarks to be created when the file is exported to PDF.

When you first open the dialog box, you may not see any items in the TOC entry list box. The value for List only TOC entries over [nn] characters long defaults to 20. If your table of contents definitions are less than 20 characters long, you won't see any entries listed. You can enter a new value (in the example I used 2 for my field entry) and then click the Relist button. A new list will be generated that displays all the entries within the total number of characters you supplied in the field box (see Figure 6-23).

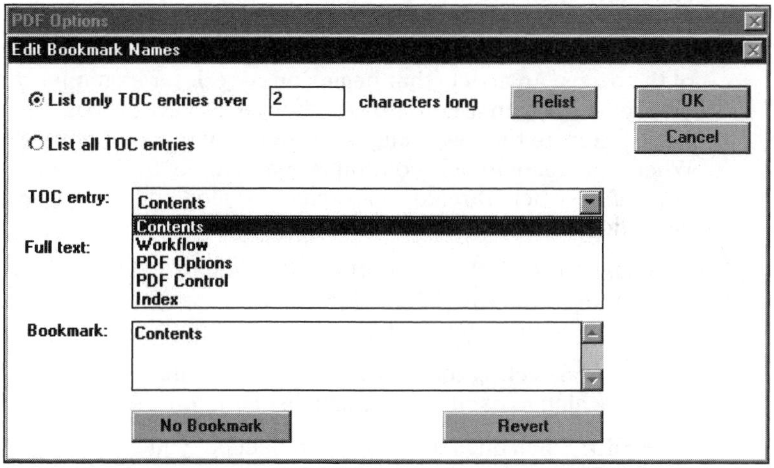

Figure 6-23: When I first opened the Edit Bookmark Names dialog box, no TOC entries were listed. I changed the List only TOC entries value to 2 and then clicked the Relist button. When I opened the TOC pull-down menu, all TOC entries of two or more characters were listed.

The example shown in Figure 6-23 will eliminate all TOC entries below two characters. To display all TOC entries, regardless of the number of characters, you would select the List all TOC entries option.

The TOC entry pull-down menu displays all the identified contents to be converted to bookmarks when the PDF is created. If you wish to rename the bookmark, you can select it in the TOC entry field and edit the text in the Bookmark box. Changes you make here will only affect the PDF bookmark names.

At times you may create a table of contents and not wish all items in your list to become bookmarks in the PDF file. You can select a TOC entry and click the No Bookmark button to eliminate it from the bookmarks to be generated. Click the Revert button to return the list of TOC entries to the state it was in when the dialog box was first opened.

- **Destination magnification:** The magnification view for the bookmark links can be set in the same manner as the magnification view for hyperlinks, as was described previously.

✦ **Create Articles:** In Chapter 8, I discuss more about article threads in Acrobat. Creating articles is usually left to Acrobat, for no other application supports creating articles before distillation. Unique to PageMaker, however, is the capability to create articles, while working in a publication, that can be exported as PDF and viewed in an Acrobat viewer. Article threads help the end user to sequentially view articles and body copy regardless of the order of the pages. An article that begins on page 1, for example, can be continued on page 4. With an article thread, the viewer clicks the last paragraph on page 1 and jumps to the beginning of the continuation of the article on page 4. When the Create Articles option is enabled, the Define button becomes active. You define article threads in a separate dialog box that appears when you click the Define button.

- **List:** Clicking the List button will recognize the Stories in the publication. From within the publication you may create many article threads from all noncontiguous text blocks.

- **New:** Selecting the New button will prompt you with another dialog box in which to establish the article definition.

- **Edit:** When an article has been defined, you select it in the list, click Edit, and the dialog box where the article was originally defined will reappear. In this dialog box, you can make changes to the defined article.

- **Remove:** Selecting a defined article in the list and clicking the Remove button will eliminate the article thread. When the PDF file is created, only the defined articles existing in the list box will appear in the Acrobat viewer.

- **One per story over [*nn*] text block(s):** PageMaker Stories can have many different text blocks. If you have one- or two-line text blocks, you may wish to eliminate them from your list. You can limit the number of text blocks in a story by supplying a value in this field. For example, entering the value 5 in this field will result in only a list of stories that contain six or more text blocks.

Clicking the New button in the Define Articles dialog box will open the PageMaker Stories dialog box, shown in Figure 6-24.

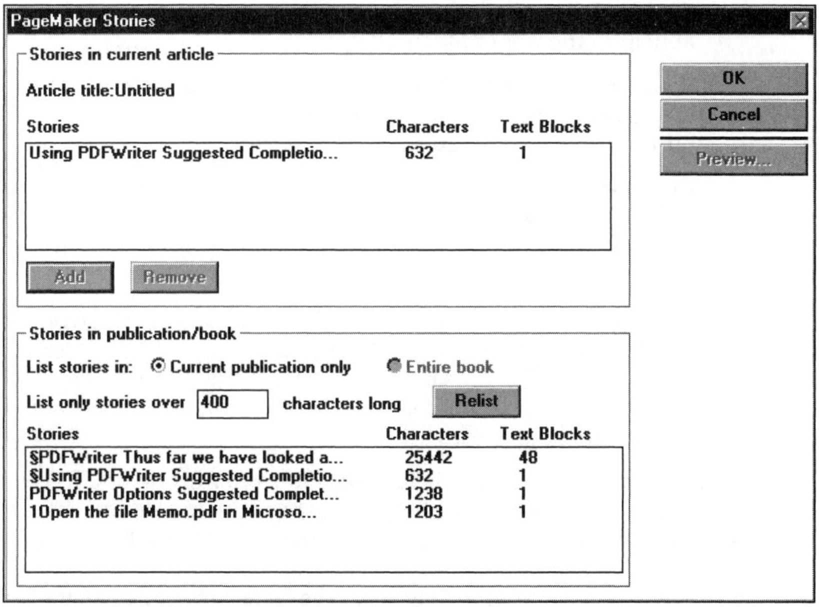

Figure 6-24: I listed all the PageMaker Stories containing over 400 characters to determine which text bodies I wanted to define as articles.

✦ **Stories in publication/book:** In defining stories, you begin at the bottom of the dialog box. PageMaker recognizes the current stories within the open publication or a book containing several PageMaker documents.

- **List stories in:** You can select the current publication or a book that has been defined just as you would when working with hyperlinks. The Entire Book option will only be available if you have created a book publication.

- **List only stories over [nnn] characters long:** The default for the field box is 400. Any stories less than 400 characters will not appear in the Stories list. You can reduce the value in the field box to reveal shorter stories. If you change the value, you need to select the Relist button, and PageMaker will recalculate the list according to the stories containing the new value.

- **Stories:** The list appearing in the Stories box is among those that can be defined as articles. To define an article, you must select a story listed in the lower box and add it to the upper list.

✦ **Stories in current article:** From the Stories list in the lower box, you add a story or several stories to an article. All stories in the upper Stories list will become part of the article you define. Whereas multiple stories can become part of an article thread, only one article thread can be defined at a time.

- **Add:** The Add button is used to place a story in the upper Stories list. Select a story in the lower box and click the Add button. You can also double-click a story name in the lower Stories list, and the story will appear in the upper Stories list.

- **Remove:** Clicking the Remove button will remove a selected story from the upper Stories list. A story must be selected before the Remove button can become active.

- **Preview:** When you select a story in either the upper or lower Stories list, the Preview button will become active. If you select Preview, a separate window will open to show you the story contents. You can preview the story before you define it as an article.

Often you will have only a single story listed in the current article story list. If multiple stories are contained in the list, all stories will be threaded in the article. When you click the OK button in the PageMaker Stories dialog box after listing a story or several stories, another dialog box will appear for defining the article properties.

✦ **Article Properties:** The fields for Title, Subject, Author, and Keywords are items searchable by Acrobat Search. Just as with the document information discussed in Chapter 2, all the search criteria apply to these fields.

Whenever creating articles in PageMaker, be certain to provide all the article property information. If you want to develop a true PDF workflow, the time you take supplying information for article properties will be much less than having to edit the properties in Acrobat.

When you click OK in the Article Properties dialog box, your article will be defined, and you will be returned to the PDF Options dialog box.

✦ **Add Document Information:** Document information, like article properties, should be provided when creating PDFs from PageMaker. As with the properties just discussed, you will save time by supplying field data here rather than later in Acrobat. To enter document information, click the Edit Info button in the PDF Options dialog box.

✦ **Add Note to first page:** When this option is enabled, the Edit Text button will become active. If you select the Edit Text button, you can add a note to the first page of the PageMaker file. Note attributes are defined in the dialog box that will appear. The display of your note can be open or closed depending on which radio button is selected in the Edit Text dialog box. Notes are all developed in a fixed position. You can't control the location of the note or create notes on other pages. For these controls, look at the last section of this chapter, where I discuss pdfmark.

PDF Control options

Exit the PDF Options dialog box, and you will return to the Export Adobe PDF dialog box where you may access additional options by selecting the Control button (see Figure 6-25).

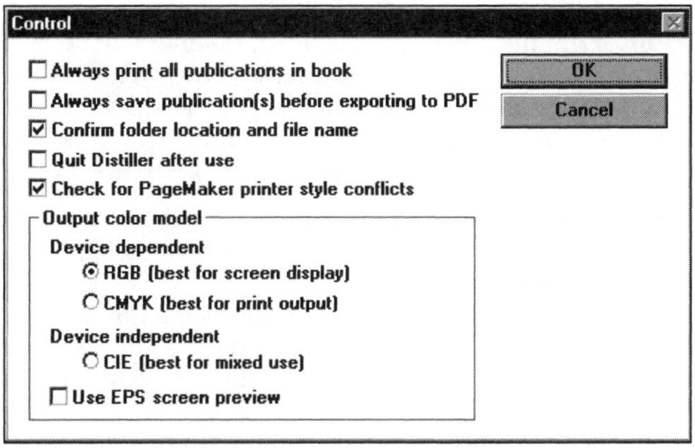

Figure 6-25: From the Export Adobe PDF dialog box, select the Control button to open the Control dialog box.

✦ **Always print all publications in book:** In PageMaker, you can create separate files to be contained within a book. When you're ready to index, develop a table of contents, or print, you can have PageMaker include all separate files into a logical book order via the Book command. When you select Utilities ⇨ Book in PageMaker, a dialog box will appear that offers the opportunity to select the chapters to be contained in the book.

When this option is enabled, all chapters identified as part of the book will be printed to disk as a PostScript file. If disabled, the current open document will be printed to disk.

✦ **Always save publications(s) before exporting to PDF:** PageMaker is notorious for prompting you to save a publication regardless of whether you have edited a page or not. You just look at the PageMaker file, and the program will prompt you for a save before closing the file or exporting to PDF. When this enabler is active, PageMaker will automatically save the document, and then export it to PDF.

✦ **Confirm folder location and file name:** By default the PostScript file and the resultant PDF file will be saved to the folder from which you opened the PageMaker document. When this check box is disabled, and you select the Export button in the Export Adobe PDF dialog box, your PDF will be created without confirmation for the directory path and filename. PageMaker will use the same filename as your application document and make the extension .ps for the PostScript file and .pdf for the PDF file. When enabled, a confirmation dialog box will appear, enabling you to change the final PDF name. In Windows, you need to type in the directory path if you wish to change folders. On the Macintosh, you can use the navigation dialog box to reroute your PDF file.

✦ **Quit Distiller after use:** PageMaker's export to PDF procedure is a two-step process. After the PostScript file has been produced, Distiller will be launched in the background. If you wish to quit Distiller after creating the PDF file, enable this option. If disabled, Distiller will remain open. The Distiller window may appear hidden behind a PageMaker document, but it will still be open. If you have several PageMaker documents to distill, leave the option disabled.

✦ **Check for PageMaker printer style conflicts:** PageMaker provides you the opportunity to capture all the attributes for printing to devices. The printing attributes are determined in the Print dialog box. You can select a PPD, page size, screening, and many other attributes in the Print dialog box and capture these settings to a printer style. When you wish to use the same style, rather than return to the Print dialog box and make all the choices again, select the printer style and print. If there are any conflicts, such as selecting the wrong page size, PageMaker will open a warning dialog box when this option is enabled.

As a default, you should leave this option enabled. Any conflicts will be reported, which can save time in having to redistill files. You should be aware, however, PageMaker is notorious for reporting some problems that do not exist. When the option is enabled, you will commonly see a dialog box appear, informing you the blank pages will not print. Even when no blank pages exist nor are any bookmarks, articles, or hyperlinks established, the warning dialog box still appears. When you see the warning dialog box appear, click the Continue button, and your PDF will print properly — even the best PDF producer on the planet has a few nuances.

✦ **Device dependent:** Two radio buttons appear under this heading in the Output color model section. These choices relate to the color viewing of the PDF documents. If using the PDF for screen views, select the RGB color model. When outputting to color devices or film separations, select the CMYK color model.

✦ **Device independent:** Enable the CIE option under this heading in the Output color model section and, if using a device-independent color system, the PostScript file maps directly to device color, and no color conversion will be produced in the PDF file.

✦ **Use EPS screen preview:** Viewing documents on screen will be defined according to the operating system and the language used to express the screen image. If you select EPS preview, the screen image will look more crude and less polished than the view displayed when using the operating system language. Inasmuch as the printed document will look much better than the EPS preview, you can use this view to see some potential problems with a printed document.

After clicking the OK button in the Control dialog box, you will once again return to the Export Adobe PDF dialog box. All of the settings discussed thus far involve the attribute choices you can make for the PDF file produced from the Export Adobe PDF dialog box. By default, you print the PostScript file to disk using a printer style for Acrobat that has been defined as the default printer style PageMaker uses to create the PDF document. If you want to make changes to the printed PostScript file, which will ultimately be converted to PDF, you may need to select options from Pagemaker's Print dialog box. For example, suppose you make all your choices in the Export Adobe PDF dialog boxes, but want the file to be printed as separations, or you wish to select a halftone frequency. These printer attributes are established in PageMaker's Print dialog box, not with the export dialog boxes.

Creating printer styles

When poking through all the export options, you can't get to the Print dialog box in PageMaker while working in the Export Adobe PDF dialog box. In this dialog box, you can choose printer styles from a pop-up menu. Before you can access a printer style, you need to create it in the Print dialog box. Once a style has been created, it will appear as a choice from the pop-up menu in the Export Adobe PDF dialog box. To create a printer style, let's walk through the steps needed for setting print attributes, which will ultimately be used in exporting to PDF.

STEPS: Creating Printer Styles in PageMaker

1. **Select File ➪ Printer Styles ➪ Define.** To create a new style, you need to open the Define Printer Styles dialog box. When you open the dialog box, the Acrobat printer style will have been developed for you and appears as a listed style, as shown in Figure 6-26. The current settings for printed documents will be specified in the lower half of the dialog box when [Current] is selected in the Style list.

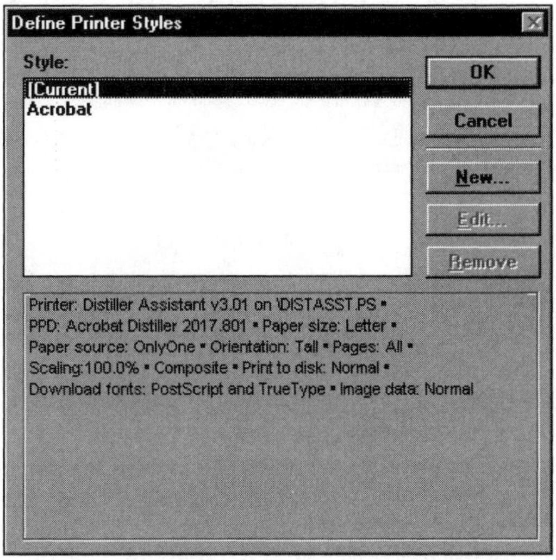

Figure 6-26: When you select File ➪ Printer Styles ➪ Define, the Define Printer Styles dialog box will appear, listing all previously defined styles and affording you an opportunity to create a new style.

Continued

2. **Select New.** To define a new style, click the New button appearing in the Define Printer Styles dialog box.

3. **Name the style.** When you select New in the Define Printer Styles dialog box, you will be prompted to supply a name for your new style. Use a descriptive name so the style can be easily identified when you wish to access it in the Export Adobe PDF dialog box.

4. **Define document attributes.** After supplying a name and clicking the OK button in the Name Printer Style dialog box, the first of several dialog boxes presenting printing options will appear. The Document specifications dialog box enables you to select the PPD, page range, and orientation of the printed file. Be certain to select the Acrobat Distiller PPD and select All for the page range.

Note

You need not be concerned about a page range for the settings in this dialog box. When you export to PDF, the Export Adobe PDF dialog box offers an opportunity to select a page range that will override the settings in the Print dialog box. The same holds true for the Print all publications in book setting.

5. **Define paper attributes.** Paper attributes have to do with paper sizes, and whether you wish to have crop marks and printer's marks, tiling, and sizing. If you have a bleed in your document and wish to display crop marks so you know where to cut the paper when printed, click the Printer marks option to enable it. For this example, I decided to set up a style where printer's marks will be displayed, as shown in Figure 6-27. Because the printer's marks would have appeared outside the page range otherwise, I also needed to set up a new page size. By selecting Custom from the pop-up menu, I could determine what size the paper should be to accommodate the image and printer's marks.

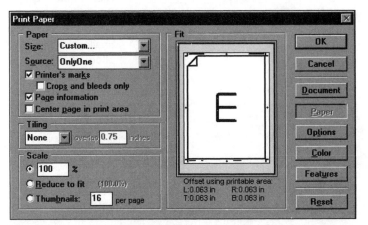

Figure 6-27: In the Print Paper dialog box, I specified that printer's marks and page information be included in my final PDF document.

Note

When you ask for crop marks or any of the printer's marks and select Custom from the Size pop-up menu, PageMaker will automatically supply a recommended value for a page size large enough to accommodate all data without clipping the image.

Note

If you prepare files for output to imaging centers, always be certain to ask the technicians if they want the document transversed. If you select the Transverse check box, the document will be rotated 90° when printed on an imagesetter. Transversing documents saves media on roll-fed machines. Many imaging centers will use media optimization features on their machines that automatically transverse portrait images to print landscape. If you select Transverse, you may be transversing transversed media – that is, like a double negative, the effect will be canceled out, and the image will be clipped. To avoid such problems, always inquire about transversing before you deliver your job to the imaging center.

6. **Print options**. After clicking OK in the Print Paper dialog box, select the Options button. Options in this dialog box enable you to specify attributes for placed images, encoding methods, font inclusion, and the type of PostScript file to be printed. Be certain to select binary for the data encoding method from the pop-up menu. Also, be certain to not select EPS. You need to print a PostScript file — not an EPS file — to disk (see Figure 6-28).

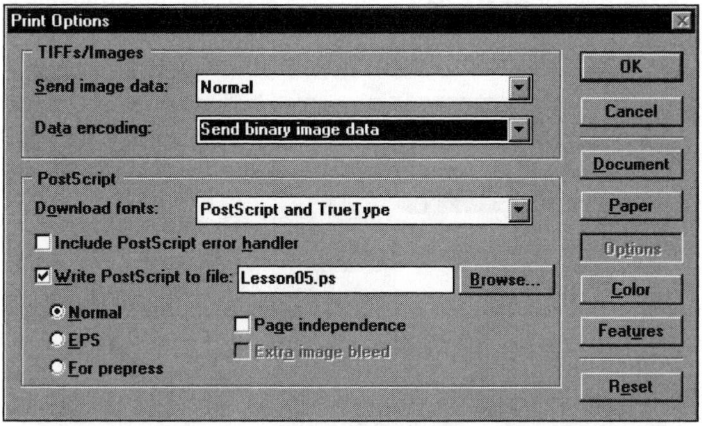

Figure 6-28: In the Print Options dialog box, I selected Send binary image data from the Data encoding pop-up menu and the Write PostScript to file option.

7. **Color settings.** Click the Color button to open the Print Color dialog box. This dialog box is used to establish the halftone frequency in the PostScript file. You can make choices for printing either composite color or separations as well as choose specific colors to print.

8. **Resolution settings.** Click the Features button to open the Print Features dialog box. You can make a choice for resolution output from within this dialog box.

Note

In almost all cases, the output resolution is not necessary to establish in the Print Features dialog box. If outputting to high-end devices, the device resolution will typically override any selections you may make here. On a rare occasion, such as when using older software in which the number of gradient steps is determined from output resolution, these settings might make a difference. However, because PageMaker doesn't use such methods, it's not necessary.

9. **Verify your settings.** When you click OK in the Print dialog box, you will be returned to the Define Printer Styles dialog box. When your new style name is selected in the Styles list, the lower half of the dialog box will display all the settings that PageMaker will use when printing with this style. Review the style attributes to be certain all settings you expect are listed in the dialog box.

10. **Export Adobe PDF with a new printer style.** When you click OK in the Define Printer Styles dialog box, shown in Figure 6-29, the new style will appear when you select File ⇨ Printer Styles. New styles are added to the submenu. If you select File ⇨ Export ⇨ Adobe PDF, the pop-up menu for PageMaker's printer style will list all your new defined styles.

Note

In addition to the printer style you select, be certain to choose the Apply printer styles settings from the Page size(s) pop-up menu in the Export Adobe PDF dialog box.

Define Printer Styles

Style:
[Current]
Acrobat
PDF 133lpi
PDF Custom/crops

OK
Cancel
New...
Edit...
Remove

Printer: Distiller Assistant v3.01 on \DISTASST.PS •
PPD: Acrobat Distiller 2017.801 • Paper size: Custom •
Paper source: OnlyOne • Orientation: Tall • Pages: All •
Crop and registration marks • Print page information •
Scaling:100.0% • Composite • Angle: 45.0° • Ruling: 133.0lpi •
Print to disk: Normal • Download fonts: PostScript and TrueType •
Image data: Normal • Resolution: 2400dpi

Figure 6-29: I defined a new style, opened the Export Adobe PDF dialog box, and selected the pop-up menu for printer's styles. My new style name appears in the menu list.

To test your new style, select it from the list, as displayed in Figure 6-27, and click the Export button in the top-right corner of the dialog box. When distillation is completed, view the document in an Acrobat viewer to be certain it exported as you expected.

Export Adobe PDF version 3.01

A newer plug-in for exporting PageMaker files to PDF is available for downloading from Adobe's Web site. Version 3.01 of the Export Adobe PDF was created to offer a more *print like* user interface. All the controls in the Export dialog boxes presented earlier in this chapter are available with version 3.01, but the structure and display of the dialog boxes are quite different. If you use PageMaker and other Adobe products regularly, you'll want to upgrade to the newest plug-in for exporting PageMaker files to PDF. The user interface and design of the dialog boxes will be consistent with newer releases of other Adobe software.

Note As of this writing, Adobe has not yet released a newer version of the Export to PDF plug-in for PageMaker, which would deal with attributes more consistent with Acrobat 4.0. If you regularly use PageMaker and Acrobat, you should plan on making frequent visits to Adobe's Web site. When an update is released, you can download it off the Web site.

Installing Export Adobe PDF version 3.01

When you download version 3.01 of the Export Adobe PDF plug-in, you need to decompress the downloaded file. Double-clicking the file will launch the installer utility and decompress the files. On the Macintosh, you need to move the Export Adobe PDF.add file to your PageMaker folder and place it in PageMaker:RSRC:Plug-ins. This file must be in your plug-ins folder to change the export dialog boxes.

In Windows, when you decompress the file as noted previously, find the Exppdf.add file and copy it to Pm65 (your PageMaker application folder)\Rsrc\<language>\ Plug-ins folder. The <language> item denoted is the language you determined upon installation. If the language was USenglsh, then the directory path would be Pm65\Rsrc\USenglsh\Plug-ins.

You must copy these files to the respective folder on your system and restart PageMaker to have the plug-in take effect. If you run into any problems after installing the plug-in, trash the old plug-in and reinstall by following the preceding steps.

Using the 3.01 Export plug-in

When you open a PageMaker document and select File ➪ Export ➪ Adobe PDF, the Export dialog box will appear. This dialog box more closely resembles a dialog box you'd expect to see when printing a document, rather than the Export dialog box that was discussed earlier.

Note Note the buttons for PDF Options and Control have been removed. All the options available to you are accessed by choosing the various categories listed in the pop-up menu at the top of the dialog box. The default category is General, as displayed in Figure 6-30. Any of the items on the pop-up menu can be selected, or you can navigate through the dialog box views for these categories by selecting the Next or Previous buttons on the right side of the dialog box.

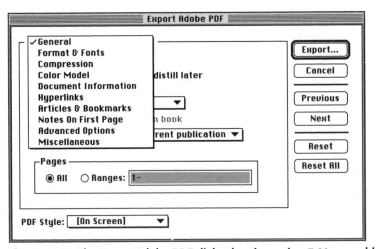

Figure 6-30: The Export Adobe PDF dialog box in version 3.01 resembles a print dialog box rather than earlier versions of the Export dialog boxes. The pop-up menu is revealed to present options similar to the ones you have with the earlier export to PDF version.

General settings

Several options appear in the General settings view of the Export Adobe PDF dialog box that are the same as those discussed in context of the earlier version of the export plug-in. Printer styles have been relocated and now appear below the choices for distillation and PostScript printing. A new addition to this plug-in is the PDF type pop-up menu. Two predefined styles have been established for your use. The PDF style for [On Screen] is consistent with ScreenOptimized in Acrobat 4. The second choice, [Print], is consistent with PrintOptimized in Acrobat 4. You can define new styles, save the styles to exchange with other users, and load styles developed locally or from other systems. Also, the new printer style, Same as Current Publication, uses only print styles available in the current publication.

Formats & Fonts

Compatibility and font embedding is determined in the Format & Fonts view of the Export Adobe PDF dialog box. You can choose to move to this view from the General view by selecting Format & Fonts from the pop-up menu, clicking the Next button, or pressing the down arrow key on your keyboard.

Compression

The compression settings have been reorganized in version 3.01 of the plug-in. You have the same choices for automatic and manual compression as were available in the earlier version of the plug-in; however, all the automatic and manual choices have been contained in one pop-up menu. Also, when choosing the Acrobat 3 format, you have two additional choices for ZIP compression.

In addition to the two ZIP compression choices, note the options for downsampling have changed. The Same as original option has been introduced as a pop-up menu choice for the Resolution setting. This modification was made to help make it more clear as to when no downsampling is used.

Color Model

The same choices for device-dependent color and device-independent color as well as the EPS preview option are contained in the Color Model view.

Document Information

Rather than clicking a button to open a new dialog box, the document information can be supplied via the Document Information view of the Export Adobe PDF dialog box. Entries in this dialog box are the same as discussed earlier in the chapter (see Figure 6-31).

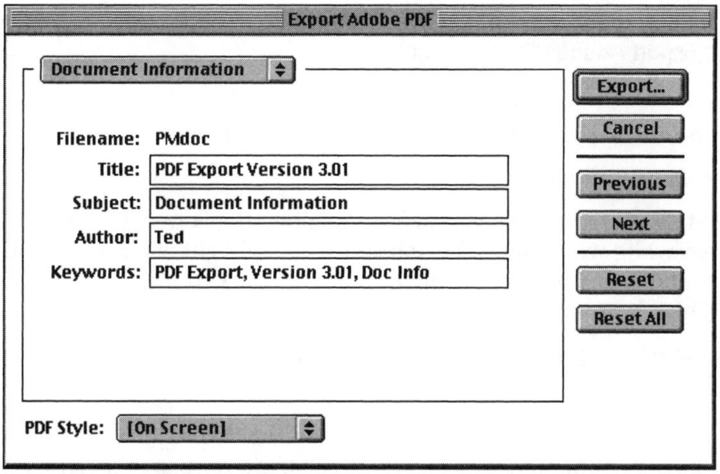

Figure 6-31: Document information is provided in the Document Information view of the Export Adobe PDF dialog box, which appears after the Color Model view.

Hyperlinks

In addition to the options for exporting links for tables of contents, the Hyperlinks view of the Export Adobe PDF dialog box (see Figure 6-32) introduces new options not found in the earlier version of the export plug-in. The items available under Default Appearance include the following:

✦ **Type:** Two options are available from the pop-up menu: Visible and Invisible. When Visible is selected, the Width, Color, and Style pop-up menus will become active. A visible link can be displayed with a rectangular box around the defined link.

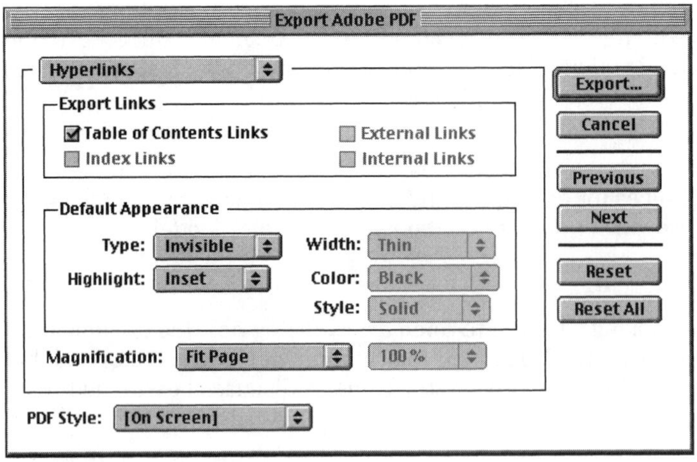

Figure 06-32: New additions to the Hyperlinks settings include attributes for link appearance that are defined in the Hyperlinks view of the Export Adobe PDF dialog box.

✦ **Highlight** provides four options for highlighting a link when selected:

- **None** will deliver no highlight.

- **Invert** displays the link with inverted colors. Black text, for example, will appear white when the link is clicked. The highlight will remain until the mouse button is released, which returns the link to the view before the highlight and invokes the link action.

- **Outline** will display a link with an outline surrounding it when that link is selected.

- **Inset** will make the link appear embossed or recessed when clicked.

✦ **Width** options include Thin, Medium, and Thick. An outline of a visible link can be illustrated with these three line widths. These views are similar to a hairline, 1-point, and 2-point strokes, respectively.

✦ **Color** enables you to select from a number of preset colors for the link rectangle, or you can choose a custom color. When you select the Custom option from the Color pop-up menu, your system color picker will appear. Selecting a color in the color picker and clicking OK will define a custom color for the link appearance.

✦ **Style** enables you to choose between either a solid line or a dashed line for your link border. Solid is the default. To make the link border a dashed line, select the choice from the pop-up menu.

The last pop-up menu provides choices for the magnification view of the page when the link action is invoked. The five viewing options are the same as those discussed earlier; however, the magnification settings are only available when selecting the Fit Top Left of Page option from the Magnification pop-up menu.

Articles & Bookmarks

Options for articles and bookmarks appear in the same view. To define articles, select the Define button in the Articles & Bookmarks view of the Export Adobe PDF dialog box. Subsequent dialog boxes for defining articles, the same as those discussed earlier, will appear. The separation of hyperlink settings from article and bookmark options make the dialog box organization in version 3.01 a bit neater than the earlier version of the export plug-in.

Note If you have difficulty in accessing the Create Index Bookmarks option, it may be due to a loss of the index attributes. If you disturb the index in any way, all the index definitions will be lost, and you won't be able to create bookmarks from an index. For example, cutting the index text block and pasting it on another page will lose the index attributes. If this happens, you may need to create another index by selecting Utilities ➪ Create Index.

Notes On First Page

Adding a note to the first page of the exported PDF from PageMaker is handled through a separate view in the dialog box. When you leave the Articles & Bookmarks view by selecting Next or pressing the down arrow key, the Notes On First Page view appears. The same options for notes exists in version 3.01 as in the earlier version of the plug-in.

Advanced Options

In the earlier version of the export plug-in, the advanced options were accessed from the PDF Job Options dialog box. Now in version 3.01, advanced options appear in a separate view. All settings here are the same as those discussed for the earlier version of the plug-in.

Miscellaneous

The last view in version 3.01 of the Export Adobe PDF dialog box is Miscellaneous. The new version streamlines the various choices you have for exporting PDFs. Options that were found in several different dialog boxes in the earlier plug-in are now collected in this dialog box.

Saving a PDF Style

After you travel through all the views in the Export Adobe PDF dialog box, you can save the attribute choices you make and capture them in a style. The style will be saved as a separate file that can be exchanged among computer users. Different styles can be created by users in an office environment on either Macintosh or PC platforms and the styles exchanged across platforms. By importing standard style formats for your PDF exports from PageMaker, you can develop PDF workflows for publication needs and document repurposing throughout your company. Here's an example of how I created a PDF style on a Macintosh for use on my NT workstation.

STEPS: Creating PDF Styles for Cross-Platform Use

1. **Create the style attributes.** From a PageMaker application document, I selected File ⇨ Export ⇨ Adobe PDF. Using the 3.01 export plug-in, I set the attributes in the resultant dialog box to create a PDF document for output to high-end digital prepress. I used the Acrobat 3 format, subset fonts at 100 percent, set the image compression to the lowest JPEG compression, and made other choices for prepress considerations.

2. **Save the PDF style.** After all the attribute choices were made in the Export Adobe PDF dialog box, I selected Save PDF Style from the pop-up menu in the export dialog box.

Note

The Save PDF Style option from the pop-up menu can be selected from any of the views in the Export Adobe PDF dialog box. Provide a descriptive name when saving the style. If you work in Windows, the style name does not need to adhere to standard DOS conventions. In the example, I used Prepress PDF Style.

3. **Review the settings.** When the Save PDF Style pop-up menu choice was made, a dialog box appeared with a list of all my attribute choices, as shown in Figure 6-33. I reviewed the list and clicked the Save button.

Save PDF Style

Save PDF Style as:

`Prepress PDF Style`

[Save]   [Cancel]

Target: Distiller
Printer style: Acrobat
Do not include all publications in book
Page size(s): Same as current publication
Compatibility: Acrobat 3.0
ASCII format: OFF
Embed all fonts
Subsample fonts below 100%

Figure 6-33: When you select Save PDF Style in any of the views of the Export Adobe PDF dialog box, another dialog box appears with a list of all your current attribute selections.

---

4. **Locate the PDFStyles.cnf file.** I located my PDFStyles.cnf file in the Adobe PageMaker:RSRC:Plug-ins folder on my Macintosh computer.

5. **Copy the PDFStyles.cnf file to another computer.** I used Miramar Systems MacLan Connect to network my PC and Macintosh and mounted the PC Volume using AppleShare on my Macintosh. I opened the destination folder on my NT workstation from the Macintosh mounted volume and navigated to PM65 (PageMaker directory)\Rsrc\Usenglsh\Plugins and copied my PDFStyles.cnf file to the plug-in folder.

6. **Select the PDF style in the Export Adobe PDF dialog box.** I launched PageMaker in Windows NT and opened a PageMaker document. I then selected File ⇨ Export ⇨ Adobe PDF. When the Export Adobe PDF dialog box appeared, as shown in Figure 6-34, I selected Prepress PDF Style, which was the name I provided when the style was saved on the Macintosh.

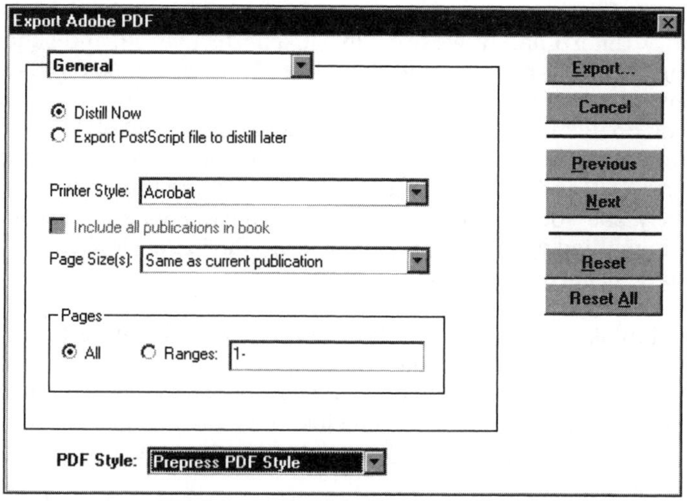

Figure 6-34: The style(s) you create on one system can be used on another system when the PDFStyle.cnf file is copied to the PageMaker plug-ins folder.

Removed features from the version 3.01 Export Plug-in

Some features that were available in the earlier export plug-in have been removed from the newer version, including the following:

✦ **Bookmark definitions for TOC Entries:** In version 3.01, you cannot change bookmark names. If you wish to change bookmark names, you need to either use the older version of the export plug-in or make those changes in Acrobat.

✦ **View PDF Using (Windows):** Windows users can view a PDF document after distillation by using Windows Explorer and selecting View ⇨ Options ⇨ File Types. From the menu, you can choose to view the PDF before returning to PageMaker.

✦ **Watched folders:** When reviewing the views for the Export Adobe PDF dialog box for version 3.01 of the export plug-in, you may have noticed there was no option to use watched folders. Watched folder definitions have been removed from version 3.01. For PDF workflow, you can print the PostScript files to a watched folder directory and use Distiller for all PDF file attributes set up for the watched folders.

pdfmark

If you're thumbing through the pages ahead wondering when I'm going to finish up this chapter, hold on — there is still more to work through when creating PDF files from various applications. All of what was discussed in the preceding section is fine if you are a PageMaker user or if you're willing to learn PageMaker. In a perfect world, we would all be up to speed on the tools needed to produce documents with ease and clarity. Unfortunately, we don't live in a perfect world, and I know getting some of you users of Quark, Microsoft Publisher, Ventura, and so on to even look at PageMaker might be a challenge. In some cases, it would be downright impossible. So what do you do if you're not willing to take advantage of all of PageMaker's PDF export controls, and you create massive catalogs in some layout application that doesn't support TOC and index entries? Fortunately, there is an option for you. It may not be easy, and you may need to poke around with some programming steps, but just about anything you can do to a PostScript file in PageMaker can also be accomplished by using a pdfmark annotation.

If you stop and think about it, anything you see as a graphic image on your screen could be created in a text editor using PostScript programming code. You certainly wouldn't want to create graphics by code. It takes over 185 pages of raw text and over 100,000 characters in PostScript code just to create a page that has the word *text* on it when printed. Imagine what you might have to do just to draw an object, let alone an entire layout?

Fortunately, you don't have to begin editing a PostScript file by starting from scratch. You can supply edits to PostScript code in the form of annotations known as pdfmark annotations. A pdfmark operator can be used to identify a TOC entry, add a note to a PDF file, add a bookmark, create a transition, or add almost any kind of element you desire. You can add pdfmark annotations in two ways. You can write the code in a text editor and concatenate two PostScript files; or you can create an EPS file that can be placed on a page to create elements and effects you wish to have appear in the PDF file. The EPS file you place contains the pdfmark annotations needed to produce the desired effect. To see how all this works, let's first explore editing PostScript code and then look at placing EPS files with pdfmark annotations.

Annotating PostScript Code

Technical information on pdfmark annotations is provided in the Help files contained on your Acrobat Installer CD. When you install Acrobat and include all the Help files in the installation, the PDFMARK.PDF document will be included in the Help folder. This document is the PDFMark Reference Manual provided by the Adobe developer team, and it explains how to use pdfmark annotations. For a complete review of pdfmark and the syntax used for adding notes, bookmarks, links, and many other features in PDF files, refer to the technical manual.

To help understand how annotating PostScript code is handled, let's take a look at adding a note to a PDF document during distillation. When working with Adobe PageMaker, a note can be added to the first page of the PDF when using the Export Adobe PDF command. The note will appear in the PDF in a fixed position on the first page. However, you cannot use this command to change the note position on page 1 or to have a note or several notes appear on pages other than page 1. Furthermore, when using programs such as QuarkXPress, Microsoft Publisher, or other applications, you won't have opportunities to create notes until you add them in Acrobat.

In a PDF workflow environment, you may wish to set up files that can automatically create notes when distilling PostScript files with Acrobat Distiller. Whereas document information is limited to some description of the PDF file, notes provide you opportunities for adding descriptions to individual document pages. Furthermore, notes can be customized to display different colors and titles that can be set up to be unique for each individual PDF author. In a workflow environment, you can exercise control over who's adding note information and easily identify the contributors.

Once you create a PDF file from a program such as Adobe PageMaker, QuarkXPress, or any other application capable of generating multiple pages, you may wish to have a note or several notes added to the PDF file. Notes can be added in Acrobat; but, in order to do so, individual authors need to have Acrobat loaded on their computers and add notes manually on the desired pages. By using pdfmark, you can create a separate PostScript file with the note contents and note color, and specify the document pages on which you want the notes to appear. When you open the PDF in an Acrobat viewer, the note(s) will appear as you defined them.

Note attributes

To add a note with pdfmark, you need to be precise about coding the information in the PostScript file you write, which will be concatenated with the document PostScript file. There are several note attributes to be addressed. Some of these attributes are required and others are optional. Table 6-3 describes the note attributes available for definition with pdfmark. In Table 6-3 several *types* are associated with the attributes:

✦ **string:** An alphameric string of characters. Typically strings will include text, — for example, the contents of the notes.

✦ **array:** A mathematical expression — will consist of numeric values. A quadrant would be composed of four numeric values in an array to define the *x, y* coordinates of the opposite diagonal corners.

✦ **integer:** Always a whole number.

✦ **Boolean:** A conditional item. May be a switch such as on or off, expressed as *true* for on and *false* for off.

✦ **name:** A specific reference to a procedure or call. Must be expressed as /Name. For example, Page /Next would proceed to the next page in a PDF document.

✦ **Required:** Not among the types already listed. You will find a reference to required in relation to pdfmark semantics in the technical manual. When required is indicated, a value for the procedure must be included.

✦ **Optional:** The opposite of required. If an optional reference is made, you don't need to include the procedure for the key in question.

Table 6-3
Note Attributes

Key	Type	Options	Syntax/Semantics
Rect	array	Required	Rect is an array describing the note boundaries beginning from bottom-left corner to top-right corner. Measurement is in points, with the page boundary at the lower-left corner defined as 0, 0 for the *x, y* coordinates. Syntax for the /Rect key is something like [/Rect 117 195 365 387]. In this example, the lower-left corner of the note is 117 points to the right of the left side of the page and 195 points up from the bottom. The top-right corner of the note is 365 points from the left side and 387 points up from the bottom. The array data must be contained within brackets as shown in the syntax example.
Contents	string	Required	The contents string is what you wish to appear as the note message. The maximum number of characters you can include in the note is 65,535. The text string will scroll within the note boundaries. If you wish to add paragraph returns, enter \r where the return should appear. An example of the syntax for the contents is /Contents (This is my first note with examples in using pdfmark annotations.) Notice the text is contained within parentheses.
SrcPg	integer	Optional	By default, notes will appear on the first page in the PDF file. Eliminate the SrcPg key, and the note will appear as you define using the Rect and Contents keys. If you have multiple pages, you can choose to place a note on any page in the document. An example of the syntax for SrcPg is /SrcPg 2, which specifies the note is to appear on page 2. When identifying a page in a PDF file, you should be aware all pages begin with page 1. Do not use page 0 as the first page when counting the pages.
Open	Boolean	Optional	By default, all notes will appear open. If you wish to have a note appear collapsed, you can use the Open key to do so. The syntax for closing a note is /Open false.
Color	array	Optional	Note colors can be determined prior to conversion to PDF. A three-character array is used with the acceptable values of 1 and 0 (zero). There are eight total permutations for color choices. An example of the syntax for the color array is /Color [1 0 0]. Notice the array values must be contained within brackets.

Key	Type	Options	Syntax/Semantics
Title	string	Optional	The title string will appear in the title bar for the note. You can add any text up to 65,535 characters. If you want to be practical, you would limit the number of characters to display a short descriptive title. An example of the syntax for the Title key is /Title (My Personal Note). Notice the text string is included within parentheses.
ModDate	string	Optional	The date can be described in terms of the month, day, year, hour, minute, and second. Any one or all of the above can be included. Unless you have a need for time stamping, use only the year, month, and day dates. Syntax is either yymmdd or yyyymmdd—for example, /ModDate (20000101) would be used to specify January 1, 2000. Notice the date field is contained within parentheses and no spaces are entered between year, month, and day. When you view the note in an Acrobat viewer, the date stamp will not appear. You need to summarize the notes in the PDF in order to view the date.
SubType	name	Optional	A subtype will commonly not be used with notes. A subtype for something like a link might look like /View [/xyz n n n], where the contents within the bracket is an array describing the view magnification. Another example is /View /Next, which specifies the next page will be viewed when the link button is selected.

Creating a pdfmark annotation

The keys and syntax described in Table 6-3 must be saved in a text file to be distilled by Acrobat Distiller. You can create a pdfmark annotation with a text editor or word processor. If using a word processor, be certain to save the file as text only. You can then combine the text file with the application document that is printed to disk as a PostScript file—just use the RunDirEx.txt file, discussed earlier in this chapter, to concatenate the two files. To see how all this is accomplished, let's walk through the steps to produce a note on page 2 in a two-page document.

STEPS: Using pdfmark to Add a Note to a PDF File

1. **Print a document to disk.** Create a two-page layout in an application such as a layout program or a word processor. After creating the layout, print the file to disk. If using PageMaker and the Export Adobe PDF command, be certain to select the option Prepare PostScript for distilling separately and not the option Distill now.

Continued

2. **Add a comment.** Open a text editor and supply a comment line for your file. All comments begin with %. In my example, I use these three comment lines:

> % Custom Note pdfmark annotation
>
> % Created by Ted Padova
>
> % Places note on page 2

Comments are optional. You don't need the comment line, but it will be helpful if you create many different files for pdfmark annotations. Try to use a comment line so you can return to the file later and know what to expect after distillation.

3. **Define the note boundary.** Your first attempt to create a note and locate it precisely on a page may be awkward. If the coordinates are not supplied properly, your notes may not appear where you expect them. To aid you in the process, try to use a program such as Adobe Illustrator that can provide you with information about coordinate values for an element created on a page. In my example, I used Illustrator 8 to determine where I wanted the note to appear and recorded the coordinates.

Note

When recording coordinate values, do not use a rectangle boundary as your assessment device. The top-right corner of the rectangle will be the coordinates from lower left to upper right for the rectangle and not the page. You need to record coordinate values for the lower-left and upper-right corners respective to the page. To determine these values, use rulers and guides in your application program and read the coordinates from an info palette.

When I drew the guidelines in Illustrator, I used the Info palette to determine the coordinates for each x and y position. In Figure 6-35, the x, y position for the lower-left corner of the note can be read in the Info palette.

4. **Enter the coordinates in the text file.** Once you determine the coordinates for the note position, enter those values for your first line of code. In my example. I entered the following:

[/Rect 117 195 365 387]

You must include all the data within brackets [].

5. **Enter the note contents.** The next line of code will be the note content you wish to appear when the note is open. Add text as you desire and use the /r operator when you wish to provide a double-space. In my example, I added these lines:

/Contents (This document was created by Ted Padova

/rThe document was originally a multiple page QuarkXPress file and the note was added to page 2.)

Note

All carriage returns used in coding the PostScript file will be retained in the note text.

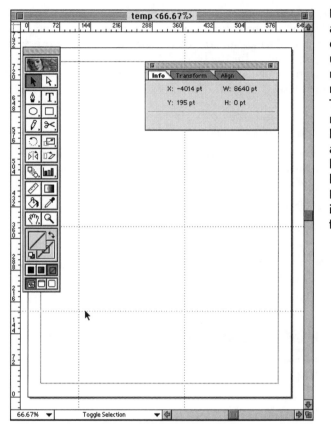

Figure 6-35: When assessing *x, y* coordinates, do not use elements as a measuring tool; use rulers and guidelines. The *x* position will be measured from the left side of the page, and the *y* position will be measured from the bottom of the page. Here, the *x, y* position is measured for the first *x, y* values.

6. **Identify the source page.** If you only have a single-page PDF, or you wish to use the default placement of the note on page 1, you don't need to use the SrcPg value key. In my example, I decided to place the note on page 2, so I added the following line:

/SrcPg 2

7. **Opening and closing notes.** If you wish to collapse the note, use the Open key value and enter false. By default, the Open key will be true, which produces an open note. If you wish to have the note appear open, you can omit the Open key. In my example, I used the Open key, as shown here, just so I could review it at a glance:

/Open true

8. **Enter a title for the note.** The Title value key allows you to specify a string of text to appear in the note title bar. In my example, I included the following line:

/Title (pdfmark Note)

Be certain all the text to appear in the note title is included within the parentheses.

9. **Enter a color value for the note color.** The note will adhere to the defaults set up in the Acrobat viewer unless you make changes, such as choosing another color for the note. To examine the colors available for the note, you can change the array values for the three data fields, by toggling 1s and 0s, and then distill each change. I wanted to change the note color for my example, so I included the following line:

/Color [1 0 0]

These values produced a red note.

10. **Date stamp the note.** Enter a date for a creation date for the note. The date can be viewed when you summarize notes in Acrobat. In my example, I included the following line:

/ModDate (20000101)

When the note is viewed as a summary, the date will read January 1, 2000 (01/01/00).

11. **Save the file as text only.** The file must be saved in text format and not as a native word processor file. In my example, I saved my file as note.ps (see Figure 6-36).

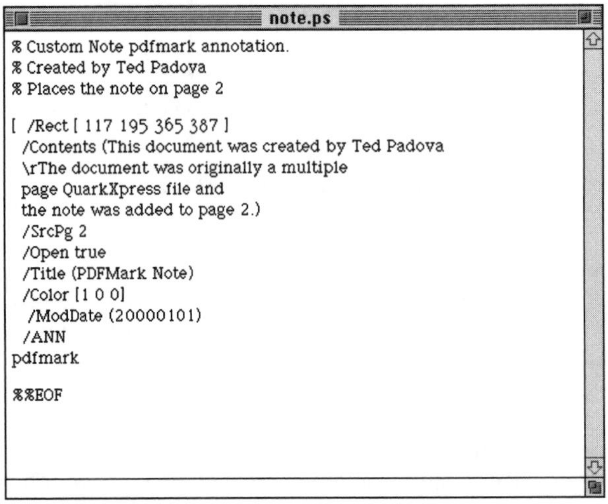

```
note.ps

% Custom Note pdfmark annotation.
% Created by Ted Padova
% Places the note on page 2

[ /Rect [ 117 195 365 387 ]
  /Contents (This document was created by Ted Padova
  \rThe document was originally a multiple
page QuarkXpress file and
the note was added to page 2.)
  /SrcPg 2
  /Open true
  /Title (PDFMark Note)
  /Color [1 0 0]
  /ModDate (20000101)
  /ANN
pdfmark

%%EOF
```

Figure 6-36: The final file was saved as a text-only file from Microsoft Word.

12. **Edit the RunDirEx.txt file.** Open the RunDirEx.txt file from the Adobe Acrobat installer CD and edit it to include the directory path for the files to be distilled in Acrobat Distiller. In my example, I edited the file for the directory path where both my .ps files were saved and named it Run.txt — remember, if you name this file Run.ps, it will be distilled and add another page to the PDF file (see Figure 6-37). To avoid distilling the RunDIREx.txt file, always use an extension that is different from the extensions of the files you are distilling.

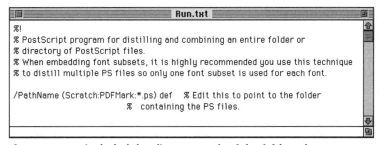

Figure 6-37: I included the directory path of the folder where my PostScript files were saved and renamed RunDirEx.txt as Run.txt.

13. **Distill the RunDirEx.txt file.** Open the new Run.txt file in Acrobat Distiller and save the PDF to a directory of your choice. In my example, I saved the RunDirEx.txt as Run.txt. I opened Run.txt in Acrobat Distiller.

14. **View the PDF in an Acrobat viewer.** In an Acrobat viewer, verify the note appears on the page where you expect it (see Figure 6-38).

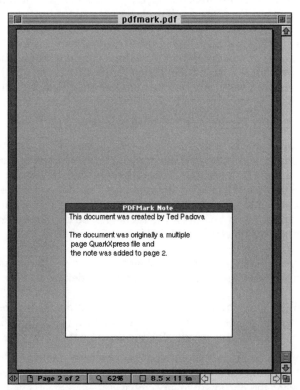

Figure 6-38: I opened my PDF file and navigated to page 2, where the note was to appear.

Annotating EPS files

The preceding exercise for creating a note for a single PDF document may seem laborious. You could easily open Acrobat and draw a note box, enter the text, and be done with it. Unless you have some workflow that uses notes on specific pages in a series of PDF files, it may not be worth your while to try and get the programming code exactly right to produce the effect you want.

Editing in Acrobat does have some limitations that can be downright frustrating. One thing I really miss in Acrobat is having a master page in which you can create a navigational link that will move you forward and back through a document. If you have a hundred page document and want to add a button to move you forward and back, you need to create the link on each page. Of course, the toolbar can be used, but some folks want to use buttons as a design element. Navigational buttons can be a real pain — especially when you consider the fact that you can't copy and paste buttons between pages. Each one needs to be created individually. This is a major limitation within Acrobat. Fortunately, pdfmark provides an alternative.

If you use a layout application that offers master pages, you can create a link to move forward and back on the master page, and that link will be visible on all other pages in your document. To create links on master pages and have the link active in the PDF document, you need to create a pdfmark annotation for the master page link. Placed EPS graphics need to have the EPS file edited for the link action to be included. EPS images can be created in any application you may use for illustration that includes the capability to export to the EPS format. To understand the steps involved in creating such links, I use Adobe Illustrator to create a link in the following example, and then I show you how to annotate the PostScript file.

STEPS: Creating EPS Links with pdfmark Annotations

1. **Create a link icon.** You can create an illustration anywhere on the Adobe Illustrator document page. After the illustration has been created, draw a box around the illustration. The box you draw will represent the hot spot for the link. When the cursor is moved over the rectangle you define for the hot spot, the cursor will change to a hand icon with a pointing finger, indicating an active link is present. When you draw the rectangle, be certain to define the element attributes with no stroke and no fill (see Figure 6-39).

   Note   If you work in keyline mode (Artwork in Illustrator), you can see the invisible rectangle. Use this mode while drawing the rectangle, which defines the link size.

2. **Set the zero point.** Display rulers in your drawing program and move the 0, 0 origin to the lower-left corner of the rectangle you drew (see Figure 6-40). Once again, this will be easier if you are viewing the document in a keyline mode.

   Note   This is a critically important step. If you don't set the ruler origin and leave the default origin at the lower-left corner of your document page, the link won't appear when viewing the document in an Acrobat viewer.

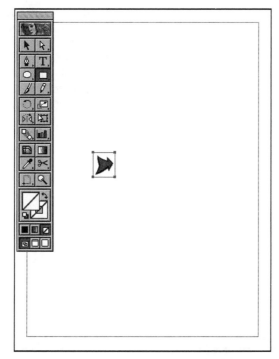

Figure 6-39: I created a brush stroke with one of Illustrator 8's brush patterns and drew a rectangle around the shape. The rectangle attributes were defined with no stroke and no fill.

3. **Record the link size.** The rectangle you draw will form the link boundary. Actually, you can make the link boundary larger or smaller than the rectangle, but keep in mind this rectangle is drawn as a guide to help you assess the link size. With the rectangle selected, view the element information. In Adobe Illustrator, the Info palette will display the size. Make a note of the physical size of the rectangle before exiting Illustrator.

Note

If your document display is in units of measure other than points, you will need to change the display to points. In Adobe Illustrator, select File ➪ Document Setup and change the Units option to points.

4. **Save as EPS.** Save your file in EPS format. If using Adobe Illustrator, you can save the file as EPS with the newest compatibility. All versions of Illustrator EPS files can be annotated with pdfmark.

5. **Open the EPS file in a text editor.** All EPS documents are PostScript code and can be edited in the same manner as was the text file created in the pdfmark annotation example earlier. In this example, rather than creating a separate file, I annotate the EPS file exported from the illustration program.

6. **Locate the placement for the pdfmark annotation.** In the EPS document, find the line of code beginning with %%PageTrailer. This line of code will appear at the end of the file (see Figure 6-41).

Continued

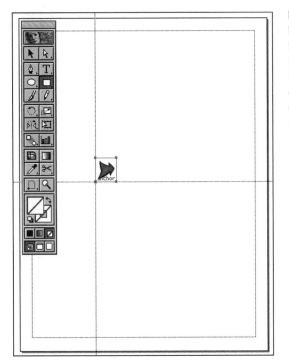

Figure 6-40: In Adobe Illustrator, I selected View ➪ Rulers to display my rulers. From the top-left corner of the ruler well, I dragged the point of origin to the lower-left corner of the invisible rectangle.

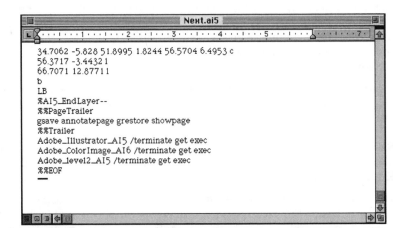

Figure 6-41: At the end of the EPS file, find the line of code beginning with %%PageTrailer.

7. **Enter PostScript code for the pdfmark annotation.** Immediately after the line %%PageTrailer, I entered the lines of code displayed in Figure 6-42.

The /Rect line of code contains the array for the bounding area of the link. These values will have been recorded when you created the link in your illustration program. In my example, the link rectangle was 59 points wide and 45 points high. Therefore, the array values read 0 0 59 45, where 0 0 is the lower-left corner and 59 45 is the top-right corner of the rectangle.

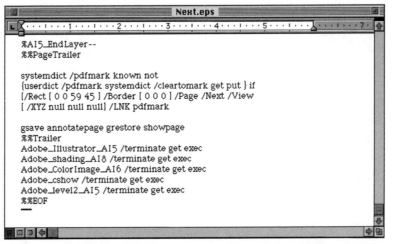

```
%AI5_EndLayer--
%%PageTrailer

systemdict /pdfmark known not
{userdict /pdfmark systemdict /cleartomark get put } if
[/Rect [ 0 0 59 45 ] /Border [ 0 0 0 ] /Page /Next /View
[ /XYZ null null null] /LNK pdfmark

gsave annotatepage grestore showpage
%%Trailer
Adobe_Illustrator_AI5 /terminate get exec
Adobe_shading_AI8 /terminate get exec
Adobe_ColorImage_AI6 /terminate get exec
Adobe_cshow /terminate get exec
Adobe_level2_AI5 /terminate get exec
%%EOF
```

Figure 6-42: With the EPS document open in a word processor, enter the lines of code for the pdfmark annotation as illustrated in Figure 6-41.

The /Page /Next value keys indicate the page destination for the link. If you wish to supply a fixed page number, you can change this line to /Page 2, in which case the link will take the user to page 2.

Notice /Showpage is not included. The showpage operator will create a blank first page. Be certain not to include showpage in the code you supply.

8. **Save the file as text only.** From your text editor, be certain to save the file as text only. The file still has EPS attributes and can be opened in your illustration program or placed as an EPS graphic in a layout application.

If you reopen the file after adding the pdfmark annotation and save it, all the annotated code will be removed from the file. You will need to reopen it in a text editor and rewrite the code.

9. **Place the EPS graphic.** You can place the EPS file saved from your text editor in any application that accepts EPS imports. Be certain to place the image and not *open* it in an PostScript editor. If using a layout application, you can place the EPS file on a master page. All subsequent pages in the final PDF document will display the graphic and retain the link attributes. In my example, I placed the EPS file on a PageMaker master page (see Figure 6-43).

10. **Create a PDF document.** If you place the EPS in QuarkXpress, print the file to disk as a PostScript file and distill it in Acrobat Distiller. If using PageMaker, you can export the file to PDF.

11. **Test your links.** If all the code you entered was correct, clicking a link will advance you to the next page in an Acrobat viewer. When positioning the cursor over the link, you'll immediately notice the cursor change to a hand with the forefinger pointing upward (see Figure 6-44).

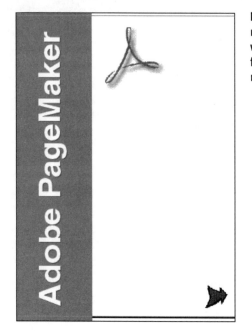

Figure 6-43: EPS links placed on master pages in layout applications will appear on all pages in the PDF file with the image and link attributes retained.

As you might suspect, using pdfmark annotations for EPS links saves you much more time than creating them individually in Acrobat. There are almost infinite opportunities available with pdfmark annotations. You can create libraries of buttons and place them in documents when needed for the actions you wish to include in your PDF documents. As part of the files available to you with your Acrobat Installer CD, you will find a folder containing transitions. Transition effects are pdfmark annotations that enable you to create wipes, venetian blind effects, dissolves, and a host of others for screen viewing. In addition to the transitions, the Distiller:Xtras folder contains the pdfmrkEx.ps file, which provides some samples of different pdfmark annotations for creating document information, cropping specifications, bookmarks, articles, borders, links, and more. The single file contains PostScript code for various pdfmark annotations and comment lines describing each annotation.

Figure 6-44: Each page in the final PDF file contains a link, which was defined on the master page in the layout application. When positioning the cursor over the graphic, the cursor shape will change, indicating a link is present.

Summary

✦ Adobe Photoshop can export directly to PDF. Photoshop 5 can open single and multiple PDF documents created by any producer.

✦ Adobe Photoshop 5 offers a batch processing action that can convert a folder of PDF files to Photoshop files.

✦ Illustration programs such as Adobe Illustrator, Macromedia FreeHand, and CorelDraw can export directly to PDF. Although these capabilities exist, distilling EPS art files in Acrobat Distiller is often preferred.

✦ Adobe Illustrator can open PDF files and access all elements. Individual elements such as text and vector objects can have the attributes changed in Illustrator.

✦ The Adobe PageMaker Export to Adobe PDF command will automatically create a PostScript file, launch Distiller in the background, distill the PostScript file, and return you to PageMaker.

✦ PageMaker offers more PDF control without the use of special plug-ins or XTensions than any other application. PageMaker can create notes, bookmarks on indexes and tables of contents, article threads, and hypertext links, and exercise total control over Distiller's Job Options.

✦ RunDirEx.txt and RunFilEx.txt can be used to concatenate a PostScript file containing pdfmark annotations and multiple application document PostScript files.

✦ You can develop pdfmark annotations in independent text files, have them contained within a PostScript or EPS file, or save them as an EPS graphic and placed in an application document. These annotations can add many different features to a PDF document when those features are not supported in the authoring application.

✦   ✦   ✦

Using Acrobat Exchange

✦ ✦ ✦ ✦

In This Chapter

Using Acrobat
preferences

Editing document
information

Saving PDF
documents

Securing PDF
documents

✦ ✦ ✦ ✦

It's time to now switch gears. The last few chapters looked at creating PDF files. This chapter covers the many ways available to edit and change PDF documents. Acrobat is unique compared with other authoring applications. It's not a page layout program, but you can make some changes to PDF files similar to what layout programs do to application documents. It's not a multimedia authoring tool, but you can import sound, video, and create hypertext links. It's not a database management program, but you can create, import, and export data fields and records. In short, it's hard to describe Acrobat compared to the many software programs we use today.

The Acrobat Environment

With respect to Adobe Acrobat, the Acrobat application is the center of the Adobe Acrobat universe. Each of the other Adobe Acrobat components performs dedicated functions related to their respective duties. These components are specific to a single task and disciplined to perform duties within a narrow scope. Acrobat, on the other hand, is the eclectic workhorse in its capacity to perform many varied tasks, either through core features or add-ons using a plug-in architecture. Through the addition of many different third-party plug-ins, Acrobat's capabilities are continuing to expand. As you begin exploring Acrobat in this chapter, you first examine the Acrobat environment and learn about the many different preferences and document controls that can be customized.

Many preferences for Acrobat are identical to Acrobat Reader. Acrobat adds more to the preference settings, however, and the differences between the Reader and Acrobat preferences are covered here. If you need to refer to preference settings not amplified in this chapter, look back to Chapter 3 for an explanation of preferences that are identical between the two programs.

General preferences

Preferences in Acrobat, like Reader, are accessed when you select File ➪ Preferences. A submenu will appear, displaying either eight menu options (on the Macintosh) or twelve options (in Windows) for different preference settings. Through the use of the Acrobat plug-in architecture, as you add additional plug-ins, you may see preferences appear in the same submenu. If no plug-ins are installed that use preference settings, you'll only see General, Annotations, Full Screen, Forms Grid, Paper Capture, Search, TouchUp, and Weblink on the Macintosh. In Windows, the additional options Digital Signatures, Self-Sign Signatures, Table/Formatted Text, and Web Capture appear (see Figure 7-1).

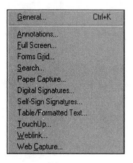

Figure 7-1: The default preference settings for Acrobat on Windows contain twelve items in a submenu accessed by selecting File ➪ Preferences.

The first item available in the Preferences submenu, General, provides you with options for general preference settings. When you select File ➪ Preferences ➪ General, the General Preferences dialog box will appear. Note when comparing the general preference options of Acrobat with those of Acrobat Reader that only a single option differs between the two programs. At the very bottom of the dialog box appears a check box for Skip Editing Warnings, as shown in Figure 7-2.

Enabling the Skip Edit Warnings option will prevent a warning dialog box from appearing when you delete an annotation, bookmark, thumbnail, and so on. If you don't wish to have these dialog boxes appear, click in the check box to enable it. By default, Skip Edit Warnings is disabled—this means a warning dialog box will appear when you perform deletions.

Caution

Be careful when disabling the warning dialog boxes, as most actions you perform in Acrobat do not have an Edit ➪ Undo available. Undos in Acrobat are much less frequent than other applications and quite different than you might expect. If, for example, you accidentally delete an item, you'll need to close the PDF without saving and then reopen it to return to the same place before you deleted any items. A nice new addition to Acrobat 4.0 is the Revert command, found under the File menu. When you wish to return to the last saved version of your document, select File ➪ Revert. A confirmation dialog box will appear that enables you to cancel the command or click Revert to close the current document and reopen the file without the last edits. When Skip Edit Warnings is checked in the General Preferences dialog box, it won't stop the confirmation for reverting a file. This is good—you don't want the Revert command invoked without warning.

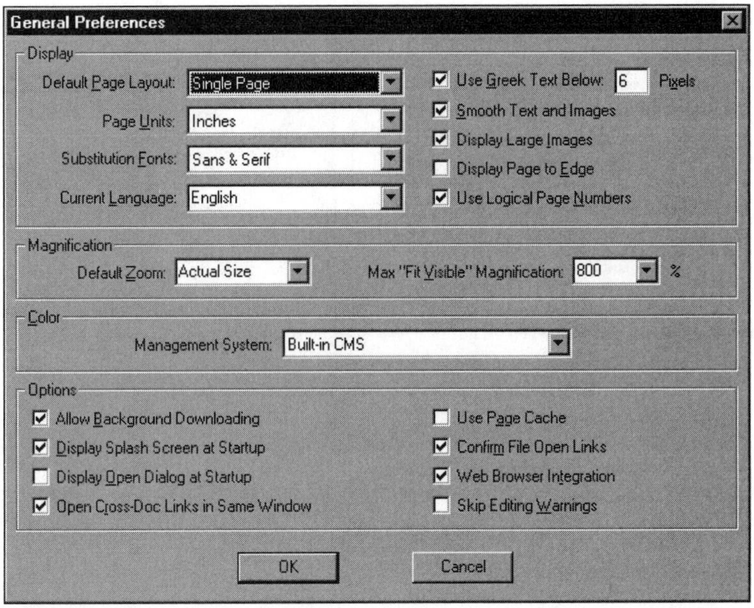

Figure 7-2: The General Preferences dialog box in Acrobat contains the same controls as Acrobat Reader except for the last check box item under Options.

Annotation preferences

With Acrobat Reader, annotation preferences were available for font and font point size only. In Acrobat, you can author several different types of annotations; therefore, additional attributes relative to authoring appear in the Annotation Preferences dialog box (see Figure 7-3). The Author field will default to the username supplied when Acrobat was installed. This field is matched to the individual who is the registered user of the product. If you wish to change the Author name, enter a new name in the field box. You can supply up to 31 characters for the default name, which will appear in the note title bar on all notes associated with annotations. A choice for fonts used within the note text can be selected from your system-installed fonts. Additionally, font sizes can be selected from a pop-up menu. You can choose point sizes for any of the seven preset values. Acrobat does not permit you to make point size selections other than the preset values.

Three additional settings in the Annotations Preferences dialog box can be toggled on or off. These settings relate to the note behavior attached to annotation marks and icons. Notes are associated with almost all annotations you create in Acrobat. A few attribute choices for note attachments are controlled by these three settings:

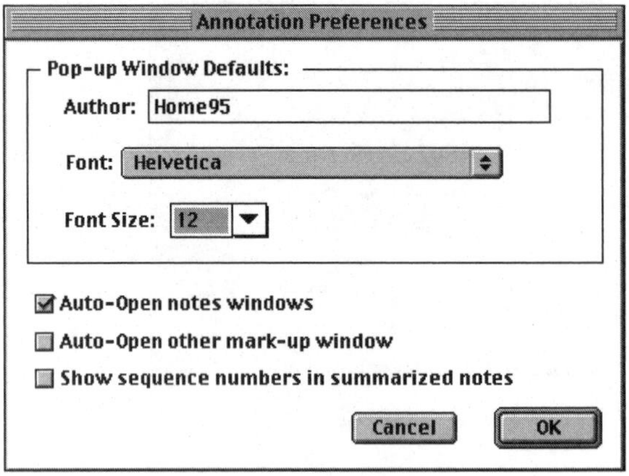

Figure 7-3: The Annotations Preferences dialog box appears when you select File ⇨ Preferences ⇨ Annotations.

✦ **Auto-Open notes windows:** When this option is enabled, the note window where the note text was created in a document is automatically displayed. By default, this option is enabled.

✦ **Auto-Open other markup windows:** Graphic annotations can be made with the Graphic Annotation tools, which also have note attachments. When the check box is enabled, the note windows will also automatically open. By default, this option is disabled.

✦ **Show sequence numbers in summarized notes:** When you enable this check box, all annotations will be numbered according to their creation order. The sequence number will appear on each note icon. By default, this option is disabled.

The preferences available for notes and other preference settings discussed in this chapter will become clearer when you actually work with them. Insofar as annotations are concerned, Chapter 8 takes a look at all the annotation options available to you in Acrobat 4.0.

Full Screen, Search, and Weblink preferences

All the settings for Full Screen, Search, and Weblink preferences are the same as those you have available with Adobe Acrobat Reader. Turn back to Chapter 3 if you need a refresher on these preference settings. Full Screen mode and Adobe Acrobat Search work the same in Acrobat as they do in Reader. Web integration in Acrobat 4.0 is no less than very amazing stuff. The preferences for Weblink are the same for both viewers, but additional features for Web Capture are only available to Windows users. The Web Capture preferences and features for Windows users are discussed in Chapter 14.

Forms Grid preferences

The Forms Grid feature is a new addition to Acrobat 4.0. Those who have used Acrobat in earlier versions will remember how difficult it was to create forms neatly in Acrobat. Form fields were all over the place, and it was difficult to precisely position fields on the same horizontal or vertical plane. Grids are displayed in the View menu when you select View ➪ Show Forms Grid. From the View menu, another option for snapping forms to a grid exists. When View ➪ Snap to Forms Grid is selected, form fields created will snap to a horizontal or vertical grid line or to an intersection of the horizontal and vertical grid lines. You can choose not to display grids but still use the Snap to Forms Grid command. The grid unit of measure is confined to points. Even if you select inches as your unit of measure in the General Preferences dialog box, the grid units will not change. All the grid lines viewed on screen will not print when outputting the PDF file.

When File ➪ Preferences ➪ Forms Grid is selected, the Grid Settings dialog box opens. From these preference choices, you can select attributes for the grid coordinates, point of origin, and grid line colors, as shown in Figure 7-4.

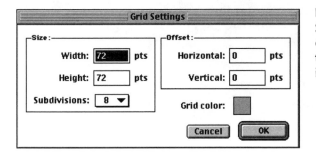

Figure 7-4: The Grid Settings dialog box enables you to customize the grid displayed in the viewer.

The Size side of the Grid Settings dialog box deals with the display of grid lines. You can enter values in the field boxes for major grid lines and then choose the number of subdivisions to be contained within the major lines. Subdivision choices are confined to the preset values available from the pop-up menu. If your number of major grid lines are small and the subdivisions are many, you may lose the minor division views when zooming out in the document window. The acceptable range for the field entries for the Width and Height options range between 1 and 10,000 points.

The offset side of the dialog box enables you to position a zero point for the major gridline intersection from the top-left corner of the PDF page. You need to examine the results carefully because gridline subdivisions will appear to all page edges. If you enter any value other than 0,0 for the horizontal and vertical offsets, the major grid lines will be relocated to the new distance specified in the dialog box. Acceptable values range from 0 to 10,000 points.

A color swatch like the one for the Grid color you see in the Grid Settings dialog box will be displayed in many other dialog boxes for a number of tools. Whenever you see this color swatch appear in a dialog box, the current color selection will be used for the element created. The swatch does not always appear in preferences dialog boxes, but you will run into it when you create such elements as form fields, links, annotations, and so on. The current color choice can be changed in the Grid Settings dialog box and all the other dialog boxes by clicking the swatch. When you release the mouse button, your system color picker will appear. From the color picker, select a new color and click OK (see Figures 7-5 and 7-6). When you return to the dialog box from which the swatch was selected, the new color value will be displayed in the swatch.

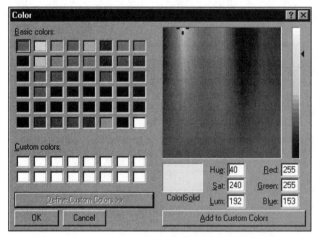

Figure 7-5: The Windows color picker is opened when the color swatch is selected. The dialog box is expanded when the Define Custom Colors button is selected.

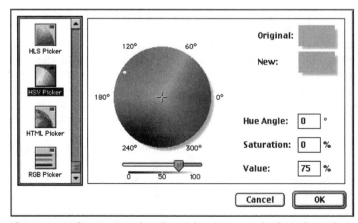

Figure 7-6: The Macintosh color picker is opened when the color swatch is selected on a Macintosh.

Whenever you wish to change colors for any element created in Acrobat or for items in preferences dialog boxes, click the color swatch and make your selections. With preferences dialog boxes, the colors will remain in effect until you change the color during an Acrobat session. Many preference color changes will not be preserved with the application or document. If, for example, you change grid color preferences with an open PDF file, the colors will return to defaults after you quit Acrobat and later reopen the same file. For individual elements, they will also continue to use the same color selection until another choice is made in the respective windows and dialog boxes. However, any colors associated with items created in Acrobat will be preserved after quitting the application and reopening the file.

Paper Capture preferences

Paper Capture preferences do not appear in Reader. Acrobat Capture is an optical character recognition (OCR) application that converts image scans to recognizable text. (The use of Capture is discussed in Chapters 13 and 14.) Earlier users of Acrobat will note the change from Capture to Paper Capture in the Preferences submenu. Now with the addition of Web Capture for Acrobat in Windows, the distinction is made between document OCR recognition with Paper Capture and Web Capture. As you're examining Acrobat preferences here, let's take a brief look at the Paper Capture preference settings. (I cover the Web Capture preferences in Chapter 15.)

When you select File ➪ Preferences ➪ Paper Capture, the Acrobat Paper Capture Preferences dialog box will appear, as shown in Figure 7-7. Choices you can make for Paper Capture preferences include the following:

✦ **Primary OCR Language:** Capture comes with several language dictionaries. You can select a dictionary from the eight listed in the pop-up menu.

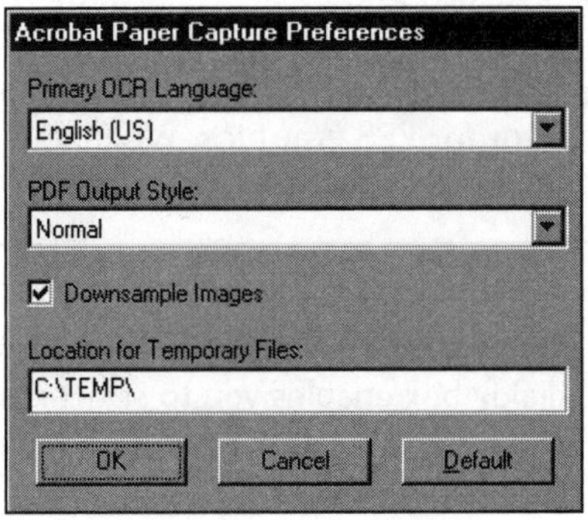

Figure 7-7: Paper Capture preferences are used to determine language and PDF style.

✦ **PDF Output Style:** Two styles are listed in the pop-up menu. The Normal choice will scan your PDF document and convert all recognizable text characters from an image into text. Text characters may change from their original appearance, depending on how Capture interprets them. The second choice is Original Image with Hidden Text. When this option is selected, the original data will not be changed by Capture. Capture's interpretation of the text will appear on a hidden layer so the document maintains display integrity and the text layer can be searched with Acrobat Search. This output style would be useful in cases where the original scan needs to be preserved but the contents need to be searchable, such as with legal documents

✦ **Downsample Images (Windows only):** When the check box is enabled, bitmap images over 300 dpi will be downsampled to 200 dpi. Grayscale and color images over 255 dpi will be downsampled to 150 dpi.

✦ **Location for Temporary Files (Windows only):** A temporary directory for temporary files can be identified by entering the path designation in the Acrobat Paper Capture Preferences dialog box. On the Macintosh, temporary files are stored in a Temporary Files folder, which resides in the Capture folder inside the Acrobat folder.

Tip

Capture will use a folder to temporarily store files while the Capture Server is running. If you wish to relocate the Temporary Files folder on a Macintosh to another drive or drive partition, open the Capture folder inside your Acrobat folder. Make an alias of the folder by selecting it and choosing File ⇨ Make Alias. Leave the alias folder inside the Capture folder and move the Temporary Files folder to your second drive or partition.

TouchUp

Two TouchUp tools are available in the Acrobat toolbox; the TouchUp Text tool and the TouchUp Object tool. This preference setting relates to the TouchUp Object tool. When you select the tool from the viewer toolbox, click a graphic to select it, press the Option/Ctrl key, and then double-click the mouse button, the authoring application for the graphic will be launched. By default, Adobe Photoshop will be used for raster images and Adobe Illustrator for EPS graphics. When you open the TouchUp Preferences dialog box, you can choose to change the defaults to other applications (see Figure 7-8).

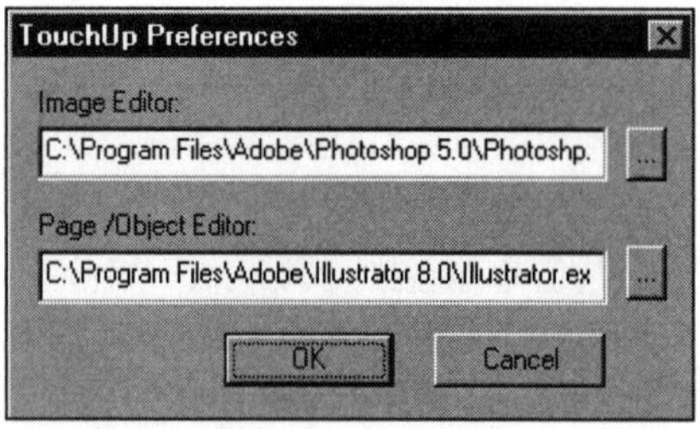

Figure 7-8: The TouchUp Preferences dialog box enables you to select editing applications for raster and EPS images embedded in the PDF file.

Note Adobe Photoshop 5 and Adobe Illustrator 7 and 8 are the only versions of Adobe products supported. Earlier versions of these applications won't work. To change to another application (such as Macromedia FreeHand), click the button on the right side of the Page/Object Editor field. A navigation dialog box will appear that enables you to navigate your hard drive and select another editor.

PDF Document Control

Whereas changes to preferences affect the Acrobat environment globally (that is, any PDF file you open after making various attribute changes will display those changes), document information is document specific. Many of the items available within the Document Info submenu are informational, but some can be changed. Changes you make in the dialog boxes appearing from the submenu after choosing File ⇨ Document Info can be saved with the PDF file. Subsequently opening the PDF document in an Acrobat viewer will show the settings you made were retained when the file was saved.

General Info

The first item in the Document Info submenu is General Info (see Figure 7-9). As mentioned in the discussion of Acrobat Reader preferences in Chapter 3, the General Info fields for Title, Subject, Author, and Keywords cannot be changed in Reader. Because you can't save a PDF file from Reader, there is no need to make these fields editable. In Acrobat, the first four fields can be user-supplied and saved with the file. Remember, you can invoke searches on any of the field data in this dialog box (as first detailed in Chapter 2). Searches require building an index, which is covered in Chapter 12.

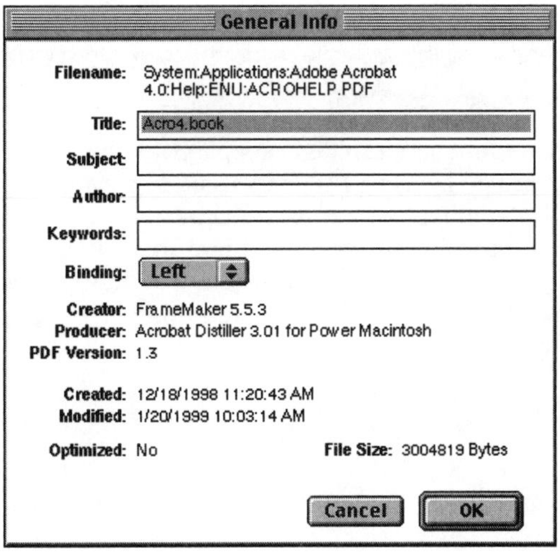

General Info	
Filename:	System:Applications:Adobe Acrobat 4.0:Help:ENU:ACROHELP.PDF
Title:	Acro4.book
Subject:	
Author:	
Keywords:	
Binding:	Left
Creator:	FrameMaker 5.5.3
Producer:	Acrobat Distiller 3.01 for Power Macintosh
PDF Version:	1.3
Created:	12/18/1998 11:20:43 AM
Modified:	1/20/1999 10:03:14 AM
Optimized:	No **File Size:** 3004819 Bytes
	Cancel OK

Figure 7-9: The General Info dialog box contains document information that can be supplied by the user in Acrobat. All changes in this dialog box can be saved and searched using Acrobat Search.

Document information can be supplied in many ways when PDF files are first created. You can enter data in the four fields with PDFWriter, supply data with direct PDF exports from many programs, and even specify data using PDFMark. Key value pairs for PDFMark would be expressed as follows:

/Author (*string*)

/Title (*string*)

/Subject (*string*)

/Keywords (*string*)

You can also add data for fields not editable in Acrobat with PDFMark. Other key value pairs include the following:

/CreationDate (*string*)

/Creator (*string*)

/Producer (*string*)

/ModDate (*string*)

Notice in Figure 7-9 that the date and producer information appears in the dialog box — these items are automatically supplied when the PDF is created.

In some instances, you won't have an opportunity to enter document information when distilling PostScript files unless PDFMark is used. This information can't be supplied with the current version of Distiller. If you use programs without direct PDF export options and create PDF files by printing a PostScript file to disk and distilling the PostScript file, you'll need to add document information in Acrobat. If you create many documents in this manner, you will need to allot quite a bit of time to make all your edits.

Supplying Document Information in a PDF Workflow

If you use programs where document information can't be supplied at the time the PostScript file is created, you will be best served by using PDFMark to hand code the information. Your workflow will move along faster when you can easily copy and paste redundant information to set up new PostScript code for the document information fields. The advantage of using PDFMark is it eliminates the need to resave the PDF from Acrobat, which alone can save quite a bit of time. The precise coding for supplying all document information acceptable for PDF files is illustrated here:

✦ /Title (Acrobat PDF Document)

✦ /Author (Your Name)

✦ /Subject (This is a test document)

✦ /Keywords (author, title, subject, keywords, PDFMark)

✦ /Creator (PostScript code programmed)

✦ /ModificationDate (D:20000101184502)

✦ /DOCINFO

✦ PDFMark

The preceding date field will result in January 1, 2000 at 6:45:02 p.m. Any of these fields can be eliminated. For example, if you wish to use the system clock for time and date stamping, you can eliminate the /ModificationDate value. After coding the preceding information in a text editor, save the file as text only. Use the RunDirEx.txt file to concatenate the application document PostScript file and this file. When distilled with Acrobat Distiller, the information will appear when you select File ⇨ Document Info ⇨ General.

Open Info

When you save a PDF document, you can also save any changes to various attributes that specify how you wish the PDF file to appear when viewed in an Acrobat viewer. The Open Info dialog box, which is accessed by selecting File ⇨ Document Info ⇨ Open, contains many different viewing parameters that can be changed, as shown in Figure 7-10 and listed here:

✦ **Initial View:** The radio buttons on the left side of the Initial View section enable you to specify what will appear on screen when you initially open a PDF file. The Page Only option will display the open PDF document without bookmarks or thumbnails. The options Bookmarks and Page and Thumbnails and Page will display the PDF file with either bookmarks or thumbnails opened, respectively, in the Navigation Pane. When you select one of these options and save the PDF document, the specified display will take effect every time the PDF file is opened in an Acrobat viewer. This section also gives you the following choices for your initial view:

   • **Page:** The document will open on the page specified in the field box. The default is page 1 or the first page in the document. Any other page can be displayed as a new default by supplying a page number here.

   • **Magnification:** Magnification options are selected from the pop-up menu and correspond to those viewing options discussed back in Chapter 2.

   • **Page Layout:** The Page Layout pop-up menu provides choices for Single Page, Continuous, and Continuous — Facing Pages (also discussed in Chapter 2). The default is Single Page view.

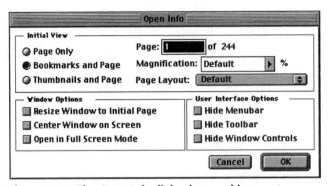

Figure 7-10: The Open Info dialog box enables you to establish viewing parameters that can be saved with the PDF document and take effect when the file is opened in an Acrobat viewer.

✦ **Window Options:** Notice the options provided in this part of the dialog box appear beside check boxes instead of radio buttons. Unlike a set of radio button options, which allow you to specify only one option in that set, you can enable any or all of the following options by clicking their respective check boxes. When none of the options have been enabled, the PDF file will open at the default view, with the Acrobat viewer window occupying a full screen.

  • **Resize Window to Initial Page:** When you set a view, the contents of the PDF document will be displayed in a window, and that window will be sized to fit the document. If, for example, you set the magnification to 50 percent, the document will be viewed at 50 percent and the Acrobat window will be sized down to fit around the page.

  • **Center Window on Screen:** An image that is smaller than full screen will be centered on your monitor. Using the preceding example, the 50 percent window will appear centered on screen.

  • **Open in Full Screen Mode**: Regardless of what you check in the other selections, the PDF file will be opened in Full Screen mode without menus or tools exposed. To bail out of this mode, press the Esc key or Cmd/Ctrl+L.

✦ **User Interface Options:** Once again, the check boxes for these options enable you to select one or more for combined effects. If you wish to hide the menu bar, Tool Bar, and window controls, enable all three check boxes. You might wish to create a PDF document for screen viewing by including all the navigational buttons within that PDF document. If you wish to have the end user use buttons you created and not those on the Tool Bar, you might elect to have the Tool Bar hidden upon opening the document in an Acrobat viewer.

The end result of enabling the various user interface options should not be confused with what you get in Full Screen mode. When the menu bar, Command Bar, Tool Bar, and window controls are hidden, you won't see the same view as when using Full Screen mode. The background color for the viewer window will not change as it does when viewing in Full Screen mode. If you enable the Hide Menubar option and save your PDF file, you won't have access to the menus with the mouse. You'll need to use keyboard modifiers when available. If you want to disable the Hide Menubar option, you must remember to use the F7 key to bring back the menu bar. Once the menu bar has returned, you can select File ➪ Document Info ➪ Open to disable the option.

Fonts and Security

The options for the Fonts and Security items in the Document Info submenu are the same in Acrobat as they are in Acrobat Reader (refer back to Chapter 3 for specifics). Acrobat also offers you the same options for viewing font names, as discussed earlier.

Prepress

The prepress preferences available through the Prepress Options dialog box are informational and permit you to inform imaging personnel whether prepress controls related to trapping or ICC profile embedding are contained in a PDF file (see Figure 7-11).

✦ **Trapping:** The first item in the Prepress Options dialog box is the Trapping drop-down menu, which offers three choices:

• **Yes:** Informs anyone opening the PDF that trapping has been applied to the file. Trapping may be applied to the PostScript file prior to distillation or trapping controls may have been used in authoring applications.

• **No:** Informs the user that no trapping has been applied to the PDF.

• **Unknown:** The default setting is Unknown, which implies the PDF author is not certain whether trapping has been applied to the PDF document. If you are in doubt, always keep this setting at Unknown. Only use the No setting if you are the author of the document application and the PDF file and you are certain these controls have not been applied to the PDF.

✦ **Print 4 color ICC profiles as Device CMYK:** When files are sent to service centers that use calibrated devices, the output is most often device dependent, relying on the calibrated device settings for consistent color reproduction. When this check box is enabled, you are informing the service center to use device-dependent color. Checking this box bypasses a color management system and preserves the original gray and CMYK values in the PDF document. A situation in which you may want to use device-dependent color is when you receive a scan generated from a service center's calibrated scanner and then send the file back to the service center for imaging to their calibrated image or plate setter. Essentially, you are ignoring your monitor color and do not compensate by using your own calibrated profiles. If you used ICC profiles, they will be ignored and the device's calibrated color will be used. By default this option is disabled, which assumes you use a Color Management System (CMS) and wish to have any profiles you use remain undisturbed.

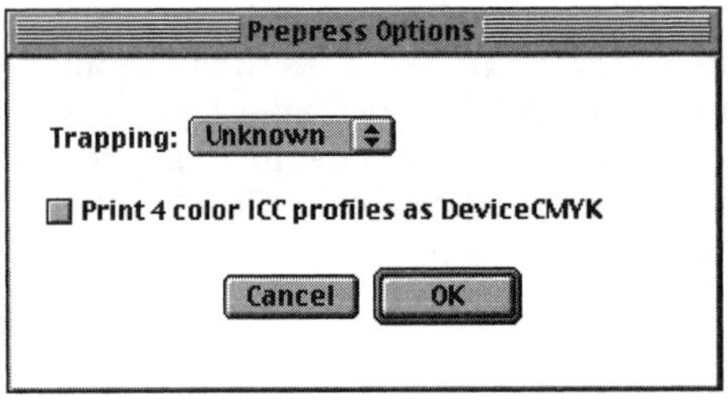

Figure 7-11: The Prepress Options dialog box offers selections for supplying service centers information on trapping and color handling.

Index

The Index setting enables you to identify an index file for an open PDF file. Once you associate an index with an open PDF document, you won't need to load the index in the Acrobat Search Window, as was discussed in Chapter 2. The index associated with your PDF document is volatile and will only be available during a given Acrobat viewer session. When you quit the Acrobat viewer and reopen the file at a later time, you need to once again reassociate the index with the open document. However, if you identify an index and then save your PDF file in Acrobat, the index file will be associated with that PDF file. In this regard, the index file won't need to be loaded in Acrobat Search whenever the PDF is opened.

By default, no index file is associated with a given PDF document at the time it was created. When you select File ➪ Document Info ➪ Index, the Auto Index Info dialog box appears, as shown in Figure 7-12.

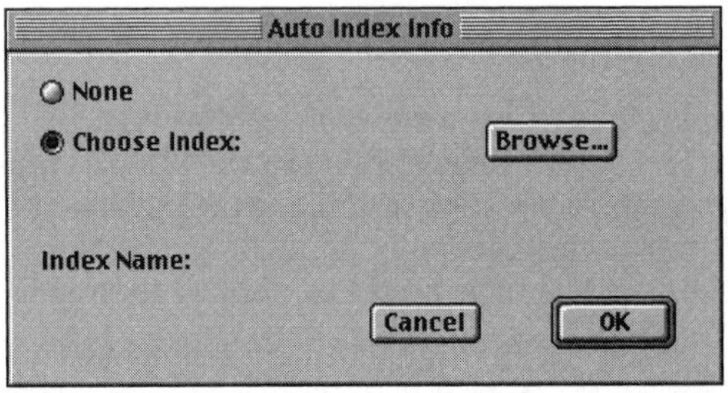

Figure 7-12: By default, no index file is associated with a PDF file, as indicated by the Auto Index Info dialog box shown here.

In the Auto Index Info dialog box, notice a radio button option labeled Choose Index. When this option is enabled, as illustrated in Figure 7-12, the Browse button will become active. If you select Browse, a navigation dialog box will appear that enables you to locate an index file on your computer.

Index filenames default to .pdx when created with Acrobat Catalog. Once you navigate to the directory and find the .pdx file you wish to use with the open PDF document, select it and click the Open button. After clicking Open, you will be returned to the Auto Index Info dialog box, which will now display the index filename and directory path for the index you selected.

Base URL

The Base URL (the acronym for Uniform Resource Locator) feature is designed to make it easy to manage links to the World Wide Web. If URLs to other sites change, you can simply edit the Base URL for the PDF files and not have to change individual links that refer to the site. If the HTML code contains a link with a complete URL, the Base URL in the PDF is not used. To specify a URL for the PDF file, select File ⇨ Document Info ⇨ Base URL.

The complete URL address needs to be identified in the dialog box shown in Figure 7-13. When you exit the file, be certain to save the updated changes. When creating links to the Web, you especially need to optimize your PDF files before uploading to a server. More details on the Web and Acrobat files are presented in Chapter 15.

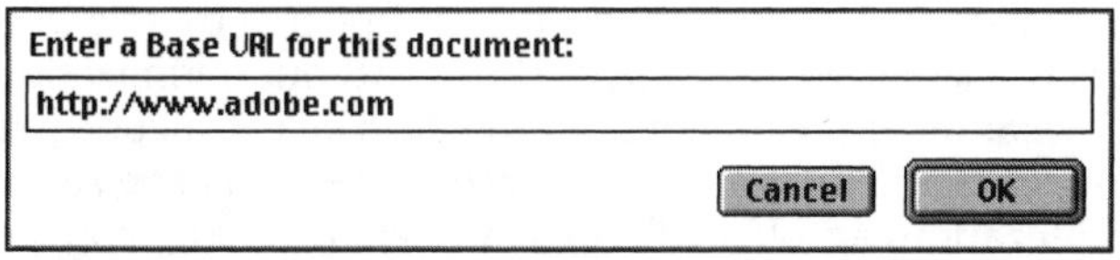

```
Enter a Base URL for this document:
http://www.adobe.com
                                    Cancel        OK
```

Figure 7-13: The Base URL is used to make it easy to manage hypertext links to the World Wide Web. When entering a URL, be certain to include the full URL information.

Saving PDF Files

It stands to reason that no file saves can occur with Acrobat Reader. Because Reader doesn't have any of the editing tools or commands that Acrobat has, it should be obvious that all saved PDF file changes occur in Acrobat. When you open the File menu, you will notice a Save command and a Save As command. If no edits have been performed on a PDF file in an Acrobat session, the Save command will not be available. Save As, however, can be selected any time a PDF file is open (see Figure 7-14). The reason is twofold: You can optimize PDF files and you can add security in the Save As dialog box. If you select File ⇨ Save, these options will not be available.

If you are a Windows user, the Optimize check box is disabled by default. On the Macintosh, the Optimize check box is enabled by default. As you work on a PDF file in Acrobat and perform editing tasks such as removing and adding pages, Acrobat will keep redundant information in the PDF file. When you optimize a PDF file, the file is completely rewritten and streamlined to contain only the necessary data needed to support the PDF format. The file is reorganized and consolidated, which ultimately reduces file size.

Figure 7-14: The Save As dialog box appears with an Optimize check box option and a button for accessing security settings.

As you work on a PDF document in Acrobat and save your updates by selecting File ⇨ Save, Acrobat keeps track of the saves you perform without optimization. A save will append new information at the end of the PDF file. The extra code needed to record the changes you make will increase the file size. After you have saved a file ten times without optimization, Acrobat will open a warning dialog box reminding you to optimize the PDF file.

Optimization is particularly important for Internet and CD-ROM replication. Optimized files can take advantage of byteserving, which enables Internet downloads for a single page within a multipage PDF document. I talk a little more about PDF files and the Internet in Chapter 15, but for now you want to know that any time you use PDF files with the Web you'll want to optimize the file before uploading it to a server. If you have several files to optimize, the command invoked by selecting File ⇨ Batch Optimize will open a dialog box that enables you to choose many options for saving the file (see Figure 7-15).

Figure 7-15: The Batch Optimize command opens a dialog box that enables you to identify the folder containing PDF files you want optimized.

✦ **Select "*folder name*":** The button below the file list is used to select the folder containing the PDF files to be optimized. Navigate to a folder and click the Select button. If you view the folder or open it, the Select button will remain active. This button should be the last you select from the dialog box. When you click the Select button, the optimization process will begin.

✦ **Process All Subfolders:** When enabled, the subfolders contained below the selected folders will also be optimized.

✦ **Optimize:** When enabled, all the files in the batch process will be resaved with optimization.

✦ **Thumbnails:** When you select the Thumbnails option, the pop-up menu to the right becomes accessible. You have a choice to add thumbnails to all files in the folder or remove them.

✦ **Passwords:** When this option is enabled, you have access to the Passwords button. Clicking Passwords opens a dialog box in which you can specify a password for opening a document or changing security options.

✦ **Security:** When the check box beside the Security button is enabled and you click that button, the Security dialog box will appear. You can also enter passwords for opening a document and changing security options in this dialog box. The Security dialog box also affords the opportunity to select which actions can be prevented.

✦ **Open Info:** When you enable the check box next to the Open Info button and click that button, you will see the Open Info dialog box, as discussed earlier in this chapter. This new addition to Acrobat 4.0 enables you to batch process many PDF files, which can be controlled by all the Open Info dialog box options covered earlier.

Sometimes you may forget whether a file has been optimized. If you create large PDF documents, saving large files with optimization can take quite a bit of time. You can determine the optimized status by selecting File ➪ Document Info ➪ General. In the dialog box, Acrobat will display the current status. If the file has not been optimized, you'll see No appear adjacent to Optimized: at the bottom-left of the dialog box.

If you select File ➪ Save with an optimized file, the optimization will disappear, and as a result, Acrobat will immediately update the General Info dialog box whenever the optimization has been changed.

Security

You can add security to PDF files that can restrict either opening a file or editing a file. The encryption method used with Acrobat is the RC4 method of security from RSA Corporation. The method may not be important to you, but keep in mind you will have little chance of breaking password security if you lose or forget your passwords. A PDF file can't be opened in any application if the open access has been secured without the password.

Security settings are accessed through the Save As command. In the Save As dialog box, click the Security button. The Security dialog box opens, as shown in Figure 7-16.

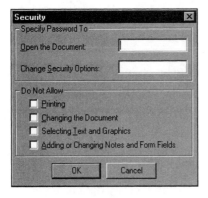

Figure 7-16: The Security dialog box is accessed from the File ⇨ Save As command.

The Security dialog box provides several options:

✦ **Open the Document:** In this field, you supply a password that allows access to the PDF file in an Acrobat viewer. You can enter as many as 255 characters in the field box, but for practical purposes you'll probably want to keep your password to the length of the field box.

✦ **Change Security Options:** In this field, if you enter a password that is identical to the Open password, an end user who knows the Change password can open *and* change your document. If you enter two different passwords in the field boxes, you can have two levels of security—one to open a PDF file and the other to change the PDF file. Once a PDF document is secure, when you attempt to open that document in an Acrobat viewer, the Password dialog box appears, as shown in Figure 7-17. If you enter the password correctly, the PDF will open. If you enter the password incorrectly, a dialog box will open informing you the password is incorrect.

If a document is opened with the Open password, and the capability to change items has been secured, the editing tools and menu commands will be grayed out (Figure 7-18). If the user supplies the Change password, he or she will have access to all editing tools (Figure 7-19).

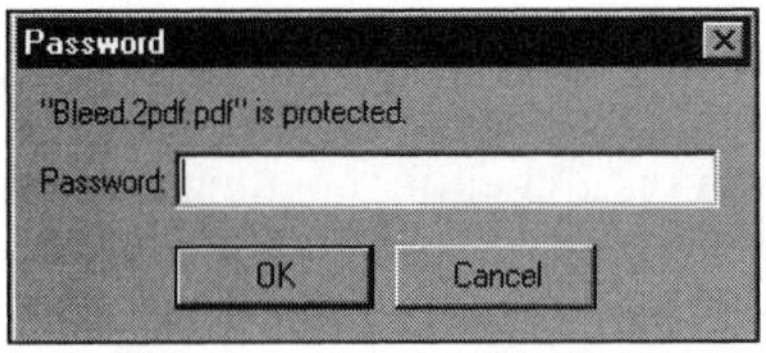

Figure 7-17: When a secure PDF is opened in an Acrobat viewer, a dialog box will first appear requesting a password entry. If the password is not exact, another dialog box will appear indicating the password was improperly entered.

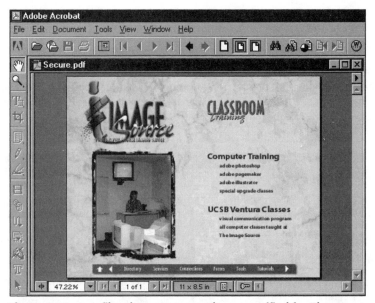

Figure 7-18: In a file where a password was specified for Change Security Options, all the editing tools appear grayed out on the left-hand side of the window.

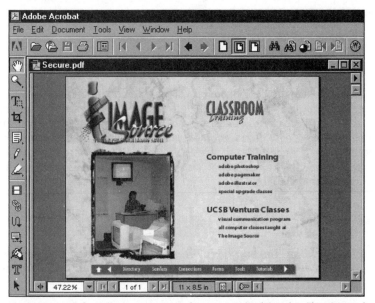

Figure 7-19: The Change password was supplied for the file pictured in Figure 7-18, and all editing tools now appear active on the left-hand side of the window.

✦ **Do Not Allow:** The options can be enabled individually or in combination. If all options are enabled, maximum restriction to editing will be secured. (These four items are discussed in Chapter 3.)

When you supply a password (or passwords), enable the check boxes for the respective items you wish to restrict, and click OK, another dialog box will appear to confirm your password. If two passwords were entered, a separate confirmation dialog box will appear for each password.

About Passwords

The password security method used in Acrobat is the RC4 method from RSA Corporation. You should understand some basic issues related to passwords when using them:

✦ Passwords are optional for either field.

✦ Documents can be opened with either password.

✦ If the Change password is used when opening a file, all tools and menu commands can be selected.

✦ Passwords are case sensitive.

✦ Passwords are limited to 255 characters.

✦ Password-secured files from Acrobat 4.0 cannot be viewed in Acrobat viewers prior to version 2.0.

✦ Forgotten passwords cannot be recovered.

Note   If a warning dialog box appears after you enter a confirmation password, you did not enter it exactly as you did the original password. If you see the warning dialog box a second time, try to cancel the dialog box and start over—you may have entered the first password in error. Be certain to write your passwords down and store them in a place other than electronically on your hard drive. If your drive crashes and you have a number of passwords on the drive, you may run the risk of never recovering the files.

Summary

✦ Preferences set up the viewer environment. Many preference settings, when saved with a document, will be preserved when viewing that document in an Acrobat viewer.

✦ Whereas preference settings are more global, document information settings are document specific. Document information items can also be saved with the PDF file.

✦ Saving PDF files with the Save As command will enable you to apply optimization and security settings.

✦ The Batch Optimize command will optimize a folder of PDF files and optionally all subfolders contained therein.

✦ Security can be provided on two levels — either for opening a PDF document or for changing it. If you use the Change password, you can open *and* change the PDF document.

✦   ✦   ✦

Enhancing PDF Documents

Chapter 8
Annotations, Text,
and Graphics

Chapter 9
Articles, Bookmarks,
and Thumbnails

Chapter 10
Creating Hypertext
Links

Chapter 11
Working with Forms

Chapter 12
Creating Search
Indexes with Acrobat
Catalog

Chapter 13
Scanning in Acrobat

Chapter 14
Converting Scans to
Text

Annotations, Text, and Graphics

◆ ◆ ◆ ◆

In This Chapter

Understanding
Acrobat tools

Working with
Annotation tools

Working with
Graphic Markup
tools

Working with Text
Markup tools

Editing text
in Acrobat

Working with
graphics

◆ ◆ ◆ ◆

In Chapter 2, I covered many tools in the Acrobat Reader Command Bar. This chapter covers tools found in the Acrobat Tool Bar. The tools used in Acrobat are one of many features that greatly distinguish Acrobat from Acrobat Reader. In this chapter, I cover the tool uses, associated properties for each tool, and how tools relate to various palettes and menu commands.

Acrobat Tools

The Command Bar in Acrobat appears similar to that in Reader, with a few differences. Acrobat's Command Bar includes the Save tool, whereas the Reader's does not. The Reader Command Bar has the Hand tool, Zoom tools, and Text/Graphic Select tools, which in Acrobat are located on the Tool Bar instead of the Command Bar. The remaining tools at the top of the viewer window are the same for both viewers.

The vertical Tool Bar along the left side of the Acrobat window is where the many editing tools that help you edit, modify, and customize PDF documents appear (see Figures 8-1 and 8-2). The Tool Bar contains several pop-up toolbars that contain more tools. The small arrow icon appearing beside a particular tool indicates that more tools are available in the pop-up toolbar. Position the cursor over any of the tools containing the arrow and click and hold the mouse button to display additional tools. Move the cursor across the pop-up toolbar and stop at the tool you wish to select. When the mouse button is released, the selected tool will occupy the position where the first tool appeared. When you select a tool, the tool will appear recessed in the tool palette to indicate that tool is currently active.

Tip   Use the Option key (Mac) or Ctrl key (Windows) to select a tool for only one use. After using the tool, you will be returned to the previously selected tool. When a tool is selected, press the Control Key (Mac) or right mouse button (Windows) in the document to open a context-sensitive menu for the respective tool.

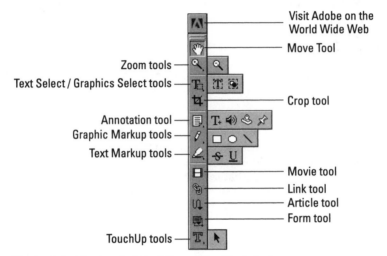

Figure 8-1: The Acrobat Tool Bar on the Macintosh

Figure 8-2: All the tools for Acrobat on Windows appear identical to those for the Macintosh with the exception of the Digital Signature tool.

Working with Annotations

Acrobat 4.0 has introduced many ways to create annotations in your documents. Annotations can take many forms — for example a note, a sound, a mark, a graphic, or an underline beneath a body of text. One attribute common to most of the annotation types is an attached note. The annotation in many cases is a visual on the PDF document page. The note associated with the annotation mark can contain explanatory text. Often you'll want to open the annotation and insert such text in a note.

Annotations are used to help office workflow environments assist groups of people working together on projects. PDF documents can be placed on servers or intranets where office personnel can access the document and create annotations to offer opinions, suggestions, and approvals for office projects and correspondence. Office groups with satellite facilities in several countries can download PDF files in Web browsers, make annotations, and upload them to the server. The annotations can be summarized and collected by a PDF author for compiling opinions of people around the world.

Notes in Acrobat are like the Post-Its you might attach to printed documents. To create a note, you need Acrobat. Reader can open and close notes, but no authoring is available to the Reader user. If you intend to use notes for electronic document reviews, all the users who contribute notes will need to install Acrobat on their systems.

Annotations can be used in different ways. Information feedback from office workers, as just described, is but one means of using annotations. You can also use annotations for instructional purposes. On CDs, a note can contain instructions to the end user on last-minute information, how to view the PDF file, and other types of informational items. With outputting PDF files, annotations can also supply information. Annotations exist on a layer independent of the PDF content. When you print a file containing notes, the notes will not appear on the printed page. This makes for an ideal method of providing information specific for output.

The tools for making annotations in Acrobat are grouped in three categories. The first category, the Annotation tools, consists of tools for notes, text, audio, stamps, and file attachments. The next group contains the Markup Annotation tools, which include the pencil, rectangle, elliptical, and line annotation marks. Finally, the Text Markup tools are used for text highlights, text strikethroughs, and text underlining.

Using the Annotation tools

The Annotation tools form the first group of tools used in annotating a PDF document. Annotation tools are used to attach to a document notes that contain comments, descriptions, audio commenting, or file attachments. When you use an Annotation tool, you may create a note description in a pop-up window, or you may create the annotation without any note description. Note windows may appear open or closed in the PDF file depending on what the author decides when saving the file in Acrobat. When notes are open and the PDF file is saved, all subsequent opening of the document will display the open notes. Some notes may be open and others closed. In such cases, the saved file will also save the note attributes, including the note locations within the PDF document window.

Note attributes

All notes attached to annotations have the same attributes. The maximum size for a note is 4 inches wide by 6 inches high. You can't size a note window larger than these dimensions in a viewer window. A note window can contain up to a maximum of 32,000 roman characters. Text in the note window can be copied, cut, and pasted. Text can be selected with the cursor, and the Edit ⇨ Select All command will select all text in the note window. Text can also be copied from a word processor or text editor and pasted into the note window. Graphic images cannot be pasted into the note window.

Notes are resized by dragging the size box in the lower-right corner in or out to size down or up, respectively. Notes resized will reflow text according to the word wrap in the text body. Carriage returns will begin new paragraphs and keep hard breaks between paragraphs. When a note window is open, the note can be collapsed by clicking the cursor in the close box in the top-left corner. When a note is collapsed, the icon for the type of annotation created will be displayed. Double-clicking most of the annotation types will open the note window.

Note window preferences are established by invoking the File ⇨ Preferences ⇨ Annotations menu command, as discussed in Chapter 7. When the font and font size are changed in the Annotations Preferences dialog box, the text will change in all note windows. When the author name is changed in the Preferences dialog box, the name change will not affect previously created annotations. Multiple author names can appear in the same PDF document. Note properties can be edited for each annotation in the PDF document so unique attributes such as title bar color and author name can be established for each note.

Notes tool

Before using the Notes tool to create a note, you may wish to first examine the Notes preferences, discussed in Chapter 7. If several users are contributing notes to a given file, you may wish to preassign colors and/or labels individualized for each user. If you change Notes preferences while working on a PDF file, the preference changes will only affect any notes created subsequent to the preference change. Any existing notes will appear with their original attributes.

To create a note, select the Notes tool from the Acrobat Tool Bar. The cursor will change to the icon displayed at the beginning of this section, which enables you to draw a rectangle in the Acrobat window. Drag open a rectangle and release the mouse button. The note will appear where you drew the rectangle and a text cursor will appear in the note content area, indicating you can now enter text. Notes can be created on a document page, as shown in Figure 8-3, or they can be created outside the document window.

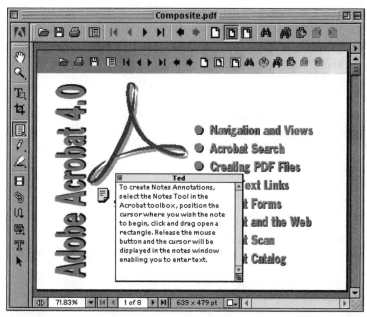

Figure 8-3: Notes can be drawn on the PDF document page and off the page within the Acrobat window.

Collapsing, expanding, and deleting notes

In Chapter 6, I demonstrate how to use the /Open true (or false) value pairs with PDFMark to have a note appear as open or closed in the PDF file when distilled with Acrobat Distiller. If the Open key is true, the note will appear expanded, as illustrated in Figure 8-3. To collapse a note, you click the small close box in the top-left corner of the note. Collapsed notes can be moved and rearranged in the document window by clicking the icon and dragging it to another location. If the note window is open, you can drag the title bar of the window to relocate it. While the note window is open, you can move the icon for the note to another location. These two elements are independent of each other. A moved icon will have no effect on the location of the note window and vice versa.

If you wish to delete a note from a PDF file, select the note icon. A note can be deleted either when open or when collapsed. With the note icon selected, press the Backspace (Delete) key on your keyboard or select Edit ⇨ Clear. If all notes or other elements are deselected, the Clear menu command will be grayed out. When a note is deleted, a warning dialog box will appear, asking you to confirm the note deletion.

Caution

If in your General Preferences dialog box the Skip Edit Warnings option is enabled, a warning dialog box will not appear. If the option is enabled and you press the Backspace (Delete) key on your keyboard, the note will disappear. Like so many other edits you make with Acrobat, you won't be able to select Edit ⇨ Undo. Acrobat presents very few undo opportunities when you use it to edit a PDF.

Note properties

Note properties can be selected from the Edit menu or by opening a context-sensitive menu. When the context-sensitive menu is used, Properties appear as one of several menu items, as shown in Figure 8-4. Other attribute settings are also listed in the pop-up menu.

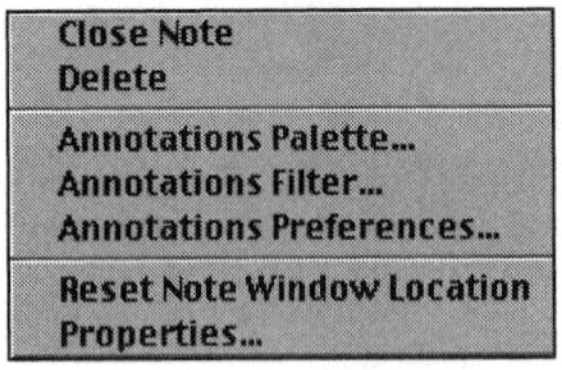

Figure 8-4: Context-sensitive menus provide menu commands for accessing all the annotation attribute settings.

The commands available when opening a context-sensitive menu by Control+clicking (Mac) or pressing the right mouse button (Windows) include the following:

✦ **Open/Close Note:** This command produces the same results as double-clicking the Notes icon. When the note is closed, the note will open by selecting the first menu command, displayed as Open Note, or double-clicking the icon while the Hand tool or the Notes tool is selected in the Tool Bar. When the Note is open, Close Note will appear as the first menu option.

✦ **Delete:** This command produces the same result as selecting Edit ⇨ Delete. As long as the Skip Edit Warnings preference setting in the General Preferences dialog box is disabled, a warning dialog box will appear asking for confirmation for the deletion.

✦ **Annotations Palette:** Selecting the Annotations Palette command will open the Navigation Pane just as if you had clicked the Show/Hide Navigation Pane tool in the Command Bar. The Annotations tab will appear in the foreground in the Navigation Pane.

✦ **Annotations Filter:** When this command is selected, the Filter Manager window will appear. From the choices available in the window, you can make selections for the kinds of annotations to be displayed. The left side of the window lists the authors of the annotations. The right side of the window contains all the annotation types to be displayed in the PDF window. If an author or type is selected, the bullet adjacent to the author/type will disappear. Choices can be made for which annotation authors and which types of annotations are to be viewed. When items are deselected, click OK, and the choices made in the window will be updated on the PDF page. When you return to the Filter Manager window, click the Select All buttons, and all authors and types will be displayed. If you select an annotation type such as Notes and choose to hide this type of annotation, when you return to the PDF window, the notes will be hidden. If you need to return to the Filter Manager to regain the display of notes, you can't use the context-sensitive menu because no note will be in view. When items are hidden, select Tools ⇨ Annotations ⇨ Filter Manager to access the options for making those hidden items visible (see Figure 8-5).

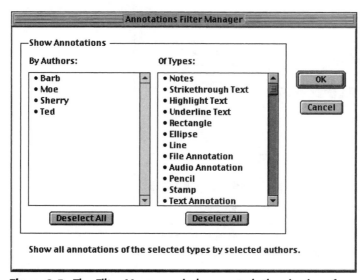

Figure 8-5: The Filter Manager window controls the viewing of annotations by author and type.

✦ **Annotations Preferences:** When invoking this command, the same dialog box will open as when File ➪ Preferences ➪ Annotations is selected. From the Annotations Preferences dialog box, you can make choices for font and font size.

✦ **Reset Note Window Location:** Moving notes, title bars, and note icons are discussed earlier in this chapter. When a note is created, the default location of the note window when opened will be above the top-left corner of the note icon. If you move the note window to another location, you can return it to the default position by selecting this command.

✦ **Properties:** Notes properties control the icon appearance when a note is collapsed. The Notes Properties window can be opened by selecting this command from the context-sensitive menu or by selecting Edit ➪ Properties. When the Notes Properties window appears, as shown in Figure 8-6, make a choice for a note's icon appearance by selecting from the list.

The Notes Properties window also provides options for changing the author name and selecting colors for the icon and notes title bar. The color swatch behaves as discussed earlier — click the icon, and the system color palette in which the color selections are made opens.

You can choose from the note icons shown in Figure 8-7. The icons need not be specifically associated to the items after which they are named. For example, you can specify a Paragraph icon be displayed on a graphic. However, so as not to confuse the user, you may wish to make a logical choice for the icon display.

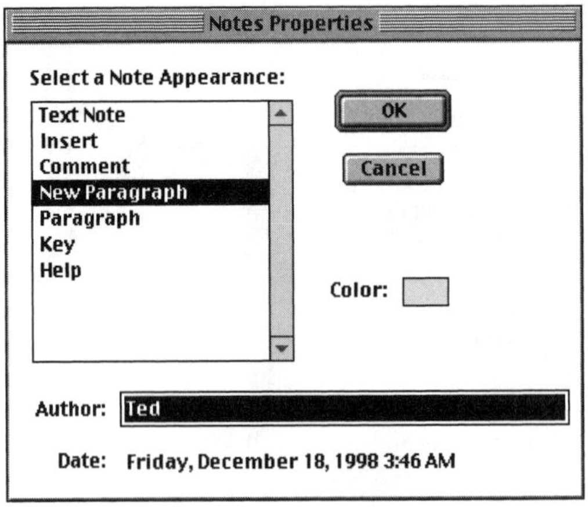

Notes Properties

Select a Note Appearance:

| Text Note |
| Insert |
| Comment |
| **New Paragraph** |
| Paragraph |
| Key |
| Help |

OK

Cancel

Color:

Author: Ted

Date: Friday, December 18, 1998 3:46 AM

Figure 8-6: The note icon and note icon color can be changed in the Notes Properties window.

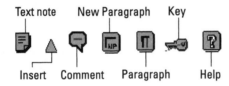

Text note   New Paragraph   Key

Insert   Comment   Paragraph   Help

Figure 8-7: The note icons, despite their names, can be associated to any type of item you specify.

Text Annotation tool

The Text Annotation tool creates a text block on the PDF page. Rather than having an icon that can be opened or collapsed to reveal text, text annotations offer a means of displaying a message. Because the annotation contains text, there isn't a note window associated with this type of annotation.

Text annotations are created by selecting the Text Annotation tool from among the Annotation tools in the Acrobat Tool Bar and dragging open a rectangle in the document window. Like note annotations, text annotations can also appear on the PDF page or the pasteboard. When the mouse button is released, a blinking I-beam cursor appears in the rectangle. Enter text and click the Hand tool to select the annotation. Once selected, the rectangle box containing the text can be sized and relocated. Click and drag any of the corner handles to resize the text box.

The options for deleting and moving text annotations are the same as those used with note annotations. The only differences in menu commands between the note annotations and text annotations are items listed in the respective Properties windows. Properties for text annotations are selected by choosing the same commands for note properties (via the Edit menu or a context-sensitive menu).

Text annotations properties

The Text Properties dialog box, shown in Figure 8-8, enables specification of font and font size measured in points. Additionally, you'll find in this dialog box options for a border frame that can appear around the text block rectangle. The Border pop-up menu features choices for border line widths of point sizes ranging from 1 to 7. When None is selected from the pop-up menu, no border will appear around the annotation.

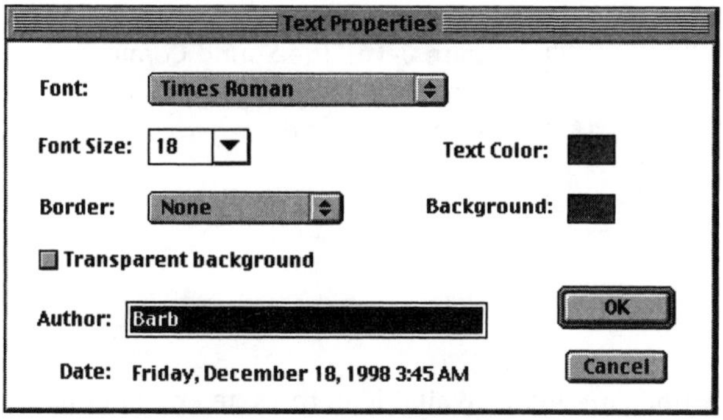

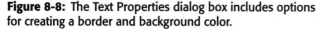

Figure 8-8: The Text Properties dialog box includes options for creating a border and background color.

The rectangle containing the text annotation can be transparent or filled with a color. You make selections for transparency and color within the Text Properties window. In order to apply a color fill to the text annotation background, deselect the Transparent background option, as shown in Figure 8-8. The Background color swatch will appear. Click the swatch to open the system color palette where the color selections are made. If the Transparent background option is enabled, the Background color swatch will disappear.

Audio annotations

Audio annotations are recorded from within the PDF document. In order to create an audio annotation, you must have a microphone connected to your computer. Audio annotations are created by selecting the Audio Annotation tool in the Acrobat Tool Bar and clicking in the document window. A click of the mouse button is all that is needed to open the Sound Comment dialog box (see Figures 8-9 and 8-10). When the dialog box opens, click the start button and speak into the microphone connected to your computer. When you've finished recording the sound, click the Stop button. The Save option will be active after you click Stop.

Audio annotations are saved as a WAV file (.wav) in Windows and as an AIFF (.aiff) file on the Macintosh. When Save is selected in the Sound Comment dialog box, you will be returned to the PDF document window, in which the sound icon will now appear. The audio annotation becomes embedded in the PDF file when saved. As the sound becomes part of the PDF document, you can transport the PDF across platforms without having to include a sound file. All sound will be audible on either platform after saving the file.

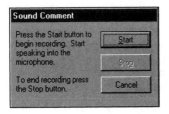

Figure 8-9: The Sound Comment dialog box in Windows is opened after the Start button is selected.

Figure 8-10: The Sound Comment dialog box as it appears on the Macintosh

Audio properties

Properties for audio annotations are made available in the same manner as with other annotations. Right-click the mouse button (Windows) or use the Control+click combination (Mac) to open the Audio Properties window, shown in Figure 8-11. The Audio Properties dialog box offers selections for choosing the icon color and editing the author name. By default, the Description field will be left blank. You can supply a description, which will be listed in the Annotations tab within the Navigation Pane when opened.

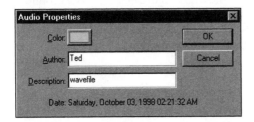

Figure 8-11: The Audio Properties window provides choices for author name, color for the audio icon, and a Description field.

Stamp annotations

The Stamp tool enables you to add an image icon to a PDF file. In an office environment, it's like a rubber stamp you might slap on a document to indicate it has been approved or that it is confidential, or you might use a stamped signature in place of a written one, among other uses. When the Stamp tool is used, Acrobat automatically navigates to a directory within the Acrobat Plug-ins folder called Stamps. Four of the PDF files contained in this folder have multiple pages, with each page containing a different graphic (see Figure 8-12). These PDF files and their respective pages are the Adobe-supplied stamp images. In addition, the folder contains the ReadMe.pdf and AdobeStudios.pdf files. All the files can be opened in an Acrobat viewer. The ReadMe.pdf file explains how you can create your own stamp files containing custom images to be used with the Stamp tool. The AdobeStudios.pdf offers information about collections from Adobe Studios, from which CDs containing fonts, images, video, and stock photography can be purchased.

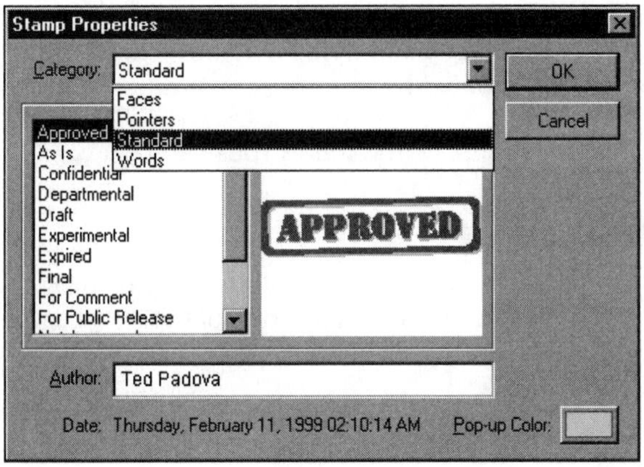

Figure 8-12: Stamp images are selected from among the four PDF files installed with your Acrobat application. You can select a category from among those appearing in the pop-up menu in the Stamp Properties dialog box.

To use the Stamp tool, select the tool in the Acrobat Tool Bar, move the cursor to the document window, and drag open a rectangle. When the mouse button is released, a dialog box will appear defaulting to the Stamps folder inside the Plug-ins folder. The pop-up menu for Category enables you to select one of the four PDF files containing images. The list of images for a given category appears in the left pane. When an image is selected in the left pane, a large thumbnail will appear in the right pane displaying the image that will be used when the OK button is selected.

When a stamp has been created in the PDF document window, you can supply a text note in the associated note window. Double-click the Stamp icon or Control+click (Mac) or right-click (Windows) to open the context-sensitive menu and select Open Note. The text window adheres to the same rules used with note annotations.

Stamp properties

When you select a Stamp image upon creating a stamp annotation, the choice is displayed in the Properties window. At the time the stamp is created, you can specify a name in the Author field or the color for the title bar of the associated note. After a stamp has been created, you can change the image by returning to the Stamp Properties dialog box. Accessing this dialog box is handled the same way as for other annotations. Select the stamp, and then select Edit ➪ Properties or open a context-sensitive menu and select Properties.

Creating custom stamps

Acrobat provides a means for creating custom stamps. You can create images in illustration programs or photo-imaging applications. The files must eventually be converted to PDF. PDF conversion can be performed through the PDFWriter, Acrobat Distiller, or by exporting to PDF from within applications. Photoshop images can be exported to PDF by using the Save As command from within Photoshop. After the PDF file has been created, you must open the file in Acrobat and create a page template. Page templates are created by selecting Tools ⇨ Forms ⇨ Page Template. A name must be supplied for the template. After creating a page template, the category is determined by supplying a name or description in the Document Info dialog box for the Title field.

To understand how creating custom stamps work, follow these steps:

STEPS: Creating Custom Stamps

1. **Create a graphic.** Use your favorite illustration or photo-imaging program to create an icon or illustration. In this example, I use one of the new custom brushes in Adobe Illustrator 8 (see Figure 8-13).

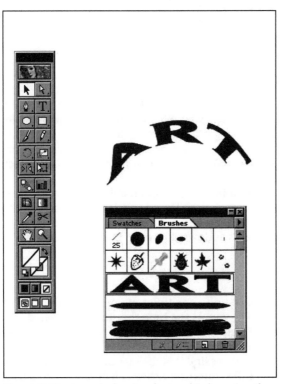

Figure 8-13: I created a simple graphic by using the Paintbrush tool in Adobe Illustrator.

Note

When creating stamps, the behavior of placed images is consistent with what occurs in other graphic applications you may use. EPS and vector-based images can be created on large paper sizes, but the placed image appears cropped to the bounding box of the artwork. Raster images retain the entire page size when placed in another application. Acrobat's stamp images conform to the same principles. If you create an EPS file and convert it to PDF, the imported stamp is cropped to the bounding box of the original artwork. If you create a stamp from a Photoshop image and save it to PDF, the entire Photoshop canvas area becomes part of the stamp. To reduce file sizes and manage your stamps more efficiently, crop raster images in either the host application or Acrobat.

2. **Convert to PDF.** If you create an image in a program that exports directly to PDF, use the Export command to convert the file to PDF. If you have access to PDFWriter, you can create the PDF file by printing to PDFWriter. If using Distiller, print the file to disk as a PostScript file and then distill it.

3. **Create a document template.** Open the PDF file in Adobe Acrobat. When the PDF file is in view in Acrobat, select Tools ⇨ Forms ⇨ Page Template. The Document Templates window will open.

4. **Provide a template name.** In the Name field in the Document Templates dialog box, enter a descriptive name for your new template file. The name supplied here will appear in the Stamp Properties dialog box for this image within a category you identify in the Document Info dialog box (see Figure 8-14).

Figure 8-14: Stamp images are selected from among the four PDF file categories installed with your Acrobat application. The page template name will identify the filename within a given category.

5. **Close the Document Templates dialog box.** After supplying a name, be certain to click the Add button. When Add is selected, the new name will appear in the list window. Click Close to return to your PDF document.

Continued

6. **Open the Document Info dialog box.** Categories appear in the Category pop-up menu when the Stamp Properties dialog box is opened. To create a new category, select File ⇨ Document Info ⇨ General or press Cmd/Ctrl+D.

7. **Supply a name for the category.** Click the cursor in the Title field and type a name for your category. Click OK after entering the name (see Figure 8-15).

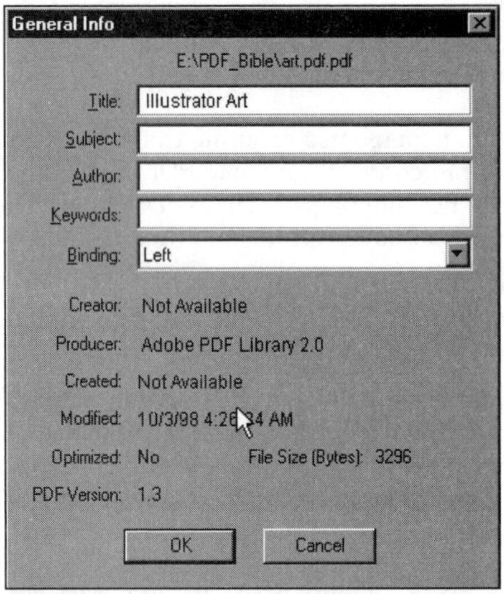

General Info

E:\PDF_Bible\art.pdf.pdf

Title: Illustrator Art
Subject:
Author:
Keywords:
Binding: Left

Creator: Not Available
Producer: Adobe PDF Library 2.0
Created: Not Available
Modified: 10/3/98 4:26:34 AM
Optimized: No   File Size (Bytes): 3296
PDF Version: 1.3

[OK]   [Cancel]

Figure 8-15: Category names in the Stamp Properties dialog box will appear from the name(s) you supply in the Title field of the General Info dialog box.

8. **Save the PDF file.** Additions made with Acrobat must be saved. Select File ⇨ Save As and save the modified PDF file to the Stamps folder inside your Acrobat Plug-ins folder. The filename you provide for the PDF file will have no effect on the names displayed in the Stamp Properties dialog box. The name used for the Title field in the Document Info dialog box will be used for the category name. The name created when you added a page template will be used to identify the page in the PDF file to be used for the stamp (see Figure 8-16).

Note

When you open the Stamps Properties dialog box and select a category from which to choose individual images, you'll notice no navigation dialog box appears. The Category pop-up menu adds names automatically when the PDF file is placed in the Stamps folder with proper assignment of page template and document information. If the PDF file is saved anywhere other than the Stamps folder, you will have no means of navigating to the file.

9. **Open a PDF file.** In order to use the new stamp, a PDF file must be opened in Acrobat. Select File ⇨ Open and open a PDF document.

10. **Add a stamp annotation.** Acrobat will recognize your new category without quitting the program. New categories you add to the Stamp folder will immediately become available when adding a stamp annotation. To add a stamp annotation, select the Stamp tool in the Acrobat Tool Bar. Click and drag open a rectangle.

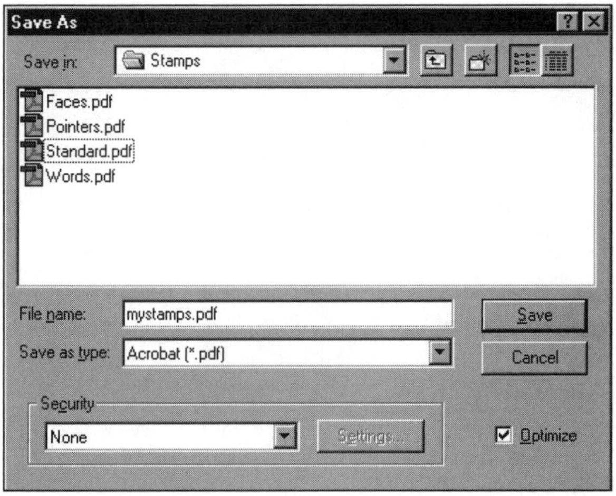

Figure 8-16: The PDF file must be saved to the Stamps folder inside your Acrobat Plug-ins.

11. **Select your new category.** If you performed all the steps correctly, you will see the new category name appear in the Category pop-up menu in the Stamp Properties dialog box. Click the pop-up menu and select the category name (see Figure 8-17).

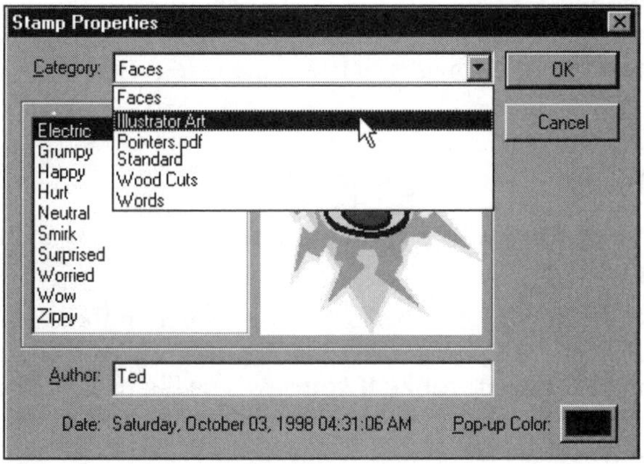

Figure 8-17: The new category name will appear in the Category pop-up menu if the stamp and category have been properly created.

12. **Select the new stamp.** Once the category has been selected, all stamps created with the page template will be visible in the list box. Because only a single stamp was created for this category, only one option should appear in the list. Select the stamp you created and click OK (see Figure 8-18).

Continued

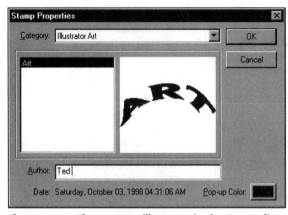

Figure 8-18: The stamp will appear in the Stamp list after the category has been selected.

13. **Observe the new stamp in the PDF document.** Notice the stamp should occupy just enough space to include the graphic image. If you created your illustration on a larger document page, the page will be cropped to accommodate the graphic.

Adding images to a stamp file

A PDF file can include many stamps from which to choose in a given category. If you want to continue adding additional images to the same category, Acrobat can accommodate this.

STEPS: Adding Images to a Category

1. **Create another stamp.** Use an illustration or photo-editing application and create a new stamp image.

2. **Convert to PDF.** Convert the image to PDF as described in the earlier exercise. You can eliminate the PDF conversion if the program you use supports files recognized by Acrobat. If you save the file to TIFF, JPEG, or a number of other formats, you can select File ➪ Import to add a page to an open PDF document. Before importing, follow Step 3.

3. **Open the PDF file from the Stamps folder.** In Acrobat select File ➪ Open and navigate to the Stamps folder to locate the file you created. Select the filename and click Open.

4. **Insert a page in a PDF.** Select Document ➪ Pages ➪ Insert. Locate the new image file created and double-click the filename. If you import a file other than a PDF file, a dialog box will appear informing you Acrobat is converting the image to PDF. Wait until the dialog box disappears. The next dialog box appearing will be the Insert Page dialog box. Click OK to import the image into your existing PDF file.

5. **Create a page template.** Any new images added to your PDF file must have individual pages identified as page templates. The page templates segregate the images so they will appear listed in the Stamp Properties dialog box. Navigate to the newly added page and select Tools ➪ Forms ➪ Page Templates.

6. **Name the page template.** When the dialog box appears, supply a name in the Name field box and click the Add button. Select Close to return to the document window.

7. **Save your updates.** The name in the Title field in the Document Info dialog box will remain the same as you specified when the file was first saved. No further editing is required in the Document Info dialog box once you have created a name for the Title field. Select File ➪ Save to update the edits for the imported page and page template name.

8. **Test the stamp.** Open a PDF document and select the Stamp tool. Click and drag in the document window to add a stamp annotation. From the Category pop-up menu, select the PDF file you created for your stamp archives. If the stamp was properly added to the original PDF file and you provided a name for the page template, you should see a list with two names (see Figure 8-19).

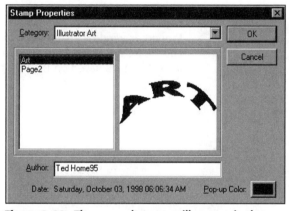

Figure 8-19: The second stamp will appear in the Stamp list after the category has been selected.

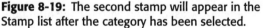

Tip

PDF documents can contain pages of different sizes. If you have several images contained in a single PDF file and some contain more page space than others, you can individually crop pages to different sizes in Acrobat. Select the Crop tool in the Acrobat Tool Bar. Navigate to the page to be cropped, and use the Crop tool to trim the page close to the edges of the illustration. If you created a vector art image in a program such as Adobe Illustrator, select Bounding Box from the Margins pop-up menu. Be certain to select only the page you desire to crop when the Crop Pages dialog box appears. In addition, pages with different dimensions can be inserted in a PDF, and they will hold their dimensions after the insertion. If you have an opportunity to crop a page before insertion, you can perform cropping in the host application.

File annotations

The last of the Annotation tools in the Acrobat Tool Bar is the File Annotation tool. File attachments enable you to attach any file on your hard drive to the current document. Once attached, the file will be embedded in the PDF document in which you create a file annotation. Embedding a file will provide other viewer users the capability to view attachments on other computers and across platforms. At first it may appear as though the attachment is a link. However, if you transport the PDF document to another computer and open the annotation, the embedded file will open in the host application. Users on other computers will need the original authoring application to view the embedded file.

To use the File Annotation tool, select the tool and click in the document window. The first item appearing will be a navigation dialog box. Acrobat opens this dialog box for you to locate a file on your hard drive to be attached to the PDF page in view when the file annotation is created. When the file to be attached is selected, click the Attach button to open the File Annotation Properties window, shown in Figure 8-20. By opening the context-sensitive menu, shown in Figure 8-21, for a file annotation, you'll notice some similar commands and several others not found with the Annotation tools noted earlier.

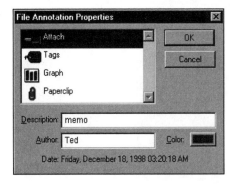

Figure 8-20: The File Annotation Properties window enables you to choose from four different annotation icons to be displayed on the PDF page.

✦ **Open Note:** Opens a note window associated with the file attachment.

✦ **Delete:** Will delete the file attachment in the same fashion as occurs when pressing the Delete (Backspace) key. The icon and the embedded file will both be deleted. A warning dialog box will appear asking for confirmation if the preferences are set to not skip the edit warnings.

✦ **Annotations Palette:** Same as discussed earlier with the note annotations.

✦ **Annotations Filter:** Same as discussed earlier with the note annotations.

✦ **Annotations Preferences:** Same as discussed earlier with the note annotations.

✦ **Properties:** The File Annotation Properties window offers some choices similar to the stamp annotation. In this window, you may select from four different file annotation icons, as shown in Figure 8-21. The behavior of the annotation is the same regardless of which icon you choose. These choices only have to do with the display of the icon as it appears on the PDF page. A Description field box is provided for supplying a short description. Other properties for author name and color selection for the pop-up text window are handled the same as with all other annotations.

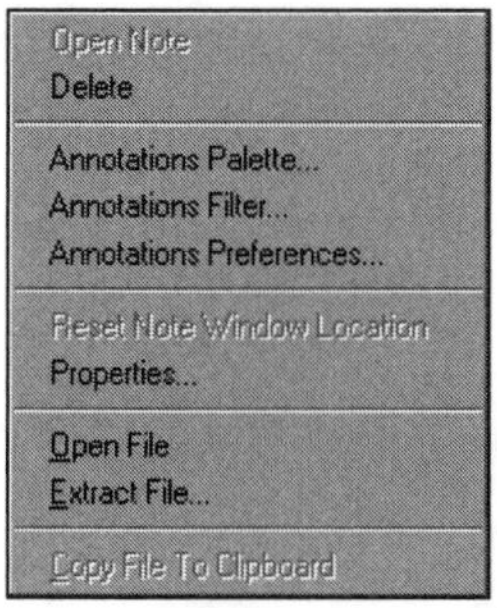

Open Note
Delete

Annotations Palette...
Annotations Filter...
Annotations Preferences...

Reset Note Window Location
Properties...

Open File
Extract File...

Copy File To Clipboard

Figure 8-21: The context-sensitive menu displays several commands not found with the other types of annotations.

✦ **Reset Note Window Location:** If the attached note is moved, selecting this item will return the note window to the default location.

✦ **Open File:** When the Open File command is selected, the attached file will open in the producer application. You may notice a momentary hesitation while the application is launched and the file is opened. Be patient, especially if you have a slower computer. When the producer application is launched, it will run concurrently in memory. This enables you to toggle back and forth between Acrobat and the open application.

Note

File annotations can be attached to any file. Attachments are not limited to documents. You can make attachments to applications as well as data files.

✦ **Extract File:** When Extract File is selected from the pop-up menu, the file attached (embedded) to the file annotation will be selected and a Save As dialog box will appear. In essence, the file is extracted from the PDF and saved back to the original file format. Extracting a file will not delete the embedded file from the PDF—it acts more like a copy-and-paste than a cut-and-paste operation.

✦ **Copy File To Clipboard:** The file will be copied to the Clipboard, which can then be pasted into documents capable of accepting the Clipboard contents. File formats other than text will be copied as Windows Metafile in Windows and PICT on a Macintosh.

When a file annotation has been created in a PDF document, positioning the cursor over the annotation icon will display the name of the file in a Tool Tip. All file annotations are labeled according to the document name you specify when you save the file to disk.

Working with Graphic Markup tools

Graphic Markup tools are the electronic equivalent of using a highlighter on paper documents. There are four Graphic Markup tools in the Acrobat Tool Bar appearing below the Annotation tools. To select a tool, click the Pencil tool icon and hold the mouse button down until the pop-up toolbar appears. Selections are made in the same way as was discussed with the Annotation tools. Like many of the tools discussed previously, each of the Graphic Markup tools can have an associated note (see Figure 8-22). The note attributes for these tools are the same as found when using the Notes tool.

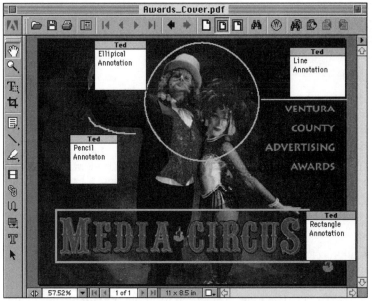

Figure 8-22: Graphic Markup tools are used to mark up PDF files for comments, suggestions, and editing. The Annotation marks can all be removed on the final document.

Pencil tool

The Pencil tool is used for freeform marking and following irregular paths. Select the tool in the Acrobat Tool Bar and draw as you would with a traditional pencil. After completing the mark, a rectangular box with handles at four corners will appear. These handles can be used to resize and reshape the mark. When you release the mouse button, a text window appears. You can enter the text note information or close the note widow to reposition the mark. Use the Hand tool to click and drag a mark to a new location. Double-clicking the mark will reopen the text window.

Rectangle tool

Rectangles are used to encompass an area with a rectangular pattern. Draw a rectangle and release the mouse button. The rectangle will be displayed with four handles, enabling you to resize and reshape the rectangle. Squares are created by pressing the Shift key and then clicking and dragging outward.

Ellipse tool

The Ellipse tool works like the Rectangle tool. The final result is an elliptical shape or circle. Circles are created using the same method to create squares with the Rectangle tool. Use the Shift key when opening a circle.

Line tool

The Line tool is used to draw straight lines horizontally, vertically, and diagonally. Use the Shift key to draw diagonal lines at 45°. When the line is drawn, a rectangle will appear around the line. If you draw lines horizontally or vertically, offset the line slightly so the rectangular box will appear large enough to enable you to use a context-sensitive menu. If the line is a small point size, you may not be able to select the line and then subsequently open the Properties window.

Graphic Markup tool properties

When you open the context menu associated with any of the Graphic Markup tools, the menu options will all be the same. All the options are the same as those discussed with other annotation types earlier, except for the options available in the Properties dialog box. Figure 8-23 illustrates the Ellipse Properties window. To bring up the Properties dialog box, Control+click (Macintosh) or right-click (Windows) inside a selected markup annotation.

Note When opening a context-sensitive menu or selecting one of the Graphic Markup tools, the Hand tool from the Acrobat Tool Bar must be used. If the TouchUp Object tool is used, you will not be able to select the marks made by these tools nor open the Properties or Notes dialog boxes.

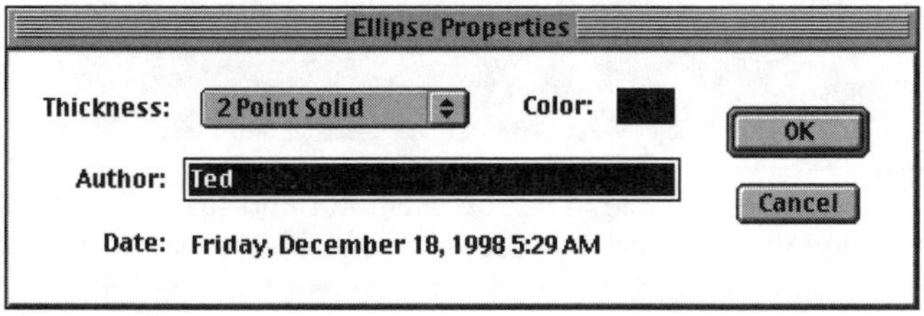

Ellipse Properties

Thickness: 2 Point Solid   Color:

Author: Ted   OK

Date: Friday, December 18, 1998 5:29 AM   Cancel

Figure 8-23: The Properties dialog boxes for all the Graphic Markup tools are identical with the exception of the name in the title bar.

The Properties window enables you to change author name, line color, and point sizes for line weights. From the Thickness pop-up menu, you may select a 1-point dashed line, or a solid line ranging in width from 1 point to 7 points. (Dashed lines are only available at the 1-point size.)

Tip   To create line weights and change line attributes, create the line(s) you wish to use in a program such as Adobe Illustrator and save the file as a PDF. You can import the PDF file into a custom stamp library you create. Select the Document ⇨ Pages ⇨ Insert command in Adobe Acrobat to insert the new page in your library. Select tools ⇨ Forms ⇨ Page Templates to name the page. Using the Stamp tool, create a stamp annotation and select the line you created. You can associate a text window the same as you would when using the Line tool (see Figure 8-24).

Figure 8-24: I created a 4-point dashed line in Adobe Illustrator and saved the file to PDF format. I then imported the PDF into my custom stamps library by selecting Document ⇨ Pages ⇨ Insert. With the newly inserted page in view, I selected Tools ⇨ Forms ⇨ Page Templates and named my new image Dashed Line 4 Point. When I created an annotation with the Stamp tool, I selected my custom stamps file and chose Dashed Line 4 Point from the list in the Stamp Properties dialog box.

Working with Text Markup tools

The next set of tools for annotations are the Text Markup tools. Three tools appear from the submenu associated with the Text Markup tool icon on the Tool Bar. The Highlight Text tool, Strikethrough Text tool, and Underline Text tool all work with text in a PDF document (see Figure 8-25). When any of the Text Markup tools is positioned in the document window, the cursor will change to an I-beam, indicating text now needs to be selected. To use any of the tools, click and drag across a character, word, sentence, or through a paragraph.

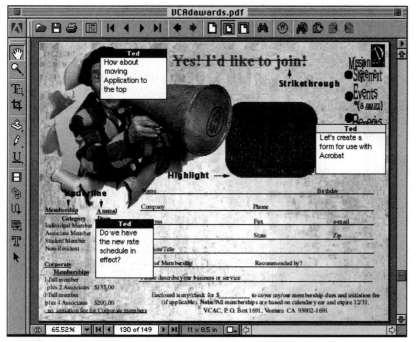

Figure 8-25: Text Markup tools are used to highlight, strikethrough, and underline text.

Highlight Text tool

Using the Highlight Text tool is like using a highlighter on paper. When you apply the highlight, a transparent display enables you to see the text behind the highlight. Working in Acrobat creates the same results on a monitor display. Highlights are drawn by selecting the Highlight Text tool in the Acrobat Tool Bar and dragging the cursor over a line of text. Horizontal movement highlights a line. Drag down to highlight text down the page. The movement of the cursor behaves similarly to the way the cursor moves when the Text Select tool is used, as discussed in Chapter 3. If you want to select a column in a multiple-column document, press the Ctrl key as you drag down the column. Adjacent columns will be left undisturbed. Highlighted text won't appear the same on a printed document as you see on screen. The screen version will appear with a transparent overlay. The printed version appears with a rectangle box around the highlighted text.

Strikethrough Text tool

Strikethrough text is handled much as it is in applications such as Microsoft Word. Selecting text is handled the same for all three of the Text Annotation tools. Use the Ctrl key to place a marquee around columns of text as described previously. Horizontal and vertical movement produces the same results as with the other tools.

Underline Text tool

The last of the Text Annotation tools is the Underline Text tool. This tool enables you to add underlining to text, as the name suggests. The selection of the text is the same as the methods used with the two previous tools and produces the same effects. All three tools support associated notes that can be accessed by double-clicking the annotation mark. Note properties are the same for all three tools.

Text Annotation tool properties

Use the same methods for opening the Properties dialog box as you do with other annotations. You can select the Properties command in the Edit menu or use the context-sensitive pop-up menu to open the Properties dialog box. The attributes are the same, but the title in the Properties dialog box will change according to the tool you are using. From the Highlight Properties dialog box, for example, you can select the color for the mark or edit the author name. Results of using each of the Text Markup tools are shown in Figure 8-26.

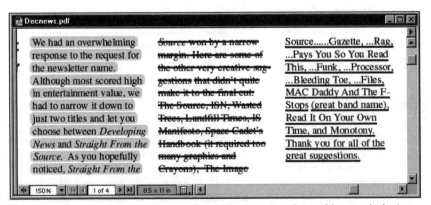

Figure 8-26: Columns of text are selected by pressing the Ctrl key and placing a marquee around the column to be marked. In this example, the three columns were marked, left to right, with the Highlight Text tool, Strikethrough Text tool, and Underline Text tool.

To help understand some of the differences in the properties for all the annotation types, look at Table 8-1. Unique characteristics in the properties for annotations are listed as well as whether the annotation supports changing color/author name and attaching notes.

Table 8-1
Annotation Properties

Annotation	Unique Properties	Color/Author Changes	Add Notes
Notes	Icon choices	Yes	Yes*
Text	Font/Font Size; Text/Background and Transparency; color choices	Yes	No
Audio	Description field	Yes	No
Stamp	Category/List; Thumbnail view; custom icon choices	Yes	Yes
File	Icon choices; Description field; Open file; Extract file	Yes	Yes
Pencil	Line weight choices	Yes	Yes
Rectangle	Line weight choices	Yes	Yes
Ellipse	Line weight choices	Yes	Yes
Line	Line weight choices	Yes	Yes
Highlight		Yes	Yes
Strikethrough		Yes	Yes
Underline		Yes	Yes

* The annotation itself is a note. No additional note window can be associated with the original note.

When annotating documents and viewing the PDF files in Acrobat versions earlier than 4.0, all the icons you create in Acrobat 4.0 will be displayed in the PDF file. The only notes you can see, however, are note windows created with the Notes tool. All other note attachments will not be visible. If the notes are all opened when the PDF file was saved, the notes likewise will not be displayed in Acrobat viewers earlier than version 4.0. When using Acrobat Reader version 4.0, all note attachments will be visible by double-clicking the annotation. Context-sensitive menu choices for opening the properties is not available in Reader.

Using the Annotations palette

You can imagine with all the types of annotations available, one could easily become lost in a maze of notes. If PDF files are distributed across networks or the Web and input is solicited among many individuals, the number of annotations in a document could easily become confusing. To help develop an organized view for displaying annotations, the Annotations palette is used. There are a number of controls in the Annotations palette to help organize, view, summarize, and display annotations. To open the Annotations palette, select the Show/Hide Navigation Pane button in the Command Bar or press the F5 key. If the Annotations tab is not available in the Navigation Pane, select Window ➪ Show Annotations. When the tab is displayed in the Navigation Pane, click it to bring the annotations list to the front of the palette.

The Annotations window in the Navigation Pane will display the annotations included in your document. From the top-right corner a palette menu can be opened to offer several commands when working with annotations. The first order of business is to be certain all annotations are listed in the palette. If you have created annotations in your document and they are not displayed in the palette, you must tell Acrobat to scan your document and load the annotations in the palette. Loading all the annotations in the palette is handled by selecting the right arrow at the top-right corner of the Annotations palette to open the palette menu and scrolling down to select Rescan Document. Acrobat will pause momentarily while the document is being scanned for annotations. After the scan is complete, the annotations will be listed in the palette.

You can also scan annotations by selecting the Start annotation scan icon in the status bar. The icon appears as a broken page positioned to the right of the Trash icon. The icon will only appear when the Annotations tab appears in the foreground in the Navigation Pane. The text to the right of the Start annotation scan icon displays the sort used by Acrobat to create the list. In Figure 8-27, the sort was created on the date field, which indicates when the annotations were created.

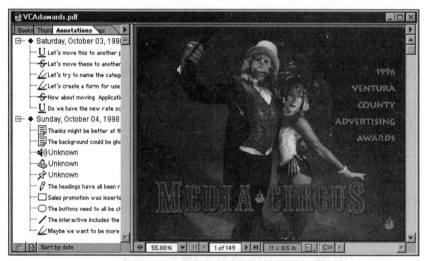

Figure 8-27: If annotations are not visible in the Annotations palette, select Rescan Document from the palette menu or click the Start annotation scan button in the status bar.

Notice also in Figure 8-27 you can see an icon display of the annotation type. When you sort annotations by any sort order other than by Type, the icons can assist you in finding the annotation you may wish to view.

Annotations palette hierarchy

The display in the Annotations palette will appear as an outline or file listing similar to your operating system's display. In Windows, the familiar hierarchical structure displays the + (plus) and – (minus) symbols denoting collapsed and expanded views, respectively (see Figure 8-28). Click the plus symbol to expand the list, and click the minus symbol to collapse the list. On the Macintosh, you'll see the right-pointing arrow displayed when the list is collapsed (see Figure 8-29). Click the arrow to the left side of the Annotations palette to expand the list. The arrow will appear pointing downward when the list is expanded. Click the down arrow to collapse the list.

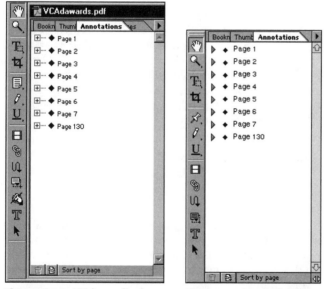

Figure 8-28: Widows display collapsed

Figure 8-29: Macintosh display with annotations with annotations collapsed

As you view Figure 8-27, you can see the display of the Annotations palette when the list is expanded. The top order of the list adjacent to the diamond lists the title of the sort order. In Figure 8-27, the list was sorted by date. Therefore, the top order for each group lists the date. All annotations created on a given date will be displayed in one group. The group changes with each date change. The date item is not an annotation and does not refer to any page number in the PDF file.

Sorting annotations

Annotations can be sorted by four fields: Type, Author, Page Number, or Date. Sorts occur in one of two ways: Select the right arrow in the Annotations palette and choose one of the sort orders, or open a context-sensitive menu in the Annotations palette. To open a context-sensitive menu, position the cursor in a space between or beside the annotation name and Control+click (Mac) or right-click (Windows). If you try to open a context-sensitive menu over the name of an annotation, other menu options will be displayed, and sort orders won't be available. Descriptions of the four sort orders are as follows:

✦ **Type:** Annotations will be sorted according to the type of annotation created. The order of the types will be sorted alphabetically. (For example, Ellipse will precede Rectangle, which both precede Sound.)

✦ **Author:** The sort order will be displayed according to author. All annotations created by an author will appear nested below the author name. Authors will be sorted alphabetically.

✦ **Page Number:** Annotations will be sorted by page number. All annotations appearing on page 1 will appear listed below the Page 1 category. Page 2 will display another category if annotations have been created on the page. If no annotations appear, the next page number will not appear in the Annotations palette. Only pages containing annotations will be listed. Regardless of whether the logical page number is used, Acrobat will display page order beginning with the first page in the PDF. If you renumber sections, the order will not conform to the new page numbers.

✦ **Date:** The sort order is displayed according to the date the annotation was created. All annotations on a given date will be nested below the date display in the Annotations palette regardless of type, author, or page number.

Navigating annotations

The Annotations palette can be used as a navigational tool. To open a page where an annotation has been created, open the Annotations palette and rescan the document. Open the annotations list if it is collapsed. Move the mouse cursor over an annotation name and double-click. The page where the annotation appears will be displayed in the viewer window.

To navigate through annotations, you must click an annotation name. If you try to double click any of the category headings (Type, Author, Page Number, or Date), no new page will be displayed. Acrobat does not associate any pages to the category headings.

In the Annotations palette, you'll notice the command Select Annotation appears on the context-sensitive menu when you Control+click or right-click an annotation name . When you choose Select Annotation, no navigation will occur. The command is reserved for selecting an annotation but not navigating to it. To use this command effectively, first navigate to the page where the annotation appears and then open the context-sensitive menu. Choose Select Annotation, and the annotation will appear selected. The use of this command helps if you have difficulty clicking an annotation to select it (see Figure 8-30). If the context-sensitive menu is opened without selecting an annotation, different menu options will appear, as shown in Figure 8-31.

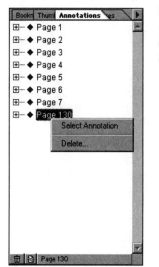

Figure 8-30: Control+click (Mac) or right-click (Windows) on an annotation name to display a context-sensitive menu used for selecting and deleting annotations.

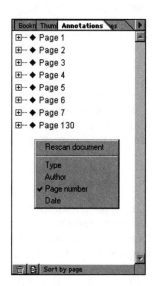

Figure 8-31: Control+click (Mac) or right-click (Windows) in an area other than on an annotation name to open a context-sensitive menu used for rescanning the document and choosing the sort order.

Finding annotation data

If a document contains many different annotations, you may wish to use the annotation search capabilities in Acrobat. Finding information in annotations is limited to Acrobat; you can't use the Find command with annotations in Reader. To use the Find command with regard to annotations, open the Annotations palette menu. There are three find commands contained in the menu:

- ✦ **Find Annotation:** The author name, type, or keywords for notes can be searched to find a particular annotation. If Find Annotation is not active in the Annotations palette, select Rescan Document. When annotations are listed in the Annotations tab, the Find Annotation command will become active. When the Find Annotations dialog box appears, enter the word or words to be searched and click OK.

- ✦ **Find Next:** Once you determine what data is to be searched among the annotations in the open document, select Find Next to search for the next page meeting the same search criteria as specified the first time you searched for the data using the Find Annotation command.

- ✦ **Find Previous:** When you invoke the Find Annotations command from the Annotations palette menu, the first find will stop on the next page forward in your document that meets the search criteria. You can retrace your steps by searching backward through the document for the same criteria.

Importing and exporting annotations

The commands for importing and exporting annotations exist in the Annotations palette menu. You'll also notice the File ➪ Export ➪ Annotations command is available. Whether you choose to export annotations from either command, Acrobat will export annotations in the same order as viewed in the document from which you invoke the Export command. When exporting annotations from Acrobat, only the annotations will be exported. The data on each page will not be exported with the annotations. As a result, the file sizes for exported annotations will be considerably smaller than your original PDF documents.

 Exporting annotations is particularly helpful when distributing a file to many users and asking for input. Each user can export his or her annotations, which can then be collected by the PDF author. Subsequently, the export files can all be imported back into the original document. When importing the data, all page sequences and annotation types will be preserved.

Deleting annotations

Annotations can be deleted by selecting the annotation on a page and pressing the Backspace (Delete) key on your keyboard. If you have a few annotations on a page and wish to delete them, this method works well. However, if you wish to delete annotations from different pages, the Delete command in the Annotations palette will be more efficient. If you select Delete from the palette menu, and notice nothing happening on a document page or the list in the Annotations palette, the reason is no annotation was selected for deletion in the palette. Acrobat requires you to select an annotation in the Annotations palette and then choose the Delete command. If you want to delete multiple annotations, you can select them in the Annotations palette. To delete an annotation, click the one you want to delete and choose Delete from the palette menu or press the Backspace (Delete) key on your keyboard. Multiple selections are handled by the following methods:

✦ **Contiguous list selection:** To select multiple annotations in the Annotations palette in contiguous order, click the first annotation, move the cursor to the last annotation to be deleted, and hold the Shift key down while clicking the mouse button.

✦ **Noncontiguous list selection:** To select multiple annotations in the Annotations palette in a noncontiguous order, click the first annotation, move the cursor to the next annotation to be deleted, and hold the Ctrl key down while clicking the mouse button.

With either selection method, you can use either the palette menu command or the keystroke equivalent. If you wish to delete all annotations from your document, you can use another command. Select Tools ➪ Annotations ➪ Delete All. All the annotations created in the document will then be deleted.

Be certain to double-check your preference settings in the General Preferences dialog box. If Skip Edit Warnings is enabled in this dialog box, you will not be warned by Acrobat before the deletion occurs. This action cannot be undone. If you inadvertently delete all annotations and wish to regain them, select File ➪ Revert. Acrobat will only revert to the last saved version. If you save the file before reverting, all your annotations will be lost forever.

Summarizing annotations

When exporting annotations, you create a PDF file with annotations placed on pages where they appeared in the original document. If a note is contained on page 1 in the top-left corner of the page, the exported file will display the same view without the document page contents. In essence, the annotation will be placed on a blank page. Exporting annotations is great if you want to import them in an example as suggested previously. However, if you wish to review a summary of the annotation notes, a more efficient means of export is handled with the Summarize Annotations command. To access the command, you have to leave the Annotations palette and select Tools ➪ Annotations ➪ Summarize Annotations. When the command is invoked, a new PDF document will be created and automatically placed in view in Acrobat. The summary will list the annotations in page order and supply information respective to the associated notes. The information displayed includes the following:

✦ **Page number:** The logical page number will be displayed with all annotations listed below the page number in the order appearing on the page. Acrobat won't pay attention to the date of the annotations, even if the time and date for one annotation appears earlier than another. The physical position of the annotation (from top-left corner) determines the order.

✦ **Annotation *n*:** Annotations will be numbered by Acrobat beginning with Annotation 1, followed by Annotation 2, and so on. These numbers are assigned to the listed order on each page.

✦ **Label:** The author title determined in the Properties dialog box and appearing on the associated note title bar is denoted in the summary as Label.

✦ **Date:** The date the annotation was created appears in the Date item of the summary. The date field will be reported in the format *mm/dd/yy* and *hh:mm:ss*.

✦ **Text:** The text contained in the associated note will appear below the three preceding items. In Figure 8-32, a line or several lines of text display all the information that was supplied for each note.

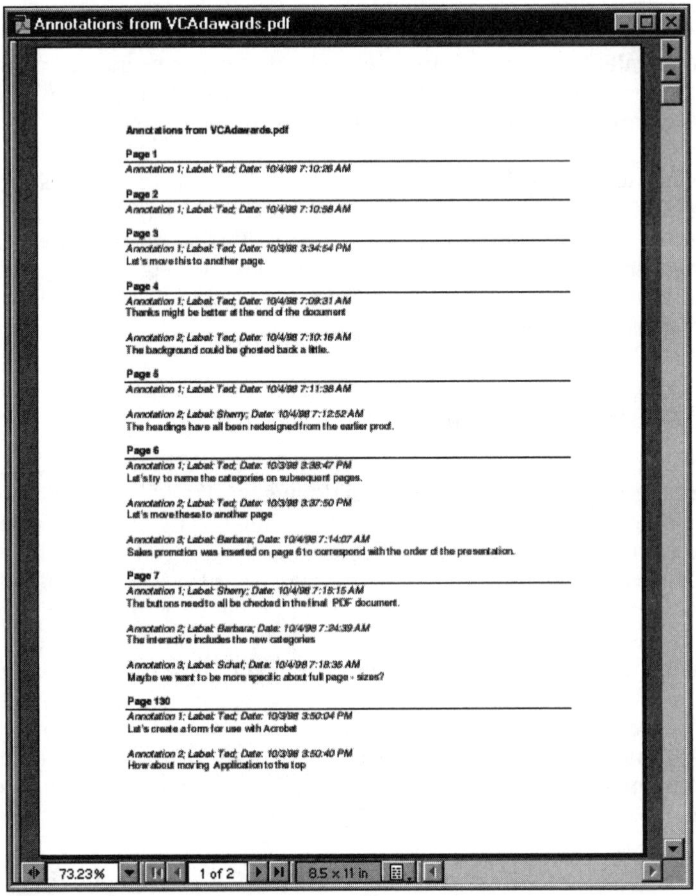

Figure 8-32: Select Tools ⇨ Annotations ⇨ Summarize Notes to create a new PDF file containing a note summary.

Using the Filter Manager

Another item listed in the Annotations menu appearing under the Tools menu is the Filter Manager command. Acrobat's Filter Manager can be selected by choosing Tools ⇨ Annotations ⇨ Filter Manager, or you can bring up the context-sensitive menu for an annotation item in the document window. Either method will produce the same dialog box.

The Filter Manager enables you to selectively determine which annotations will be displayed in your document. When you eliminate from view some annotation types, the list in the Annotations palette will be updated to conform to the selections made in the Filter Manager. Furthermore, when you elect to summarize notes, the current notes display will be included in the summary while excluding those that were omitted in the Filter Manager.

To get a feel for how annotations are created, sorted, managed, and summarized, let's walk through some steps that you can perform on your own computer.

STEPS: Creating and Summarizing Selective Notes

1. **Open a PDF document.** Choose a document with several pages (at least three). You can use one of the Help files in the Acrobat folder, if necessary.

2. **Create annotations.** Try to use several different annotation types. Don't use the audio or stamp annotations.

3. **Create notes for each annotation.** Double-click the annotation icon or use the context-sensitive menu and choose Open Note. In the note window, enter a few lines of text.

4. **Change the properties.** Try to create about a dozen different annotations. Change the author field twice, producing four notes for additional authors. The total will be 12 notes with three different authors. You can use the Edit ⇨ Properties command, the context-sensitive menu, or double-click the note title bar to access the Properties dialog box. When the Properties dialog box appears, change the author name field.

5. **Summarize the annotations.** Select Tools ⇨ Annotations ⇨ Summarize Annotations. A PDF document will be created and opened in Acrobat.

6. **Select the original file.** Select Window ⇨ *filename*, where *filename* will be the name of the original PDF you opened to create the annotations.

7. **Open the Filter Manager.** To open the Filter Manager, Select Tools ⇨ Annotations ⇨ Filter Manager; or bring up the context-sensitive menu by Control+clicking (Mac) or right-clicking (Windows) an annotation icon. When the menu appears, select Annotations Filter. The Filter Manager dialog box will open, as illustrated in Figure 8-33.

Continued

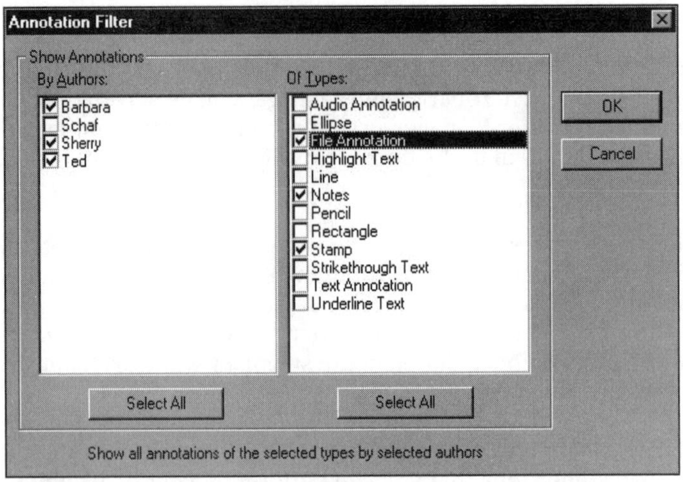

Figure 8-33: The Filter Manager displays the authors and annotations contained in the document.

8. **Eliminate two authors.** To eliminate two of the three authors you identified when the annotations were created, click the author names for those authors you wish to eliminate. The check mark to the left of the author name will disappear.

9. **Click OK.** Click OK to leave the Annotation Filter dialog box.

10. **Summarize the annotations.** Select Tools ➪ Annotations ➪ Summarize Annotations or press Cmd/Ctrl+Shift+T.

    Compare the difference between the first summary and the last. You should see only the annotations associated with one author appear in the second summary.

Printing annotations

I'll cover printing PDF documents more thoroughly when discussing printing and digital prepress in Chapter 16. I should mention printing respective to annotations here, though, in case you want to output them to hard copy. Printing annotations can be performed in either Reader or Acrobat by selecting either the Print tool in the Command Bar or by selecting File ➪ Print. Be certain to access the Print dialog box and not the Page Setup dialog box when printing annotations.

When you access the Print dialog box, a check mark will appear adjacent to the Annotations option, as shown in Figures 8-34 and 8-35. By default, the viewer will print annotations from your PDF files. If you don't want to have the annotations printed, disable this option.

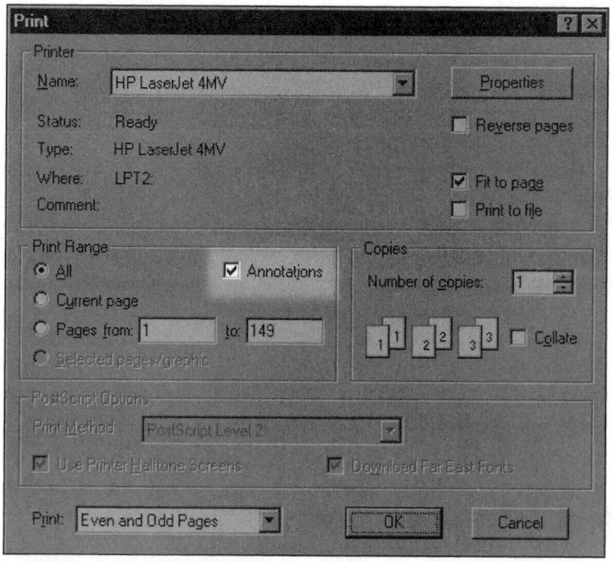

Figure 8-34: The Print dialog box in Windows with the Annotations option enabled.

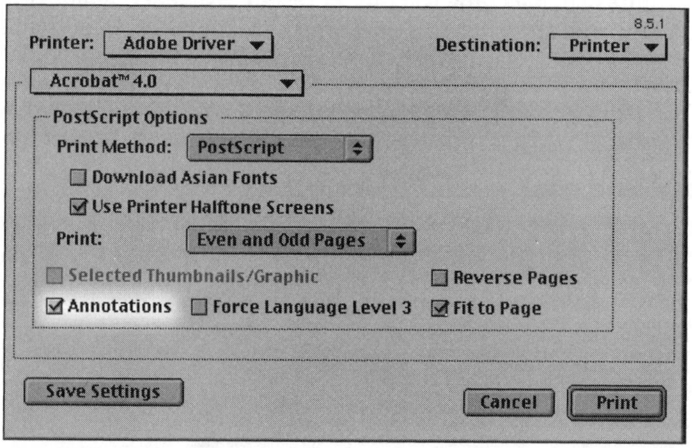

Figure 8-35: The Print dialog box on the Macintosh with the Annotations option enabled.

Editing Text

Creating text in note windows is one of the few means of adding text to PDF files. Acrobat is not a layout or word processing program, and doesn't come close to functioning like those applications without the use of third-party plug-ins. If you need to create copy that you wish to have appear on a page in a PDF document, you typically will want to return to the authoring application and set the type, and then redistill the file. Whereas earlier versions of Acrobat offered little in regard to adding text to the PDF page, Acrobat 4.0 provides somewhat more functionality in this area.

Before moving on to examining how text can be edited in Acrobat, let me start by telling you text editing with Acrobat tools is intended to only slightly modify documents. In rare cases, you may be able to correct typographical errors, but reworking a paragraph of text will be out of the question. Another matter to deal with in editing text is the availability of fonts. If fonts are subset in the PDF file, you won't be able to edit the text. Acrobat will prompt you if you attempt to edit subsetted fonts. A dialog box will appear asking if you wish to unembed the subsetted font. If you select Yes, font substitution will be used, and the edited text may not appear exactly like the other text on the page. If you think you may need to do some text editing in Acrobat, distill your files without font subsetting.

Using the TouchUp Text tool

The tool used for text editing in Acrobat is the TouchUp Text tool. When you use the TouchUp Text tool, Acrobat enables you to edit text in a single row at a time. Paragraphs with multiple lines are not recognized by Acrobat, something you may have already observed if you've ever worked with Adobe Illustrator and PDF files. Paragraph attributes such as tabs will often present problems. When you select the TouchUp Text tool and click in a line of text, the boundaries of the text block will appear with a rectangular border, as shown in Figure 8-36.

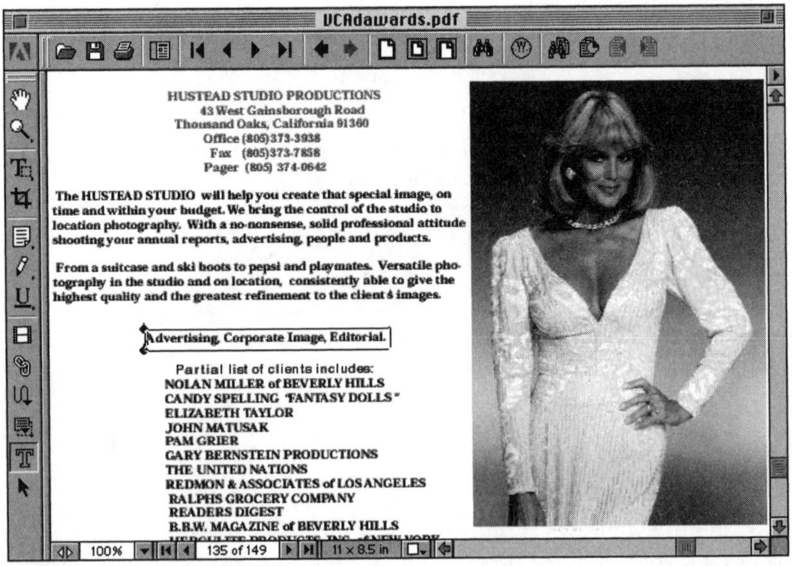

Figure 8-36: When the TouchUp Text tool is clicked over a word or character, the text block containing that word or character will appear within a border.

If you wish to reposition a text block, you are limited to horizontal movement only. By dragging the small arrow icons on the left side of the text block rectangle, you can move left or right. This movement will relocate the text within the rectangle border. Vertical movement is not possible in Acrobat without the use of third-party plug-ins.

Acrobat may display a warning dialog box indicating there is hidden information in the document when using the TouchUp Text tool. Acrobat can reference the document attributes with information that is hidden from the user. If you elect to proceed, the hidden information will be removed. An example of hidden information would be the text block formatting for character positions. If you create a document with tabs, for example, Acrobat uses a different means to describe where the text is tabbed. Because tabs are not available when creating text in Acrobat, if you proceed from this point, you can potentially encounter problems with where the characters will be displayed in a tabbed line of text. If you proceed to editing the text, you'll lose the tab attributes and won't be able to retab the line.

To edit text, select the TouchUp Text tool from the Acrobat Tool Bar and click the line of text you wish to edit. If text is contained within a link, press the Ctrl key down when clicking the text. The Ctrl key will enable you to pierce the link to select the text behind it.

Moving text

When you select text with the TouchUp Text tool, a rectangular border appears around the text. On the left side of the text border are line markers appearing as a down and up arrow. Line markers are visible by default when you select a line of text. If the markers are not visible, select Tools ➪ TouchUp ➪ Show Line Markers. To move text, position the cursor above a line marker. Click and drag the mouse left or right. You cannot position text up or down.

Fitting text to a selection

You can choose to fit the text to a selected area, which will either stretch the text or condense it to the area you select. If you change a word in a single line, and choose to fit the text to the selection, it may appear as though a second text block is created separate from the original text block. The display will be misleading, because all the text will remain in a single line. To fit text to a selection, choose Tools ➪ TouchUp ➪ Fit Text to Selection or use a context-sensitive menu, shown in Figure 8-37, by Control+clicking (Macintosh) or right-clicking (Windows).

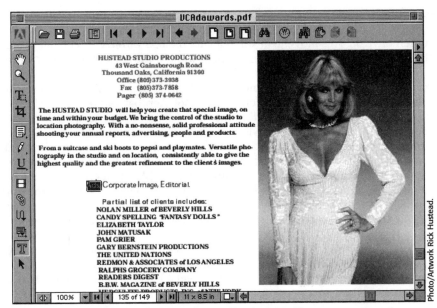

Figure 8-37: When you select Fit Text to Selection, it will appear as though a separate text block has been created. Here I edited the text block from Figure 8-36. The view is temporary. When I drag the cursor over the text, the complete text block from Figure 8-36 will be selected.

Text attributes

You can change some of the text attributes by using the Text Attributes palette, shown in Figure 8-38. To open the Text Attributes palette, select Tools ➪ TouchUp ➪ Text Attributes, or use the context-sensitive menu and select Attributes from the pop-up menu.

Figure 8-38: The Text Attributes palette enables text editing for font formatting, character formatting, and line spacing.

✦ **Font fills and strokes:** Fonts are selected when the Font tab is forward in the palette. If it is not in view, click the Font tab to bring it forward. The pop-up menu displays fonts loaded in your system. The items to the right of the point size box, represented by a solid fill box on the left and a diagonal line on the right, control the font fills and strokes. If you click the color swatch or the box with a diagonal line, the system color palette will open, enabling you to assign custom colors. The down arrows enable you to choose from preset color values without needing to go to the system color palette. The last item in both pop-up menus for color selection is Other. When you select Other, the system color palette will open.

In order to legally change attributes of fonts in a PDF document, you must own a copy of the font to be edited or have permission from the font manufacturer.

✦ **Character spacing:** There are four controls for editing character widths and spacing. All four field boxes accept values ranging from –32767 to 32767; however, values less than 50 or more than 500 are impractical. The first item is the horizontal scale specifications. The item below the Horizontal Scale option is for baseline shifts. The top-right corner is for character spacing, and the bottom-right corner is for word spacing.

✦ **Line formatting:** Line formatting controls the horizontal position of the text line. You can select either the Left, Right, Center, or Full Justification options in the tab.

Text editing controls

Moving around text blocks in Acrobat can be simplified by using keystrokes on your keyboard. Following is a list of keystrokes and how they relate to text editing:

✦ Click and drag across a line of text to select it.

✦ Double-click a word to select it (Macintosh only).

✦ Triple-click in a line of text to select the line (Macintosh only).

✦ Shift+click to select text from the first cursor position to the second click position.

✦ Use Shift+right arrow to select one character to the right; the selection is extended as long as the Shift key is pressed.

✦ Press Shift+left arrow to select one character to the left; the selection is extended as long as the Shift key is pressed.

✦ The up arrow moves the cursor to the preceding line of text.

✦ The down arrow moves the cursor to the following line of text.

✦ Cmd/Ctrl+A selects all the text in a line.

✦ Del (Delete key) on Mac and Windows numeric keypad deletes one character after cursor position OR all selected text.

✦ Delete on Mac and Backspace in Windows deletes one character to the left of cursor position *or* all selected text.

✦ Pressing any key when text is selected deletes the current selection and replaces the text with the keystroke.

✦ Pressing the right mouse button (Windows) opens a context-sensitive menu where the commands Cut, Copy, Paste, Delete, Select Line, Fit Text to Selection, and Attributes are available.

✦ Control+clicking a text block (Macintosh) opens context-sensitive menu and offers same choices as right-clicking in Windows.

✦ Edit ⇨ Clear deletes selected text.

✦ Edit ⇨ Deselect all deselects selected text.

Editable text

Depending on particular attributes of the PDF file and the application used to create the original file, you may find at times text cannot be edited. Guidelines for what is editable or not editable in Acrobat follow.

Text can be edited under the following conditions:

✦ Text created in layout, word processing, and illustration programs

✦ Text created in spreadsheet and database programs

✦ Text created in Microsoft Chart

✦ Embedded EPS graphics distilled with Acrobat Distiller

✦ PDF exports from Adobe Illustrator

✦ PDF files created from Adobe PageMaker

✦ Text rotated in any of the preceding applications

Text cannot be edited under the following conditions:

✦ Graphic file formats, including EPS, embedded in other documents and exported via PDFWriter*

✦ Text in raster image files (Photoshop)*

✦ Screen captures*

✦ Embedded fonts with subsetting

*You can perform workarounds with the Capture plug-in on these file types

As you work with text edits in Acrobat, I'm certain you'll quickly come to believe that all but minor changes require editing the PDF file in the producer application and redistilling the file. The TouchUp Text tool will be best employed when you use Acrobat Scan and make corrections to text recognized by Acrobat's optical character recognition (OCR) program, as discussed in Chapter 14.

Working with Graphics

Until Acrobat 4.0, any alterations for graphic elements were almost not existent. If you wanted to do anything other than copy or import a graphic, no other options were available unless you purchased some plug-ins from third-party manufacturers.

Now in version 4.0 of Adobe Acrobat there are some major changes to the handling of graphics from within the application. You can move graphics on a PDF page and you can edit graphics. Editing of graphic images is not directly handled within Acrobat. But the way the program handles graphic image editing is much preferable than having a bunch of imaging tools added to more palettes.

Chapter 3 demonstrated how to use the Graphics Select tool in Acrobat Reader. The same tool exists in Acrobat, and the way it's used in Acrobat is the same as it is handled in Reader. With Acrobat, the Tool Bar contains another tool to be used with graphic objects. The TouchUp Object tool is like a selection tool you may have used in other applications.

Using the TouchUp Object tool

The TouchUp Object tool appears as the last tool in the Acrobat Tool Bar. The tool is used for selecting objects within a PDF page. You won't find any attribute settings for the TouchUp Object tool in menus or palettes. Once an object is selected, you can choose to copy it or move it. If copying the object, the data will be stored on the Clipboard. Copied data can be pasted on a PDF document page or into other applications.

To select objects with the TouchUp Object tool, select the tool from the Acrobat Tool Bar and click an object in the document window. The object will be defined as a selection with handles appearing around the edges. Click and drag the object to relocate it on the PDF page.

When an object is selected, you can open a context-sensitive menu with Control+ click (Macintosh) or a right-click (Windows). The pop-up menu will appear with many of the same commands as those accessible in the Edit menu. The only item not accessible in the Edit menu is Edit Object, which appears as the last command in the pop-up window that appears for selected objects.

Editing objects

When an object is selected, choose Edit Object from the context-sensitive menu or hold down the Option key (Macintosh) or Ctrl key (Windows) and double-click the mouse button. Either action produces the same result. At this point, you will momentarily lose control of your computer. Acrobat will launch by default Adobe Illustrator 7 or Illustrator 8 if installed on your computer when vector objects are selected. If both Illustrator 7 and Illustrator 8 are installed, Illustrator 8 will be opened. These programs are determined in the TouchUp Preferences dialog box. For raster-based objects, the default is Adobe Photoshop 5. If you have earlier versions of either application, they won't be compatible with Acrobat 4.0.

When either Illustrator or Photoshop is launched, the object selected in the PDF document will appear in the application window for the program launched. As you work in either Illustrator or Photoshop, you can make any editing changes you would normally make before the file was converted to PDF. The only caveat when working with Illustrator involves fonts. If your object is text, you must have the proper font installed on your computer. If security settings have been specified for the PDF document, the Edit Image command won't be available. Neither using the context-sensitive menu nor double-clicking the object will enable you to modify it.

Using Acrobat's Edit Image command is much better than copying and pasting text. When you copy data and edit an image, the page must then be produced as a PDF file. Acrobat won't let you paste data back into the page. When Edit Image is used, the PDF document will be dynamically updated if any object edits are made.

To gain an understanding for how all this works, let's walk through the steps for editing an image.

STEPS: Editing an Image

1. **Open a PDF file.** Use a PDF file of your choice. If you do not have a file handy, create a page in a page layout application with a graphic image from either Adobe Illustrator or Adobe Photoshop. Print the file to disk and distill it in Acrobat Distiller.

2. **Select the object.** Use the TouchUp Object tool and select the image you wish to edit (see Figure 8-39).

3. **Verify preferences.** Select File ⇨ Preferences ⇨ TouchUp. In the Preferences dialog box, be certain the image editing program you intend to use appears listed in the dialog box. If it does not, click the Select button (Macintosh) or Ellipsis button (Windows). Navigate your hard drive to find the application you wish to use.

Note   If you opened an Illustrator file in Photoshop or vice versa, and then saved the file, the producer application will become Photoshop (or Illustrator). Keep in mind, Acrobat will open the file in the application from which the document was last saved.

4. **Select Edit Object.** Choose either the context-sensitive menu command for Edit Object or hold the Option key (Macintosh) or Ctrl key (Windows) down while double-clicking the selected object.

5. **Edit your image.** Perform some editing tasks that will be easily observable in Acrobat like applying a filter, changing color, and so on.

6. **Select File ➪ Save.** Be certain to click the Save button. If you provide another name for the image, it won't be updated properly in Acrobat. The Save command will save a temporary file to the location where the PDF document was opened.

7. **Quit the application.** After saving, quit the application where you edited your image. You will be returned to the Acrobat window, and your newly edited image will appear in the PDF file (see Figure 8-40).

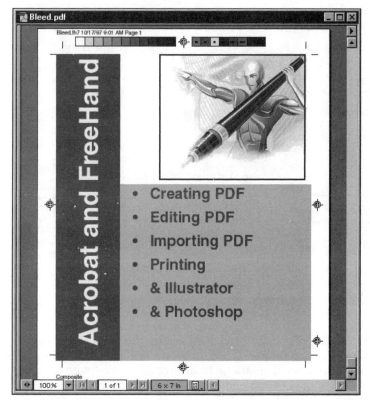

Figure 8-39: I created a PDF file from Macromedia FreeHand. The file included an image from Photoshop in the layout. Here the image to be edited is selected.

Continued

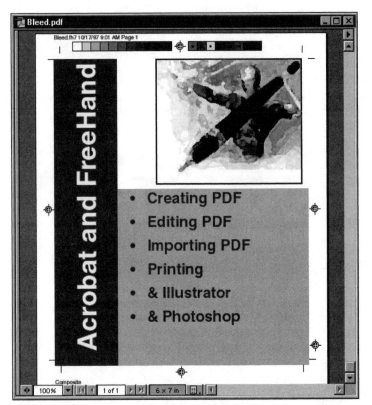

Figure 8-40: I applied the Watercolor filter in Photoshop to the image, saved my file, and quit the program. When I returned to Acrobat, the PDF document was updated with my edited image.

Now, isn't this pretty cool stuff? Dynamic image updates is a new feature in Acrobat 4.0 that can save much time when either vector or raster images need updating. If you use programs other than Adobe Illustrator or Adobe Photoshop, you need to test these steps with your application. Many programs will not work, especially in older versions.

Summary

✦ The Acrobat Tool Bar offers many tools for editing PDF files that are not available in Acrobat Reader.

✦ Annotations can be developed from among three major categories: Annotation tools, Graphic Markup tools, and Text Markup tools.

✦ Most annotations created in Acrobat have associated notes where descriptions of the annotation can be supplied.

✦ Annotations all have Properties dialog boxes in which unique options can be defined for the annotation type.

✦ Annotations can be exported from and imported back into PDF files. Additionally, annotation summaries can be created that immediately open as a new PDF document.

✦ The Annotations palette lists all the annotations in a document. Double-clicking an annotation in the palette will move you to the page where the annotation appears.

✦ Annotations can be sorted by Type, Author, Page Number, and Date.

✦ The Filter Manager enables you to selectively choose the annotations you wish to view in the PDF document. When selected annotations are eliminated from view, the annotation summary will only list the annotations visible in the document.

✦ The TouchUp Text tool is used for very minor edits to text in a PDF file. Text can be altered only one line at a time, although many different text attributes can be changed through the Text Attributes palette.

✦ The TouchUp Object tool enables you to select and move graphic elements on a PDF page. When you choose the Edit Image command, the selected image will appear in an editing program where changes can be made. When the file is saved from the editing program, the PDF page will be dynamically updated to reflect the edits.

✦   ✦   ✦

Articles, Bookmarks, and Thumbnails

✦ ✦ ✦ ✦

In This Chapter

Working with article threads

Using bookmarks

Working with thumbnails

Editing PDF pages

Working with destinations

✦ ✦ ✦ ✦

Part II covered all you need to know about editing text on a PDF page. In this part, you begin with viewing text in articles and learn how you can link to different views within a document.

Working with Articles

Acrobat offers a feature to link text blocks to provide easy navigation through columns of text. User-specified ranges of text can be linked together, thereby forming an article. Articles can be created in Acrobat and subsequently viewed in an Acrobat viewer. Articles can help you jump at warp speed through a PDF file, enabling you to read continuing sequences of paragraphs throughout a document. Working with articles is particularly helpful when you view PDF files on the World Wide Web. PDF files can be downloaded a page at a time in a Web browser, even if the PDF file is a multiple-page document. (There are some requirements at the server end, which I discuss in Chapter 15.) When the requirements are satisfied, however, you can browse PDFs on the Web without waiting for an entire file to download. Therefore, if you have a column or group of paragraphs of text that begins on page 1 and continues on page 54, an article thread can assist you in jumping from page 1 to page 54.

Article viewing and navigation

When you first open a PDF document, you'll want to determine if articles are present in the file. If articles are included in the PDF, you'll need to know a few basics on navigating through an article. To determine if articles exist in a PDF file, select Window ➪ Show Articles. A palette opens with tabs for Articles and Destinations, as shown in Figure 9-1. If you wish to move the Articles palette to the Navigation Pane, click the tab and drag to the top of the open Navigation Pane (see Figure 9-2).

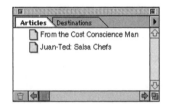

Figure 9-1: When you select Window ➪ Show Articles, a palette opens with the Articles tab displayed.

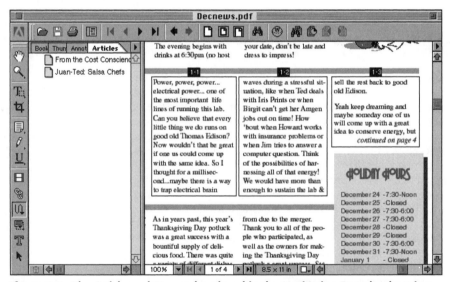

Figure 9-2: The Articles palette can be placed in the Navigation Pane by dragging the tab and dropping it on top of the open pane.

When the Articles palette is in view, any articles existing in the PDF file will be displayed in the palette list. If you select the Article tool from the Acrobat Tool Bar, the article definition boundaries will be displayed. In Figure 9-2, the Article tool is selected. The defined article is contained within rectangular boxes. If another tool is selected in the Tool Bar, the rectangles will disappear.

Article properties

The article properties are contained in a dialog box accessible by clicking an article with the Article tool. To open the Article Properties dialog box, select Edit ⇨ Properties or open a context-sensitive menu by Control+clicking (Macintosh) or right-clicking (Windows) and select Properties from the pop-up menu. The Properties dialog box is informational. When you view Properties, information supplied at the time the article was created is displayed for four data fields. The Title, Subject, Author, and Keywords fields are the same as those found in the Document Information dialog boxes. Inasmuch as the data for these fields is identical to that found in document information, Acrobat Search does not take advantage of the article properties information. When you use properties, they are designed to help you find information about an article before jumping to the page where the article is contained. All the fields can be edited when the Article Properties dialog box is opened, as shown in Figure 9-3. You can at any time change the data in the fields.

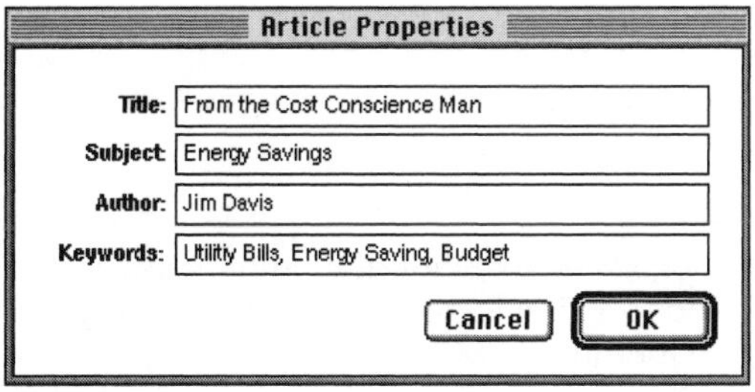

Article Properties	
Title:	From the Cost Conscience Man
Subject:	Energy Savings
Author:	Jim Davis
Keywords:	Utiltiy Bills, Energy Saving, Budget

[Cancel] [OK]

Figure 9-3: The Article Properties dialog box displays user-supplied information for Title, Subject, Author, and Keyword fields. These fields are not searchable through Acrobat Search.

Viewing articles

Before moving about a document to explore articles, the first item you should always check is the maximum view defined in the General Preferences dialog box. The default magnification view is 800 percent. When articles are viewed, this zoom may be much too high for comfortable viewing. Depending on your monitor size and your vision, you may find zooms of even 200 percent to be too large or too small. If you use a small monitor, a 200 percent zoom will usually lose columns adjacent to the column being read. Find a comfort zone for your own viewing preferences and set them up in the General Preferences dialog box.

Once the zoom is established, open the Articles palette by selecting Window ⇨ Show Articles. The Articles palette can remain as an individual palette, or you can drop it into the Navigation Pane. The palette menu in the Articles palette offers only one option. If you select Hide After Use from the palette menu, the palette will disappear. If you wish to have the palette remain but want more viewing area in the document, double-click the tab in the palette to collapse it. This choice offers the best viewing opportunities for articles while keeping the palette open.

To bring the palette back up you'll need to return to the Window menu and select Show Articles or double-click the tab in the palette. When articles are displayed in the palette, double-click an article. Acrobat will place in view the top corner where the article begins. You will immediately see a right-pointing arrow blink on the left side of the first line of text. Once an article is in view, select the Hand tool and position the cursor over the article. The cursor will change to a hand with an arrow pointing down. As you read articles, the cursor will change according to the direction Acrobat will take you when reading an article. For example, if viewing a column backward or up instead of down, the cursor will change display to inform you which direction will be navigated. The different cursor views are shown in Figure 9-4.

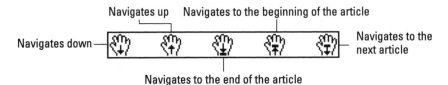

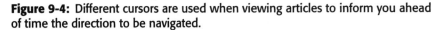

Navigates up   Navigates to the beginning of the article

Navigates down   Navigates to the next article

Navigates to the end of the article

Figure 9-4: Different cursors are used when viewing articles to inform you ahead of time the direction to be navigated.

To help navigation with the Article tool, several keyboard modifiers assist you when using the mouse. When the Hand tool is selected and the cursor appears over an article, use the following keyboard modifiers:

✦ **Click:** First click zooms to the Max Fit Visible preference setting. When the mouse cursor is placed at the end of a column, the cursor will display a down arrow. Click at the end of an article, and the view will take you to the beginning of the next column. Figure 9-5 displays the cursor icon when appearing over the end of a column.

✦ **Shift+click:** Moves backward or up a column. The cursor display will appear as shown in Figure 9-6.

✦ **Option/Ctrl+click:** Moves to the beginning of the article.

✦ **Option/Ctrl+Shift+click:** Moves to the end of an article

✦ **Return or Enter:** Moves forward down the column or to the top of the next column.

✦ **Shift+Return or Enter:** Moves up or to the previous column.

✦ **Cmd/Ctrl+Shift+click:** When the cursor is placed over a link, the link will be ignored and the article navigation will move the same as the first entry in this list.

The Image Source of Ventura and Thousand Oaks is opening a facility in Bakersfield. Our new location at 5472 California Avenue is expected to open by October 1, 1998.

The Image Source is a complete Digital Imaging and Photofinishing center providing digital output, High tech imaging and commercial photofinishing services. As the largest digital imaging/photofinishing center between the San Fernando Valley and Silicon Valley, The Image Source offers many unique services not currently available locally. For example, we have the only Kodak Photo CD system in Central California. We also have the only On Demand printing system with variable data in Central California.

Our commitment to keeping our customers informed on advanced digital methods is evidenced by our resident classroom where applications software training is offered. We offer classes

Our 20+ employees are well-trained experts in high-tech imaging and provide answers to digital imaging problems.

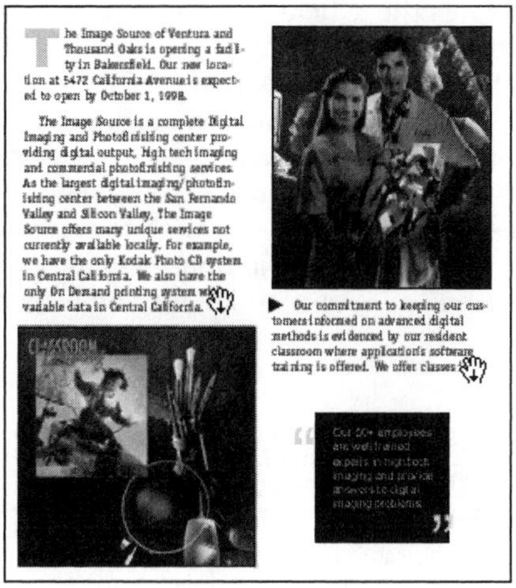

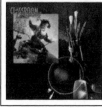

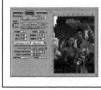

Figure 9-5: When the cursor is placed at the end of a column and the mouse button is clicked, the view will jump to the top of the next column and a right-pointing arrow will flash.

popular applications as well as provide free seminars on such topics as PostScript printing, Acrobat PDF Development, and Resolving Color Problems in Photoshop 5.0.

Scanning Issues

Questions about scanning are among the most frequent my customers usually ask. When to use a flatbed or drum scanner, what resolution is sufficient, how do we control dot gain, how can I improve my scans and what is the best scanner around are some of the questions I often encounter. Let's look at a few of the common questions posed on scanning and try to demystify the process.

Resolution

One of the first questions about scanning is usually *what resolution do I use?* Although this question is usually the first asked, it should be number two on your question list. Resolution is dependent upon frequency. What frequency will be used when your photographs are imaged? For color and grayscale work the safe zone is to use frequency X 2 (twice the halftone frequency). In many cases you can use 1.2 or 1.5 times the frequency which will provide excellent results. However, to be safe, you can always use frequency times two and be done with it. Therefore, if you plan on developing a grayscale display ad for a newspaper, you will typically use an 85 line screen. Resolution of your image should then be 170dpi. If you intend to print a color separation on coated stock with a 150 line screen, use 300dpi images.

Downsampling

Should I scan at a higher resolution and downsample my image to twice the halftone frequency? Everytime you resample images in Photoshop, you will be interpolating your image. Downsampling, transformations, etc. will employ interpola-

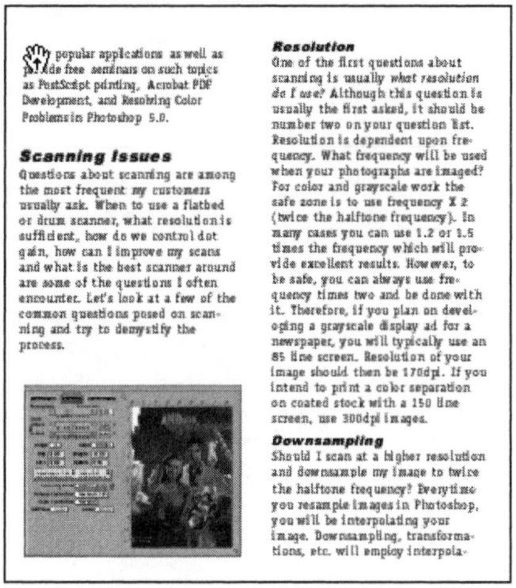

Figure 9-6: When the Shift key is pressed, the cursor icon will change, denoting the navigation will move backward.

Defining articles

Articles are defined by drawing rectangular boxes around the text within the article. While using the Article tool, the rectangular boxes will be visible. When the tool is not active, the rectangular boxes will become invisible.

Click and drag open a rectangle surrounding the column to appear as the first column in the article. When the mouse button is released, the rectangular box will be visible. At each corner will appear a handle that can be used to reshape the rectangle, and an article number will be visible at the top of the rectangle, as shown in Figure 9-7. The lower-right corner will contain a plus (+) symbol. The number appearing at the top of each box indicates the article number in the document (first article, second article, and so on) and the column order for the article. Therefore, a number such as 2-3 would represent the second article in the PDF file and the third column for the second article. The second digit indicates the order of forward movement as the article is read. The plus symbol appearing in the lower-right corner for each box indicates the article thread is continued. The plus symbol at the bottom right of the rectangle is used for linking. If you wish to return to Acrobat after deselecting the Article tool, you can continue to add more columns after reselecting the tool. Click the plus symbol, and Acrobat knows you want to extend the article thread.

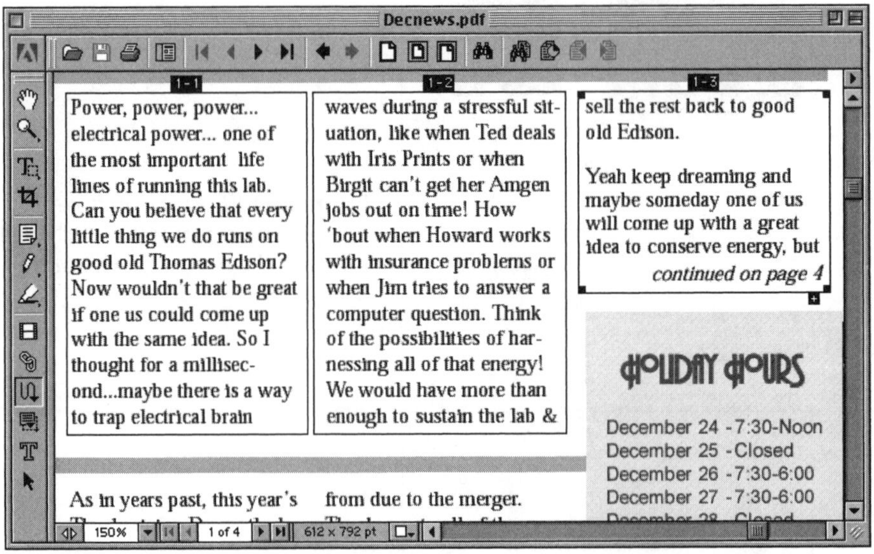

Figure 9-7: Article threads are indicated with rectangular boxes.

Ending an article thread

When the end of the article is included within a rectangle box, Acrobat needs to know you are at the end of the article. To end an article thread, press Return, Enter, or Esc. Acrobat will prompt you with a dialog box for supplying the Title, Subject, Author, and Keyword fields for the article properties. This dialog box appears immediately after defining an article. It's a good idea to supply the information at the time the dialog box is opened. The task will be completed, and you won't need to worry about returning to the Article Properties dialog box for last minute clean up.

Deleting articles

If an article has been created, you might wish to delete a portion of the article thread or the entire article. To delete either, select the Article tool in the Acrobat

Tool Bar and click a rectangle box where an article has been defined. Press the Delete (Backspace) key on your keyboard. A dialog box will appear that provides options for deleting the currently selected box or the entire article, as shown in Figure 9-8.

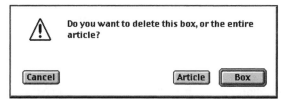

Figure 9-8: The Delete Article dialog box enables you to choose between deleting an article segment or the entire article.

If the Box button is selected, the deletion will eliminate the box within the article thread you selected when the Backspace (Delete) key was pressed on the keyboard. Clicking the Article button will delete all boxes used to define the article thread.

A context-sensitive menu can also be used to delete articles, as shown in Figure 9-9. Place the Article tool over a box and press the Control key (Macintosh) or the right mouse button (Windows). From the pop-up menu select Clear. The Clear command can also be chosen from the Edit menu when an article is selected. In either case, the same dialog box illustrated in Figure 9-8 will appear, asking if you want to delete the box or the entire article.

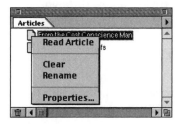

Figure 9-9: A context-sensitive menu can be opened for a selected article in the Articles palette with a Control+click (Macintosh) or right-click (Windows). When the Clear command is selected, the entire article will be deleted.

If you know you wish to delete the entire article, open the Articles palette and, using the context-sensitive menu described previously, click the article to be deleted. From the pop-up menu select Clear. If your Skip Edit Warnings preference setting is enabled in the General Preferences dialog box, the article will be deleted without warning. When the setting is disabled, a confirmation dialog box will appear. Either way, the entire article will be deleted. If the article is selected in the Articles palette and you choose Edit ➪ Clear, the same result will occur.

Combining articles

At times you may wish to join two articles to create a single article. The reader can then continue a path through all contents of the former two articles, which will now be in a single thread. To join two articles, you must first have them defined in the PDF document. Move to the last column of the first article and click the plus symbol in the last box. This click will load the Article tool. Next, move to the beginning of the article to be joined to the first article, and Option/Ctrl+click inside the first box. While the modifier key is pressed, the cursor icon will change, as illustrated in Figure 9-10.

 Figure 9-10: When the Option/Ctrl key is pressed, the cursor will change to an icon informing you the articles selected will be joined.

The numbering at the top of each box in the second article will change. For example, if you have two articles, the first numbered 1-1, 1-2, 1-3 and the second article numbered 2-1, 2-2, the new numbering for the second article will be 1-4 and 1-5. Article 2 takes on the attributes of Article 1 and assumes the next order of the columns. In addition, the properties identified in the second column will be lost. Because the continuation of the thread is from Article 1, all attributes for Article 1 will supersede those of Article 2.

> **Tip**   If you wish to combine two articles and assume the properties of a given article, always start with the article attributes to be retained. For example, in the preceding case, begin with article 2. Select the plus symbol at the end of the last column and click. Option/Ctrl+click in the first box for Article 1. When the two articles become combined, the attributes of Article 2 will be retained.

To gain an understanding of creating and joining articles, follow through the steps that appear next.

STEPS: Creating and Combining Articles

1. **Open a PDF file with multiple columns and multiple pages.** Try to use a file with at least three pages and several columns of text on each page. If you do not have available a PDF file you created, use one of the help files installed with Acrobat.

2. **Create an article thread.** Select the Article tool and draw at least two rectangular boxes around columns of text appearing on a page. Navigate to a second page and draw at least one column of text to continue the article.

3. **Complete the properties information.** Press Return, Enter, or Esc to end the article. The Article Properties dialog box will appear. Supply information for the Title, Subject, Author, and Keywords fields.

4. **Create a second article thread.** Repeat Steps two and three. Locate a few columns of text on a page and produce another article. Complete the Properties dialog box information after ending the thread.

5. **Browse your articles.** Select the Hand tool from the Acrobat Tool Bar and review the article. Check the navigation for article 1 to be certain it follows the thread and moves you from one page to another.

6. **Compare the articles properties.** Open the Articles palette. You should see the two new articles listed. Review the Properties dialog boxes with a context-sensitive menu or by selecting Edit ➪ Properties. You must close one Article Properties dialog box before viewing the other.

7. **Combine the articles.** Select the Articles tool and click the plus symbol at the end of article 1. Position the cursor in the first box for article 2. Hold down the Option/Ctrl key and click.

8. **Review the Properties.** If the articles have been joined successfully, you should see only one article listed in the Articles palette. Open the Article Properties dialog box and review the properties. You'll note the properties for Article 1 prevail.

Working with Bookmarks

Bookmarks work the way a table of contents does in PDF documents. Bookmarks can be created from layout programs, as mentioned in Chapter 6, or they can be created in Acrobat. Whereas tables of contents in publications are static, bookmarks in Acrobat viewers are dynamic; they enable you to jump to sections and views within an open document or links to files stored on a computer or server.

Bookmarks are viewed in the Navigation Pane. Open a PDF file, click the Show/Hide Navigation Pane icon in the Command Bar, and bookmarks will appear as the default view. If no bookmarks are included in the document, the window will appear empty. The Navigation Pane will list bookmarks individually, or you may see them nested in groups. The display looks similar to what you'd see for annotations. A right-pointing arrow (Macintosh) or plus symbol (Windows) indicates the bookmarks are collapsed. Clicking the icon will expand bookmarks.

On the status bar at the bottom of the Navigation Pane, several icons appear for editing bookmarks. The Trash icon will delete a selected bookmark. If no bookmark is selected, the Trash icon will appear grayed out. The Page icon appearing to the right of the Trash icon will create a new bookmark. The bookmark created will mark the current page and the zoom view. By default, the name will appear as *Untitled* and remain so until you provide a bookmark name. The last icon in the status bar is the Find current bookmark button. When you click this icon, Acrobat will find a bookmark associated with the page you are viewing. If the current page has no bookmark, the bookmark preceding the page will be selected. In bookmark terms, selected bookmarks will appear in bold type in the bookmark list (see Figure 9-11).

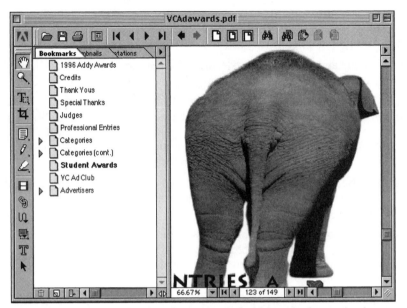

Figure 9-11: Selected bookmarks appear in bold type in the Navigation Pane. Nested bookmarks will appear with a right-pointing arrow (Macintosh) or plus symbol (Windows). To expand a bookmark list, click the arrow/plus icon.

Adding and deleting bookmarks

Bookmarks are added to PDF files in several ways. Regardless of the tool or command used to create a bookmark, you should first navigate to the page and view before creating it. Creating bookmarks is like capturing a page view. When the bookmark is created, it is associated to the page and current zoom level displayed in Acrobat. Therefore, if you wish to have page 22 marked with the page fitting within the window, you go to page 22, select Fit in Window from the View menu, and then click the Page icon in the status bar. Bookmarks can also be created by selecting Cmd/Ctrl+B or bringing up a context-sensitive menu in the bookmark list window. The bookmark will appear in the Navigation Pane in the bookmark list. By default the name will be *Untitled*. *Untitled* will be highlighted, so you can immediately provide a descriptive name for the new bookmark. When finished naming a bookmark, press the Return or Enter key.

Deleting bookmarks is also handled in several ways. When you wish to delete a bookmark, select it and press the Delete (Backspace) key on your keyboard. You can also use the context-sensitive menu or the Trash icon in the status bar. Regardless of which method is used, if the Skip Edit Warnings setting is enabled in the General Preferences dialog box, the bookmark will be deleted without warning.

Ordering bookmarks

Bookmarks created in a document will appear in the order they are created, regardless of the page order. For example, if you create a bookmark on page 15, and then create another on page 12, the bookmarks will appear with page 15 listed before page 12 in the bookmark list. At times you may wish to have the bookmarks list displayed according to page order. Additionally, bookmarks may appear more organized if they are nested in groups. If you have a category and a list of items to fit within that category, you may wish to create a hierarchy that will expand or collapse on selection of the right arrow/plus symbol discussed earlier. Fortunately, Acrobat enables you to change the order without recreating the current bookmark order. Additionally, you can categorize the bookmarks in groups.

To reorder a bookmark, select the page icon adjacent to the bookmark name in the list and drag it up or down. A highlight bar represented by a horizontal line will appear when you drag to a location where the bookmark may be relocated, as shown in Figure 9-12. As you move the bookmark, a "do not" symbol, like the one shown in Figure 9-13, will first appear until you drag the bookmark to an acceptable location. To nest a child bookmark below a parent bookmark, drag up or down and slightly to the right, as shown in Figure 9-14. Wait for the highlight bar to appear before releasing the mouse button.

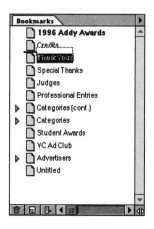

Figure 9-12: A bookmark repositioned to appear directly below another bookmark will display a highlight bar when Acrobat accepts the new location.

Figure 9-13: A "do not" symbol such as this one will appear until you move a bookmark to an acceptable location.

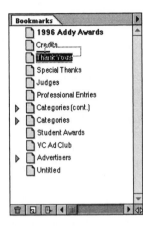

Figure 9-14: To make a child bookmark nested below a parent, move the bookmark slightly to the right until you see the highlight bar.

If you have a parent bookmark with several child bookmarks nested below it, you can move the parent to a new location. Drag the parent bookmark, and all subordinate bookmarks below it will move with the parent. If you wish to remove a subordinate bookmark from a nest, click and drag the bookmark to the left and either down or up to the location desired. Multiple nesting is also available with bookmark organization. A bookmark can be subordinate to another bookmark that is itself nested under a parent bookmark. To subordinate a bookmark under a child bookmark, use the same method as described previously for creating the first order of subordinates. As you drag right and up slightly, you can nest bookmarks at several levels.

Multiple bookmarks can also be relocated. To select several bookmarks, Shift+click each bookmark to be included in the group. As you hold the Shift key down, you can add more bookmarks to the selection. If you click one bookmark at the top or bottom of a list and Shift+click, all bookmarks between the two will also become selected. Once selected, drag one of the bookmarks to a new location in the list. It doesn't matter which bookmark is dragged—their selected order will remain in effect.

To understand a little more about creating and organizing bookmarks, follow these steps:

STEPS: Creating and Organizing Bookmarks

1. **Open a multiple page PDF document.** Use one of the help files if you don't have a PDF document of your own creation.

2. **Open the Bookmark palette.** Click the Navigation Pane and select the Bookmark tab to bring it forward.

3. **Create a bookmark on page one.** Try to become familiar with the keystroke modifiers. Use Cmd/Ctrl+B to create the bookmark. Keep in mind, the current zoom view will also be recorded with the bookmark. If you wish to fit the document in the window, select the appropriate view before creating the bookmark.

4. **Name the bookmark.** When the bookmark is created, it will need to be named. Type a descriptive name.

5. **Register the bookmark.** To inform Acrobat you have finished typing the bookmark name, press the Return or Enter key.

6. **Create three more bookmarks.** Navigate your document and select the views you wish to appear when the bookmarks are selected. Create a bookmark on three individual pages. To simplify the example, I'll use Page 1, Page 2, and so on, for my bookmark names.

7. **Organize the bookmarks.** Move the second bookmark up slightly and to the right. Release the mouse button when the highlight bar appears offset to the right below the first bookmark. Move the fourth bookmark below the third in the same manner, as shown in Figure 9-15.

Figure 9-15: After the bookmarks are created, reorganize them by dragging the bookmarks up and to the right of each parent.

8. **Reorder the bookmarks.** Drag Page 3 up above Page 1 to reorder the bookmarks, as shown in Figure 9-16. When the highlight bar appears, release the mouse button.

Figure 9-16: The bookmarks were reordered by dragging the Page 3 bookmark straight up above Page 1.

Tip

When the Navigation Pane is closed, a bookmark can be created and the Navigation Pane opened in one step. Create the bookmark by pressing Cmd/Ctrl+B on the page you wish to bookmark. The Navigation Pane will open and your bookmark, named *Untitled,* will appear. The bookmark will be created after the last bookmark listed in the Navigation Pane.

By default, new bookmarks will appear at the end of a bookmark list. If you wish to place a bookmark within a series of bookmarks, select the bookmark you wish the new bookmark to follow. When you select New Bookmark from the palette menu in the Bookmarks palette or press Cmd/Ctrl+B, the new bookmark will appear after the one you selected.

Renaming bookmarks

If you create a bookmark and wish to change the bookmark name at a later time, select the bookmark to be edited in the Bookmarks palette. From the palette menu, select Rename Bookmark. Acrobat will highlight the name in the Bookmarks palette. Type a new name and press the Return/Enter key on your keyboard.

Structured bookmarks

Structured bookmarks retain document structure in files generated from Microsoft Word and Web pages. Microsoft Word headings and certain Web page content such as URLs for links contain such structure. When pages are converted to PDFs, the structure from the files are converted to bookmarks. Structured bookmarks can be used to navigate PDF pages, reorganize the pages, and delete pages. Conversion of files containing tables, images, HTML table cells, and other such items can be bookmarked with a structured bookmark. More on using structured bookmarks appears in Chapter 15.

Bookmark properties

Many more options for bookmark navigation exist with settings available for bookmark properties. Accessing the Bookmark Properties dialog box is handled by first selecting the bookmark in the bookmark list. If a page action is associated with the bookmark, press the Ctrl key while selecting the bookmark. You can open the context-sensitive menu by Control+clicking (Macintosh) or right-clicking (Windows), or select Bookmark Properties from the palette menu, as shown in Figure 9-17. If you Control+click the bookmark name, you can also open the Bookmark Properties dialog box by pressing Cmd/Ctrl+I. When the dialog box opens, select the pop-up menu for Type. You can choose from a number of options for the type of bookmark property. For now, let's restrict the discussion to the Open File option on this menu. (The remaining options are discussed in Chapter 10.) Select Open File from the Type pop-up menu.

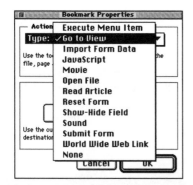

Figure 9-17: The Bookmark Properties dialog box enables you to define a number of different actions accessible when selecting a bookmark.

When Open File is selected from the Type pop-up menu, the button below Type will appear as Select File. Click this button, and a navigation dialog box will appear, enabling you to select a file. When you find a file to be opened, select it and click the Select button in the navigation dialog box. When you return to the PDF document, click the bookmark and the file identified will open. If the option Open Cross-Doc Links in Same Window is enabled in the General Preferences dialog box, Acrobat will prompt you to save your file if not yet saved. When you click Save, the file will be saved and then closed. The selected file will subsequently open. If you wish to keep both documents open, disable the Open Cross-Doc Links in Same Window preference setting.

Working with Thumbnails

Thumbnails are mini-views of PDF pages that can be displayed in two sizes. Thumbnails are not only views of the pages, but are also navigational links and can be used in ordering your pages. When used as a tool for ordering pages, thumbnails work like a slide organizer in which you can see all the slides and move them around. When you saw how to reorganize bookmarks earlier, you may have noticed that moving bookmarks around has no effect on page order. Thumbnails, on the other hand, retain links to pages, and moving thumbnails changes the page order of a document. In order to view thumbnails in a document, they must first be created.

Creating and deleting thumbnails

Adding thumbnails to a PDF document will increase its size. Thumbnails add approximately 3K to each page. If you want to keep your PDF files small, you'll want to save the final file without thumbnails. Fortunately, you can create thumbnails, edit your PDF file, and then delete the thumbnails after you finish editing. When viewing thumbnails, Acrobat provides you with two different views. You can select Small thumbnails or Large thumbnails from either the context-sensitive menu or the palette menu.

Thumbnails can be created by batch-processing PDF files, at the time of distillation, or within an open PDF document. When you select File ➪ Batch Process, a dialog box will open containing an option for creating thumbnails. In Distiller's General Job Options, there will also be an option for creating thumbnails. When a PDF document is opened in Acrobat, you can use either the palette menu or a context-sensitive menu to create thumbnails. All said, Acrobat provides many different ways to create thumbnails (see Figure 9-18).

 Thumbnails can also be deleted from PDF documents either individually in Acrobat or by using the Batch Process command. If your work environment is such that you do a lot of editing in Acrobat and often use thumbnails, you may wish to create them during distillation. When you finish up the jobs and want to post PDF files on the Web or create CD-ROMs, you can batch-process the files for optimization and delete the thumbnails. When the Batch Process command is used, a pop-up menu enables you to create or delete thumbnails.

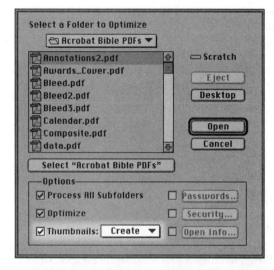

Figure 9-18: Acrobat provides several ways to create thumbnails. Selecting File ⇨ Batch Process enables you to create thumbnails for a folder of PDF files (a). When distilling PostScript files in Acrobat Distiller, Distiller's General Job Options has an option for creating thumbnails (b). When working in Acrobat, you can use a context-sensitive menu or the Thumbnail palette menu (not shown) to create thumbnails (c).

Regardless of whether the thumbnail is created, you can navigate the PDF document by double-clicking a thumbnail to jump to the respective page. Obviously the navigation will be easier if the thumbnails have been created — but they are not necessary. You can also change views in the Thumbnail palette. The small rectangle displays a handle in the lower-right corner. Drag the handle to reshape the rectangle, and the view will correspond to the rectangle size.

Editing PDFs with thumbnails

Your first clue to the editing capabilities Acrobat provides when working with thumbnails is the palette menu in the Thumbnail palette. Open the palette menu by clicking the right arrow in the top-right corner of the palette. Palette choices provide many options for page editing. These same choices are also available when Document ⇨ Pages is selected. Commands for creating and deleting thumbnails are not available from the menu choices, but the remaining page editing commands are the same as on the palette menu.

Reordering pages

Thumbnails can be used with drag-and-drop actions for several of the commands listed in either of the menus just described. One thing the menu choices don't provide you is a command for changing page order. With menu commands, you would have to extract a page, and then move to a location to insert the extracted page. This method of page editing requires several steps. When thumbnails are used, you can perform the series in one step. To reorder pages using the drag-and-drop method, open the Navigation Pane and click the Thumbnails tab to bring the palette forward. Select Small thumbnails from the palette menu. Select the page you wish to reorder and drag it to the left or right of the thumbnail where the page is to appear. A vertical highlight bar will appear where the page will be relocated. When pages are reordered, all the links on the page will be preserved.

Copying pages

Pages can be copied within a PDF document or between two open PDF documents. To copy a page with thumbnails, hold the Option/Ctrl key down as you drag a page to a new location. Within a PDF file, drag the page to a new location and release the mouse button when you see the vertical highlight bar appear. To copy a page between two documents, open the PDF files and view them tiled either vertically or horizontally. The Thumbnails palette must be in view on both PDF documents. To copy a page from one PDF document to another, click and drag the thumbnail from one file to the Thumbnail palette in the other document. The vertical highlight bar will appear where the new page will be located when you release the mouse button. If viewing Large thumbnails, a horizontal bar will appear.

Removing pages

The previous example performs like a copy-and-paste action. You can also create a cut-and-paste action whereby the page is deleted from one PDF document and copied to another document. To remove a page and place it in another PDF file, hold the Option/Ctrl key down, and then click and drag the page to another Thumbnail palette in another file. The page will be deleted from the original file.

Caution   Be certain not to confuse the modifier keys. When Option/Ctrl+click+drag is used with a PDF file in view, the page will be copied. When using the same keys between two documents, the page is deleted from the file of origin and copied to the destination file.

Editing Pages

In this context editing pages refers to the PDF page as an entity and not the page contents. Rather than look at changing individual elements on a page, this section examines some of the features for structuring pages as an extension of the commands found in the Thumbnails palette. Page editing in this regard relates to the insertion, deletion, extraction, and replacement of PDF pages. Additionally, cropping and rotating pages are covered.

Before you go about creating a huge PDF document with links and buttons, it is imperative to understand how Acrobat structures a page and related links. Bookmarks and other links are specified within a PDF document and are user defined. Thumbnails and the link to the respective pages are handled by Acrobat. You have no choice with a link from a thumbnail to a page. With regard to links and bookmarks, think of Acrobat as having two layers. One layer contains the page and its contents, and the layer hovering over the page contents is where all the links appear. When viewing a PDF file, you don't see the layers independent of each other. This said, when you delete a page, all the links to the page will be lost. Acrobat makes no provision to go to the page following a deleted page that may be the target view of a link. Therefore, if you set up a bookmark to page 4 and later delete page 4, the bookmark has no place to go.

When editing pages in Acrobat, you can choose to insert a page, delete a page, extract a page, and replace a page. If you understand the page structure, you'll know when to use one option versus another. Each of the options is accessed by choices available in the Thumbnails palette menu, by selecting Document ⇨ Pages, or by using a context-sensitive menu while clicking a thumbnail in the Thumbnails palette.

✦ **Inserting Pages:** When you select this option, a dialog box appears in which you can navigate to another PDF file and select it for insertion. The Insert dialog box, shown in Figure 9-19, enables you to choose the location for the insertion regardless of the current page viewed. You can choose to insert a page either before or after the page determined in a field box. Inserted pages will not affect any links in your document. All the pages will be *pushed* left or right depending on whether you select the Before or After option. If you attempt to insert a secure PDF document, Acrobat will prompt you for a password. This action applies to all the options listed below.

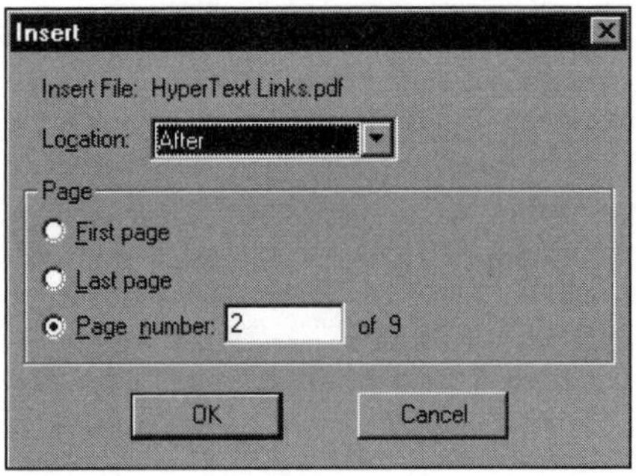

Figure 9-19: The Insert dialog box enables you to locate the page that will precede or follow another page that you specify.

✦ **Deleting Pages:** When you delete a page, you delete not only its contents but also its links. If a bookmark or other link is targeted for the deleted page, all links to the page will be inoperable. When creating a presentation in Acrobat with multiple pages, you must exercise care when deleting pages to be certain no links are made to or from the page.

✦ **Extracting Pages:** Extracting a page is like copying it and then pasting it into a new PDF document. Extracting pages has no effect on bookmarks or links. The new PDF page created in the new PDF document will not retain any of the links of the page from which it was extracted.

✦ **Replacing Pages:** This option only affects the contents of a PDF page — the link layer is unaffected. If you have links going to or from the replaced page, all links will be preserved. When editing PDF documents where page contents need to be changed, redistilled, and inserted in the final document, always use the Replace Page command.

Cropping pages

Acrobat has a tool in the Tool Bar for cropping pages. You can select the tool and draw a marquee in the document window to define the crop region, or the Crop Pages command can be selected from either the Thumbnails palette menu or by using the context-sensitive menu. Regardless of which manner you select to crop pages, Acrobat will open a dialog box (see Figure 9-20) that can provide you some additional choices for cropping pages. If the Crop tool from the Acrobat Tool Bar is not used, the crop dimensions can be specified in the dialog box. When the Crop tool is used, the cursor will change to a scissors icon when moved inside the marquee created with the tool. When you click the mouse button, the Crop Pages dialog box will open. On selecting either of the other two methods, the Crop Pages dialog box will open. The Crop Pages dialog box offers several options from which to choose when cropping pages:

✦ **Margins:** Choices for margins are available in this pop-up menu. The Custom Margins option enables you to define the margins in the four field boxes below the pop-up menu. You can use the up or down arrows and watch a preview in the thumbnail at the left side of the dialog box. As you click the up or down arrow, the margin line will be displayed in the thumbnail.

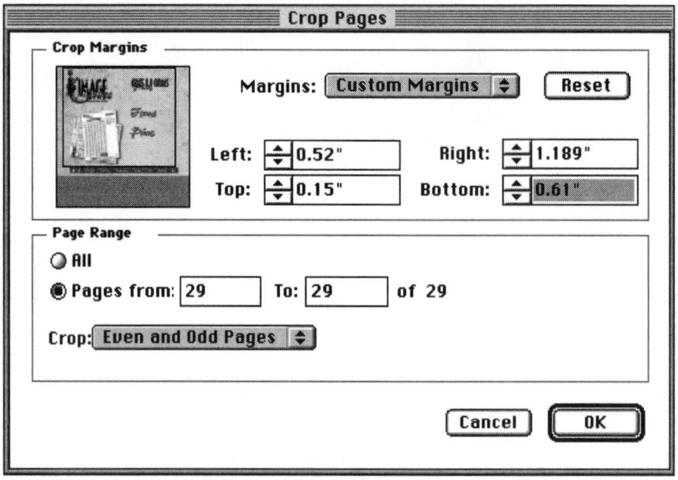

Figure 9-20: The Crop Pages dialog box displays a thumbnail image of the document page and offers options for crop margins and page ranges.

✦ **Bounding Box:** Clips to the content on the page. If text or graphics appears inside some white space, the crop rectangle will move to one pixel outside the page data on all four sides. If you have a background filling the entire page, the crop bounding box will be determined by the size of the background image.

✦ **None:** Resets the crop margins to zero. If you change the dimensions with either of the preceding settings, and then select None from the pop-up menu, all field boxes will return to zero.

✦ **Page Range:** Pages identified for cropping can be handled in the Page Range options. If All is selected, all pages in the PDF file will be cropped as defined. Specific pages can be targeted for cropping by entering values in the Pages from and To field boxes. Choices for Even and Odd Pages, Even Pages Only, and Odd Pages Only are selected from another pop-up menu.

✦ **Reset:** The Reset button in the top-right corner of the dialog box is different from the None margin option. When you select None with a previously cropped document, the original document size will be restored. Reset only applies to changes while the Crop Pages dialog box is open. When the dialog box is open, it appears as if these two options are identical. Reset, however, will not restore the original page from cropped pages.

Cropping pages does not eliminate data from the PDF document even when resaved. If you crop a page, the printed page will appear as it is viewed on screen with the data cropped. If you return to the Crop Pages dialog box either after cropping or after saving and reopening the file and select None from the Margins pop-up menu, the PDF page will be restored to the original size.

Tip   If you wish to crop pages to the same values in two different PDF documents, crop the page(s) in your first document using the menu command or Crop tool. From the Thumbnails palette select Insert Pages and select the second file to be cropped to the same dimensions. Note the page numbers for the inserted pages. Move to the page you cropped and select the Crop Pages command from the Thumbnails palette menu. The page dimensions for the cropped region will be listed in the field boxes. Enter the values for the new inserted pages in the Pages from and To field boxes. Select OK and the pages will be cropped to the same dimensions. Select Delete from the Thumbnails palette menu and enter the number for all but the new inserted pages. Select the File ➪ Save As command and rename the file. Your second document will now be cropped to the same dimensions as the first document.

Rotating pages

PDF documents can contain many pages with different page sizes. You can have a business card, a letter-sized page, a tabloid page, and a huge poster, all contained in the same file. Depending on the authoring program for an original document, at times there may be some problems with pages appearing rotated or physically inverted. At other times, you may wish to print duplexed material and need to rotate a page 180° to accommodate two-sided printing. Regardless of whether you wish to overcome a limitation or suit a design need, Acrobat enables you to control page rotations.

Rotating pages is handled in either the Document ➪ Pages submenu or by using the Thumbnails palette menu or context-sensitive menu. When you select Rotate Pages through any of these methods, the Rotate Pages dialog box will appear. The direction of rotation is determined in a pop-up menu, which enables you to rotate either clockwise or counterclockwise. Pages targeted for rotation are specified in the field boxes in the dialog box, and you can supply a range if you want multiple pages rotated. The default value will be the current page viewed in the PDF document. When you select OK, a warning dialog box will appear if the Skip Edit Warnings option in General Preferences is not enabled.

Understanding Destinations

Destinations work similarly to bookmarks. The advantage in using destinations is the capability to sort the destination names by either the name or page number. Unlike bookmarks, destinations have no properties. You can't create actions associated with the destination as you can with bookmarks, and destinations will only work within a PDF document, not across multiple PDF files.

Destinations are made visible in the Destinations palette. To open the palette, select Window ➪ Show Destinations. The palette, which has some similar attributes as the other palettes covered in this chapter, will appear. The status bar contains icons for actions such as trashing a destination, creating a new destination, and rescanning the document for destinations included in the file. To determine whether destinations exist, open the Destinations palette by selecting Window ➪ Show Destinations and click the Scan document icon in the palette status bar. Acrobat will scan the document and list all destinations in the palette.

Creating destinations

Creating a destination works the same as creating bookmarks. First zoom to the view on a document page you wish to define as a destination. When the page and view are specified, click the Create new destination icon in the Destinations palette. Acrobat will automatically name the destination *Untitled*. The destination name should be descriptive of the location. Enter the text you wish to call the destination and press the Return or Enter key on your keyboard.

Creating destinations can also be handled in the palette menu appearing in the Destinations palette or by using a context-sensitive menu. If you use a context-sensitive menu, be certain to click in an empty area of the Destinations palette. If you open the menu while Ctrl+clicking (Macintosh) or clicking the right mouse button (Windows) on a destination name, you won't see the New Destination command appear. Renaming destinations can be handled by opening the context-sensitive menu while clicking a destination name. Additional destinations are subsequently created by navigating to new pages, selecting the desired view, and selecting the New Destination command. As each destination is named, the corresponding page number will appear in the Destinations palette.

Sorting destinations

As destinations are created, they will be listed in the Destinations palette. If you open a PDF file and the destinations do not appear, click the Scan document icon in the status bar or select Scan Document from the palette menu in the Destinations palette. When the destinations appear, you can choose to display the list according to an alphabetical order, as shown in Figure 9-18, or according to the page number associated with the destination, as shown in Figure 9-19. To sort destinations according to name, click Name, which appears below the palette tab. To sort by page number, click Page, which is adjacent to Name in the palette. Acrobat will sort the list accordingly.

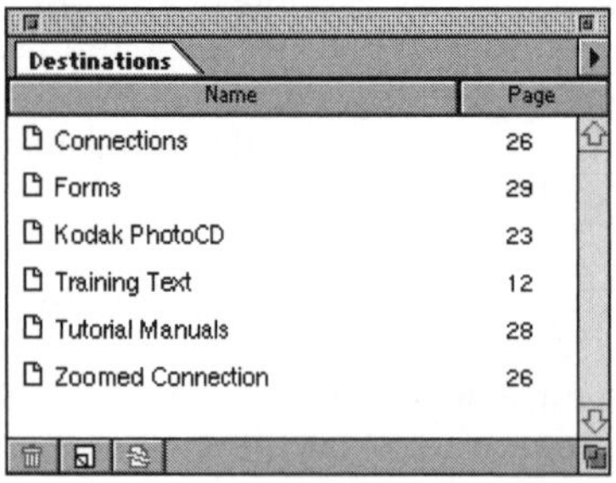

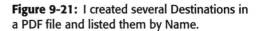

Figure 9-21: I created several Destinations in a PDF file and listed them by Name.

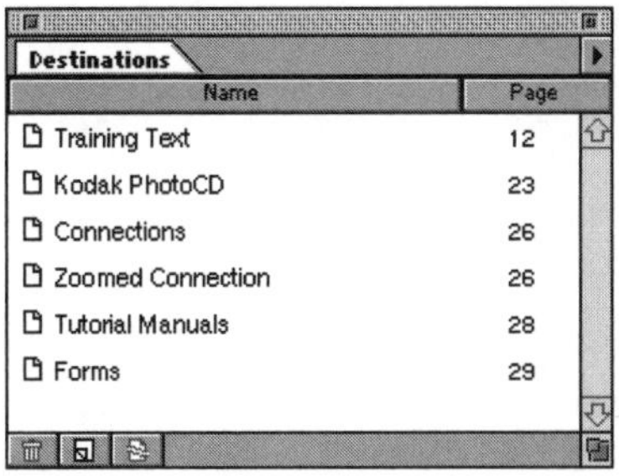

Destinations	
Name	Page
🗋 Training Text	12
🗋 Kodak PhotoCD	23
🗋 Connections	26
🗋 Zoomed Connection	26
🗋 Tutorial Manuals	28
🗋 Forms	29

Figure 9-22: When I clicked Page in the top of the palette, my list was re-sorted according to page number.

Depending on how you last sorted destinations, any new destination names will appear according to the last sorted order. For example, if your current view is according to page number, and you create a new destination on page 100 called *aardvark*, the name will appear after page 99 in the list. When you re-sort according to name, *aardvark* will appear at the top of your list.

Summary

✦ Article threads facilitate navigation across a body of text in a PDF file. Articles can be created with Acrobat and viewed in any Acrobat viewer.

✦ Articles can be joined after they have been created. Article properties help identify key information related to the article contents.

✦ Bookmarks in PDF documents are like tables of contents with links to the pages where they are created. Bookmarks can link to a page or a specific view, or enable many different link actions.

✦ Thumbnails can be created in a PDF document, at the time of distillation, or by batch-processing multiple PDF files. Thumbnails are represented in two sizes in the Thumbnails palette.

✦ Thumbnails can assist the PDF author in manipulating and editing page orders. Thumbnails can be dragged and dropped between PDF files to insert, copy, and remove pages.

✦ Pages can be inserted, deleted, extracted, and replaced in a PDF file either by using a menu command or the Thumbnails palette. When pages are deleted, links to the pages are removed. When pages are replaced, all links to and from the page are preserved.

✦ Destinations work like bookmarks in that links to pages and views within a PDF file can be created. Destinations can be sorted by name or page number.

✦   ✦   ✦

Creating Hypertext Links

✦ ✦ ✦ ✦

In This Chapter

Creating hypertext links

Creating page actions

Importing sound and video

✦ ✦ ✦ ✦

If you've been following along up to this point, your first glimpse of links appeared in Chapter 8, where I discuss bookmarks and thumbnails linking to pages and views. In addition to bookmark and thumbnail links, Acrobat affords many opportunities to create links and link actions. This chapter covers tools found in the Acrobat Tool Bar and menu commands used specifically for creating links.

About Hypertext Links

"Okay Scotty, beam us over." Ahh — if Kirk had only used Acrobat, just think of what the Star Date Logs would have looked like? Why, the whole Star Fleet Command would have been on a PDF workflow. Well, maybe hypertext links are not quite the same as traveling warp speed, but in our own little world, links in Acrobat enable us to navigate the PDF universe. The celestial bodies of PDF planets can be explored via links, page actions, sounds, movies, and JavaScripts. Links in Acrobat can have many different action types. You can simply jump to a new location or view, or add more sophistication through associated menu commands, scripts, data handling, and launching external applications. In short, buttons and links add an enormous variety to how you may navigate and view PDF documents on monitors and via the World Wide Web. In this chapter I show you the many different benefits of creating and using buttons and links.

Link actions

A *link action* is the result of executing a defined task. The task is identified within the properties of a particular link and most often associated with the movement of the mouse cursor. A link action can occur when the mouse button is clicked, released, or moved over a button. Links can be created with the Link tool, Movie tool, Form tool, bookmarks, and page actions. Most often, links and buttons have associated actions. It is possible, however, to create a link with no associated action. A situation in which this type of link is helpful is when you want to use a bookmark as a space holder where a title, subsection or section heading appears. The bookmark name will appear in the bookmark list, but no action will occur when the bookmark is selected. All other action types invoke a step or series of steps that are executed when the button is either selected or approached by the mouse cursor.

Link properties

Choices for action types are handled in a Properties window. From this window, you can make choices for different action types and attributes of the associated link. The edit mode for a particular type of link becomes active when the respective link tool is selected in the Acrobat Tool Bar. After selecting either the Link tool, Movie tool, or Form tool, the respective Properties window is accessed by selecting Edit ⇨ Properties or using a context-sensitive menu that appears when you Control+click (Mac) or click the right mouse button (Windows) over a link. By default, when new links are created, the Properties window appears when the mouse button is released.

Link properties can also be accessed by selecting the respective link tool and double-clicking the link rectangle. Links are created by selecting the appropriate link tool and drawing a rectangle around the area where the link button is to appear. All the content within the rectangle will become the hot spot for the link. When the Hand tool is placed within the rectangle drawn to define the link periphery and the mouse button is clicked, the link action will be invoked. When you wish to create a link from text, hold the Option/Ctrl key down over a text block. The cursor will change to an I-beam, which indicates the text has been selected. When the mouse button is released, the Properties window will appear.

Removing links

To delete a link from the PDF document, first select the link with the respective link tool, and then press the Delete/Backspace key. Links can also be deleted through a menu choice in a context-sensitive menu or by selecting Edit ⇨ Clear. When the Skip Edit Warnings option is disabled in the General Preferences dialog box, a warning dialog will appear before the link is deleted.

Link environment

Links reside on a *layer* independent of the PDF page contents. When a link is created, it is associated with the page but behaves like an independent element. As independent page elements, links can be repositioned and moved about a page. If a page is deleted from a PDF document, the page contents and the associated link are removed from the file. When using the Replace Pages command, the page contents will be replaced, but all links on a given page and their actions will be preserved. This is particularly important when you create PDF documents with links to and from pages. If you inadvertently delete a link, all navigation to and from the link will be lost.

Buttons created with the Link tool and Movie tool cannot be copied and pasted in a PDF document. Form links can be copied and pasted in the same document or between different PDF documents. When a movie is "imported" into a PDF document, the PDF is linked to the movie file, which must remain in its original location to be found on the source drive. Sound files imported into PDF documents are converted and embedded in the PDF file. Therefore, when transferring PDF files with movie clips, both the PDF and movie file must be transported together. PDF files with sound clips embedded in the document don't require transport of the original sound file.

Creating Links

Navigational buttons and link actions are created with the Link tool from the Acrobat Tool Bar. The area defined for the button will be the hot spot. To invoke a link action, use the Hand tool and move the cursor over the button. When the cursor enters the defined area for the link, the Hand tool cursor icon will change to a hand with the forefinger pointing upward. Whenever this cursor view appears, you'll know a link action will be activated on the click of the mouse button.

To create a button, select the Link tool from the Acrobat Tool Bar and draw a rectangle in the document window. When the mouse button is released, the rectangle will display four handles, one appearing at each corner. The handles are used to reshape the rectangle. While in the edit mode (that is, the Link tool remains selected), you can place the cursor inside the rectangle and drag it around the document to relocate it.

If you wish to create a button and return to the navigation mode, select the Option/ Ctrl key and click the Link tool in the Acrobat Tool Bar. After creating the link and setting the properties, you will exit the edit mode and can then navigate your document. When the Link tool is selected in the Acrobat Tool Bar, all links created on the PDF page will appear with rectangular borders, as shown in Figure 10-1.

When the Link tool is used to draw the rectangle and the mouse button is released, the Link Properties window will appear. The Link Properties window is where you specify the type of link action to be associated with the link.

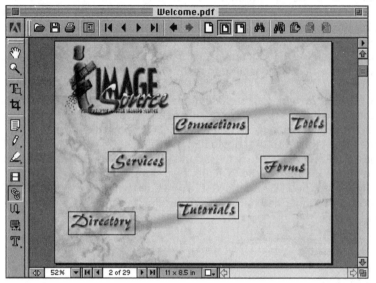

Figure 10-1: When the Link tool is selected in the Acrobat Tool Bar, all links will be displayed with rectangular borders.

Link properties

Acrobat affords you many options for creating link actions, which you can choose from in the Link Properties window. Among the many choices for link actions, you also have choices for modifying the appearance of the link rectangle and specifying the highlight view that appears when the link is selected. To open the Link Properties window, select the Link tool from the Acrobat Tool Bar, draw a rectangle, and release the mouse button. The Create Link window opens immediately, as shown in Figure 10-2.

Note
When you first create a link, the properties window is titled Create Link. When you edit a previously created link and select Properties from the Edit menu, the same window appears, but it is now called the Link Properties window. Both windows offer the same attribute choices. The rest of this section shall refer to this window as the Link Properties window.

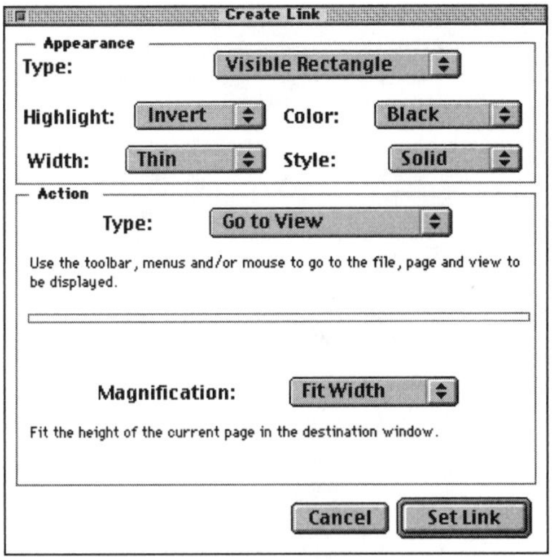

Figure 10-2: After drawing a rectangle with the Link tool and releasing the mouse button, the Create Link window is displayed.

The Link Properties window contains all the properties available for the link display and link action. The first attributes in the window relate to the appearance of the link rectangle:

✦ **Invisible Rectangle:** When the link is drawn, the link rectangle will only appear in the edit mode. When you return to the navigation mode, the rectangle will disappear. To display the link rectangles, you need to select the Link tool in the Acrobat Tool Bar. Below the Invisible Rectangle option appear four other pop-up menus. Only the Highlight option will be available if the Invisible Rectangle option is selected. This option is also available when the Visible Rectangle option is selected. Highlights include the following:

- **None:** When you click the link, no highlight will be displayed (see Figure 10-3).

- **Invert:** When you click the link, the reverse color of the link contents will appear as the highlight. The mouse (button) down action will display the highlight, which informs the user the button is selected. If you click down and drag the mouse away from the button, the highlight will disappear (see Figure 10-4).

- **Outline:** The mouse down action on the link will display a rectangle border similar to the view you see when the Link tool is selected from the Acrobat Tool Bar (see Figure 10-5).

Figure 10-3: When None is chosen as the highlight type, a link will
show no highlight when selected.

Figure 10-4: When Invert is chosen as the highlight type, a link will
appear reversed out when selected.

- **Inset:** On the mouse down action, the link will look like an embossed or
  recessed button, slightly offset (see Figure 10-6).

Figure 10-5: This link demonstrates the Outline highlight.

Figure 10-6: This link demonstrates the Inset highlight.

✦ **Visible Rectangle:** When the Visible Rectangle option is selected from the Type pop-up menu, the pop-up menus for Width, Color, and Style become available in the Link Properties window. A visible rectangle will appear in the document window when you return to the navigation mode. To set the attributes of the rectangle border, choose from the four pop-up menus below the Visible Rectangle option.

- **Width:** The choices Thin, Medium, and Thick are available from the pop-up menu. The keyline border will be displayed with a rule thickness as determined by these choices.

- **Color:** Preset color choices for the outline border are available from the pop-up menu as well as the Custom option, which enables you to specify a particular color. When choosing Custom, the system color palette will open so that you can define a custom color.

- **Style:** Choices for solid or dashed lines appear in the pop-up menu.

After you make your choices for the options that relate to the link button's appearance, the next step is to select the particular link action to be associated with the link. A number of different actions reside within the Type pop-up menu under the Action section of the Link Properties window.

Execute menu item

A link action can execute a menu selection. Almost all menu commands are available in the Execute Menu Item dialog box, including commands for bookmarks, thumbnails, articles, and destinations. When Execute Menu Item is selected from the pop-up menu for the Action type, the button in the lower portion of the Link Properties window displays the label Edit Menu Item. Click this button, and the Acrobat menu items will be displayed in another window, titled Menu Selection. The Menu Selection window lists the menus and menu items available from the Acrobat menu bar. Select a menu and scroll down to the desired command. When the command is selected, click OK in the Menu Selection window to return to the Link Properties window. Click Set Link in the Link Properties window, and the menu command will be associated with the link. The Menu Selection window is displayed in Figure 10-7 with all pull-down menus opened.

Figure 10-7: Any of the commands listed in the pull-down menus in the Menu Selection window can be selected for the associated link action.

One example of using the Execute Menu Item command might be to navigate a PDF document. If you have a contents page and wish the user to click a button that opens another PDF document, the Go to Previous View menu command will return the user to the contents document. Menu commands associated with links will eliminate the need for a user to be familiar with Acrobat tools. If you wish to have the display appear in Full Screen mode, such navigational buttons created from menu commands can be quite helpful.

Go to View

Go to View is a very common link action used frequently when preparing PDF files for screen viewing. The Go to View action type works similarly to the bookmark feature discussed in Chapter 9. To create a button that navigates to another page, another view, or another page and new view, select Go to View from the Action Type pop-up menu. While the Link Properties window is open, navigate to another page and/or view using the Acrobat Command Bar tools or keyboard modifiers. Select the desired view magnification from the menu options or status bar, and then click the Set Link button. Acrobat returns to the page where the link was created. If you use the Option/Ctrl key when selecting the Link tool, you will be ready to test the button by moving the cursor inside the link rectangle and clicking.

Magnification options are available from the pop-up menu for Magnification when the Go to View option is selected. The magnification items are the same as those discussed in earlier chapters. What's important to remember is to first navigate to the page and view desired before you click the Set Link button.

Import Form Data

When the Import Form Data option on the Action Type pop-up menu is selected, the Select File button appears, enabling you to select the file from which the data will be imported. This action type works with forms, which I cover in the next chapter.

JavaScript

Acrobat 4 supports JavaScript. When the JavaScript action type is selected, an Edit button appears in the Link Properties window. Click the Edit button, and a window will appear where the JavaScript code can be entered. You can type the code in the window, or copy and paste JavaScript code from a text editor.

Movie

To select the Movie action type, a movie must be present in the PDF file. Movies are not imported with this command, they are imported with the Movie tool. Once a movie is contained in a PDF file, you can create a button that will invoke one of four action types when the button is selected. These options are available in a pop-up menu named Select Operation. You may choose to play a movie, stop a movie, pause the movie during the play, and have it resume after it has been paused. If more than one movie is contained in the document, you can select which movie will be associated with the action from the Select Movie pop-up menu, shown in Figure 10-8.

Figure 10-8: Select Movie is available when a movie file is linked to the PDF document. When choosing Movie from the Action Type pop-up menu in the Link Properties window, you can choose one of the four operations shown here.

Open File

Open File works differently from using the Execute Menu Item option and selecting the File ➪ Open command. When File ➪ Open is selected, only PDF documents can be opened. If you use the Link Properties window and choose Open File, any application document can be opened. Acrobat will launch the host application and open the document. For example, if you wish to open a Microsoft Word file, you can select the Word document by clicking the Select File button in the Link Properties window. When the link is invoked, Microsoft Word will be launched and the document opened in Word. Using this action type requires you to have the host application installed on your computer.

Read Article

On specifying Read Article as the action type for a particular link, the Select Article dialog box will open (see Figure 10-9). If no articles are present in the PDF document, you won't be able to use this link action. When articles are present, select from the listed articles the one you wish to associate with the link. When the link is selected in the navigation mode, Acrobat will open the page where the article appears. Additionally, the cursor will change to the Article tool, which enables continuation in reading the selected article.

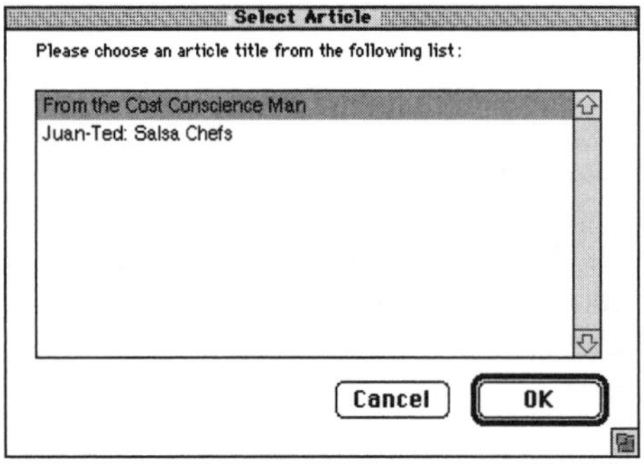

Figure 10-9: After selecting the Read Article option, the Select Article dialog box opens, enabling you to select the article you want associated with the link.

Reset Form

The Reset Form link action relates to PDF documents with form fields. When a form is filled out, you can reset the form, which will remove all the data contained in the form fields. Acrobat provides an opportunity to clear the data from all fields or those fields you identify individually. A Field Selection dialog box appears, enabling you to select the fields to clear. (The Field Selection dialog box is covered in more detail in Chapter 11.)

Also related to forms in Acrobat, the Show/Hide Field type enables the user to hide selected fields. Forms can be created to permit users to fill out selected data and preserve some fields where data is not to be completed by the end user. If a field has been hidden, it can be made visible by returning to the Show/Hide Fields dialog box. Within this dialog box the options for hiding and showing fields are enabled through radio buttons.

Select Sound

A button can be created to play a sound in a PDF document. When the Select Sound type is chosen, a dialog box will appear enabling you to navigate to the sound to be imported. Acrobat will pause a moment while the sound is converted. Once imported in the PDF, the sound can be played across platforms. The button will be associated with the sound import. When the button is selected, the sound will play.

Submit Form

Forms can be contained in PDF documents and distributed on the World Wide Web. When the form data is completed, the data can be submitted as a data file. The PDF author can then collect and process the data. Using form data with Web servers has some requirements you'll need to work out with the ISP that hosts your Web site. If you use forms on PDF Web pages, you'll want to include a button that, when clicked, will submit the data after the user completes the form. Using the Submit Form type enables you to identify the URL where the data is to be submitted and determine which data type will be exported from the PDF document. When identifying URLs, be certain to use the complete URL address (see Figure 10-10).

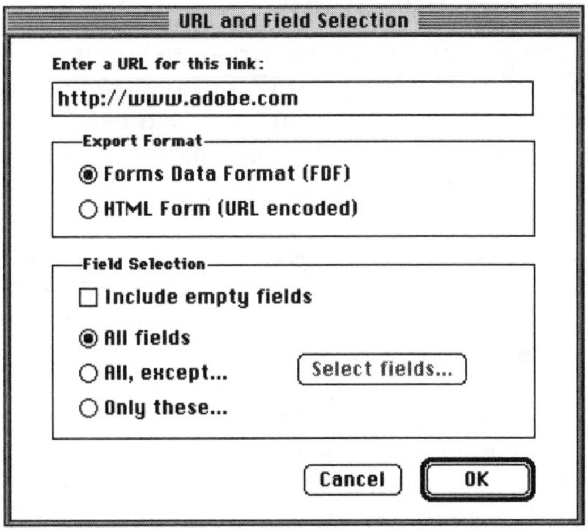

Figure 10-10: The Submit Form link enables you to submit form data to a particular URL on the World Wide Web.

World Wide Web Link

The World Wide Web Link option enables you to associate a link action to a Web address. Web links can be contained in PDF documents viewed on screen or within a PDF page on the World Wide Web. If a Web link is contained in a PDF document, selecting the link will launch the browser configured with Acrobat and establish a Web connection. Acrobat will remain open in the background while the Web browser is viewed in the foreground. Like the Submit Form requirements mentioned previously, always use the complete URL to identify a Web address.

None

Buttons with no associated link action will produce no effect. You may use this type of action with bookmarks, as explained earlier in this chapter.

Creating Links

Creating links will add some interactivity to your PDF designs. Without having to learn complex programming code for interactive presentations, Acrobat provides a simple and effective means for creating dynamic presentations. In addition, you can add some functional applications for file management with Acrobat through the use of links. One particular application for link actions I use is cataloging documents on external media cartridges or CD-ROMs. I often take a screen shot of a directory or folder on a media cartridge or before I replicate a CD-ROM. The screen shot is imported into Acrobat where links to the files are made. When the link is selected, the document opens in the application used to create the file. In addition, I add information related to the document such as purpose, creation date, and comments about the contents. The following steps explain how to organize such documents.

STEPS: Creating Links in a PDF Document

1. **Assemble files in a folder and capture the screen.** Organize files in a folder either by icon view or as a list. When the organization is the way you like, capture the screen with a utility such as Capture on the Macintosh (or press Cmd+Shift+4) and marquee the area to be captured. In Windows, use a utility such as Corel Capture.

   Tip

   Macintosh users can easily capture a window by pressing the Caps Lock key on the keyboard and then pressing Cmd+Shift+4. The cursor will change to a circle, or "target," icon. Click inside the open folder window you wish to capture. The screen capture will include the folder window and the contents.

2. **Import the file into Acrobat.** Open Adobe Acrobat and select File ⇨ Import ⇨ Image. If you capture the entire screen, you may wish to crop the image in a program such as Adobe Photoshop before importing, or use the Crop tool in Acrobat. I captured an open folder on the Desktop that contains multiple file types (see Figure 10-11).

3. **Create a link.** For any file type other than PDF, use the Link tool from the Acrobat Tool Bar to draw a rectangle around the file icon or name.

4. **Define the properties and establish the link attributes.** Determine what appearance you wish the link to have. In my example, I wanted a keyline to appear around the document icons. For the appearance type, I selected Visible Rectangle and changed the appropriate option settings to specify a red, medium-width border (see Figure 10-12). For all non-PDF file types, use the Open File action from the Type pop-up menu choices.

Figure 10-11: In my example, I captured an open folder that contains multiple file types.

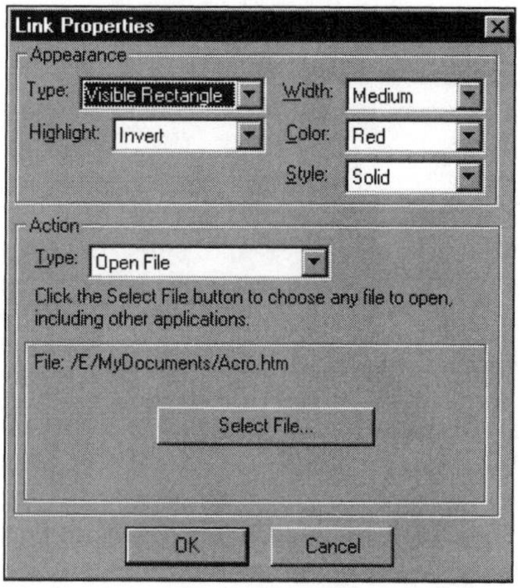

Figure 10-12: I drew a link rectangle around the first icon in my screen capture and specified Medium Width, Red, and Visible Rectangle for the link appearance. I set the Action Type to Open File.

5. **Set the link action.** If the file you link to is not a PDF document, and you use Open File as the Link Action, click the Select File button in the Link Properties window. In my example, I selected the file on my hard drive contained in the folder where the screen dump was taken.

6. **Create an annotation.** For this example, I used the Note Annotation tool and created a Note, which provides some information about the file. In Figure 10-13, I created multiple links with note annotations.

Continued

Figure 10-13: When the note for a link is expanded, the note contents are revealed.

If you want to create a link to a PDF document, rather than selecting the Open File link action as described in the preceding example, you would have to choose Go to View from the Action Type pop-up menu. While the Properties window remains open, select File ➪ Open from the Acrobat menu bar and then open the PDF document. Select the desired view magnification, and click Set Link in the Link Properties window. When you use Link Properties, all the navigation tools will be available while the Properties window remains open.

> **Tip** With Acrobat, you can't use the Find command or Acrobat Search to find text contained within a note. If you wish to search note information, select Tools ➪ Annotations ➪ Summarize Notes. The PDF created from the note summary can be saved along with the PDF document created from the screen dump. A link can be created from the note summary file to the captured page to facilitate finding the note data.

Each of the link properties works with buttons you create on PDF pages. The actions associated with the buttons need to have a response from the end user to invoke an action. At times, you may wish to have your PDF pages automatically executed without user input. In some cases, creating a page action may be more desirable to implement the views you wish to be displayed.

Creating Page Actions

Page actions invoke a link action when the page is viewed in a PDF document. A page action does not require the user to click a button or issue a command for the action to execute. Page actions can be supplied on any page in a PDF document. Most often you may find page actions helpful when viewing the first page in a file. A page action might be used when you wish to display a credit page, and then have the document jump to the contents page for the user to select links to other pages. The contents page will display momentarily, and then scroll to the next page identified in the page action.

Navigation is only one means of associating a page action with a PDF page. When creating page actions, you have available to you all the link actions available found in the Link Properties window discussed earlier in this chapter. Menu commands, URL links, sounds, movies, and so on are all available with page actions.

To create a page action, select the Document menu and choose Set Page Action. A dialog box appears that enables you to select either a Page Open or Page Close item for invoking the page action, as shown in Figure 10-14. If Page Open is selected, the action type will be employed when the PDF page opens. Page Close will invoke the action when the page is closed. You first determine which item will invoke the action and then select the Add button in the Page Actions dialog box. Unlike the Properties window for Links, you cannot navigate pages while the Page Actions dialog box is open. If you wish to use a page action to scroll to another page, you must do so through the Execute Menu Item command instead of navigating to a page and setting the link.

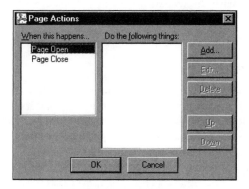

Figure 10-14: When setting page actions, first select either Page Open or Page Close, and then click the Add button to identify the link type.

Editing page actions

Care must be exercised when setting page actions on pages in a PDF file. If you set a page action to a page with an action type that moves to another page, you won't be able to return to the page where the action type was created. Even when looking at pages in a continuous or facing pages view, the page where the action has been created cannot be selected. If the page is selected, the action will be invoked, thus moving you to another page. Other types of actions where the page remains in view can be edited by selecting Document ➪ Set Page Action. If you wish to remove an action, select it in the Do the following things list and click the Remove button. To edit an action, select the action type in the list and click the Edit button. Clicking the Edit button will open the Edit an Action dialog box, in which you can change the action type.

Tip

To remove a page action that jumps to another page, select Extract Pages from the Document menu. In the Extract Pages dialog box, select Delete Pages After Extracting. The extracted page will appear in Acrobat. Select Document ➪ Set Page Action and delete the action type from the Page Actions dialog box. Save the extracted page to disk. Select the original document from the Window menu, select Document ➪ Insert Pages, and insert the saved file back into your original document.

Using transitions with page actions

One effective use of page actions is to introduce transition effects. Transitions are available when you view PDF documents in Full Screen mode and scroll pages with the transitions applied. If you wish to view a PDF file without the Full Screen mode in effect, you can create transitions with pdfmark. While in the normal viewing mode, any transitions associated with pages when the file was distilled with pdfmark annotations will be viewed. One circumstance where such an effect might be useful is in creating an opening page with a credit or company logo that uses a transition effect when jumping from the credit page to the second page in the document. Creating such an effect is a two-step process. First, you use a pdfmark annotation and distill a PostScript file with the transition. Next, you create a page action in Acrobat that will move the user to the second page after the transition effect. Let's take a closer look at how you might work through this example.

STEPS: Creating Transitions with pdfMark

1. **Create a document in a layout application.** For this example, create a document with multiple pages in a program such as Adobe PageMaker or QuarkXPress. The document should have several pages so the first page can accept a page action that moves the user to the second page in the file.

2. **Import a transition effect.** Acrobat ships with transitions that are EPS files you can place on a page with the pdfmark code contained in those files. If you wish to view the code, simply open the file in a text editor. It's not necessary to know any programming code to use the transitions; they are placed the same way you would place any graphic image. The transitions are available on the Acrobat Installer CD-ROM located in the Utility:Transitions directory.

Note

To see a sample of the transition effects, open one of the sample PDF documents in Acrobat and scroll through the pages. The sample PDF documents are contained in the Transitions folder on your Acrobat installer CD-ROM. The transition types will be displayed as you view the different pages.

3. **Print the file to disk as a PostScript file.** After importing the transition on the desired page, print the file to disk as a PostScript file. If using Adobe PageMaker, you can select File ➪ Export ➪ Adobe PDF. For this example, I included the glitter transition (GLTR_0.EPS) on Page 1 in a PageMaker file.

4. **Distill the PostScript file.** Open Acrobat Distiller or select Distill now in the Adobe PageMaker Export Adobe PDF dialog box and distill the PostScript file. For this example, you can use the ScreenOptimized Job Options in Acrobat Distiller.

5. **View the PDF document.** Open the PDF document created with Acrobat Distiller in Acrobat. After the transition is completed, the page will be displayed in the viewer, as illustrated in Figure 10-15.

Figure 10-15: I created a credit page that includes a ghosted-back version of my company logo and a transition effect imported into PageMaker. After I set a page action, this page will be momentarily displayed when the PDF file is opened, and then the second page will be viewed.

To display the page momentarily and then move to the second page in the document, set a page action to go to the next page.

STEPS: Creating a Page Action

1. **Create a page action.** Using the PDF document described in the preceding example, select Document ➪ Set Page Action. In the Page Actions dialog box, shown in Figure 10-16, select Page Open and click the Add button to open the Add an Action dialog box. In this dialog box, select Execute Menu Item.

Continued

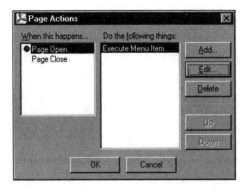

Figure 10-16: To add a page action, select the Page Open item and click Add. A second dialog box appears in which you can select an action type.

2. **Select the menu item for navigating the page.** In the Execute Menu Item dialog box, select Document ➪ Next Page. The item you select will be identified in the dialog box adjacent to Selected:, as shown in Figure 10-17.

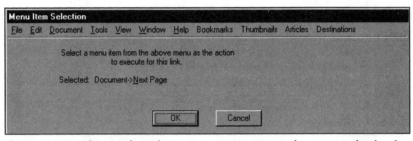

Figure 10-17: When I selected Document ➪ Next Page, the menu selection item was identified in the dialog box. If the identified item is different from what you want, return to the menus and make the proper selection.

3. **Accept the changes and return to the document window.** Click OK after making the selection, and you will return to the Page Actions dialog box. Click OK again to return to the PDF document window.

4. **Save the file and reopen it.** Save your new edits and close the file. Select File ➪ Open and open the saved file. If all the edits you made were correct, you should see a glimpse of the first page with the transition applied, and then the second page will be displayed (see Figure 10-18).

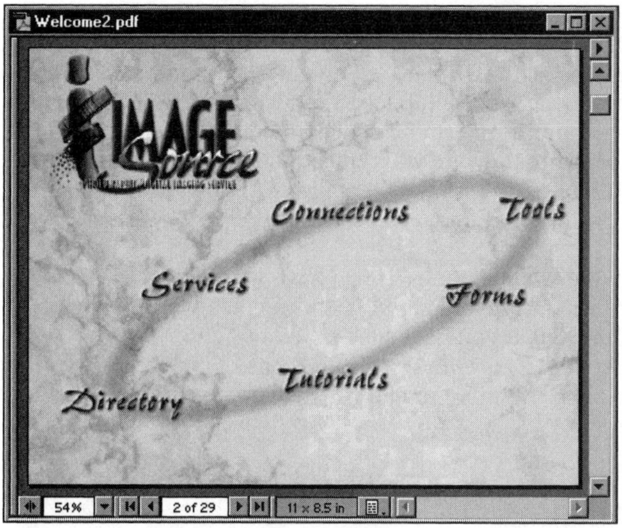

Figure 10-18: When I opened my file, the first page, viewed in Figure 10-15, was displayed with the transition I imported in my PageMaker document. After the transition completed, the page action displayed the next page in my document.

Nesting page actions

Page actions are not limited to a single action type. You can add additional page actions to the list in the Page Actions dialog box. After adding an action, select either the Page Open or Page Close item and click Add to add another action. If you wish to jump to a view upon opening a page and then return to another view when leaving the page, you can add actions for the Page Open and Page Close items. Acrobat will jump to the view you associate with the action when the page is opened. After you move from the page to another page, the view level you associate with the Page Close item will be displayed.

Multiple page actions can be applied to either or both the Page Open and/or Page Close items. When applying multiple page actions, be certain to think through your work. If you attempt to create actions that conflict with each other, the last action type associated with the page will be used by Acrobat. In some cases, you may not see an action type if it is overridden in the page display.

Importing Sound and Video

Acrobat supports several different sound and video formats. For sound files, Mac users can import AIFF files, and Windows users can import WAV file formats. Once a sound file has been converted by Acrobat, the sounds can be played in a PDF file on either platform.

Movies can be imported from files saved in Apple QuickTime or Windows AVI format. Because these files are linked to the PDF document, you need to be certain the linked files are compliant with the platform in which you intend the files to be viewed. Apple QuickTime, which is available on the installer CD-ROM for both Windows and Macintosh computers, can be viewed on either platform as long as QuickTime is installed. Macintosh users will typically have QuickTime installed because it comes with the operating system installer. Windows users will need to install QuickTime from the Acrobat installer CD-ROM.

AVI format is native to Windows machines. If you have video files saved in AVI format, Macintosh users will not be able to view these files on their Macs unless they upgrade to QuickTime 3.0. If you have files saved in AVI format and wish to enable cross-platform use for users with earlier versions of QuickTime, you can use a video editor such as Adobe Premiere to export the video in a QuickTime format compatible to all users.

Importing sound files

Earlier in this chapter, I mentioned using a link to activate a sound in a PDF document. Sounds can be handled in several ways and with several link types. You can, for example, import a sound via the Movie tool, set a page action to play a sound, or create a link button to a sound. If a sound file is imported via the Page Action command, the sound will become part of the PDF document. If, on the other hand, you import a sound via the Movie tool, the PDF document will link to the external sound file. In this case, if you transport the PDF document to another computer, you would need to transport the sound file as well.

When you use a page action, any sound added to your file will not be page dependent — that is, the sound will be heard on all pages as you scroll through the PDF file. The sound will begin playing on opening the page where the sound import page action has been identified and will continue to play until completion. Pressing the Esc key will not stop the sound, nor will the sound stop when the file is closed. Setting a page action to play a sound won't require a user selection to invoke the action — play will be automatic. The only way to stop the sound will be to quit Acrobat.

To import sound in Acrobat via a page action, select Document ➪ Set Page Action. Select Page Open and click the Add button. When the Add an Action dialog box appears, as shown in Figure 10-19, select Sound from the Type pop-up menu and click the Select Sound button. A navigation dialog box appears, enabling you to identify the sound file. When you select the sound file, Acrobat will pause momentarily while it converts the sound. Once converted in Acrobat, the sound will be embedded in the document and can be transported across platforms.

If you elect to use the Link tool and select Sound from the Link Properties window, the user will need to click the link button to activate the sound. If a sound file is imported via a link, the sound can be stopped in the middle of play by pressing the Esc key on the keyboard.

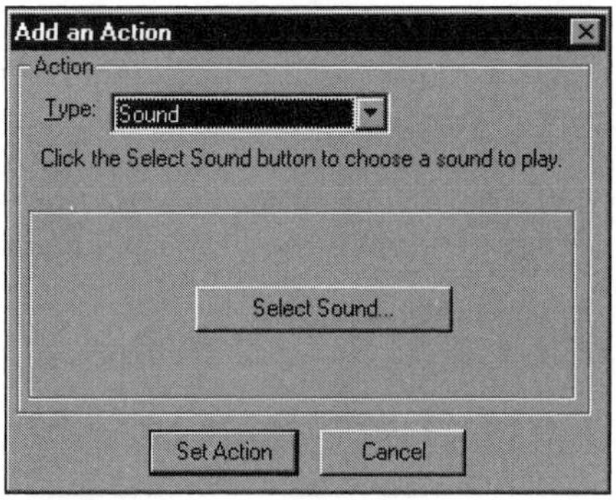

Figure 10-19: To associate a page action with a sound file, select Sound from the Action Type pop-up menu. Click the Select Sound button to locate the sound file on your hard drive.

Importing movies

The Movie tool in the Acrobat Tool Bar is used to import movies. To import a movie, you create a movie link similar to other links. Select the Movie tool from the Tool Bar and click the mouse button or click and drag open a rectangle. When you release the mouse button, the Movie Properties dialog box will appear. In the Movie Properties dialog box, shown in Figure 10-20, you can select from a number of attributes for how the movie will be displayed and the types of play actions that can occur with the movie file.

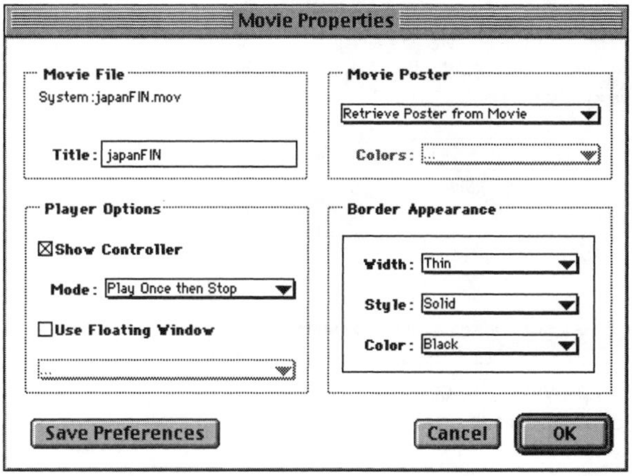

Figure 10-20: The Movie Properties window provides attribute settings for the display and play actions of movie files.

Tip

When you click the mouse button, the imported movie will be placed in the PDF document at the size the movie file was originally created. The spot you click in the PDF page will be where the movie frames are centered. If you click and drag with the Movie tool, most often the movie will appear at a different size than it was created, resulting in a distorted view. Use a 100 percent view of the PDF page and click to import the movie. View the size on screen to determine how large the movie file will be displayed.

Movie File

The first item in the Movie Properties window displays the name of the movie file you import in Acrobat. The Title field displays the filename. Above the filename appears the directory path for the linked file. Because movie files are linked to PDF documents, the directory path can help you manage your movie imports. If the file is relocated on your hard drive, you will need to redirect Acrobat to the location of the linked file.

Player Options

Player Options enable you to choose between displaying the controller for a movie file or hiding the controller. When the controller is visible, as shown in Figure 10-21, buttons for playing the movie, stopping play, setting the volume, and scrolling through the movie frames will appear. The controller becomes visible while the movie is in play. When not playing, the controller disappears.

Figure 10-21: While a movie is playing, the controller will be visible when the Show Controller option is enabled in the Movie Properties window.

Mode

The Mode option offers choices from a pop-up menu for the play action. You can elect to play the movie, and then stop when the film clip reaches the last frame by selecting the Play Once then Stop option. After finishing the last frame, the display will eliminate the controller and return to the first frame in the movie. Play Once and Stay Open is the second choice available from the pop-up menu. When the film clip reaches the end, the controller remains in view, and the movie is stopped at the last frame. Repeat Play will play the clip from beginning to end and then continue to replay the movie. Such a choice might be used when setting up a kiosk containing a computer on which you want to play the clip continuously. The final choice is to Play Forward and Backward. Once the clip completes the play, it plays backward from end to beginning. When the clip comes back to the beginning, it will play forward again, then back, and so on.

Use Floating Window

If this option is enabled, a floating window will display the movie clip centered on your monitor screen irrespective of where the movie clip rectangle is drawn in the PDF document (see Figure 10-22). When choosing a floating window as your movie display, you can choose a size for the floating window from the pop-up menu appearing below the Floating Window check box. Size options are available for ratios according to the size of the originally created movie clip. 1/4x size will display the movie clip at one-fourth the actual size, whereas 2x displays the movie at twice the actual size. For almost all circumstances, a 1x choice will be the best view. Movies displayed at larger sizes will be pixelated when viewed.

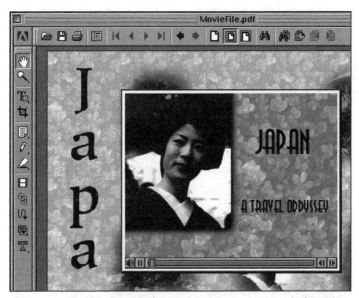

Figure 10-22: Floating windows appear as separate windows in which the movie is played independent of the movie link.

Movie Poster

The display of a stopped movie is called a *movie poster*. The movie poster is typically the first frame in the film clip. You can choose from three options for poster display. Don't Show Poster will eliminate the video frame from view while the movie is stopped. The second option, Put Poster in Document, will display the first or halted frame in the film clip. When this option is selected, you can choose the color bit depth for the video display. Choosing 256 colors will display the movie in 8-bit color. You might wish to use this option when the end user views videos on 8-bit monitors. Selecting Millions of colors from the pop-up menu will display the video clip in 24-bit color. You can manually choose from either color views when you've selected Put Poster in Document. If either of the other two choices from the first pop-up menu are selected, you won't have a choice for the color bit depth. Choosing the Retrieve Poster from Movie option in the first pop-up menu will display the poster with the color bit depth used in the movie file.

Tip   When the movie poster is hidden, the rectangle drawn with the Movie tool will be the hot spot for playing the movie. At times, the user may not intuitively know where to click to play the film clip. You can create a hot spot covering the entire PDF page by drawing the Movie rectangle around the document page. Choose Don't Show Poster and enable the Floating Window option so the movie will not appear degraded. No matter where the cursor rests on the page, the movie icon will be displayed, informing the user a movie file can be played. If an icon is desired, you can create an icon for a movie by shrinking the movie link to the size of a custom thumbnail (as shown in Figure 10-23) and choose the Put Poster in Document option. Drawing a keyline around the movie poster can help the end user find the hot spot to click to play the movie. When using such an icon view of the movie poster, choose the Use Floating Window option for the video clip display.

Figure 10-23: To create this movie link, I used the Movie tool to draw a small rectangle and chose the Put Poster in Document option. A blue border was added so the end user would know a link button exists on the page. The Use Floating Window option was selected so the video would play at normal size independent of the link button.

Border appearance

Borders can be drawn around the film clip when the Use Floating Window option is not active. Floating windows have a keyline automatically drawn around the poster; however, you can't control the line weight or color. If a floating window is not used, you can create a keyline border in one of three sizes available from the Width pop-up menu. First select one of the width options — Thin, Medium, or Thick — and then select a style for the lines, such as dashed or solid. The Color pop-up menu enables you to select from preset colors or choose a custom color. When the Custom option is selected, the system color palette will appear, enabling you to make a color choice.

Save preferences

After specifying options in the Movie Properties window, the choices you made can be saved so you can apply them to subsequent movie imports. Choose Save Preferences when you need to keep the options all the same for PDF documents where consistency is to be maintained. If you wish to edit the preferences for additional movies, select Edit ➪ Properties while the Movie tool is selected in the Acrobat Tool Bar. You can edit the movie properties and then click Save Preferences to update the default properties.

If developing many PDF documents with links, you'll need to think out your design very carefully. Individual links on PDF pages can take some time, as each page will require individual authoring. You can cut down the time by using pdfmark annotations, as I explained in Chapter 6 in the context of creating navigational buttons and link actions. Navigational buttons, as explained in Chapter 6, can be added to master pages in layout programs. You can also add links to documents in Acrobat and use the Replace Pages command when common links will be used across many different PDF files. Short of these examples, your PDF workflow may require extensive changing when custom links are used.

Summary

✦ Hypertext links add interactivity to PDF documents for screen and presentation designs.

✦ Links can be created for different views within a PDF document, across PDF documents, and to document files from other authoring programs.

✦ Links can be made to execute most of the menu items available in Acrobat.

✦ The Link Properties window provides different attribute settings for determining link choices, views, and link button displays.

✦ Page actions can be established to invoke an action or series of actions when opening and closing pages.

✦ Sounds can be imported into PDF files via links or page actions.

✦ A movie import is a linked file in Acrobat and requires the movie file to accompany the PDF document to be viewed. Apple QuickTime movies can be displayed across Mac and Windows platforms.

✦   ✦   ✦

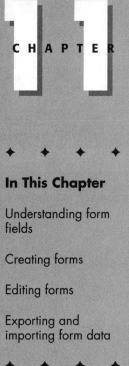

CHAPTER

In This Chapter

Understanding form
fields

Creating forms

Editing forms

Exporting and
importing form data

Working with Forms

The use of forms is a powerful feature for managing document flow in office environments or using them on the World Wide Web. Acrobat is not a database manager, but comes close when we use forms. We can create forms in Acrobat that will enable office personnel or consumers to complete forms for adding to our information databases.

What Are Acrobat Forms?

Forms in Acrobat are PDF files with data fields that can contain user-supplied data. In Acrobat, you can use text string fields, numeric fields, date fields, calculation fields, signature fields (Windows only), and a variety of custom fields created with JavaScripts. The advantage of using forms in Acrobat is it enables you to maintain design integrity. Rather than using a database manager, which may limit your ability to control fonts and graphics, Acrobat can preserve all the design attributes of a document while behaving as a data manager. In this chapter, you get the opportunity to explore creating, modifying, and using forms.

Forms are created and filled out in Acrobat. The Acrobat Reader software can edit field data, but there are no provisions for saving the edited form, nor is there an opportunity to export form data. In developing PDF workflows for a company or organization, all users expected to complete forms in Acrobat will need to be individually or site licensed for the Acrobat software.

Understanding Form Fields

Forms use different types of data fields that can hold data, act as buttons that invoke actions, and call scripts to execute a series of actions. Form fields can assume different appearances as well as possess the capability to include graphic icons and images to represent hot links that invoke actions. Acrobat forms are more than a static data filing system — they can be as vivid and dynamic as your imagination. When designing a form in Acrobat, you are well advised to plan your work ahead of time. As you shall see, with the many different choices available for field contents and appearances, creating form fields offers an enormous number of options.

Form contents

To learn how forms function in Acrobat, you need to understand how forms are developed and, ultimately, how you will go about creating forms. Because Acrobat cannot be effectively used as a layout application, nor can it be used to draw rules and design elements, creation of a form begins in another application. You can use illustration or layout software for designing a form, which ultimately is converted to PDF. In Acrobat, the form data fields are created with the Form tool, and options are selected from the Field Properties window. Form fields can be of several different types:

✦ **Text:** Text fields are boxes in which text will be typed by the end user when the form is filled out.

✦ **Check boxes:** Check boxes typically appear in groups to offer the user a selection of choices. A Yes box or a No box is often used in forms.

✦ **Button:** A button is usually designed in an illustration or layout application as a graphic element and saved as a PDF file. When you create the field in Acrobat, you add the button as a transparent item so the original design element appears as though it's the item executing the action.

✦ **Combo box:** When you view an Acrobat form, you may see an arrow similar to the arrows appearing in palette menus. Such an arrow in a PDF form indicates the presence of a combo box. When you click the arrow, a menu will appear containing two or more choices.

✦ **List box:** A list box will display a box with scroll bars, much like windows you see in application software documents. As you scroll through a list box, you can make a choice of one of the alternatives available by clicking it.

✦ **Radio buttons:** Radio buttons perform the same function in PDF forms as they do in the dialog boxes of other applications. Usually you have two or more choices for a category. When you click a radio button, it enables the associated option, a bullet (or other symbol you choose) is placed inside the circular shape, and any other radio button in the group is turned off.

✦ **Signature fields (Windows):** A digital signature field is available only to Windows users. Digital signatures can be applied to fields, PDF pages, and PDF documents. A digital signature can be used to lock out fields on a form.

All these form field types are available to you when you create a form in Acrobat. From the end user point of view, one needs to examine a form and understand how to make choices for the field types in order to accurately complete a form. Fortunately,

Acrobat field types relate similarly to the metaphors used by most applications designed with a graphic user interface. An example of an Acrobat form with several form field types is shown in Figure 11-1.

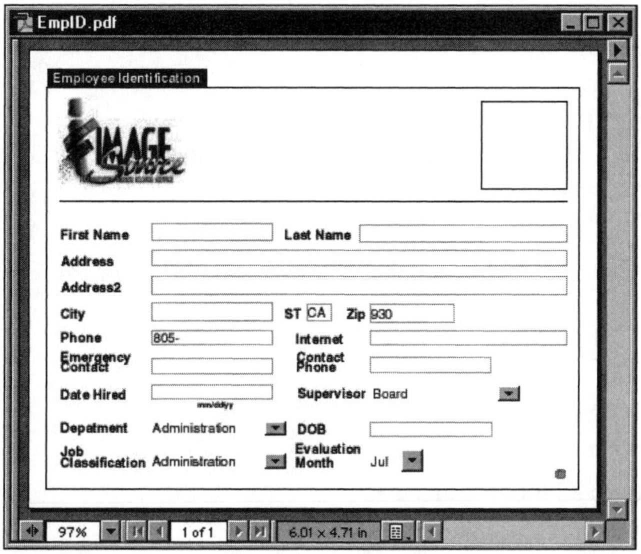

Figure 11-1: An Acrobat form with several form field types

Navigating text fields

As you view the form shown in Figure 11-1, notice it contains several text fields and a few combo boxes, as signified by the arrows in the form. To fill out a text field, you need to select the Hand tool, place the cursor over the field, and click the mouse button. When you click, a blinking I-beam cursor will appear, indicating text can be added by typing on your keyboard.

To navigate to the next field for more text entry, you can make one of two choices: Click in the second field or press the Tab key on your keyboard. When you press the Tab key, the cursor jumps to the next logical field, according to an order you specify in Acrobat when you design the form. Be certain the Hand tool is selected and a cursor appears in a field box when you press the Tab key. If any of the Annotation tools are selected or the cursor is not blinking in a field box, striking the Tab key will toggle the tabs in the Navigation Pane.

When selecting from choices in radio button or check box fields, click in the radio button or check box. The display will change to show a small, solid circle or an X within a box, respectively. When using a combo box, click the arrow appearing in the field and select one of several pop-up menu choices.

When you finish completing a form, you will usually submit the data. This can be accomplished in one of several ways: exporting the form as data, sending the data to an Internet server, exporting to a Form Data File (FDF), or simply saving the filled-out PDF form under a new name so the original form, serving as a template, remains without any field entries. Forms can include buttons to execute actions similar to those specified by the Execute Menu Item command that appears when creating hypertext links (see Chapter 10). When designing a form, you will often include a button for the user to click that will export the data through one of the export methods just listed.

Form field navigation keystrokes

As mentioned earlier, to move to the next field you need to either click in the field or press the Tab key. Following is a list of other keystrokes that can help you move through forms to complete them:

✦ **Shift+Tab:** Moves to the previous field

✦ **Esc:** Ends text entry

✦ **Return:** Ends text entry

✦ **Shift+click:** Ends text entry

✦ **Double-click a word in a field:** Selects the word

✦ **Cmd/Ctrl+A:** Selects all the text in a field

✦ **Left/right arrow keys:** Moves the cursor one character at a time left or right

✦ **Up arrow:** Moves to the beginning of the text field

✦ **Down arrow:** Moves to the end of the text field

You'll notice I used Acrobat to demonstrate completing a form. Because Reader users cannot save or export data, form data can only be submitted from hard copy if the user has not purchased Acrobat. Forms can be completed in Reader and printed. The printed copy can then be faxed or filed.

Creating Forms

Now that you know something about filling out a form, let's move on to creating a form and setting up the form fields in Acrobat. Creating forms in Acrobat begins with a template or PDF document and requires use of the Form tool. With the Form tool, you can create actions very similar to those created with the Link tool (see Chapter 10). Rather than creating a link to a view or page, the Form tool creates a data link whereby data fields are identified and choices for expressing the data are defined.

To help create precise placement of data fields, the Grids and Guides attributes should be defined in the Preferences dialog box. Major and minor gridlines can be identified in the Grid Settings dialog box by selecting File ➪ Preferences ➪ Forms Grid. Showing Forms Grid and Snapping to Forms Grid are enabled by selecting the

View menu and choosing the respective option. When creating forms, it is advised that you show the forms grid and use the snap to feature. Without these features turned on, accurately placing forms on fields will be difficult.

All form fields are created with the Form tool. Select the tool in the Acrobat Tool Bar and draw a rectangle. When the Snap to Forms Grid option is enabled, the rectangle created will snap to the gridlines. The moment you release the mouse button after drawing a rectangle, the Field Properties window will appear, in which all the field attributes are defined.

Field properties

The field properties have six general categories, which include Appearance, Options, Actions, Format, Validate, and Calculate. The Appearance tab is the default tab that appears in the Field Properties window. The items appearing in the default window relate to the appearance for the form type you have selected from the pop-up menu in the upper-right corner of the Field Properties window. The Type pop-up menu in the Field Properties window identifies several types of fields that can be used in your form. As you scroll through the tabs in the Field Properties window, different options can be selected for the type of field you create. All options above the tabs are independent of the tab options. Some choices need to be made before you go about scrolling through the tabs and selecting different options. The first choice is to provide a name for the field created.

Naming fields

The Name item in the dialog box enables you to enter a name for the field. The name that appears here will be used to provide a name for the field irrespective of the field contents. You can identify your field name as anything you like. In practice, it's best to use an identifier that closely resembles the contents of the field — something such as *First* or *First Name*. You could use any other identifier such as *1*, *F1*, *First Field*, and so on. The name you enter will be used to identify the field when the data is exported or imported. If you use forms for the Web or import data into other PDF forms, the Name field will play an important role in setting up the proper import and export criteria. It's critical that you understand the importance of field names and keep naming conventions and case sensitivity consistent among files and applications.

Type

The types of fields available for use in PDF forms are accessed from the Type pop-up menu on the top right of the Properties window, as shown in Figure 11-2. When you click the pop-up menu, you can see the available choices.

A brief description of the form types were discussed earlier in this chapter. The default field type is Text. Text is a generic field that can accept data in the form of alphanumeric characters. After naming a field, choose from the pop-up menu the field type you wish to create.

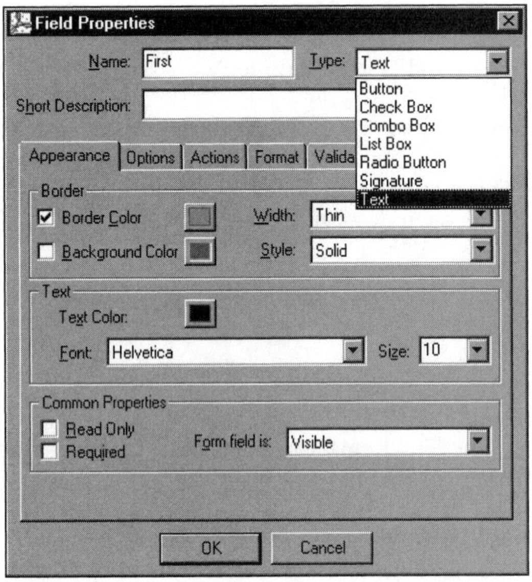

Figure 11-2: The Field Properties window enables you to identify the attributes for form fields. Here the pop-up menu for the various field types is open.

Short description

As previously stated, the Name item in the Field Properties window identifies a particular field and plays an important part in the import and export of forms. You must supply a field name when creating a field. Short Description, located beneath the Name item, is optional. When you add a descriptor to this field, the field name you supply will appear in the display of a Tool Tip. The Short Description field can be helpful to the user when completing the form. For example, you could name a field 1A, which you intend to be the field in which users type in their first name. In the Short Description field, enter the text *First Name*. Then when a user moves the cursor over the field box, First Name will appear as a Tool Tip. As fields are encountered by the mouse cursor, the Tool Tip will change to the short description supplied for the respective field.

Appearance

The Appearance tab relates to the form field appearance. Much like links, you can create a rectangle in a form with the rectangle border either invisible or visible. When made visible, you have access to border attribute options as well as options for the text appearance, as listed here:

✦ **Border Color:** The keyline created for a field can be made visible with a rectangular border appearing in a color selected from the color swatch adjacent to the Border Color option. To specify a border color, enable the option and click the color swatch. When the swatch is selected, the system color palette will appear, enabling you to select a custom border color. (No preset color choices are available for this item.)

✦ **Background Color:** The field box can include a background color. If you wish the field box to be displayed in a color, enable this option, click the color swatch next to it, and choose a color the same way you would for the border. When the check box is disabled, the background will appear transparent, and the field name will be visible in the field box. If you wish to eliminate the field name, choose a color for the Background.

✦ **Width:** The Width options include the same options available for link rectangles. Select the pop-up menu and choose from Thin, Medium, or Thick.

✦ **Style:** There are five style types to choose from this pop-up menu. The Solid option will display the border as a keyline at the width specified in the Width setting. Dashed will display a dashed line; Beveled will appear as a box with a beveled edge; Inset makes the field look recessed; and Underline will eliminate the keyline and supply an underline for the text across the width of the field box. See Figure 11-3 for an example of these style types.

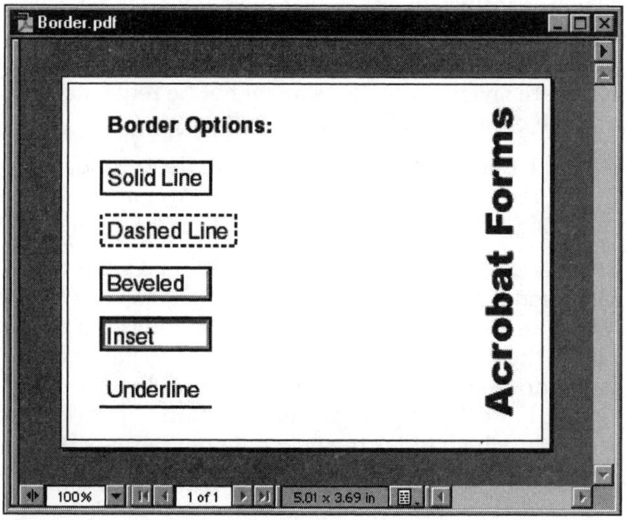

Figure 11-3: Five options for choosing a border style are available in the Field Properties window.

✦ **Text Color:** The text appearing for the field name defaults to black. If you identify a color for text by selecting the swatch adjacent to Text Color, the field contents supplied by the end user will change to the color chosen. The field name, however, will remain black.

✦ **Font:** From the pop-up menu, select a font for the field data. Regardless of the fonts installed in your system, Acrobat only permits use of the Base 13 fonts and Zapf Dingbats for data fields. Because Acrobat ships with the Base 13+1 fonts, you can be certain all users will be able to complete the forms you design with the same font sets. When designing forms, try to use Sans Serif fonts. They will display better on screen than Serif fonts. The default for the font used with Acrobat Forms is Helvetica. In most cases, this choice will provide the best results when viewing PDFs on screen.

✦ **Size:** Depending on the size of the form fields you create, there may be a need to choose a different point size for the text. The default is 12 points, which may be too large if your data fields are small in height. Choices for manually setting the point size for text range between 6 and 18 points. If you select Auto, the text will be automatically sized to fit within the height of the field box. When Auto is used, the point sizes for text can be smaller than 6 point and larger than 18 point, depending on how large the vertical height of the field box is sized.

✦ **Read Only:** Below the text attribute choices are the Common Properties settings. The first item deals with a read only item. When Read Only is selected, the field will not accept user input — it "locks" the field box. If no background color is used, the name of the field will appear within the field box. Likewise, the border color and style will also appear. If a background color is used, the field name will not be visible. In either case, no cursor can be placed inside the field box, and no entries can be made. Read Only might be used to display information in a field where no user input is required. Or you might create a series of forms where given populations might not be requested to fill in some data fields, in which case this option comes in handy.

✦ **Required:** When the Required option is enabled, the form data won't be submitted until all required fields are completed. You might use this field option for something like a date field or Social Security number field.

✦ **Form Field is:** Several options for displaying individual fields are available from this pop-up menu. The default is Visible, which displays the field and permits entry. The second choice is Hidden, which hides the field from view and does not print the field when the form is output to hard copy. The third item is Visible but doesn't print, which makes the field visible on screen and enables user entry, but will not print the field to hard copy. The last item is Hidden but printable, which hides the field data but permits printing the field on hard copy.

Regardless of which choice you make for the field type, the Appearance tab will contain most of the items discussed in the preceding list. Subtle changes to options might include different defaults as you select from the Type pop-up menu. For example, the default font for the various form types is Helvetica. However, when you specify the Radio Button type, the font will default to Zapf Dingbats. For the most part, Appearance options are consistent with the field types used. The other tab settings options, however, will change depending on which type is selected.

Options

The Options tab provides selections for specific attributes for the field to be created. Options settings are dependent on the field type selected from the Type pop-up menu, so let's take a moment to look at the Options tab attributes for each of the types.

Text options

When Text is selected from the Type pop-up menu and the Options tab is clicked, the Field Properties window will appear as illustrated in Figure 11-4.

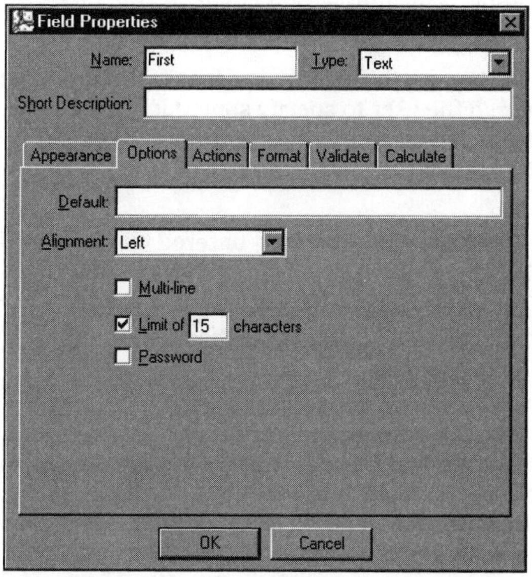

Figure 11-4: The Options settings for Text field properties

Each of the attribute settings, listed here, are optional when creating text fields:

✦ **Default:** The Default field in the Field Properties dialog box for a text item can be left blank, or you can enter text that will appear in the field when viewing the form. The Default item has nothing to do with the name of the field. This option can be used to provide helpful information when the user fills out the form data. If no text is entered in the Default field, when you return to the form, the first field will appear empty. If you enter text in the Default field, the text you enter will appear inside the field box when you return to the form.

✦ **Alignment:** The Alignment pop-up menu has two functions. First, any text entered in the Default field will be aligned according to the option you specify from the pop-up menu choices. Alignment choices include Left, Centered, and Right. Secondly, regardless of whether text is used in the Default field, when the end user fills out the form the cursor will be positioned at the alignment specified in the Field Properties window. Therefore, if you select Centered from the Alignment options, the text entered when filling out the form will be centered within the field box.

✦ **Multi-line:** If your text field contains more than one line of text, select the Multi-line option. When you press the Return key after entering a line of text, the cursor will appear on the second line, ready for text entry. Multiline text fields may be used, for example, as an address field to accommodate a second address line.

✦ **Limit of [__] Characters:** The box for this option provides for user character limits in a given field. If you wish the user to specify something in a date field, for example, where the field would be expressed as *mm/dd/yy*, you might use a limit of eight characters. If the user attempts to go beyond the limit, a warning beep will sound.

✦ **Password:** When this option is enabled, all the text entered in the field will appear as a series of asterisks when the user fills in the form. The field is not secure in the sense that you must have a given password to complete the form; it merely protects the data being typed from being seen by an onlooker.

Check box and radio button options

Check boxes and radio buttons have two data options for Export Value: Yes (on) or Off. When a mark is placed in the form field, the default will be Yes (or on). When no check is placed in the field box, the data will be read as Off. From the options available for check boxes or radio buttons, you can choose a style for the check mark or radio button from the available pop-up menu choices. Check boxes and radio buttons have identical choices for appearance attributes. (See Figure 11-5.)

In the Options tab for the check boxes or radio buttons, the item denoted as Default is checked; when enabled, this option will place a mark in all data fields that have been identified with this default. When the user fills out a form, he or she would need to click a check box field to toggle the check mark off. Radio buttons behave a little differently. If the user clicks to select a radio button, another click will not deselect it. Toggling radio buttons is a little different, as is explained later in this chapter. The six check styles available for the check box are illustrated in Figure 11-6. The same icons are also available for radio buttons.

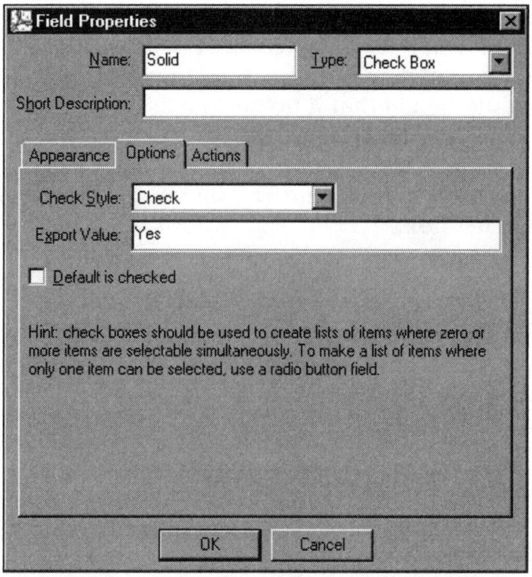

Figure 11-5: The Options settings for check box fields include a pop-up menu for the style of the check mark to be used and an identifier for the data value exported. The same choices are also available for radio buttons.

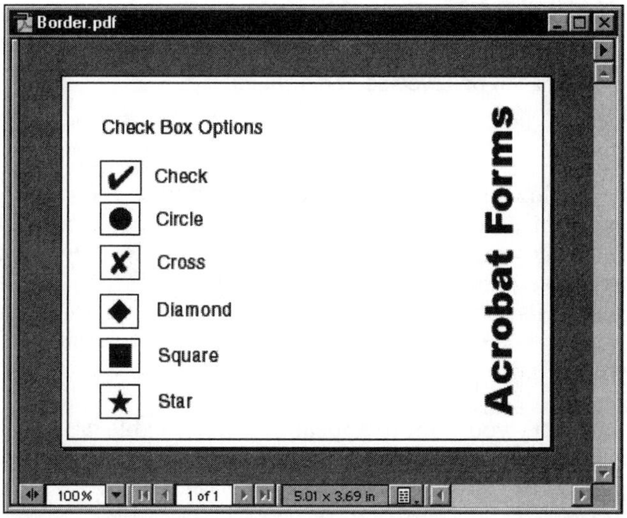

Figure 11-6: These six icon options are available for check boxes and radio buttons.

Combo box and list box options

Combo boxes enable you to create form fields in which a list of selections appears in a scrollable window. The user completing a form can make a selection from the list. A list box is similar to the combo box in that it presents a list that is also scrollable when some items are hidden. However, the list for a combo box only displays one item at a time from the scrollable list, whereas a list box will display as many items as can appear in the form field. Figure 11-7 illustrates the differences between a combo box and a list box.

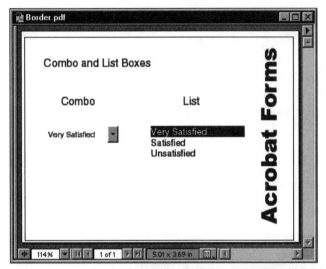

Figure 11-7: A combo box and a list box are displayed beside each other. The combo box items can be revealed and scrolled by selecting the down arrow.

The data exported with the file will include the selected item from the combo box or list box. When creating a form, restricting a user to specific items from which to choose is preferred over allowing open-ended comment lines. Restricting data choices to a few options makes it easier to analyze and categorize the final data. When the combo box item or list box item is selected from the Type pop-up menu, and you click the Options tab, the Options window enables you to define various field attributes, as shown in Figure 11-8.

✦ **Item:** The name of an entry you want to appear in the scrollable list is entered in the Item field. This value can be identical to the export value, or a different name than the export value can be used.

✦ **Export Value:** When the data is exported, the name entered in this field box will be the value appearing in the exported data file. As an example of when you may want to make the values for the Item and Export Value fields different, let's say you created a consumer satisfaction survey form. In that form, the user may choose from list items such as Very Satisfied, Satisfied, and Unsatisfied, and you've specified the export values for these items to be 1, 2, and 3, respectively. When the data is analyzed, the frequency of the three items would be tabulated and defined in a legend as 1=Very Satisfied, 2=Satisfied, and 3=Unsatisfied.

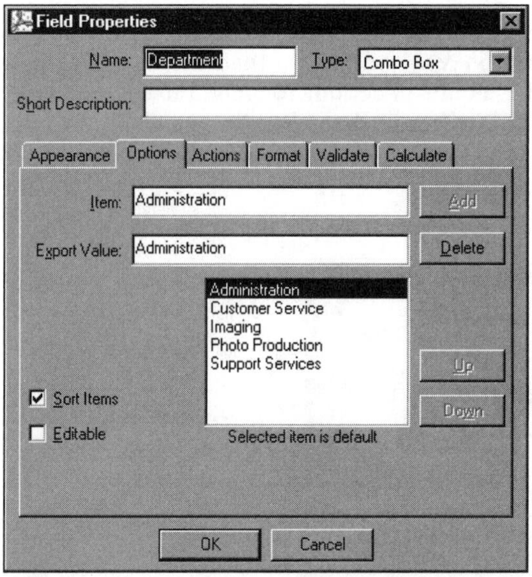

Figure 11-8: The Options settings for combo boxes provide an opportunity to specify how items in the combo box list will appear. List box options are the same, except for the Editable item option.

✦ **Add:** After the Item and Export Values have been entered, clicking the Add button will place the Item in a list box appearing below the Export Value field. After adding an item, you can return to the Item field and define a new item and, in turn, a new export value.

✦ **Delete:** If an item has been added to the list and you wish to delete it, first select the item in the list. Click the Delete button to remove it from the list.

✦ **Up/Down:** Items are placed in the list according to the order in which they are entered. The order displayed in the list will be duplicated in the combo box or list box when you return to the PDF document. If you wish to reorganize items, select the item in the list and click the Up or Down button to move one level up or down, respectively. To enable the Up and Down buttons, the Sort Items option must be disabled.

✦ **Sort Items:** When checked, the list will be alphabetically sorted in ascending order. As new items are added to the list, the new fields will be dynamically sorted while the option is enabled.

✦ **Editable:** The items listed in the Options tab are fixed in the combo box on the Acrobat form by default. If Editable is selected, all items in the combo box can be changed by the user. Acrobat makes no provision for some items to be edited and others not. The Editable option is not available for list boxes. When you create a list box, the data items cannot be changed.

Button options

Buttons differ from all other fields when it comes to appearance. You can create and use custom icons for button displays. Rather than entering data or toggling a data field, buttons typically execute an action. You might use a button to clear a form, export data, or import data from a data file into the current form. When the Button type is selected, the Options tab attributes will change to those illustrated in Figure 11-9.

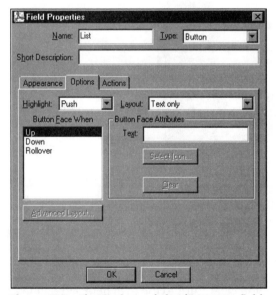

Figure 11-9: The Options tab for the Button field properties includes highlight settings and three options for mouse behavior: Up, Down, and Rollover.

When the Button type is selected, you can make choices on the Options tab for the highlight view of the button, the behavior of the mouse cursor, and choices for text and icon views. The Options attributes for buttons are as follows:

✦ **Highlight:** The Highlight options affect the view when the button is clicked. The None option specifies no highlight will be applied to the button when it is selected. Invert will momentarily invert the colors of the button when selected. Outline will display a keyline border around the button, and Push will make the button appear to move in and out.

✦ **Button Face When:** The three choices on this list become available when a highlight option has been specified. Up will display the highlight action when the mouse button is released. Down displays the highlight action when the mouse button is pressed. Rollover offers an opportunity to use a second icon; when the mouse cursor moves over the button without clicking, the image will change to the second icon you choose.

✦ **Layout:** Several views are available for displaying a button with or without the field name you provide in the Name field. The choices from the pop-up menu for layout offer options for displaying a button icon with text (specified in the Text field within the Button Face Attributes section) appearing at the top, bottom, left, or right side of the icon. Figure 11-10 illustrates the different Layout options.

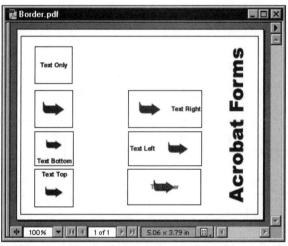

Figure 11-10: The Layout options include, from top-left down, Text only; Icon only; Icon top, text bottom; Text top, icon bottom. On the right, from the top are Icon left, text right; Text left, icon right; and Text over icon.

✦ **Select Icon:** When an icon is used for a button display, click Select Icon to open the Select Appearance dialog box, shown in Figure 11-11. In this dialog box, a Browse button will open a navigation dialog box in which you can locate a file to be used as a button. The file must be a PDF document. The size of the PDF can be as small as the actual icon size or a letter-size page or larger. Acrobat will automatically scale the image to fit within the form field rectangle drawn with the Form tool. When an icon is selected, the icon will be displayed as a thumbnail in the Select Appearance dialog box.

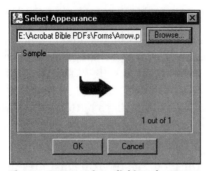

Figure 11-11: After clicking the Browse button and opening the PDF file to be used as an icon, the image will be displayed as a thumbnail in the Select Appearance dialog box.

An icon library can be easily created from drawings using an Adobe font such as Zapf Dingbats or Carta or patterns and drawings from an illustration program. Create or place images on several pages in a layout application. Distill the file to create a multiple-page PDF document. When selecting an icon to be used from the PDF file, the Select Appearance dialog box enables you to scroll pages. Each icon will be viewed in the thumbnail. When the desired icon is displayed, click the OK button. The image viewed in the thumbnail will be used as the icon.

✦ **Clear:** When an icon is selected, it can be eliminated by clicking the Clear button. Clear will eliminate the icon only. The text identified in the Button Face Attributes section will remain.

✦ **Advanced Layout:** Clicking the Advanced Layout button will bring up the Icon Placement dialog box, which provides attributes related to scaling an icon (see Figure 11-12). You can specify that the icon always be scaled, never be scaled, scaled down when it is too big to fit in the form field, or scaled up when it is too small to fit in the form field. The Scale How option offers choices between proportional and nonproportional scaling. Sliders provide a visual scaling reference for sizing the icon.

To gain a better understanding of creating buttons, let's take a look at some steps used to create a rollover effect with two different icons.

STEPS: Create a Button That Includes a Rollover Effect

1. **Create the icons.** You can use type characters from Zapf Dingbats, two Photoshop files, or two illustrations from any illustration application. In my example, I created two Adobe Illustrator files.

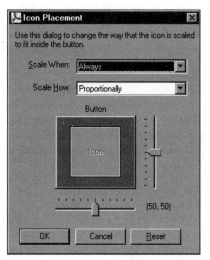

Figure 11-12: The Icon Placement dialog box offers options for scaling icons.

2. **Convert to PDF.** The files used must be converted to PDF. If you set type in a layout or illustration program, create two different characters on two separate pages. If importing graphics to a layout application, use a separate page for each graphic. If using programs that permit direct export to PDF, export two files to PDF. In my example, I exported the Illustrator drawings to PDF.

3. **Open a PDF document.** You need a PDF file in which to create the form field. You can use an existing file or create a blank page in an application and export to PDF.

4. **Create the form field.** From the Acrobat Tool Bar, select the Form tool and draw a rectangle.

5. **Select the Appearance tab in the Field Properties window.** When the Field Properties window appears, set the Type to Button and specify settings for border display, text font, and size. In my example, I chose a thin black border, Helvetica for the font, and 18-point type.

6. **Enter a name for the field.** Provide a name for the field by entering text in the Name field.

7. **Choose the layout.** Select the Options tab to move to the Options settings. For layout, select the option desired. In my example, I chose Text top, icon bottom.

8. **Select the icon to be used.** Click the Select Icon button. In the Select Appearance dialog box, select the icon to be used for the default display and

Continued

click OK. If using text as part of the button display, enter the text in the Text field. In my example, I used Forms are Tough for my text.

9. **Set the attributes for the rollover.** While still in the Options tab of the Field Properties window, select Rollover from the Button Face When list (see Figure 11-13). Click Select Icon to choose the second icon to be displayed when the mouse cursor moves over the field.

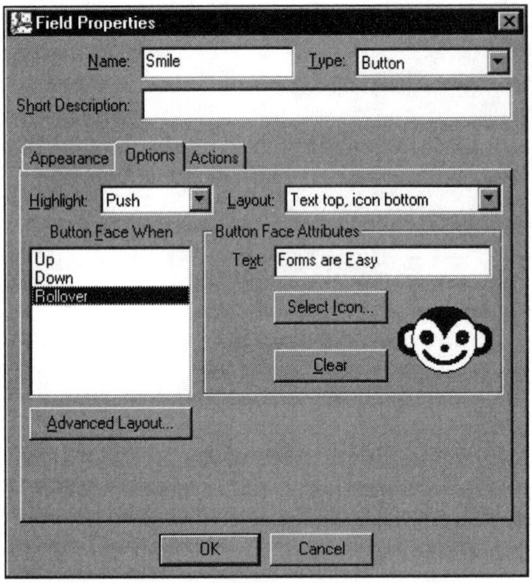

Figure 11-13: In my example, I chose the second icon to be displayed and entered the text, "Forms are Easy."

10. **Click OK.** To accept all the attributes and return to the Acrobat document window, click the OK button.

11. **View the results.** To display the icon, a tool other than the Form tool must be selected in the Acrobat Tool Bar. Click the Hand tool to view the results (see Figure 11-14).

12. **View the rollover effect.** Move the cursor over the form field. If the steps were properly executed, you should see the icon change to the second image defined for the rollover effect (see Figure 11-15).

In this example, no action was identified for the form field. The result is simply a change in the icon view for the button. In most cases, buttons are created to invoke actions. Actions are handled in the Field Properties window when you select the Actions tab.

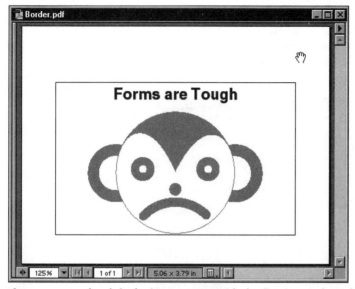

Figure 11-14: The default view appears with the first icon selected for the button. The associated text for this view appears at the location defined through the Layout option. Notice the cursor rests outside the form field.

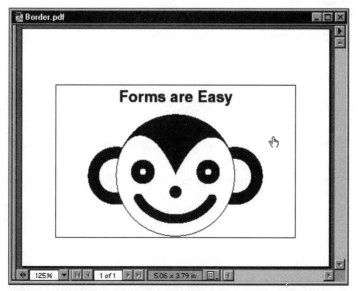

Figure 11-15: When I moved the cursor over the form field, the second image and the new text were both displayed within the field boundaries.

Actions

The Actions tab, shown in Figure 11-16, enables you to set an action when you click the field, when the cursor appears over a field, when the cursor exits a field; or, you can have no action associated with the field.

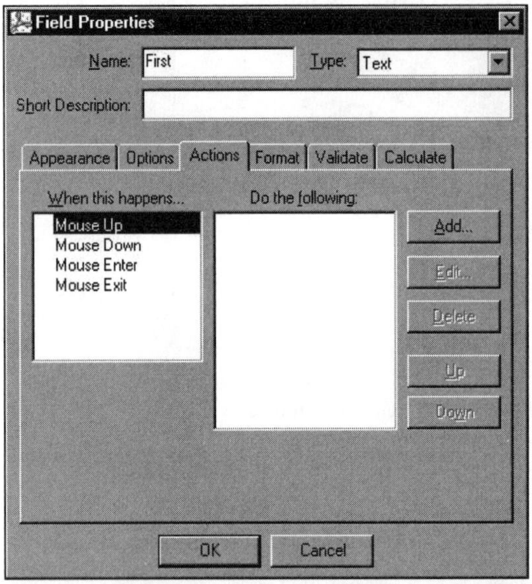

Figure 11-16: The Actions tab provides options for invoking an action dependent on the mouse behavior.

The four mouse behavior items in the Actions tab are as follows:

✦ **Mouse Up:** When the user releases the mouse button, the action will be invoked.

✦ **Mouse Down:** When the user presses the mouse button, the action will be invoked.

✦ **Mouse Enter:** When the user moves the mouse cursor over the field, the action will be invoked.

✦ **Mouse Exit:** When the user moves the mouse cursor off the field, the action is invoked.

Actions for the cursor movements are similar to those discussed in the context of creating links in Chapter 10. You can specify menu commands and deal with some specific items for working with forms. All the actions are accessed by clicking the Add button in the Actions tab.

The action will be associated with the mouse cursor option selected when you click Add. The default is Mouse Up, so when Mouse Up is selected, the action will be invoked when the mouse button is released.

When you select the Add button, the Add an Action dialog box will appear, as shown in Figure 11-17. The actions listed in this dialog box are the same as the those in the Link Properties dialog box discussed in Chapter 10. Turn back to Chapter 10 for examples of how the following action types work: Execute Menu Item, Go to View, Movie, Open File, Read Article, Sound, and None. The remaining action items relate more specifically to the task of creating a form, and so are discussed in detail in the text that follows.

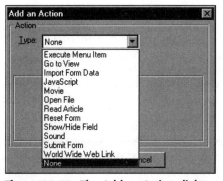

Figure 11-17: The Add an Action dialog box offers a pop-up menu with options for the action type to be associated with the mouse behavior.

Import form data

You can export the raw data from a PDF file, which creates a Form Data File (FDF) that can later be imported into other PDF forms. To import data, you can use a menu command or set an action on a field and execute the Import Form Data command. Data can be imported locally on your hard drive. You cannot import data into a PDF file from a Web site. Rather than retyping the data in each form, you can import the same fields into new forms where the field names match. Therefore, if a form contains field names such as First, Last, Address, City, State, and so on, all common field names from the exported data will be imported into the current form. Those field names not matching exactly will be ignored by Acrobat.

The Importing Form Data command enables you to develop forms for an office environment or Web server where the same data used can easily be included in several documents. In designing forms, it is essential that you use the same field names for all common data. If you import data and some fields remain blank, recheck your field names. Any part of a form design or action can be edited to correct errors.

Acrobat's Data Search

When a data file is identified for an import action, Acrobat will look to the location you specified when creating the action. Acrobat also searches other directories for the data. On the Macintosh, Acrobat looks to the Reader and System:Preferences directories for the data file. On Windows, Acrobat looks to the Acrobat directory, Reader directory, current directory, and the Windows directory. If Acrobat cannot find the data file, a warning dialog box will appear containing a Browse button to prompt the user to locate the data file.

Reset form

This is a handy action for forms that need to be cleared of data and resubmitted. When the Reset Form action is invoked, all the data fields are cleared. When you use this action, it's best to associate it with Mouse Up to prevent accidental cursor movements that might clear the data and require the user to begin over again. Reset Form can also be used with the Set Page Action command. If you want a form to be reset every time the file is opened, the latter will be a better choice than creating a button. Regardless of where you identify the action, it will be performed in the same manner.

The Reset Form command offers an option for clearing the entire form or selected fields. When I discussed radio buttons earlier, I mentioned clicking a radio button or check box will not clear the data. If you use a radio button or check box for making a decision from among two or more items, the selection for one option must be cleared to toggle back and forth. Because of this, radio buttons or check boxes are ideal for enabling the user to choose among certain categories of information, such as gender, or age range.

Let's take a look at some steps for using the Reset Form option to select fields and demonstrating how the Add an Action option is used.

STEPS: Resetting Form Fields

1. **Open a PDF document in Acrobat.** Use an existing PDF file, or create a blank page and convert to PDF.

2. **Create a form field.** For this example, you'll use two radio buttons — one for Male and the other for Female. When the user clicks on Male, the Female field will be reset and vice versa.

3. **Select the Form tool and draw a rectangle.** Select the Form tool from the Acrobat Tool Bar and draw a field rectangle in the document window. When the mouse button is released, the Field Properties dialog box will open.

4. **Set the Appearance tab and choose the field type.** In the Field Properties dialog box, select the Appearance tab. Name the first field *Male* and choose Radio Button from the Type pop-up menu. Select Border and choose a color for the border. Select the Options tab and choose a radio button style. For this example, choose Circle from the pop-up menu. Click OK to accept the properties and return to the Acrobat document window.

To reset the form, you need to tell Acrobat to clear the opposite field when this button is selected. Because you only have one form field, there is not yet an opportunity to identify the field to be cleared. Therefore, the action cannot yet be created.

5. **Create a second form field.** With the Form tool, draw another field rectangle. Name the field *Female* and choose Radio Button from the Type pop-up menu. Choose the same style for the radio button as selected in Step 3.

   At this point, you can add an action because two fields are now present.

6. **Add an action.** Click the Actions tab. The default selection is Mouse Up. Leave this item selected in the list. Click the Add button to open the Add an Action dialog box. Select Reset Form from the pop-up menu.

7. **Select the fields.** In the Add an Action dialog box, click the Select Fields button. The Field Selection dialog box appears, providing choices for field selections (see Figure 11-18). If more fields are to be preserved than cleared, check the All, except button. If only one or a few fields are to be cleared, check the Only these button. In this example, only one field is to be cleared, so check Only these and click OK.

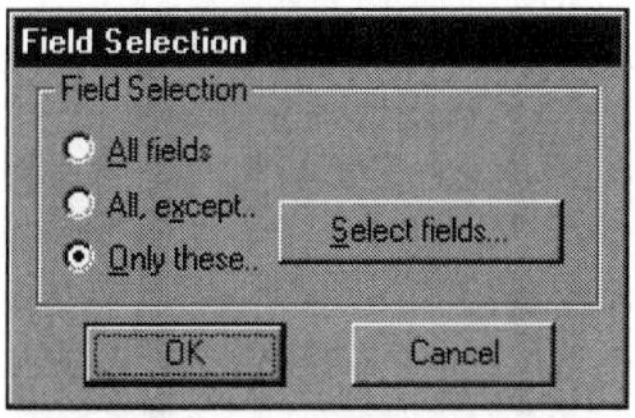

Figure 11-18: The Field Selection dialog box offers choices for clearing all fields when resetting a form, selectively clearing all but specific fields, or limiting the Reset Form option to fields you select individually.

8. **Identify the field to be cleared.** Another Field Selection dialog box will appear, which enables specific field selections to be cleared. Notice the left column is labeled "Excluded fields" and the right column is labeled "Included fields." All fields listed in the left column will not be cleared, whereas all fields listed in the right column will be cleared.

   Because the current field is Female, you want to clear the Male field when this button is selected. Therefore, the Male field needs to be moved to the right column, which will be included when the form is reset. To move a field, select the field name in the list on the left and click the arrow button (chevron) at the bottom of the list, as illustrated in Figure 11-19.

Continued

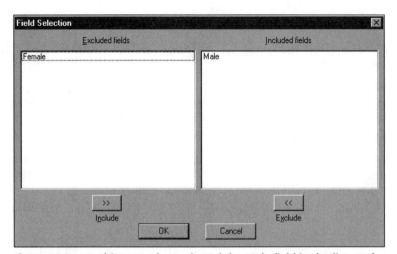

Figure 11-19: In this example, I selected the Male field in the list on the left side of the dialog box, and then clicked the right chevron appearing above the word *Include* at the bottom of the list. Male was then moved to the Included fields list, which means this field will be cleared when the form is cleared. Because Female remains in the Excluded list, clicking the Female field will exclude it from clearing in the form.

9. **Click OK in all dialog boxes.** To accept the edits, click OK in all the dialog boxes until you return to the PDF document window.

10. **Add a second action.** You added the action for the Female field, and now need to perform the same steps for the Male field. To do so, double-click the Male field with the Form tool to open the Field Properties dialog box. Select the Actions tab and click the Add button. Choose Reset Form for the action type and move the Female field to the Included fields list. Click OK in all dialog boxes to return to the PDF document window.

11. **Test the results.** If you performed the steps accurately, when you select Male, the Female field should clear and the Male field will display a circle inside the radio button border. The opposite effect should occur when the Female button is selected.

Format

The first three tabs — Appearance, Options, and Actions — are available for all field types but the digital signature. Options and Actions attributes change, but the tabs for these three general categories appear. The tabs for additional options vary significantly depending on which field type is used. Table 11-1 illustrates categorical choices for the field types used.

As illustrated in Table 11-1, the Format, Validate, and Calculate tab options are only available for Combo Box and Text field types. To access the Format tab, select either of these field types. The Format options will be the same for both types.

Table 11-1
Tab Options for Field Types in the Field Properties Window

Field Type	Appear-ance	Options	Actions	Format	Validate Change	Calcu-late	Selection Change	Signed
Button	X	X	X					
Check Box	X	X	X					
Combo Box	X	X	X	X	X	X		
List Box	X	X	X				X	
Radio Button	X	X	X					
Signa-ture	X	X						X
Text	X	X	X	X	X	X		

When the Format tab is clicked, Acrobat displays multiple choices for formatting either combo box or text fields, as shown in Figure 11-20. To define a format, select from the Category list displayed in the window. As each item is selected, various options pertaining to the selected category will appear on the right side of the window..

The Category list displays seven choices for format category:

✦ **None:** No options are available when None is selected. Select this item to use Acrobat defaults for the field type.

✦ **Number:** Options for display of a numeric field include defining the number of decimal places, specifying any currency symbols used to express currency fields, and indicating how the digits will be separated (for example, by commas or by decimal points). The Negative Numbers Style list provides choices for displaying negative numbers, which can include parentheses or a different display color.

✦ **Percentage:** The number of decimal places you wish to display for percentages is available from the Decimal Places field when Percentage is selected as a category. Acrobat will accept values from 0 to 10 decimal places. Choices for Separator Style are the same as those available with the Number category.

✦ **Date:** The date choices offer different selections for month, day, year, and time formats.

✦ **Time:** If you wish to eliminate the date and identify only time, the Time category enables you to do so, offering choices to express time in standard and 24-hour units.

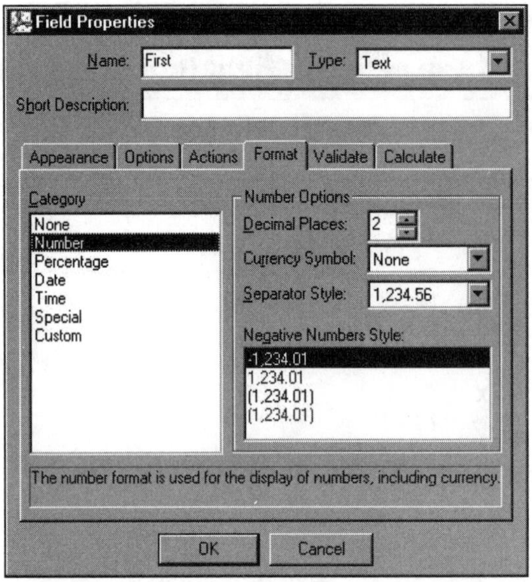

Figure 11-20: When either Combo Box or Text is chosen as the field type, the Format tab will appear. Format options provide selections from seven categories.

✦ **Special:** The Special category offers formatting selections for Social Security number, zip code, and phone number fields.

✦ **Custom:** Custom formatting can be edited by using JavaScript. To edit the JavaScript code, click the Edit button to provide a custom format script. Another window will appear in which the code is created.

Validate

Validate can help ensure proper information is completed in a form. If a value must be within a certain minimum and maximum range, check the radio button for validating the data within the accepted values (see Figure 11-21). The field boxes are used to enter the minimum and maximum values. If the user attempts to enter a value outside the specified range, a warning dialog box will appear informing the user the values entered on the form are unacceptable.

The Custom validate script radio button enables you to enter JavaScript code. Scripts that you may want to include in this window would be those for validating comparative data fields. A password, for example, may need to be validated. If the response does not meet the condition, the user will be denied entry for supplying information in the field.

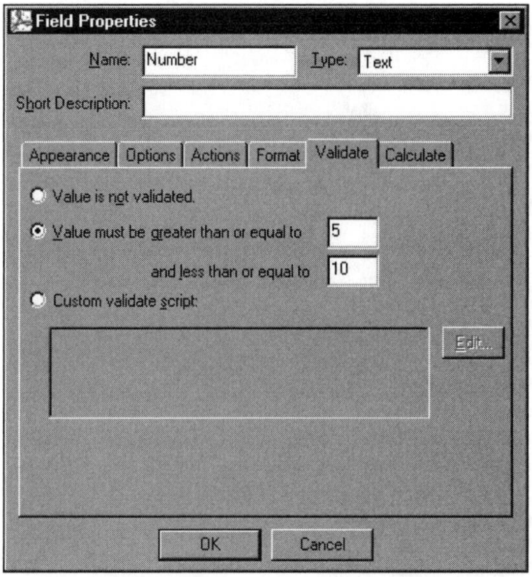

Figure 11-21: Validate can be used with Combo Box and Text field types to ensure acceptable responses within two values.

Calculate

The Calculate tab in the Field Properties window enables you to calculate two or more data fields (see Figure 11-22). A good example of when calculations may be used is to figure out sales tax. A subtotal field might add together the contents of multiple fields, and a tax rate field can be specified. If the form is submitted to different areas where tax rates vary, you can set up multiple fields for choosing a tax rate or an open text field — the contents of which can be supplied by the user. The tax rate would be multiplied by the subtotal to calculate the tax amount.

If you wish to calculate tax and add the tax to the subtotal, you might use JavaScript code to make the calculations and place the resultant data in a single field box.

Selected change

The Selected Change tab is only available for the List Box field type. If a list box item is selected, and then a new item from the list is selected, JavaScript code can be programmed to execute an action when the change is made. Like the other dialog boxes, an Edit button will open the dialog box in which the JavaScript code is created (see Figure 11-23).

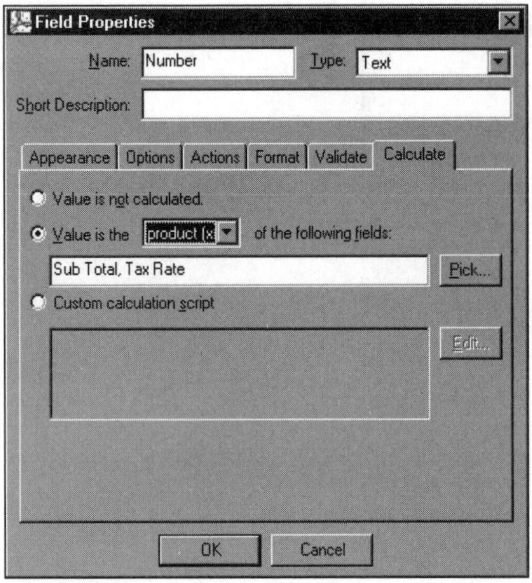

Figure 11-22: The Calculate tab offers options for calculating fields for summing data, multiplying data, and finding the average, minimum, and maximum values for selected fields.

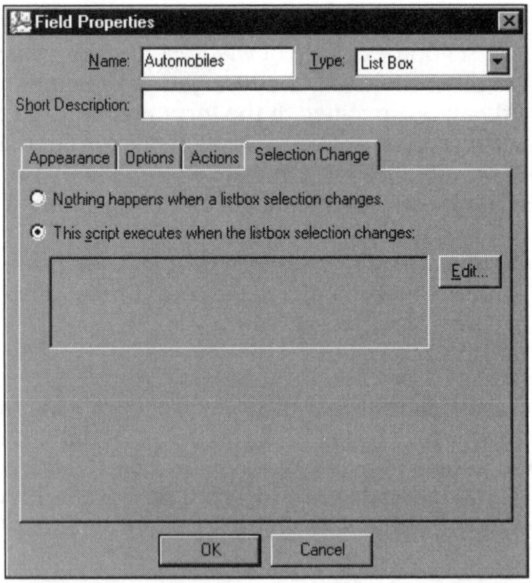

Figure 11-23: The Selected Change tab is only available for List Box field types. When using a Selected Change option, you'll need to program JavaScript code to reflect the action to be made when a change in selection occurs.

There are a variety of uses for the Selected Change option. You might want to create a form for consumer response to a given product — something such as an automobile. Depending on information preceding the list box selection, some options may not be available. For example, a user specifies for "four-door automobile" as one of the form choices; and then from a list, that user selects "convertible." If the manufacturer does not offer a convertible for four-door automobiles, through use of the appropriate JavaScript code in the Selected Change tab, the user would be informed this selection cannot be made based on previous information supplied in the form. The displayed warning could include information on alternate selections that can be made.

Signature fields (Windows only)

Digital signatures, which are only available to Windows users, enable you to create a field that is filled in with a signature. The signature may have one of three appearances:

✦ **Field Signing:** The signature is filled out as part of the form and appears as a printable item. Field signing is intended for entry fields.

✦ **Blind Signing:** The document is signed with a signature with no printable appearance. Blind signing is used when the document needs to be signed, but no printable appearance is necessary.

✦ **Manual Signing:** The PDF page is signed by dragging open a rectangle. Manual signing is used to sign a page when no fields have been identified for signatures and the page needs approval from a user or author. The signature will be generated on the page.

Digital signatures may appear as secured data fields, and they can also be used to indicate approval from users or PDF authors. Actions commonly associated with signatures on forms can individually lock out selected data fields. To create a digital signature field, use the Form tool and select Signature from the Type pop-up menu. Two radio buttons exist in the Signed tab, which is shown in Figure 11-24. You can elect to choose to do nothing or invoke an action when the field is selected. The action items available are the same as those with other field types.

To execute the action, you need to double-click the signature field. Acrobat requires a double-click operation to help prevent inadvertently selecting the signature. When you double-click the signature field, an option to choose a signature handler will be available. Adobe provides you with one signature handler when Acrobat is installed. You can accept the default handler and click OK, which will open the Acrobat Self-Sign Signatures – Sign Document dialog box in which you can specify a reason for signing the document from a list in a pop-up menu (see Figure 11-25). You can choose an optional field for location and another option for the appearance of the signature, which offers the choices None and Text Signature. At the bottom of the dialog box appears a field where you enter your password. Passwords are supplied when you log on by selecting Tools ➪ Self-Sign Signature ➪ Log On. When you click OK, Acrobat will prompt you with a navigation dialog box in which the file can be saved with a new filename. Once saved, the fields you identified to be locked will not be editable.

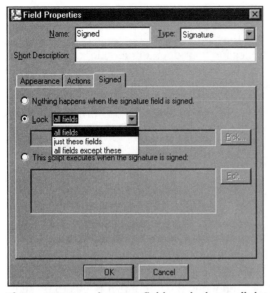

Figure 11-24: A signature field can lock out all data fields or those you select from the Signed tab in the Field Properties window.

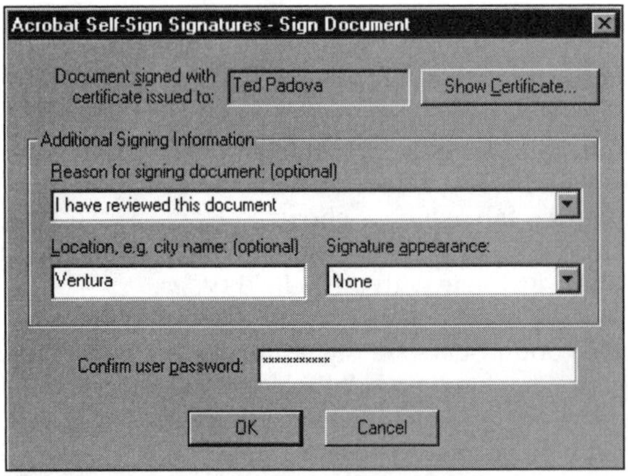

Figure 11-25: The Acrobat Self-Sign Signatures – Sign Document dialog box requires a password from a logged on user permit adding a signature. Without the proper password, another user cannot sign a document with the certificate profile issued to you.

Editing fields

For purposes of explanation, I'll use the term *editing fields* to mean dealing with field duplication, deleting fields, and modifying field attributes. After a field has been created on a PDF page, you may wish to alter its size, position, or attributes. Editing form fields in Acrobat is made possible by using one of several menu commands or returning to the Field Properties window.

To edit a form field's properties, use the Form tool from the Acrobat Tool Bar and double-click the field rectangle. The Properties window will reappear. You can also use a context-sensitive menu, accessible by Control+clicking (Macintosh) or right-clicking (Windows). At the bottom of the context-sensitive menu will appear the Properties command. Select Properties to open the Field Properties dialog box. To select multiple fields, Shift+click each field to be selected with the Form tool. When multiple fields are selected and Properties is chosen from the context-sensitive menu, the appearance for the selected fields can be changed. For example, if you use a keyline border for the selected fields, the border style and color can be changed for those fields.

Tip   If the fields you want to select are located next to each other or many fields are to be selected, use the Shift key (Macintosh) or Ctrl key (Windows) and drag with the Form tool to place a marquee around the fields to be selected. When the mouse button is released, the fields inside the marquee and any fields intersected by the marquee will be selected. The marquee does not need to completely surround fields for selection — just include a part of the field box within the marquee.

Duplicating fields

You can duplicate a field by selecting it and holding down the Option/Ctrl key while clicking and dragging the field box. Fields can also be copied and pasted on a PDF page, between PDF pages, and between PDF documents. Select a field or multiple fields, and then choose Edit ➪ Copy. Move to another page or open another PDF document and select Edit ➪ Paste. The field names and attributes will be pasted on a new page.

Moving fields

Fields can be relocated on the PDF page by selecting the Form tool in the Acrobat Tool Bar, and then clicking and dragging the field to a new location. To constrain the angle of movement, select a field with the Form tool, press the Shift key, and drag the field to a new location. For precise movement, use the arrow keys to move a field box left, right, up, or down.

Deleting fields

Fields can be deleted from the PDF document in two ways. Select the field and press the Delete key (Mac) or Backspace key (Windows). You can also select the field and then select Edit ➪ Clear. In either case, Acrobat will prompt you with a confirmation dialog box. Be certain the Skip Edit Warnings option is disabled in the General Preferences dialog box to view confirmation dialog boxes.

Aligning fields

Even when the grids are viewed on the PDF page, aligning fields can sometimes be challenging. Acrobat simplifies field alignment by offering menu commands for aligning the field rectangles at the left, right, top, and bottom sides as well as for specifying horizontal and vertical alignment on the PDF page. To align fields, select two or more fields and then select Tools ➪ Forms ➪ Align. The options for left, right, top, bottom, horizontal, and vertical alignment will appear in a submenu. The same commands are also available in a context-sensitive menu. Acrobat will align fields according to the first field selected. This is to say, the first field's vertical position will be used to align all subsequently selected fields to the same vertical position. The same holds true for left, right, and top-alignment positions. When using the horizontal and vertical alignments, the first field selected will determine the center alignment position for all subsequently selected fields. All fields will be center-aligned either vertically or horizontally to the first field selected.

You can distribute fields on a PDF page by selecting multiple fields and choose Distribute from the Tools ➪ Forms ➪ Fields ➪ Distribute menu or the context-sensitive menu. Select either Horizontal or Vertical for the distribution type. The first field selected will determine the starting point for distribution.

Center alignment is another menu command found on both the menus just discussed. A single field will be centered in the PDF page either horizontally, vertically, or both horizontally and vertically, depending on the menu choice made. If multiple fields are selected, the alignment options will take into account the extreme positions of the field boxes and center the selected fields as a group on the PDF page.

Sizing fields

Field rectangles can be sized to a common physical size. Once again, the first field selected determines the size attributes for the remaining fields selected. To size fields, select multiple field boxes and then choose Tools ➪ Forms ➪ Fields ➪ Size or use the context-sensitive menu. Size changes can be made horizontally, vertically, or both horizontally and vertically. To size field boxes individually in small increments, hold the Shift key down and move the arrow keys. The left and right arrow keys will size the field box horizontally, while the up and down arrow keys will size the field box vertically.

Setting field tab orders

When you design a form and create form fields, Acrobat will record the sequence of the field order beginning with the first field you create and continue in logical order through the last field created. The first field becomes Field 1, the next Field 2, and so on. This sequence dictates the *field tab order*—which is the order of fields the user will move through when tabbing through the form. If you move a field from one spot to another in the document, Acrobat does not change the order relative to location. In many cases, you will want to reorder the fields to facilitate easy movement through the fields when tabbing through the document. To change field tab order, use the Tools ⇨ Forms ⇨ Fields ⇨ Set Tab Order command or select the same command from the context-sensitive menu. When Set Tab Order is selected, the form fields will appear in the document window with the tab order indicated by number on each field, as shown in Figure 11-26.

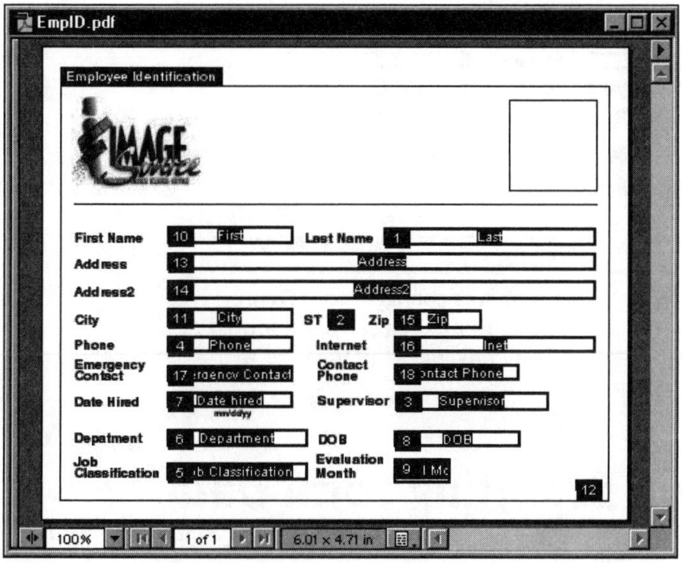

Figure 11-26: When Set Tab Order is selected, the fields will be displayed with a number that describes the tab order. Here, the order is without a logical flow to ease the user in moving around the form.

Unlike previous versions of Acrobat, setting a tab order in Acrobat 4.0 is much more intuitive. In earlier versions of Acrobat, you had to click a field first to identify the beginning of the order, and then click the first field to be renumbered. Not so in version 4.0. After selecting Set Tab Order, the cursor will appear as a selection arrow with the # symbol. To reorder the tabs, click the field you want to appear as number 1, then click the field you want to appear as number 2, and so on — successively clicking each field following a logical order. As you click each field, Acrobat will dynamically update the display to reflect the order you select. If a mistake is made, click the cursor outside a field and choose Set Tab Order again. Clicking outside a field box will deselect the tab order mode. Figure 11-27 illustrates the previous figure reordered.

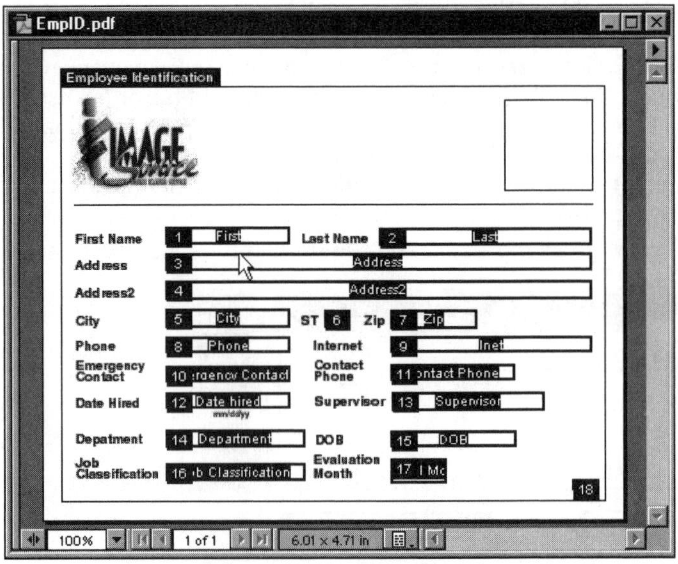

Figure 11-27: The order for the tabs was changed from Figure 11-26 to reflect a more logical flow for the user to complete the form. Pressing the Tab key after completing a field entry will send the user to the next successively numbered field.

Importing and Exporting Form Data

The field boxes in an Acrobat form are placeholders for data. Once data has been entered in a form, it can be exported. When the data is exported from Acrobat, it is written to a new file as a Form Data File (FDF). These files can be imported in a PDF document or managed in an application that can recognize the FDF format. When submitting data to a Web server, the server must have a Common Gateway Interface (CGI) application that can collect and route the data to a database. Using form data on the Web requires advanced programming skills and use of the Adobe FDF Toolkit. You can acquire more information about this via the Web, at `http://beta1.adobe` `.com/ada/acrosdk`. On the Adobe Web site, you'll find samples of CGIs and information for contacting Adobe's Developer Support program (see Figure 11-28).

Exporting data

If you intend to export data to a Web site or intranet, you would add to your form a button used to execute a Submit action. This action type can be handled by either a hypertext link or a form field. In order to collect the data, the Web server must have on it a CGI application that will be used to collect and route the data. Assuming you obtain assistance from a Web administrator for developing such an application, the only thing you would need to know is the URL for the site where the data will be submitted.

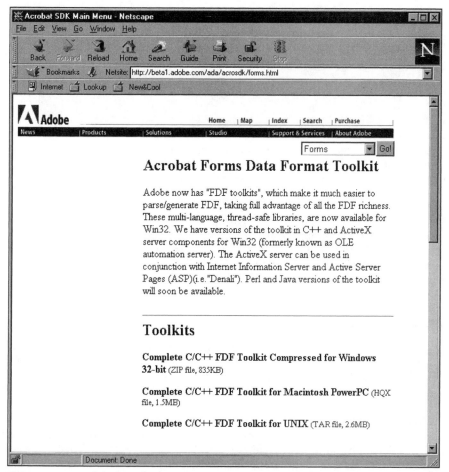

Figure 11-28: Adobe's Web site contains information and samples on exporting form data to a Web site or intranet. From this Web site, you can download samples of CGIs and obtain information on contacting Adobe's Developer Support program.

The other means for exporting data can be handled locally on your computer or network. Exporting form data can be performed directly from a menu command or by developing a form field with a button to execute the Export command. In most cases, the latter would be used for forms distributed to users. To define an action to export data, create a form field. The field can be a text field or a button. For the action, click the Actions tab in the Field Properties dialog box, select Mouse Up, and click the Add button. Select Execute Menu Item from the Action Type pop-up menu, and in the Menu Item Selection dialog box (shown in Figure 11-29), select File ⇨ Export ⇨ Form Data. When the user clicks the field used to export data, a navigation dialog box will appear, prompting you to save the file and supply a name and location.

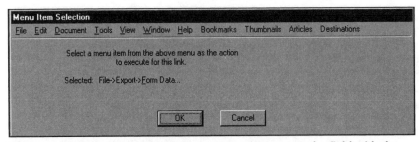

Figure 11-29: To create a form field to export data, create the field with the Form tool and choose Execute Menu Item as the action type. In the Menu Item Selection dialog box, select File ➪ Export ➪ Form Data.

When the data is saved, it will be written to disk as an FDF. The format is not recognized by data managers and needs to be parsed. Therefore, using the data other than in PDF files will need special programming. With regard to PDF files, however, the data can be imported into a PDF document in which common fields share the same names and formats.

Importing data

Importing data is handled in a similar manner as exporting it. You can select the appropriate command in the File menu or create a form or hypertext link to import data. Acrobat will recognize FDFs and import from those files the fields that meet the same conditions as the fields in the PDF document to which you are importing. When the field or button is selected, a navigation dialog box will prompt you to identify the file to be imported. Regardless of which means you use to import data, the file must be selected in the Properties window. When using a form field, the Select File button in the Actions tab enables you to identify the file to be imported. When using a hypertext link, the same button appears in the Link Properties window.

To gain a better understanding of how form data might be imported and exported, here are some steps I followed to manage a form that can export common identifying information to other forms.

STEPS: Export and Import Form Data

1. **Create two forms with a number of fields using common data.** For this example, I created a form, illustrated previously in Figure 11-27, that is used to collect personnel information—name and contact information for an employee, date of hire, department and supervisor, job classification, and evaluation date. Some of the information appearing in this form might be used with other personnel forms. For instance, the employee's name and address will likely be used on various forms. Rather than retyping this information, I created a second

form, illustrated in Figure 11-30, that would be used for the primary identifying information. When creating the new form, I had to ensure all field export names were identical to the names appearing in the import form. Figure 11-31 illustrates the field names used in both forms. Note the field names are different from the short description names appearing in Figure 11-30; however, the field names in Figure 11-31 are identical to the field names in the form shown in Figure 11-27.

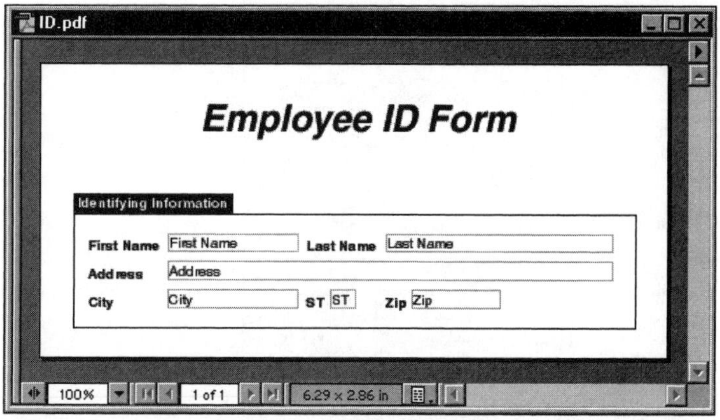

Figure 11-30: I created a form with fields used for the employee name and address only.

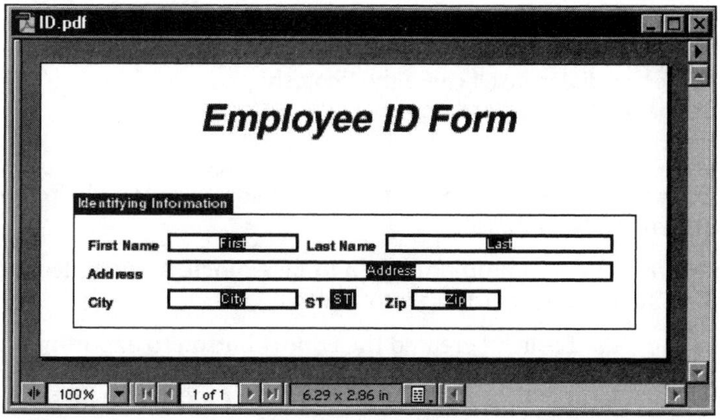

Figure 11-31: When the Form tool is selected from the Acrobat Tool Bar, the field names are displayed. These names must precisely match those in the first form, shown in Figure 11-27.

Continued

2. **Create an Export button.** Depending on the type of button used, draw a link rectangle or form field rectangle. In this example, I created a form field rectangle. I chose Button for the field type and selected Icon only for the layout (see Figure 11-32). For the icon, I imported a Photoshop text image titled *Export*. I then selected the Actions tab and clicked the Add button with Mouse Up selected. In the Add an Action dialog box, I selected Execute Menu Item and then selected File ⇨ Export ⇨ Form Data.

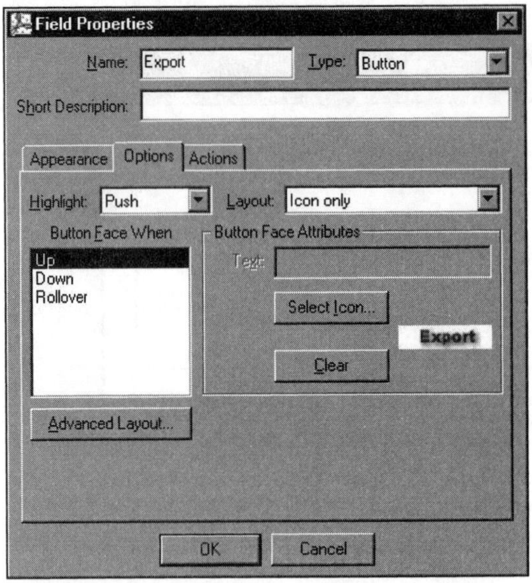

Figure 11-32: I created text in Photoshop and saved the file to PDF. In the Options tab for the Field Properties dialog box, I chose the Photoshop image to be displayed as Icon only.

3. **Save both files.** After creating all the form fields, save the file from Acrobat. I saved my new file as ID.pdf.

4. **Fill out the form containing the data to be exported.** I completed the ID.pdf form containing the identifying information.

5. **Export the data.** Earlier, I created the Export button to export my form data. After I filled out the form, I clicked the Export button, which opened a navigation dialog box. In the dialog box, I named my FDF file id_data.fdf.

6. **Import the data.** The same type of link can be created to import data as was used when exporting data. If no link or form field has been created, then use the File menu and select Import ⇨ Form Data. In this example, I opened the EmpID.pdf form and used the menu command. I selected the id_data.fdf file to import. When the data was imported, those fields common to both forms were filled in, as shown in Figure 11-33.

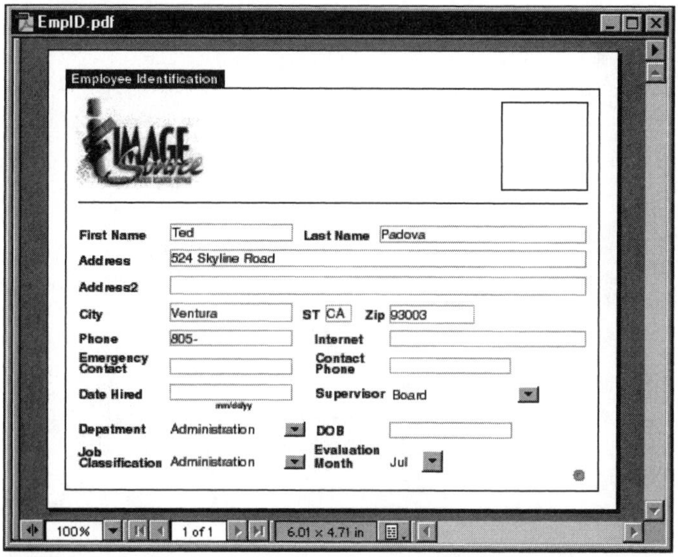

Figure 11-33: The data was imported for all fields with common field names.

Summary

✦ Acrobat forms can be created that contain different form fields, which act as data placeholders or execute different actions.

✦ Data fields can be of several types, including Text, Icons, Lists, and Signatures (Windows only).

✦ All data field attributes are handled in the Field Properties window. Properties can be described for the field by selecting the tabs labeled Appearance, Options, Actions, Calculations, or any of the tabs associated with specific field types.

✦ More functionality with many field types can be created with JavaScripts. The Field Properties window enables the user to supply JavaScript code for several field types.

✦ Once data fields are created, they can be copied and pasted to a PDF page, between pages, and between PDF documents.

✦ Editing fields can be accomplished with menu commands and using context-sensitive menus. Acrobat has several editing commands used for aligning fields, distributing fields, and centering fields on a PDF page.

✦ Data can be exported from a PDF document to Web servers and Form Data Files (FDFs). FDF data can be imported into other PDF files with matching field names.

✦   ✦   ✦

Creating Search Indexes with Acrobat Catalog

✦ ✦ ✦ ✦

In This Chapter

Working with
Acrobat Catalog

Using Catalog
preferences

Creating a catalog

Creating dynamic
indexes

Setting up network
catalogs

✦ ✦ ✦ ✦

Acrobat Catalog is a separate program installed with your Acrobat suite of software. Catalog is used to develop indexes of PDF files. You can have a simple catalog for a few PDF files, or you can create many indexes for a collection of PDF files accessible on an Intranet or office server. Catalog is robust and provides many options for creating and modifying indexes. You can automate the process to have index files automatically created at specified intervals for all PDFs added to a collection. The version of Catalog for the Macintosh differs greatly from the version for Windows computers; the process of cataloguing information is relatively the same across platforms, but there are some distinct differences in how you can change the many options.

In this chapter, you see how to work with Catalog on both platforms, with particular attention devoted to the differences between Catalog on the Macintosh and Catalog in Windows.

Structure of Catalog files

When you produce an index with Acrobat Catalog, there will be several files and folders created automatically by Catalog. The index file by default will have a .pdx extension. You should get in the habit of using this extension for all index files to keep them organized and recognizable. Catalogs can be created inside folders, drive partitions, or on entire hard drives. There will be a total of nine subfolders created by Catalog when the index is produced (see Figure 12-1). Each of these subfolders must remain intact in order to use an index for searching with Acrobat Search. If you eliminate or relocate individual folders, Search won't be able to use the index file.

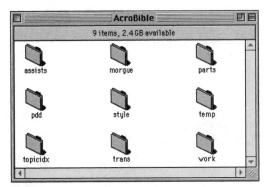

Figure 12-1: When an index file is created by Catalog, nine folders will also be created. These folders must be included in the same folder as the index file when the file is used by Acrobat Search.

Hierarchy of indexed files

You can index a file, folder, or hard drive. When you identify a folder to index, Catalog will include all PDF files inside the given folder and all nested folders inside the target folder. Therefore, you can index all the PDF documents contained in several levels of folders. Catalog will include for indexing all the PDF documents within the identified folder and all PDF documents in folders nested below the root folder.

Relocating indexes

You can move an index and the subfolders to another hard drive or server, or write the index and subfolders to a CD-ROM. When you move an index file, you need to move all subfolders with the index file in order to perform searches on the index. If you fail to copy the index and all related folders, the index will need to be rebuilt.

Using Catalog Preferences

Preference settings are handled in different ways on Macintosh and Windows computers. On the Macintosh, a Preference file is located in the Preferences subfolder of the System Folder, and this is where all the preference settings are recorded. Preferences are accessed on the Macintosh by selecting Edit ⇨ Preferences. When the preference changes are made, they are recorded to the Preference file in the System folder. In Windows, a menu command for preferences is not available. The preference settings in Windows are changed in the Acrocat.ini file. On Windows 95 and 98, the Acrocat.ini file is located in the Windows folder. On Windows NT, it is located in the Winnt folder. To change preferences, you need to edit the Acrocat.ini file in a text editor. Because the handling of preferences in Catalog is so different between platforms, let's look at each scenario individually.

Note   When opening the Acrocat.ini file in a text editor in Windows, be certain to show all files and either the .ini or all extensions (that is, *.ini or *.*) for the filename in the Open dialog box.

Macintosh Catalog preferences

Before launching Acrobat Catalog, you may wish to trash the preference file, identified as Acrobat Catalog Preferences, that is located in the System Folder: Preferences folder. Catalog will build a new preference file when the program is launched. If errors occur, such as a drive or folder not being found after creating an index, you may need to trash the Catalog preference file and create a new index.

Index

To set up preferences for Acrobat Catalog, select File ⇨ Preferences after launching Catalog. The Catalog Preferences dialog box will open, as shown in Figure 12-2. The Preference settings are made by selecting a category item in the left column, and then choosing from the options on the right side of the dialog box. By default, the first category is Index.

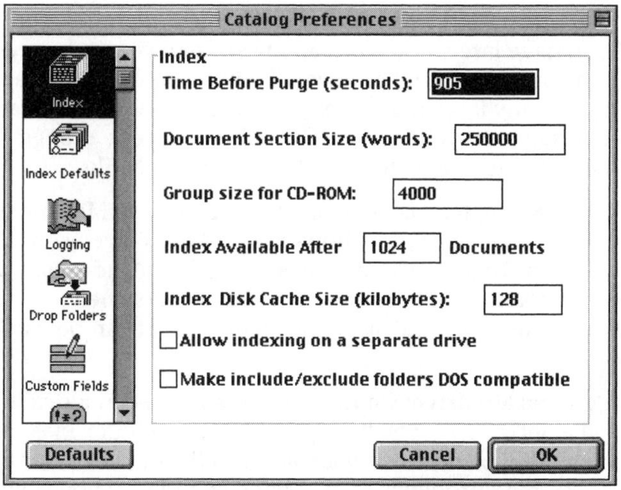

Figure 12-2: Catalog preferences on the Macintosh are accessed in a dialog box available when selecting Edit ⇨ Preferences. When an icon on the left side is selected, the respective preference options will be displayed in the window on the right side of the dialog box.

Index preferences offer several selections to determine the nature of the index file to be created and acceptable locations for the file:

✦ **Time Before Purge (seconds):** Purging involves eliminating unnecessary information from an index. I cover purging in more detail a little later and discuss why it is performed. For now, note the setting you see identified as Time Before Purge (seconds) is a user-definable item that sets up a warning for when a purge will begin. If users on your network are conducting a search, a warning dialog box will appear before the purge begins. The default time for when the warning is posted prior to the purge is 905 seconds, or roughly 15 minutes. You can determine another time period and change the setting as desired.

✦ **Document Section Size (words):** This item is limited to the amount of memory installed on your computer. If you have 32 megabytes of free RAM available, the maximum document section size you can use is 3,200,000 (or 3.2 million) words. The amount of memory required to process a document is approximately ten times the number of words in the document. For faster updates, use the largest size your computer can handle. The acceptable range is 5,000 to 1,000,000.

✦ **Group size for CD-ROM:** This setting has to do with the reliability of the total number of documents indexed. The maximum recommended is 4000. Catalog will permit ranges up to 64,000,000; however, any number above 4000 may be unreliable.

✦ **Index Available After [_] Documents:** This setting will be dependent on the size of your index and how soon you may wish users to access an index after updating it. When you have small index files and want fast searches, set the number to 1024. If you have large index files and wish to have quick access to partial indexes, set the number to 100 or lower. If you need to perform a thorough reindexing of many large index files, set the number higher than 1024 and let it run overnight on your server. Catalog will accept a range between 16 and 4000 PDF documents to be indexed in a single file.

✦ **Index Disk Cache Size (kilobytes):** Disk caching is available to Macintosh users only. A disk cache is a memory location on your hard drive used for frequently accessed items. To increase the speed of updating indexes, increase the cache size. Catalog will use the extra disk space when reorganizing the index. The range of disk cache memory that can be used is between 64 and 2048K.

✦ **Allow indexing on a separate drive:** On the Macintosh, you can index files on different drives or on a network server. If you plan to create index files on remote systems, you should plan your organization well and not move the indexes. Doing so may create problems in accessing an index. If you wish to perform such a task, you need to enable this option.

✦ **Make include/exclude folders DOS compatible:** If you are a Macintosh user who wants your files to be shared by Windows users and you want to build a cross-platform index, all your files and folders need to be named with standard MS-DOS naming conventions (that is, a filename of up to eight characters with an extension of up to three characters). If you have folders that do not conform to MS-DOS conventions, this option will exclude the folders from the index. Filenames not conforming to these conventions are acceptable. In order to alleviate any potential problems, you will be well advised to name all your Macintosh files according to MS-DOS conventions regardless of whether you plan on using cross-platform indexing or not. You never know when a need will arise to make your files DOS compliant.

Index Defaults

The second category in the Catalog Preferences dialog box is Index Defaults, which includes several items for determining the contents of the index file (see Figure 12-3). You'll also find optimizing controls and compatibility options in these settings.

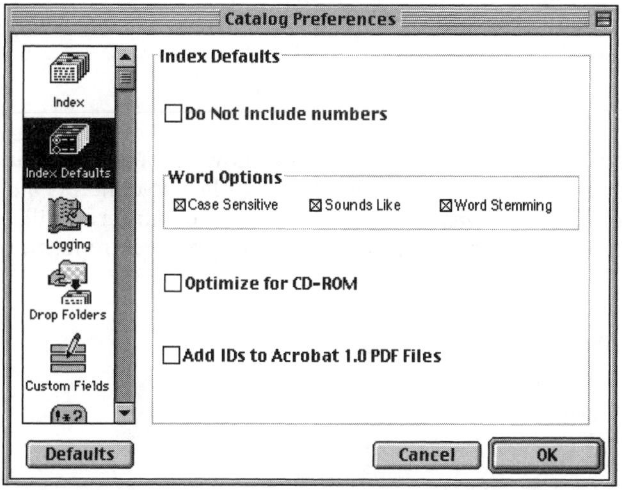

Figure 12-3: The Index Defaults category provides options that determine content attributes of the index file.

✦ **Do Not Include Numbers:** The size of your index files relate dramatically to the speed of updating indexes and performing searches. To speed up both processes, you can exclude some information from the index file. By enabling the Do Not Include numbers option, you can reduce file size from 10 to 20 percent. If numbers are excluded from the index, you will not be able to perform searches for numbers.

✦ **Word Options:** As discussed in Chapter 2, search options provide additional capabilities for narrowing down the search. These include searching by case sensitivity, synonyms, and roots of words. If you feel these options are not necessary, you can choose to exclude any one, two, or all of the options by clearing the respective checkbox. When any of these items are excluded from the index file, they will be disabled when performing a search in an Acrobat viewer.

✦ **Optimize for CD-ROM:** When you choose this option, the searches performed on an index file contained on a CD-ROM will finish much faster. This option can also speed up searches of indexes on your hard drive. When a file is modified, and you perform a search, a warning dialog box will appear informing you the index has been changed. You need to choose to use the index or not by so signifying in the warning dialog box. When you optimize for CD-ROM, activating a search will prevent such warning dialog boxes from appearing.

✦ **Add IDs to Acrobat 1.0 PDF Files:** Earlier versions of Acrobat Distiller and PDFWriter did not include document identifiers as were later added to Acrobat Pro in version 2.0. If you want these identifiers added to PDF files created with either Distiller or PDFWriter from the earlier versions, enable this option.

Logging

When an index is created, Catalog will create a text file known as a log file. The log file will record the progress of creating the index. The log file also contains a date and time stamp for when the index was created. Any errors encountered will be written to the log file. Figure 12-4 shows the choices for logging preferences.

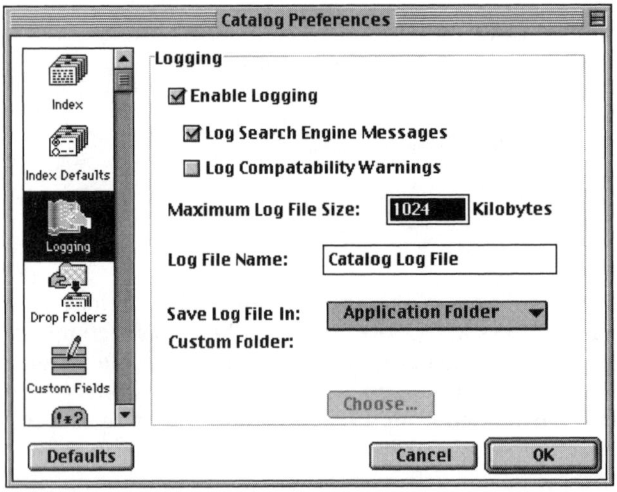

Figure 12-4: Choices for location and filename are established, among other options, in the Logging category of the Catalog Preferences dialog box.

✦ **Enable Logging and associated options:** The Enable Logging option is the first item in the dialog box. When this option is turned on, a log file will be written. If you disable this option, a log file will not be written. The two options under Enable Logging let you include or exclude search engine messages and compatibility warnings.

✦ **Maximum Log File Size:** The default file size for the log file is 1MB. When the log file grows to a size larger than what is specified in this field box, the file will automatically be deleted. The auto-deletion is provided so you don't have a random file on your hard drive grow to extreme sizes. After the log file is deleted, a new log file is created. You can specify a log file size in the range of 16 to 16,384 kilobytes.

✦ **Log File Name:** The default name for the log file is Catalog Log File. If you wish to use another name, enter it in this field box.

✦ **Save Log File In:** By default, the log file is located in the Catalog folder. You can choose a new location by selecting one of the options in the pop-up menu for the log filename. When Custom is selected from the pop-up menu, the Choose button will become active. Click Choose to identify the folder on your hard drive where the log file is to be saved.

Drop Folders

The Drop Folders feature works on the Macintosh only. A folder or multiple folders containing PDF files can be dragged and dropped on top of the Catalog application icon. When the mouse button is released, Catalog is launched and begins indexing the PDFs in the folder and subfolders. The resulting index file and nine subfolders will be placed inside the folder dragged to the Catalog application if Inside Dropped Folder is selected from the Save Index pop-up menu (see Figure 12-5). Alternatively, if Outside Dropped Folder is selected, the index file and subfolders will be placed one level above the dropped folder in the hard disk hierarchy. Indexes created through this drag-and-drop method will assume the attributes of the current preference settings. If you wish to change preferences, launch Catalog and make the changes. Catalog can remain open in the background when the Drop Folders feature is used.

If a folder contains an index file when it is dragged and dropped on the Catalog icon, Catalog will use the definitions of the PDX file found in the dropped folder. If no PDX file is located in the dropped folder, a new index file will be created using definitions prescribed in the Catalog Preferences dialog box.

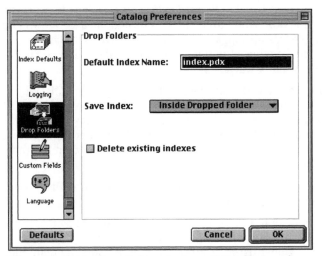

Figure 12-5: The Drop Folders feature of Catalog is only available on the Macintosh. Indexes can be placed inside or outside the dropped folder.

Custom Fields

The Custom Fields settings, shown in Figure 12-6, are used when customizing Acrobat with the Acrobat Software Development Kit. This item is intended for programmers who wish to add special features to Acrobat. To make changes to the Custom Fields settings, you should have a strong command of the PDF format. There are three field types that can be used with the Custom Field settings:

✦ **DocType:** A string field that can accept up to 256 characters of data

✦ **DocNumber:** An integer field that can accept values between 0 and 65,535

✦ **DocDate:** A date field

Each of the field data types are available from a pop-up menu in the Custom Fields dialog box. To identify a type, enter the field name in the field box and select the data type from the Field Type pop-up menu. If you wish to edit a field or data type, the field must be removed and the new edits added again.

Language

Depending on the language(s) installed with Acrobat, you may have choices for a language type from the Language pop-up menu (see Figure 12-7) for the Language category. If only a single-language version has been installed, no options other than the default language will be available.

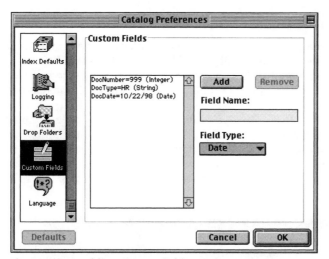

Figure 12-6: Adding custom fields requires a strong knowledge of the PDF format and programming skill. Custom data fields can be added to Acrobat with the Acrobat Software Development Kit.

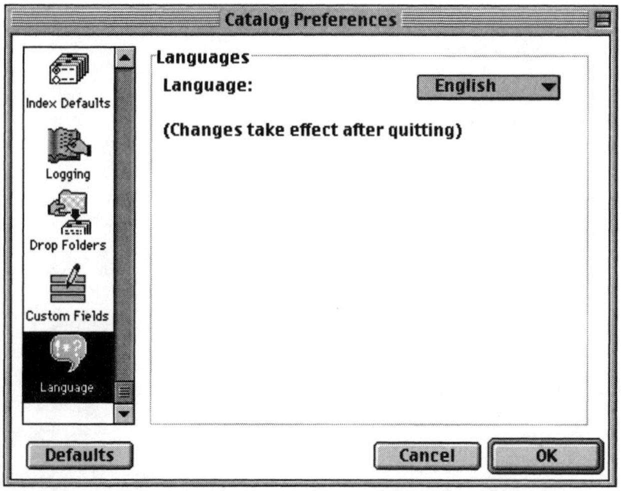

Figure 12-7: When multiple languages are installed, the available language choices will appear in the Language pop-up menu shown here. Once another language has been chosen, you must quit Catalog and then relaunch it.

Windows Catalog preferences

Windows does not have a preference setting dialog box for Acrobat Catalog. All preference settings are edited in a text file found in the Windows (or Winnt) directory. Before you edit the file, it's a good idea to make a backup copy. Use Wordpad or any text editor. Always be certain to save the edited file as text only.

When the file is viewed in a text editor, you will see many lines of code beginning with a ; (semicolon), as shown in Figure 12-8. These lines are comment lines and have nothing to do with the preferences you change. Below each section will begin a line of code not preceded by a semicolon. These lines describe your preference settings. To change the settings, edit the lines and save your changes.

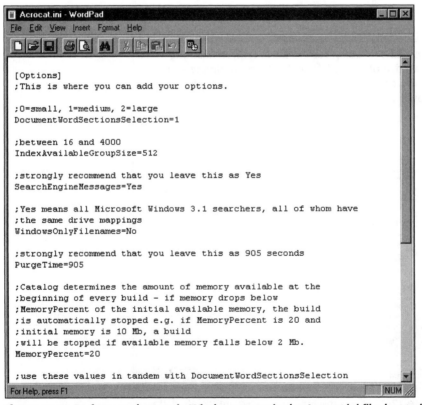

Figure 12-8: Preference changes in Windows occur in the Acrocat.ini file, located in the Windows directory (or Winnt for Windows NT). Changes to the preferences are made in a text editor.

DocumentWordSectionsSelection=1

The DocumentWordSectionsSelection setting provides for three choices. The default is DocumentWordSectionsSelection=1. As noted in the comments section in the example shown in Figure 12-8, you can choose 0, 1, or 2 for the value. This value determines the maximum size in words a catalog will hold for a single document before additional catalogs are created for the same document.

IndexAvailableGroupSize=512

The result of this setting is the same as it is on the Macintosh. The default, shown in Figure 12-8, is 512. The Macintosh default, as mentioned earlier, is 1024. You can use any number ranging between 16 and 4000. This is the number of total files that will be processed before a partial index is created or the current index is updated.

SearchEngineMessages=Yes

You have the choice of entering either Yes or No at the end of this line of code. As indicated in the comment section in the example file, it is recommended that the default, Yes, be used.

WindowsOnlyFilenames=No

The default for WindowsOnlyFilenames is No, which means the file mapping is not set up for performing searches in Windows 3.1 searchers. As a matter of rule, you'll probably keep the default unless in some extreme exception you find someone running a Windows 3.1 machine.

PurgeTime=905

The purge time setting is the same as identified in the discussion of the Catalog preferences in Macintosh, and the default is the same in Windows. You can edit the value to add more or less warning time before the purge begins.

MemoryPercent=20

If you leave this line of code at the default, twenty percent of available memory or less will stop the index build. This is a safe percentage, and it is not recommended you use a lower value. Too low of a memory envelope may cause a crash on your system.

DocumentWordSection(Small, Medium, Large)

If you look back to the value choices for DocumentWordSectionsSelection, the values 0, 1, and 2 relate to the memory identified here: 0 is small, 1 is medium, and 2 is large. In lower memory configurations, use the smaller settings. If you have more than average memory installed (64MB or more), set the large value to a higher setting.

MaxLogFileSize=1000000

This setting is the same for the Macintosh preference for log file size. The default is 1MB. A 1-megabyte file size for text is more than ample. You shouldn't need to change this setting. If you have a text editor that takes a lot of time loading larger file sizes, you can reduce the amount significantly.

[Fields]

The last lines of code in the file relate to the Custom Field settings noted in the Macintosh preferences. As mentioned previously, these settings are used by programmers when modifying Acrobat with the Acrobat Software Developer's Kit.

Creating an Index

When creating an index, it is always a good idea to review your preference settings. Be certain to toggle through the various dialog boxes on the Macintosh or review the Acrocat.ini file in Windows. Before creating index files, you should also make a habit of reviewing the folder where the PDFs to be indexed reside. Be certain all the files intended to be indexed are contained in the same directory or subdirectories for the designated index location.

Creating a new index is handled in Acrobat Catalog by selecting File ⇨ New (Macintosh) or Index ⇨ New (Windows). Be certain not to confuse the New command with the Build command located under the Index menu on both platforms. Before builds can be made, an index file must first be created. When the New command is selected, the New Index Definition dialog box will appear in which you establish the definition, as shown in Figure 12-9. Some important information needs to be supplied in this dialog box before the build can be accomplished.

Index title

On the Macintosh, the default index title, Untitled, appears in the Index Title field; this field is blank in Windows. The title you place in this field will be a title for the index, but not the name of the file you build. The name you enter here does not need to conform to any naming conventions, because it won't be the saved filename. The title will be viewed in the Search Results window when a search is performed. The more descriptive the name, the easier it will be for users to find the information for which they are searching.

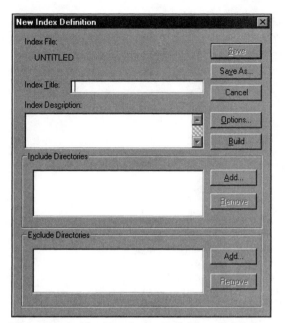

Figure 12-9: The New Index Definition dialog box is used to define the definitions for the Index file and provides the means for selecting the directory where the index will be created.

Index description

You can have as many as 255 characters in the Index Description field. Descriptive names and keywords should be provided so the end user knows what this particular index contains.

To the right of the Index Description box is a button labeled "Options". Click this button, and the Options dialog box appears, in which you can make several exceptions to the index file (see Figure 12-10). Some of these options are similar to those discussed in the context of the Preference settings. Any edits you make here will supersede any preferences.

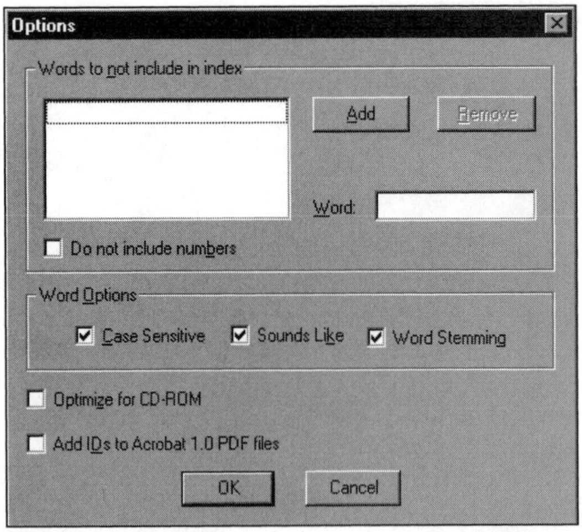

Figure 12-10: Clicking the Options button adjacent to Index Description opens the Options dialog box. Here, the various word options can be enabled and made available when using Acrobat Search.

Excluding words

You may have words such as *the, a, an, of,* and so on that would typically not be used in a search. You can choose to exclude such words by typing the word in the Word field box and clicking the Add button in the Options dialog box. To eliminate a word once it has been added, select the word and click the Remove button. Keep in mind every time you add a word, you are actually adding it to a list of words to be excluded. Regardless of the order in which you enter the words, Catalog will alphabetize them.

Below the settings for exclusion of words is an option for excluding numbers. By selecting the Do not include numbers option, you can reduce the file size, especially if data containing many numbers is part of the PDF file(s) to be indexed. Keep in mind, though, if numbers are excluded, Acrobat Search won't find numeric values.

Word options

The Word Options section in this dialog box present the same choices as discussed in Chapter 2 in the context of Acrobat Search. If you wish not to use these options, you can deselect any or all of the checkboxes.

Optimize for CD-ROM

The Optimize for CD-ROM option is included here, as well as in the Catalog Preferences dialog box. This option is disabled by default. If you want to optimize the search of an index on CD-ROM, enable this option. Like the preceding settings, if you enable this option, it will supersede the preference setting in the Preferences dialog box.

Add IDs to Acrobat 1.0 PDF files

Once again, this setting is the same as you find for Index Defaults in the Catalog Preferences dialog box. Because Acrobat is now in version 4.0, it may be rare to find a need to add the IDs for Acrobat 1.0 files. If you have older files, it would be best to batch-process the older PDFs by saving them out of Acrobat 4.0. As software changes, many previous formats will not be supported with recent updates. To ensure against obsolescence, update older documents to newer file formats.

After determining Options settings, click OK in the Options dialog box, and you will be returned to the New Index Definition dialog box. Before building an index, information must be provided for one more important option. At this point, Catalog does not yet know which directory to include in the index.

Include directories

If you add nothing in this field, Catalog won't build an index because it won't know where to look for the PDF files to be included in the index. Adding the directory path(s) is critical before you begin to build the index. Notice the Add button on the right side of the dialog box in Figure 12-9. When Add is clicked, a navigation dialog box will appear, enabling you to identify the directory where the PDFs to be indexed are located. Many directories can be added to the Include Directories list. These directories can be in different locations on your hard drive. When a given directory is selected, all subfolders will also be indexed for all directory locations. When the directories have been identified, the directory path and folder name will appear in the Include directories field.

Exclude directories

If you have files in a subdirectory within the directory you are indexing and wish to exclude the subdirectory, you can do so in the Exclude Directories field (see Figure 12-11). The folder names and directory paths of excluded directories will appear in that field.

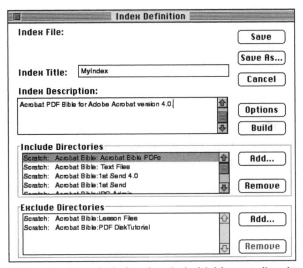

Figure 12-11: Included and excluded folders are listed in their respective order with directory paths specified.

Removing directories

A folder can be deleted from either the Include Directories or Exclude Directories list. To remove a folder, select the name of the folder in whichever list it appears in and click the Remove button adjacent to the list box.

Building the index

After all the attributes for the index definition have been set, the index file is ready to be created. Notice in Figure 12-11 the Save, Save As, and Build buttons. The Save and Save As buttons will not produce an index file — they are used instead to save the index definition created by specifying settings for the preceding options. If you wish to return to the Index Definition dialog box, select File ⇨ Open (Macintosh) or Index ⇨ Open (Windows) and the attributes will appear as they were identified.

Creation of an index is executed via the Build button. Click the Build button, and Catalog will display the progress of the build (see Figure 12-12). Depending on the speed and memory of your computer and the size of the folder to be indexed, it may take several minutes to complete the build. When the build is finished, the last line in the Messages field of the Acrobat Catalog window will appear as shown in Figure 12-13 if the build was successful.

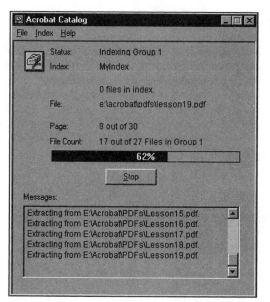

Figure 12-12: When Catalog builds an index file, a progress bar displays the percentage of completion for the build and a list of PDF documents being added to the index appears.

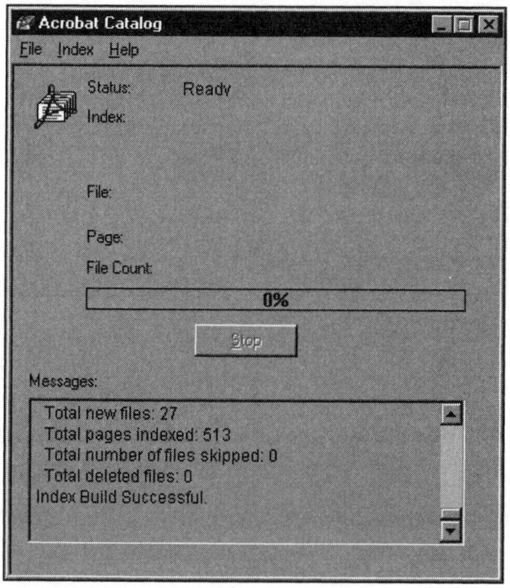

Figure 12-13: When Catalog finishes creating the index, the Catalog window will display the number of files included in the index, number of pages and any skipped or deleted files. The last line will display the message "Index Build Successful" if the index has been created.

Creating Dynamic Indexes

Dynamic indexes are maintained in an automated fashion; Catalog will update the index at intervals you specify. When you add files to the folder where Catalog looks to update your index file, builds will be created as long as Catalog is open. You need to have Catalog launched and running in the background in order to automate the process. If you have a network server, you may want to keep Catalog and Distiller open on the server to update files in watched folders. Automated updating of files are handled in the Schedule Builds dialog box. On both the Macintosh and in Windows, select Index ⇨ Schedule to open the Schedule Builds dialog box, shown/ in Figure 12-14.

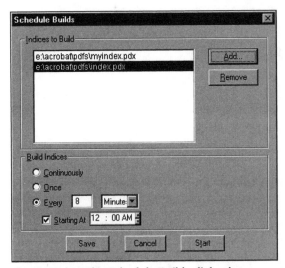

Figure 12-14: The Schedule Builds dialog box enables you to select automatic intervals for rebuilding index files.

Identifying indexes

In the top of the Schedule Builds window, a list box will display all the indexes to be scheduled. The default is a blank list. You add an index to the list box by clicking the Add button. Clicking Add will open a navigation dialog box that enables you to locate the index to be added to the schedule. The list box will display the path and filename for any index files you've added to the list. If you wish to delete an index from the schedule, select it and click the Remove button.

Locating indexes on the Macintosh

On the Macintosh, index files won't appear in the list box until you select the Add button. A second dialog box will appear in which all PDX files will be displayed. If you select Show All Files, all file types will be displayed in the dialog box.

Locating indexes on Windows

In Windows, when you first look at the dialog box appearing after you select Add, the file list will automatically seek out the PDX files. The file types are noted in the dialog box when you open it.

Building indexes

Indexes are built according to the interval defined in the Schedule Builds dialog box. The default is to build the index file once with no scheduled maintenance. You have several choices for when to build an index:

✦ **Continuously:** Indexes are built immediately when you select Continuously and click the Start button at the bottom of the Schedule Builds window. As files are added to the watched folder(s), the indexes are built and appended.

✦ **Once:** The default is to build an index file once with no scheduled updates. If you return to the dialog box after scheduling index builds and select Once, all updating will stop, and you will need to reschedule builds or manually update indexes.

✦ **Every [_]:** You can schedule builds at specific intervals and at a specific time to start the maintenance. When you select Every, the pop-up menu to the right of the value field offers choices for minutes, hours, and days. Fractions of minutes (for example, .5 for 30 seconds) are not permitted. Below the Every radio button is a Starting At option that enables you to define the start time. If you select the box and the unit, you can make changes with the up and down arrow keys on the keyboard (Macintosh only). Changes can be made by selecting the field and keying in the new value or clicking the up and down arrows in the dialog box (Macintosh/Windows).

As you add files to the directory, they will be included in the index. It is important to note that new files do not need to be added for the scheduled build to occur. This interval build will be invoked as long as Catalog is open and running.

Stopping the scheduled build

While a build is in progress, the build can be stopped by clicking the Stop button in the Build Progress dialog box. Click Stop, and the dialog box shown in Figure 12-15 will appear displaying the progress of the stop.

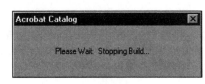

Figure 12-15: After clicking Stop in the Build Progress dialog box, Acrobat will display this dialog box to indicate the status of the stop.

Purging data

The last menu item available in Catalog is the Purge command. As indexes are maintained and rebuilt, you will need to perform routine maintenance and purge the data. A purge will not delete the index file; it simply recovers the space used in the index for outdated information. Purging is particularly useful when you remove PDF files from a folder and the search items are no longer needed. Purging can only occur manually, so you can't schedule a purge to occur after a specified interval. Before purging data, it's a good idea to review your preference settings and observe the Time Before Purge (seconds) field box. The Default is 905 seconds, which means Catalog will wait 15 minutes and 5 seconds before purging data. The delay is adjustable for users in workgroups who may be accessing an index file to be purged. While the file is open, the purge cannot be performed. A warning dialog box will appear to users when a purge has been invoked (see Figure 12-16). By default, users have over 15 minutes before the purge begins, which should be ample time to quit Catalog and move on to other tasks. If you wish to stop a purge, click the Stop button in the purge process window, shown in Figure 12-17.

If you are working in an independent environment and have no other users sharing files on a network, you may wish to reduce the amount of time in the Time Before Purge (seconds) field box so you don't have to wait for Catalog to begin purging data.

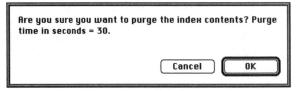

Figure 12-16: I set my preferences to begin a purge after 30 seconds in the Catalog Preferences file. When I selected Index ⇨ Purge, Catalog displayed a warning reflecting the new time the purge would begin.

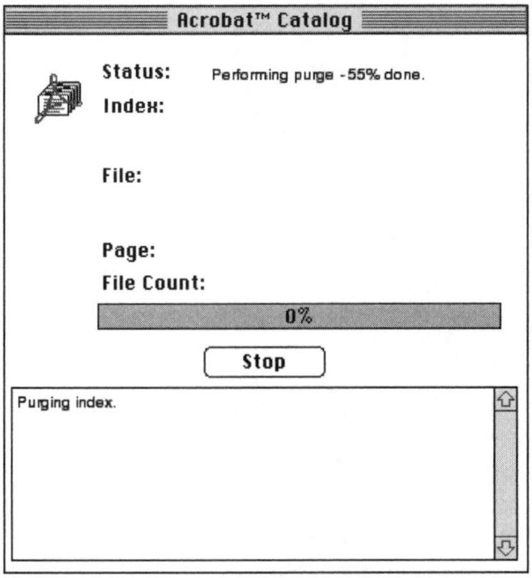

Figure 12-17: After clicking OK in the Purge warning dialog box, the Catalog window will display the purge progress. If you wish to stop a purge, click the Stop button.

After purging data in an index file, select the Index menu and choose the Build option again. Catalog will rebuild the index. Index files that are purged after data has been removed provide for smaller file sizes and faster searches.

Setting Up Network Catalogs

If yours is a PDF workflow environment, you may wish to dedicate Acrobat Catalog to a server or host computer that performs the cataloguing functions and also distillation of PDF files. Automated PDF creation and cataloging can be performed immediately after files have been printed to disk in PostScript format. To help you envision such a workflow, in this section I move through a series of steps to set up a network configuration for distillation and cataloguing. If you are not connected to a network, try following the steps on your own computer.

STEPS: Cataloguing PDF Documents on a Network

1. **Configure the network server.** Both Acrobat Catalog and Acrobat Distiller should be installed on the server. A directory, drive partition, or entire drive should be identified as a watched folder in Acrobat Distiller. You can also specify a folder for Distiller to watch. In my example, on my Windows machine I created a folder on the D drive and named it *PDF_Docs*.

2. **Establish the watched folder.** Distiller needs to be configured to watch a folder. When identifying the folder, two subfolders will be created for In and Out. In my example, I located the PDF_Docs folder in Distiller's Watched Folder dialog box and selected it (see Figure 12-18).

Continued

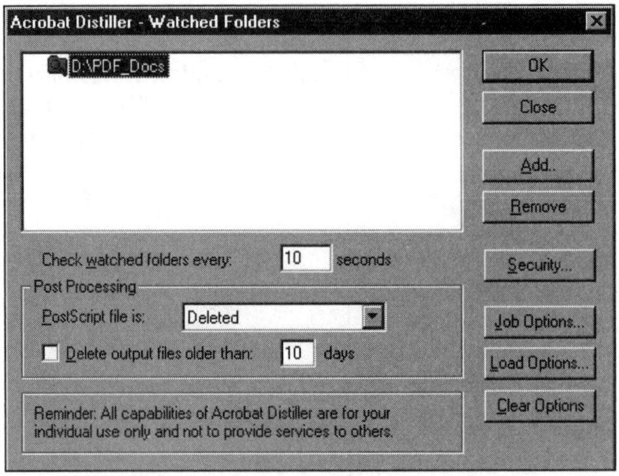

Figure 12-18: In Distiller's Watched Folder dialog box, the folder is identified and the distillation interval is established.

Set the interval to check the watched folder and select Deleted from the pop-up menu below the interval setting.

3. **Create a PDF file.** Before Acrobat Catalog can accept a schedule, an index file needs to be created. To create an index file, you need to first create a PDF document. When a PostScript file is printed to the In folder inside Distiller's watched folder, Distiller will automatically distill the file and move the PDF to the Out folder. Because I enabled the Deleted option in the Distiller Watched Folder dialog box, the PostScript file will be deleted.

4. **Create an index file.** Launch Acrobat Catalog and create a new index file. In the Index Definition dialog box, include the directory where the PDF documents will be located. In my example, I identified the Out folder.

5. **Save the index file.** When you select Build in the Index Definition dialog box, another dialog box will appear prompting you to name and identify a location for the index file. You can save the index file either inside the Out folder, at the root level of your drive, or in the watched folder.

6. **Schedule the builds.** In Acrobat Catalog, select Index ⇨ Schedule. For this example, I added the index file created from the first PDF document to my Build list, shown in Figure 12-19. Also, I selected Continuously for the interval to test my scheduled builds.

7. **Add a PDF file to the watched folder.** To create a PDF file, you can print a PostScript file to disk and save it to the In folder inside the watched folder (see Figure 12-20). You should have both Distiller and Catalog open.

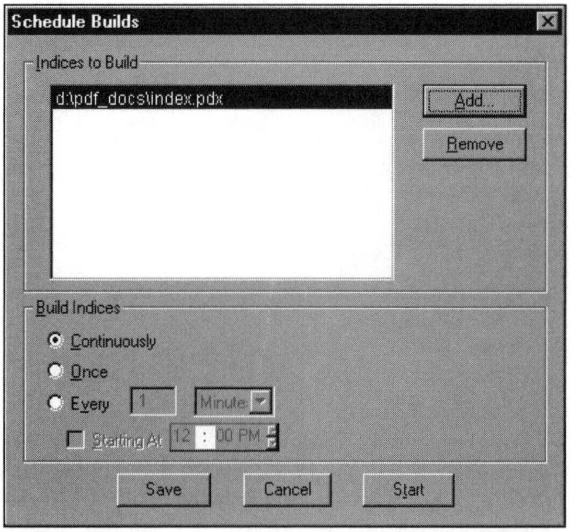

Figure 12-19: In the Schedule Builds dialog box, I set the interval to Continuously in order to test the schedule. If you wish to alter the interval, you can always return to the Schedule Builds dialog box and choose another option.

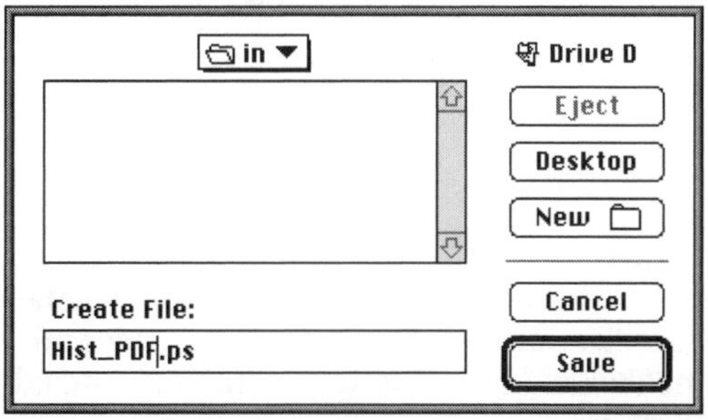

Figure 12-20: I printed a file to disk and saved it to my In folder. After creating the PostScript file, Distiller produced the PDF document and moved it to my Out folder. As soon as the PDF was located in the Out folder, Catalog updated the index file.

In Figure 12-21, the details of the build are observed in the Acrobat Catalog window. In this example, another PDF document was catalogued. The display indicates two files are in the index.

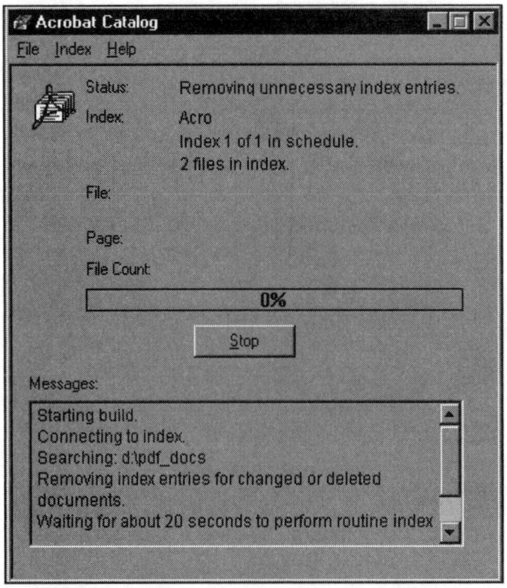

Figure 12-21: The updated build is detailed in the Messages window of the Acrobat Catalog window.

 When using a network for PDF workflows, be certain to keep the Catalog application and the index file(s) on the same system. The process will move faster than it does when cataloging indexes on remote drives.

Summary

✦ Preference settings on the Macintosh are established through a menu command in the Catalog application. On Windows, preferences are established by opening the acrocat.ini file inside the Windows directory and editing the text, which defines the attributes.

✦ Indexes are created in Acrobat Catalog by selecting File ➪ New and specifying Index Definitions. When the definitions have been selected, the index is created by selecting the Build option.

✦ Indexes should be periodically purged to eliminate outdated information. Purging the index file will not delete the index, but rather make it smaller and more efficient.

✦ Indexes can be updated and scheduled for builds automatically by using the Schedule Builds options available in Acrobat Catalog.

✦   ✦   ✦

Scanning in Acrobat

♦ ♦ ♦ ♦

In This Chapter

Configuring scanners

Understanding scanning essentials

Configuring computer systems

Using Acrobat Scan

♦ ♦ ♦ ♦

If you haven't gotten your fill of Acrobat features, then hold on — here you have the opportunity to explore more of what you can do by taking a look at scanning and capturing pages. Among other things, Acrobat enables you to use a plug-in — Acrobat Scan — for accessing a desktop scanner. Once the scanned image is created, you can capture the scanned page and have all the text read through an optical character recognition (OCR) algorithm.

Acrobat Scan is a plug-in module that enables you to access your scanner without leaving the Acrobat program. To work properly, the Scan plug-in needs to be installed in your Acrobat plug-in folder, and the scanner needs to be configured by accessing the Scan plug-in in Acrobat. Once a paper document is scanned and appears in Acrobat, Acrobat Capture converts the scanned image to text via OCR. By default, when you install Acrobat, the Scan plug-in and Capture application will also be installed. In this chapter, I cover scanning documents with Acrobat Scan, and the next chapter takes a look at using the Paper Capture command to convert scanned documents to editable text using Acrobat Capture.

Accessing a Scanner

Your scanner must be properly attached to your computer and capable of working independent of Acrobat. Be certain the scanner manufacturer's software for scanning images is properly operating before attempting to scan in Acrobat. Access to your scanner is made through the aid of either the Automatic Scanner Interface Standard (ISIS) software or a TWAIN (short for *Technology Without An Important Name*, and also now known as *The spec With An Important Name*) scanner module.

ISIS software

Adobe supplies ISIS software for Windows. (The ISIS software is not available to Macintosh users.) With ISIS, you need to have the profile available for your particular scanner, or you'll need to use the TWAIN software. To determine whether the profile for your software is available, select File ➪ Import ➪ Scan. The Adobe Acrobat Scan dialog box will appear offering several options, as shown in Figure 13-1:

✦ **Device:** Your scanner device should appear on this pop-up menu. If it is not visible, recheck your scanner installation to ensure it is properly installed.

✦ **Profile:** Acrobat will have installed profiles for many common scanner types. If your scanner profile does not appear in the pop-up menu, you may need to contact your scanner manufacturer and ask if they have a profile available. Some manufacturers may have updated profiles on their Web sites available for downloading.

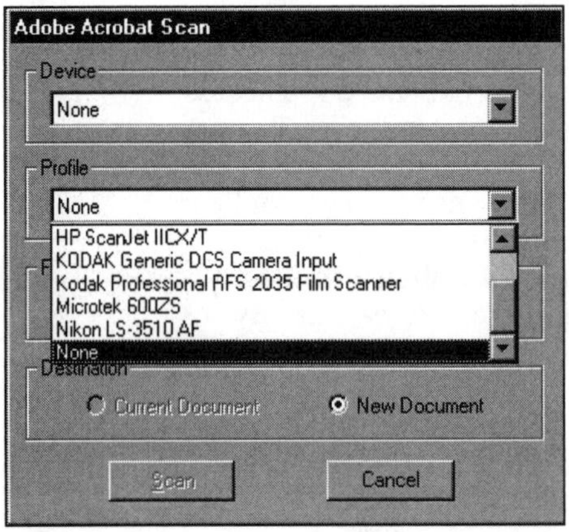

Figure 13-1: The Adobe Acrobat Scan dialog box enables you to specify your scanner and its profile in the Device and Profile pull-down menus.

✦ **Format:** If your scanner and software permit double-sided scanning, you can select Double sided from the pop-up menu. If not, the default format will be Single sided. Leave the default choice if your scanner does not have double-sided capabilities.

✦ **Destination:** When a PDF file is open, you can select between adding the scanned page to your document or creating a new PDF file. When no file is open, you can access the Scan plug-in, but the destination is limited to a new document.

TWAIN software

TWAIN software is manufacturer supplied and should be available on the floppy disk or CD-ROM you receive with your scanner. On the Macintosh, you'll have two files for TWAIN, and they both belong in the Preferences folder inside your System folder. They should also be inside a TWAIN folder, which resides inside the Preferences folder. When the TWAIN components are installed in the Preferences folder, your scanner name should appear in the Acrobat Scan Plug-in dialog box, as shown in Figure 13-2. From the pop-up menu, select the device name for your scanner.

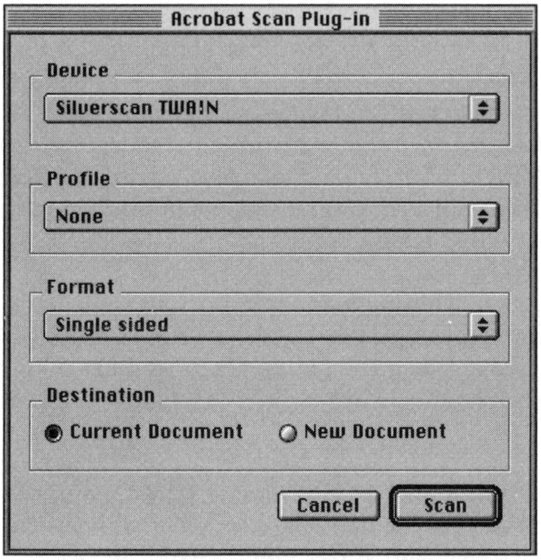

```
┌──────────────────────────────────────────┐
│          Acrobat Scan Plug-in             │
│ ┌─ Device ───────────────────────────────┐│
│ │ Silverscan TWAIN                    ▲▼ ││
│ └────────────────────────────────────────┘│
│ ┌─ Profile ──────────────────────────────┐│
│ │ None                                ▲▼ ││
│ └────────────────────────────────────────┘│
│ ┌─ Format ───────────────────────────────┐│
│ │ Single sided                        ▲▼ ││
│ └────────────────────────────────────────┘│
│ ┌─ Destination ──────────────────────────┐│
│ │ ● Current Document   ○ New Document    ││
│ └────────────────────────────────────────┘│
│                    [ Cancel ]  [  Scan  ] │
└──────────────────────────────────────────┘
```

Figure 13-2: When TWAIN components are installed, your scanner name will be available in the Device pop-up menu.

There are many scanner manufacturers that produce equipment but use third-party developers to write the software. Adobe has certainly not tested the Scan plug-in with all scanner manufacturers and all software developers. Theoretically, the TWAIN software should work in most cases. If you have problems accessing your scanner from within Acrobat, but can perform scans in Photoshop, then you most likely have a problem with the TWAIN software. If this is the case, contact your scanner manufacturer and see if they have an upgrade or if you can get some technical support. In many cases, you can download upgrades for registered software on the Internet.

HP AccuPage software

Hewlett-Packard developed the HP AccuPage software to optimize scans for OCR and text scanning. The HP AccuPage software works with the ISIS profile, which is available by installing the driver from the Acrobat CD-ROM. If you have an HP scanner supporting the technology, be certain to install the driver. Errors listed as exceptions in Acrobat Capture will be much fewer than with traditional grayscale scanning.

Scanning Basics

At this point you should have your scanner and Acrobat Scan configured properly. Before I begin discussing how to use Acrobat Scan, let's take a moment to understand some of the essential issues to deal with in performing clean, accurate scans. Several items need to be discussed: first, the hardware and hardware-related issues; second, the types of scans to be produced; and third, the document preparation for which the scan will be made. A few moments here will save you much time in producing the best scans you can expect from your equipment.

The first hardware item is your scanner. The single most important issue with scanner hardware is keeping the platen clean. If you have dust and dirt on the glass, these particles will appear in your scans. Keep the platen clean, and use a lint-free cloth to clean the glass. If you use a solvent, always apply the solvent to the cloth and not the scanner glass.

The second item to consider is your computer. When running Acrobat and the Scan plug-in, try to allocate as much memory as you can spare to Acrobat. If you have multiple applications open simultaneously and subsequently experience crashes, then by all means try using Acrobat alone when performing scans. Also related to your computer is the hard drive free space. Double-check the free space on your computer's hard drive before attempting to scan. Scans will eat up memory fast, so be certain you have ample space before engaging in a scanning session.

Understand your scanner and the technology used to manufacture the device. Flatbed consumer-grade scanners use charge coupled devices (CCDs), tiny little sensors placed along a horizontal plane in number equal to the optical resolution of your scanner. Therefore, a 600-dpi scanner has 600 CCDs per inch. Each of these sensors will pick up a pixel when the scanner pass is made. Where these sensors begin and end along the horizontal plane is important for you to know. If you experience some edge sharpness problems or degradation in your image at the edges, try placing the scanned source material a little farther from the edges of the scanner platen and toward the middle. When doing so, be certain to keep the material straight on the scanner bed.

Understanding Acrobat scan types

There are several different types of scans you can produce with your Acrobat Scan plug-in. Each of the scans you produce will have different requirements and need some special attention when scanning.

Text recognition

If you scan directly in Acrobat, more often than not your requirements will be for text and OCR scanning. Given the fact that PDF pages are usually created in applications such as layout, illustration, and photo editing software, it would be rare to attempt to create PDF documents by scanning them into Acrobat. If you compose a layout, you're more than likely going to use Photoshop as the scanning source, as it will enable you to enhance and optimize your image quality. The area Acrobat excels in is the creation of search indexes from text-heavy documents. In such a case, using Acrobat enables you to have easy access to your stored PDFs, and you can find information fast. For this situation, you would use the Scan plug-in and then the Capture software to recognize the text. When scanning text, you'll want to follow a few simple rules.

Image mode

Image modes range from 1-bit line art or black-and-white scans to 24-bit color. The higher the bit-depth, the larger the file size. For text scans, you only need 1-bit line art to recognize text. If your scanner software has a line art mode, use it to perform scans for text recognition.

Resolution

Resolution for text recognition needs to be high enough for good, clean scanning and tight pixels on the edges of characters, but not as high as you would need for output to high-end devices. As a general rule, you can scan normal body text at 300 dpi. Large text sizes might be sufficiently scanned at 200 dpi. For small text of 8 points or lower, you may wish to raise the resolution to 600 dpi. In many cases, you may wish to run some tests for the target resolution for your particular type of scanner, software, and typical documents scanned. The maximum resolution supported by Acrobat is 600 dpi, and the maximum document size is 14 inches by 14 inches.

Grayscale scanning

Once again, scanning images will often be the task of Photoshop. However, you may find grayscale scanning necessary or helpful when scanning for text recognition. The most important attribute of a scanned image for OCR software is sharp contrast between the text and the background. If your line art scans aren't producing enough contrast, try scanning in grayscale and apply contrast settings in your software before completing the scan. Many software applications provide controls for brightness and contrast settings. Most software will display previews of the adjustments you make, which greatly speeds up the entire process.

Grayscale photos

If you wish to scan photographic images in grayscale, be certain to lower the resolution. Try 200 dpi or lower. You should plan on testing resolutions to achieve the lowest possible resolution that will maintain a good quality image. If you scan grayscale images in Acrobat, they should be for screen view only. To create PDF files that will ultimately be printed, you should use Photoshop and a layout or illustration application, and then distill the images with Acrobat Distiller.

Color scanning

If you have color documents and wish to capture text from the pages, you might want to use a color mode if you can build up enough contrast during the scan. Large type in color images can be effectively recognized in 200 dpi scans.

Color photos

Color images will occupy the largest file sizes and should almost always not be scanned using Acrobat Scan. If you use a color image for text recognition, you can optimize the image in several ways by either printing the image to a PostScript file and distilling the file with Distiller's compression settings or by replacing an image with a grayscale or color scan you create in Photoshop. In either case, you should be prepared to not leave the original scanned image in the PDF file. The size burden defeats much of the purpose of the PDF file format.

Font embedding

When scanning for OCR, you want to be certain to not embed or subset fonts. Acrobat Scan determines font handling from the PDFWriter preferences. Before scanning any documents, open the Page Setup dialog box in PDFWriter. In the Page Setup dialog box click the Fonts button. When the Acrobat PDFWriter Font Embedding dialog box appears, as shown in Figure 13-3, disable Embed all Fonts and disable the Subset items.

Note

PDFWriter cannot be accessed from within Acrobat. Open any application or change defaults from your system's Desktop. On the Macintosh, press the Control key and select File ➪ Page Setup. Click the Fonts button at the bottom of the dialog box to open the Acrobat PDFWriter Font Embedding dialog box. Disable Embed All Fonts and the subsetting options.

In Windows, open the Control Panel and open the Printers folder. Right-click Acrobat PDFWriter. From the pop-up menu, select Document Defaults. In the Acrobat PDFWriter Default dialog box, shown in Figure 13-4, click the Font Embedding tab. Disable the same items in this dialog box as described for the Macintosh configuration.

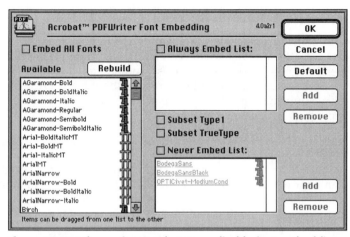

Figure 13-3: When using Acrobat Scan, disable font embedding and font subsetting in the PDFWriter Page Setup dialog box.

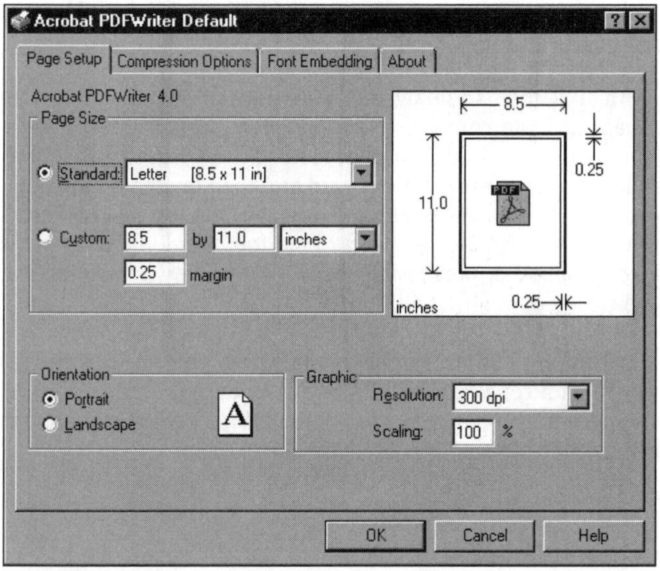

Figure 13-4: Right-clicking the Acrobat PDFWriter printer driver will open a pop-up menu in Windows. Select Document Defaults from the menu to open the Acrobat PDFWriter Default dialog box. Click the Font Embedding tab to disable font embedding and subsetting.

Preparing a document

Just as your scans can benefit from paying careful attention to your scanner, exercising a little care with the source material can help prepare for clean scans. Bits of dust, improperly aligned pages, poor contrast, and degraded originals will affect your ability to create scans capable of being read without many errors by Acrobat Capture. A little time in preparation before scanning will save you much time in trying to clean up poorly scanned images.

Photocopying originals

Sometimes you can improve on the contrast adjustments by photocopying original documents. If you can improve image and text contrast by photocopying material, try some experiments to test your results. If you have large, bulky material, photocopies placed on the scanner bed will ultimately result in better scans.

Straight alignment

If you have documents with frayed edges or pages torn from a magazine, then you should trim the edges and make them parallel to the text in the page. Precise placement of pages on the scanner bed will facilitate clean scans. Even though Acrobat has a recognition capability within a 7° rotation, the straighter the page, the better the results.

Tip

A method I use with all flatbed scanning is to tape the source material to a large piece of poster board or foam core (illustrated in Figure 13-5). I have a piece of poster board laminated on one side. On the poster board, I used a T-square to draw a horizontal line across the top of the board and then laminated the board. I align my page top to the line on the board and tape it at the top two corners. The board is larger than my scanner top, so I can rotate the board without removing material from the scanner. After previewing scans, I make new adjustments until the image is straight.

Try to remember the axiom "garbage in, garbage out" when you approach any kind of scanning. The better the source material, the better your scanned results will appear. Exercise a little care in the beginning, and you'll find your Acrobat scanning sessions will move along much faster.

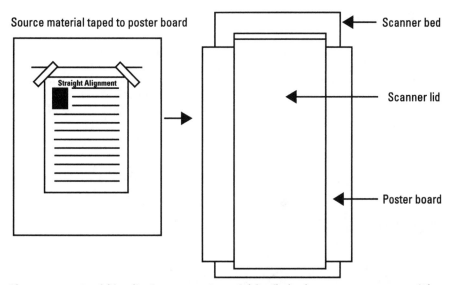

Figure 13-5: To aid in aligning source material for flatbed scanners, tape material to a poster board larger than your scanner lid. Place the poster board on the scanner bed and preview a scan. Rotate the board after each preview to adjust alignment. The horizontal line at the top of the page should appear straight on the scanner preview thumbnail when aligned properly.

Memory Configurations

When using Acrobat for scanning, there are two considerations with memory requirements. You must have enough RAM to operate both Acrobat and Acrobat Capture, and you must have enough hard disk space for work files to be created during the scan. Each of the memory requirements must be satisfied to work efficiently when you attempt scanning.

Macintosh memory requirements

The total RAM recommended to run Acrobat on the Macintosh is 18.5MB. When you add the Scan plug-in, the memory requirements grow another 8.8MB. Therefore, the total memory to run Acrobat Scan is 27.3MB.

Assessing memory

On the Macintosh, your first step to determine whether you can run Acrobat Scan is to assess how much available RAM you have after your system starts. From the Desktop, select Apple ➪ About This Computer. The About This Computer dialog box that appears will inform you if you have enough free memory to run your applications, as shown in Figure 13-6. Look for the item designated Largest Unused Block. If the amount of free memory does not exceed 20MB of free RAM, you'll need to use virtual memory.

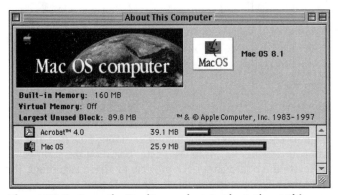

Figure 13-6: From the Desktop, select Apple ➪ About This Computer and look at the largest unused block to determine the amount of free memory.

Virtual memory

To allocate more RAM for applications, you can use virtual memory. Virtual memory uses a portion of the free hard drive space and treats that portion of free space as an extension of RAM. Virtual memory will never operate as fast as RAM, but you may need to use it if your hardware is not sufficient to run Acrobat Scan. Refer to your system manual for configuring your computer with virtual memory.

Allocating memory to Acrobat

On the Macintosh, you need to allocate enough RAM to an application in order to take advantage of the RAM available to you. By default, software manufacturers have preset allocations of memory assigned to a software application. In order to increase the memory assigned to the application, you will need to manually make that assignment.

You should have a minimum of 24MB free when setting the preferred size to 20MB. I like to allow at least 1MB of latitude between the computer's available memory and the maximum size you may assign to an application. If you have more available RAM, then by all means try to allocate more memory to Acrobat. The preceding is only a guideline for the most conservative assignment with limited hardware memory.

Hard disk space

The other memory issue of concern is the amount of free hard drive space after you assign virtual memory. Whether virtual memory is assigned or not, you do need ample space for creating scans in Acrobat. When you scan an image with Acrobat Scan, the file is saved to your hard drive in PDF form. When you then invoke Acrobat Capture to recognize text, Capture will require some work space on your hard drive. The average amount of required space will be approximately three times the file size. Hence, if your scan is 4MB, 12MB of free space will be required. If you intend to scan with resolutions of 300 dpi, you'll need to compensate for larger size images.

Windows memory requirements

Application memory requirements in Windows are similar to those discussed for the Macintosh. Windows users don't need to be concerned with assigning memory to specific applications, but those users do need to work with allocating virtual memory to foreground applications of which the open application will take advantage.

Assessing memory

You probably know how much RAM you currently have installed on your computer. If you're working on an office system or shared computer, you may not be aware of how much RAM is installed. In Windows 95, 98, or NT, by default, your system will be named My Computer. If the name has been changed, you should see the icon for your system, bearing the changed name, in the top-left corner of your screen. Right-click the icon and select Properties from the pop-up menu. The System Properties dialog box appears, as shown in Figure 13-7.

You should see a view similar to the one displayed in Figure 13-7. In the bottom of the dialog box, note the total amount of installed RAM on the computer. You should have at least 24MB of RAM installed and preferably 32MB. If you're running Windows 95, anything less than 24MB of RAM will be a problem when running Acrobat and Scan.

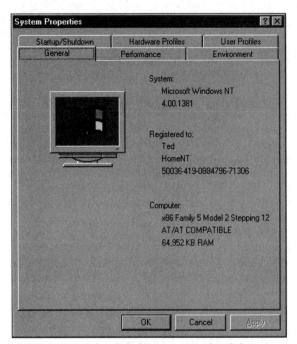

Figure 13-7: Right-click the computer hard drive to open a pop-up menu. Select Properties from the menu to determine how much RAM is installed in your computer.

Virtual memory

Virtual memory is adjusted by selecting the Performance tab in the System Properties dialog box. Notice the item identified as Virtual Memory and the button to the right labeled Change (see Figure 13-8).

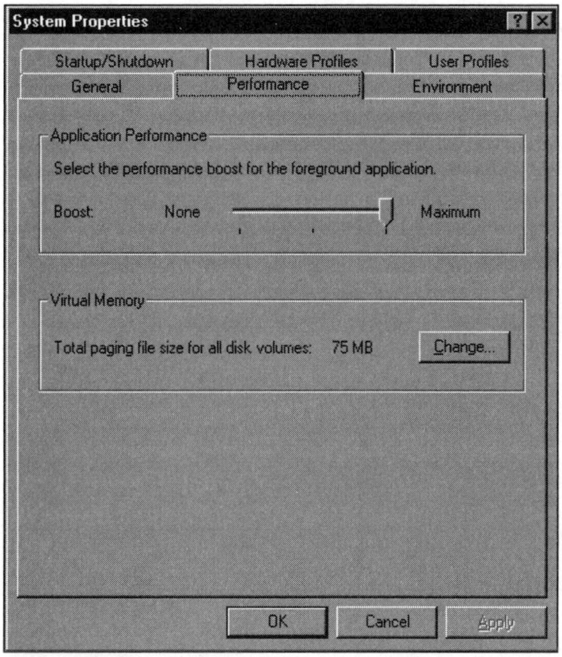

Figure 13-8: For virtual memory configurations in Windows, click the Performance tab in the System Properties dialog box.

If you have multiple drives or partitions, you can assign a virtual memory space to any of the drives or partitions. In the example shown in Figure 13-9, there are two drives, one of which is partitioned. The C drive is partitioned into two volumes, and the E drive is a separate drive. To change the virtual memory, select the drive for the virtual memory space and enter a value in the Initial Size (MB) field. For the Maximum Size (MB) field, enter a slightly higher value. When the values have been entered, click the Set button in the Virtual Memory dialog box, shown in Figure 13-9.

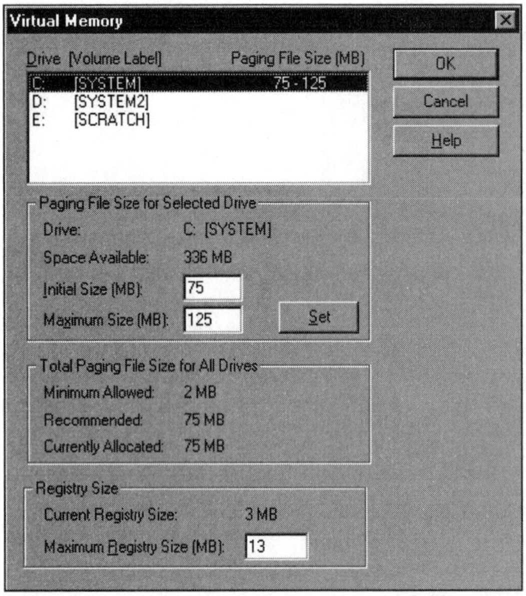

Figure 13-9: Changing virtual memory in Windows is handled in the Virtual Memory dialog box, which is accessed by clicking the Change button in the Performance tab of the System Properties dialog box.

Allocating memory to Acrobat

The Performance settings also include an adjustment for application performance. You'll see a slider with adjustments ranging from None to Maximum. This setting applies to any software loaded in Windows. Background tasks take secondary position over the foreground application. If you move the slider to the far right, the foreground application will take advantage of all the memory Windows can provide it. When working in Acrobat and Acrobat Scan, you should keep the performance boost for the foreground application to a maximum.

Hard disk space

Hard drive free space will be of equal concern to Windows users as it is Mac users. To determine how much free space you have on your hard drive(s), select the System Properties again. You should see the available drive(s). If you have only one hard drive and a single partition, only one drive letter will appear. Note the area designated Free Space. Be certain you have enough free working space available on your hard drive. Like the Macintosh users, you'll need 10MB to 15MB of free hard disk space as a minimum.

Using Acrobat Scan

When you perform a scan with Acrobat Scan, the scanned image will appear as a PDF document in Acrobat. You can choose to leave the scan as an image and save it as a PDF file. However, to do nothing more than scan images with Acrobat Scan would be less efficient than scanning images in Photoshop and saving the Photoshop image as a PDF file. Acrobat Scan is only half of the equation related to scanning in Acrobat. The real power of using Acrobat for scanning images lies in its capability to convert all scanned text into readable and searchable text with Acrobat Capture. Raw image files with no text are referred to in Acrobat terms as *PDF Image Only* files. When you distill documents with Acrobat Distiller, save with PDFWriter, or capture scanned pages with the Capture plug-in, the files contain text that can be indexed, searched, and selected. These files are known in Acrobat terms as *PDF Normal* documents. When Acrobat Scan is used to import a scan into Acrobat, the file will be a PDF Image Only document.

Scanning images

After you verify proper configuration for both your scanner and computer hardware, prepare your document, and configure the PDFWriter, the rest of the scanning process is easy. To scan an image with Acrobat Scan, select File ⇨ Image ⇨ Scan. The Acrobat Scan Plug-in dialog box discussed earlier will appear. Select the proper Device and Profile choices from the pop-up menus. If you do not have a profile for your scanner available, select None from the Profile pop-up menu. Choose the Format option and Destination, and then click the Scan button.

Acrobat Scan will open the scanner plug-in from your device manufacturer. You should have a clear understanding of the various options available in the scanning software for adjustments made before scanning images. If you have contrast and brightness adjustments in the application, you may need to perform tests on which adjustments work well when scanning for text recognition. Typically, sharp contrast will always be a criterion when scanning for optical character recognition. I use a LaCie Silver Scanner IV on my personal computer. When the Scan button is selected in the Acrobat Scan Plug-in dialog box, my Silver Scanner software appears, as shown in Figure 13-10. From this window I make changes for image resolution, color mode, and preview selections. Brightness controls are made from a menu appearing when the Silver Scanner software is opened.

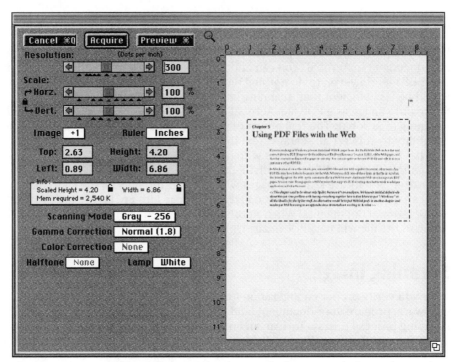

Figure 13-10: From this window I make changes for image resolution, color mode, and preview selections.

When adjustments are made in the scanning software, click a preview button if your scanning software supports a preview. Examine the alignment and contrast. Adjust the margins for the scan area and click the appropriate button to begin scanning. When the scanning is completed, the Acrobat Scan Plug-in dialog box will appear enabling you to continue scanning, as shown in Figure 13-11. You can choose to replace the source material with another page and continue scanning or select the Done button to terminate scanning. If Next is selected, your scanner software dialog box will reappear. You can change resolutions, create another preview, and adjust brightness before continuing.

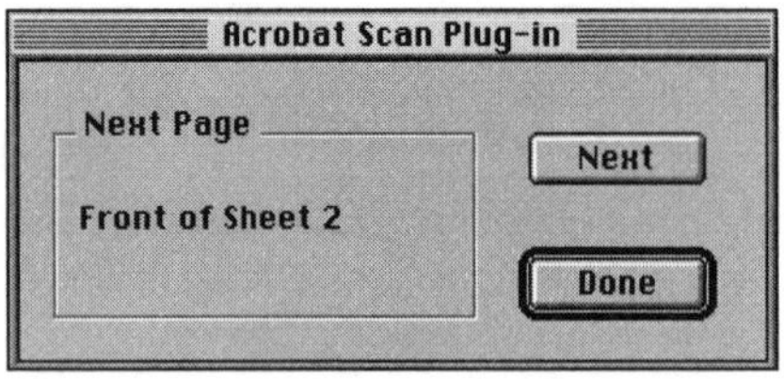

Figure 13-11: After completing a scan, Acrobat opens the Acrobat Scan Plug-in dialog box, prompting you to either continue or terminate scanning.

When you've finished scanning, click the Done button in the second dialog box. If you scanned several pages, they will appear in the same document. Once you have the scan imported as a PDF Image Only file, you can use Acrobat Capture to convert the scan to a PDF Normal image or Original Image with Hidden Text. Both of these terms will be explained in the next chapter.

Summary

✦ Acrobat Scan uses ISIS software for Windows or TWAIN software for either Macintosh or Windows. ISIS software is distributed on the Acrobat Installer CD-ROM, and TWAIN software is acquired from a scanner manufacturer.

✦ When preparing documents for scanning in Acrobat, proper preparation of the scanner and documents will improve the quality of the scans. The scanner platen should be clean, the documents should be straight, and the contrast should be sharp.

✦ If using scanned images with Acrobat Capture for text recognition, font embedding and subsetting should be disabled. Acrobat Scan uses the PDFWriter font embedding and subsetting defaults when scanning images. Disable these items before scanning.

✦ System memory requirements are critical to Acrobat and Acrobat Scan. Be certain to allocate enough memory to the programs, and clear enough hard drive space to accommodate scans.

✦ When scanning images in Acrobat, use the scanning software to establish resolution, image mode, and brightness controls before scanning. Test your results thoroughly to create a formula that works well for the type of documents you scan.

✦   ✦   ✦

Converting Scans to Text

◆ ◆ ◆ ◆

In This Chapter

Capturing scanned
pages

Editing Suspects

Importing images

◆ ◆ ◆ ◆

In the last chapter, I discussed scanning images into Acrobat. Once a file is either scanned into Acrobat or imported via the File ➭ Import ➭ Image menu command, the page can be converted to text. Acrobat Scan retains the data as image data. In order to convert image data to text, you need to use Paper Capture. Paper Capture is not a plug-in, but rather a command in Acrobat. When the command is invoked, the Capture Server (Macintosh) or Capture.exe (Windows) application is launched and appears in the foreground, while the PDF page remains in the background. To launch the Capture Server, select Tools ➭ Capture ➭ Capture Pages.

Note   In Acrobat 4, Capture is referred to as Paper Capture in the Tools menu and the Preferences submenu. This term was introduced to avoid confusion with Web Capture (Windows only). Capture Server remains the name of the application launched to perform the OCR conversion. When references to Capture in this chapter appear, they refer to Paper Capture and not Web Capture.

Using Acrobat Paper Capture

Capture Server requires proper installation and a few conditions must be met for it to launch and properly perform the OCR conversion. If you fail to adhere to the following requirements, the Capture Server may not launch.

   ✦ **Font limitations:** If the total number of installed fonts in your system exceeds 128, you will receive an error message while launching Capture Server. If you encounter problems with warning dialog boxes related to fonts, uninstall some fonts and try to launch Paper Capture again.

✦ **Font requirements:** When Acrobat is installed, a number of fonts will be installed on your system. Acrobat will operate with the Base 13 fonts, Adobe Sans Serif and Adobe Serif fonts. Paper Capture, however, requires additional fonts to create recognized characters during operation. If you remove any of the fonts installed with Acrobat, Paper Capture may not be able to recognize text in the document you attempt to capture. For Macintosh users, be certain not to use font management utilities for the Acrobat fonts. If you use Suitcase, MasterJuggler, or ATM Deluxe for loading and disabling fonts from a fonts folder, don't manage the Acrobat fonts with these utilities. Leave the Acrobat fonts in your System:Fonts folder. The same holds true for Windows users — leave the fonts located in the installed directory.

✦ **Dictionaries:** There are eight different dictionaries in the Capture folder for text recognition in eight different languages. US English is one of the dictionaries. Additionally, a custom dictionary is accessible in Windows where words can be added for individual user needs. On the Macintosh, there is no custom dictionary available to which to add words.

Paper Capture preferences

To change preferences for Paper Capture, select File ➪ Preferences ➪ Paper Capture. In the Acrobat Paper Capture Preferences dialog box, shown in Figure 14-1, there are options for selecting a supported language; the output format for the captured page; and, in Windows, a choice for selecting a directory for temporary files.

✦ **Primary OCR Language:** By default, Acrobat will install multiple languages in the Capture folder, which resides inside the Acrobat folder. Eight different language dictionaries are included during installation. If you scan documents from any of the supported languages, select the appropriate language in the pop-up menu in the Acrobat Paper Capture Preferences dialog box, which is shown in Figure 14-2.

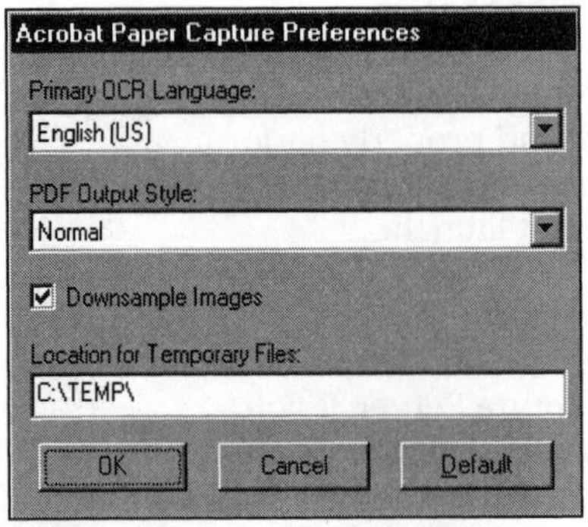

Figure 14-1: To open the Acrobat Paper Capture Preferences dialog box, select File ➪ Preferences ➪ Paper Capture.

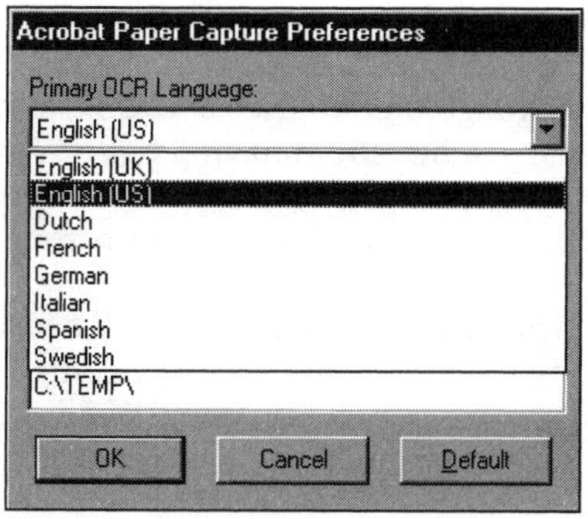

Figure 14-2: The Primary OCR Language pop-up menu provides eight choices for supported language.

✦ **PDF Output Style:** You have two choices for PDF Output Style. Normal will scan the text in the image, and the scanned text will be converted to text characters appearing in the document when viewed in an Acrobat viewer. When you select Original Image with Hidden Text, the appearance of the scanned image will not change. Text will be supplied on a hidden layer, which gives you the capability of creating indexes and performing searches. Use this option when you don't want to change a document's appearance, but you do want to be able to search the text of that document. Something on the order of a legal document or a certificate might be an example of such a document.

✦ **Downsample Images:** This option enables or disables downsampling of images. When the check box is enabled, images are downsampled as follows:

  • **Black and White:** Black-and-white images are downsampled to 200 dpi. If the line art mode was used and the scan resolution was 300 dpi, the image won't be downsampled.

  • **Grayscale and Color:** These types of images are downsampled to 150 dpi. If an image was scanned as grayscale or color at a resolution of 225 or less, the image will not be downsampled.

✦ **Location for Temporary Files:** The last item in the Preferences dialog box is not functional on the Macintosh. In Windows, select the directory Paper Capture will use for temporary space while converting the PDF page(s) to one of the formats listed previously. On the Macintosh, the Temporary folder is located inside the Capture folder.

Tip

If you are a Macintosh user who wishes to have temporary files located on another drive or partition, do the following: Make an alias of the Temporary folder by selecting the folder and then selecting File ⇨ Make Alias (Cmd+M). Leave the alias in the Capture folder, and drag the original Temporary folder to the drive or partition in which you wish to place it. The file will be copied when dragging to another drive or partition. Delete the original folder. When Capture uses temporary disk space, the original folder copied to your second drive or partition will be used to store the data.

Custom dictionaries (Windows)

Windows users have the same foreign language dictionaries available as do Mac users. However, Windows users have an extra benefit in having the option to add words to a custom dictionary. The custom dictionary resides in the Capture folder and is labeled Custdict.spl. To add words, you need a text editor or word processor.

When you attempt to open the file in a program such as Microsoft Word, a dialog box will appear prompting you to identify the file format. Use Text Only as the file format option. If you can't open the file in your editor, try to use Windows WordPad or another text editor. With the file open, you should see a list of words added to the custom dictionary.

To add a word, you can place the new word in alphabetical order by placing the cursor to the right of the word preceding your new word and pressing the Return key. Enter the word and double-check the spelling. Save the file as Text Only. If you decide to edit the Custom Dictionary, as illustrated in Figure 14-3, always make a backup copy of the last saved version. If the new save becomes corrupted or doesn't work, reinstall the last working version of the dictionary.

Figure 14-3: I opened the Custdict.spl file in Windows WordPad on my PC and added some words to the custom dictionary.

Note   Words in the custom dictionary must be in alphabetical order and each word must be on a separate line. Use a carriage return after entering the new word(s) in the alphabetical list.

Capturing a Page

Once the file has been scanned and preferences have been established, the PDF page(s) is ready to be converted to a paper capture. When you capture a page in Acrobat, the text will be converted from an image file to a rich text file. The text can be edited with the TouchUp Text tool, which was covered in Chapter 8. When you select the Paper Capture command, the Acrobat Capture Plug-in dialog box appears, as shown in Figure 14-4, offering you some choices about the page(s) to be captured. If you wish to capture the page in view, select the Current Page radio button. If all pages are to be captured, select the All Pages radio button. The Specified Range(s) item enables you to identify the page numbers to be captured in a document.

Figure 14-4: The Acrobat Capture Plug-in dialog box will appear when you select Tools ⇨ Paper Capture ⇨ Capture Pages.

If you select the Preferences button, a dialog box will appear identical to the Preferences dialog box discussed previously. This button can be used to alternate between selecting the Normal and Original Image with Hidden Text options as you work with Paper Capture. The Preferences button in this dialog box eliminates the need to keep returning to the File menu to select the Paper Capture preferences. After setting the preferences, click OK. Acrobat will pause and load the Capture Server. Depending on the speed of your computer, you may wait some time for the server to load. Be patient. Eventually the Acrobat Capture Server window will appear, as shown in Figure 14-5.

Note When the Capture Server dialog box appears, the name of the PDF file being captured appears in the top-right corner of the window. At the bottom-right corner a display will appear identifying the image resolution, bit depth of the image, and the memory the file occupies. This information can be helpful in organizing files to be captured. If you have multiple files with similar names, they can be easily distinguished while Capture is running.

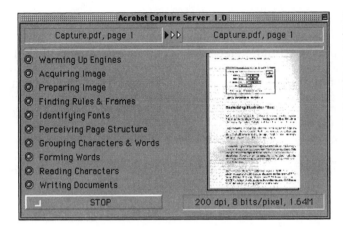

Figure 14-5: The Acrobat Capture Server window appears after a few seconds following the specification of Paper Capture preferences.

Capture Suspects

After Paper Capture completes its task, the page will have been converted to text. However, not all text may have been recognized by Paper Capture. To see if any words have been misunderstood, you need to look at the Capture Suspects. Suspect words will not appear until you select Tools ⇨ Paper Capture ⇨ Show Suspects. When the command is selected, the PDF page in view will be displayed with red borders to indicate suspects (see Figure 14-6). A Capture Suspect displays because Paper Capture is not certain whether the suspected word has a match in the Capture dictionary. You can choose to accept the guess Capture provides or edit the text to correct it. All of the editing of Capture Suspects is accomplished with the TouchUp Text tool.

When you select the first suspect with the TouchUp Text tool, a window will appear, as illustrated in Figure 14-7. The window displays the original scanned text and two buttons. The buttons offer choices for Accept & Next and Find Next. If you select the first option, any text you have edited will be changed, and you will be sent to the next suspect. Find Next leaves the currently selected suspect as it appears and moves to the next suspected word. If you edit the suspect and click Find Next, the edit will not be accepted and the text will return to the original suspect. To make a change, you need to edit the text and click the Accept & Next button.

When you view the document and see the marked suspects, Capture only displays the items in question. Capture's interpretation of the suspect is only revealed when you select the suspect. Therefore, if a word is identified as a suspect, Capture's interpretation is not yet displayed. When a word is selected by pressing Tab or clicking the TouchUp Text tool, Capture's interpretation is revealed. What's important to note here is you won't know how the word has been interpreted until it is selected.

You'll want to commit the keyboard modifiers to memory when correcting suspects. On the Macintosh and in Windows, Accept & Next is invoked with the Tab key. Find Next is applied with Cmd+Tab on the Macintosh and Shift+Tab in Windows. The Tab key will accept the first suspect and send you to the next.

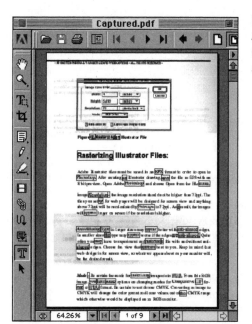

Figure 14-6: I captured a page in Acrobat and selected Tools ➪ Paper Capture ➪ Show Suspects to display all the suspected words.

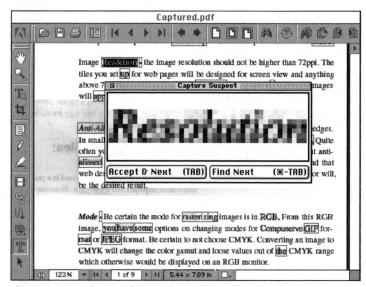

Figure 14-7: When I selected the word *Resolution,* Capture displayed its interpretation, *Res&tion*. To correct the word, type in the correct spelling, and then click the Accept & Next button or press the Tab key on your keyboard. If Find Next is selected, the word will remain unchanged from Capture's interpretation.

To correct the suspect, you can enter the text while the suspect is selected, or position the cursor inside the selection and press the Backspace key, or enter text from the cursor position.

Capture performance

If you work in environments with multiple computers and have machines of different platforms, you may wish to make several tests on Paper Capture's performance from one machine to another. When you have text that is difficult to read, such as what you may find on faxes and degraded photocopies, Paper Capture's performance will suffer. You'll want to use the fastest computer in your environment for converting documents to text, and you'll want to use the system that reports the fewest Capture Suspects. Correcting long documents with many errors can be more time consuming than retyping documents. I have found Capture performance to be better running under Windows NT than other computers in my environment.

If you wish to develop a workflow in an office environment, you might wish to have the function of scanning documents performed on several machines and use other computers to capture suspected words. Acrobat can import images that are not in PDF form. Therefore, you can scan images in software other than Photoshop and save your files in a format such as TIFF. Acrobat can import TIFF images via the Import Image command. Once scanned, you can set up workstations or servers to import images and save them as PDF files. The PDF files can be routed to workstations capturing pages. In this scenario, you won't need to purchase Acrobat for all your computers, and the time savings will be significant.

Capturing Imported Images

Files saved as PDFs are opened in Acrobat. If you use Photoshop with your scanner, images can be saved as PDF files. If you have scanning software that does not support PDF formats, you can save your files in a number of other formats. Formats acceptable to Acrobat include those listed here:

✦ **Amiga IFF:** This format is almost defunct because there are very few Amiga image editors around. In most cases, you'll never use it. However, Acrobat can import the file type if you find any old images in this format.

✦ **BMP:** Most often, this format will be used in exchanging files between the Mac and PC. BMP can be imported into Acrobat on either platform.

✦ **GIF:** This format originally was developed for CompuServe to exchange files between computer systems linked to their on-line services. Web graphics saved in this format can be imported.

✦ **JPEG:** Saving files with JPEG compression will reduce file sizes considerably. The same file compression can be applied when distilling PDFs. A compressed JPEG will import into Acrobat.

✦ **PCX:** A format very common to the PC. Files created in some Windows paint programs support the format. Once saved as PCX, they can be imported into Acrobat on either the Mac or PC.

✦ **PICT:** If you create screen dumps or use native drawing programs on the Mac operating system, they will be saved as PICT files. Once exported to PICT, they can be imported to Acrobat.

✦ **Pixar:** Pixar workstations are high-end modeling computers capable of generating 3-D rendering much faster than even the fastest of the current Macs or PCs. This format can also be imported into Acrobat directly.

✦ **PNG:** Developed for the World Wide Web as an alternative to GIF, this format holds 256 colors and has great compression of a lossless type. When imported into Acrobat, it will be compressed according to the compression levels mentioned in Chapter 13.

✦ **Targa:** Targa format was developed by Truvision for their line of Nuvista video boards. Many PC users have used the Targa format to capture still frames from a video board. The format supports 32 bits — 24 bits for the image, and an extra 8 bits for an alpha channel used for chroma keying. When Targa files are imported, the alpha channel will be lost.

✦ **TIFF:** This format is most often used for importing images into other programs, such as QuarkXPress, Adobe PageMaker, Macromedia FreeHand, CorelDraw, and Adobe Illustrator, across platforms to a number of different operating systems. Most scanning software will enable you to export in TIFF format, which can subsequently be imported into Acrobat.

✦ **Not supported:** File formats not supported by importing directly into Acrobat include EPS, Photoshop native format, RAW, and ScitexCT.

To import any of the acceptable formats, select File ⇨ Import ⇨ Image. The Import Image dialog box will appear, enabling you to identify the location and images to be imported. In the Import dialog box, you'll find an option for adding multiple images. You can select the Add All option, which will specify a folder of images to be imported into a single PDF file. You can select an individual image by clicking its filename and then clicking the Add button. As files are added, they will appear in a list below Select Files to Import, as shown in Figure 14-8. If you inadvertently add a file to the list, select the file and click the Remove button. When finished identifying the files, click Done.

After importing images, you can choose the Capture command to convert the files to PDF Normal or Original Image with Hidden Text. When selecting the Original Image with Hidden Text option, you still need to clean up the document if you wish to use the text for searches. The document integrity will be preserved according to the scan, but the hidden layer of text can contain many suspects.

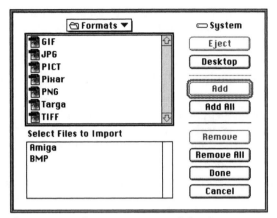

Figure 14-8: The Import Image dialog box enables you to import multiple images, which can be imported into an existing document or a new document. If multiple images are selected, they will appear in the same PDF file on different pages.

Summary

✦ Acrobat Paper Capture is an optical character recognition program used for converting scanned images into editable text.

✦ Text can be captured and saved as a PDF Normal image, which will modify the text appearance of the original scan. Text can be captured and saved using the Original Image with Hidden Text option, which preserves the scan appearance and contains a text layer independent of the scan. The latter format can be used where document integrity is necessary for legal and archival purposes.

✦ users can access a custom dictionary containing additional words specified by the user. When Capture scans a document, it will use a language dictionary and custom dictionary to convert the image to recognizable text.

✦ Capture Suspects are used to correct interpretation problems when Paper Capture does not properly identify a word. Text editing is performed with the TouchUp Text tool. When changes to text are made, the Tab key is used to accept changes and move on to the next suspect.

✦ Acrobat can import images from a number of different file formats. Imported images can be captured in the same manner as scans are created with Acrobat Scan.

✦   ✦   ✦

Advanced Acrobat Applications

Chapter 15
PDF and the Web

Chapter 16
Printing and Digital
Prepress

Chapter 17
PDFs and CD-ROMs

Chapter 18
Using Acrobat
Plug-ins

PDF and the Web

◆ ◆ ◆ ◆

In This Chapter

Understanding Web page construction

Understanding PDF versus HTML

Configuring your Web browser

Capturing Web sites

Working with captured PDF files

◆ ◆ ◆ ◆

If you've read the book up to this point, by now you should be aware of the many advantages PDF has over other document formats. The integrity of a PDF file can also be maintained when accessed by a Web browser or viewed as a Web page. By tradition, Web page design is handled with a programming language.

If you are new to designing Web pages, a few preliminaries should be understood. The first thing to know about Web page design are the tools used to create the pages. Web pages are created in a coding language called Hypertext Markup Language (HTML). HTML coding can be created in a text editor whereby raw formatting code is used to position elements and text in a file known as a Web page. You can also create Web pages in WYSIWYG (What You See Is What You Get) graphics applications. When pages are created in a Web page design program, there is usually a means of working in a graphic environment and switching to the HTML code within the application. If you want to add all the bells and whistles available for Web pages, you will need to become skilled at the programming level. Even the most sophisticated design applications cannot offer the same results as programming in HTML. You can, however, create very impressive Web pages without knowing any program code and struggling with the syntax for HTML.

HTML Programming

Programming in HTML is handled by a text editor. Text editors are not the same as word processors, so don't attempt to write code in programs such as Microsoft Word or WordPerfect. Text editors designed for writing HTML will always be a better choice. Like anything available related to the Internet, you have many choices for the text editor you wish to use. Most of what is available can be found in the public domain. Therefore, you can download software from the Internet and use freeware applications for writing your HTML code.

Macintosh text editors

On the Macintosh, one of the most popular text editors available is BBEdit or BBEdit Lite. The latter is a freeware application available from BareBones Software. You can download BBEdit Lite from the BareBones Software Web site at www.barebones.com. Although you can code HTML in a text editor such as SimpleText, a more sophisticated editor will be a better choice. Many editors, such as BBEdit Lite, offer special features for coding HTML.

Windows and NT editors

One of the best compilations of shareware listings for PC users is available at www.tucows.com. You can go to one of Tucows' many mirror sites by entering this URL and then clicking a location. You will enter the contents page, where a button appears labeled "HTML Editors - Text". Click this hypertext link, and you'll end up at a listing of text editors. For Windows, you can use Windows WordPad; or you can use one of the many editors found on the Tucows site, all of which are rated from 1 to 5 cows (5 being the top rating). Of the many editors available, the best one will be the one that meets your personal preference. Download a few with high ratings and see which one appeals most to you.

Coding in HTML

If you have browsed a bookstore lately, you'll notice the incredible number of volumes in print on Web page design and HTML programming. This book is not intended to teach HTML or Web page design. If you need to know more, I suggest you look at one of the many volumes out there that appeals to you. Try something easy to start with such as *HTML 4 For Dummies* (IDG Books Worldwide, Inc., 1998). For a great resource in designing Web pages, pick up a copy of *Web Design Studio Secrets* (IDG Books Worldwide, 1998). For a bare bones, basic exercise in HTML programming, let's look at some steps for creating a Web page that embeds a PDF document.

STEPS: Embedding PDFs in Web Pages

1. **Open a text editor of your choice.** If using a Macintosh, you can use SimpleText as a text editor. Windows users can use WordPad or any text editor on hand.

2. **Enter the following code:**

```
<HTML>
<BODY BGCOLOR="#FFFFFF">
<BODY>
<CENTER>
```

The BODY BGCOLOR line is used to create a white background instead of using the default background of the Web browser. The <CENTER> tag is used to center-align the contents below the tag. Although you can use alternatives for aligning objects and text, for this exercise simply move on after the last line of the preceding code is entered in the text editor.

At this point, you need to add the code for importing the PDF file. PDF files are placed in HTML in two ways. You can use the EMBED tag, or you can use FRAME SRC tag for adding PDFs to a page with frames. You can't use the IMG SRC tag because the browser won't see your PDF as a graphic file. In this case, use the EMBED tag to import a PDF file into the Web browser via HTML. To follow the example, you'll need a PDF document. In my example, I used a file titled web.pdf. Use any PDF document you may have on hand or one contained on the CD-ROM accompanying this book.

3. **Assess the file size.** Open Acrobat and select File ⇨ Preferences ⇨ General. In the General Preferences dialog box, select Points from the Page Units pop-up menu. (You need to know the physical dimensions of the PDF document before proceeding.) View the status bar in the Acrobat window after changing the units to points and record these values (see Figure 15-1).

4. **Enter the following code below the <CENTER> tag.** Back in the text editor, continue coding your document. The next line of code will contain the measurements assessed on the status bar in Acrobat.

```
<EMBED SRC="web.pdf" WIDTH=385 HEIGHT=368>
</CENTER>
</BODY>
</HTML>
```

The EMBED tag syntax is <EMBED SRC =*"filename.pdf"* WIDTH=*nn* HEIGTH=*NN*>, where *nn* and *NN* are equal to the width and height measurements in pixels, respectively. The final code in the text editor appears as illustrated in Figure 15-2.

5. **Save the text file.** Save your file as text-only from the text editor. Be certain to save the file in the same directory as the PDF file embedded in the HTML. In my example, I saved the file under the name sample.htm.

Continued

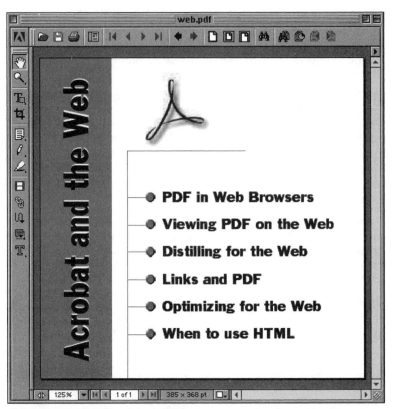

Figure 15-1: The size of the PDF document can be viewed in the status bar appearing at the bottom of the Acrobat window. In this example, the size reads 385 by 368 points.

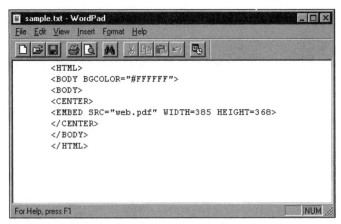

Figure 15-2: The final code in the text editor

This file can now be displayed in a Web browser as an HTML document. Keep this file around to be viewed in your browser. If you wish to examine it now, jump to the section where I discuss configuring the Web browser. The Web browser will need to be properly configured to see the PDF file within the browser window. Before moving on to configurations, though, it may be a good idea to understand the advantages and disadvantages of using PDF over HTML, and vice versa.

PDF Versus HTML

Inasmuch as you haven't viewed your PDF files in a Web browser yet, the preceding steps explain how to successfully import them in the page design. If your Web site is to contain PDF documents, a clear understanding of when to use PDF and when to use HTML will be helpful. Most of the Web sites you see on the World Wide Web are created in HTML. PDF support has been slow with Web graphics; however, many of the new features related to Acrobat 4.0 may inspire more people to use Acrobat with Web pages.

PDF advantages

PDF can provide some advantages over HTML. Because Acrobat Reader is a free application distributed by Adobe, the viewing of PDF files on the Web can be made available to all Internet users without cost. For more extensive use of PDF, the end user would need to purchase Acrobat. Regardless of what Acrobat viewer is used, there are some advantages to using PDF files on the Web:

✦ **File integrity:** PDF files maintain total file integrity and appear as they were originally designed. When fonts are embedded in the file, the end user will see all text formatting as it was intended, complete with fonts and typographical design.

✦ **Resizing windows has no effect on the layout:** In HTML, when you resize a window, the window content may conform to the window size. This may be undesirable if your page is intended to be viewed at a standard size. With PDF, resizing windows has no effect on the design. Users need to use horizontal or vertical scrolling to see more of the page contents when the browser window is not sized large enough to accomodate the layout.

✦ **Ease of design:** For the design community, designing a PDF document is nothing more than outputting the design from a layout or illustration application. Therefore, the design requirements are within the knowledge base of the author, because no special software or coding needs to be learned to create the Web page. In addition, if your workflow includes document repurposing, the same files you may use for screen or print displays can be converted to PDF, thus reducing the amount of time to create Web pages.

✦ **Access speed:** In some cases, PDF files can be faster than HTML if the files have been prepared properly. By optimizing PDF files, using progressive display, and relying on servers with byteserving capabilities, the PDF file can sometimes download faster. The progressive display will show text first, then images, and finally the embedded fonts. The end user will see text immediately and can begin reading the page while waiting for the download to complete. Because font compression is used, the text display will appear faster than with HTML.

✦ **Annotating pages:** This can be handled on the Web within a PDF document. Rather than using e-mail for correspondence, a company can create PDF files and viewers can add comments, approvals, and other annotations to the same file downloaded from the Web site. The annotations can be collected and summarized from the original document receiving the comments. This feature is not interactive and requires downloading the document to a local computer for supplying annotations, and then uploading the edited file.

HTML advantages

HTML is a standard on the Web. It has been continually developed for a single purpose, which is simply to display Web text and graphics. Many of the various features commonly found on Web sites for more advanced designs are all programmed in HTML. The advantages of using HTML over PDF include the following:

✦ **Robust programming:** HTML has more robust programming opportunities than PDF. Pages on the Web can include many displays designed to be spectacular. As a markup language, you have much more flexibility in combining page elements than with PDF.

✦ **Consistent page display:** With PDF, the page always appears inside the browser window. Irregular page sizes may look awkward. With HTML, the page size is determined by the user and the view can be made consistent for all HTML Web pages.

✦ **Navigation:** Navigation with HTML can be handled within the page with hypertext links or the browser toolbar. If you wish to go back a page, the browser will display the last page viewed in HTML. If you view PDF, the Page Back command in the browser will take you back to the page viewed before the PDF was displayed. This will often not be the previous page in the PDF document.

✦ **Search engines:** These often build indexes from HTML pages on the Web. Few of them can search PDF contents to add keywords to their indexes.

Combining PDF and HTML

The items listed in the preceding section are a few of the reasons to use either PDF or HTML as well as some reasons not to use one over the other. There are many tools and applications available in Web design, and most people do not find a single solution with a single utility. Much like Java scripting or Shockwave usage, PDF files are yet another means of displaying information. Rather than looking for a single solution, the Web designer will be well advised to pick the right tool for the job at hand. In some cases, combining the advantages of PDF with those of HTML will be your answer.

Configuring Your Web Browser

There are four ways to view PDF files when working on the Internet. You can have the PDF file imported into the Web browser window so it appears like an HTML page. The PDF can be viewed inside the browser window, with viewer tools accessible (as if Acrobat were *inside* the browser). You can save the PDF file to disk and later look at the it in an Acrobat viewer. Or, you can have the Acrobat viewer open and view the PDF file in the viewer as a window beside your browser window. Depending on how you wish to view PDF files, you'll need to configure your browser accordingly. Improper browser configuration is perhaps the problem most often experienced by users attempting to view PDF files.

Viewing configurations

If you have an Internet connection, you most likely already have a browser installed on your computer. In order to take full advantage of Acrobat, a version of Netscape Navigator 3.0 or greater or Microsoft Internet Explorer version 3.0 or above is needed for either the Macintosh or Windows PC.

Configuring Netscape Navigator

Netscape Navigator uses a plug-in architecture similar to Acrobat. To view PDF files within the Netscape browser window, the plug-in needs to be properly installed. These plug-in names will differ according to computer platform.

PDF viewing configurations on the Macintosh

After installing an Acrobat viewer, the PDFViewer plug-in needs to be moved from the Acrobat Reader or Acrobat Web Browser Plug-in folder to the Netscape:Plug-ins folder. A complete installation of Acrobat will include the plug-in with the other installed files.

The PDFViewer plug-in will appear inside the Acrobat Web Browser Plug-in folder. If you do not have the folder or plug-in, you'll need to copy it from the Acrobat installer CD-ROM. Once the files are appropriately located, you can use the PDFViewer to view PDF files on the Web.

PDF viewing configurations in Windows

The logic applied to the plug-ins for Windows is the same as that for the Macintosh plug-ins; however, you need to find the right files, and these have to be copied to the Netscape plug-ins folder. The two files to be copied to the Netscape plug-ins folder are nppdf32.dll and ewh32.api. Before you copy the files, a word of caution: There are two versions, a 16-bit version and a 32-bit version, of the plug-in files for both Netscape Navigator and Adobe Acrobat. If you are using Windows 95, Windows 98, or Windows NT, then be certain to use the 32-bit versions of both the files, which I've listed above. If you find files named nppdf16.dll and/or ewh16.api, you know you are using a 16-bit version. By all means, do not mix a 16-bit version of one application with a 32-bit version of another.

In most cases you won't see anything residing in the browser folder. In order to view the file, you may need to view all hidden files on your system. When you return to the browser folder, the nppdf32.dll file will appear. When all hidden files are viewed, both the necessary files can be copied to the Netscape plug-ins folder.

Configuring Microsoft Internet Explorer

Microsoft Internet Explorer also supports the plug-in architecture; however, Microsoft has devoted more of their development time to ActiveX components, which is an alternative to plug-ins. When using Explorer, you will benefit more by using ActiveX. Adobe has written an ActiveX control to allow handling of PDF files in Explorer. Fortunately, you don't have to relocate or copy the file. Just be certain the pdf.ocx file is installed in the ActiveX folder on Windows machines. When Adobe released earlier versions of Acrobat, an ActiveX component had not yet been developed for the Macintosh. If you use Microsoft Internet Explorer on a Mac, visit Adobe's Web site at www.adobe.com/acrobat for release information on the latest updates.

Helper configurations

Netscape Navigator has some preference settings referred to as *helper applications*. A helper application is designed to communicate a given file type from the server to the end user's computer. When the transfer occurs, a file conversion will be made to the helper application attributes. This conversion will enable you to view or load a file in a given application. In order to completely understand the configurations for helper applications, you need to look at a few of the attribute settings.

MIME types

In Netscape Navigator version 3.0, select Options ➪ General Preferences. In Netscape Navigator/Communicator version 4.0 and above, select Edit ➪ Preferences and open the Preferences dialog box. Select Applications from the preference choices to list the helper applications.

In the list, you'll find many preset applications defined. Some of these items are handled by plug-ins, and others are identified with some settings available when you select the Edit button. At the top of the list, you should see Acrobat PDF, Acrobat, or Portable Document Format. Select the item as listed, click the Edit button, and the Edit dialog box will appear (see Figure 15-3). In the Edit Type dialog box, several settings will require your input, beginning with the first three field boxes. The first item, Description, will identify the name in the description list of the helper applications. Whatever you enter here is up to you; this item is simply an identifier.

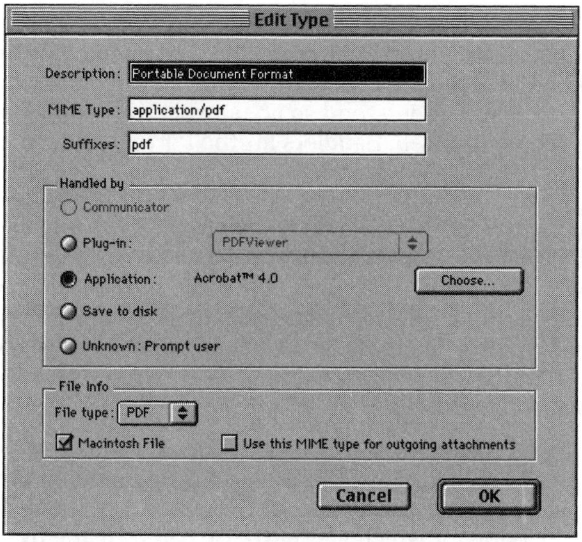

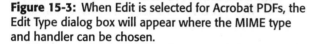

Figure 15-3: When Edit is selected for Acrobat PDFs, the Edit Type dialog box will appear where the MIME type and handler can be chosen.

The second item you need to specify is MIME type. MIME stands for *Multipurpose Internet Mail Extensions*. A mail extension is an attachment to a link or file that ultimately gets downloaded from a server to your computer. In the transfer process, the file needs to be converted. MIME supplies the necessary information for the conversion. In this case, you need to be certain the MIME type description is defined for an Acrobat PDF file.

MIME type specifications follow a certain convention. For example, if you were to establish a file type for a Microsoft Excel spreadsheet, you would enter application/excel; a graphic might be identified as graphic/jpeg; HTML files are identified as text/html; and so on. The information you need to supply in the MIME Type field box for PDF files is application/pdf.

Suffixes

Naming conventions typically involve a three- or four-character suffix. Although DOS doesn't recognize a four-character extension, UNIX does. Most often you will find your files identified with three characters as the suffix. On the Mac, you may find JPEG used for .jpg and PICT used for .pic.

Handlers

In the next area of the Edit dialog box, choices for how a file is to be handled are available. Choosing the right handler will be important to PDF viewing. It is essential that the handlers are clearly understood so no unexpected results occur when PDF files are encountered on the Web. Handlers for the Portable Document Format include the following:

✦ **Plug-in:** When Plug-in is selected, the PDFViewer plug-in will be used by Netscape. This choice places the PDF page within the browser window much like a GIF or JPEG image. If the HTML uses the EMBED tag, the PDF page will be viewed like other images in an HTML document. If the URL addresses a PDF page, the Acrobat viewer tools will appear below the browser window and the PDF page will reside within the viewer inside the browser. The latter is commonly referred to as *inline viewing*.

✦ **Application:** If Application is selected, the PDF page will be downloaded and a viewer application will be launched. The PDF page will then appear in the Acrobat viewer window. If both Acrobat Reader and Acrobat are installed on the same computer, a selection for which viewer to use can be made by selecting the Browse button. When Browse is selected, a navigation dialog box will appear enabling you to locate the viewer desired.

✦ **Save to Disk:** The PDF page from the Web will be downloaded and saved to disk. The PDF can be saved and viewed in an Acrobat viewer after disconnecting from the Internet.

✦ **Unknown: Prompt User:** If this item is selected, a dialog box will appear prompting for selection of an application to be used for viewing the PDF page. In most cases, one of the preceding choices will be preferred.

You should note if the Plug-in option is not available for selection, you haven't installed the plug-in properly. You will need to perform the steps previously outlined for installing the plug-in in the Netscape plug-ins folder.

Viewing PDFs in a browser

I discussed earlier how to embed a PDF page in an HTML document and how to configure Web browsers for viewing. As yet, you haven't looked at a PDF page through a browser. The configuration discussed in the preceding section is important because there are several ways to handle PDF files on the Web. Become familiar with the following options so you know how to set up your viewing.

Viewing PDFs embedded in HTML

If you include a PDF file as part of the HTML code, you won't have to do much in the way of configurations. A Web page using the EMBED tag will display the PDF file inside the browser. This treatment will be similar to the way you view graphic images in HTML documents. To view a Web page with a PDF document contained in the HTML code, take a look at the file created earlier. Launch your browser and open the sample.htm page. When you open the page, the display of the PDF document inside the browser window will appear as shown in Figure 15-4.

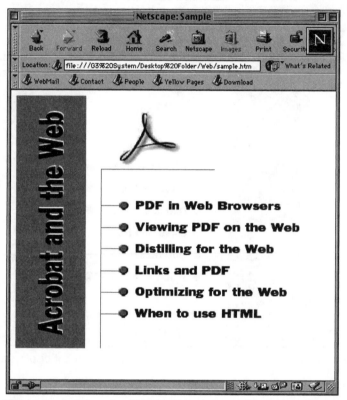

Figure 15-4: When the EMBED SRC tag is used in HTML, the PDF document will be displayed as if it were an <IMG SRC> link (a graphic image).

In this example, the PDF file is embedded in the HTML code. You can choose to include PDF files inside a Web page as in this example, or you can open PDF files directly in the Web browser. It is important to understand the difference, so let's move on to looking at opening PDF files directly in Netscape.

Viewing PDF documents in a browser

Opening PDFs in a browser cannot be accomplished by opening a file as you would an HTML document. You need to specify a URL and filename to view the PDF directly in the browser. For example, logging on to www.provider.com/file.pdf would result in the display of the PDF page inside the browser window — as mentioned earlier, this is referred to as inline viewing (see Figure 15-5). Look carefully at the difference between the example in Figure 15-4 and this example.

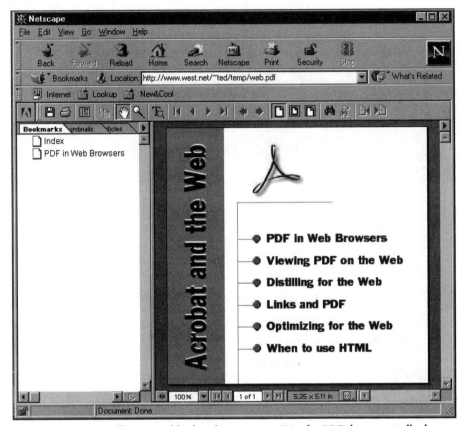

Figure 15-5: A PDF file opened by logging on to a URL of a PDF document displays an inline view.

Notice the Acrobat toolbar appears inside the browser window. The active Acrobat tools can be used when viewing PDF documents directly in the browser. Notice the bookmarks appear in the Navigation Pane. The Netscape window will display the page linked to the bookmark.

Article threads can also be followed directly within the Web browser. If an article exists, the cursor will change to indicate the copy contains an article. As the mouse button is clicked, the thread will be followed the same as in Acrobat. When the Web server has byteserving capabilities, only the page viewed will be downloaded, which will save time exploring PDF documents inside the browser window. With both bookmarks and articles, as another page is selected, the respective page downloads, permitting viewing.

Viewing PDFs directly in a browser requires the proper configuration, as suggested earlier. Without the plug-in and the MIME type appropriately defined, you wouldn't be able to view the file as illustrated in Figure 15-5.

PDF documents downloaded to an Acrobat viewer

Up to this point, PDF documents have been viewed through the Netscape window. In Netscape, you can't take advantage of Acrobat's menu commands, and there may be times when you wish to use various commands in Acrobat or Reader. For example, you may wish to see documents in Full Screen view, add annotations, import data, and so on. The browser can be configured to display the PDF in an Acrobat viewer, where all of Acrobat's menu commands can be made available.

To use an Acrobat viewer, the preferences must be changed to Application. When the Application radio button is selected, the Browse button can be used to select the viewer. When logging on to the URL, the entire PDF document will be downloaded and displayed inside the viewer.

Saving PDF files

At times you may wish to retrieve a file and view it at a later time. You can elect to save a file by choosing the Save radio button in the Helper or Preferences dialog box. When the Save item is enabled, a progress bar will be displayed that indicates the download status. A dialog box will appear prompting you to save the file. Be certain the plug-in is disabled to save the PDF to disk.

Viewing preferences in the browser

Some support for viewing document information and accessing the General Preferences dialog box is available when viewing PDFs in a browser. If the browser is set up for inline viewing, several menu commands are made available from a fly-away menu in the Acrobat window. From the fly-away menu, choices can be made for viewing information relative to the PDF by accessing the menu commands (see Figure 15-6).

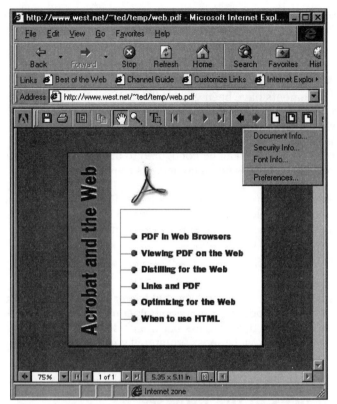

Figure 15-6: When the right arrow is selected in the inline Acrobat window, a fly-away menu will display menu choices for document viewing.

The menu choices, listed here, provide access to the same information as the related choices found in the Acrobat viewer:

✦ **Document Info:** The PDF General Info dialog box will appear when the Document Info command is selected from the fly-away menu. From within the browser, the viewer can display Document Info without downloading the PDF file and opening it in an Acrobat viewer (see Figure 15-7).

✦ **Security Info:** Secure files can be downloaded from the Internet. Once viewed in an Acrobat viewer, the security features saved with the file will be effective. If you need to know whether security has been applied to a PDF document, you can determine this by examining the Security level prior to saving a file (see Figure 15-8).

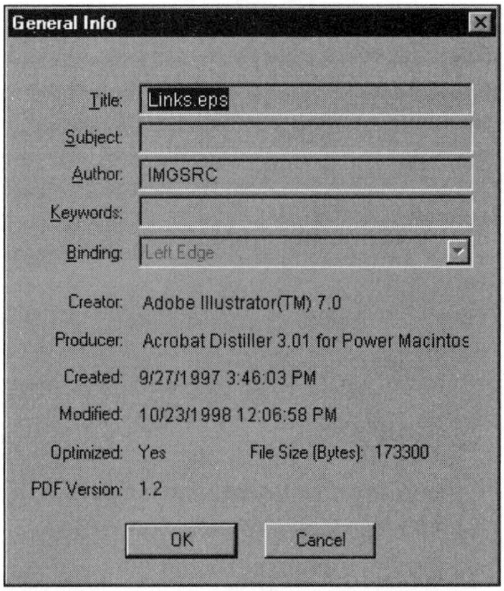

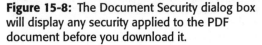

Figure 15-7: General information is accessed by bringing up the fly-away menu and choosing Document Info.

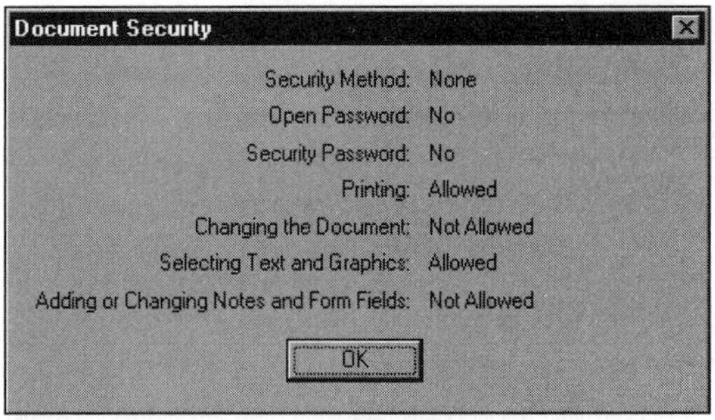

Figure 15-8: The Document Security dialog box will display any security applied to the PDF document before you download it.

✦ **Font Info:** Font usage and font embedding can be assessed before saving the PDF file to disk by selecting the Font Info option from the fly-away menu. The List All Fonts button in the dialog box functions as it does in an Acrobat viewer. When the button is selected, all the fonts in the document will be included in the Original Font list—even for the pages not yet viewed in the browser window (see Figure 15-9).

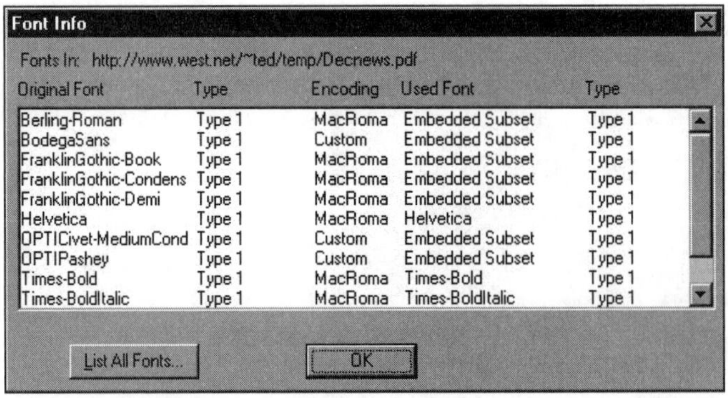

Figure 15-9: The Font Info dialog box lists all fonts contained on the current page. To view all fonts in the entire PDF document, click the List All Fonts button.

✦ **Preferences:** All the general preference settings available in Acrobat are displayed from the inline Web browser view with the exception of Skip Edit Warnings. Preferences can be selected from this dialog box to customize viewing PDFs on the Web (see Figure 15-10).

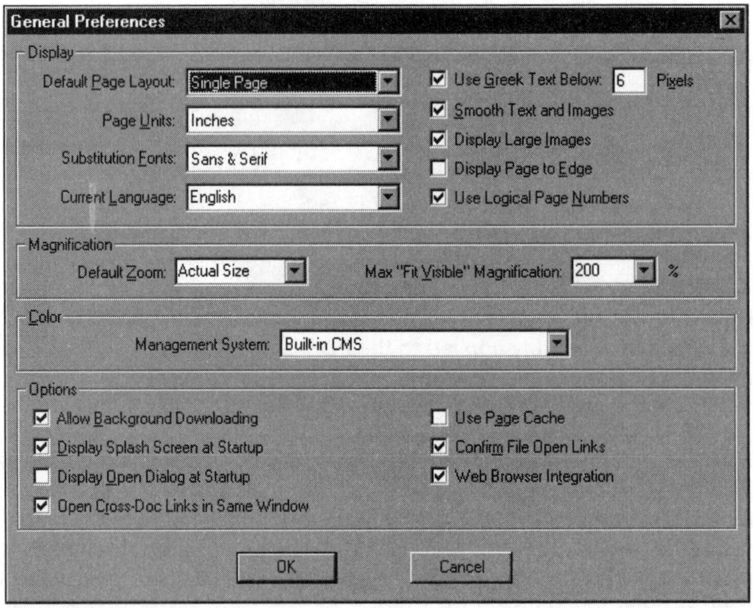

Figure 15-10: General preferences setting are available by selecting the Preferences option from the fly-away menu in the browser window.

Viewing PDF links in the Web browser

Hypertext links in a PDF document can be navigated while viewing embedded PDFs or through inline viewing. Associated links will open other HTML documents or PDF files. If page actions are created in a PDF document, the page actions will execute in the Web browser. Transition effects can also be viewed in the browser window. In terms of navigational links, there are three options available for viewing inline PDF documents: hypertext links, Web links to URLs, and bookmarks as links.

Hypertext links

Any link to another PDF page or another PDF document is handled in the Web browser the same way it is in an Acrobat viewer. Click a link, and the browser will display the page and view created with the Link tool in Acrobat. You can create links to video and sound as well as PDF pages. Once again, these link actions will behave similarly to the way they do in an Acrobat viewer. Not all interactive features are available to Netscape. If you have problems viewing links, you'll need to switch to Microsoft Internet Explorer.

Web links

A Web link can be made to another PDF document or a Web address. When linking to a PDF document on the Web, an address and filename are required. An example of such a link is www.company.com/myfile.pdf. If the link were www.company.com, the link would open the Home page for the domain site.

To create a Web link in Acrobat, the Link tool in the Acrobat Tool Bar is used. Once the Properties window is open, select World Wide Web Link from the Type pop-up menu. The Weblink Edit URL dialog box will appear, and this is where you enter the URL, as shown in Figure 15-11. In the field box, be certain to include the complete URL.

Figure 15-11: Web links are created through the Link Properties window. From this window, select World Wide Web Link from the Type pop-up menu. Another dialog box will open in which you enter the URL.

The Web link can be activated from a local hard drive in an Acrobat viewer or as a Web page on the Internet. If the file is opened locally, activating the link will create an Internet connection, launch the Web browser, and connect to the URL. If viewing the PDF on a Web page, the link will open the URL associated with it.

Bookmarks and thumbnails

Bookmarks created in a PDF that link to other pages, views, other PDF documents, or Web sites are also available when viewing PDF documents on the Web. When inline viewing is used, you'll have access to the Acrobat Command Bar. Selecting the Navigation Pane will open the pane where the bookmarks are displayed as they are in an Acrobat viewer, as shown in Figure 15-12.

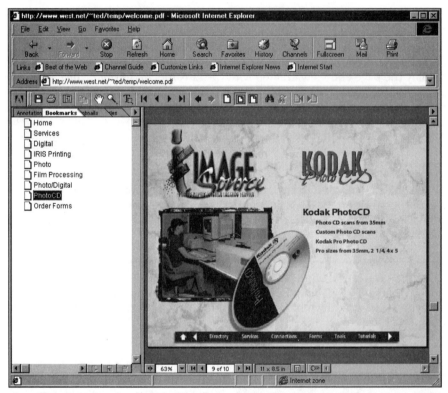

Figure 15-12: When bookmarks have been created in a PDF document, they will be displayed in an open Navigation Pane in the Web browser.

Bookmark links created to other pages or views will behave as they do in the Acrobat viewers. Click a bookmark, and the associated view will be displayed. The same applies to thumbnails within a PDF document. In the Navigation pane, select the thumbnail icon to view thumbnails. If thumbnails have been created in the PDF, they will be displayed in the Navigation Pane. If no thumbnails appear, the page borders will be displayed. Regardless of the view, double-clicking a thumbnail will move to the respective page.

Capturing Web Sites (Windows Only)

The previous section covered views and navigation that can be made on both the Mac and Windows platforms in either Netscape Navigator or Microsoft Internet Explorer. Much more power with PDF and Web integration is unfortunately, as of this writing, reserved for the Windows user and those who install Microsoft Internet Explorer. Several features appear in Acrobat for Windows that do not appear in Acrobat running under the Mac OS. Web Capture and Send Mail are menu commands unique to Windows. Web Capture appears under the Tools menu in Acrobat, and it provides different options for capturing a Web page, Web site, or multiple sites and converting all HTML documents to PDF. A captured Web site will convert HTML, text files, and images to PDF, and each Web page will be appended to the converted document. PDF files will also be appended to the document. Send Mail is a menu command that enables you to send a PDF document as an e-mail attachment from within Acrobat. Once an e-mail program is configured properly, an open PDF document can be attached to an e-mail message by selecting File ➪ Send Mail.

Web site structure

To understand how capturing a Web site and converting the documents to PDF is handled, you need a fundamental understanding of a Web page and the structure of a site. A Web page is a file created with the Hypertext Markup Language. There is nothing specific to the length of a Web page. A page may be a screen the size of 640 × 480 pixels or a length equivalent to several hundred letter-sized pages. Size in terms of linear length is usually determined by the page content and amount of space needed to display the page. PDF files, on the other hand, have fixed lengths up to 200 inches by 200 inches. You can determine the fixed size of the PDF page prior to converting the Web site from HTML to PDF. Once the PDF page size is determined, any Web pages captured will adhere to the fixed size. If a Web page is larger than the established PDF page, the overflow will automatically create additional PDF pages. A single Web page, converted, may result in several PDF pages.

When Web sites are designed, they typically follow a hierarchical order, as shown in Figure 15-13. The home page rests at the topmost level, whereas direct links to this page will occupy a second level. Subsequently, links from the second level will refer to pages at a third level, and so forth.

When pages are captured with Acrobat, the user can specify the number of levels to convert. Be forewarned, though, even two levels of a Web site can occupy many Web pages. The amount of time needed to capture a site will be determined by the number of pages to convert and the speed of your Internet connection.

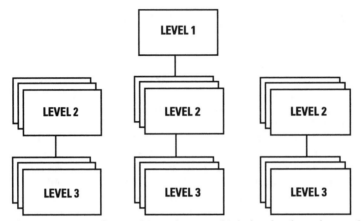

Figure 15-13: Web Page hierarchy at multiple levels. The volume of Web pages at any level other than the first level can be extensive.

Converting Web pages

When using the Web Capture command, Web pages will be converted to PDF. One or more levels can be captured from a Web site, and this action downloads pages and converts them to PDF. PDF pages can be converted and placed in a new PDF file or appended to an existing PDF file. The pages are converted by accessing a URL on the Internet from within Acrobat. The converted pages can then be viewed in Acrobat or linked directly to a Web browser for viewing on the Internet, but only with Microsoft Internet Explorer. File types that can be converted to PDF include the following:

✦ **HTML documents:** HTML files such as the Web page created earlier in this chapter can be converted to PDF. The hypertext links from the original HTML file will be active in the PDF document as long as the destination documents and URLs have also been converted.

✦ **Text files:** Any text-only documents contained on a Web site, such as an ASCII text document, will be converted to PDF. When capturing text-only files, you have the opportunity to control many text attributes and page formats.

✦ **JPEG images:** Images used in the HTML documents will also be captured and converted to PDF. JPEGs may be part of the converted HTML page. When captured, they can be part of a captured HTML page and can also appear individually on PDF pages.

✦ **GIF images:** GIF images, as well as the first image in an animated GIF, will also be captured when converting a Web site. GIFs, like JPEGs, will appear in the HTML file and can also appear on separate PDF pages.

✦ **FDF:** Form Data Files will also be converted to PDF. If Form Data appears in a database file, the entire file will be converted.

✦ **Image maps:** Image maps created in HTML will be converted to PDF. The links associated with the map will be active in the PDF as long as the link destinations are also converted.

✦ **Password-secure areas:** A password-secure area of a Web site can also be converted to PDF. In order to access a secure site, however, you'll need the password(s).

✦ **HTML attributes:** Pages containing frames, tables, background and text colors, and forms can be converted, and the attributes will be preserved in the PDF document.

Accepted file types and links

If a Web page link to another Web page or URL exists, it will be preserved in the converted PDF document. Links to pages, sites, and various actions will work similarly to the way they do directly on the Web site. If a PDF document contains a link to another PDF document, the converted file won't preserve the link. When the site is converted, the captured pages will reside in a single PDF document. In order to maintain PDF links that open other PDF documents, the destination documents will need to be captured as individual pages or extracted and saved from the converted pages.

Links to another level will also be inactive if they have not been converted during the capture. Individual linked pages can be appended to the converted PDF document by viewing Web links and opening a dialog box. Selections for converting individual links will be made available. One or more links can then be appended to the converted document. Specifics on how to accomplish this task will be explained when you look at appending links a little later in this chapter.

JavaScripts cannot be downloaded when capturing a Web site. For executed animation, such as an animation from a GIF file or other programming application, the download will only contain the first image in the sequence. A mouseover effect that changes an image will be preserved in the converted PDF document as long as both the original image and the image associated with the mouseover are downloaded. Additionally, sounds contained in documents can be captured.

For Web pages that contain non-English characters, you need to have the appropriate resources loaded in order to download and convert the files. Japanese characters, for example, require installation of the Far East language files and additional system files.

Bookmarks in converted pages

Once a Web site has been converted to PDF, you can edit the document in Acrobat like you would any other PDF. Links to pages will become editable links — that is, their properties can be changed and modified. When a site has been converted to PDF, all the PDF pages will contain bookmarks linked to the respective pages, as shown in Figure 15-14. The first bookmark will be a regular (unstructured) bookmark, which will contain the name of the server from which the site was captured. All bookmarks appearing below the server name will be structured bookmarks linked to the converted pages. With the exception of specific Web applications, these bookmarks can be edited and modified like any other bookmarks created in Acrobat.

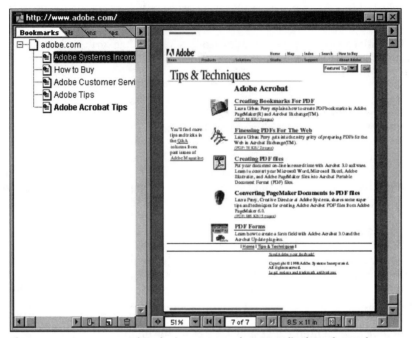

Figure 15-14: A captured Web site converted to PDF displays the Web server name as a normal bookmark at the top of the list. All bookmarks below the server name are structured bookmarks linked to the converted pages. The bookmark names refer to HTML filenames, PDF document names, and URLs.

Bookmarks contained in the converted PDF document can be edited and reorganized like unstructured bookmarks created in Acrobat. By opening a context-sensitive menu (Control+click on the Mac, or right-click in Windows), you can display options for bookmark behavior (see Figure 15-15). Some of the options available for structured bookmarks are not available for the unstructured bookmarks created in Acrobat (see Figure 15-16).

Figure 15-15: By opening a
context-sensitive menu on a
structured bookmark, options
for bookmark editing will appear.

Figure 15-16: Some bookmarks appearing
on captured pages will fall in the category
of unstructured. The context menu
commands for unstructured bookmarks
offer fewer options.

The options available in the context-sensitive menu for structured bookmarks
include the following:

✦ **Go to Bookmark:** The same option exists with bookmarks created in Acrobat.
Selecting this option enables you to navigate to the page linked to the
bookmark. When the Web site is converted to PDF, links to the pages are
automatically created.

✦ **Print Page(s):** The page related to the bookmark will be printed. No options
exist for specifying page ranges when using this command from the context-
sensitive menu.

✦ **Delete:** The selected page will be deleted. All subordinate bookmarks will be
deleted with the parent bookmark. This option appears the same for
structured and unstructured bookmarks.

✦ **Delete Page(s):** When Delete Page(s) is selected, both the bookmark(s) and
associated page(s) will be deleted. A dialog box will appear, enabling you to
supply the page range for deletion.

✦ **Extract Page(s):** A page range can be specified for extraction. This feature may
be used if PDF links to other PDF documents were included in the capture.
When saving the extracted pages, be certain to use the same name as the link
uses to identify the document.

✦ **Rename:** Selecting Rename enables renaming of the bookmark name. This
option appears with both structured and unstructured bookmarks.

✦ **Append Next Level:** When a site is captured and the level is defined so not all of the site contents appear in the resulting document, additional pages can be appended to the open PDF document. When Append Next Level is selected, Acrobat will convert all PDFs below the last level captured.

✦ **View Web Links:** When View Web Links is selected, the Select Page Links to Download dialog box will appear, providing options for page links to be selected and subsequently downloaded. (See the following section, "Select Page Links to Download" for more about this dialog box.)

✦ **Open Web Page in Browser:** When a bookmark is selected and Open Web Page in Browser is chosen from the context-sensitive menu, the URL associated with the bookmark will open in the Web browser. This behavior is similar to a bookmark in a Web browser. When you select the bookmark, the browser will display the respective Web page.

✦ **Properties:** The last item available from the context-sensitive menu is the Properties command. When Properties is selected, the Bookmark Properties dialog box appears (see Figure 15-17), presenting the same properties options that are available for unstructured bookmarks. The properties for all the structured and unstructured bookmarks on converted documents can be edited the way they are any other PDF.

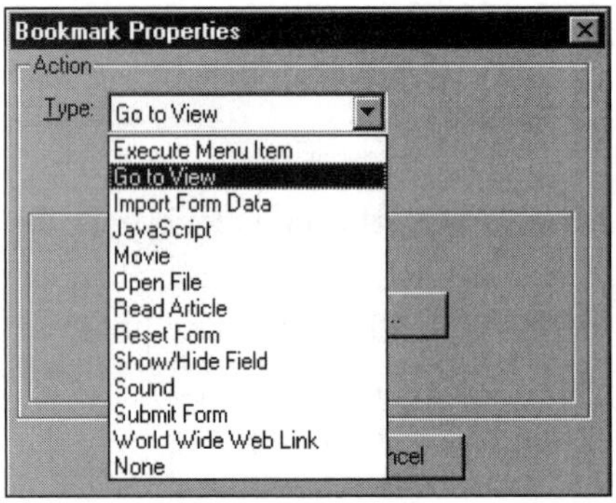

Figure 15-17: The Bookmark Properties dialog box is displayed with the Type pop-up menu in view. The bookmark links for structured bookmarks can be edited for the same actions as apply to unstructured bookmarks.

Select Page Links to Download

The Select Page Links to Download dialog box appears when the View Web Links option is selected from the context-sensitive menu shown in Figure 15-15. From this dialog box, shown in Figure 15-18, you can select attribute options for the downloaded page.

Click the link to be viewed and select the Properties button to gain access to the attribute settings for that link. Following is a run-down of each attribute settings tab:

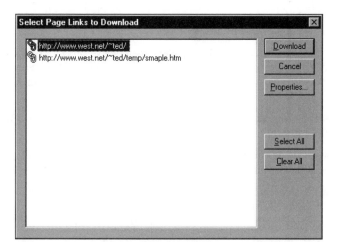

Figure 15-18: When View Web Links is selected, this dialog box appears, listing the available links contained within the page associated with the bookmark. Select a link to gain access to the properties for the respective link.

✦ **Download Tab:** The default view for the link properties contains attribute choices for the linked download (see Figure 15-19). When additional files are downloaded, they will be appended to the open PDF document.

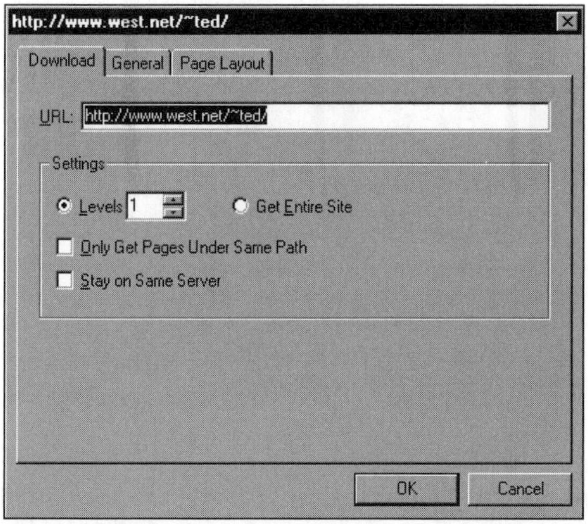

Figure 15-19: The Download tab in the link properties dialog box contains options for the URL and levels to be downloaded.

- **URL:** The URL will be placed in a field box that can be edited. If you wish to change the URL, edit the field box.

- **Levels:** Appended pages can contain more than one level. The URL link may go to another site or stay within the same site. Select the levels to be downloaded by clicking the up or down arrows, or enter a numeric value in the field box.

- **Get Entire Site:** When the radio button is selected, all levels on the Web Site will be downloaded.

- **Only Get Pages Under Same Path:** When this option is enabled, all documents will be confined to the directory path under the selected URL.

- **Stay on Same Server:** If links are made to other servers, they will not be downloaded when this option is enabled.

✦ **General Tab:** Select the General tab from the link properties dialog box displayed in Figure 15-20 to view content-type specific options and general content options. From the options available in this dialog box, choices are made for the converted PDF content.

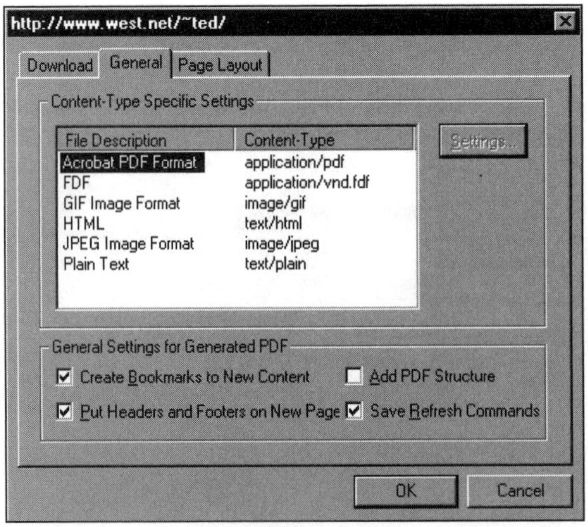

Figure 15-20: The General tab in the link properties dialog box provides options for specific content items to appear in the converted PDF document.

- **Content-Type Specific Settings:** A list of file types appear in the dialog box within this section. The content type is listed adjacent to the file description. All the items are fixed except the HTML and plain text files. Fixed file descriptions will be downloaded with the content preserved from the Web pages.

• The content of HTML pages and ASCII text pages can have specific attributes changed by selecting the file description and clicking the Settings button. To change the HTML page attributes, select HTML in the File Description list and click the Settings button. The HTML Conversion Settings dialog box appears, as shown in Figure 15-21. Here HTML conversion settings can be selected for the layout appearance and font usage.

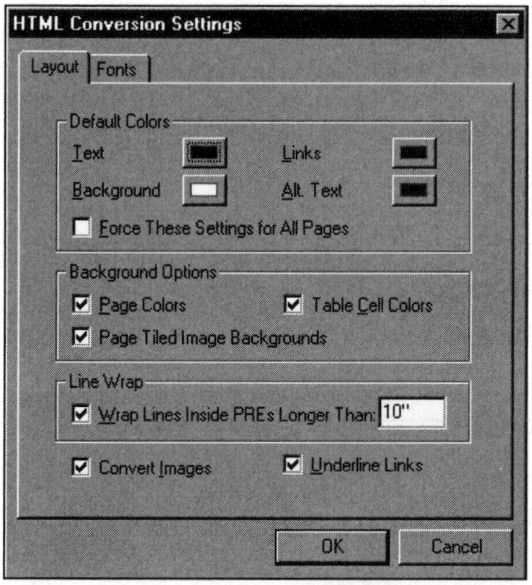

Figure 15-21: When HTML is selected in the General options dialog box and you click the Settings button, the HTML Conversion Settings dialog box will appear. From this dialog box, attribute settings for the HTML conversion to PDF are made.

• Layout attributes are made from choices in this dialog box. *Default colors* can be identified for the text, background, links, and ALT tags used in the HTML file. To change a color, click the respective swatch. When Force These Settings for All Pages is enabled, all the linked pages will adhere to the same layout attributes.

• *Background Options* include settings for the background colors used on the Web page, tiled image backgrounds, and table cells. When these check boxes are enabled, the original design will be preserved in the PDF document.

• *Line Wrap* enables you to choose a maximum distance for word-wrapping the text in an HTML file. When the <PRE> tag is used in HTML, the text will be preformatted to preserve line breaks and indents. The field box for this option enables controlling the maximum length for text lines.

- *Convert Images* will convert images contained in the HTML to separate PDF pages. If the option is disabled, the JPEG and GIF images will not be converted to separate PDF pages, but will appear on the HTML converted page.

- *Underline Links* will display the text used in an <A HREF...> tag with an underline. This option can be helpful if the text for a link is not a different color than the body copy.

- Fonts for body copy, headings, and text defined with the <PRE> tag in the HTML file can be changed globally by selecting the Fonts tab in the HTML Conversions dialog box, as illustrated in Figure 15-22. Click the Choose Font button for the respective item to display your installed system fonts, and select a font to be used during conversion. When the Embed Platform Fonts check box is selected, the fonts will be embedded in the PDF document much as they are embedded in Distiller.

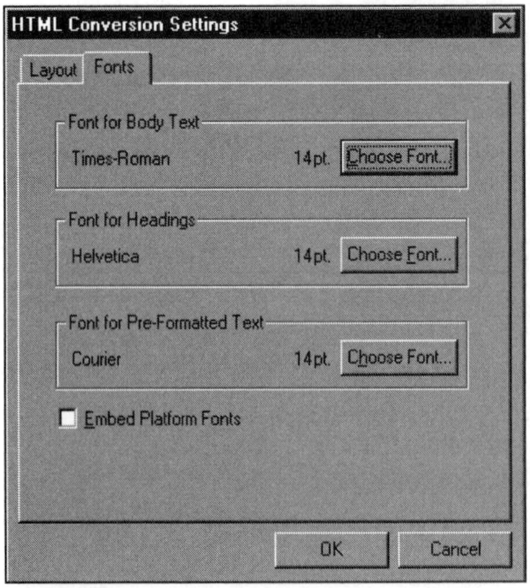

Figure 15-22: The second tab in the HTML Conversion Settings dialog box provides choices for changing text attributes from the HTML file to the converted PDF.

- Text documents refer to ASCII text files contained on a Web site. These files do not contain HTML code and can be treated differently from the HTML documents. When you select Plain Text in the General settings dialog box (shown in Figure 15-20) and click the Settings button, the Text Conversion Settings dialog box in which you define attributes for text documents will appear (see Figure 15-23).

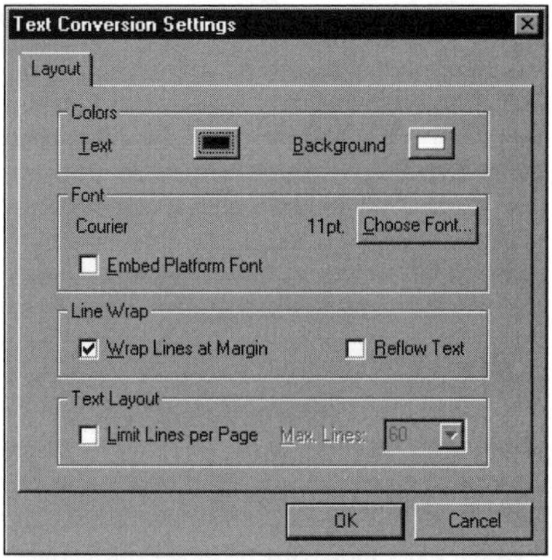

Figure 15-23: The Text Conversion Settings
dialog box will appear when you select Plain
Text in the General Settings dialog box and
click the Settings button.

- Choices for font, font embedding, and font color appear as attribute
  options in the dialog box and work the same as those described for the
  HTML settings. For specifying line wrap, there are two options. You can
  wrap the text lines at the page margins, or you can choose to reflow the
  text to follow the line breaks and margin guides. The last item in the
  dialog box enables you to limit the number of lines per PDF page
  according to the values supplied in the Max Lines box.

- **Create Bookmarks to New Content:** Back in the General settings dialog
  box illustrated in Figure 15-20, notice this option is enabled. This results
  in appended pages converted to PDF having structured bookmarks
  created for each page captured. The bookmark name will be the same as
  the title referenced in the HTML document.

- **Put Headers and Footers on New Page:** A header and footer will be
  placed on all converted pages if this option is enabled, as it is in Figure
  15-19. A header in the HTML file consists of the page title appearing with
  the <HEAD> tag. The footer will retrieve the page's URL, the page name,
  and a date stamp for the date and time the page was downloaded (see
  Figure 15-24).

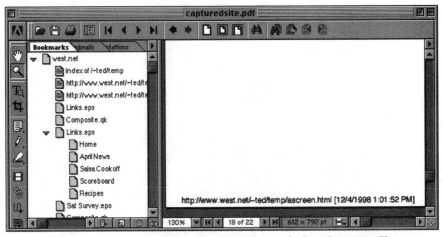

Figure 15-24: A page footer displays the page URL, including the HTML filename, and a time and date stamp for when the file was downloaded.

- **Add PDF Structure:** The structure of the converted PDF will match that of the original HTML file. Items like list elements, table cells, and similar HTML tags will be preserved. The PDF document will create structured bookmarks for each of the structure items converted.

- **Save Refresh Commands:** When enabled, a list of all URLs in the PDF document converted will be saved. When the capture is refreshed, these URLs will be revisited and new PDF pages will be converted for additional pages added to the site.

✦ **Page Layout Tab:** The Page Layout tab from the link properties dialog box, as shown in Figure 15-25, provides options for the size of the PDF page created from the converted file. Because HTML documents do not follow standard page lengths, you'll want to review these settings periodically when capturing a site.

- **Page Size:** A pop-up menu with default page sizes provides selections for a variety of different sizes. Acrobat supports page sizes from 1-inch square to 200-inches square. You can supply any value between the minimum and maximum page sizes in the Width and Height field boxes to override the fixed sizes available from the pop-up menu.

- **Sample Page:** The thumbnail displays a view of how the converted page will appear when sizes are established for the Width and Height settings.

- **Orientation:** Choices for portrait or landscape orientation are selected from the radio button options. If a site contains all Web pages that conform to screen sizes such as 640 by 480, you might wish to change the orientation to landscape.

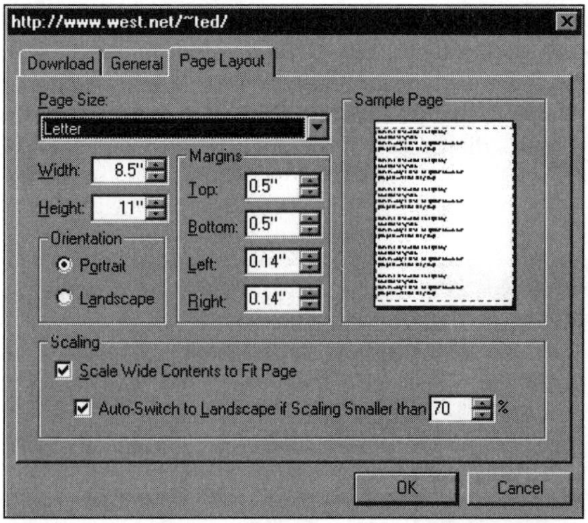

Figure 15-25: The Page Layout tab in the link properties dialog box provides options for changing the physical size of the converted pages.

- **Scaling:** Once again, because HTML documents don't follow standard page sizes, images and text can be easily clipped when converting to a standard size. When this option is enabled, the page contents will be reduced in size to fit within the page margins.

- **Auto-Switch to Landscape if Scaling Smaller than:** The percentage value is user definable. When the page contents appear on a portrait page within the limit specified in the field box, the PDF document will be automatically converted to a landscape page, and vice versa.

Preferences for converting PDFs

There are two menu commands related to preference settings for capturing Web sites. When File ➪ Preferences is selected, Weblink and Web Capture appear as submenu selections. Weblink relates to preferences for links in the converted file and Web Capture offers choices for showing the progress of the conversion and attributes of the converted file. In addition, there are several options available as menu commands under the Tools menu for controlling downloads. Although the latter are not preferences, there exists some choices you'll want to understand. Navigating around all the attribute choices can be downright confusing, so let's take these one step at a time. I'll first introduce the preference settings, and then move on to menu choices. When all is said and done, you have a chance to explore the steps in making your preference choices and then look at downloading a Web site.

Weblink preferences

Weblink preferences provide options for the display and behavior of Web links either while converting a document or after the document is converted. Depending on the option selected, the Web link behavior will be applied to one or the other. To open the WebLink Preferences dialog box shown in Figure 15-26, select File ➪ Preferences ➪ Web Link.

Figure 15-26: The WebLink Preferences dialog box provides options for determining the behavior of Web Links.

The WebLink Preferences dialog box contains the following attribute settings for Web links:

✦ **Link Information:** Choices are available from a pop-up menu for displaying the URL while the Option key (Macintosh) or Ctrl key (Windows) is pressed. The other choices include Always display or Never display the URL. The default is to display the URL with the Option/Ctrl key. When the Option/Ctrl key is pressed, the URL for the Web link will appear in a Tool Tip–like display below the cursor (see Figure 15-27).

Tip

When appending to a captured site, clicking a link to another level will append the newly converted pages to the open PDF document. If you wish the new converted pages to appear in a separate and new PDF document, keep the Ctrl key pressed when clicking a link. The converted pages will appear in a new document and leave the original PDF undisturbed.

Note

Inasmuch as you cannot capture Web sites on a Macintosh, a converted site performed in Windows can be opened on a Macintosh. The structure of the PDF document will appear the same, including all internal links, links to the Web, and structured bookmarks. The PDF can be edited on either platform. Options for structured bookmarks will be limited to editing PDF documents without the inclusion of options requiring downloading or updating sites (see Figure 15-28).

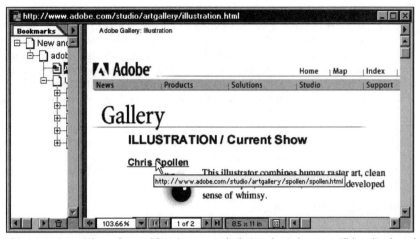

Figure 15-27: When the Ctrl key is pressed, the Web Link URL will be displayed if the cursor is placed over a link. In order to display the URL, the Link Information option in Web Link Preferences must be set to Control Key to Display or Always display.

Figure 15-28: When a converted PDF document from Windows appears on the Macintosh, options for structured bookmarks will be limited to editing locally on the saved PDF document.

✦ **Show Toolbar Button:** The Toolbar Button is used to open the default Web browser. The tool icon appears in the Command Bar at the top right of the Acrobat window. Don't confuse this tool with the Open Web Page button, which appears on the left side of the Command Bar (Windows only). When the option is disabled, the tool for Open Web Browser will be removed from the Command Bar.

✦ **Show Progress Dialog:** When Acrobat downloads Web pages, a status information dialog box will appear when this option is enabled. The download time and amount of data transferred from the server to your computer will be displayed.

✦ **Web Browser Application:** You can use either Microsoft Internet Explorer or Netscape Navigator to view the Web page links. Click the Browse button to select your browser of choice. A navigation dialog box will appear, enabling you to locate a browser installed on your computer.

Note Some interactive features of PDF links require the use of Microsoft Internet Explorer. For example, when viewing a PDF document in a Web browser and clicking a link to another PDF file, the link won't open the second PDF document when using Netscape. Nor will embedded PDF documents in the HTML code contain active links in Netscape. Links for inline PDF documents will open other pages in Netscape, but not other PDF files. The browser application selected in the Web Link Preferences dialog box for viewing Web links, however, can be either Netscape or Internet Explorer.

✦ **Connection Type:** This pop-up menu provides choices for either Microsoft Internet Explorer or Netscape Navigator/Communicator. If you use another type of browser, select the Standard option, also available from the pop-up menu.

Web Capture preferences

The Web Capture preferences are available by selecting File ⇨ Preferences ⇨ Web Capture (see Figure 15-29). The attribute settings further identify Web Link behavior as well as options available for converting a Web site to PDF. The choices appearing in the Web Capture Preferences dialog box are listed here:

✦ **Verify Stored Images:** From the pop-up menu, options are available for verifying images stored on a captured Web site once per session, always, or never. When the default setting, Once Per Session, is selected, Acrobat will check the Web site to see if stored images have changed on the site. If changed, the new files will be downloaded.

✦ **Open Weblinks:** You can elect to open Weblinks in either Acrobat or the default browser, which was identified in the WebLink Preferences dialog box. When the browser is used, clicking a Web link in the converted PDF document will launch the browser and open the URL for the associated link. Inasmuch as the link originated from the PDF document, the view will appear on the Internet.

Tip Regardless of which option you elect to use for opening Web links, the alternate method can be used by pressing the Shift key and clicking the link. For example, if the preference setting is used to display the link in the Web browser, Shift+click will display the link in Acrobat and vice versa.

✦ **Consolidate Menu Items in Top-level Menu:** At first, this option may seem a bit redundant. When this item is enabled, the menu options found by selecting Tools ⇨ Web Capture (see Figure 15-30) are reorganized and included in a new menu titled Web. The new menu is added to the menu bar and appears to the right of the Tools menu (see Figure 15-31). Rather than having to use a submenu, which includes only one keyboard modifier for one of the options, the new menu makes for easier access to the commands.

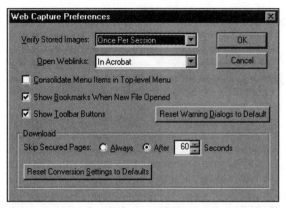

Figure 15-29: The Web Capture Preferences dialog box opens when selecting File ➪ Preferences ➪ Web Capture.

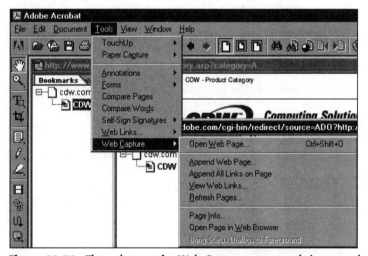

Figure 15-30: The submenu for Web Capture commands is opened by selecting Tools ➪ Web Capture. Navigating to these commands takes a little more time because you need to select the menu and then choose the desired command from among the submenu items.

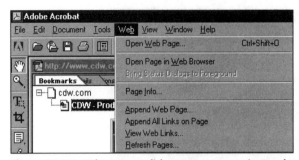

Figure 15-31: When Consolidate Menu Items in Top-level menu is enabled in the Web Capture Preferences dialog box, a new menu appears with the same commands illustrated in Figure 15-30. The order for the commands appears different, but the menu choices are identical.

✦ **Show Bookmarks When New File Opened:** When this option is enabled, the converted PDF file will be displayed with the Navigation Pane open and the structured bookmarks appearing in the Bookmarks tab. When this option is disabled, the Navigation Pane will be closed, but the bookmarks will still be created.

✦ **Show Toolbar Buttons:** The button on the top left of the Command Bar is the Open Web Page button. When this item is enabled, the button is displayed.

✦ **Reset Warning Dialogs to Default:** When you first capture a site in an Acrobat session, a warning dialog box will appear, informing you the operation may take a long time to complete (see Figure 15-32). An option in the dialog box enables you to eliminate the warning during subsequent downloads. To regain access to this or other warning dialog boxes, enable Reset Warning Dialogs to Default. The next time the same command is invoked, a warning dialog box will reappear.

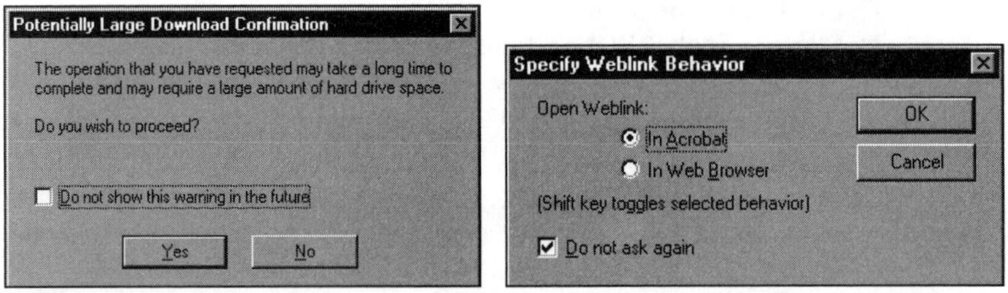

Figure 15-32: Warning dialog boxes like these can be eliminated from further display by enabling the Do Not Ask or Do Not Show option. To have the warning boxes reappear, select Reset Warning Dialogs to Default in the Web Capture Preferences dialog box.

✦ **Skip Secured Pages:** Secured areas of a Web site can be downloaded, but you must have permission to access the secured areas. If you inadvertently attempt to download a secure area, you can elect to always skip secured pages or skip secured pages at specified intervals ranging between 1 and 9999 seconds.

When you enter a secure area of a Web site, Acrobat provides an opportunity to supply a login name and/or password. The dialog box shown in Figure 15-33 will automatically open for secure sites.

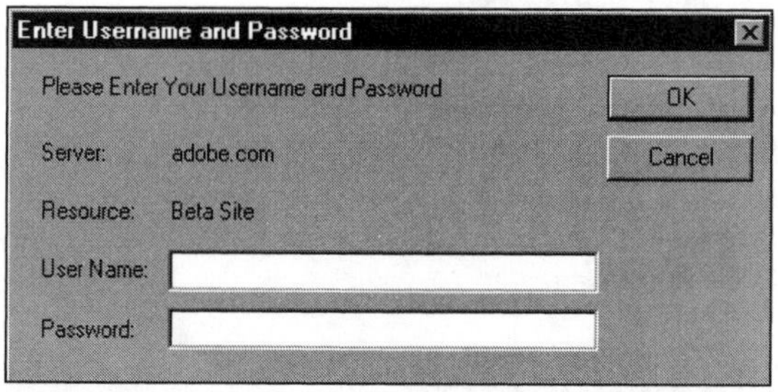

Figure 15-33: When attempting to capture Web pages on a secure site, you'll need to access the site with a username and password.

Acrobat will continue to try to gain access to a secure site until the time interval established in the Web Capture Preferences dialog box has been reached. In the dialog box that appears when you try to download secured pages, notice the time remaining in the specified interval is displayed. When no access is granted, an error dialog box will open, displaying an error message and the URL where the access attempt was made (see Figure 15-34).

✦ **Reset Conversion Settings to Defaults:** Clicking this button will reset all options in the Web Capture Preferences dialog box back to the default positions established when Acrobat was first installed.

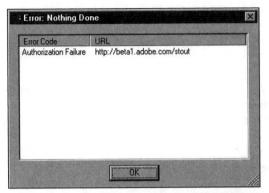

Figure 15-34: An error dialog box will appear when access to a secure site has failed. Adjacent to the error code, notice the display of the URL where the download attempt was made.

Web Capture menu commands

In the preceding section, you had a glimpse of the commands available for capturing a Web site. The commands appear in the Tools submenu; or, if you've turned on the Consolidate Menu Items in Top-Level Menu option in the Web Capture Preferences dialog box, the commands will appear in the Web menu. Regardless of the menu display, the attribute choices from the dialog boxes appearing for the respective menu command will appear the same. The menu commands enable more options for Web Link behavior and converting Web pages to PDF. The commands displayed in the Web menu include the following:

✦ **Open Web Page:** This menu command offers the same options as are available by clicking the Open Web Page tool in the Command Bar (see Figure 15-35). Before the site is captured, you'll have an opportunity to choose the URL and the number of levels to be converted. The Conversion Settings button is also available, which brings up a dialog box that enables you to determine the general conversion options and page layout specifications for the converted pages.

✦ **Open Page in Web Browser:** The page viewed in the converted PDF document will have a URL link. When Open Page in Web Browser is selected from the Web menu, the currently viewed PDF page will open in the default Web browser from the URL address.

✦ **Bring Status Dialogs to Foreground:** When downloading a site, a status dialog box will appear, displaying the download status. After the first level is downloaded, the status dialog box will move to the background and be hidden behind the newly converted PDF document as the download continues. While the download continues, you can work in Acrobat on the downloaded file or any other PDF document. If you wish to see the download status, you can select this menu item to bring the status dialog box to the foreground.

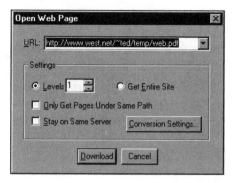

Figure 15-35: The Open Web Page command enables you to make choices for the URL to be converted and the levels to be downloaded. The Conversion Settings button will open a dialog box in which general conversion and page layout attribute choices are made.

Tip

If you wish to determine whether the download is continuing without moving the status dialog box to the foreground, observe the Open Web Page tool in the Command Bar. When the globe appears to be turning, Acrobat is still downloading files. When the globe stops turning, the download will be complete.

✦ **Page Info:** Document information applies to the entire PDF document. When pages are converted from a Web site, the General Document Info dialog box only includes a generic name for the Title field — the other field boxes are left empty. Page information, on the other hand, can be assessed for each individual page in the converted PDF document (see Figure 15-36) by issuing the Page Info command. Information for each page will include the URL address where the page was captured, a filename, date, and content type.

✦ **Append Web Page:** Pages can be appended to the converted PDF document while it remains open by selecting this command. When the Append Web Page command is invoked, a dialog box containing the same options as the Open Web Page dialog box appears. To review these attribute settings, see Figure 15-35.

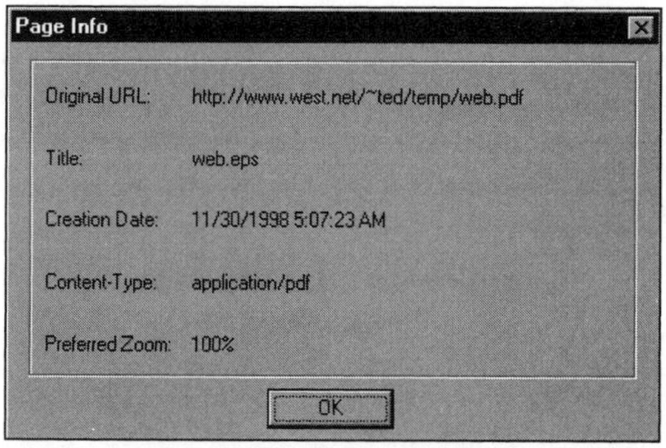

Figure 15-36: The Page Info command displays an information dialog box containing the URL address from which the Web page was downloaded.

✦ **Append All Links on Page:** If you download a site and choose one or several levels for the conversion, some links may be left without destinations. This can occur if the destination is another level, or if you instructed Acrobat to stay on a server and the links are made to other servers. When Append All Links is selected from the Web menu, only those pages with direct links to the currently viewed page will be appended. A status report for this command will appear in the Download Status dialog box, as illustrated in Figure 15-37.

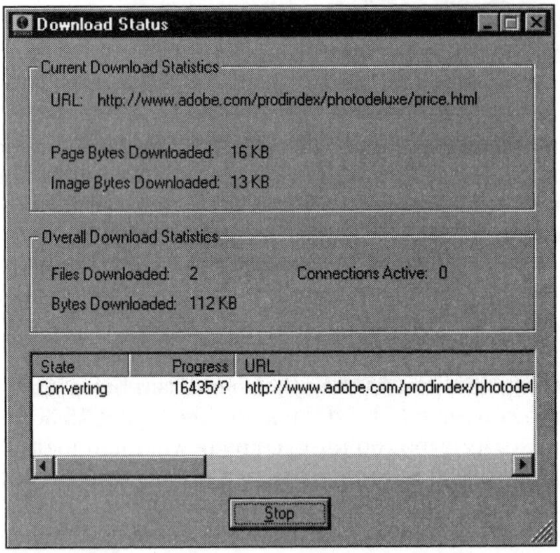

Figure 15-37: When appending links to a PDF page, the Download Status dialog box will display the download progress. This dialog box is the same as the one viewed when downloading a Web site or appending pages to the PDF file.

✦ **View Web Links:** Web Links can be viewed from individual pages in the converted PDF document. To view a page's links, navigate to the PDF page and select View Web Links from the menu options. The Select Page Links to Download dialog box will appear with the link URLs listed, as shown in Figure 15-38. This command also lists any structured bookmarks that may be contained on the page viewed.

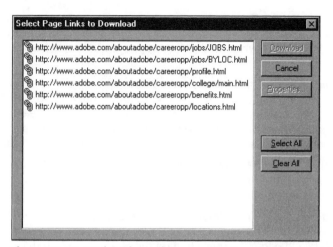

Figure 15-38: Web Links to the currently viewed PDF page and any structured bookmarks contained on the page will be listed in the Select Page Links to Download dialog box. The Download and Properties buttons will appear inactive when no link is selected in the list box.

In the Web Link list box, you can select a listed link and download the page individually. You can select multiple links in contiguous order by using the Shift+click method in the list box and then download the selected pages. A group of pages listed noncontiguously can be selected by using the Ctrl+click method. When no pages are selected in the list box, the Download and Properties buttons will be inactive.

✦ **Refresh Pages:** The Refresh Pages command will update all structured bookmarks along with the converted PDF pages. When you select the menu command, the Refresh Pages dialog box will appear, offering several attribute choices for the updated bookmarks and pages, as shown in Figure 15-39.

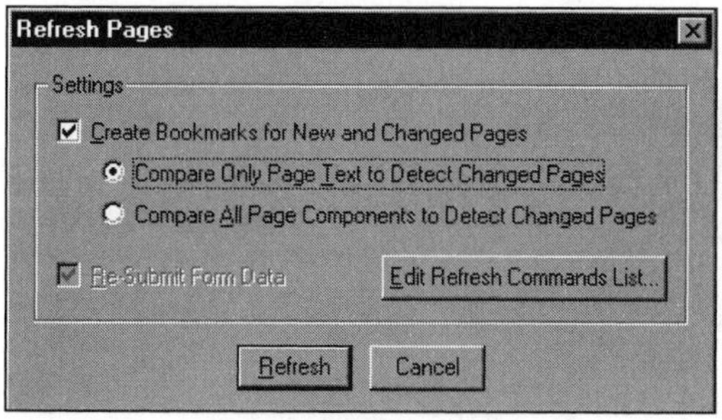

Figure 15-39: The Refresh Pages dialog box provides options for updating structured bookmarks and PDF document pages.

✦ **Create Bookmarks for New and Changed Pages:** To enable this option, you must also select one of the two choices listed below the item. Regardless of which item is selected, when enabled, the update will create bookmarks for new and changed pages.

• **Compare Only Page Text to Detect Changed Pages:** The criteria for assessing a changed page will be compared against the text in the Web page to determine whether it will be updated. If images are changed, but not text, the page won't be updated. However, depending on the way images are saved, some updates can occur with image changes.

• **Compare All Page Components to Detect Changed Pages:** Any changes to Web page contents and/or formatting code will update the page and structured bookmarks.

✦ **Re-Submit Form Data:** This option will only be active if a form and query results appear on the PDF pages. When the option is active, resubmitting the query for data will occur. Changes in data fields will be updated.

✦ **Edit Refresh Commands List:** When you select the button for this item, a dialog box will open similar to the one in Figure 15-38. You can select individual links to include in the update from the list.

✦ **Refresh:** When all attributes for the updates are made, click Refresh to update the pages. Only pages conforming to the options settings will be updated.

Menu commands rearranged from the Tools ➪ Web Capture submenu all appear under the Web menu when the Consolidate Menu Items in Top-Level Menu option is active. Two other menu commands exist under the Tools ➪ Weblink submenu that remain as submenu items. Because these commands don't move to the Web menu, to access them you'll need to select Tools ➪ Weblinks ➪ Create (or Remove).

✦ **Create:** When Tools ➪ Weblinks ➪ Create is selected, links to the URLs embedded in the open PDF document will be created. In order to access the command, a PDF file must be open in Acrobat. When the command is invoked, all Web links in the file will be created for the pages you specify in the Create Web Links dialog box, shown in Figure 15-40.

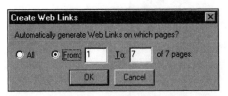

Figure 15-40: The Create Web Links dialog box enables you to select the range of pages in the PDF document from which the links are to be created.

✦ **Remove Weblink:** Conversely, when Tools ➪ Weblinks ➪ Remove is selected from the menu, all associated links to the Web will be removed from the document. Links to other internal PDF pages will remain in effect. If you wish to view a link in a browser that has been removed, you'll need to go back to the Create Web Links dialog box and reestablish the link. When either Create or Remove is selected from the submenu, a second dialog box will appear, displaying the results of either creating or removing links (see Figure 15-41).

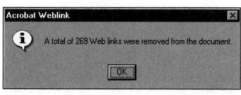

Figure 15-41: Through the Weblinks submenu command Remove, I elected to remove the links for seven captured pages. The second dialog box that appeared informed me of how many links were removed.

Capturing a Web site

The number of options available for converting Web pages and controlling the behavior of Weblinks may seem overwhelming when you first attempt to capture a site. There is no substitute for practice; the more you use the tools and options discussed earlier, the more proficient you'll become at converting Web sites to PDF documents. To help simplify the process, let's take a look at some steps for converting Web pages. In order to perform these steps, you need to be working in Windows 95, Windows 98, or Windows NT and with Microsoft Internet Explorer as your Web browser.

STEPS: Capturing a Web site

1. **Set the Web Capture preferences.** Before attempting to capture a site, review all the preference settings. To open the Web Capture Preferences dialog box, select File ➪ Preferences ➪ Web Capture. In the dialog box, click the Reset Warnings to Default button and click Reset Conversion Settings to Default. Use Acrobat's default settings for this capture. Click OK after making the changes.

2. **Set the Web link preferences.** Select File ➪ Preferences ➪ Weblink. The default settings should display Control Key to Show for the Link Information option, and both check boxes below Link Information enabled. If your default Web browser is not Internet Explorer, select it from the pop-up menu or click the Browse button and find Explorer on your computer. Click OK when the attributes have been defined.

Continued

3. **Click the Open Web Page tool.** Because the default preference settings include showing the Open Web Page tool in the Command Bar, you should see the globe icon appear on the top left of the Command Bar. Click the globe icon to display the Open Web Page dialog box.

4. **Enter the URL for the site to be captured.** You can use any site on the World Wide Web. If you have a company Web site, use the URL for your site. If not, pick a site. The URL must be complete, so verify the address before proceeding.

5. **Enter the number of levels to capture.** If working with a modem connection, you should first attempt to capture only a single level, especially if you are not familiar with the site structure. If you have a faster connection, try capturing two levels. Enable the options for downloading files under the same path and staying on the same server (see Figure 15-42).

6. **Click the Conversion Settings button in the Open Web Page dialog box.** You can elect to use Acrobat's default settings, or make some choices for bookmark attributes and how the HTML and plain text files will be converted. When the Conversion Settings button is clicked, the Conversion Settings dialog box will appear.

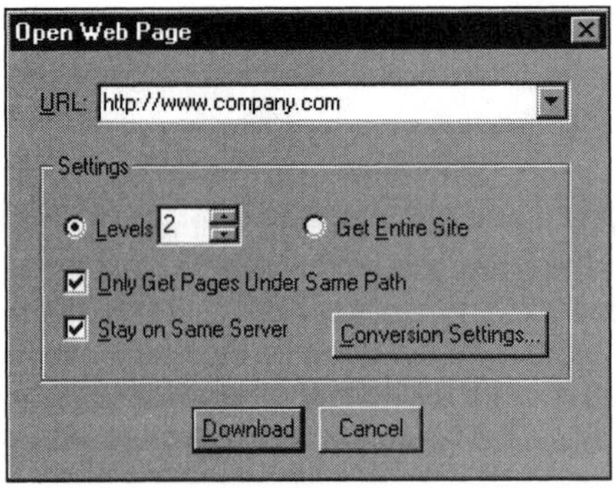

Figure 15-42: The Open Web Page dialog box for this example includes the option choices shown here.

7. **Determine Bookmark attributes.** Enable all options in the Conversion Settings dialog box (see Figure 15-43). In particular, the Add PDF Structure will add the HTML structure to the structured bookmarks, which Acrobat will create.

8. **Define the HTML conversion attributes**. You can customize the conversion from HTML documents to PDF. To open the HTML Conversion Settings dialog box, select HTML in the Conversion Settings dialog box illustrated in Figure 15-43 and click the Settings button.

   Choices made for Layout and Font attributes are up to you. You can elect to change fonts and colors, backgrounds, and line wraps or leave them at the default values. The settings I used in my example appear in Figure 15-44. After completing changes to layout and fonts, click OK in the HTML Conversion Settings dialog box.

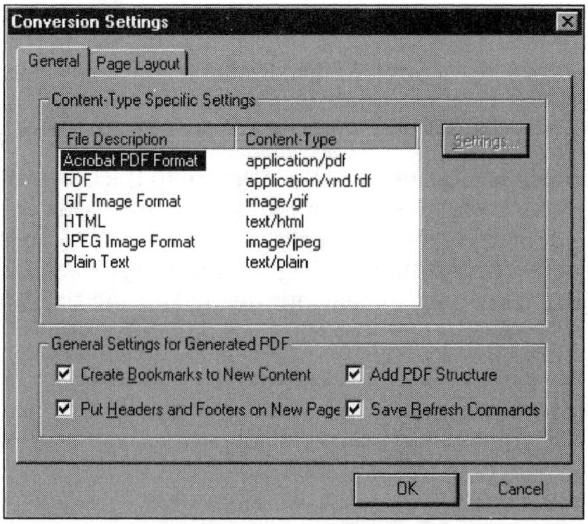

Figure 15-43: The Conversion Settings dialog box provides options for several general settings related to the bookmarks created and information that will appear on the PDF pages.

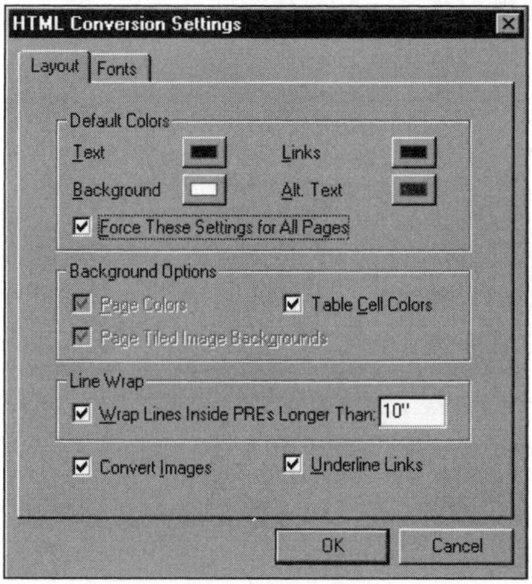

Figure 15-44: The HTML layout attributes used in my example are illustrated in Figure 15-44. I elected to force the settings on all pages and use underlining for the Web links.

Continued

9. **Define the plain text conversion attributes.** Select Plain Text in the Conversion Settings dialog box and click the Settings button. In the Text Conversion Settings dialog box, define the attributes you wish to use for text conversion. You can elect to use either the default settings or change fonts and colors and use font embedding. Click OK after making the changes.

10. **Define the page layout attributes.** When you return to the Conversion Settings dialog box, click the Page Layout tab (see Figure 15-45). Set the page attributes for your converted files. If you want the page size to be less than a letter-sized page, define the Width and Height for the page sizes. Use scaling to keep the data within the page dimensions defined for the size. Click OK when finished.

11. **Capture the site.** After all the attributes have been defined for the conversion, click OK in the Conversion Settings dialog box. You will be returned to the Open Web Page dialog box. Click the Download button to begin downloading the site.

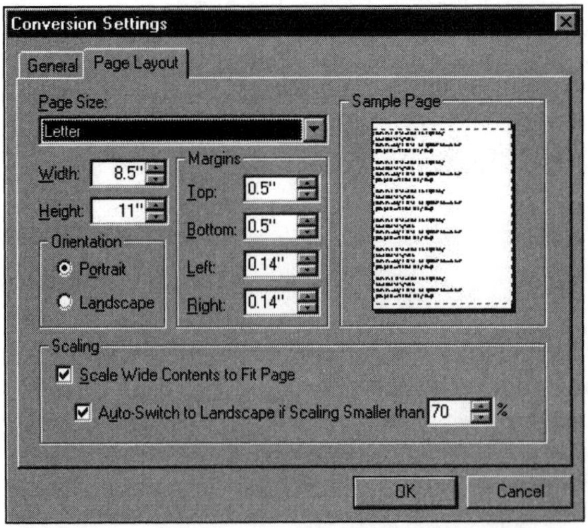

Figure 15-45: The Page Layout dialog box provides options for page size and scaling for the converted pages. In my example, I defined the attributes as illustrated here.

12. **View the download progress.** If your connection is slow, and it appears as though the computer is sluggish, files are continuing to download. You can easily determine whether files are downloading by observing the globe for the Open Web Page tool. To display a progress dialog box, select Tools ➪ Web Capture ➪ Bring Status Dialogs to Foreground.

13. **Stop the progress.** If an inordinate amount of time passes and you wish to stop the download, click the Stop button in the Download Status dialog box. Acrobat will display all PDFs converted from Web pages before the Stop was invoked.

Regardless of whether you downloaded the entire site or stopped the download progress, you'll end up with the converted pages appearing in Acrobat. The PDF document can be edited or saved for further use. If you save the file, appending Web pages can be accomplished in other Acrobat sessions at a later time. If you performed the preceding steps, save the file to use it later for working through some editing steps.

Converting pages locally

Capturing a Web site can be done locally from your hard drive. Because a hard drive won't have a URL that can be found with the Open Web Page tool, another method must be used. To convert a Web page or a site, first be certain all the files for the Web site are contained in a single directory. Open the home page or Level 1 page in a Web browser directly from the hard drive. To convert the file, the view of the Acrobat icon or a shortcut created in a folder or on the desktop must be visible. From the browser window, you need to find the Web site icon. The icon will usually be located next to the location URL listed in the browser window. Different browsers and different versions of browsers may have the icon located in different places. In Microsoft Internet Explorer version 4.x, the icon, displayed as the Explorer icon, is located adjacent to the address line.

To capture the site, drag the icon just described to the Acrobat application icon or a shortcut icon. When you release the mouse button, Acrobat will be launched and the conversion will commence (see Figure 15-46).

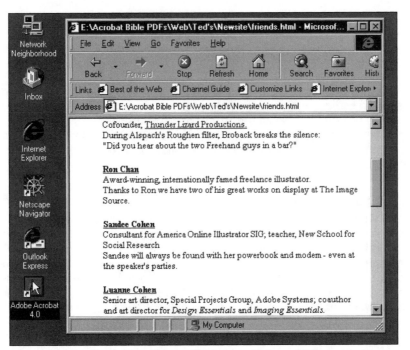

Figure 15-46: I dragged the icon adjacent to address, which appears next to the URL location in the Explorer window, to the shortcut for Acrobat resting on my desktop. When the mouse button was released, Acrobat was launched and the HTML document was converted to PDF.

Comparing Captured documents

Links can be followed from a PDF and a download executed to place the new conversions into a second PDF document. If you capture a site and later capture the same site, you can compare the PDF pages with a menu command in Acrobat. Acrobat will analyze all pages and report back any discrepancies found. To compare documents, you must have two files open together in Acrobat. Select Tools ⇨ Compare Pages. If the documents are long, it will take some time to analyze the files. When Acrobat completes the assessment, a new document will be created with the identical pages displayed as facing pages in a single new file. The original files will be left undisturbed. The first two pages in the new document will contain information found during the analysis (see Figure 15-47). If discrepancies were found, they will be reported on the first page. All subsequent pages will include the page matches, which can be viewed as facing pages (see Figure 15-48)

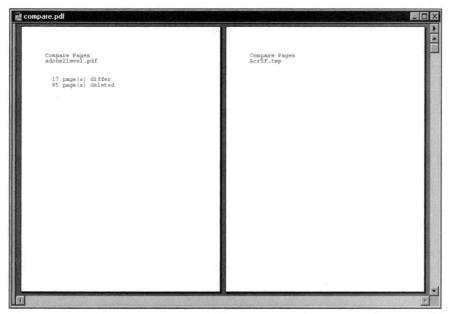

Figure 15-47: When the Compare Pages command is invoked, a new document will be created. The first two pages in the document will report the comparison between the files.

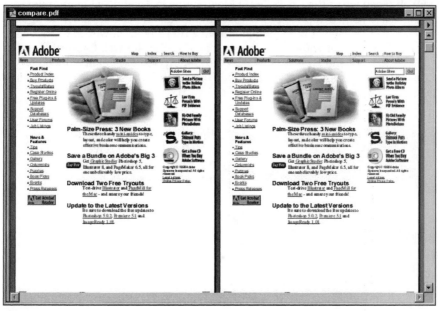

Figure 15-48: The following pages in the resultant document will contain all the page matches.

Working with Captured Web Sites

After a Web site has been captured, you may wish to return to the PDF document to update information, make changes to the file, or follow some Web links, which will also be converted. Acrobat provides several means for appending and editing PDF documents converted from Web sites. Both menu commands and structured bookmarks offer options for editing captured pages. Page modifications within Acrobat can be performed on either the Macintosh or Windows. Appending pages, however, will require the use of Acrobat running under Windows.

Appending Web pages

There are several reasons to use the Append Web Page command. If you download a single level for a site in one Acrobat session and later wish to add more converted pages from the same site, you might append the newly downloaded pages to the existing document. Another reason for appending pages might be to follow a series of links to other sites where information related to the original site can be found. Acrobat offers several methods for dealing with appending pages to a captured document.

Using the Append Web Page command

The Append Web Page command is found in the Tools ⇨ Web Capture submenu (or the Web menu when the Consolidate Menu Items in Top-Level Menu preference setting is active). To append pages to a PDF document, the file must be open in Acrobat. You can select the command from either menu, however, it will be more convenient for you if you enable the Web menu from the Web Capture preferences. When Web ⇨ Append Web Page is selected, the Append Web Page dialog box will appear. The same options offered in the Open Web Page dialog box appear in the Append Web page dialog box (see Figure 15-49).

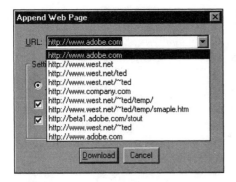

Figure 15-49: The Append Web Page dialog box features a pop-up menu containing a list of URLs last visited.

The first item to select is the URL. If you wish to append pages to the existing document from the same server, you need to verify the URL is correct. When the

URL pop-up menu is selected, as shown in Figure 15-49, the URLs last visited will appear. If the URL is not listed in the pop-up menu, you can obtain the correct URL in several ways. One method would be to copy the URL from a link on the page and paste it in the URL field box in the Append Web Page dialog box. To perform this task, cancel the Append Web Page dialog box and find a link on one of the pages. If you know the order of the pages and the related links, navigate to a page where a logical link to another level might appear.

Move the mouse cursor over a URL link and right-click the mouse button. A context-sensitive menu will appear, as shown in Figure 15-50. From the menu choices, select Copy Link Location. Reopen the Append Web Page dialog box and press Ctrl+V. The URL will be pasted into the field box for the Web address.

Note When the Append Web Page dialog box is open, you don't have access to the menu commands. Therefore, you will not be able to select Edit ⇨ Paste. Use the keyboard modifiers to paste the data (Ctrl+V).

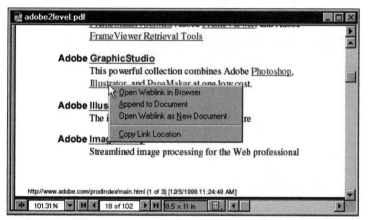

Figure 15-50: When the cursor appears over a Web link, right-click the mouse button and select Copy Link Location. The copied URL can then be pasted into the URL address list in the Append Web Page dialog box.

From the context-sensitive menu, you can also select the Append to Document command. When this command is selected, you won't have a choice for specifying the number of levels or the attributes for the conversion. Acrobat will use the last attribute definitions supplied in the Open Web Page or Append Web Page dialog box.

Another method for obtaining the URL for converted pages is to examine the footer. If Put Headers and Footers on New Page was enabled in the General Conversion Settings dialog box when the original document was captured, the footer data will include the URL for respective pages.

Once the URL is supplied, you can make choices for the general settings, the attribute choices for HTML and plain text files, and the levels of the site you wish to append to the current document. When the attributes have been determined, click the Download button. As the download occurs, all new pages will be appended to the end of the document.

Let's look at adding to the captured site created in the last series of steps:

STEPS: Append HTML Pages to a PDF Document

1. **Open the PDF document created in the preceding exercise.** If you don't have a document available, you'll need to convert a site, as explained earlier.

2. **Select Web ➪ Append Web Page.** If the Web menu is not available, select Tools ➪ Web Capture ➪ Append Web Page.

3. **Select the new level to capture.** If you captured a single level during the last series of steps, select a second level by entering 2 in the Levels field box, as shown in Figure 15-51.

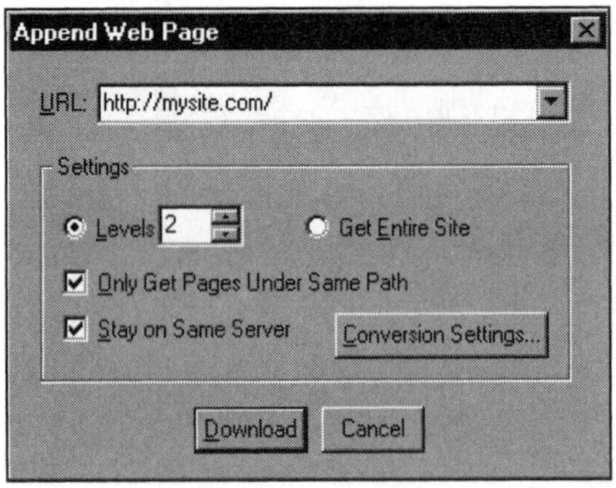

Figure 15-51: I selected a second level of pages for appending to my existing PDF document by entering 2 in the Levels field box.

4. **Select the conversion attributes.** Once the attribute settings have been made in the Conversion Settings dialog boxes, the same settings will be used for all additional captures. If you wish to change any attributes, you can make them by clicking the Conversion Settings button. In my example, I want the appended pages to adhere to the same options, so I left the settings as they were last identified.

5. Click Download in the Append Web Page dialog box. When you click the Download button, Acrobat begins to download Web pages and starts the conversion. All newly converted pages will be appended to the existing document.

Appending pages with structured bookmarks

Another method for appending more converted pages to the open PDF document is to use a structured bookmark. Open the Navigation Pane to display bookmarks. To append pages using a bookmark command, the bookmark must be a structured type. Unstructured bookmarks won't provide a choice for appending pages. In the Navigation Pane, the structured bookmarks will appear with an icon or mini-thumbnail beside them. Unstructured bookmarks will appear as thumbnails with blank pages. Move the mouse cursor over a structured bookmark and right-click the mouse button. From the context-sensitive menu, select Append Next Level. Acrobat will then begin capturing the next level below the selected bookmark and related URL.

When you use a structured bookmark for capturing Web pages, you don't have an opportunity to define the levels to be captured. Using the command from the context menu will capture all files one level below the related URL. Append Next Level can also be selected from the Bookmark palette menu. Be certain a structured bookmark is selected and click the right arrow to open the palette menu. Append Next Level will appear as a menu item.

Appending pages by following a link

If you first convert pages and set the attributes for the Only Get Pages Under Same Path and/or Stay on Same Server options, links to other servers will be ignored. If you wish to return to the PDF document and append pages by following a link, you can capture pages contained in different directory paths and on different servers. To follow one or more links, use the Web menu, a context-sensitive menu for a structured bookmark, or the Bookmark palette menu.

From any one of these menus, select View Web Links. The Web links will be displayed in the Select Page Links to Download dialog box, as shown in Figure 15-52. The list of links relates to the page in view in Acrobat or the bookmark that was selected from either the context-sensitive menu or the palette menu. Therefore, be certain to navigate to the page or bookmark that contains the link you wish to follow before opening the dialog box.

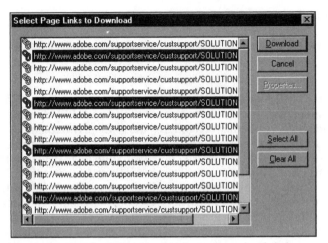

Figure 15-52: The Select Page Links to Download dialog box will display all links on the current viewed page or selected structured bookmark.

In the list of URLs, select the link(s) you wish to follow. Multiple noncontiguous selections are made by Ctrl+clicking among the listed items. When finished with the selection, click the Download button to begin the conversion. To illustrate following a link further, walk through these steps:

STEPS: Convert Pages by Following a Link

1. **Open a converted document in Acrobat.** If you followed either of the exercises in earlier sections, use the file converted to PDF. In order to follow these steps, you'll need a document containing links. If you don't have one available, try downloading another site.

2. **Select Web ➪ View Web Links.** You can use either the Web menu or Web Capture submenu. When the menu selection is made, the Select Page Links to Download dialog box will appear.

3. **Change the properties for the download.** If you make more than one selection in the list of links, the Properties button will become inactive. When choosing two or more links to follow, you need to change the properties individually. Select a single link in the list box and click Properties.

4. **Change the properties to enable following the link.** As illustrated in Figure 15-53, make the appropriate choices in the dialog box. If more than two links

are to be included, change the properties for the second link. Click OK in the dialog box after making the changes to the properties.

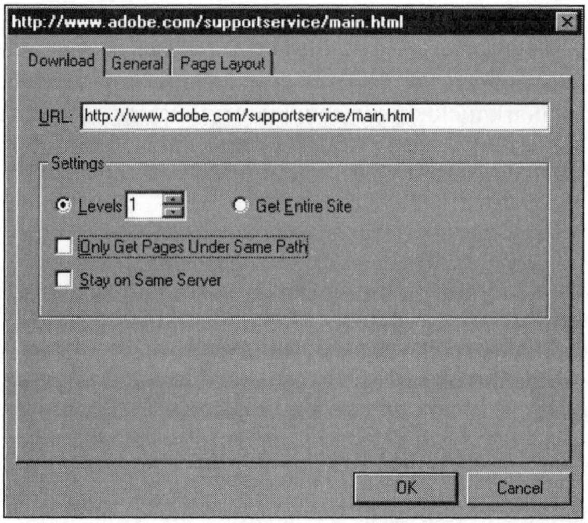

Figure 15-53: After clicking the Properties button, deselect Only Get Pages Under Same Path and Stay on Same Server. When these items are enabled, you won't be able to follow a link to other servers or directories.

5. **Click Download to begin the conversion.** When you return to the Select Page Links to Download dialog box, click the Download button. Acrobat will begin the download and conversion. The converted pages will be appended to the open document.

Tip   When downloading files from a site, be certain to let Acrobat continue its download before attempting to download additional sites or links. If a download is in progress and you click a link, a second download will occur simultaneously. Several simultaneous downloads may create a system crash, or they may not be easy to stop. If you try to stop a download and the download still continues, close the Acrobat window. Your file will be lost, but you may be able to recover without a system crash. If the download status dialog box still displays a download progress, quit Acrobat. Wait until the status dialog box disappears, and then relaunch Acrobat. Try to download fewer levels on your next attempt.

Editing with bookmarks

Bookmarks can be used to organize captured pages, delete unwanted pages, and edit properties associated with the bookmark. Both structured and unstructured bookmarks can be used for editing the PDF document. When downloading files, it will be best to ensure bookmarks are created during the download or when appending pages to the document. The Open Web Page and Append Web Page dialog boxes control bookmark inclusion in the general settings. Keep these options enabled and also verify the Add PDF Structure item is checked in the General Settings dialog box. By default, it will most often be a feature you'll use.

Ordering pages

When a Web site is captured, files are downloaded and appended to the last converted page. The page order may or may not be logical or the way you wish to have them appear. Pages can be reordered with the bookmarks created during the download. Bookmarks follow the same logic as was discussed in Chapter 9. Any structured or unstructured bookmark can be a subordinate to a parent bookmark.

Moving bookmarks

Bookmarks are repositioned and reordered by selecting them in the Navigation Pane and dragging up or down the bookmark list. To create a subordinate bookmark, move it up or down and slightly to the right of the parent bookmark.

Nested bookmarks can be moved while maintaining the same family relationships (see Figure 15-54). A parent and one or more child bookmarks are moved by dragging the parent up or down the bookmark list.

Moving bookmarks and pages

By default, when you move a bookmark, the page order will not be affected. The bookmark list will change according to the order you drag the items in the list but will still link to the same pages. If you want to move bookmarks and reorder pages together, press the Ctrl key and then click and drag the bookmarks. The associated pages will move to the same position in the document as reflected in the bookmark order.

Deleting bookmarks

Bookmarks can be deleted from the Navigation Pane by selecting the bookmark and striking the Del (Delete) key. As long as Skip Edit Warnings is not enabled in the General Preferences dialog box, a warning dialog box will appear requesting confirmation for the deletion. If you select OK, the bookmark will be deleted. Bookmarks can also be deleted from a context-sensitive menu or by using the Bookmark palette menu. Select the menu command for Delete or Delete Bookmark(s), respectively.

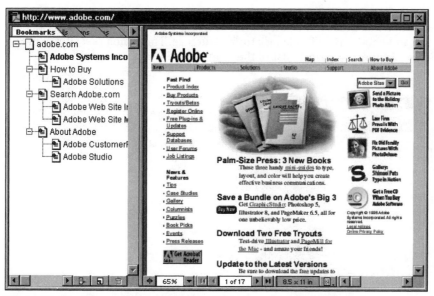

Figure 15-54: When a site is captured, all bookmarks will appear at the same level. You can nest bookmarks and create subordinates by dragging the bookmark up or down the list and slightly to the right of first-level bookmarks.

Deleting bookmarks and pages

When a bookmark is deleted, the bookmark will be eliminated, but the associated page will remain in the document. You can use bookmark deletions to also delete the respective pages. To delete both items, select one or more bookmarks and choose Delete Page(s) from either a context-sensitive menu or the Bookmarks palette menu.

Adding structured bookmarks

A bookmark can be added to the converted document by selecting the New Bookmark command from a context-sensitive menu or the Bookmarks palette menu. When bookmarks are created from these menu choices, they are created as unstructured bookmarks. If you enabled the option Add PDF Structure in the converted files, you can also create new structured bookmarks. Adding a PDF structure will include many HTML tags along with the conversion. When structured bookmarks are added to the converted document, Acrobat looks at the converted page and determines what HTML structure was used. If, for example, a table was used in the document, you may have an option to link the bookmark view to zoom in on the table. The same applies for hypertext references, titles, heads, preformatted text, and so on.

To create a bookmark from a structure, select a structured bookmark in the Navigation Pane. Use either the context-sensitive menu or the bookmarks palette menu and choose New Bookmark from Structure. The dialog box shown in Figure 15-55 will appear, offering a list of the items found in the structure.

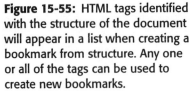

Figure 15-55: HTML tags identified with the structure of the document will appear in a list when creating a bookmark from structure. Any one or all of the tags can be used to create new bookmarks.

When the dialog box for New Bookmarks from Structure appears, select the items you want to have included as bookmarks. When a checkmark is applied to a list item, bookmarks will be created for the associated tags found in the original HTML file. Acrobat will begin to create bookmarks from the structure interpreted in the document. When you view the Navigation Pane, as shown in Figure 15-56, the new bookmarks will appear below the bookmark selected when the command was invoked. Clicking one of the new bookmark items will display the page and zoom view associated with the bookmark.

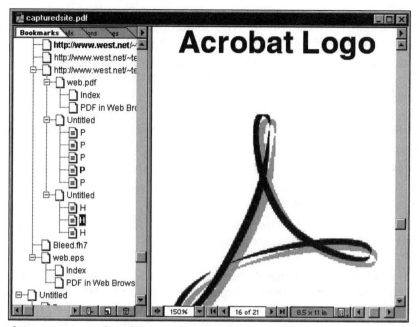

Figure 15-56: Bookmarks created from structure are listed in the Navigation Pane. When a bookmark is selected, the page will be displayed at the zoom level associated with the bookmark.

Summary

✦ Web pages are created in the Hypertext Markup Language. HTML has some advantages over PDF for Web page display, whereas PDF has some distinct advantages over HTML. Web site designs can be effective when using both PDF and HTML.

✦ PDF pages can be displayed and/or downloaded from the Web in several ways. A PDF file can be embedded in the HTML document by using the <EMBED> tag. PDF documents can be viewed by accessing the URL and viewing the page as an inline image, which provides access to many Acrobat tools inside the Web browser. And PDF pages can be saved to disk for viewing after disconnecting from the Internet.

✦ In order to view PDFs as embedded or as inline images, the Web browser must be properly configured.

✦ Many interactive features are available only with Microsoft Internet Explorer. Some features for PDF links and interactivity are not available with Netscape Navigator.

✦ HTML documents and many of their associated links can be captured by Acrobat and converted to PDF. When capturing a site, it is important to know the structure of Web sites and the many levels of Web pages.

✦ Web Capture is only available when running Acrobat under Windows 95, Windows 98, or Windows NT. Web Link and Web Capture are not available for the Macintosh.

✦ Weblink and Web Capture preferences provide many options for changing the behavior of Web links and defining attributes for converted pages.

✦ Web pages can be converted to PDF with all links and Web addresses preserved in the PDF document.

✦ Captured pages can have structured bookmarks assigned to each page. The bookmarks can be reorganized in Acrobat and used to order the PDF pages.

✦ Web pages can be appended to converted PDF documents, and individual links can be followed to append additional pages from other servers and directories.

✦ Unstructured and structured bookmarks can be used to modify page orders. Structured bookmarks can be used to create new bookmarks from the page structure.

✦   ✦   ✦

Printing and Digital Prepress

In This Chapter

Distilling PostScript files for printing devices

Printing PDF files

Printing color separations

Using transfer functions

Printing for variable data devices

By now you might feel that Acrobat is quite an amazing product. It has many uses, as discussed in the previous chapters. To add to Acrobat's amazing capabilities, Acrobat is an exceptional application for printing and prepress imaging. Many of the problems experienced in imaging centers can be overcome if Acrobat PDF files are prepared properly. For the end user, any streamlining of files intended for high-end output will save time and money. In this chapter, you'll look at printing PDF files and high-end output, which is defined as printing to equipment such as imagesetters, large inkjet printers, dye-sublimation printers, film recorders, on-demand printing systems, and high-quality color devices. In short, you'll look at preparing files for office printing and commercial imaging usually found at service bureaus and print shops.

Preparing Files for Printing

There are several steps necessary to image PDF files on high-end devices. The first of these steps is to ensure proper distillation of the file from which the document was created. In this chapter I only discuss distilling PostScript files as a method of creating PDFs, since this method is the only recommended means for outputting your documents. In Chapters 5 and 6, creating PDF files is discussed and the various settings for Distiller's Job Options are explored. In this chapter, I discuss the recommended Job Options for using Distiller to create PDFs for specific output devices. The first step in preparing files for output begins with the design elements and subsequently continues with creating the PostScript file.

Layout design

Assuming you may later want to take files originally created for printing proofs to desktop instruments and have them imaged on high-end devices at imaging centers, you can create a single PostScript file that can be repurposed by Distiller for several different devices. In this scenario, it will be best to create your design using images suited for the most high-end device through which you intend to send output. This is to say, if the final output is a film separation at a 150-line screen, use images in the original layout that will support such output. Three hundred dpi images would be used in this example. If the file is to be proofed on a desktop printer, you can let Distiller handle the downsampling for the original PostScript file and then redistill the file for the more high-end device.

Preparing the PostScript file

In many cases, a single PostScript file can be printed and redistilled for output to several different devices. In some cases, you may need to create two different PostScript files for imaging. To be certain your PostScript file will be usable for multiple PDFs created for different devices, follow these simple guidelines for generating the PostScript file:

✦ **Proper PPD selection:** If a device PPD is chosen when printing the PostScript file, some attributes may not be available when redistilling the file. For example, if you choose an imagesetter PPD, and wish to redistill the PostScript file for output to a color printer, in some cases, the color information may not be retained in the PostScript file.. To avoid such problems, use the Acrobat Distiller PPD. If you experience any problems when imaging the PDF, you may need to return to the authoring program and print to PostScript using the device PPD. Most printing devices will accept the Acrobat Distiller PPD, so try this one first and use it if no problems are experienced.

✦ **Include fonts in the PostScript file:** There may be times when you might print the PostScript file from one computer and distill the same PostScript file on another computer. If the same fonts used in the original file are not available in a folder that Distiller monitors for font inclusion, the fonts will not be embedded in the PDF file. To avoid such a problem, always include fonts in the PostScript file.

✦ **Use the proper encoding and PostScript level:** As a default, use binary encoding and PostScript Level 2 when they appear in the Print dialog box. Use these as defaults unless you encounter any problems with special devices preferring PostScript Level 1.

✦ **Set the halftone frequency:** Choose the halftone frequency for the device with the highest level of output. Distiller can control preserving the halftone frequency or not preserving it. By not preserving frequency, the file will be imaged at the device default. With desktop printers and almost all composite printing devices, the output device will use a device default frequency. Imagesetters, on the other hand, can have the frequency default changed manually by the imaging personnel. If you distill a file for an imagesetter, you can use the PostScript file frequency to create the PDF, which will preserve what you set up in the authoring application and override any defaults established by technicians at the imaging center.

✦ **Accommodate bleeds and page sizes:** If files contain bleeds and oversized pages, you have two choices when imaging to different devices. Create two PostScript files or create a single PostScript file for the device that can handle bleeds and larger page sizes. For example, if a letter-size page contains a bleed, you won't be able to print the entire page on a desktop proofer that only permits printing on 8.5-×-11-inch paper. If you wish to create a single PostScript file, you can use an option in Acrobat's Print dialog box to shrink the page size to fit on the paper supported by your printer.

✦ **Downsampling with Distiller:** Distiller can downsample images to the sampling size you specify in the Compression Job Options. My recommendation to you is to do all your sampling in Photoshop for the imagesetter requirements prior to printing the PostScript file. When distilling the PDF to be used at the imaging center, don't use Distiller's downsampling. When outputting to proofing systems requiring less resolution, use the downsampling available in Distiller's compression settings. For example, assume you wish to color-separate a file for a 150-line screen. Sample all your images to 300 dpi in Photoshop and print the file to disk as a PostScript file. If you wish to see a color proof generated from a machine such as a desktop color proofer, distill the PostScript file using downsampling to 150 dpi. If the proof looks fine, redistill the original PostScript file without downsampling for the color separations. In Acrobat 4.0, you can easily save Custom Job Options for each device used. Just keep the PostScript file handy for redistillation when you need to print to a different device.

✦ **Separating duotones:** The one thing Acrobat can't successfully handle is duotone separations. If you wish to print separations from duotone images, you need to perform the separation at the time the PostScript file is printed. In this case, you can't use the PostScript file for printing composites and separations, so two different PostScript files would be needed. For the imagesetter output, print separations with printer's marks and separation angles defined in the authoring application. When the PDF files are viewed, a different page will contain each individual color.

✦ **Don't convert colors in Distiller:** Distiller affords you an opportunity to convert CMYK colors to RGB. Some printing devices like desktop color printers and large format inkjet printers prefer RGB images over CMYK. Film recorders always use RGB. If you know your device prefers RGB, don't use Distiller's Job Options to convert the colors. Use RGB images in the authoring program and distill the PostScript file without color conversion.

✦ **Use proper formats for the imaging device:** In some cases, TIFF images will appear better than EPS. When separating files on imagesetters or platesetters, EPS will often be the choice. Knowing which image format is best for the device used will require some testing. RGB TIFFs tend to be better for large inkjet printers. CMYK EPS files are best for IRIS printers, imagesetters, and platesetters. When sending files to an imaging center, ask the technicians which color mode and file format is preferred for the devices they have.

Not all imaging solutions can be specified in a definitive recipe. If you use the preceding guidelines as a starting point, you can make some changes as you encounter problems with specific devices. Regardless of the designs you create and the service center used, some periodic testing will be needed.

Distilling PostScript Files

Once the PostScript file attributes are known, the file needs to be distilled with Acrobat Distiller. Acrobat Distiller 4.0 offers three options among which you choose a default for selecting different Job Options. When outputting to printing devices, the PressOptimized and PrintOptimized Job Options can be used as a starting point. However, you may wish to make some custom changes to these settings and save the settings as a Custom Job Options file. When preparing a PDF for output to a specific device, load the Custom Settings as needed.

Customizing Job Options

The high-end output Job Options settings are those identified for the PressOptimized Job Options. As you view the tabs in the Distiller Job Options window, you'll see the defaults shipped with Acrobat and recommended for printing files to devices like imagesetters and platesetters. Let's walk through these Job Options and review the settings.

General Job Options

The first tab in the Job Options settings is where you will find the General Job Options, shown in Figure 16-1. From this dialog box, you make selections for compatibility and some format choices.

✦ **Compatibility:** The default is Acrobat 4.0. Leave this option unchanged. The PDF file will be created in the newer version 1.3 format.

✦ **ASCII Format:** The check box is disabled and should be left as is. Because this example uses binary encoding, this option shouldn't be enabled.

✦ **Optimize PDF:** When enabled, the file will be optimized. Leave this setting unchanged to produce smaller file sizes.

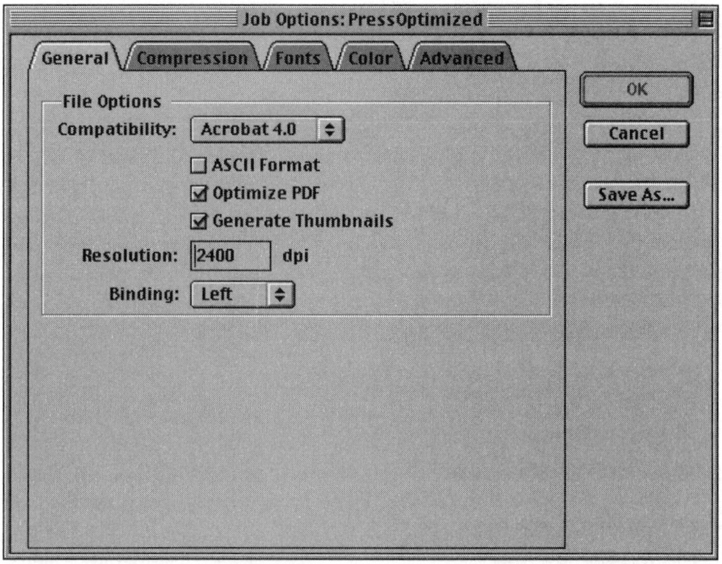

Figure 16-1: The General Job Options defaults are first displayed when you open Acrobat Distiller.

✦ **Generate Thumbnails:** The default is enabled. Disable this check box. Thumbnails will add approximately 3K for each page in the PDF file. They will be unnecessary when printing PDF files.

✦ **Resolution:** The default is 2400. A 2400-dpi resolution will add about 3K to the file size over a 600 dpi resolution setting. As a rule, leave it at 2400.

✦ **Binding:** The default is Left. Leave this item unchanged. Binding will have no effect on the printed image.

Compression

The next tab controls the compression settings, as shown in Figure 16-2. If files are prepared properly in Adobe Photoshop, you won't have a need for downsampling when imaging to prepress systems, but be certain to use the proper compression. If a PostScript file was created for prepress and is to be repurposed for desktop output, use the PrintOptimized Job Options and change the settings for downsampling and compression as needed for the output device.

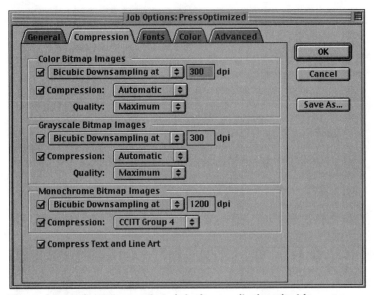

Figure 16-2: The Compression defaults are displayed with downsampling for images set at 300 dpi and compression set to maximum quality.

✦ **Color Bitmap Images:** If the proper sampling was applied in Photoshop, there will be no need to use any downsampling. The first check box can be on or off. If your images are sampled at 300 dpi, and downsampling is checked with a 300-dpi resolution, the PDF file will be created without any downsampling.

Compression should be left at Automatic and Maximum Quality. In some cases, you can compress files more than the Maximum Quality without loss in detail. But rather than take any chances, always use Maximum when sending files for digital prepress.

✦ **Grayscale Bitmap Images:** The same applies for Grayscale as Color Downsampling and Compression. Use the same settings as mentioned above.

✦ **Monochrome Bitmap Images:** Photoshop line art that is a monochrome bitmap follows one simple rule for determining resolution. Image resolution should equal device resolution. When printing files to imagesetters at 1200, 2400, or 3600 dpi, you won't need more than 1200 dpi for the image resolution. If you sampled the file in Photoshop at 1200 dpi for imagesetter output, you need not be concerned about whether this check box is on or off. Just like the bitmaps above, no downsampling will occur when the resolution is equal to the number placed in this field box. As a default, use CCITT Group 4 for the compression method.

✦ **Compress Text and Line Art:** This option should almost always be on. If you find any fallout with rules with point sizes less than .5 points — especially at diagonal intersections, then disable the option before distilling the file. Also, any small fonts (that is, smaller than 6 point) with tiny serifs may also need to be distilled without this compression. You may find this necessary when the print is used for creating paper plates from RC paper printed at 1200 dpi.

Fonts

The Fonts tab, shown in Figure 16-3, enables font selection for embedding in the PDF file. You can identify font directories for Distiller to watch for finding fonts to be embedded in the file. If the fonts were included in the PostScript file, the file can be distilled without the fonts resident on the machine using Distiller.

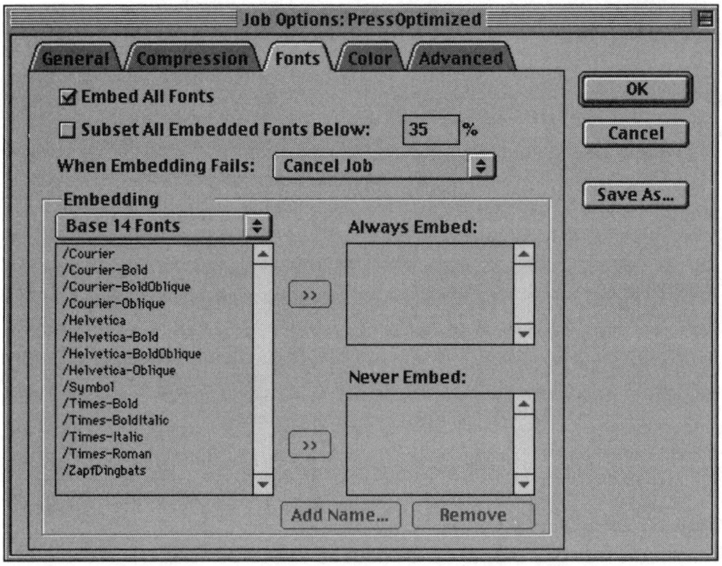

Figure 16-3: The default settings for fonts include embedding fonts without subsetting.

✦ **Embed All Fonts:** The option is enabled by default and should be left as it appears. You always want to have the fonts embedded in the PDF, especially when the file is printed at the service center.

✦ **Subset All Embedded Fonts Below:** The default is off. Check this box and set the percent field to 99%. The entire character set for a given font will ultimately be embedded in the PDF, as opposed to only the characters used below the 35% default setting.

✦ **Always Embed and Never Embed:** These two list boxes are blank by default. It is rare that the same font contained in the PDF and on the PostScript RIP presents any problem. Therefore, you need not be concerned about listing fonts to not embed. When the Embed All Fonts option is enabled, you don't need to identify any fonts to be included by listing them in the Always Embed list.

Color

The color settings enable you to control color profiles and various options for press-ready conditions. The defaults first encountered in these Job Options are identified in Figure 16-4.

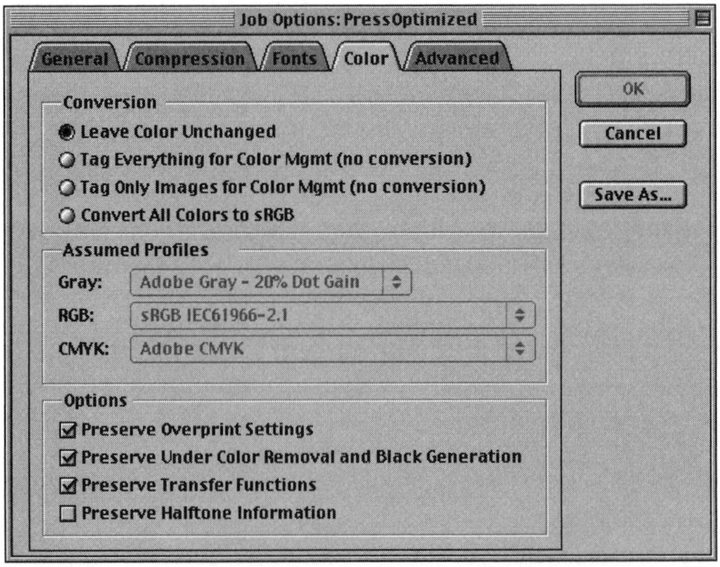

Figure 16-4: The default for color handling is to leave the color unchanged. If profile tagging is desired, you can select from any ICC profiles created or installed on your system.

✦ **Leave Color Unchanged:** The default is enabled for not changing color in the images to be distilled. Regardless of whether you use a Color Management System (CMM), leaving the color unchanged will always work well when printing files. If you define an RGB color working space in Photoshop and embed an ICC profile, leaving the color unchanged will handle the color output as it would be handled in any other application. If confused about all the color handling variables, just leave this option enabled as a default.

✦ **Tag Everything for Color Management (no conversion):** If you use device-independent color and wish to select from a monitor display and a CMYK ICC profile, you can select from the pop-up menus the color system you use.

✦ **Tag Only Images for Color Management (no conversion):** You can elect to tag files for either all graphics and color selections in a document or only imported images. This option only tags the images. Use the same guidelines as mentioned previously if image tagging is desired.

✦ **Convert all Colors to sRGB:** For printing and prepress, don't use this option. This conversion is suited for screen displays or Web use.

✦ **Assumed Profiles:** If color is left unchanged, no options will be available for selecting profiles. If you use ICC profiles, make the appropriate selections from the available choices in the pop-up menus for Gray, RGB, and CMYK.

✦ **Preserve Overprint settings:** Trapping is usually best handled at the imaging center. If there are some cases where manually set overprints are used in a file, it is necessary to leave this enabler on. As a default, leave it enabled.

✦ **Preserve Under Color Removal and Black Generation:** Unless you have included UCR/GCR in a Photoshop file, this item will have no effect on the printed document. As a default, the enabler is checked. Leave it at the default.

✦ **Preserve Transfer Functions:** Also, unless Transfer Functions have been embedded in images, this item will have no effect on the final printed page. As a general rule, leave it at the default.

✦ **Preserve Halftone Information:** If preparing a file for imagesetters and platesetters, and the PostScript file was printed with halftone frequency choices, enable this option.

Advanced

Advanced settings offer a number of miscellaneous attribute choices used for creating PDF files for prepress output. The defaults are displayed in Figure 16-5.

✦ **Use prologue.ps and epilogue.ps:** This option is disabled by default. As a matter of rule, drag the prologue.ps and epilogue.ps files from the Distiller:Data folder to the same level as Distiller. In the event you edit either file in a text editor, make a copy of the originals and relocate the copies to the Distiller folder. Enable the option to use these files when running Distiller. Keep this option enabled as a default.

✦ **Allow PostScript File to Override Job Options:** This option is enabled by default. When Distiller encounters a difference between settings embedded in the PostScript file and those from Distiller's Job Options, the PostScript file will supersede Distiller's Job Options. If you wish to have Distiller's Job Options take precedence, disable the option. Because it was recommended earlier that PostScript files be created for the highest level of output, as a default, leave this option enabled. Only those options conflicting between Distiller and the PostScript file will be changed.

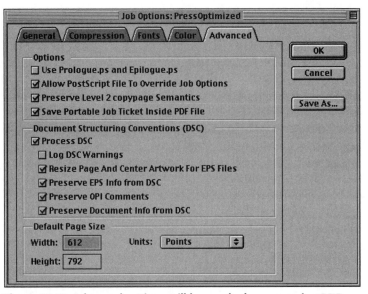

Figure 16-5: Advanced settings will be used when preparing PDF
files for PressOptimized jobs.

✦ **Preserve Level 2 copypage Semantics:** You should check with the imaging
center to find out if they are using PostScript Level 2 or PostScript 3 RIPs.
When the imaging device uses a Level 2 RIP, enable this option. If the imaging
center uses a PostScript 3 RIP, disable the option.

✦ **Save Portable Job Ticket Inside PDF File:** For all output on high-end devices,
leave this option enabled. Job tickets contain information about page sizes,
frequencies, resolution, and so on.

✦ **Process DSC:** Document structuring conventions contain information about
the file such as originating application, creation date, page orientation, and so
on. Keep this checkbox enabled as a default.

✦ **Log DSC Warnings:** Enable this option to have any errors written to a log file.
This will help diagnose any problems in distilling the PostScript file. In many
cases, if a file can't be distilled, it won't be printed on a PostScript device. You
can open the log file in a text editor to review any distillation errors.

✦ **Resize Page And Center Artwork For EPS Files:** Leave this option enabled.
Centering EPS artwork will avoid problems with clipping and centering the
EPS bounding box.

✦ **Preserve EPS Info From DSC:** Leave this option enabled. As a rule, don't
distill EPS files directly. It's best to place an EPS file in a layout program to
create the final PostScript file.

✦ **Preserve OPI Comments:** Leave this option enabled for output to service centers.

✦ **Preserve Document Info From DSC:** For printing files, enabling this option won't have any effect. As a default, leave it on in the event you need to review the document information.

✦ **Default Page Size:** Changing page sizes only relates to EPS files. If you place EPS files in layout applications and then create the PostScript file, you won't need to manually set the page size. You can leave the defaults as they appear.

The preceding recommendations for Distiller Job Options were made for prepress systems. If printing to desktop printers, use the same settings as just listed, but change the downsampling and compression to meet the requirements of your printer. Save the settings made for each device where the Job Options change, and load them as needed when distilling PostScript files.

Printing PDF Documents

If PDF files are created for printing to desktop proofers or laser printers, the printing can be performed from within Acrobat. If PDFs are printed to prepress devices, other methods will be needed. If PDFs are printed to PostScript 3 devices, they can be sent direct to the imaging system. Depending on the device and the tools installed on your computer, you have several options from which to choose. The preparation and distillation of the file must be appropriate to the device used, as explained previously.

Printing to desktop printers

Desktop printers and low-end color proofers will most often be the first step in printing a PDF document. If files are prepared for digital imaging at a service center, you'll want to print the file first on your desktop system, and then send the file to the imaging center. Desktop systems come in many different varieties. PostScript printers are the most common among laser printers, whereas desktop color printers are more common as non-PostScript devices. If you have a desktop color printer, you may have an option to purchase a PostScript interpreter for your printer. Ideally, using a PostScript printer will be a better choice when printing a proof that will eventually end up at an imaging center. However, Acrobat PDF files can be successfully printed to non-PostScript devices. When the Print Setup and Print dialog boxes are opened, several options are made available to accommodate different printing devices.

Printing to PostScript printers

Printing from Acrobat is similar to printing from application files. First you open the Print Setup (Windows) or Page Setup (Macintosh) dialog box. In Windows, the printing device selection is handled in the Print Setup dialog box. Macintosh users need to select the Chooser and identify the printer driver before opening the Print dialog box. On Windows, the port for your printer should be set up to print directly to the device. If the port is set to print to File:, then a PostScript file will be created. Choosing this option defeats the purpose of using a PDF file. In Windows, you can also make the page size selection from the Print Setup dialog box. Click OK after making this selection, and you're ready to move to the Print dialog box.

On the Macintosh, when the Page Setup dialog box opens, click the Options button. The next dialog box displays several options for the printer selected in the Chooser dialog box (see Figure 16-6). Under Printer Options, several check boxes will be toggled on by default. Be certain to disable Substitute Fonts, Smooth Text, and Smooth Graphics. If Larger Print Area is enabled, the image can appear about $1/8$ inch closer to the page border. Select this options a default. If your printer generates a PostScript error by downloading too many fonts, try disabling this option.

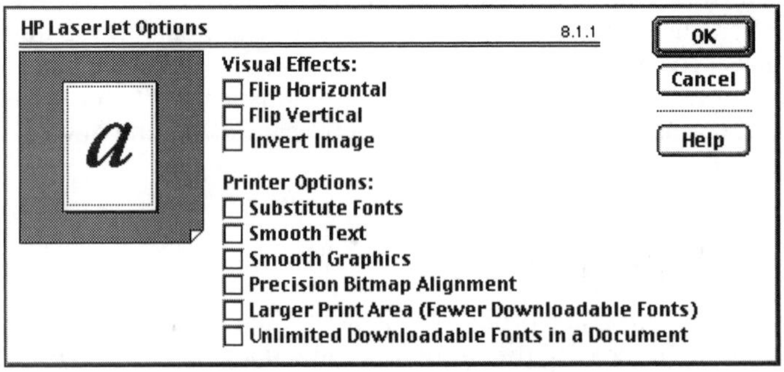

Figure 16-6: On the Macintosh, disable the check boxes for Substitute Fonts, Smooth Text, and Smooth Graphics in the Page Setup dialog box.

After the Print Setup (Windows) and Page Setup (Macintosh) options are selected, open the Print dialog box by selecting File ➪ Print. The Print dialog box on both platforms provides the same options from which to choose. (Figure 16-7 shows the Windows Print dialog box; Figure 16-8 shows the same dialog box on the Macintosh.) A few of these options will be important when printing PDF documents.

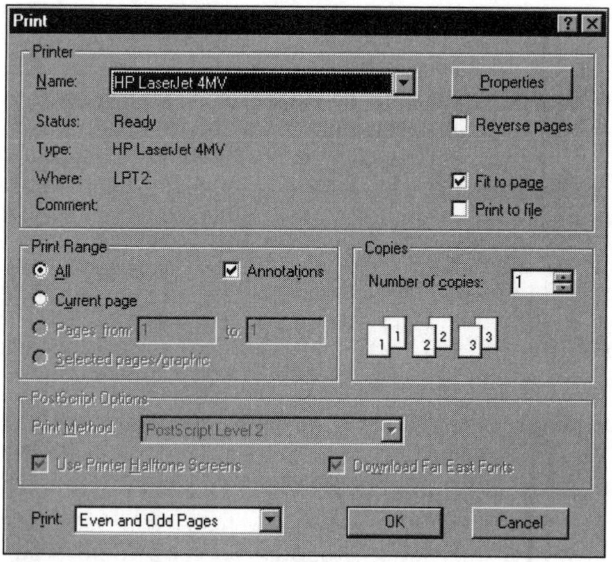

Figure 16-7: The Print dialog box is displayed for an HP LaserJet PostScript printer.

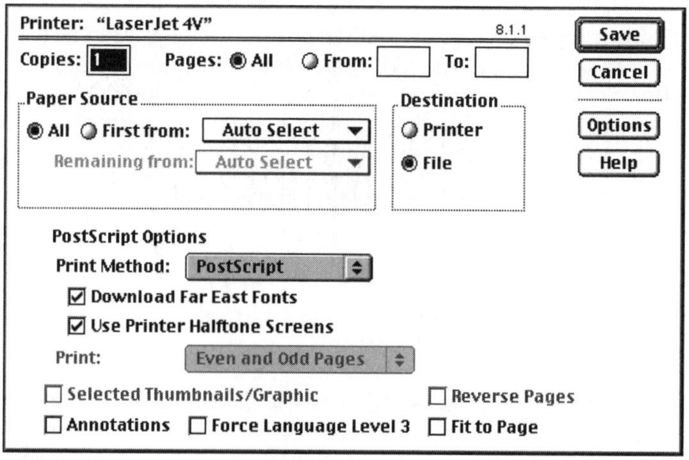

Figure 16-8: The same options are available for the same printer in the Macintosh Print dialog box.

Options to choose in the Print dialog box when printing from Acrobat include the following:

✦ **Fit to Page:** If the file was prepared for a device with a larger page size, you can select the Fit to Page options, which will reduce the printable area to the page size selected for your printer. If a PDF has been created for output at an imaging center where the page size may be larger, you can proof the page on your laser printer to see a smaller print, which would include any bleeds and printer's marks.

✦ **Print to file:** Leave this option disabled. You should have your printer on line and print the PDF directly to the device. Printing to file would be redundant, as you could download the original PostScript file directly to your printer before the file is distilled.

✦ **Annotations:** For printing files as proofs for imaging, deselect the option to print annotations. If PDF documents are created for displays, and you wish to prepare prints for proofing screen views, you can print annotations created in the PDF.

✦ **Print Method:** Some devices may not offer options for the print method. If a PostScript printer is used, Acrobat may automatically choose the PostScript method for your printer. If you have a PostScript 3 printer, you may have a choice for selecting PostScript Level 2 or PostScript 3. If the choice is made available, choose the method corresponding to the level of your printer.

✦ **Use Printer Halftone Screens:** If the PostScript file has been prepared with a higher screening than accommodated by the printer, and the distillation included the PostScript file screening, be certain to enable this option. Laser printers use screening. If the screening is higher than can be accommodated by the device, the images will appear muddy.

✦ **Download Far East Fonts:** If character sets from the Far East have been used, you will want this option enabled. The check box can be left disabled when such fonts are not used.

The remaining choices for page order and the pages to be printed are handled the same in Acrobat as they are in other applications.

Tip If you have a low-end PostScript printer that has limited RAM, PostScript errors may be encountered when too many fonts are downloaded to the printer during printing. To help alleviate the problem, try printing fewer pages when printing the file. If the problem persists, try printing one page at a time. Downloading fewer fonts to the printer may eliminate a RAM overload.

Printing to non-PostScript printers

Many low-end desktop color printers do not ship with a PostScript interpreter. The color printers you can purchase for $600 or less will typically not be PostScript printers. Many of these printers can be outfitted with a PostScript hardware interpreter or a software RIP. If you haven't purchased a PostScript interpreter or RIP for a desktop color printer, you can often print PDF documents without the use of PostScript. There are many different models of non-PostScript printers, and each model ships with a different printer driver. It is important to review the printer documentation to understand the different options available in both the Print Setup/Page Setup and Print dialog boxes. Depending on the printing device and software shipped with the printer, choices for various print options will vary significantly.

Desktop color printers are continuous tone devices, so you need not worry about screening when printing the PDF. Other choices may be available for using device profiles and special attributes for ink choices, page sizes, and dithering. If the printer driver permits choices for the print method, you may have a selection to choose PostScript or Print as Image. If the PostScript method does not produce the print, try using the Print as Image method. Some errors generated while printing a PDF can be overcome by one or more of the following:

✦ **Print one page at a time:** In a multipage PDF file, try printing one page at a time. If the print buffer gets overloaded, you may experience problems.

✦ **Disable Fit to Page:** If Fit to Page is enabled, it may require more processing time to reduce the image size. Try turning this option off when printing. To print oversized pages, you can crop the pages to your output size in Acrobat before printing.

✦ **Use fewer fonts in the native file:** Font downloads and substitutions can overload the printer memory. If you experience problems with multiple fonts, try reducing the number of fonts in the authoring application and redistill the file.

✦ **Downsample images:** Be certain to sample images at optimum sizes for the device. Because desktop printers are continuous tone, you can't follow rules for image sizes related to frequencies. Most color desktop printers will have a recommended file resolution to be used. Downsample images to the recommended sizes or lower when printing PDF files.

✦ **Rasterize the PDF in Photoshop:** If PostScript is difficult to print, you can rasterize the PDF in Photoshop. Desktop color printers print raster images usually without a problem. Open the PDF in Photoshop and rasterize to the image resolution optimized for the printer.

✦ **Convert images to the proper color mode:** Some desktop color printers may prefer RGB images as opposed to CMYK. If the printer uses RGB, save the Photoshop files as RGB TIFFs and distill the PostScript file. If the same document is to be printed at an imaging center, two files will need to be produced. Be certain the high-end output PDF file uses CMYK images from the authoring application.

Regardless of the device used, you'll need to become familiar with the driver software and run some tests. Also, if you have an Internet connection, be certain to visit the Web site for your printer manufacturer. Many drivers are updated regularly, and the latest printer driver can often be downloaded from the manufacturer's Web site.

Printing to high-end devices

When files are printed to imaging devices at service centers, the controls for page sizes, screening, rotations, emulsion, and other such attributes require the use of a PostScript Printer Description (PPD) file. Acrobat does not permit PPD selection in the Print dialog box. Therefore, high-end imaging requires printing through other means. You have two choices when PPD selection is required. Either export the PDF as an EPS file that ultimately will be printed from another program, or use a third-party plug-in to print from within Acrobat.

Exporting EPS files

Acrobat offers an option to create an EPS file from within the application. EPS files exported from Acrobat will appear as though they were created in an EPS authoring application such as Adobe Illustrator or Macromedia FreeHand. The exported file will contain all the file attributes of the PDF, including embedded fonts and image links. To export an EPS file from Acrobat, select File ➪ Export ➪ PostScript or EPS. A dialog box will appear, prompting you for the attribute choices for the EPS file, as shown in Figure 16-9.

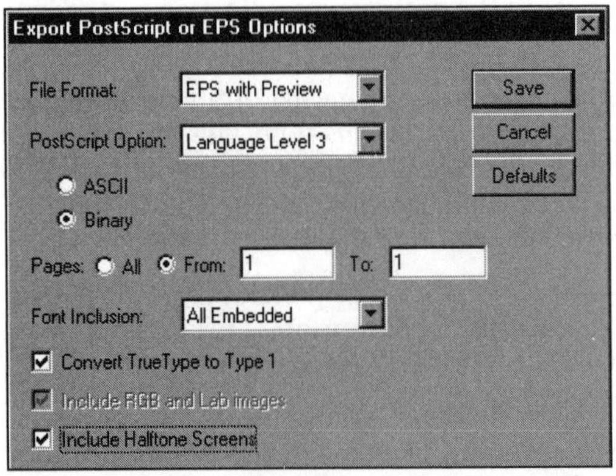

Figure 16-9: By selecting File ➪ Export ➪ PostScript or EPS, a dialog box will appear offering options for exporting the file to PostScript or EPS.

The Export dialog box enables writing the file either as PostScript or EPS. When you select EPS with Preview from the Format pop-up menu, a screen image of the EPS file will be saved with the file. If you don't include the preview, the file will appear as a gray box when viewed as an imported EPS. You can print it, but you won't be able to see the image.

> **Tip**
>
> Whereas printing PostScript files are best handled by using binary encoding and PostScript Level 2, quite often exporting EPS files may require ASCII and PostScript Level I. If you have trouble importing EPS files or printing them properly, return to Acrobat and export as ASCII, PostScript Level I.

Page ranges can be included, enabling you to print more than one page at a time to EPS. Each page exported will be a separate EPS file, which makes the task difficult if a lengthy document has been converted to PDF. Ultimately, the EPS file will be imported into a program for printing or individually sent directly to the imaging system.

The Include Halftone Screens option behaves similarly to screening, as I discussed earlier. If the Include Halftone Screen option is disabled, screening can be controlled in the application from which the resultant EPS is printed.

The EPS file created from exporting to EPS will appear as though you created it from an illustration program. The file will print, separate, and accept the print specifications entered from the program that ultimately prints the file. You can choose to use a layout, illustration, or color-separating program for printing.

Several advantages exist with exporting EPS files from Acrobat. You can specify printer type and PPD, image output resolution, paper sizes, and halftone frequencies. When all the printing attributes are established, you can print the file. In the Print dialog box, selections for composite or separation, printer's marks, specifying colors, and so on can be made. All these controls will be necessary if printed to prepress systems.

Plug-ins supporting printing

Third-party manufacturers have special add-on software that make many printing attributes available without your needing to export a file as EPS. A plug-in designed for high-end output of PDF files is Crackerjack, from Lantana Research Corporation. More information about Crackerjack can be obtained from the Lantana Web site at www.lantanarips.com.

Crackerjack performs all the tasks necessary for printing PDFs directly from within Acrobat. When you open a PDF file in Acrobat, Crackerjack is available by selecting File ➪ Crackerjack. The plug-in loads separately under the File menu. When accessing the plug-in, a Print dialog box will appear, enabling you to select a PPD and perform all the print selections needed for imaging. There are four tabs in the dialog box for selecting print attributes relative to the document, pages, output, and color, as shown in Figure 16-10.

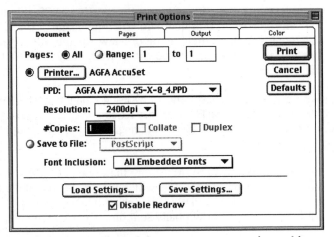

Figure 16-10: Crackerjack from Lantana Research provides for PPD selection and all the attribute settings needed for imaging PDFs to all devices.

This plug-in is a vital supplement to Acrobat for anyone needing the print controls from PPD options. With Crackerjack, printing color separations, choosing emulsion, converting colors to CMYK, and so on can all be performed in Crackerjack's dialog box (see Figure 16-11). The same print options appear as you find in applications such as Adobe PageMaker or QuarkXPress.

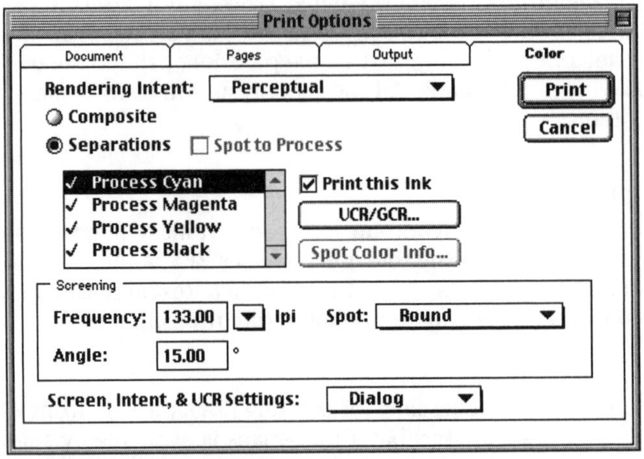

Figure 16-11: Among other attribute settings, Crackerjack permits printing color separations from PDFs and converting spot color to process color.

To help automate workflow, settings made in the Print dialog box for Crackerjack can be saved as a custom settings file. When documents requiring the same printing attributes are imaged, the custom settings can be loaded in Crackerjack's Print dialog box.

Tip When PostScript files are printed from an authoring application as separations then distilled in Acrobat Distiller, the final PDF should be printed as a composite with Crackerjack. When printing separated files, be certain to view the Color window in Crackerjack and manually set the proper color angles.

Printing to PostScript 3 devices

One of the great benefits of PDF and PostScript 3 is direct imaging of the bitmap created by Distiller. Rather than working through the PostScript interpreter, PDFs can be accepted directly on a PostScript 3 RIP. These RIPs are not exclusively found at imaging centers. Many new desktop models are being introduced with PostScript 3. In order to submit a PDF to a PostScript 3 RIP, the device manufacturer needs to supply a utility for sending the PDF to the RIP or support the delivery of PDF files to hot folders. If you use any of the Print dialog boxes discussed previously, then the PDF is not being sent directly to the RIP, and you won't notice any difference in printing speeds.

PDF files submitted directly will almost always print faster than printing through a print dialog box. To give you an idea of the kind of time you can save, I recently printed a 1 gigabyte PostScript file on a PostScript 3 RIP that took two hours to image eight plates. The same file was distilled and printed, and the film was processed and cut all in 20 minutes. Because PDF will reduce file size, eliminate redundancy, and print faster when submitted directly to PostScript 3 RIPs, you'll often find similar time savings with almost all files.

Imaging centers will have utilities for controlling screening, resolution, and emulsion on their RIPs. Therefore, none of these controls need be embedded in the PostScript file. Of course, many service centers vary in how they handle printing to their devices. In some cases, a service center may ask you to control all these attributes before sending them the file. Additionally, if the file is to be separated, then the PDF will need to be printed as a separation prior to being submitted directly to a PostScript 3 RIP. When working with service centers, be certain to inquire about how the files should be assembled before submitting them and ask what level of PostScript is used on the devices.

Printing Color Separations

PDFs designed for color separation require some knowledge of separating documents, the device that will produce the separation, and the level of PostScript used. Process color separations can be handled without special attention to the PDF created, whereas spot color requires more care. If you are the author of the PDF and follow the guidelines suggested in this chapter, then printing color separations from a PDF should be of no problem. If, on the other hand, you receive a PDF file from another who has not followed essential guidelines for preparing files for digital prepress, there may be some need to find a workaround to image the file properly. There are three areas to examine for separating color: printing process color, printing spot color, and dealing with files that have color improperly identified in the PDF file.

Printing process color separations

Process color separations can easily be handled by exporting a PDF as an EPS file or printing through a plug-in like Crackerjack. When printing process color, always be certain to verify all colors in the document contain either cyan, magenta, yellow, or black. If a spot color exists in the file, then the spot color must be converted to process color. Color conversion can be performed either in the program that prints the EPS file or directly within Crackerjack.

Process color separations are printed as four separate plates containing the values for cyan, magenta, yellow, and black. Each plate prints with the halftone dots at separate angles. Cyan is printed at $15°$, magenta at $75°$, yellow at $0°$ (or $90°$), and black at $45°$. Printing each color at separate angles is as important as printing with proper frequency, page size, and emulsion settings. If two or more plates are printed at the same angles, a moiré pattern will appear. To ensure against moiré, imaging RIPs often use special screening and filters to make certain the colors will print at separate angles. Application software capable of printing separations will usually support the standard printer's angles. With regard to printing process color separations, you most likely will not need to be concerned about controlling these angles. Spot color, on the other hand, is a different matter.

Correcting process color problems

In a perfect world, you could leave the process color discussion at this point and move on to a lesson about printing spot color. Unfortunately, with the vast number of software applications out there and the crazy things people do with them, the world is far from perfect. Take desktop publishing, for example. "Why, give me a computer and I'll be a real graphic designer," cries the end user. Meanwhile, down at the imaging center, you'd think Godzilla had just terrorized the staff. Probably the single most dangerous element in high-tech imaging is the person who visits the local CompUSA, purchases a computer, buys a software application with a coupon clipped from the daily throw-away, works half the night, and then takes his or her file to the imaging center for a color separation. "Why I think I'll design my own business cards direct from my new computer, by gosh!"

Well, maybe I should not be so hard on the uninformed. The fact of the matter is many people will often use whatever tools they have at hand. If they are not aware of the technical issues related to digital imaging, they may not be informed about prepress and proper assembly of files. Regardless of where you are in the imaging world, you will no doubt at one time or another have a need to help resurrect a file that someone may have spent countless hours assembling in the wrong program. The most common problem experienced with regard to color-separating files is improper identification of color. This problem occurs with both process color and spot color, which I'll get to in a moment.

Business applications and the low-end layout programs do not provide the same level of sophisticated features as do professional applications like Adobe PageMaker and QuarkXPress. The former is used primarily with office documents designed for output to office printers. Professional applications, on the other hand, are designed for everything up to and including high-end imaging. Many of the more low-end programs support RGB color and do not offer the printing controls afforded by the high-end layout applications. So the eventual occurs — someone creates a design in an application that either can't image to a prepress system or needs to be modified for correct output.

Regardless of the program used to create a design, there is often a way to deal with this situation. You can try to correct some problems with program documents not supporting high-end output by printing the file to disk as a PostScript file. Because the controls for printing these files may not be available as I recommended earlier in this chapter, the PDF file you create from the PostScript file won't be used for printing. You need intervention from another source.

One of the best rescuers for such problems is Adobe PageMaker. In version 6.52 of PageMaker, you can import PDF files much like you import images. To import PDF files into PageMaker, you'll need to acquire the PDF Import Filter version 1.0 or higher. If you have PageMaker 6.5, an updater for version 6.52 as well as the PDF Import Filter can be found on Adobe's Web site. Follow the guidelines described in the readme file for installing the Import filter. If you have the new PDF Import QuarkXTension, you can use the same methods for separating color with QuarkXPress.

Once you have the 6.52 update and the PDF Import Filter installed, PDFs can be imported into PageMaker via the File ⇨ Place command. Imported PDFs are handled like raster images and vector EPS files. If a PDF contains improper color identification, such as RGB color that needs to be converted to CMYK, you can perform the conversion in PageMaker's print dialog box. To see how to make use of the PDF Import plug-in and print such a file, follow these steps:

STEPS: Color-Separate Placed PDF documents from Adobe PageMaker

1. **Create the PostScript file.** Business applications such as word processors, Microsoft Publisher, AMI Pro, and so on are often used in the office for document publishing in business environments. Sometimes these files need color separation. The preparation for digital prepress is limited by the tools available in the programs and the inability to print with the proper controls for separations. However, documents created in such applications can all be printed to disk as PostScript files. Print the file to PostScript.

2. **Distill the PostScript file.** Use Distiller's Job Options for font embedding and compression appropriate for the device. Follow the guidelines for the prepress recommendations listed earlier in this chapter.

3. **Place the PDF in PageMaker.** Select File ➪ Place and choose the PDF you wish to import when the navigation dialog box appears.

4. **Select the page to import.** Any page from a multiple-page PDF can be imported. In the PDF Import dialog box, shown in Figure 16-12, navigation controls appear at the bottom of the thumbnail preview for the page to be placed. You can scroll through the document by selecting the forward and back arrows. As each page is selected, a preview of the page will be displayed in the thumbnail.

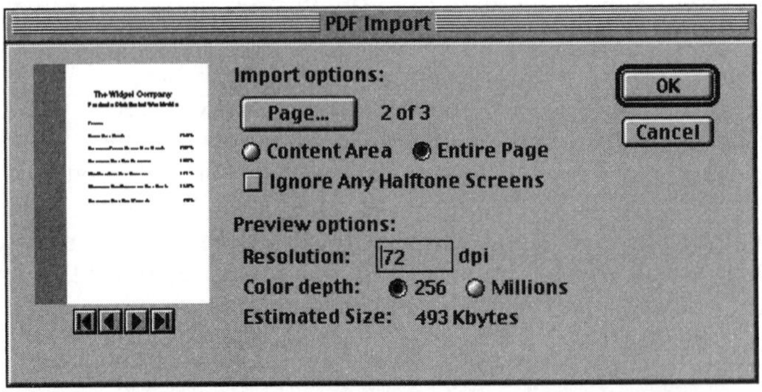

Figure 16-12: The PDF Import dialog box enables scrolling through pages that are previewed as a thumbnail display.

5. **Select the preview resolution.** Under Preview options, you will find choices for the display resolution. Values entered here will have no effect on printing. If you use a higher display resolution than 72 dpi or choose Millions for the colors, the PDF import will take more time. The default settings will import and display the PDF much faster than higher settings. Leave the defaults as they appear and click OK.

6. **Center the page.** The loaded graphic gun will appear when you click OK in the PDF Import dialog box. Click to drop the PDF in the document window and center the artwork on the page.

7. **Convert to process color.** Select File ➪ Print and choose the PPD for the device to be used. Select all the options in the Print dialog box as you would for printing directly to the device used. When you come to the Print Color dialog box shown in Figure 16-13, select Separations and click Convert to Process. PageMaker's algorithm for RGB-to-CMYK conversion will be used to convert the colors.

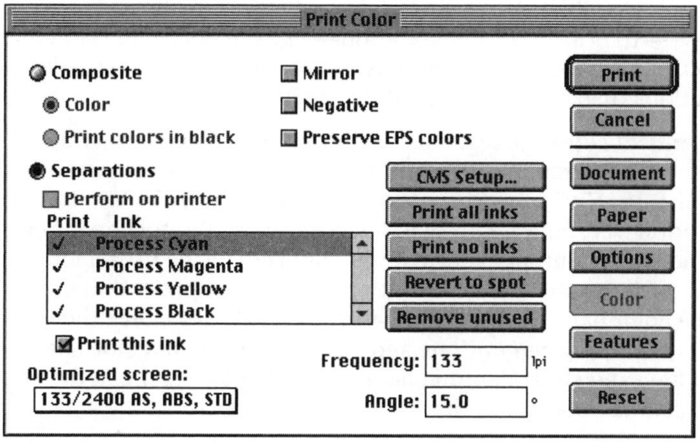

Figure 16-13: In PageMaker's Print Color dialog box, RGB color can be converted to process color by selecting Separations and then selecting Convert to Process.

If a composite proof is desired, click the Composite button after converting to Process and print the proof.

Note

If the final image prints as a grayscale during color separation, the images might have used indexed color when originally imported in the authoring application. PageMaker can't convert indexed color to CMYK. If this happens, you'll need to return to the original images and rescan them or convert to CMYK in Photoshop. Reimport, print to PostScript, and then redistill the file.

Printing spot color

Spot color cannot be printed from PDF files nor can you create a PDF with spot color and export to EPS for separations. Spot color is not handled by Acrobat. In order to submit a spot color file to an imaging center, the PDF must be created from a PostScript file that was printed as a separation. When PostScript files are prepared, the spot color angles need to be manually set in the authoring application prior to printing. Because a composite PDF cannot be delivered to the imaging center for printing separations, the user needs to preseparate the file. When printing the separations, the angles must be controlled manually.

Layout applications such as Adobe PageMaker and QuarkXPress are well suited to print color separations, and they provide all the controls needed to properly separate both process and spot color. When preparing duotones, tritones, quadtones, or using two or more spot colors, be certain to follow these important guidelines:

✦ **Use the device PPD:** As separated files will typically be used for only one purpose — to print a color separation — use the device PPD to create the PostScript file. The device PPD may offer more control over color-handling separations than the Acrobat Distiller PPD.

✦ **Use identical color names:** If using files imported from other applications, be certain the color naming conventions are identical. A spot color identified as PANTONE 167 CVC from Photoshop and PANTONE 167 CV in the layout application will separate on two different plates. Photoshop supports using long and short Pantone names. If the imported image uses a long name and the elements created in the layout or illustration application use short names, edit the color names to be identical. You can always check the print dialog box when printing separations and examine the list of color names. If you see both a long and short Pantone name, edit the color name in the application before printing the PostScript file.

✦ **Change spot color angles to process angles:** The default will print all spot color angles at 45°. If duotone images or a layout with two spot colors contain black and a spot color or two different spot colors, they will both print by default at 45°. Use the Color editing dialog box or the print dialog box in your separating application to change the angles (see Figure 16-14). In QuarkXPress, you can edit the colors and change spot color angles to a process angle. For example, change a spot color to the cyan angle, which prints at 15°.

In PageMaker, color angles are edited in the Print dialog box by selecting the Print Color options (see Figure 16-15). When selecting individual colors, the angles can be manually supplied in the field box for Angle.

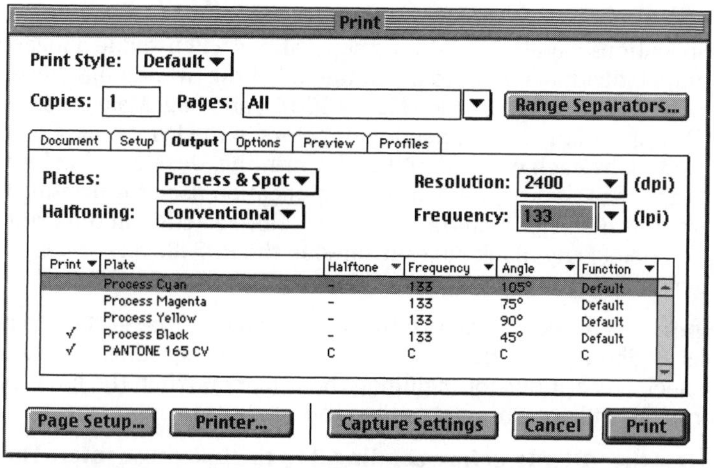

Figure 16-14: In QuarkXPress, spot color angles can be changed to process angles by selecting Edit ➪ Color and then editing the spot color angle. As shown here, changes were made in the Default Color dialog box in order for the spot color to assume the cyan angle, which will print at 15 degrees.

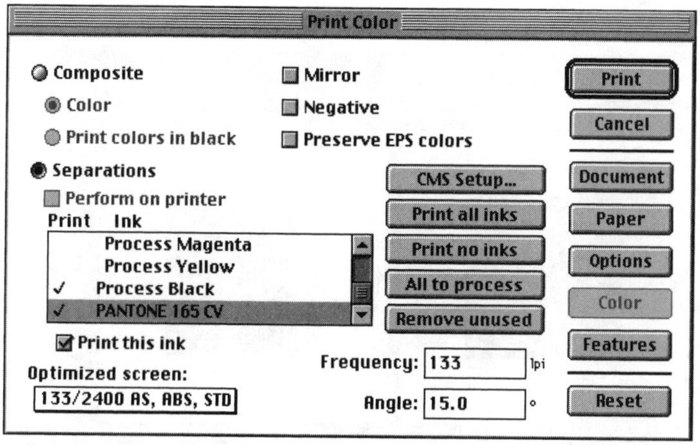

Figure 16-15: When separating spot color in PageMaker, select the color and edit the value for Angle appearing in the Print Color dialog box.

✦ **Only print the colors contained in the document:** The more recent releases of applications capable of printing separations will provide a means for selecting individual colors to be contained in the printed file. Both QuarkXPress version 4.03 (see Figure 16-14), and PageMaker 6.52 (see Figure 16-15) support individual selection of colors in the Print dialog box. Notice the check mark by each color identified for printing. Deselected colors will not be printed in the PostScript file. If some application used for printing the separations does not include individual color selection in the Print dialog box, you can delete any blank pages printed in the PDF file after opening the document in Acrobat.

✦ **Use printer's marks:** When printing a separated file, be certain to include crop marks, registration marks, and color names. In separating applications, you'll see check box options for including these marks. When the file is printed, the color name will appear outside the crop marks for each plate.

✦ **Preview the PDF file before sending it to the imaging center:** The advantage of using PDF is the final display you'll see in Acrobat for correctly separated colors (see Figure 16-16). You can't examine the angles, but you can see how the spot color separates. If you have more pages than you expected, something went wrong with your color identification. This is an easy proof method that will help diagnose problems before sending files to service centers.

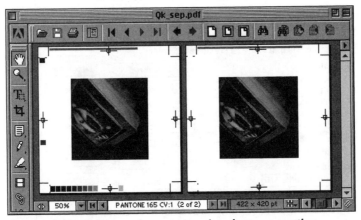

Figure 16-16: A duotone image was printed as a separation. When viewed in Acrobat, both colors contained in the duotone are displayed as they will print.

At the imaging center, a separated PDF document will print much like a composite. The PDF can be exported as an EPS or printed with a plug-in such as Crackerjack.

With regard to spot color separations or even process color that was separated in the PostScript file, the PDFs can also be sent directly to PostScript 3 devices.

Using Transfer Functions

Perhaps the use of PDF documents for imaging was first heavily supported in the newspaper industry. Major publication houses receiving display ads from people in a particular locale or from around the world are asking their customers to submit PDF files. If you want to send a display ad to a major metropolitan newspaper, a national magazine, or the local newspaper office, chances are you'll need to send your ad as a PDF file. Publication houses adopted PDF early to resolve many problems experienced by imaging centers. Due to extremely tight deadlines, these organizations had no time to contact an artist for submitting lost image links. Nor did they wish to invest enormous amounts of money to purchase font libraries to accommodate every advertising agency or graphic design firm. The solution was obviously PDF, whereby such problems would be eliminated.

Newspaper display ads often require some special attention with halftones. Because the paper is highly absorbent, heavy dot gain will tend to plug up the shadows in images. If you're not careful, the photo of the CEO of your client can become a muddy mess when it prints in *The New York Times*. To avoid problems with plugging and muddy images, control needs to be established in the image editing program for adjusting tonal values along the gray levels.

Not all publications adhere to the same standards for image preparation. Therefore, it will always be best to ask the publication art department for a document recommending how the PDF file should be prepared and what controls you need to exercise with halftone images. Many publications have prepared documents recommending how files should be created for printing on their web presses. If such a document is available from your vendor, by all means ask for it and follow their guidelines.

There may be times when you need to submit a display ad to several publications, or maybe your vendor does not yet have recommended guidelines to follow. If this is the case, try some of the following recommendations for preparing PDFs with halftones designed to be printed on newsprint by web presses.

Embedding transfer functions

Dot gain in halftones will be most apparent in high-contrast areas of a photograph. The image that looks great on your monitor screen or as a photographic print will usually be a mess when printed in the newspaper or yellow-page directory of the phone book. The halftones will actually print better when the image has a flatter look on your monitor with less contrast. You can control image contrast in

Photoshop by adjusting Levels and the Output Levels, adjusting Curves, or changing the ink percentages in the transfer functions. Adjustments will vary depending on the publication center you use. My personal preference is to use the transfer functions in Photoshop because it gives me a measurable value in 10 percent increments for adjusting the dots and amount of ink to be applied. The lower range tones need more dots to display grays in lighter shades, whereas the dark tones usually print total black ink much lower than the black point in the photograph.

If your publication center does not have a recommended guideline for adjusting image tones for their presses, use the following as a starting point. Keep in mind not all presses and all papers are identical, so you may need to make some adjustments for different publications.

STEPS: Embedding Transfer Functions in the PDF Document

1. **Open a grayscale image in Photoshop.** Assuming you have a halftone image to be used in a display ad for the newspaper, open the image file in Photoshop.

   When scanning for halftone output, scan color images on flatbed scanners in RGB mode. Make level adjustments for each of the three RGB channels. (On the Macintosh, hold the Option key down as the black-and-white input levels slider is moved, and release the mouse button upon the first appearance of black and white, respectively.) Convert the RGB image to Lab color. Delete the a and b channels to produce a multichannel image. Select Image ➪ Mode ➪ Grayscale. Sharpen with the Unsharp Mask filter. The final grayscale image will print much better than an RGB image converted to grayscale.

2. **Open the Transfer Function dialog box.** Select File ➪ Page Setup. In the Page Setup dialog box, click the Transfer button.

3. **Enter the Transfer Function values.** The zero point is the absence of a dot. As you go up the scale, the minimum dot that represents the smallest dots in the halftone image are at the lower end of the scale. The maximum dot that represents black is at the 100 percent end of the scale. To define more detail in the subtle tones toward the minimum dot, you need to raise the values for the lower percentages to include a little more ink. By contrast, the maximum dot will print 100 percent black somewhere above 85 percent on many newspaper presses. Therefore, no distinction of tones will be made between 85 and 100 percent, and this will result in plugging (filling up with black ink). As such, you need to bring the maximum dot down in size to reduce the plugging. Finally, because you remap the image from zero to about 86 percent, the total curve will shift left toward the minimum dot. The midtones should be set less than half the range—somewhere around 35 percent. The final settings would be applied as illustrated in Figure 16-17.

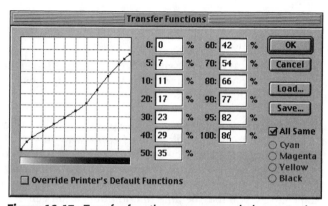

Figure 16-17: Transfer functions recommended as a starting point for printing images to newsprint on web presses.

4. **Save the file.** Embedding of the transfer functions in the Photoshop file only occurs when saving the file in Photoshop EPS format. In Photoshop, click OK to accept the new transfer functions and OK in the Page Setup dialog box. Select File ➪ Save As and save the file as Photoshop EPS. When the EPS Options dialog box appears, shown in Figure 16-18, select Include Transfer Functions.

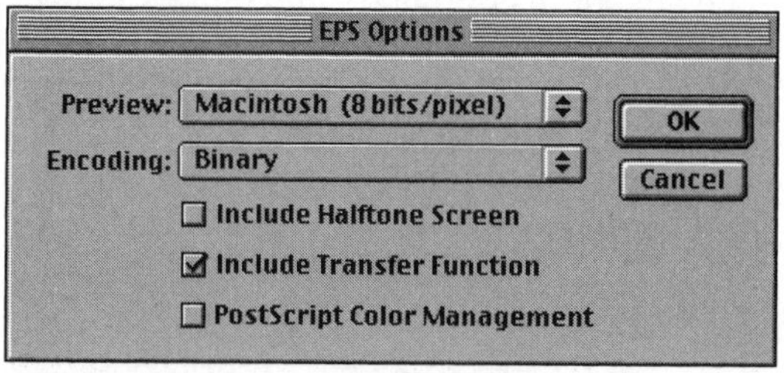

Figure 16-18: Transfer functions are embedded in the Photoshop file when you save file as EPS and select Include Transfer Functions in the EPS Options dialog box.

Tip

Publications will image files you submit at halftone frequencies they determine. If you wish to have your images print at a different frequency or with a different dot shape, you can control the frequency and dot shape by selecting the Page Setup dialog box and clicking the Screen button. When changing frequency or dot shape, select Include Halftone Screen in the EPS Options dialog box. Once embedded in the Photoshop file, Acrobat cannot change the frequency during printing.

5. **Print the PostScript file.** To complete the ad, import the image into the application to be used and set the type. When finished, print the file as a PostScript file for distillation.

6. **Distill the PostScript file.** When choosing Job Options in Distiller, be certain Preserve Transfer Functions is selected in the Color Job Options. Distill the file when all Job Options have been set.

There is no substitute for inquiry and testing. Before preparing a PDF document for any source, always be certain to ask for guidelines. People who operate the devices they own know the capabilities of those devices best — sometimes even better than the manufacturers. Listen to their recommendations and follow them. If you need to tweak files for your own design requirements, be certain to run tests and record your findings. In some cases, you may be able to find publication centers and service bureaus to assist with the testing and offer advice along the way.

Variable Data Printing

Marketing and advertising is currently traveling through a revolution with regard to the messages sent to prospective customers. If you stop and think about it, development of printed communication was static for almost two hundred years. From the time of Guttenburg until recent times, we have printed massive documents and tossed them about through the mail system — something we have come to call *junk mail*. With the advent of computers and more sophisticated data analysis, we began to create demographic makeups of households and target marketed mail to vertical populations, and then to segments within populations. Today, we are experiencing target marketing to an audience of one. Whereas printing technology in past years only made producing identical pieces affordable, several new on-demand printing systems are capable of printing with variable data. Variable data printing can customize a printed piece, with both the change of text and graphics for each piece passing through the imaging system.

In the early stage of development, variable data printing was delivered by some publication houses as contest entry forms to massive mailing lists. How many times have you received a piece in the mail asking you to join the sweepstakes entry from a form that had your name printed in 36-point bitmapped red type? These sweepstakes entry forms were the beginning of variable data that offered a new approach to marketing for the individual. As crude as they were, they paved the way to a much more sophisticated form of printing from high-tech imaging systems that could handle the exchange of high-resolution images along with PostScript type.

Variable data printing is similar to a mail-merge program. There are two sources used in variable data printing. The document file, which is like a letter in the mail-merge process, and the data file. In a mail merge, as each letter passes through the laser printer, it picks up several fields of information from a new record. These fields are identified in the document as data fields, and this identification brings the field contents from the data file into the letter. With variable data printing, the same process occurs. Instead of using a word processor for the authoring application, a layout program such as PageMaker or QuarkXPress is used. These programs have plug-ins or XTensions developed from third-party manufacturers to program the code necessary to swap images and text as each piece reads a new data record and imports the data field contents. With regard to image files, the database may contain codes or names of image files that reside in the same directory as the database. When the data is imported, the database refers to the images by code or name, and these are subsequently imported on new pages in the layout.

Variable data and PDF

PDF documents use embedded data and as such cannot swap images or text on-the-fly. To understand how variable data printing can be used with PDF, you need to know more about the eventual document that will be printed. First, the data file for variable data printing is created. The data file can be created in any application capable of exporting ASCII text with delimited fields. You can use a database management program, spreadsheet application, or a word processor. I personally like using Microsoft Excel. It's fast, easy, and enables me to reorganize data quickly and visually (see Figure 16-19).

	A	B	C	D	E	F	G
1	Company	Address	City	St	Zip	Code 1	Code 2
2	ACE Advertising	4130 Ardmore Ave	Springfield	MD	10009	3	AA
3	ADVantage marketing	P.O. Box 82573	Springfield	MD	10009	5	AA
4	ADs R US	2020 17th Street	Springfield	MD	10009	6	AA
5	Adpro Advertising	2030 17th Street	Springfield	MD	10009	7	AA
6	Ann's Design	9302 Chesaw Ct.	Springfield	MD	10009	15	AA
7	Beck's Advertising	4716 District Blvd.	Springfield	MD	10009	34	AA
8	Breakthru Marketing	2712 Judith St.	Springfield	MD	10009	43	AA
9	Creative Concepts	5329 Office Center Ct.	Springfield	MD	10009	64	AA
10	Creative Marketing Ideas	5101 Marcy St.	Springfield	MD	10009	65	AA
11	CYP Communciations	1800 30th Street	Springfield	MD	10009	69	AA
12	D'Olson Advertising	1400 Easton Dr.	Springfield	MD	10009	74	AA
13	Design Sketch	5401 Business Park South	Springfield	MD	10009	77	AA
14	Griffin Graphics	1930 Truxtun Ave	Springfield	MD	10009	106	AA
15	Hometown News	3400 Incline Dr.	Springfield	MD	10009	115	AA
16	Jake's Advertising Agency	1626 19th Street	Springfield	MD	10009	122	AA
17	James Productions	2205 Westminister Dr.	Springfield	MD	10009	124	AA
18	Mark Bribey Advertisement	1401 19th Street	Springfield	MD	10009	157	AA
19	May New Services	29 Oleander Ave	Springfield	MD	10009	161	AA
20	McAllister & Associates	1590 Strebor Dr	Springfield	MD	10009	162	AA
21	McMahon & Associates	1716 Oak Street #11	Springfield	MD	10009	163	AA
22	Multi-Media Advertising	401 E. Truxtun Ave	Springfield	MD	10009	179	AA
23	Newer Associates Marketing & Advertising	1004 H St. Ste.F	Springfield	MD	10009	180	AA
24	Nelson Web Concepts	3703 Savannah Avenue	Springfield	MD	10009	181	AA
25	Parliment Advertising	2030 17th Street	Springfield	MD	10009	199	AA
26	Scott Smith Advertising Agency	801 S. Mount Vernon Ave	Springfield	MD	10009	238	AA
27	Sutter Advertising Inc.	4806 W. Mineral King Ave	Springfield	MD	10009	261	AA
28	The Partners	5401 Business Park South	Springfield	MD	10009	277	AA
29	The Robley Agency	13501 Spring Mountain Ave	Bakersfield	CA	93312	279	AA

Figure 16-19: I created a database file in Microsoft Excel with the first record identifying my field names. Code 1 and Code 2 at the top right of the spreadsheet contain the names of some of my Photoshop images.

The next step is to create the layout. One distinct advantage in using customized variable data printing is only one layout needs to be assembled for the piece. The overall design is the same, but the personalization comes with unique images and text targeted for individuals that are imported during the merge. The layout would be assembled similarly to any other layout created for a marketing piece (see Figure 16-20).

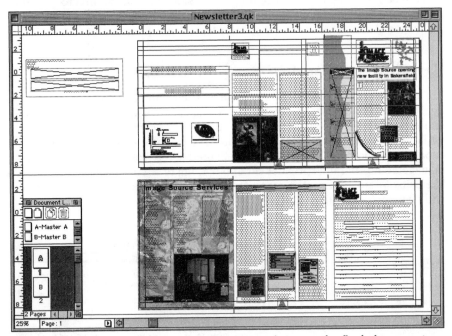

Figure 16-20: I created a newsletter layout in QuarkXPress. The final piece was to be printed two-sided with variable data appearing on both sides. The box on the pasteboard to the left of the layout holds the variable data code similar to what might be used with mail merges.

In order to assemble a variable data piece, a plug-in or XTension is needed to support the merging of the data. In the examples illustrated previously, I used Xdata from EM Software, Inc. Xdata is a QuarkXPress XTension that supports XPress versions 3.3 or higher. The XTension enables merging data the way a mail-merge utility does. Data fields are identified and programming code can be created for many different conditions. If . . . else statements are supported as well as Boolean expressions. Figure 16-21 illustrates the code that will be used to change text fields and two graphic fields.

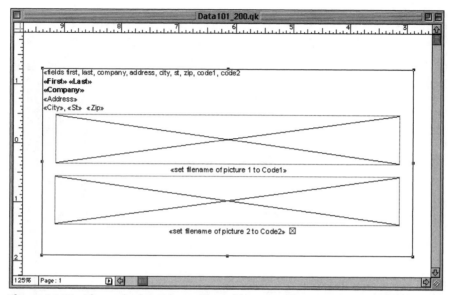

Figure 16-21: The code that Xdata will read is created in a separate text box in QuarkXpress and rests on the pasteboard. When Xdata is opened, the text box will be identified as the source from which the data will be read.

In the layout, the placeholders are positioned on the document master pages and linked. When the data is imported, it starts with the first placeholder on the first page and reads the first field from the database. The second field is read next, and so on. When the record finishes with a carriage return, a new page is automatically created, the new data is placed on the second page, and then another page is created, and so on. The constant data in the document layout (the graphics and text that remain constant and don't change) is suppressed from printing when the data is imported. Therefore, all new pages contain only the variable data (see Figure 16-22).

Creating the PDF file

After the layout is complete and the variable data is imported, three documents will be produced in the example I just illustrated. One file will include the front and back side of the layout. The second and third files will include just the variable data for pages 1 and 2, respectively. If you create similar files on your computer, there would be no way to print the final piece to a laser printer when this kind of file is created. When these files are submitted to an imaging center, the RIP software used with on-demand systems will separately rip the three different files and then use their software to match the ripped data files with the ripped layout file.

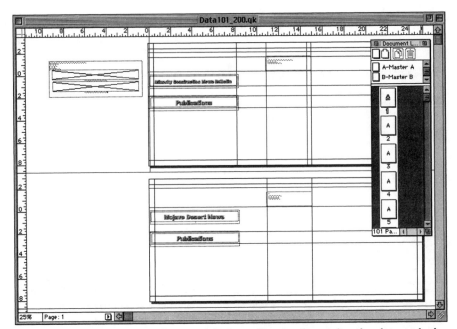

Figure 16-22: When I viewed my QuarkXPress file after importing the data, only the variable data was placed on new pages in the document. This particular file included 869 records, which produced the same number of pages after merging the data.

The three files in this example can be submitted to an imaging center either as a native file, a PostScript file, or a PDF file. The advantage of using PDF will be the same as those for other imaging solutions. Linked images will be embedded in the PDF as well as fonts. More importantly, the file sizes can grow enormously with variable data. Sending PDFs instead of either native or PostScript files will conserve much memory. Here are a few of my recommendations for preparing files for variable data on-demand systems:

Printing the PostScript File:

✦ **Use the device PPD:** Variable data files will only serve a single purpose. What's more, many on-demand printing systems use web-fed paper, which can accommodate many sizes not available with other PPDs. You'll need to acquire from the service center the PPD for their device. Always use the device PPD when printing to these machines.

✦ **Use the proper color mode and file size:** As you would expect from any other device, be certain to use the proper color mode. On-demand systems are CMYK devices, and all images should be converted to CMYK. Image resolution may vary between devices, so be certain to inquire what resolution is best suited for the equipment.

✦ **Center the artwork on the printed page:** Especially when two-sided printing is used, be certain to center the artwork on the page. This option will be available in both PageMaker and QuarkXPress when you print the PostScript file. If the artwork is not centered, you may experience problems with alignment for the front and back sides on the printed piece.

✦ **Always use printer's marks:** Regardless of whether you use a bleed, the paper will eventually need to be cut since it's web-fed. The service center staff will need crop marks to know where the cuts are to be made. When creating crop marks, use the print crop marks in the layout application and don't draw them manually on the pages. If folds are to be used, you can draw fold lines outside the page boundaries.

✦ **Identify bleed distance:** Programs such as Macromedia FreeHand and QuarkXPress 4.0x require you to define the bleed area. When using bleeds, be certain to enter a value large enough to accommodate any bleeds or fold lines.

✦ **Preview in the Print dialog box:** Both PageMaker and QuarkXPress 4.0x offer a preview before the file is printed. Double-check the preview box to ensure all crops, bleeds, and page sizes will print properly.

Distilling the PostScript File:

✦ **Choose the optimum compression:** You may find excellent results from using the Medium quality setting or lower instead of High quality. These devices are continuous tone and print at resolutions like 600 dpi. Try to find the best compression suited for the print without image degradation. If you have large documents with many different images, the file sizes can grow significantly. Any memory saved through compression will significantly reduce image sizes.

Viewing the PDF:

✦ **Preview the PDF pages:** Be certain to review the PDF pages before submitting the job to the imaging center. If you find irregular rotations of pages, correct them before sending the file.

✦ **Check the data flow:** A careful review of the PDF pages will save you time and money. Be certain to review the data fields to be certain no text overflows have occurred. PDF is one of the best ways to deliver these jobs because you can preview exactly what will be printed in the variable data fields. Carefully check your work.

✦ **Save the ripped files:** At an imaging center, ripped files can be saved, eliminating reripping the file and sometimes saving money for set up and RIP times. Once a master page has been ripped, you can send new data files that can be printed with the same master pages. If you expect to add to your database and print additional pieces, ask the service center to save the files.

Printing to Large Format Inkjet Printers

Earlier versions of Acrobat supported a maximum page size of 45 inches by 45 inches. With Acrobat 4.0, PDFs can be created that are up to 200 inches by 200 inches in size. Support for larger sizes makes it possible to output to large inkjet printers. When using larger formats, the likelihood of repurposing the document for any other source is slim. If PDFs are to be created for a single source, use the device PPD when preparing the PostScript file. Also, many of the large format inkjets use PostScript clones rather than true Adobe PostScript RIPs. Many of these RIPs designed with special dithering algorithms will prefer RGB TIFF images. Resolution is often much lower than you would find with other devices — 70 to 150 dpi at one-to-one ratios is often optimum. There's no substitute for testing, so be certain to ask the imaging center what their specifications are, and run some tests to find the file attributes and Distiller Job Options best suited for the device used.

Summary

✦ Printing PDF files to all imaging devices requires careful preparation of the PostScript file to be distilled by Acrobat Distiller. When repurposing documents for several devices, create the original document for the most high-end device to be used and print to PostScript. Distill the PostScript file with Job Options suited for the imaging device.

✦ Custom Job Options can be saved from Distiller and loaded as files are distilled for specific devices.

✦ Printed PDFs from Acrobat can only be used with desktop and composite printers. For imaging equipment at service centers, imagesetters, and platesetters, PDFs need to be exported as EPS or a third-party plug-in such as Crackerjack should be used.

✦ PDFs can be sent directly to PostScript 3 devices. To image PDFs on PostScript 3 printers, a software utility or support for hot folders is needed to send the file to the device.

✦ Spot color separations are not supported by Acrobat 4.0. To print spot color separations, print the PostScript file as a separation. Each plate will appear on a separate page in the PDF file.

✦ PageMaker version 6.52 and QuarkXPress version 4.02 and above accept PDF imports. PageMaker or QuarkXPress can be used to convert RGB color to CMYK from a placed PDF document.

✦ When preparing PDFs for newspapers and publications, ask the publication art department for guidelines on creating PDFs and controlling image contrast and tonal corrections. Transfer functions embedded in Photoshop files can be preserved in PDF documents.

✦ PDFs can be used with on-demand printing systems for variable data printing, which will significantly reduce file sizes. When printing to these devices, always use the device PPD when creating the PostScript file.

✦ Acrobat 4 accepts page sizes up to 200 by 200 inches. Support for these sizes enables you to output PDF files to large-format inkjet printers.

PDFs and CD-ROMs

✦ ✦ ✦ ✦

In This Chapter

Preparing PDFs
for CD-ROM

Distributing the
Acrobat Reader
software

Preparing artwork for
CD silk-screening

✦ ✦ ✦ ✦

Knowing that PDF files have many uses, you will often find a need to archive many types of documents on a storage device. Additionally, you may wish to publish a catalog, self-promotion piece, service directory, or any other type of information you need to make available to many users. One of the most cost-effective means of publishing large volumes of data and information is through a CD-ROM. CD-ROMs are inexpensive (under $1.00 each when published in volumes of 500 to 1,000) and can be distributed much more easily than printed documents. Furthermore, the volume of information a CD-ROM is capable of containing is exceptionally large when you consider the file compression and storage requirements of PDF files. In this chapter, I present some guidelines you should follow when storing PDFs on CD-ROMs.

CD-ROM Publishing

CD ROMs are created from a master disc at a CD-ROM replication center. The originally developed CD is referred to as a *CD Master*, and in replication houses the process of duplicating the original CD is referred to as *mastering*. From the master, the duplicate CDs are developed, and this process is referred to as replication. When you place an order at a CD replication service center, they will master the CD, which will cost you a mastering fee, and then replicate it according to the number of copies you wish to receive. Once the CD has been mastered, you can reorder additional copies without paying the mastering fee again. If you change any of the CD contents for subsequent orders, you will incur another mastering fee.

CD-ROM replication

Considering all the material you can write to a CD, the cost of replication is much less than printing. You can place thousands of four-color PDF pages on a CD, and the cost of replication can be as little as less than $1.00 per CD, including a four-color silk screen for the CD design and a CD jewel case.

Costs

Depending on which service center you use, you can expect to pay between $300.00 and $750.00 for having a CD mastered and anywhere between $.80 and $2.00 per CD. Jewel cases will cost you another $.10 to $.20 per case. The average cost of replicating 500 CDs complete with a four-color silk screen and jewel cases is around $1,000.00 — that's $2.00 per CD.

Replication centers

There are several replication centers located in many major metropolitan communities around the country. You may not have one in your local community, so you may need to send your files out for replication and deal with a service center via phone and mail. You can search the phone books or Internet for a service center close to you.

Tip   If you can't find a center, I recommend you use Technicolor Optical Media Center in Camarillo, California. Although they have a huge facility and replicate CDs for companies worldwide, they treat the small account with the same degree of service as the large accounts. Technicolor's address is 3301 East Mission Oaks Boulevard, Camarillo, California, 93012, and they can be reached at 805-656-8667.

CD-ROM jackets

Some CD-ROM jacket designs are actually copyrighted, so if you have a CD-ROM jacket printed, you need to be certain you do not violate any copyrights. If you have any CDs enclosed in jackets with no flap, peek inside the cover. You may see some with a Romvelope stamp. These designs are copyrighted, and your printer would need permission to replicate the design. Before you plan the artwork, have your printer research the jacket design and inform you of those types of designs that can be used without copyright infringement. A good commercial print shop with sales staff will be able to assist you in the research. Be certain to do this before you start your artwork. If you plan on using a jewel case instead of a printed jacket, you can have an insert printed to slide into the jewel case. Costs of printing will be added to the replication costs mentioned previously.

Planning the content design

Since the CD mastering will be the most expensive part of your replication process, you'll want to determine all the contents to be included on your CD ahead of time. There are several elements that need to be on your CD in addition to your PDF files and the directories you create for them.

Welcome file

When the CD is opened on a PC desktop, you'll want the user to see a README or Welcome file. This file should be immediately accessible and visible when the CD is opened on the desktop. If you have Acrobat PDF files on the CD, the user may not be able to read any of them until the Acrobat Reader is installed. The Welcome file can guide the user through the installation process. On the Adobe Acrobat Reader installer CD, you'll find README files for the Macintosh, Windows, and UNIX systems. These README files can be used as templates for creating your Welcome file. The Reader CD is a hybrid CD and can be read by a Macintosh, Windows, or UNIX computer (see Figure 17-1).

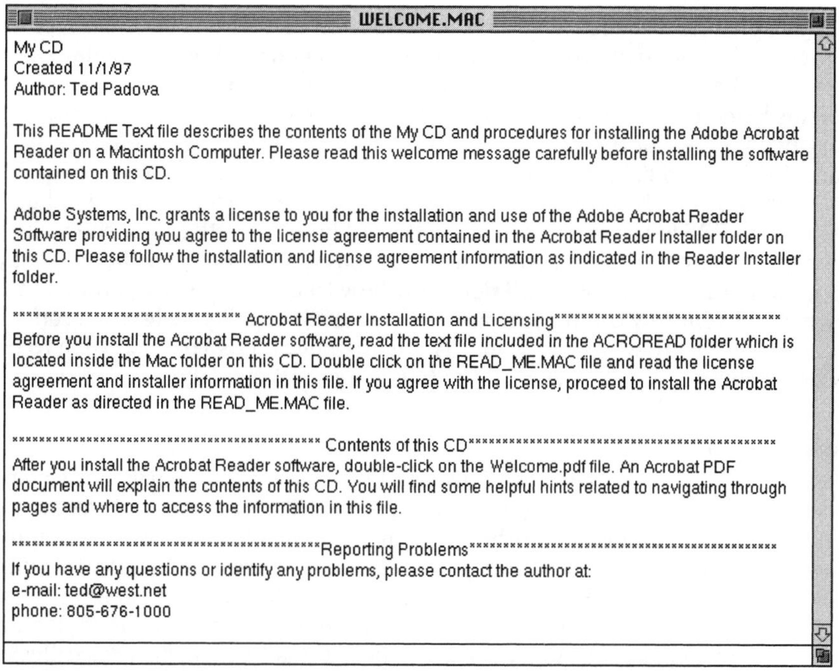

WELCOME.MAC

My CD
Created 11/1/97
Author: Ted Padova

This README Text file describes the contents of the My CD and procedures for installing the Adobe Acrobat Reader on a Macintosh Computer. Please read this welcome message carefully before installing the software contained on this CD.

Adobe Systems, Inc. grants a license to you for the installation and use of the Adobe Acrobat Reader Software providing you agree to the license agreement contained in the Acrobat Reader Installer folder on this CD. Please follow the installation and license agreement information as indicated in the Reader Installer folder.

******************************** Acrobat Reader Installation and Licensing********************************
Before you install the Acrobat Reader software, read the text file included in the ACROREAD folder which is located inside the Mac folder on this CD. Double click on the READ_ME.MAC file and read the license agreement and installer information in this file. If you agree with the license, proceed to install the Acrobat Reader as directed in the READ_ME.MAC file.

** Contents of this CD**
After you install the Acrobat Reader software, double-click on the Welcome.pdf file. An Acrobat PDF document will explain the contents of this CD. You will find some helpful hints related to navigating through pages and where to access the information in this file.

Reporting Problems
If you have any questions or identify any problems, please contact the author at:
e-mail: ted@west.net
phone: 805-676-1000

Figure 17-1: I created a README file for my CD, which explains the licensing details for Acrobat Reader, how to install the Reader software, and where to begin exploring the CD contents.

PDF Welcome file

The text files should be limited to a brief description of your CD contents and simply guide the user to complete the Reader installation. You'll want to get the end user into Reader as soon as possible because you have much more opportunity for providing information in a PDF file than in a text file. The first file the user opens should be a Welcome PDF document that should serve as a central navigator for all your CD contents. You can include multiple files and folders on the CD without the user having to search through them if the navigation is simple and logical in the PDF files. The hypertext references can be used to access all your PDF files. If you are distributing a CD to people who may not be familiar with Acrobat Reader, you may wish to include a brief description of how PDF navigation is handled in Reader. In doing so, you'll want to keep the instruction simple and restricted to only a few tools and keystrokes. Don't bother with all the viewing options. Users will soon learn some navigation features on their own.

File preparation

When you plan on developing a CD for distribution to clients, consumers, or employees of a company, you need to always keep in mind your personal logic may not be shared by the masses. If you plan as you create, users may run into problems when they attempt to browse your CD contents. The first step in preparing PDF files for distribution on CD-ROM is to plan it out carefully and ensure the flow and navigation is easy and makes sense to the novice computer user. There's probably nothing more irritating to the end user than to wind up in some remote PDF location and not know how to go back to the path she or he was following. Acrobat 4.0 has helped greatly with navigation, but you should always keep in mind that many users will not know how to use all the navigation methods. They may rely entirely on the buttons you create with the hypertext references within the PDF file they are browsing. There are a few steps you may wish to use in your planning, which I discuss in the following sections.

Draw a diagram

Before you begin a project, draw a flow chart describing all the PDF files to be created and the folder hierarchy you intend to use. The end user may never know when a new file is opened or another page in the same file is used. You should also be aware that some users may change preference settings and disable the Open Cross Document Links in Same Window check box in the General Preferences dialog box. If this item is disabled, the end user will wind up with several open documents on screen. You can plan ahead by setting page actions to close files regardless of how the preferences are set. A flow chart will help you identify the page actions and overall structure of the PDF organization.

Optimizing files

As you create PDFs for distribution on CD-ROM, you should employ all optimizing tasks for the files you create. There are two specific items to deal with when preparing your files. In Acrobat Catalog, you will always want the Optimize for CD-ROM option enabled in the Index Default preferences.

Also, be certain the last save for all PDF files occurs with the Optimize feature enabled. As a matter of habit, use the Batch Process feature in Acrobat to optimize all the PDF files just before sending them off to the replication house. You may also wish to delete all thumbnails to conserve space and bring file sizes down. Both the Batch Optimize and Delete Thumbnail options are available when you select File ➪ Batch Process in Acrobat. If security is desired to prevent users from changing or printing your files, you can establish security settings in the Batch Process dialog box, as shown in Figure 17-2. Be certain to not use security for opening files. You'll go crazy trying to explain to users how to view the files on the CD.

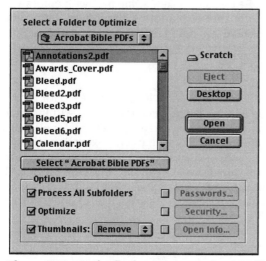

Figure 17-2: As the final step in preparing PDF files for CD-ROM replication, use the Batch Process command to optimize all the documents.

Font issues

During your PDF development, you should double-check some sample files on a few different computers. When you distill files in Acrobat Distiller and use any font outside the Base 13 font sets, you should embed the fonts during the distillation. Be certain to print the files to disk as PostScript files, and then use Acrobat Distiller to convert them to PDF. In the Distiller Job Options, enable the Embed All Fonts option.

Double-check a few PDF files containing a sampling of all the fonts you intend to use on both a Macintosh and in Windows before creating all your PDF files. If Acrobat Reader is installed properly, the font substitution should display the pages without any font problems.

Also, be certain to comply with licensing requirements when embedding fonts. If uncertain whether a particular font manufacturer permits font embedding in PDF files, contact the vendor and ask for permission.

Color issues

When you create a PDF document on one platform and view the file on another platform, you may see great disparity in color viewing. The range of 256 colors in the system palette on each machine only has a maximum of 216 colors that are common across platforms. For colors specified in illustration programs, you should use colors within the 216 color palette that are common to cross-platform viewing. When using Photoshop images, you can employ Photoshop 5's new color handling features to embed profiles or export the images in a GIF89a format with a color palette drawn from the 216 colors. Be certain to view some files with colors you intend to use and some sample photos on two platforms before completing your project. A little planning ahead will save you much time in creating your presentation.

File naming

This is of particular importance to Macintosh users. If you write a CD for cross-platform use, you will want to keep all the file naming conventions within ISO 9660 standards. Be certain your file names have from one to eight characters (using only alphanumeric characters), a dot, and one- to three-character extensions. If you supply a replication house with a file outside these character limits and ask for a hybrid CD to be read cross-platform, the filenames will be truncated. Macintosh users should avoid preceding a filename with blank spaces or including spaces within the name of the file. When blank spaces are desired, use an underscore (file_doc.txt).

Supplying the data

How your CD is organized should be determined by you and not left to the replication center. I strongly recommend you do not use low-capacity storage disks in a situation where you need several disks for your CD contents, and then send those disks to the replication house to be copied to a single source. Find a service bureau that can put all your files on a Jaz cartridge, or write a single CD that appears exactly as you intend to have it mastered. Having all files copied to a single source allows you to organize the files and folders without leaving this organization to the replication center.

Folders and icons

The views you save with your files will appear the same on the CD as they do on your computer. If you wish to have your folders viewed as a list, you should display all the folders in a list view before the data is submitted to the replication center. Icon views, shown in Figure 17-3, should be set before the master data disk is sent to the replication center. On the Macintosh, you should place your folder windows in the top-left corner of the screen. If your design was created on a 20" monitor and the folder appears in the lower-right corner, the end user may not see the folder on a 13" monitor.

Folders should also be opened or closed according to how you wish them to appear. If all your folders are opened and you send off your data disk to be replicated, when you receive your CDs back from the service center, all the folders will appear opened. The best way to organize your folders and views is to open them one at a time, view them in the desired view, and size the folder window to the desired size. Close each folder after the views have been set and close or open the final disk. The last step depends on whether you want the CD icon to appear on a desktop or a window to be opened that shows the root directory of the CD (see Figure 17-3).

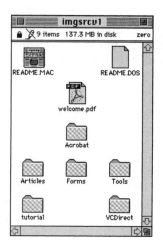

Figure 17-3: The last CD I had replicated shows the two README files at the top of the root level of the CD. The Acrobat folder contains the installers for Acrobat and Search.

CD authoring software will optimize files on-the-fly during the CD replication process. It is, however, a good idea to optimize a disk before you send it off to the service center. If you have a utility program that optimizes and defragments files, use it on the final data disk before you send it to the replication center.

Distribution of the Acrobat Reader Software

Adobe Systems grants you license and distribution rights for the Acrobat Reader software. So as to not confuse the software permissible for distribution with the nondistributable software, Adobe offers you two CDs when you purchase Adobe Acrobat. The Acrobat software, including Reader, Acrobat, Scan, Capture, Catalog, Distiller, and so on, is on one CD. You do not have permission to distribute any of the software on this CD. All of these components require purchase from Adobe Systems, Inc. The Acrobat Reader CD contains the Reader software for the Macintosh, Windows, and UNIX. The installer files you find on this CD are available to you to distribute to other users, and you can include the installers on any CD you develop. You are limited to certain restrictions when distributing the CD, and you should become familiar with what you can do and what is not permissible.

Adobe License Agreement

All distribution of the Adobe Acrobat Reader software requires that you also
include the licensing information supplied on the Reader installer CD when
distributing the program for Macintosh, Windows, and UNIX. Additionally, all
the licensing information is also included within a folder on the installer CD.

Reader and Search

You may elect to limit the installer for one of two sets of folders on the installer
CD. If you open any of the folders for Macintosh, Windows, or UNIX, you'll find two
Reader folders. One of these folders contains the Reader software only, and the
other contains the Reader and Acrobat Search software.

Reader installer

The Acrobat Reader installer contains all the necessary files you need for
distribution, but only includes the Reader software. There's a README file in this
folder; however, it does not include the licensing information. When you copy the
specific installer folder to your data disk, you need to copy the respective README
file contained within the ARCOREAD folder. If you do not use Acrobat Catalog and
don't need the search capabilities within Reader, you can copy this folder and the
README to your data disk.

Reader and Search installer

The second folder inside the folder containing the Reader installer for the
respective platform is the Reader+Search (Macintosh) or RDR_SRCH (Windows)
folder (see Figures 17-4 and 17-5). This folder contains the Reader installer and
the Search installer. Like the preceding example, you need to copy the respective
license agreement to your data disk.

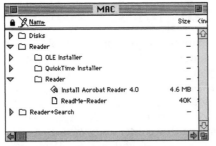

Figure 17-4: The Reader software
installation files for the Mac with the
Reader-only installer in view

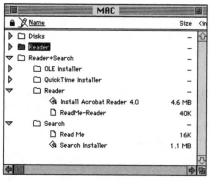

Figure 17-5: The Reader+Search files contain separate installers for Reader and Search.

Registering as a Reader distributor

Adobe Systems has provided you with a great opportunity to freely distribute the Reader software so end users may see the files you develop on your CD-ROM. Adobe encourages the distribution of the Reader software and likes to keep track of the distributors and the projects they develop with Acrobat PDF files. You gain some benefits by registering with Adobe Systems on their Web site at `www.adobe.com/acrobat/acrodist.html`. When you navigate to this page in your Web browser, you'll find a form for you to complete the registration (see Figure 17-6).

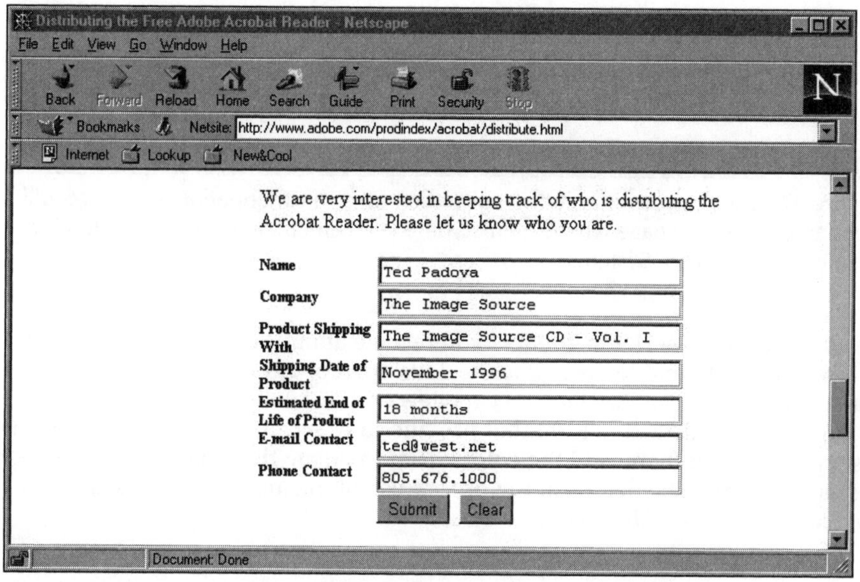

We are very interested in keeping track of who is distributing the Acrobat Reader. Please let us know who you are.

Name	Ted Padova
Company	The Image Source
Product Shipping With	The Image Source CD - Vol. I
Shipping Date of Product	November 1996
Estimated End of Life of Product	18 months
E-mail Contact	ted@west.net
Phone Contact	805.676.1000

Submit   Clear

Figure 17-6: Acrobat Reader distributors can register on Adobe's Web site.

You should plan on filling out the form and submitting it to Adobe's site by clicking the Submit button. Adobe will inform you of news related to Acrobat when you add your e-mail address. After you click the Submit button, another page will appear confirming your registration, as shown in Figure 17-7.

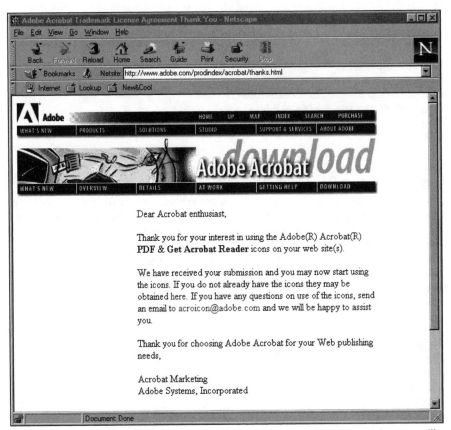

Figure 17-7: When you submit the registration form, a confirmation Web page will appear. On the Web page will be a link where you can obtain icons authorized for distribution by Adobe Systems.

In addition to the periodic updates you receive about Acrobat, you will be entitled to use many different logos and icons developed by Adobe to include in your CD packaging. There is a PDF file you can view on the Adobe Web site after you complete the registration form that provides a description of the icons you may use, where to get them, and the colors used to create the icons when printing color separations. Specific details of the proper use of the logos and icons are also included in the PDF file.

Artwork Preparation for CDs

Almost any replication center you use will include a silk-screen print on your CD cover. The CD artwork will help the user identify the CD and adds a professional look to the product. Preparing your artwork for silk-screening the top side of the CD requires you to precisely lay out the artwork on a template. When you identify the replication center that will replicate your CDs, they should be able to provide you with a template for your artwork. A template may be available in a variety of file formats, but most often you'll find the service center supporting Adobe Illustrator and/or QuarkXPress.

Printable area of a CD

A CD can have the silk-screen ink applied to its surface in limited areas only. If you examine your Acrobat CD, you'll notice the ink coverage does not extend to the edge of the disc. Your artwork must be limited to a small distance within the outer edge. You will also note a ring on the inside of the disc where no ink is applied. There has to be a blank area for this internal ring. Finally, the innermost area has a small ring where no ink is applied. This area must also be clean of artwork. The inside and outside clean areas measure one millimeter and the inside ring is two millimeters in size. In creating your artwork, you'll need to create a mask in Illustrator to confine the artwork to all but these rings.

Continuous tone images

Any Photoshop image you use should be saved with transfer functions specified by the replication center. If the service center does not provide you with the transfer functions to use, then do not include them in the Photoshop file. Transfer functions will remap the ink coverage specific to the press being used. Most of the better replication centers will be able to print CMYK color with 133-line screens. If you use a 133-line screen, you'll want to ensure no plugging will appear in your artwork. Using proper transfer functions can be helpful in laying down the right ink coverage to prevent too much ink in midtone and high-density areas.

Applying transfer functions to Photoshop files

If the replication center uses specific transfer functions, they will provide you the values, which you should include in your Photoshop files. You might also inquire as to whether the replication center will accept PDF files. If so, you can use Distiller Job Options recommended for digital prepress separations and include the transfer functions in the Advanced Job Options.

Be certain you convert your file to CMYK mode. To apply transfer functions in a Photoshop file, select File ⇨ Page Setup. In Photoshop's Page Setup dialog box, click the Transfer button. The Transfer Functions dialog box will appear in which all the values supplied by your replication center should be added. Figure 17-8 illustrates transfer functions I've used with Technicolor Optical Media Services in Camarillo, California.

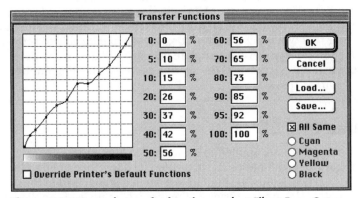

Figure 17-8: To apply transfer functions, select File ➪ Page Setup. In the Page Setup dialog box, click on the Transfer button.

Embedding transfer functions in a Photoshop file

The next step requires you to select the Save As dialog box and not select File ➪ Save. If you simply save the file, you won't have an opportunity to include the transfer functions. When selecting File ➪ Save As, choose the Photoshop EPS format. Transfer functions can only be saved with EPS formats.

After you select Replace, another dialog box will appear to enable you to control some EPS attributes. This is the dialog box that enables you to include the new transfer functions in the EPS file. After clicking the Save button in the EPS Save As dialog box, another dialog box will appear in which you embed the transfer functions. Select Include Transfer Functions in the EPS Options dialog box, as shown in Figure 17-9.

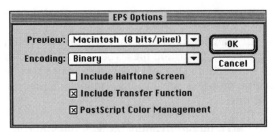

Figure 17-9: Enable the Include Transfer Functions option in the EPS Options dialog box. When this option is on, all the transfer functions will be embedded in the Photoshop EPS file.

Assembling the artwork in a template

After your images have been edited in Adobe Photoshop and saved with the proper transfer functions, you can import them into an Illustrator template. When you import the Photoshop image, you'll need to mask the image and create some compound elements in order to preserve the areas where ink will not be applied. The final image in Illustrator will appear as illustrated in Figure 17-10.

Figure 17-10: A Photoshop file was imported into an Adobe Illustrator template provided by the replication center to create artwork for a CD.

Requirements will vary for the CD silk-screening and CD cover depending on the replication house. Some replication centers may not require you to include Photoshop transfer functions. Others may perform design in house or farm out the silk-screen printing. The common denominator with all vendors is to first inquire about their needs before spending time on your designs.

Summary

✦ CD-ROM replication can provide cost-effective means of distributing PDF documents.

✦ PDF files intended for CD-ROM replication should be optimized. As a final step in transferring files to external media, use the Batch Process command in Acrobat to optimize PDFs and delete thumbnails.

✦ Adobe Systems grants you permission for distribution of the Acrobat Reader software as long as you comply with their distribution and licensing requirements.

✦ CD-ROM replication centers will vary in their requirements for silk-screening CDs and printing CD jackets. Always inquire first with your vendor before attempting to create designs for printing.

Using Plug-ins

✦   ✦   ✦   ✦

In This Chapter

Understanding plug-ins

Using Adobe plug-ins

Using third-party manufacturer tools

Contacting suppliers

Staying connected

✦   ✦   ✦   ✦

T he plug-in architecture has long been used by software manufacturers to encourage third-party developers to create mini-programs that add more features to the host application. Adobe Photoshop, Illustrator, and PageMaker all support a plug-in architecture, as do QuarkXPress and Macromedia FreeHand. Adobe refers to their add-ons as plug-ins, whereas QuarkXPress uses XTensions and FreeHand uses Xtras. Whatever you call them, they are applications that add more functionality to the host application. In this chapter, I cover many different plug-ins supported by Acrobat that were developed by third-party manufacturers.

Understanding Plug-ins

Acrobat supports a plug-in architecture. But don't think all these third-party add-ons are inexpensive little items you want to run out and purchase. Some are incredibly expensive. XTensions for QuarkXPress can run into many thousands of dollars, and some for Acrobat can be equally expensive. Before you purchase a particular plug-in for Acrobat, you can often find a demonstration version that will run for a limited amount of time after you install it. Other demo versions may disable a few features, but offer you enough usable features to thoroughly test them. If a demo version is not available for a costly plug-in, be certain to research it well. You can often find information on the Web. Visiting trade shows where products are demonstrated can also be helpful.

You will find some plug-ins supplied by Adobe Systems on the installer CD as well as some demonstration plug-ins from third-party manufacturers. You can visit Adobe's Web site at www.adobe.com/acrobat for updated announcements on available plug-ins as well as some demonstration utilities you can download. In addition, you'll find several demonstration third-party plug-ins on the CD accompanying this book.

Installing plug-ins

Plug-ins developed by third-party manufacturers often use an installer application. You can double-click the installer, which will automatically decompress and save the necessary files to the proper locations on your computer. Most often the location will be the Acrobat:Plug-ins folder. However, some plug-ins are designed to work with Acrobat and other applications, or they may need to install some system resources, so installation of other files may be in different locations on your computer. If an installer application is supplied by the manufacturer, it will be best to use the installer instead of copying files to the Acrobat Plug-ins folder.

On Windows, you can double-click the installer application or use the Run command from the status bar. In most recent versions of installer applications, double-clicking will launch the installer application for Windows 95, Windows 98, and Windows NT. Either method you choose, however, will work.

Plug-ins may be supplied by manufacturers without an installer application. If this is the case, you will often find a ReadMe file contained on the installer disk or CD. If a ReadMe file is supplied, be certain to review the installation instructions. There may be files that need to be stored in special folders on your hard drive, and the ReadMe file will describe these to you. If an installer is not supplied by the manufacturer, then you will likely need to copy some files to the Acrobat Plug-ins folder on your hard drive. When the Acrobat folder is opened on your hard drive, the Plug-ins folder will appear in the next level. Opening the Plug-ins folder as illustrated in Figure 18-1 will display subfolders containing individual plug-ins.

If you acquire a plug-in without an installer or documentation, then the plug-in will need to be copied to the Acrobat:Plug-ins folder. When copying plug-ins to this folder, copy the folder. Acrobat recognizes nested folders for plug-in usage. If several files exist for the plug-in, it will be difficult to manage your files and know exactly which files relate to which plug-ins. Therefore, copy the folder supplied by the manufacturer with all the resources contained therein to the Acrobat:Plug-ins directory.

If a plug-in is supplied by a manufacturer without a folder and only as a single item, you can copy it directly to the Plug-ins folder. You can also create a folder and place the single plug-in inside this folder. This method is a matter of personal preference. I prefer to handle plug-ins this way so I don't forget that a plug-in contains no other files, and this method helps keep my Acrobat plug-ins organized. If you make a folder and copy the plug-in to a new folder, test it out. If Acrobat can't find the plug-in, then relocate it to the Plug-ins folder level.

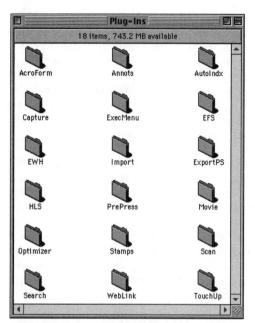

Figure 18-1: Plug-ins are stored in separate folders in the Acrobat:Plug-ins folder. Newly installed plug-ins will often be stored as subfolders in the Acrobat:Plug-ins folder.

Plug-in conflicts

Software releases at the *point zero level* (that is, 3.0, 4.0 , 5.0, and so on) often have bugs when they're shipped out the door by a manufacturer. Personally, I find Adobe applications very solid when shipped in the final version. Upon the release of Acrobat 4.0, the program went through an extensive beta period before it was finally shipped. However, no manufacturer can expect to find all bugs and inconsistencies when a program is shipped. In the case of Acrobat, several programs are being shipped together. Add the first release version of all the Acrobat components to the new or updated software offered by many plug-in manufacturers, you most definitely will find problems. Sometimes the problems can lead to system crashes, irregular behavior, or rendering a program nonfunctional. Plug-in installations can lead to problems with the performance of Acrobat. At times, you may find a conflict between plug-ins or between Acrobat and a third-party plug-in.

Diagnosing plug-in conflicts

Finding conflicts with plug-ins is not always an easy task. The first thing to look at when Acrobat misbehaves is the last plug-in installed. When installing plug-ins, keep a record of the installation order. It will often help to know exactly which application was installed last on your computer. If you know a plug-in was installed and then Acrobat experienced problems, remove the offending plug-in folder from the Acrobat:Plug-ins folder. You can simply relocate this folder to another folder on your hard drive without trashing it. If an uninstaller has been supplied with the plug-in by a third-party manufacturer, deinstall the plug-in. Sometimes installers will copy hidden files to your computer. This is particularly true for Windows users. If a .dll file has been installed in the Windows directory, unless you're a tech head, you'll never find it. Use the uninstall application if one exists.

When Acrobat is launched, it will read all the plug-ins before opening the Acrobat window. If Acrobat is launched, and the program freezes, it may relate to a plug-in problem. Watch the splash screen as Acrobat reads the plug-ins. It may display a plug-in name when it halts. Try to remove the offending plug-in as noted above.

If Reader is installed on your computer along with Acrobat and you experience problems, you may have a conflict with Acrobat attempting to read two plug-ins of the same type. Remove Reader from the Acrobat folder if you find the two programs installed in the same folder. Relaunch Acrobat after removing Reader to see if the problem is resolved.

If all the preceding attempts fail, you may need to isolate the problem by removing all plug-ins from the Acrobat:Plug-ins folder, and then add a few at a time to isolate the problem. For example, remove all plug-ins, bring three or four back to the plug-in folder, and then launch Acrobat. If everything works, quit Acrobat, move a few more plug-ins to the plug-in folder, and relaunch Acrobat. Continue this operation until you narrow down the problem. Before you attempt to reinstall Acrobat, it is a good idea to try to isolate the problem. Reinstallation won't tell you anything about where the problem existed, and you may return to it by installing additional plug-ins. Use the reinstallation method as a last resort.

Tip   To verify a problem with a plug-in when Acrobat freezes upon launching, you can temporarily disable all plug-ins without removing them from the plug-in folder. Double-click the Acrobat program icon and immediately press the Shift key. When Acrobat launches, it will bypass loading all plug-ins.

One more issue that is equally important when experiencing problems is to use the current version of Acrobat. While third-party manufacturers are updating their software, Adobe will be recording all problems reported as bugs. Whenever a software product is released, you can soon expect a *point zero one release* (for example, 4.01) to soon follow. Updates usually fix bugs found after the first release of a product. When Acrobat Distiller 3.0 was released, I remember having much difficulty running it on a Macintosh without constant crashes. By the time release 3.02 appeared, it ran flawlessly. You can check for current releases and bug fixes by visiting Adobe's Web site. Be certain to use the most updated version of the software and check out the Adobe Web site before attempting to reinstall the program.

Plug-in documentation

Manufacturers of software, especially plug-in manufacturers, are supplying their product documentation in Acrobat format. Whenever you see a PDF file accompanying a new release, be certain to review the document. The PDF document can be a compilation of last-minute notes, or it could be an entire user manual. All supported documentation can often help you understand the application usage and how to avoid problems.

If Acrobat is installed with an installer application, you may have ReadMe files and PDFs all stored in the plug-in folder. These files won't be needed to operate the program, and they can be relocated on your hard drive (or removed) if you choose to do so.

Tip   When installing several plug-ins, keeping track of the documentation can sometimes be overwhelming. To organize your documentation when it is supplied in PDF documents, create a folder on your hard drive for Acrobat documentation. Create a catalog of all the PDF files and rebuild the catalog as new PDFs are added to the folder. When you need to find information related to a particular feature, open Acrobat and use Acrobat Search for finding the keyword(s) supplied in the Query dialog box. You can combine all the help files shipped with Acrobat along with your plug-in PDFs in the same catalog for easy access.

Disabling plug-ins

At times you may wish to temporarily disable a plug-in. If you deinstall the plug-in or delete it from your hard drive, you'll need to reinstall at a later time. Deleting plug-ins is much more difficult to manage and requires more time than simply disabling them. An easy method for keeping track of your Acrobat plug-ins is to create a folder and name it Disabled, Disabled Folder, or Disabled Plug-ins. Whatever name you prefer can be used. Move the plug-in to the Disabled folder and keep this folder inside the Acrobat folder. You must, however, keep the Disabled folder at the Acrobat level or in another location on your computer. Acrobat can find plug-ins in nested folders, so if the Disabled folder resides inside the Acrobat:Plug-ins folder, it will locate the plug-ins therein. I find keeping my Disabled folder at the Acrobat folder level to work well since I know at a quick glance these plug-ins belong to Acrobat and not another application.

Adobe Acrobat Plug-ins

Acrobat requires certain plug-ins for proper performance of the program; in addition, some optional plug-ins are available to you in a folder titled Optional Plug-ins. The Acrobat plug-ins are all installed when you install Adobe Acrobat. Installation of the optional plug-ins is a personal choice. These plug-ins are not required for Acrobat to run properly, they just add more features to the program. Although all the plug-ins installed with Acrobat are not required, I'll refer to them as *standard plug-ins* for lack of a better term. Understanding each of these plug-ins and what they do will help you overcome any problems that occur when running Acrobat.

Standard plug-ins

Barring any last minute updates Adobe may decide to include with the final shipping version of Acrobat, the following plug-ins, as of this writing, are installed during the Acrobat installation. Acrobat will create the Plug-ins folder and install subfolders for each of the plug-ins described. When you first install Acrobat, open the Plug-ins folder and examine it to verify all plug-ins have been included.

AcroForm

When Acrobat is launched and you view the Command Bar, a submenu will appear for Forms. On the Forms submenu are commands for creating and working with forms in Acrobat. The tools and menu commands are supplied by a plug-in and not hard coded in Acrobat. If the AcroForm folder is not properly contained in the Plug-ins folder, the submenu will not appear in Acrobat.

Annots/Annots32.api

This plug-in handles all the new Annotation tools in Acrobat 4.0. If the Annots plug-in is not installed, you can only use the Note tool. The remaining tools will not appear in the pop-up toolbar for annotations. Likewise the Filter Manager will not be available.

AutoIndx/Autidx32.api

Auto Index enables you to identify an index with a PDF document. The index identification is determined when selecting File ⇨ Document Info ⇨ Index. If the plug-in does not load, the menu command will be unavailable, thereby prohibiting an index to be associated with the document.

Capture/Capture32.api

The Capture plug-in is used to launch the Capture Server. Capture has its own folder with some plug-ins for file formats. But to launch the Capture Server, this plug-in needs to be installed. If the Capture plug-in is not installed, the Capture Pages command will not appear on the Tools ⇨ Paper Capture menu. The Capture Suspects command will be visible, which allows showing suspects after a page has been captured.

EFS

EFS is a plug-in that permits Web connections without a Web browser. The Windows version of the plug-in is called IA32.api, and is explained in the "Windows-only plug-ins" section later in this chapter.

EWH/EWH32.api

The EWH plug-in is the External Window Handler. This plug-in enables viewing PDFs in other applications such as Web browsers. When this plug-in is disabled, you won't be able to view PDF files in external applications.

ExecMenu/Excmnu32.api

The ExecMenu plug-in handles the Execute Menu Items command in the Link Properties dialog box. If this plug-in is missing, the menu command is not available for Link Properties or Forms.

ExportPS/expps32.api

ExportPS is the plug-in used to export a PDF file to PostScript or Encapsulated PostScript (EPS). If the plug-in is not installed, the Export PostScript or EPS command will not be available.

HLS/Ahls32.api

The Highlight Server plug-in will display highlighted word hits in a PDF document from Web search engines. Without the plug-in installed, found words will not be highlighted.

Import/Import32.api

The File ➪ Import submenu is used to import various file types. When the Import plug-in is not installed, you still have access to several import filters, but the Import ➪ Image command is not available. The Import plug-in relates only to image formats to be converted to PDF.

Movie

Movie links are created with the Movie tool. When this plug-in is not loaded, the Movie tool won't appear in the Acrobat Tool Bar. If a movie file has been linked to the PDF and the Movie plug-in is not loaded, the link won't appear in the PDF document.

Ole (Mac)

Object linking and embedding (OLE) can be used to edit embedded data in one application that was created in another application. When the Ole plug-in is available, you'll notice the command Copy File to Clipboard appears in the Edit menu. This command will copy all the text in a PDF file to the Clipboard. The text can then be pasted into another document running in a different application (for example, Microsoft Word). When the Ole plug-in is not installed, the command will not be available.

Optimizer/Opt32.api

The Optimizer plug-in enables batch-processing PDFs to optimize files, add security, and create thumbnails. When the Optimizer plug-in fails to load, the Batch Process command will not be available in the File menu.

PrePress/PrePress.api

The PrePress plug-in supports adding document information to indicate whether a PDF was generated from a trapped file. The File ⇨ Document Info ⇨ PrePress command opens a dialog box in which the options for choosing whether the file contains trapping are available. Without the plug-in, the document cannot be tagged with this information.

Scan/Scan32.api

Scanning pages occurs from within Acrobat by selecting File ⇨ Import Scan. The Scan plug-in dialog box provides options for choosing a scanner and using the TWAIN module for scanning within Acrobat. When the plug-in does not load, the menu command will not be available.

Search/Asrch32.api

Acrobat Search is available for both Reader and Acrobat. If the Search plug-in does not load all search options related to identifying indexes, you won't be able to query an index and use the Search tools. When installing Acrobat Reader, be certain to install both Reader and Search to make these commands available.

Stamps

The Stamp tool enables creating stamp annotations, and the Properties dialog box defaults to the Stamps plug-in folder, where the Adobe-provided stamp libraries are located. When the plug-in is not loaded, the Properties window will be disabled, and no stamp icons can be selected for use.

TouchUp/TouchUp.api

The TouchUp Text tool and TouchUp Object tool appear in the Acrobat Tool Bar. If the plug-in does not load, neither tool will be available; as a result, text cannot be edited nor can objects be selected. In addition, the TouchUp Object tool is necessary to dynamically open an image in the host authoring program (Option/Ctrl+double-click a graphic to open in Photoshop or Illustrator). Without the tool available in the Acrobat Tool Bar, external applications cannot be launched via object linking.

WebLink/weblnk.api

The WebLink tool will appear in the Command Bar when the plug-in loads, enabling you to identify the default browser and launch a Web browser from within Acrobat. When the plug-in does not load, the WebLink tool will be unavailable in the Command Bar.

Windows-only plug-ins

Some Acrobat features are only available to Windows users. As a result, there are several plug-ins found in Acrobat running under Windows that are not found in the Macintosh version. The Windows-only plug-ins are as follows:

DigSig.api

The Digital Signature tool appears in the Acrobat Tool Bar. If this plug-in does not load, the tool will be unavailable. No digital signatures can be created when this plug-in is unavailable.

HTML2pdf.api

When using Web Capture, HTML pages can be converted to PDF. This plug-in is required when capturing HTML documents to support the conversion.

Ia32.api

The Internet Access plug-in works in conjunction with Web Capture. Without this plug-in installed, the Web Capture command and Web Capture preferences will be unavailable. The Macintosh version enables a Web connection without a browser; however, Web Capture is unavailable on the Macintosh.

ieweb32.api

This plug-in is required to access a Web browser from within Acrobat. If the plug-in is not installed and you attempt to access the default browser, an error dialog box will appear.

OpenAll.api

You can open documents created in other applications by selecting File ⇨ Open and choosing a file format from those listed in the File Type pop-up menu. The documents will be converted to PDF when opened. If this plug-in is not installed, however, only PDFs can be opened in Acrobat.

ppklite.api

The Adobe Acrobat Entrust Security plug-in works in conjunction with the DigSig.api plug-in. If neither of these plug-ins are installed, the Digital Signature tool will be unavailable in the Acrobat Tool Bar.

SendMail.api

You can send e-mail from within Acrobat by selecting File ⇨ Send Mail. The current open document will be sent as an attachment to your e-mail. If the plug-in is not installed, you can't send e-mail or attach the PDF to an e-mail document from within Acrobat.

Taps32.api

Files containing tables can be converted and opened as a PDF document. When the plug-in is installed, attributes for how tables are handled by Acrobat will appear when selecting File ➪ Preferences ➪ Table/Formatted Text. The preference settings will be unavailable when this plug-in is not loaded.

Webpdf32.api

This plug-in works together with the Ia32.api plug-in mentioned previously. Without this plug-in installed, Web Capture cannot be used.

Optional plug-ins

In addition to the standard plug-ins noted previously, Adobe ships a few optional plug-ins you may wish to include in your Plug-ins folder. The optional plug-ins will be installed in the Acrobat folder on installation of Acrobat. To use these plug-ins, you'll need to move them to the Plug-ins folder.

Using Third-Party Plug-ins and Applications

Third-party manufacturers have created many plug-ins for Adobe Acrobat, and there are many related applications designed to work with Acrobat or support the Portable Document Format. As Acrobat becomes more prolific with computer users, we can expect many new developers and more plug-ins to add to Acrobat's amazing features. In addition to plug-ins, there are some stand-alone applications designed to work with Acrobat and PDF files. It would be beyond the scope of this volume to list all plug-ins manufactured for Acrobat or applications used to work in concert with PDF documents. What follows is a fair sampling of tools designed to work with the Portable Document Format.

5D

The Rotunda
Guardian House
Borough Road
Godalming
Surrey
GU7 2AE
United Kingdom
www.5-d.com

Niknak (Windows)

Niknak is a print driver that can be used as a virtual printer to convert print files to PDF. This driver will appear as a printer selection in the Print dialog box in Windows. When this driver is selected, it works similarly to PDFWriter, converting the document to PDF. From the Desktop, you can drag and drop EPS files for automatic launching of Acrobat Distiller. Niknak converts vector-based gradient fills to image files for poster displays and printing.

Acquired Knowledge, Inc.

3655 Nobel Drive
Suite 380
San Diego, CA 92122
www.acquiredknowledge.com

EZ-PDF (Macintosh/Windows)

Acquired Knowledge is a developer of applications for the prepress industry. Their Download Mechanic application is a must for those who create PostScript files used for downloading to imaging devices. The company is also one of a few places where you can obtain advanced training in the PostScript language. The most recent program developed by the company is EZ-PDF. EZ-PDF is a stand-alone application that simplifies creating PDF documents from virtually any application. PDFs are created at the Print stage within the document authoring application, much like with PDFWriter. EZ-PDF, however, uses Distiller Job Options and provides alternatives for associating different Job Options with different printer styles. The program offers many preset PDF styles from which to choose for a number of output needs and affords the opportunity to create custom styles. With EZ-PDF, well-formed PDF documents are created with a click of the print button.

AGFA

(USA Headquarters)
Bayer Inc.
Agfa Division
100 Challenger Road
Ridgefield Park, NJ 07660
www.agfahome.com

Apogee

AGFA has been involved in the high-end imaging market with innovative new developments for over a decade. Unlike many other high-end equipment manufacturers who integrate PDF workflows with existing products, AGFA has almost bet the farm on PDF, creating a multimillion-dollar system around core PDF architecture. The Apogee system comprises components for imaging to imagesetters, platesetters, and on-demand devices. The Apogee PDF-based Workflow Production System includes Apogee PrintDrive, Apogee Viper, and the Apogee Pilot production manager. Hook these up to Avantras, Chromapresses, the AGFA Galileo Platesetter, or other output devices, and you can develop a PDF workflow unrivaled by other systems. Viper3 is a software PostScript 3 RIP that can accept PDF documents directly for output via the RIP Pilot software.

Aliant Techsystems

DocMaestro
600 Second Street NE
Hopkins, MN 55343
ais.atk.com

InfoLinker (Windows)

InfoLinker is an Acrobat plug-in used for automating hypertext links in PDF documents. First, the user specifies rules according to specific syntax requirements in a text editor. Templates can be created for documents with common rule characteristics. When the InfoLinker plug-in is used, the rules set applies link attributes according to the definitions from the text file. Links can be created within a given PDF document, between PDF documents, or to application document files.

Library Manage (Windows)

File lists in DOS syntax is limited to a maximum of eight characters with an extension of up to three characters. In order to provide more descriptive information for file lists, Library Manage will organize a file list according to PDF Title fields in which up to 60 characters can be displayed. Searches can be performed on words within the file descriptions.

LinkManager (Windows)

LinkManager is an Acrobat plug-in that helps automate the editing of hypertext links. Properties attributes can be changed globally for links within a document. Individual or multiple links can be selected for modification, enabling manipulation of notes, properties and threads.

Ambia Software

InfoData Systems, Inc.
12150 Monument Drive
Suite 400
Fairfax, VA 22033
www.infodata.com

Compose (Windows)

Compose is an Acrobat plug-in with a toolbox containing 22 tools for aiding you in PDF page composition. With Compose, you can add navigation features such as bookmarks, hypertext links, tables of contents, and more. Also included are tools for repaginating documents; validating links; setting security, printing, and file open options; creating bookmarks, hypertext links, thumbnails, and tables of contents; and more. Many of these features can be automated, which alleviates the painstaking effort of making such changes manually when using many of Acrobat's tools.

Re:mark (Windows)

Back in the Acrobat 3.01 days, Re:mark was a great tool for adding many of the annotation features now found in Acrobat 4.0. Tools for sounds, stamps, lines, text, and underlining were made available through Re:mark and provided many more features for the earlier Acrobat Exchange. Because Acrobat 4.0 has now incorporated most of these features, you may find some of Re:mark's tools a bit redundant. But before you scratch this one off your plug-in list, visit the manufacturer's Web site to find information on new updates. Ambia has proven itself to be an innovative company in the past, and therefore I suspect we'll see more new features added to Re:mark for Acrobat 4.0.

Aerial

Aerial is an Acrobat plug-in with a host of different features to add more functionality to PDF documents. It encompasses tools for pagination; extracting text; searching document indexes; tagging frequently visited pages; paper clipping page edges for quick reference; copying tables to the Clipboard while preserving formats; and building a library of PDF titles and authors for quick launching of documents. One particular feature of Aerial I find useful — and you may, too, depending on your PDF workflow — is its capability to convert form data to RTF, as illustrated in Figure 18-2. When data is exported as an FDF, examining it in Excel is a mess. When using Aerial, you can export to either RTF or Lotus Notes format for easy importing into other applications.

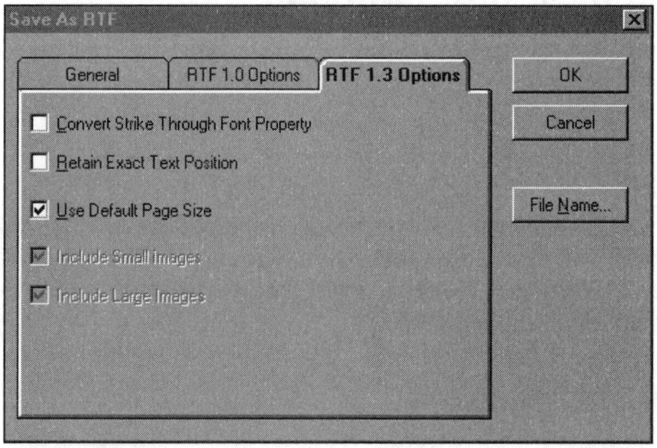

Figure 18-2: The RTF export option in Aerial enables you to find a simplified means for exporting form data that can be read in databases, word processors, and spreadsheets with delimited fields.

One nice feature provided by Aerial is the capability to display the tools you wish in the Acrobat Tool Bar. A dialog box, shown in Figure 18-3, enables you to choose from among the tools to either display or hide. Eliminating unnecessary tools will reduce the clutter in your Acrobat Tool Bar.

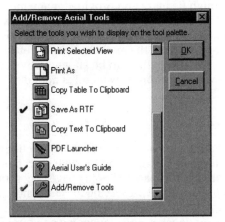

Figure 18-3: Aerial provides a dialog box that enables you to choose which tools to be displayed in the Acrobat Tool Bar.

Autologic Information International

1050 Rancho Conejo Boulevard
Thousand Oaks, CA 91320
www.autoiii.com

APS RIP3 (Windows NT)

This product is a PostScript 3 software RIP operating under Windows NT. PDF files can be delivered individually as single digital masters, which are RIPed and printed to many different devices. APS RIP3 is compliant with Microsoft Internet Explorer and Netscape Navigator for remote operations.

APS PDF AdTool (Macintosh/Windows)

PDF AdTool is designed to work with the newspaper industry's formatting and output of newspaper layouts and designs. PDF AdTool offers speedy cropping for custom ad sizes, definable in column inches for newspaper layouts, and exporting pagination formats specific to systems used in the industry. Ad size errors are flagged by comparing cropped sizes to user-defined tables. Files can be exported as EPS for both composite and preseparated ads. The preseparated ads are exported into composite EPS files.

Avenza Software, Inc.

3385 Harvester Road
Suite 205
Burlington, Ontario
Canada
www.avenza.com

MAPublisher LT (Macintosh/Windows)

MAPublisher LT is a plug-in/Xtra for Adobe Illustrator or Macromedia FreeHand, and it imports vector data from MapInfo, ARCINFO, ArcView, AutoCAD, and other formats into the respective illustration program. Included with the plug-in is an Export to PDF option, which exports the file and attaches attribute databases to the PDF. JAMBuddy (Windows) is a plug-in for Acrobat Reader that enables users to view the map file exports.

BCL Computers

650 Saratoga Avenue
San Jose, CA 95129
www.bcl-computers.com

BCL Computers developed technologies that are incorporated into the Table /Formatted Text Plug-in provided with the Acrobat Plug-ins, mentioned earlier in this chapter. BCL manufactures several plug-ins for converting PDFs to other file formats. Among those plug-ins are the following:

Magellan (Windows)

Magellan is a nifty tool for converting PDF documents to HTML. As mentioned in Chapter 12, the new Web support in Acrobat for Windows will convert HTML to PDF documents by using Web Capture. This plug-in takes us in the other direction. Mac users, don't be concerned — there's a plug-in developed by another manufacturer to do the same for you under Mac OS. In instances when HTML is preferred over PDF for Web sites, you can purchase this plug-in to do a great job in handling the file conversion.

Firebird (Windows)

This plug-in was perhaps more interesting before the introduction of Adobe Photoshop 5.0. It's used to convert PDF documents to TIFF images. Firebird is designed to work in production environments to develop PDF workflows where images need conversion up to resolutions of 600 dpi. Because Photoshop 5.0 now has a batch-process command for PDF to PSD conversion with multiple page documents, you can also set up Actions in Photoshop to accomplish similar workflows.

Jade (Windows)

Jade is another file conversion utility that enables you to convert text and data from PDF documents for use in other applications such as word processors and spreadsheets. Jade interprets the PDF data and converts it to Rich Text Format. You can drag and drop data blocks, tables, and body copy to other applications while retaining much of the formatting of the original data.

Brook House Limited

5 Gorwell
Gotlington
Oxfordshire
OX9 5QB
England
www.brookhouse.co.uk

BatchPrintPDF (Windows)

BatchPrintPDF is an executable application for printing multiple PDF documents. If you're at the office late and you need to print a lot of files, BatchPrintPDF can print a directory of documents overnight. Page ranges can't be identified, so you may need to extract pages and create new PDF documents for just the pages you wish to print. After the PDFs to be printed have been determined, copy them all to the same directory. BatchPrintPDF can print all files located in the same directory, as illustrated in Figure 18-4. Under the View menu, the Details command will display a dialog box indicating the total number of files contained in the directory. The application is available in either a 16-bit or a 32-bit version.

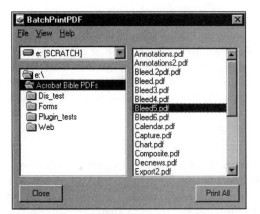

Figure 18-4: BatchPrintPDF is a Windows executable application that is used to automatically print all PDF documents contained in a directory.

Homer (Windows)

This utility adds a tool icon to the Acrobat Command Bar. An icon of a house appears that enables you to identify a home page. When installed, it also adds a plug-in with a menu command for Set Home Page. Click the tool, and you'll return to the home page you identify through the menu command.

WordMark (Windows)

There are several utilities for converting Microsoft Word files to PDF. WordMark is a utility that performs this conversion while converting headings and fields to bookmarks and links. You can download an evaluation copy of this offering from our friends in England at their Web site. In addition to their software offerings, they provide a page that displays an Acrobat tip of the month.

Callas Software GMBH

Pappelallee
D 10437 Berlin Germany
www.callas.de

pdfToolbox (Macintosh/Windows)

pdfToolbox contains several utilities, listed here, for prepress and imaging solutions to automate and cleanup PDF documents for output devices:

pdfBatchMeister

pdfBatchMeister provides for preconfiguring Distiller's Job Options. This feature of the pdfToolbox is intended to work with pdfBatchProcess. Preconfiguration can include Job Options for several output sources such as prepress, CD-ROM, and Web publishing. The disposition of the files is also determined in the pdfBatchMeister dialog box, as illustrated in Figure 18-5.

pdfBatchProcess

This utility provides batch-process distillation of PostScript files. pdfBatchProcess accepts the pdfBatchMeister preconfigured Distiller Job Options for production workflows, which is controlled in the dialog box shown in Figure 18-6. The program emulates Distiller's watched folders and enables mounting of the In and Out watched subfolders on any drive or volume. PostScript files can be repurposed for several output requirements via the pdfBatchMesiter Job Options profiles.

pdfInspektor

pdfInspektor is a preflight checker that analyzes PDF documents and submits a report for file content, including information on fonts, image resolutions, colors, and other potential imaging problems.

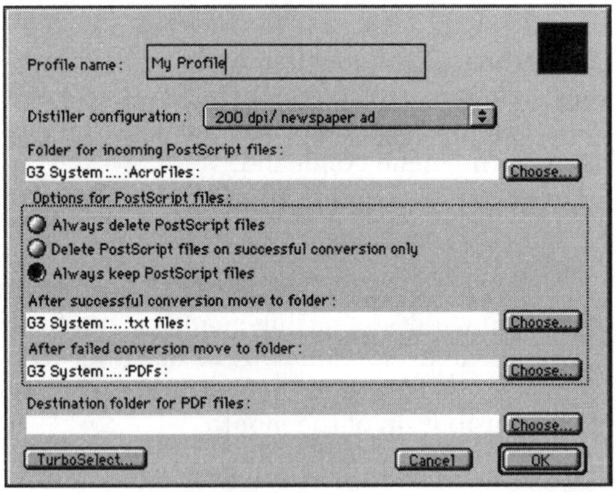

Figure 18-5: pdfBatchMeister is a stand-alone application that enables you to configure profiles for Distiller Job Options to be used with pdfBatchProcess. Disposition of the PostScript and PDF files can be routed to user-defined folders.

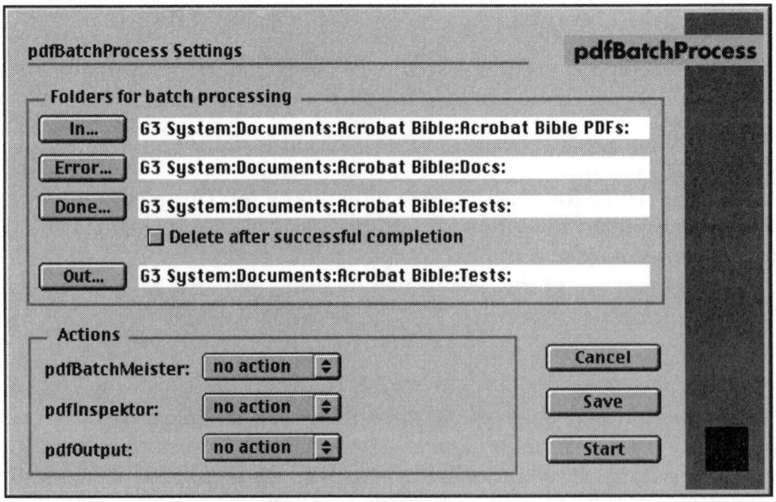

Figure 18-6: pdfBatchProcess is an Acrobat plug-in that enables you to batch-process distillation. From this dialog box, you can select the source files, destination, and disposition of the PostScript files. Errors during distillation can result in routing the PostScript files to a new directory.

pdfOutput

This utility converts PDFs to EPS files with full-image previews and font embedding. Multipage PDF to EPS conversion can be made to provide clean EPS files for importing into programs without PDF support.

pdfCropMarks

Crop and registration marks for bleeds and custom pages sizes can be added to the PDF document with this utility. Replacement of default crops ensures proper imaging for custom page sizes.

pdfCropMeasure

pdfCropMeasure provides a floating palette with a display of the x,y coordinates for crop marks. This utility enables measuring of the crop mark distances to ensure proper cropping to fixed and custom page sizes.

pdfOutputPro (Macintosh/Windows)

pdfOutputPro enables you to print composites and separations from PDF files for high-end imaging systems. In addition to the output options, a feature for adding crop marks on-the-fly with user-specified distances and positions is also available. Separations can be printed with selected colors, halftone frequency control, and dot-gain compensation settings.

MadeToPrint XT (Macintosh)

MadeToPrint is a QuarkXPress XTension that matches PageMaker's feature for direct export to PDF, which launches Distiller in the background and creates the PDF file. MadeToPrint, like PageMaker's Export to Adobe PDF controls, enables overriding of Distiller Job Options. Job Options can be set within QuarkXPress from the MadeToPrint XTension. Font embedding can be handled through a companion program offered by Callas Software called FontIncluder, which embeds all fonts, including TrueType, Type1 and Type3, in XPress documents and imported EPS files.

Cessna Publishing

www.win.net/cessnapub

cpAnnCollector (Windows)

cpAnnCollector is an application used to collect annotation data and convert the data to common separated values (CSV). The CSV data can be imported into databases or spreadsheets. Data from eleven fields, including Path, Filename, Title, Color, Date, and Time, is collected and exported. cpAnnCollector can analyze a directory of PDF files and automatically retrieve annotation data for importing into applications accepting delimited data.

Computerized Document Control, Ltd.

P.O. Box 5
Chepstow, Gwent
NP66YU United Kingdom
www.docctrl.co.uk

PDF*fusion*/PDF*aqua*/PDF*control* (Windows)

The trio of PDF support applications from Computerized Document Control are used to convert complex documents to PDF. PDF*fusion* is an advance document control management system that converts complex documents to PDF in an automated environment. Document templates can be populated with dynamic database information. PDF*aqua* is designed to add a print time watermark to PDF documents, and PDF*control* is used for controlling permissions for printing and viewing.

Local Render (Windows)

Local Render is used to convert Microsoft Office files to PDF. MS Word heading levels are converted to bookmarks and Word cross-references are converted to Acrobat and Web links. Local Render can be accessed through a toolbar button in MS Word or can operate as a command-line application for file conversion.

PDF*tools* (Windows)

PDF*tools* is used to automatically convert MS Word documents to PDF or HTML. Like Local Render, PDF*tools* converts MS Word headings to bookmarks and cross-references to hypertext links and Web links. Documents can be converted manually or batch-processed.

Computerstream Limited

70 Tamworth Road
Ashby de la Zouch
Leicestershire
LE65 2PR, United Kingdom
www.dircon.co.uk/computerstream

Computerstream Limited are specialists in Adobe Acrobat document delivery solutions. Their bureau service covers document scanning and electronic document conversion. Technical developments at Computerstream Limited embrace advances in custom plug-in technology, with their main goal to create solutions in CD-ROM, intranet, and Internet delivery methods.

Banner Print (Windows)

Banner Print is an Acrobat plug-in used to print a watermark on the printed PDF document. When viewing a PDF on screen, the banner will be invisible. Several levels of security are provided for banners. The highest security level enables you to print a standard banner or user-defined banner. Those with a lower level of security can only print the banner defined for the document.

PDF Imposer (Windows)

PDF Imposer is a full-featured imposition plug-in for Adobe Acrobat The PDF Imposer plug-in allows the user to perform the imposition functions commonly required in A4 and A3 black-and-white digital printing. PDF Imposer works entirely with the Portable Document Format and does not require the imposed document to be printed on a Postscript printer; it can be printed on any printer for which a driver is available.

The main features of this plug-in include the following:

✦ The plug-in works on a PDF file that is open in Adobe Acrobat.

✦ The plug-in changes the document in memory, after which it can be printed or stored in its imposed form.

✦ The sizes and/or positions of the logical pages in the PDF file may be changed.

✦ Several PDF pages may be arranged side-by-side on the same sheet of paper.

PDF Imposer is useful for making booklets or signatures, assembling covers, printing several copies of the same document side by side, and printing one copy of a document across several stacks. This utility also provides two additional benefits:

✦ You can inform Acrobat that the changes are temporary, so it will not prompt you to save changes to the document when you close it. The imposed document can be saved to a different file.

✦ Job-ticket files, which contain all the information for imposing the document, can be created and saved.

PDF Protector (Windows)

PDF Protector enables the user to apply (or remove) standard Acrobat security to a batch of PDF files, and to apply (or remove) a watermark on each page of a PDF document. Batch applications can be applied to files in a directory and subdirectories, as illustrated in Figure 18-7. A second dialog box is used to apply attribute settings (see Figure 18-8). PDF Protector is ideal for users who wish to publish controlled documents or publish documents on the Web (copyright notice and logo on each page). Protector has been highly acclaimed by users many of whom applaud its simplicity and the fact that it works exactly as described.

PDF Scantools (Windows)

This product features tools for scanned image "cleanup" in PDF. Eraser removes dirty edges, punch holes, and so on. Positioner allows the image to be correctly positioned on the screen (thus correcting the irritating problem when dealing with scanned documents of the pages not being properly "centered").

PDF Measure (Windows)

PDF Measure is a measurement tool allowing the precise measurement of two points on a PDF page.

Figure 18-7: PDF Protector enables you to apply or remove security to all the PDF documents within a directory and its subdirectories.

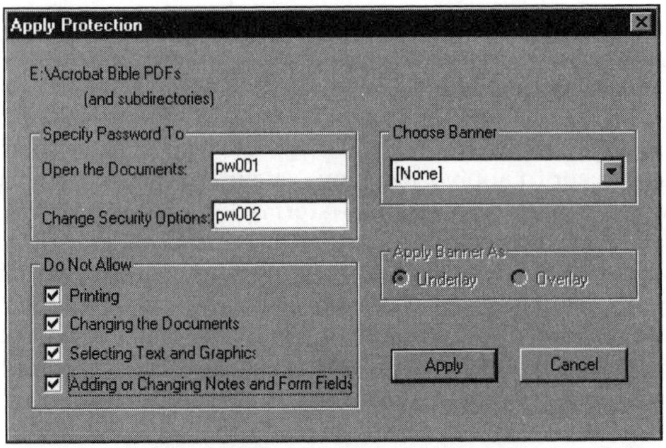

Figure 18-8: After selecting the directory to which you want to apply or remove protection, a second dialog box will appear where the passwords and security options are applied.

Consolidated Technical Services, Inc.

P.O. Box 630
New Market, Maryland 21774
www.contechinc.com

Spiffy-Pop (Windows)

Here's a neat little plug-in for Acrobat and Acrobat Reader from the folks at Consolidated Technical Services. When Spiffy-Pop is installed as an Acrobat plug-in, the Create Link properties window will display Spiffy-Pop as a link option. Select this item, and a dialog box appears in which you can specify a text message. Pop-up windows created in Acrobat can be viewed in Reader with the Spiffy-Pop plug-in installed in Reader's plug-in folder. When viewing text messages created with Spiffy-Pop, document view zoom changes will cause automatic adjustment of font sizes so that the text remains legible.

D Soft

Sparrestraat 24
B-9920 Lovendegem
Belgium
www.dsoft.be

Acrobat CD Installer (Windows)

Many plug-ins occupy a special place under the Command Bar in Acrobat, whereas others create their own menus. If a number of plug-ins are installed, they compete for space at the top of the Acrobat window. With an inordinate number of plug-ins installed, the space can become crowded and unmanageable. Acrobat CD Installer handles custom plug-ins for CDs. Only the needed plug-ins are installed, and when you quit Acrobat, the plug-ins are deinstalled.

Data Technology Group

221 East Main Street
Milford, MA 01757
www.dtgsw.com

CRF Publisher (Windows)

CRF Publisher is an application that converts patient case report forms collected during clinical studies of new drugs to PDF for submission to the U.S. Food and Drug Administration (FDA). The application performs on-the-fly conversion of text and TIFF image files and automatically generates bookmarks and tables of contents. The PDF documents created are compliant with FDA standards for electronic case report forms.

Datawatch Corporation

234 Ballardvale Street
Wilmington, MA 01887
www.datawatch.com

Redwing (Windows)

Redwing is an Acrobat plug-in designed to extract data from PDF documents. With Redwing, you can extract text and tables with total file integrity, preserving formatting codes and tabular text. Extracted data can be saved in many popular Windows application file formats for importing into databases, spreadsheets, and word processors. User-defined selections can determine which data will be extracted from the PDF document.

Digital Applications, Inc.

215 East Providence Road
Aldan, PA 19018-4129
www.digapp.com

AppendPDF (UNIX)

Back in Chapter 5, I mentioned concatenating PostScript files to create a single PDF file from multiple files printed to disk. At times, you'll want to combine several PDF documents into a single document. In Acrobat 4.0, the only way you can go about the task is to open a PDF and insert new PDFs one by one — a laborious task if you need to merge many files. If you're working on a UNIX system, AppendPDF is your answer when you have a need to combine files. AppendPDF is a stand-alone UNIX command-line application used to combine PDFs, extract selected pages to be combined in other PDFs, and add document information to the newly created files. In environments for CD-ROM publishing, on-demand printing, or Web publishing, AppendPDF can speed up your PDF workflows.

AppendPDF Pro (Windows NT/UNIX)

AppendPDF Pro is a server-based application that is built using the Adobe PDF Library. It is a command-line-driven application that combines PDF files or page ranges within files. It will also add a TOC and a cover page. AppendPDF Pro will also generate hyperlinks in the TOC, add bookmarks, and add page numbers. It is ideally suited as a Web server solution for generating customized reports.

Redax (Macintosh/Windows)

To *redact* a document is to prepare it for publication — that is, edit and revise it. The Redax plug-in for Acrobat enables you to redact text and scanned images in PDF documents. Such editing is beneficial when eliminating information from documents to comply with the Freedom of Information Act and Privacy Act. When executed, Redact will scan a PDF, tag words selected in a text file, and overlay them in the PDF with exemption codes. Text can be verified, resized, moved, deleted, and tagged for exemption. With the click of a button, a new PDF is created containing your edits.

DateD Author and DateD Viewer (Macintosh/Windows)

DateD Author permits date and time stamping of edited PDF documents. The date and time stamp can also include a text line. When the PDF file is printed, the date and time stamp and text message will be printed with it. DateD Viewer permits viewing of the date and time stamps in Acrobat Reader.

FDFMerge (UNIX/Windows NT)

FDFMerge is a server-based application that uses the Adobe PDF Library. FDFMerge runs on your Web server and fills in a PDF form with the data from an FDF file. The resultant document is the completed PDF form that your users can download from your Web site to their computer. You can reliably generate completed forms in the time it takes to save a document. Users can download the completed form to their own system where they can save it and print it at any time.

TimedOut Author and TimedOut Viewer (Macintosh/Windows)

TimedOut Author is an Acrobat Plug-in that enables you to identify an expiration date for a PDF document. When the expiration date is determined, the TimedOut plug-in can secure the file with password protection. The TimedOut Viewer is a plug-in that works with Acrobat Reader to enable you to view TimedOut documents. The Viewer plug-in is distributed free of charge.

StampPDF (Macintosh/Windows)

A plug-in for Acrobat, StampPDF is similar to the Stamp annotations offered in version 4.0 of Acrobat. StampPDF limits the stamping of a PDF document to text; however, that text can be formatted — you can make changes to fonts, size, justification, position, orientation, and so on. StampPDF can also be used to add watermarks and permanent text to the PDF.

StampPDF Batch (UNIX/Windows NT)

StampPDF Batch is a server-based application that uses the Adobe PDF Library. It is a command-line-driven application that stamps any text-based information on PDF documents in batch mode. StampPDF Batch will add the same types of information as the StampPDF plug-in, but without the need to open individual documents in order to stamp them. As with the StampPDF plug-in, new text added with StampPDF Batch becomes a permanent part of the documents.

Dionis

167 Milk Street
Suite 476
Boston, MA 02109-4315
www.dionis.com

Ari's Toolbox (Macintosh/Windows)

Ari's Toolbox is a collection of four Acrobat plug-ins used for document analysis and printing:

Ari's Crop Helper

When this plug-in is installed, three options will appear in the plug-ins menu for checking the open document's pages for crop information. You can choose to have the Ari's Crop Helper find any pages that have been cropped, pages that have not been cropped, or pages that are not cropped like the page in view. A dialog box will appear informing you of the results.

Ari's Link Checker

If you're an Acrobat evangelist and you spend a lot of time creating PDF documents for screen, Web, or CD-ROM, and you immerse yourself in links, this is a great tool for you. I find Ari's Link Checker indispensable when assembling documents with great numbers of links. The Link Checker can survey your open PDF document and report back information on links, or you can batch-process the links of all PDF documents in a directory, drive, or CD-ROM. From a pull-down menu, you make selections for the link checking (see Figure 18-9).

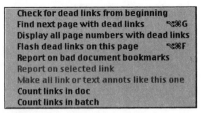

Figure 18-9: The Ari's Link Checker plug-in installs menu commands for checking links in an open PDFdocument.

When you run a check for one of the items in the pull-down menu, a dialog box such as the one illustrated in Figure 18-10 will appear displaying results or, for some selections, a PDF report will be created. For example, if you select the first menu item, Check for dead links from beginning, a dialog box will display all pages in the open PDF document in which links with no destinations appear.

If you elect to browse each page to find a bad link, Ari's Link Checker will cause the bad link to flash. Bookmarks can also be found by Link Checker.

Ari's Print Helper

Ari's Print Helper is an Acrobat plug-in that appears as an icon in the Acrobat Tool Bar. The print helper offers options typically found in layout or advanced business applications. You can select page ranges to print or print only even or odd pages, fit the data on a page, and choose the PostScript level and encoding method. Figure 18-11 displays the options available for printing.

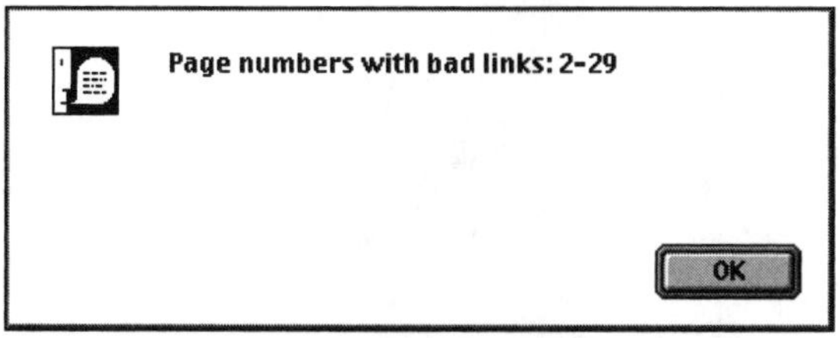

Figure 18-10: I selected Check for dead links from beginning from the Plug-ins:Link Checker Menu, and Ari's Link Checker reported all pages in my PDF where dead links were found.

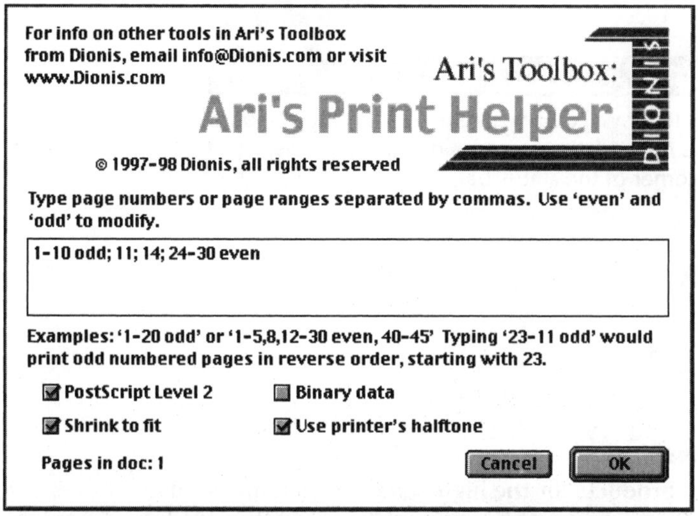

Figure 18-11: Ari's Print Helper provides more print options than are available in Acrobat's Print dialog box. Among the choices are selections for page ranges and printing even or odd pages.

Ari's Ruler

Ari's Ruler also installs a tool in the Acrobat Tool Bar. The measurement tool displays the x,y coordinates of the cursor position from origin to destination and the distance between the two points. In Figure 18-12, the x,y coordinates are displayed in the lower-right corner of the Acrobat status bar. You can measure a rectangle with all three readouts in units defined in Acrobat's General Preferences dialog box.

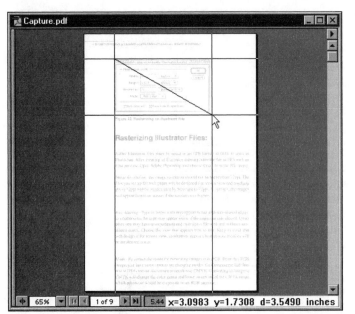

Figure 18-12: Ari's Ruler will display a ruler icon for the cursor. When a rectangle is opened, the *x,y* coordinates will be displayed in the lower-right corner of the status bar.

Doculex, Inc.

200 Avenue B, NW
Winter Haven, FL 33881
www.doculex.com

PDF-it (Windows)

Doculex produces products for the high-end OCR scanning industry. PDF-it can be used as a stand-alone product or in conjunction with other products manufactured by the company for text recognition on scanned documents. PDF-it converts TIFF images to PDF image only or PDF image plus text. This is the high-productivity tool to use when you have 10,000 to 100,000 document pages you need to conversion.

Easy Software Products

44145 Airport View Drive
Suite 204
Hollywood, MD 20636-3111
www.easysw.com

HTMLDOC (Windows)

HTMLDOC is an application that converts indexed HTML files created in any editor to PostScript or PDF. The program supports HTML version 3.2 and some markups in HTML version 4.0. From a dialog box with tab choices, you specify the attribute settings (see Figure 18-13).

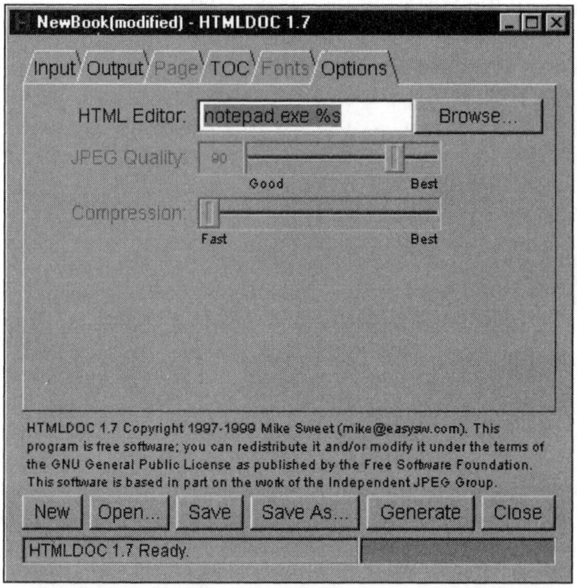

Figure 18-13: HTMLDOC offers options in a dialog box for conversion attributes of PostScript and PDF documents, including JPEG compression quality settings.

Enfocus Software, Inc.

234 Columbine Street
Suite 300B
Denver, CO 80206
USA
www.enfocus.com

CheckUp (Macintosh/Windows)

CheckUp is a preflight utility that ensures proper configuration of PostScript and PDF files. Through user-specified profiles, CheckUp analyzes a PostScript or PDF file for various types of output, which you determine in a Control Panel as illustrated in Figure 18-14. A report is generated from CheckUp's findings.

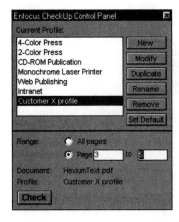

Figure 18-14: From Check-Up's Control Panel, you can determine a profile to be used in the analysis of the PostScript or PDF file. The analysis will result in a report of the findings based on the profile attributes.

PitStop (Macintosh/Windows)

Even with all the new features of Acrobat 4.0, there's no comparison to all the editing features provided with PitStop. PitStop offers a toolbox with options for editing text and graphics like those available in an art program. You can copy and paste text and images, change attributes including fonts and colors, perform transformations, add new objects with drawing tools, and more. PitStop enables you to edit in either a preview mode or keyline mode (see Figure 18-15).

Extensis Corporation

1800 SW First Avenue
Suite 500
Portland, OR 97201
USA
www.extensis.com

Collect Pro (Macintosh)

In the prepress industry, preflighting documents will always improve workflow solutions. Collect Pro does just that. It's a preflight utility that enables you to use a drag-and-drop method to collect all files associated with the document. From the window shown in Figure 18-16, you can add or delete items for collection prior to gathering them in a folder. If distillation on another computer in a workflow environment is used, Collect Pro can ensure all related files are included with the authoring application to create a PDF suitable for imaging. Collect Pro works with the major professional applications for publishing, as well as Multi-Ad Creator.

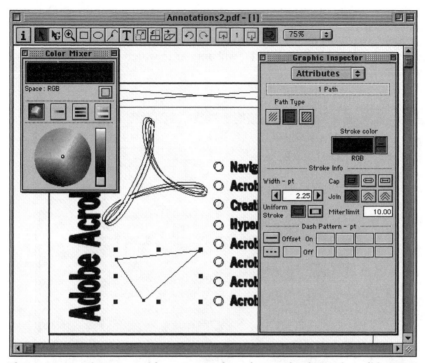

Figure 18-15: PitStop provides many tools and several palettes for editing PDF objects and text. The display can be viewed in either preview or keyline mode.

Figure 18-16: Collect Pro from Extensis Software provides user-selectable options for collecting links, fonts, and related document data. As an executable application, it is not limited to the collection options contained within applications supporting a similar command.

A nice feature provided with Collect Pro is the opportunity to supply job ticket information with the collected data. After the data is collected, a button will appear labeled Next, as shown in Figure 18-16. When you click the Next button, another dialog box, illustrated in Figure 18-17, will appear in which the job ticket information is supplied.

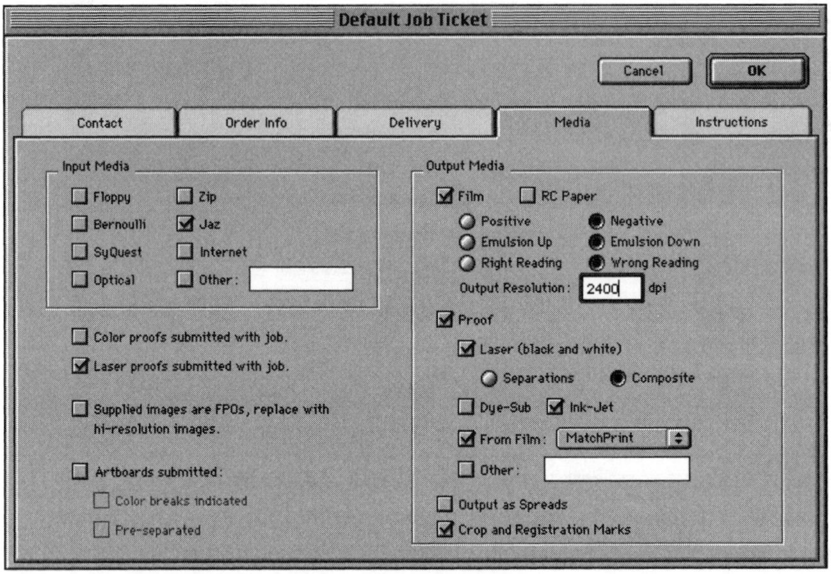

Figure 18-17: Job ticket information related to the PDF document or application file can be user specified in a dialog box after the data has been collected.

Collect Pro goes beyond a stand-alone application with support for Acrobat. It actually functions similarly to the way Distiller is launched from an application program. The Collect Pro command will appear in the Plug-ins menu. When selected, the stand-alone application is launched, enabling you to supply the preflighting and job ticket information. Extensis has a real winner with this product. If you prepare files for prepress or you work in a production environment for almost any kind of output, this product should be on your top ten list.

Preflight Pro (Macintosh)

Preflight Pro, working in conjunction with Collect Pro, will analyze the collected documents and report back any potential imaging problems such as resolution deficiencies, color modes, missing fonts, and so on. When complete, you can run scripts with customized Job Options to create PDF documents for application files that will be printed to disk.

QX-Tools (Macintosh)

QX-Tools is a QuarkXTension package that is easy to use. The QX-VectorEdit feature of the tools is used to convert EPS, PostScript, and PDF documents to QuarkXPress artwork. Once imported into QuarkXPress, the PDFs or EPS/PostScript files can be edited.

FileOpen Systems, Inc.

101 West 85th Street
Suite 1-4
New York, NY 10024-4451
www.fileopen.com

FileOpen PDF Publisher (Macintosh/Windows)

FileOpen PDF Publisher is a stand-alone, high-level security application that adds expiration dates and security to PDF documents. The application can batch-process directories of PDFs suitable for PDF workflows in the most demanding environments. PDF Publisher enables document security to control parameters for limiting printing, viewing, copying, editing, and changing annotations. Pages may be viewed and selected pages blocked from viewing, printing, editing, and so on. Documents can be locked on local drives, CDs, and Web sites.

HAHT Software, Inc.

4200 Six Forks Road
Suite 200
Raleigh, NC 27609
www.HAHT.com

HAHT Enterprise Solution Module (Windows)

HAHT is an advanced systems developer providing tools for creating and deploying dynamic data-driven PDF forms. Through their Enterprise Solution Module (ESM), HAHT provides developers a means for converting paper forms to interactive electronic forms that interface with applications software. Using the HAHT site, users can dynamically supply and retrieve data for immediate forms processing.

Handmade Software

48860 Milmont Drive
Suite 106
Fremont, CA 94538-7369
www.handmade.com

Image Alchemy PS (Macintosh/Windows)

Image Alchemy PS supports 94 different file formats and provides the capability to convert files in these formats to PostScript, EPS, or PDF. The application contains a PostScript interpreter for scaling images and RIPing without size limitation. The application is particularly valuable to those printing to large format inkjet printers where print sizes may require upscaling images with special dithering to maintain high-quality output. Clicking the More Options button shown in Figure 18-18 will open a dialog box in which sizes and resolutions can be specified.

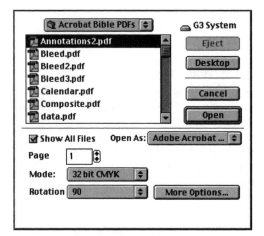

Figure 18-18: PDF files can be opened in Image Alchemy PS as individual or multiple files. By clicking the More Options button, you can make choices for input/output sizes, clipping, preloading fonts, and several levels of anti-aliasing.

Helios Software

HELIOS Software GmbH
Steinriede 3
D-30827 Garbsen, Germany
www.helios.de

PDF Handshake (UNIX)

The server software for PDF Handshake runs on many different flavors of UNIX configured for the professional and high-end print market. Macintosh clients are used with an Acrobat plug-in to print to high-end devices. Color separations, color conversions (spot to process), ICC profile support including profile tagging, and sophisticated font support with automatic TrueType to Type 1 conversion are among the features available with PDF Handshake and the accompanying applications Helios Software also markets. The product includes a number of ICC profiles for proofing systems, scanners, SWOP profiles, and newspaper presses. It also permits using PDF files as high-resolution input for an OPI workflow by creating standard EPS low-resolution placement images out of PDF originals. PDF Handshake gives prepress and printing customers all the benefits of PDF as a universal exchange format for their existing applications and their currently installed output devices, without any need for costly and time-consuming upgrades.

Iceni Technology

82 St Philips Road, Norwich, Norfolk
NR2 3BW. England
www.iceni.com

Gemini (Macintosh/Windows)

Iceni Technology develops plug-ins for converting PDFs to other file formats. The Generate HTML plug-in converts PDF documents, including images, to HTML. A companion plug-in, ExtractImages, will convert images to scalable JPEG or Progressive JPEG files. HTML-converted styles can have attributes assigned to display Web pages in the correct reading order and include fonts and font styles from the original PDF layout. During conversion, all images contained in the PDF will be extracted and converted to the formats noted above.

There's probably no easier application to use for conversion to HTML than these plug-ins. To extract images in a PDF document, select the Plug-ins menu and choose Extract Images, which opens the dialog box shown in Figure 18-19. When the OK button is clicked, the Generate HTML dialog box will appear, as shown in Figure 18-20.

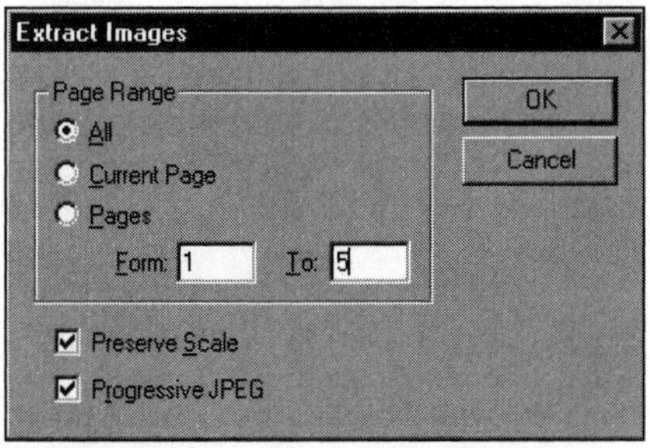

Figure 18-19: When the Export Images dialog box appears, choices for page ranges and JPEG attributes become available.

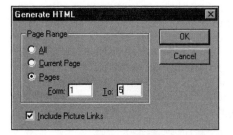

Figure 18-20: When the Generate HTML menu is selected, you can select the page ranges in the document for export. An option appears for the inclusion of picture links.

You select the page range and click OK. Gemini will open a dialog box in which you specify where the exported file will be located. A button appears for choosing HTML as the format. First navigate to the folder where the file will be saved, and then click Choose HTML. Gemini will begin the conversion. It's that easy.

If converting PDFs to HTML, use the Extract Images command first to develop the image links that will be referenced in the HTML. After extracting images, select the Generate HTML command. The final Web page will display the image links along with the text from the PDF document. In the demo version, an X will be displayed in the converted images, as illustrated in Figure 18-21. When purchasing the full product, images will be properly displayed.

Picture Extraction Plug-in (Windows)

Picture Extraction Plug-in (PEP) is a plug-in designed for image conversions. It converts images to one of several selected formats — EPS, JPEG, or TIFF. When images are converted to EPS, color spaces and profile tagging are preserved. OPI comments are also preserved in the converted files. Extractions can be batch-processed to create individual files from selected sources with unique filenames created for the converted files.

Image Solutions

101 Gibraltar Drive
Morris Plains, NJ 07050
www.imagesolutions.com

CRFScan & Trade (Windows)

CRFScan & Trade is a vertical application for the pharmaceutical industry, which requires submitted forms to comply with FDA criteria. The FDA accepts documents in PDF format for case study reports. Case report forms (CRFs) can be captured or converted from TIFF, fax, or PDF and then indexed by study, site, patient, and form number. CFRScan & Trade manages the data and verifies compliance for either internal use or submission to government offices.

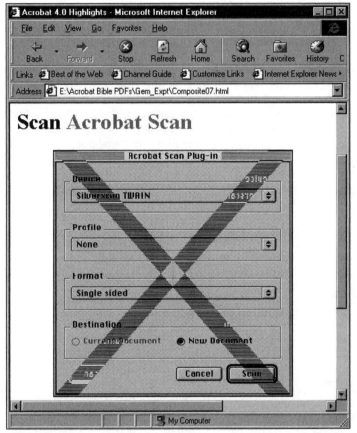

Figure 18-21: The demo version of Gemini will mark all converted images with an X.

PDFComposer (Windows)

PDFComposer is a utility used to convert scanned images, TIFF formats, and word processor files exported from Windows to PDF. When using scanned images, Composer will supply bookmarks through optical character recognition on user-specified areas. Page editing is also available, enabling page reordering, deletions, and replacements. A number of other features are included for making image enhancements, annotations, transformations, headers and footers, borders, and page numbering.

ISIFile (Windows)

Also a conversion application, ISIFile can convert multiple scanned TIFF images to PDF. Auto-integration of bookmarks, hypertext links, image enhancement, orientation corrections, keyline border editing, and more are handled.

ISIToolBox (Windows)

ISIToolBox is an Acrobat plug-in that provides many tools for the creation of book-marks and hypertext links. Text can be copied from text blocks or tables with pre-served text formatting characteristics and pasted into word processed documents or spreadsheets. Delimited text fields will be preserved when pasting data from tables. Automating a TOC to bookmarks is a feature as well as creating bookmarks globally on text attributes. Additional features include global editing of hypertext links, importing/exporting bookmarks, merging PDFs, and assigning links to page numbers.

TableMaster (Windows)

TableMaster is an Acrobat plug-in designed to convert ASCII text to PDF. During the conversion, characteristics for page breaks, font sizes, replacement of graphic symbols, and handling paper margins are user controlled. Bookmarks can capture keywords and associate the found words to their respective pages.

GraphCopy (Windows)

GraphCopy is a freeware distribution from Image Solutions. The Acrobat plug-in can copy 72 ppi images to 400 ppi images. Resolution is determined in a preference dialog box, as shown in Figure 18-22.

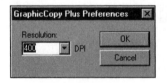

Figure 18-22: GraphCopy can copy a selected range of the PDF document at a resolution determined in the GraphCopy preferences dialog box. To use the plug-in, select File ➪ Preferences ➪ ISI GraphCopy Plus. A dialog box will appear in which the resolution can be determined.

Once the resolution is selected, choose the ISI menu from the Acrobat menu bar and select GraphCopy. The cursor will change, informing you data can be copied to the Clipboard. Draw a rectangle around the data you wish to copy. When the mouse button is released, GraphCopy will copy the data to the Clipboard. If you open Photoshop and select New from the File menu, the resolution for the new document will be retained from the GraphCopy selection.

Imation

Imation Enterprises Corp.
1 Imation Place
Oakdale, MN 55128-3414
www.imation.com

PressWise (Macintosh)

Imation PressWise is a stand-alone application designed for the high-end imaging industry for page imposition on imagesetters and platesetters. PressWise supports full integration of PDF for impositions and accommodates a mix of PDF, EPS, and PostScript for the same jobs.

INFOCON AMERICA CORP.

620 Newport Center Drive, Suite 1100
Newport Beach, CA 92660
www.INFOCONAMERICA.com

InfoLink Publishing Enhancement Software (Windows)

The InfoLink Publishing Enhancement Software is an advanced Acrobat publishing solution that uses plug-ins to support tools to enhance PDF publications and documents designed for professional publishing over the Internet, intranets, and CD-ROM. The company markets the InfoLink Publishing Enhancement Software to publishers of newsletters, journals, directories, and newspapers, educational publishers, and other industries. However, when you look at the many capabilities of the software, you can see how it would be useful for almost any market. With the advanced Acrobat publishing solution, you can preflight PDFs, add text, highlight and annotate, catalog, index, archive, and secure files. You can create links, bookmarks, and thumbnails, build tables of contents and indexes, and create overlays and watermarks. In short, if you find some of the Acrobat 4.0 features limiting, visit the INFOCON AMERICA Web site and take a quick tour of the amazing tools offered with this plug-in. INFOCON AMERICA also provides a complete electronic publishing service to create enhanced PDF files using the same InfoLink software as a service bureau.

Informative Graphics Corporation

706 East Bell Road
Suite 207
Phoenix, AZ 85022
www.infograph.com

Myriad (Windows)

The Myriad Engineering Viewer is designed to view, redline, and print a wide range of engineering CAD drawings, documents, images, and 3D models. Myriad enables inclusion of author name with redlines of drawings, time and date stamping, and exporting redlines and notes to CAD. Though a stand-alone application, Myriad can be integrated with Acrobat. Acrobat can be used inside Myriad's user interface to extend Acrobat's capabilities. The PDF views can display redlines created in Myriad, and PDF redlines can be displayed in Myriad.

Intense Software

Suite 310 - 3495 Cambie Street
Vancouver, British Columbia
Canada
www.intensesoftware.com

PDF Embedder (Macintosh)

The people at Intense Software call PDF Embedder a *digital briefcase*. This Acrobat plug-in is used to embed a file inside the PDF document. The file can be a data file or an application. When you purchase PDF Embedder, you get a serial number to permit file embedding. If you run the plug-in in demo mode (that is, without the serial number), you can unembed the file(s). The program was originally created to overcome some limitations with the prepress preparation of PDFs. But it has many other useful features available for working with almost any kind of data or application. You could, for example, embed an installer application in a PDF document and run the installer from within an Acrobat viewer. The installer would decompress and install a software application. Application document files can be embedded in the PDF, and when unembedded, they will launch the host application. If a PDF container for other documents or applications is your wish, then PDF Embedder is your ticket.

Lantana Research

39500 Stevenson Place
Suite 110
Fremont, CA 94539
www.lantanarips.com

Crackerjack (Macintosh/Windows)

I spoke of Crackerjack back in Chapter 16 when digital prepress was covered. For the imaging industry, Crackerjack is a must. The plug-in appears under the file menu when installed and opens a Print dialog box that overcomes various limitations within Acrobat. PPD selection, page sizes, orientation, color handling, emulsion, and reading as well as device-independent color spaces are all settings you can change through Crackerjack's Print dialog box. If you're tired of exporting to EPS for color separations, then visit the Lantana Web site for more on Crackerjack.

Crackerjack Pilot (Macintosh/Windows)

Pilot is a companion product to Crackerjack. Pilot enables you to develop hot folders from which Crackerjack can print. One or more hot folders (see Figure 18-23) can be developed for multiple devices so that job queues can manage the workflow. The PDF is printed by the Crackerjack plug-in, installed in Acrobat, to a user-defined hot folder. From the hot folder, the PDF is printed using the Crackerjack plug-in, and the job can be routed to the imaging device or to an Output folder.

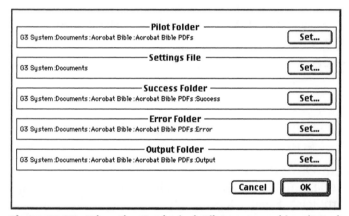

Figure 18-23: When the Crackerjack Pilot command is selected, a dialog box will appear in which the selections for folders containing jobs are made. The Output folder can be used as a hot folder where jobs to be imaged can be dragged and dropped.

OPI Doctor (Macintosh/Windows)

Acrobat allows for the inclusion of OPI comments in PDF files. However, due to Acrobat's strict compliance with the OPI 1.3 spec, the PDF will include either the low-res preview or the path to the high-res file, but rarely both. OPI Doctor is a plug-in that allows the user to add, edit, or delete OPI paths in a PDF. In addition, the user can reposition, scale, rotate, replace, subsample (convert fat PDF to skinny PDF), or extract images for editing in an external application and later replacement in the PDF.

PDF Bellhop (Macintosh/Windows)

PDF Bellhop uses a PDF document to provide full suitcase services. In addition to fonts, you can include images, Quark and PageMaker files, or other digital files. This Acrobat plug-in turns a PDF file into a portable container for prepress delivery. PDF Bellhop's easy-to-use features, such as hot folder input, make inclusion and extraction of files effortless. It's not restricted to graphic arts applications. Included files can be easily extracted using Lantana's royalty-free PDF Valet plug-in.

PDF Librarian (Macintosh/Windows)

PDF Librarian turns a PDF document into an archiving environment. With this Acrobat plug-in, you can store digital files within a PDF. PDF Librarian also provides a complete tool set for managing, extracting, and launching these files. PDF Librarian has capabilities for watched folder input, compression, encryption, version control, revision control, automated backup, and logging. It's great for engineering projects, Web site management, and graphic arts projects. Included files can be easily extracted using Lantana's royalty-free PDF Valet plug-in.

Markzware USA

1805 East Dyer Road
Suite 101
Santa Ana, CA 92705
www.markzware.com

Flightcheck (Macintosh/Windows)

Flightcheck is a preflight utility that checks application document files for potential imaging problems. Feedback is reported for fonts, color modes, links, resolution, rotations, and so on. The application is best used prior to printing a file to PostScript for distillation.

MarkzScout (Macintosh/Windows)

Whereas Flightcheck will preflight files individually, the new addition to Markzware's line of products has great benefits to true production workflows. File attributes for output requirements are user supplied. MarkzScout contains criteria for over 300 problems that might be associated with imaging errors. Files are dropped into a hot folder and then matched against attributes for preflighting, as illustrated in Figure 18-24. Files containing errors can be routed to folders, workstations, servers, and so on for holding or editing. If, for example, you wish to identify all files containing RGB images that need to be converted to CMYK for output, MarkzScout will route files from the hot folder to a user-specified folder. Or, you can have the files opened in Photoshop where an Action can perform the mode conversion. MarkzScout recognizes the popular professional layout, illustration, and photo-imaging application file formats.

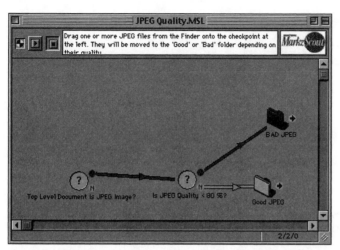

Figure 18-24: When MarkzScout is launched, you can select a profile for preflighting files and then drag and drop your files in the Scout window. The files that meet the profile attributes will be routed to the Good folder, whereas those that do not meet the attributes will be routed to the Bad folder.

Merlin Open Systems

P.O. Box 230
Nottingham
NG2ILJ
United Kingdom
www.merlin-os.co.uk

Name It/Name It Launcher (Macintosh/Windows)

Merlin Open Systems has created several nifty Acrobat plug-ins that speed up your production workflows and add some features for viewing and printing documents. The first of these is Name It, an Acrobat plug-in for creating named destinations (see Figure 18-25). This plug-in is great for anyone creating large document files or archives of information in PDF form. You can create multiple named destinations in one action for all bookmarks in a PDF file, individual pages, or multiple files in a directory. A destination is *named* according to page and view. The text name associated with the view can then be applied to links or bookmarks. Named destinations appearing as bookmarks will open the linked views within Web browsers on the World Wide Web on intranets and office servers. A companion product called Name It Launcher will open PDF documents associated with named destinations.

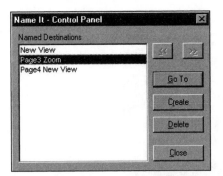

Figure 18-25: Create named destinations through the Name It - Control Panel. Double-clicking any of the destination names will take you to the view associated with the destination.

Options (Macintosh/Windows)

Options is an Acrobat plug-in designed to batch-process a selected directory of PDFs for editing of document information and security options. Nested folders can also be processed with Options. The Title, Subject, Author, and Keywords fields for PDF files in the selected directory can all be edited and saved. Secure files can be edited as long as the user has the security passwords needed to open the files.

Date Stamp (Windows)

Date Stamp is a stand-alone application; however, it only works with Acrobat Reader. When the Reader user prints a PDF document, the printed page(s) will appear with a time and date stamp as well as a user-supplied text message. The utility intercepts printing, which is how the data is supplied on the document.

Index Fixer (Windows)

Index Fixer is an Acrobat plug-in designed to work with Acrobat Catalog to create searches for password-secure files. If you password-protect a PDF document, Catalog won't be able to interpret the passwords or offer a dialog box for access to the PDF at the time the search is being built. In workflow environments where many files have been secured, users would need to resave the files without security or use a batch-process application to unsecure the files, generate an index, and then resecure the files. With Index Fixer, the PDFs will be *fixed* so indexes can be created as long as the user has the necessary password(s). After the index completes its build, the PDF password integrity will remain undisturbed.

Search Results Printer (Macintosh/Windows)

When a search is invoked in Acrobat or Acrobat Reader, the search results can be printed with this plug-in. A menu will appear, enabling user confirmation on the pages to be printed that match the query.

Muscat

The Westbrook Centre
Milton Road
Cambridge
CB4 1YG
England
www.muscat.com

Muscat PDF Document Filter (Windows)

Muscat manufactures products to search and index office automation documents including Acrobat PDFs and HTML. The Acrobat Filter allows users to search and display data stored in Portable Document Format. Indexes can be built across multiple documents and across multiple platforms, and support for multiple languages with automatic language detection is included. Searches can be performed on local systems, intranets, and the Internet.

NetFormation, Inc.

106 Montague Street
Brooklyn Heights, NY 11201
www.netformation.com

Face-It! (Windows)

NetFormation is a member of the Acrobat Certified Experts and an authorized HAHTsite Solution Provider. The company specializes in integrating Acrobat forms with databases and application servers over a network such as the Internet, an intranet, or an extranet. Among other products and services, NetFormation has developed a Web-based proofing system that combines PDF file delivery with version tracking and workflow reports. Face-It! performs a function similar to the dynamic object linking now available with Acrobat 4.0. Rather than change the embedded image in a PDF document, Face-It! uses a form field where a button image is dynamically changed to a user-specified PDF. On-the-fly customization replaces button fields with new user-defined graphics.

One Vision, Inc.

438 Davison Street
Sewickley, PA 15143
www.one-vision.com

Asura (Macintosh/Windows)

Asura is designed to work in a high-production workflow environment where files prepared as PDF, EPS, TIFF, AI, and PostScript are automatically checked and corrected for production and imaging. With Asura, you create folders for specific output devices defined with specific configurations. The output folders are associated to a resource folder where files are dropped and an error folder where problem files are routed. During user-defined time periods, files are routed to the corresponding device. Corrected errors are recorded in a log file. Corrections involve color mode changes, font problems, orientation and page sizes, sampling, compression, and more.

Solvero (Macintosh/Windows)

Whereas Asura is a tool for production workflows, Solvero is a manual editor that lets you open and correct files with potential imaging problems. Solvero works with several digital file formats and converts them to PDF, EPS, or PostScript. One unique feature of the Solvero editing model is the use of Display PostScript. Once displayed, image editing will be consistent with output to PostScript because of a more consistent WYSIWYG environment. The capability to open PDF, EPS, and PostScript files that are then viewed as Display PostScript reduces applications of different versions running under different platforms to a common denominator. Solvero provides tools for editing vector and raster artwork, fonts, color modes, sampling, and most of the attributes related to common imaging problems.

Page Technology Marketing, Inc.

12730 Carmel Country Road
Suite 120
San Diego, CA 92130-2153
www.pcltools.com

FormView (Windows)

FormView is a stand-alone application that reads, views, searches, and prints Hewlett Packard Printer Control (PCL) language files. PCL files can be converted to PDF or several other formats for printing to non–PCL printers. FormView can be configured as a Web browser helper application for storing PCL-printed documents on the Web.

PDF Solutions Limited

2 Conisborough Court
Osbourne Road
Dartford, DA26PY
United Kingdom
www.pdf-solutions.com

CloneLink (Windows)

The editing of individual hypertext links in PDFs has always been an aggravation. CloneLink is an Acrobat plug-in that eases the time-consuming, page-by-page editing of links that share common properties, letting you apply new properties to links on selected ranges of pages. With CloneLink, you can select the link properties and apply the same properties to all links within the page range determined in a dialog box. This plug-in won't let you copy and paste links, but you can globally change existing link properties, such as border, color, and highlight, and the views associated with them, as illustrated in Figure 18-26. To top it off, CloneLink is a fully functioning plug-in without a time limit offered free by PDF Solutions. The company also provides tutorials and PDF solutions. Visit the PDF Solutions Limited Web site for more information.

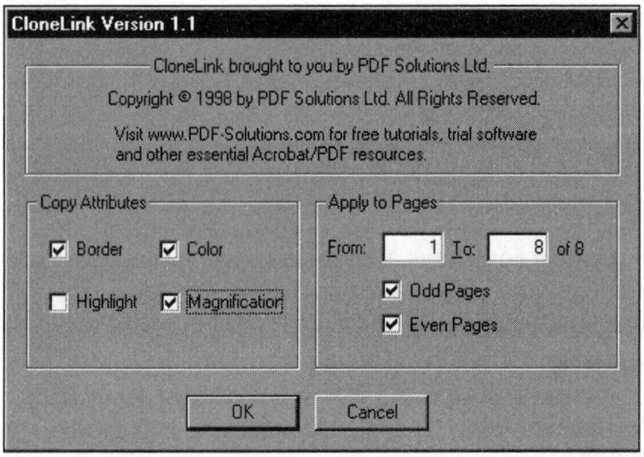

Figure 18-26: The CloneLink dialog box enables you to choose the attributes from a selected link to be applied to other links in the open PDF document within specific page ranges.

PrePress-Consulting Stephen Jaeggi

Bottmingerstrasse 92
CH-4102 Binningen
Switzerland
www.prepress.ch

Distiller Tools (Macintosh/Windows)

If you become confused about which Job Options were used when a file was distilled, PrePress Consulting has a product to help identify those Job Options. Four tools provide feedback on Job Options used to create a PDF file. DistillerNotes creates a note on the first page of the PDF document and stores the Job Option information within the note. FontNotes attaches a note to the PDF document indicating which fonts are contained therein as well as any font errors. Reports are generated in the form of notes in the PDF document, as illustrated in Figure 18-27. MakeStartup and MakePrologue create a startup and prologue file respectively for preset Distiller options, which can be defined by the user before distillation.

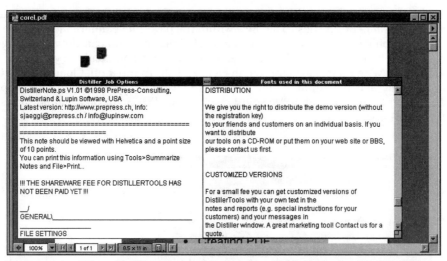

Figure 18-27: When DistillerNotes and FontNotes are placed in the Distiller Startup folder, two notes will appear closed in the PDF after distillation. When the notes are opened, the Distiller Job Options used to create the PDF and the font usage will be reported in the notes.

PubSTec Corporation

12871 Pinewood Street
Gowen, MI 49326
www.pubstec.com

PubSTec Action Plug-in (Macintosh/Windows)

The PubSTec Action plug-in is a powerful enhancement to Acrobat that possesses limitless opportunity. Designed with the PDF content provider in mind, PubSTec Action is ideal for those who create PDF-based catalogs and information archives. It is also well suited for use in many other business applications. With the action.api file in the Acrobat Plug-ins directory, the user will have access to a new link-type action when creating an Acrobat link. PubSTec Action performs in a fashion very similar to that of Acrobat's standard Open File link type, with one big exception: PubSTec Action is capable of passing text from within a link's bounding box to an external application. Among many things, this plug-in is perfect for creating catalogs with "add-to-shopping-cart" functionality or for performing database parts lookup actions.

PDFDraftsman Application (Macintosh/Windows)

PDFDraftsman is a stand-alone application that allows a user to create PDF illustrations without the need for any Adobe software. Yet the PubSTec's custom software library guarantees PDFDraftsman-created files conform to the PDF data format in every respect. Use PDFDraftsman's tools to create images and text in a manner similar to many illustration programs. These images and text items can then be formatted and sized, and moved forward or backward. In addition, the user can select to show or hide grid lines, and has a choice of different "paper" colors. When the user has finished creating the content of the file, he or she can fill in the document information fields (including Title, Subject, Author, and Keywords). Then, by simply selecting Save As PDF from the File menu, the user can treat the document like any other PDF file! PubSTec PDFDraftsman can be used to create quick and easy PDF documents such as notes, simple maps, and messages.

PubSTec Floating Text (Macintosh/Windows)

The PubSTec Floating Text plug-in is an enhancement to Acrobat designed to increase a user's personal productivity. If running Acrobat with the floattxt.api file present in the plug-ins directory, the user will have an additional button available to him or her on the Acrobat Tool Bar. The Floating Text button launches windows that float on top of the PDF file being viewed. The PubSTec Floating Text plug-in is very handy for taking notes while perusing a PDF file. The user can copy text into the floating window and copy the text into another program later. Multiple instances of PubSTec Floating Text windows can be open at one time, with each window capable of holding different text.

PubSTec PDFTree (Macintosh/Windows)

PDFTree is a stand-alone application that gives a user the ability to view a PDF file's internal data structure without using any Adobe software. Viewing the internal structure of a PDF file can be useful for software developers, end users involved in PDF-based technical support missions, or for anyone who wishes to gain a better understanding of how PDF works. Choose Open from the application's File menu and browse to the PDF tree structure to view the file's organization. This release of PubSTec PDFTree is limited in its functionality for purposes of free distribution, and as such is a viewer only. The PubSTec custom software libraries on which PDFTree is based include PDF read and write capabilities.

PubSTec PolyLink lite (Macintosh/Windows)

The PubSTec PolyLink lite plug-in is an enhancement to Acrobat designed to extend the user's ability to create hypertext links of varying shapes, sizes, and colors. If running Acrobat with the polylinklite.api file present in the plug-ins directory, the user will see an additional tool in the Acrobat Tool Bar. The PubSTec PolyLink lite tool can be activated by clicking the button in the Acrobat Tool Bar, or by selecting it from the Plug-Ins menu on the Acrobat Command Bar. This tool enables you to draw polygons capable of performing Acrobat or PubSTec link-type actions, which is a great way to create PDF image maps. For instance, a user may create PubSTec PolyLink lite links out of each state's border on a map of the United States by simply selecting the tool, drawing the polygonal links, double-clicking the newly drawn links, and then formatting their appearance and assigning them actions. PubSTec PolyLink lite ships with one action (Go To View) that is capable of linking to three page views (Fit Horizontal, Fit Vertical, and Fit Page). The commercial version of this plug-in, PubSTec PolyLink, is capable of performing all the link-type actions of an Acrobat link and contains many additional features not included in PolyLink lite.

Starter Plug-in (Macintosh/Windows)

The PubSTec Starter plug-in is an enhancement to Acrobat designed to increase a user's personal productivity. If running Acrobat, with the starter.api file present in the plug-ins directory, the user has the benefit of being able to place a new tool on the Acrobat Tool Bar and Command Bar. PubSTec Starter can be configured to launch any other application (see Figure 18-28) or a specific file. From the Acrobat Preferences menu, select PubSTec Starter, and then browse for the application or file to be launched with the Starter toolbar button. After the preferences have been configured, the new tool is ready to use; simply click the Starter from the Acrobat Tool Bar or select PubSTec Starter from the Plug-Ins menu. A favorite use of PubSTec Starter is to configure the plug-in to launch a text editor (such as NotePad or Simple Text) and then have it pop up in order to perform editorial-type tasks on PDF content.

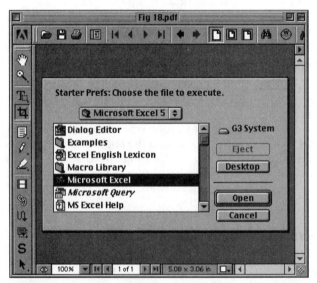

Figure 18-28: The application or document to be associated with the Starter Tool is determined when you select the File ⇨ Preferences ⇨ Starter option. The Starter Tool will be placed in the Acrobat Tool Bar. When selected, it will launch the application xor open the document within a host application you have identified in the Preferences menu.

Quark, Inc.

1800 Grant Street
Denver, CO 80203
www.quark.com

PDF Import/Export XT

The PDF Import/Export Quark XTension is Quark's answer to PageMaker's Export Adobe PDF. The XTension works with QuarkXPress version 4.02 and above. When an XPress document is exported, it is printed to disk as a PostScript file, and then Distiller is launched to convert the file to PDF with the current Distiller Job Options or an Options override. On first launching the Export to PDF XTension, QuarkXPress will prompt you for Distiller's location. A navigation dialog box will appear in which you can identify the Distiller application. The Save as PDF option enables you to provide document information prior to distillation by clicking the Document Info button, shown in Figure 18-29. When the Edit button is selected, choices appear for controlling Job Options, as illustrated in Figure 18-30.

Figure 18-29: When you select the Save as PDF command, a dialog box will appear, enabling you to supply document information, manage hyperlinks, and override Distiller's Job Options. If you choose to override Distiller's Job Options, a second dialog box will appear in which new Job Options are selected.

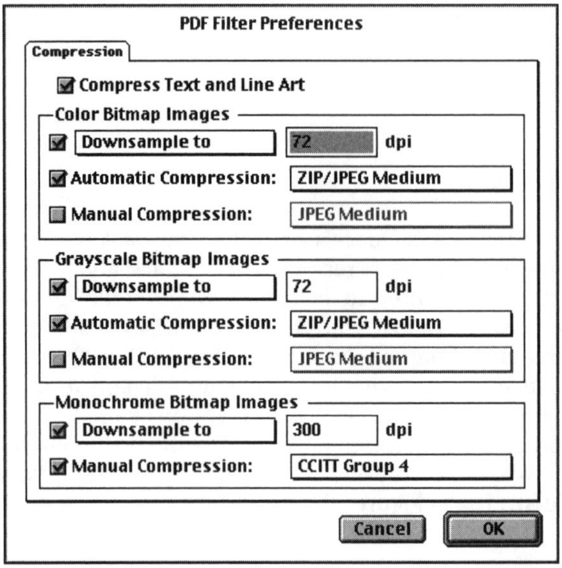

Figure 18-30: QuarkXPress can override Distiller's Job Options for Compression settings. To control the other Job Options attributes, you'll need to use the Distiller Job Options, which requires disabling the check box displayed in Figure 18-29.

The filter also enables importing of PDF files into QuarkXPress picture boxes. When you select Get Picture from the File menu, an option for PDF will appear, as shown in Figure 18-31. The imported PDF image can be printed and color-separated like any other XPress import.

Quite Software

105 Ridley Road
Forest Gate
London E7 0LX
United Kingdom
www.quite.com

Quite a Box of Tricks (Macintosh/Windows)

Cute name! And it is indeed a box of tricks. This Acrobat plug-in controls image sampling, color handling, transformations, form fields, and document information through the following features:

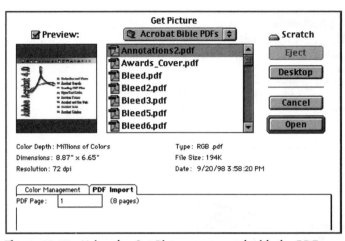

Figure 18-31: Using the Get Picture command with the PDF Import/Export XTension installed, PDF documents can be imported into QuarkXPress. Once imported, they can be treated like other imported image files.

Shrink

Shrink enables you to resample images within the PDF document without the need for redistillation. When file sizes need to be smaller than Distiller's Job Options permit, recompressing the PDF images can save even more space. This feature works particularly well with Web graphics. Shrink offers a JPEG extra option to add more compression, thus reducing file size. A restoration button enables you to restore the image if the compression creates an obvious distortion.

Colours

Those people out there in the imaging industry who have been battling with Microsoft Publisher files containing RGB images, here's the solution for you. The Colours option in Quite a Box of Tricks, shown in Figure 18-32, enables RGB and Lab conversion to CMYK. No longer do you need to place your files in PageMaker; now, with the color conversion options available with this plug-in, you can print from within Acrobat with Crackerjack to create separations. Spot-to-process color conversion is also available, and ICC profiles are used to convert the color data. ICC profile tagging is expected in a future release.

Transform

With this option, page transformations can be handled with a free transformation feature; mirroring images can also be performed for printing film; and lines in a PDF file can be thickened so they don't disappear when printed on high-resolution output devices.

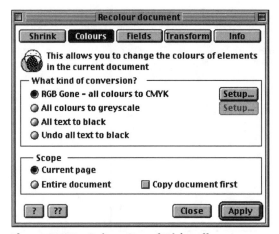

Figure 18-32: Quite a Box of Tricks offers many options for controlling image output size, color handling, form data fields, and transformations. Click the buttons at the top of the dialog box to access options for each of the categories.

Fields

Through this option, form fields can be combined or removed from a PDF document.

Info

Information can be obtained from text and images in the PDF document. Text information will report fonts and sizes, whether they are embedded or not, and whether subsetted fonts were used. Image feedback includes resolution, physical size, and compression method. Document searches can be performed for finding the largest images, RGB-only images, and other attributes that can help find potential imaging problems. Individual images can then be reduced in size or physically resampled.

Quite Imposing/Quite Imposing Plus (Macintosh/Windows)

Quite Imposing and Quite Imposing Plus both have the same core features for page impositions for digital presses, imagesetters, and platesetters. They are both plug-ins for Acrobat that offer imposition options such as booklet layouts, page numbering, trim sizes, reversing pages, and page arrangement, as shown in Figure 18-33. Quite Imposing Plus adds features for manual impositions, redefining page numbers, specifying bleeds, removing crop marks, and other similar options.

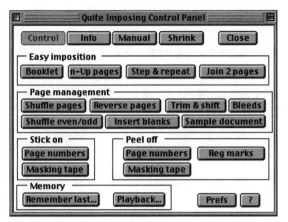

Figure 18-33: A simple and easy to use page imposition plug-in, Quite Imposing offers generous options for determining how the PDF document pages will be printed. The demo software provides complete functionality. An X is displayed on the resultant pages until you purchase and register the product.

Radtke Consulting

4707 140th Avenue North
Suite 213
Clearwater, Florida 33762
www.radtkeconsulting.com

P/Comp (Windows)

P/Comp is an Acrobat plug-in that compares PDF documents and generates bookmarks linked to pages where the differences appear. Any two PDF documents can be analyzed and reported for discrepancies. Discrepancies are reported in different colors for font usage, point sizes, position, and text contents.

RC: Splitter (Windows)

RC: Splitter is an Acrobat plug-in that searches according to user-specified criteria for changes in PDF documents. When Splitter encounters a change, a new PDF document with pages extracted from the original will be created. The new document pages will contain all pages searched up to the point of change. The title for the newly created document will appear with the user-defined text string used for the analysis. If a new file to be created finds an existing PDF document with the name string, pages will be appended to the existing file. In addition, Splitter can combine PDFs from a user-defined directory into a single PDF document.

Bookworm (Windows)

Bookworm is an automated bookmark creation plug-in for Acrobat. A search is performed in an open PDF, and when Bookworm finds a match, a new bookmark is created.

A Round Table Solution (ARTS)

Level 10, 114 Albert Road
South Melbourne, 3205
Victoria, Australia
www.roundtable.com.au

PDFWorkshop (Windows)

If you created PDFs without supplying document information at the time the PDFs were distilled, then adding data to the Title, Subject, Author, and Keywords fields for each document would be an aggravating task in Acrobat. PDFWorkshop is an Acrobat plug-in that eases this burden. You can batch-process multiple PDF documents to update fields containing document information as well as export the fields into a speadsheet. PDFWorkshop also obtains information from the PDF files for page count, page mode selected for display, and the security level. A set of Excel spreadsheet macros that enable printing, updating, and modifying the document information accompanies PDFWorkshop. PDF Workshop lets you batch-print PDF files, print PDF files to PostScript, and print PDF files to single PostScript page files. PDFWorkshop also lets you merge and copy PDF files from Excel spreadsheets.

ARTS Import (Windows)

Another Acrobat plug-in suited to batch-convert files is the ARTS Import plug-in. If you have image files in multiple formats that need to be displayed or printed, then this plug-in may help you; it permits importing of image formats such as BMP, DCX, GIF, PCX, and TIFF into an Acrobat PDF document. The plug-in allows you to select the file formats to be included, and with the click of a button converts the selected formats to individual PDF pages. This plug-in is ideal for educational facilities and organizations possessing large archives of image files.

ARTS ThumbOpt (Windows)

ARTS ThumbOpt is a batch processor for optimizing and adding thumbnails to PDF documents. Rather than opening documents in Acrobat, this utility uses the DOS command line for executing the optimization and thumbnail creation. Users who publish CD-ROMs might take advantage of ARTS ThumbOpt to run the application prior to submitting files for CD-ROM replication. One quick command-line execution will ensure all PDFs are optimized and have thumbnails for a directory of PDF files.

ARTS Duplex (Windows)

ARTS Duplex offers more control over printing PDFs from Acrobat and Acrobat Reader. The plug-in is a print utility that enables printing of duplex pages on almost any kind of printer, odd/even pages, and selected page ranges for duplex and odd/even pages. The folks down in Australia would like to see the people in North America save a few trees. So if your paper piles are mounting, try this plug-in.

ARTS Joust (Windows)

Acrobat 4.0 includes some of the features supported with ARTS Joust. This Acrobat plug-in is used for e-mailing a viewed PDF document. You can send an e-mail with the PDF attached to single or multiple e-mail addresses. The plug-in also works when using inline viewing on the Internet. When looking at a PDF file on a Web page through inline viewing, Joust enables you to save the PDF file. This feature eliminates the need to view Web PDFs with different browser configurations. The newest version works with both Acrobat Reader and Acrobat.

ARTS AcroBuddies (Windows)

AcroBuddies are now able to update listings and searchs for other buddies by using the AcroBuddies plug-in. This plug-in gives you a convenient way to maintain your description and at the same time contact other buddies for assistance. Like Duplex, it is 100 percent free.

Scitex Corporation Ltd.

Corporate Headquarters
P.O. Box 330
Herzlia Industrial Park
46103 Herzila B, Israel
www.scitex.com

Brisque Digital Front End

Now, I suspect if you're an end user, you won't rush out and purchase a Scitex system for your home office. However, you may be sending files to an imaging center using Scitex systems; or, if you own an imaging center, you might be contemplating the purchase of a Scitex system. In either case, you'll be happy to know Scitex has adopted PDF support on their high-end devices. The Scitex line of front-end systems is named Brisque, and these systems perform high-end prepress tasks for ripping, trapping, imposing, preflighting, OPI, and printing to imagesetters, platesetters, and other high-end devices. Brisque has integrated both PostScript and PDF into its infrastructure. Because of PDF's page independence, the digital front end (DFE) can image selected pages with trapping, impositions, job tickets, and other such features. If you wish to learn more about Brisque support for PDF, you may wish to attend a free seminar cosponsored by Scitex and Adobe that is currently traveling around North America. Scitex and Adobe have corroborated to provide seminars on PDF workflows in imaging environments.

Silanis Technology, Inc.

La Tour Digital
3333 Cote Vertu
Suite 305
Saint Laurent, QC
Canada
H4R 2N1
www.silanis.com

ApproveIT for .pdf (Windows)

ApproveIt, from Silanis Technology, is an off-the-shelf electronic approval software that enables any enterprise to quickly and easily convert its paper-based signing processes into an electronic environment. It automates and manages corporate approval procedures, securing the process through its electronic handwritten and digital signature components. As a snap-in to Adobe Acrobat, ApproveIt for PDF can be used as a stand-alone for the simple routing of documents via e-mail for multiple approvals, or it can be integrated into any complex solution — including those involving document management, workflow, and database or internet/intranet systems. Due to the fact that ApproveIt works seamlessly in any of these environments, many corporations, including those in government and the pharmaceutical, insurance, manufacturing and financial industries, are implementing the software in order to leverage their existing investment in information technology and to enable electronic signing across the enterprise in a cost-effective manner.

Solimar Systems, Inc.

3940 Fourth Avenue
Suite 300
San Diego, CA 92103
www.solimarsystems.com

Legacy XCHANGE (Windows NT)

Legacy XCHANGE is designed to work with Solimar's Print/Director System NT print server to convert many mainframe formats to workgroup printers. Legacy files from ASCII, EBCDIC, DJDEs, Xerox Metacode, image formats, fonts, forms, and so on can be converted to PostScript or PDF. Printing occurs from mainframe hosts and prints to the print server for file conversion. XCHANGE includes two emulation modules for file conversion: XCHANGE:PDF and XCHANGE:PostScript.

Sys-Print, Inc.

2951 Flowers Road South
Oxford Building, Suite 227
Atlanta, GA 30341
www.sysprint.com

Sys-Print (Standard) (Mainframes/Windows)

The miles of mountain-high data originating on mainframe computers and different operating systems throughout the world often present problems for companies when updating to modern systems. Visiting a mainframe computer and printing a file to disk as PostScript is unlikely to work when this data is to be converted to PDF. Sys-Print offers a solution for computers outputting to line printers in Sys-Out, Line-Out, and PCL formats. The application accepts data normally sent to a line printer and converts the file to PostScript or PDF. Sys-Print can accommodate many different vertical market applications as long as they are capable of outputting to line printers.

Sys-Meta (Xerox Mainframes)

Sys-Meta converts Metacode files to PDF. Metacode is a standard used to drive the family of Xerox printers. Many Xerox systems used to create forms can have the form designs and layouts, including color, shading, artwork, and so on, converted to PDF.

Sys-AFP (IBM Mainframes)

IBM systems using mainframe data in AFP code can be converted to PostScript or PDF. Sys-AFP emulates each command or instruction in the Page Description Language, created by the IBM systems, and converts it to PostScript or PDF. Sys-AFP converts artwork on-the-fly to TIFF format.

SYS-DJDE (Xerox Mainframes)

Another mainframe data format used by Xerox systems can also be converted to PostScript or PDF. When converting these files, bookmarks up to three levels are inserted for files created with indexes.

SYS-PCL (Windows)

Hewlett-Packard's PCL format is used on desktop printers and local area networks. When PCL-formatted documents are converted to PostScript, you can often find problems such as text reflow and repagination. Sys-PCL interprets PCL and converts it to PostScript or PDF while preserving the layout attributes.

SYS-TIFF (Windows)

Images contained on high-end systems and designed for different vertical markets can be enormous in volume. Sys-TIFF converts images to TIFF-formatted files, and Sys-Print claims the conversion is over 40 times faster than Acrobat Capture's conversion capabilities.

Tangent Software

Sabu Francis & Associates
212 Vardhaman Market
Sector 17, VashiNavi Mumbai
MAHARASHTRA
PIN: 400 703
India
www.archsfa.com/tangent

Simple-PDF (Windows)

This is a poor person's command-line utility that converts text files to PDF. If you haven't yet purchased Acrobat, use this utility to make PDF conversions on Windows machines with the execution of a command line at the DOS prompt. Text files will be converted to PDF without optimization or compression. With some coding knowledge, you can even add annotations, links, and bookmarks. You can also create vector graphics with some knowledge of marking operators in PDF.

Techno Design

Koraalrood 100
2718 SC Zoetermeer
The Netherlands
www.techno-design.com

PDF Design XT (Macintosh)

This is a QuarkXPress XTension that adds many of the features you can find with the Adobe PDF Export from Adobe PageMaker. The XTension permits automatic generation of bookmarks, thumbnails, links, and articles from XPress documents. Distiller's Job Options settings can be controlled within XPress with the XTension.

TechPool Software

2726 Loker Avenue West
Carlsbad, CA 92008
www.techpool.com

Transporter Pro (Macintosh/Windows)

Transporter Pro is a stand-alone application that RIPs PDF, PostScript, and EPS files to TIFF, JPEG, and GIF formats. Ripped EPS files can be edited in vector drawing programs and previews can be added to EPS files saved without a preview. Files can then be placed in layout applications for output to high-resolution devices. Transporter Pro also rips files at higher resolutions — over 4000 dpi. This application is particularly helpful when fonts have not been emdedded in the PDF document. You can export the PDF to EPS with font inclusion when you have the fonts stored locally on your computer. Automated ripping of files can be made through the use of hot folders for drag-and-drop execution.

Ultimate Technographics

1 Westmount Square
Suite 1700
Montreal, QC H3Z 2P9
Canada
`www.ultimate-tech.com`

Impostrip (Macintosh/Windows NT/CIP3)

Ultimate Technographics offers products for imaging solutions for high-end Web and sheet-fed printing as well as for the on-demand prepress/printing market. Their products support PDF imaging and workflows. Impostrip is a tool for imposing composite and separated files. Multiple file formats can be imposed including PDF, EPS, TIFF, and PostScript from all platforms. Impostrip supports job tickets, CIP3, OPI, and trapping for PostScript Level 2 and PostScript 3 devices. Impostrip virtual folding with Origami allows automatic creation of signatures. Impostrip client/server architecture offers Signature Server and remote control to the user for all printing occurring on the server.

IMPress (Macintosh)

IMPress is also an imposition tool that automates imposing to digital presses, imagesetters, and platesetters, as well as to digital copiers and on-demand printing systems. Hot folders can be created for drag-and-drop automation. IMPress will automatically calculate page impositions to find the best fit supporting output up to 22 x 29 inches. Automatic calculations are performed for bleeds, cut marks, paper weights, color bars, and printer's marks. Full PDF support is integrated in the workflow solution.

Trapeze (Macintosh/Windows NT)

Trapeze is Ultimate Technographic's trapping solution. Batch-trapping can be performed on PostScript, EPS, and PDF files. PDF documents can be input for trapping and output to PostScript Level 2 and PostScript 3 devices as well as to

TIFF/IT, HandShake, and DDEF formats. The Trapeze job control window can be used by an unlimited number of remote users while the processing stays with files on the server. Trapeze can work as a stand-alone product or be integrated into Ultimate's other imposition and OPI server products.

UltimateFlow (Macintosh/Windows NT)

UltimateFlow is a workflow solution designed to automate and speed up the PDF/OPI process for prepress. PDF files are accepted directly and routed to an unlimited number of job queues; or, host application documents can be accepted, and these are sent to the queue where PDF creation, trapping, and imaging are managed and automated.

Visual Software

15 Cleardene
Dorking
Surrey
RH4 2BY
United Kingdom

pcl2pdf (Windows)

pcl2pdf will convert LaserJet PCL files to PDF. Batch-mode conversions can be made from command-line access.

xman Software

350 Pacific Avenue
Second Floor
San Francisco, CA 94111
www.xman.com

xToolsOne

xToolsOne from xman Software installs a number of tools in the Plug-in menu (see Figure 18-34) as well as on the Acrobat Tool Bar. This program provides choices for editing annotations, dog-earring a page for reference, creating footnotes, identifying a Home page, making bookmarks from text selections, making links from text selections, printing a selection, and more.

One particular feature I find helpful when working with annotations is xAnnotation-Window. When xAnnotationWindow is selected from the Plug-in menu options, a window will appear displaying all annotations in the document and what types of annotations they are (see Figure 18-35). You can choose to display annotations on a given page, display common types, display only those created within a specified date, and globally edit the properties.

Figure 18-34: When xToolsOne is installed, tool options appear under the Plug-in window as well as the Acrobat Tool Bar.

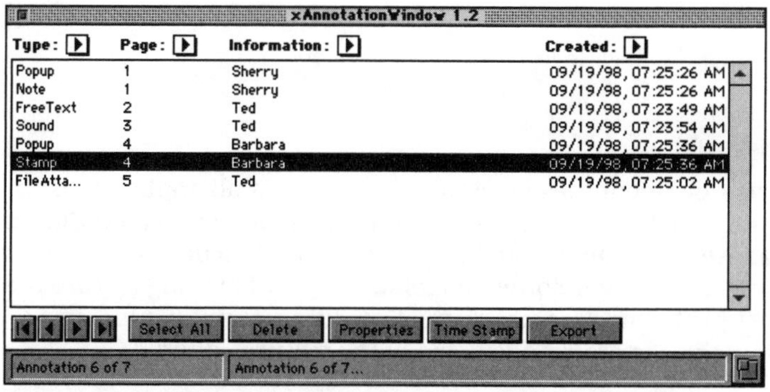

Figure 18-35: The xAnnotationsWindow offers several means for displaying annotations as well as an opportunity to edit their properties without navigating to the pages where the annotations appear.

If you create a number of annotations in a PDF document, then xAnnotationsWindow can save you much time in finding and editing annotations.

XtraMedia

1093 East Main Street #502
El Cajon, CA 92021-6247
www.xtramedia.com

AcroViewer XTRA (Macintosh/Windows)

This utility is a Lingo XTRA used with Macromedia Director. The AcroViewer Lingo XTRA enables you to have cross-platform presentations, catalogs, tutorials, and so on that are controlled from within Director using PDF rendering capabilities. You can call Lingo methods, which look for and launch Acrobat viewers, bring Acrobat or Director to the foreground, print PDF files, and quit viewer applications. It provides up to 42 features, including scrolling, zooming, going to a particular page, finding text, invoking menu commands, and so on.

Zeon Corporation

1/F, 34, Alley 4, Lane 69, Section 5
Ming Shen E. Road
Taipei, Taiwan
www.zeon.com.tw

DocuCom (Windows)

DocuCom converts document files generated from almost all applications to PDF and supports multilingual formats including traditional and simplified Chinese, Korean, and Japanese. Documents can be shared across languages and computer platforms. The Zeon font server software includes a font-handling feature that resolves many font problems. Bookmark creation, Internet publishing, image importing, and annotations are among some of the features offered.

Contacting Suppliers

A number of demonstration plug-ins are available on the accompanying CD-ROM. Most of the plug-ins are fully functioning for a limited time or may limit a single feature. Software developers are continually upgrading their products and adding new plug-ins and applications to work with Acrobat. In Table 18-1, I list those manufacturers who offer demonstration versions of their products. If the product is contained on the accompanying CD-ROM, you might first wish to visit the Web site for the manufacturer to ensure you are using the most updated version. Also, you may want to bookmark this table for future visits to the listed Web sites to investigate new developments.

Table 18-1
**Third-party Manufacturers Offering Demonstration
Software on Internet Web Sites**

Manufacturer	Product	Platform	Acrobat Plug-in	Stand-alone Application/ Other Non–Plug-in	Web Address
5D	Niknak	Win		X	www.5-d.com
Acquired Knowledge	EZ-PDF	Mac/Win	X		www.acquiredknowledge.com
Ambia Software	Aerial	Win	X		www.ambia.com
	Compose	Win	X		
	Re:mark	Win	X		
Avenza Software, Inc.	JAMBuddy	Win	X		www.avenza.com
BCL Computers	Magellan	Win			www.bcl-computers.com
	Firebird	Win			
	Jade	Win			
Brook House, Ltd.	BatchPrint PDF	Win		X	www.brookhouse.co.uk
	Homer	Win	X		
	WordMark&Trade	Win		X	
Callas Software	pdfToolbox	Mac/Win	X		www.callas.de
	pdfOutputPro	Mac/Win	X		
	MadeToPrint XT	Mac		X(XPress)	
Cessna Publishing	cpAnnCollector	Win		X	www.win.net/cessnapub
Computerized Document Control, Ltd	Local Render	Win		X	www.docctrl.co.uk
Computerstream, Ltd.	Banner Print	Win	X		www.computerstream.co.uk
	PDF Protector	Win	X		

Continued

Table 18-1 (continued)

Manufacturer	Product	Platform	Acrobat Plug-in	Stand-alone Application/ Other Non–Plug-in	Web Address
Consolidated Technical Services, Inc.	Spiffy-Pop	Win	X		www.contechinc.com
Dionis	Ari's Crop Helper	Mac/Win	X		www.dionis.com
	Ari's Link Checker	Mac/Win	X		
	Ari's Print Helper	Mac/Win	X		
	Ari's Ruler	Mac/Win	X		
Easy Software Products	HTMLDOC	Win		X	www.easysw.com
Enfocus Software	CheckUp	Mac/Win		X	www.enfocus.com
	PitStop	Mac/Win	X		
Extensis Software, Inc.	Collect Pro*	Mac	X	X	www.extensis.com
	Preflight Pro	Mac		X	
	QX-Tools	Mac		X	
FileOpen Systems, Inc.	FileOpen PDF Publisher	Mac/Win		X	www.fileopen.com
Handmade Software	Image Alchemy PS	Mac/Win		X	www.handmade.com
Iceni Technology	Gemini	Mac/Win	X		www.iceni.com
Image Solutions	ISiFile	Win	X		www.imagesolutions.com
	GraphCopy	Win	X		
Informative Graphics Corp.	Myriad	Win		X	www.infograph.com
Intense Software	PDF Embedder	Mac	X		www.intensesoftware.com

Manufacturer	Product	Platform	Acrobat Plug-in	Stand-alone Application/ Other Non–Plug-in	Web Address
Lantana Research	Crackerjack	Mac/Win	X		www.lantanarips.com
	Crackerjack Pilot	Mac/Win		X	
	OPI Doctor	Mac/Win	X		
	PDF Bellhop	Mac/Win	X		
	PDF Librarian	Mac/Win	X		
	PDF Valet	Mac/Win	X		
Markzware USA	FlightCheck	Mac/Win		X	www.markzware.com
	MarkzScout	Mac/Win		X	
Merlin Open Systems	Name It	Mac/Win	X		www.merlin-os.co.uk
	Name It Launcher	Mac/Win	X		
	Options	Mac/Win	X		
	Date Stamp	Win		X	
	Search Results Printer	Mac/Win	X		
NetFormation, Inc.	Face-It!	Win	X		www.netformation.com
One Vision, Inc.	Asura	Mac/Win		X	www.one-vision.com
	Solvero	Mac/Win		X	
Page Technology Marketing, Inc.	FormView	Win		X	www.pcltools.com
PDF Solutions, Ltd.	CloneLink	Win	X		www.pdf-solutions.com
PrePress-Consulting	Distiller Tools	Mac/Win		X	www.prepress.ch

Continued

Table 18-1 (continued)

Manufacturer	Product	Platform	Acrobat Plug-in	Stand-alone Application/ Other Non–Plug-in	Web Address
PubSTec Corporation	PubSTec Action Plug-in	Mac/Win	X		www.pubstec.com
	PDFDraftsman	Mac/Win		X	
	PubSTec Floating Text	Mac/Win	X		
	PubSTec PDFTree	Mac/Win		X	
	PubSTec PolyLink lite	Mac/Win	X		
	Starter Plug-in	Mac/Win	X		
Quark, Inc.	PDF Import/Export	Mac/Win		X	www.quark.com
Quite Software	Quite a Box of Tricks	Mac/Win	X		www.quite.com
	Quite Imposing	Mac/Win	X		
	Quite Imposing Plus	Mac/Win	X		
A Round Table Solution	ARTS Duplex	Win	X		www.roundtable.com.au
	ARTS Import	Win	X		
	ARTS Joust	Win	X		
	ARTS ThumbOpt	Win	X		
	PDFWorkshop	Win	X		
Tangent Software	Simple-PDF	Win		X	www.archsfa.com/tangent
TechPool Software	Transporter Pro	Mac/Win		X	www.techpool.com

Manufacturer	Product	Platform	Acrobat Plug-in	Stand-alone Application/ Other Non–Plug-in	Web Address
Ultimate Technographics	Impostrip	Mac/Win NT		X	www.ultimate-tech.com
	IMPress	Mac		X	
	Trapeze	Mac/Win NT		X	
	UltimateFlow	Mac/Win NT		X	
Visual Software	pcl2pdf	Win		X	www.visual.co.uk
xman Software	xToolsOne	Mac/Win	X		www.xman.com
Zeon Corporation	DocuCom	Win		X	www.zeon.com.tw

*Functions as both a stand-alone application and plug-in.

Staying Connected

About every five minutes new products and new upgrades are distributed. If you purchase a software product, you will find a revision not too long after release. Manufacturers are relying more and more on Internet distribution and less on postal delivery. If you have Acrobat and related third-party products, you should plan on making routine visits to the manufacturers' Web sites. Anyone who has a Web site will offer a product revision for downloading or give you details for acquiring the update. There are some basic steps you should follow to keep updated on Acrobat.

Registering the product

Regardless of whether you purchase Acrobat or download the free Acrobat Reader software, Adobe Systems has made it possible to register either product. You can register on the World Wide Web or mail a registration form to Adobe. If you develop PDF documents for distribution, Adobe likes to keep track of this information. You will find benefits to being a registered user. First, update information will be sent to you, so you'll know when a product revision occurs. Second, information will be distributed to help you achieve the most out of using Acrobat. Who knows — some day you may be requested to provide samples of your work for the Adobe Web site. By all means, complete the registration form.

Web sites to contact

The first Web site to frequent is the Adobe Web site. Updates become available when Acrobat components are revised. You can also find tips, information, and solutions to various problems. Visit Adobe's Web site at www.adobe.com.

A PDF newsletter is available for those with an interest in promoting the Portable Document Format. The newsletter describes products, contains interviews, and offers solutions for almost any industry. To visit the PurePDF Web site, go to www.purePDF.com.

If third-party applications and solutions are of interest, you can find a Web site that features a comprehensive list of developers. Solutions of every kind are given and direct URL links to developers Web sites are provided. Visit PDFZone at www.pdfzone.com.

The people at Brookhouse Software market Acrobat applications and plug-ins as well as maintain a Web site for describing tips on using Acrobat. You can find them at www.brookhouse.co.uk.

In addition, Acrobat tips can be found on many other Web sites, and all you need do is search the World Wide Web for Acrobat information.

Summary

✦ Adobe Acrobat uses a plug-in architecture to expand program features and enable third-party developers a means of offering expanded solutions with the Portable Document Format.

✦ Many of Acrobat's tools are made available through plug-ins installed during the installation of Acrobat.

✦ Adobe Systems provides some optional plug-ins on the installer CD that require independent installation.

✦ Plug-ins for Acrobat can be nested in folders, but those nested folders must be installed in the Plug-in folder.

✦ Disabling plug-ins may be required when there are conflicts that prohibit Acrobat from operating correctly. Plug-ins can be disabled by removing them from the Plug-ins folder.

✦ There are a great many third-party distributors of plug-ins who develop products to enhance Acrobat's performance and add specialized features.

✦ Many stand-alone applications in almost all markets have been created to work with PDF documents.

✦ If you have Acrobat and related third-party products, you should plan on making routine visits to the manufacturers' Web sites to keep on top of the latest updates and upgrades.

About the CD-ROM

The CD-ROM at the back of the book is a hybrid CD that can be read by both Macintosh and Windows platforms. The CD-ROM contains folders that include Macintosh and Windows demo software and plug-ins, sample PDF documents (including a fully searchable electronic version of this book and PDF information documents), as well as the Acrobat Reader 4.0 software.

Contents

The folders you will find on the CD-ROM are as follows:

- ✦ Acrobat
- ✦ PDFBible
- ✦ Samples
- ✦ Products
- ✦ Mac Specific
- ✦ PC Specific

Acrobat

The Adobe Acrobat Reader installers for both the Macintosh and Windows versions of Reader appear inside the Acrobat folder. In addition to the installers are ReadMe files and licensing agreements. Please take the time to read the licensing information distributed by Adobe Systems. The ReadMe files will provide installation instructions for installing Acrobat Reader on your computer. Follow the guidelines outlined in the ReadMe files for installation. You will find both Acrobat Reader and Acrobat Search available for installation. Distribution of the Reader installer is prohibited unless all licensing agreements and distribution guidelines are followed.

PDFBible

The *Acrobat PDF Bible* has been converted to a PDF document (complete with a search index) that you will find in the PDFBible folder. You can review pages and sections of the book while working in Acrobat. Search on keywords using the search options discussed in Chapter 2. Before attempting to search for information, however, you'll need to load the search index contained in the PDFBible folder. Loading search indexes is also explained in Chapter 2. As you come to the "Steps" sections in the *Acrobat PDF Bible*, you can toggle open windows in Acrobat and follow the steps described in the text to produce the results for the concepts discussed.

Samples

The Samples folder includes some sample presentations, newsletters, and PDF documents in subfolders. Here you'll find a few examples of PDF documents created for CD-ROM replication or informational items related to products and PDF workflows. All documents are copyrighted by their respective owners. Duplication of the contents is prohibited without the expressed written permission of the developer. All the contents of the subfolders contained in the Info folder can be viewed in an Acrobat viewer.

Ventura County Ad Club Awards (vcawards.pdf)

The Advertising Club of Ventura County, California, produced a CD-ROM of their annual Addy awards competition. In this presentation, the Ad Club had all entries shot with a digital camera and assembled the layout in Adobe PageMaker. The PageMaker document was exported to PDF. Categories in the layout are linked to pages where the entries are found. Browse through this document and discover how you may wish to assemble a PDF for similar events or other projects designed for CD-ROM distribution.

BassWorks (MoviePitch)

Jim Bass of Bassworks Design in Thousand Oaks, California, assembled PDF documents for the MoviePitch Web site. Within these documents is a presentation on how to sell ideas to motion picture producers. The final project was distributed on CD-ROM.

The Image Source (imgsrc.pdf)

I put together a promotional CD-ROM for distribution to my customers at the Image Source Digital Imaging and Photo Finishing Centers. Services, price lists, and links to many different documents are included on the original CD-ROM I assembled as a self-promotion piece for the company. If self-promotion is an interest, you'll find PDF and CD-ROM replication to be an affordable means of communicating product offerings and services.

AutoGraph Newsletter (AGS1298.pdf)

A bimonthly newsletter published by Automated Graphics Systems is available on the Internet at www.ags.com. The newsletter reports information related to prepress and multimedia news as well as PDF solutions. A sample of their newsletter is included in this folder.

PurePDF

A sample newsletter provided by Glyphica (purepdf.com) is included. On the purePDF Web site you can find a monthly newsletter containing articles about Acrobat and PDF solutions. This folder contains a PDF document of the newsletter published by Glyphica. (For more updated news and articles on Acrobat 4.0, view the current publication at www.purepdf.com.)

Products

Some spec sheets, product descriptions, and material related to developers is included in the Products folder according to manufacturer name. Browse through the documents to find ordering information and guides for using third-party manufacturer products.

Macintosh Software

A number of demonstration plug-ins and applications are offered by third-party manufacturers. The Mac Specific folder contains Macintosh-only items. In some cases, the plug-ins can be copied to the Acrobat plug-ins directory, as I explain in Chapter 18; other items require launching the installer application. All installers can be launched by opening the folder and double-clicking the installer icon. Distribution of the software on the CD-ROM is prohibited without authorized permission of the developer. Many software products may be upgraded by the time you first attempt to install the applications. Before installation, explore the developer's Web site to see if a newer upgrade is available for download.

An explanation of the plug-ins is also available in Chapter 18. If you wish to know what an application or plug-in is used for, first look at the brief description in Chapter 18. Following is a brief list of products, categorized by manufacturer, that appear on the CD-ROM. The names within parentheses indicate the corresponding folders on the CD-ROM.

✦ **Acquired Knowledge (Acquired Knowledge):** EZ-PDF is offered by Acquired Knowledge. A short description of the application is described in Chapter 18. EZ-PDF is an executable application. Double-click the EZ-PDF icon, and the program will be launched. A manual is available in PDF form inside the EZ-PDF folder.

✦ **Callas Software (Callas):** pdfToolbox is available from Callas Software. There are five plug-ins that can be copied to the Acrobat Plug-ins folder. You can make a subfolder within the Acrobat Plug-ins folder named Callas or pdfToolbox and copy the plug-ins to the subfolder. The pdfToolbox folder also includes pdfBatchMeister, which is an executable application. This application can be copied to any folder on your hard drive—it does not require installion in the Acrobat Plug-ins folder. In the pdfPrefs folder, you'll find several PDF files in which instructions are provided.

✦ **Ari's Toolbox (Dionis):** The Acrobat plug-ins Ari's Ruler, and Ari's Print Helper are included in the Ari's Toolbox folder. Each of these items are Acrobat plug-ins and need to be copied to the Acrobat Plug-ins folder.

✦ **Extensis Software (Extensis):** Collect Pro, Preflight Pro, and QX-Tools are all installer applications. Collect Pro is an executable application and will also appear as a plug-in within Acrobat. Preflight Pro is an executable application, and QX-Tools is a QuarkXPress XTension. Drag the QX-Tools XTension to the XTensions folder inside your QuarkXPress folder.

✦ **Intense Software (Intense):** PDF Embedder is included. Copy the plug-in to the Acrobat Plug-ins folder.

✦ **Merlin Open Systems (Merlin):** The Options plug-in appears on this CD. Double-click the installer icon for installation and licensing information.

✦ **Pubstec (Pubstec):** The Pubstec folder contains two plug-ins and two executable applications. FloatText and Starter are plug-ins you can copy to the Acrobat Plug-ins folder. Double-click PDFDraft and PDFTree to launch these applications.

✦ **Quite Software (Quite):** Quite a box of tricks, Quite Imposing, and Quite Imposing Plus are all plug-ins that can be dropped in the Acrobat Plug-ins folder. A companion PDF document is available for instructions.

Windows Software

The files for Windows applications you will find in the PC Specific folder may end in .exe, which indicates an executable application; or .api, which indicates an Acrobat plug-in. Or, you may need to run a setup file from the Windows status bar or double-click the setup file to install an application. When ReadMe files are provided in the directory for a product, be certain to read the file in Windows NotePad or a text editor. All products are prohibited from distribution without authorization from the manufacturer. As with the preceding Macintosh applications, explore the developer's Web site before attempting to install the applications. Upgrades may be available. Many of the installers for the products contained on the CD-ROM have licensing agreements noted in the installer dialog boxes. Installation will assume you agree to the manufacturer's licensing agreement. I've included the following Windows applications, as listed by manufacturer:

- ✦ **Ari's Toolbox (Dionis):** Ari's Print Helper, and Ari's Ruler are included on this CD. Copy the .api files to the Acrobat Plug-ins folder.

- ✦ **Easy Software (EasySW):** Html.doc appears in the EasySW folder. Run the htmldoc-1_7-windows.exe file and follow the installation guidelines.

- ✦ **FileOpen (FileOpen):** PDFPublisher is available on the CD-ROM. Run the fo_eval.exe program and follow the installation guidelines.

- ✦ **Iceni Technology (Iceni):** Gemini Studio, the Picture Extraction Plug-in (PEP), and several other applications are found in this folder. Double-click the zipped files to expand them. Run the Setup.exe file to install Gemini studio. Expanded folders will include manuals and user guides.

- ✦ **Lantana Research (Lantana):** Crackerjack, OPIDoctor, and Crackerjack Pilot are installer applications. Run the .exe files and follow installation directions.

- ✦ **Merlin Open Systems (Merlin):** Run the setup.exe files and follow installation instructions.

- ✦ **pdfSolutions (pdfSolut):** Copy the CloneLink.api file to the Acrobat Plug-ins folder.

- ✦ **Pubstec (Pubstec):** Pubstec contains the Windows versions of the same software noted for the Macintosh systems as well as the Float Text Acrobat plug-in. Installation is the same as noted previously for the Macintosh installations. The Float Text plug-in needs to be copied to the Acrobat Plug-ins folder.

- ✦ **Silanis Technology, Inc. (Silanis):** The Demo.exe files are demonstration-only descriptions of products available from the developer. Double-click each demo to view a self-running demonstration.

System Requirements and Installation

To install and run the programs on the CD-ROM, Macintosh users need System 7.5 or above. Windows users need Windows 95, Windows 98, or Windows NT. (The CD-ROM will not function properly with Windows 3.1.)

To gain access to the contents on the CD-ROM, follow these steps:

Macintosh

1. Insert the CD-ROM in your CD-ROM drive and wait a few moments until the CD-ROM icon appears.

2. Double-click the icon to open the CD-ROM, which will display a window in which the contents will appear.

Windows

1. Insert the CD-ROM in your CD-ROM drive.

2. Double-click the CD-ROM icon on the desktop to display a window in which the contents will appear.

✦   ✦   ✦

Index

SYMBOLS

* (asterisk), wildcard, 70
<= (back arrow, equal sign), less than or
    equal to, 70
< (back arrow), less than, 70
= (equal sign), equals, 70
!= (exclamation, equal sign), does not equal,
    70
!~ (exclamation, tilde), does not contain, 70
>= (forward arrow, equal sign), greater than
    or equal to, 70
> (forward arrow), greater than, 70
? (question mark), wildcard, 70
~ (tilde), contains, 70

A

Acrobat. *See also* Acrobat Exchange
    Acrobat Web page, 108–109
    EPS files, exporting from, 554–555
    hard disk requirements
        Macintosh, 459
        Windows, 462
    memory requirements
        Macintosh, 457–459
        Windows, 459
    Navigation Pane, 29–30
    place in Acrobat suite, 11
    Undo limitations of, 293
    usage of the term in this book, 11
    using with illustration programs
        Adobe Illustrator, 214–223
        CorelDraw, 214
        Macromedia FreeHand, 213
    using with layout programs
        Adobe PageMaker, 224–249
        QuarkXpress, 223–224
    using with Photoshop
        compression issues in, 206–207

        exporting from Photoshop, 203–207
        Photoshop PDF support, 202
Acrobat Capture
    Capture Server dialog box, 471–472
    converting scanned pages to text
        Capture Suspects, 472–474
        capturing a page, 471–474
        dictionaries, 468, 470
        editing with TouchUp Text tool, 472
        font limitations, 467
        font requirements, 468
        OCR language, selecting, 468
        PDF output style, 469
        unrecognized words, 472–474
    dictionaries, 468, 470
    font limitations, 467
    font requirements, 468
    images, importing
        Amiga IFF, 474
        BMP, 474
        formats not supported, 475
        GIF, 474
        Import Image dialog box, 476
        JPEG, 474
        PCX, 475
        PICT, 475
        Pixar, 475
        PNG, 475
        Targa, 475
        TIFF, 475
    introduction to, 13
    paper capture (the term), 467
    performance, system choices affecting,
        474
    preferences
        downsampling images, 272, 469
        location for temporary files, 272, 469
        PDF output style, 272, 469
        Preferences dialog box, 468
        primary OCR language, 271, 468–469
        (continued)

Acrobat Capture *(continued)*
　RTF, converting scanned pages to,
　　471–474
　using, 467–470
　Windows NT, running best under, 474
Acrobat Catalog
　CD-ROM publishing, uses in, 580–581
　index description field
　　adding ID's to Acrobat 1.0 files, 439
　　excluding words, 438
　　log file, 430–431
　　New Index Definition dialog box, 437
　　optimizing for CD-ROM, 439
　　word options, 438–439
　index maintenance, automating
　　building indexes, 443
　　identifying indexes for Schedule Builds,
　　　442–443
　　Purge Warning dialog box, 445
　　purging data, 444–445
　　Schedule Builds dialog box, 442
　　stopping scheduled builds, 443–444
　indexes
　　adding, 56–57
　　building, 440–441
　　creating, 436–441
　　directories, excluding, 439–440
　　directories, including, 439
　　directories, removing, 440
　　hierarchy of, 426
　　index information, 58–59
　　Index Information dialog box, 59
　　Index Selection dialog box, 57
　　introduction to, 56
　　Macintosh defaults, 429–430
　　Macintosh preferences, 427–429
　　New Index Definition dialog box, 437
　　relocating, 426
　　removing from searches, 57–58
　　restoring to searches, 57
　　structure of, 425–426
　　title, 436–437
　log file, 430

network catalogs
　cataloging on a network, 445–448
　watched folders in, 445
preferences, Macintosh
　Catalog Preferences dialog box, 430
　custom fields, 432–433
　drop folders, 431–432
　index, 427–429
　index defaults, 429
　language, 432–433
　logging, 430–431
　.pdx files, 431
preferences, Windows
　Acrobat.ini file, 434–436
　document word sections, 435
　field settings, 436
　index available group size, 435
　log file size, 436
　memory setting, 435
　purge time, 435
　search engine messages, 435
　Windows-only filenames, 435
Acrobat CD Installer plug-in, 613
Acrobat Distiller
　Acrobat Distiller Guide, 104
　Add Font Name dialog box, 165
　color job options
　　CMYK, 169
　　Convert All Colors to sRGB/CalRGB, 168
　　Gray, 168–169
　　Leave Color Unchanged, 167
　　Preserve Halftone Information, 169
　　Preserve Overprint settings, 169
　　Preserve Transfer Functions, 169
　　Preserve Under Color Removal, 169
　　RGB, 169
　　Tag Everything for Color Mgmt, 168
　　Tag Only Images for Color Mgmt, 168
　compression options
　　automatic compression, 162
　　Average Downsampling at [__], 160
　　Bicubic Downsampling at [__], 161–162
　　Compress Text and Line Art, 162
　　downsampling PostScript files, 541

Quality, 162
Subsampling at [__], 161
environment of, 156–184
font embedding, steps in, 166–167
font embedding options
Add Name, 164–165
Always Embed, 164
Embed All Fonts, 162
Embedding, 163–164
Never Embed, 164
Remove, 166
Subset All Embedded Fonts Below [__], 163
When Embedding Fails, 163
history of, 4
introduction to, 12–13
job options
advanced job options, 169–174
ASCII Format, 159
binding, 160
center artwork for EPS files, 171
compatibility, 158–159
default page size, 172
general job options, 158–160
generate thumbnails, 160
load, 172
log DSC warnings, 171
optimize PDF, 159
overriding by PostScript file, 171
overriding in PageMaker, 228–229
preserve document information from DSC, 172
preserve EPS information from DSC, 172
preserve Level 2 copypage semantics, 171
preserve OPI comments, 172
preset job options, 157–157
PressOptimized, 157
PrintOptimized, 158
process DSC, 171
resize page for EPS Files, 171
resolution, 160
saving job options, 173
saving portable job ticket in PDF, 171
ScreenOptimized, 158
use Prologue.ps and Epilogue.ps, 170
PageMaker, integration with, 224–225
passwords in, 182–183
PDFWriter, compared with, 115, 143
preferences
restarting after PostScript fatal error, 156
startup volume nearly full notification, 157
watched folders unavailable notification, 156
printing to
drag-and-drop distillation, 190
files, combining by name, 191–193
files, combining in folders, 193–194
launching Distiller, 184–185
one step distillation, 185–188
page order, 194–196
PostScript Files, combining on networks, 196–199
PostScript Files, concatenating, 190
RunDirEx.txt file, using, 191–196
RunFilEx.txt file, using, 191–196
using Windows Run command, 189–190
security
introduction to, 182–183
Security dialog box, 183–184
watched folder issues, 184
startup volume full notification, 157
uses of, 143–144
using, 143–199
watched folders
creating, 177–182
notifying when unavailable, 156–157
options, 174–177
PDF workflow, place in, 176
using in PageMaker, 227
Watched Folders dialog box, 174, 446
Acrobat Exchange
environment of, 265
grid lines, 269–271

(continued)

Acrobat Exchange *(continued)*
  PDF document control
    base URL, 279
    fonts, 277
    General Info, 273–275
    General Info dialog box, 273
    index settings, 278
    Open Info, 275–277
    prepress options, 277–278
    Prepress Options dialog box, 278
  preferences
    annotation, 267–268
    Annotations Preferences dialog box,
      268
    color, 270–271, 277
    Forms Grid, 269–271
    full screen, 268
    general, 266–267
    General Preferences dialog box, 267
    Grid Settings dialog box, 269
    initial view options, 275
    paper capture, 271–272
    search, 268
    skip edit warnings, 266
    TouchUp Preferences dialog box, 272
    TouchUp tools, 272–273
    trapping, 277
    user interface options, 276
    Weblink, 268
    window options, 276
  saving PDF files, 279–281
  security, adding to PDFs, 277, 281–284
  Security dialog box, 282
  using, 265–285
Acrobat PDFWriter Properties dialog box, 120
Acrobat Reader
  distribution issues
    registering as distributor, 585–586
    rights, 583–586
  environment controls, 77–94
  graphics
    copying to other applications, 100–102
    Graphics Select tool, 100–101
    selecting, 100
  help, getting, 104–105
  history of, 4
  licensing, 584
  menus, context-sensitive, 102–104
  Navigation Pane, 29
  preferences
    annotation preferences, 89–91
    application language, 86
    background downloading, 88
    color manager, 88
    confirm file open links, 89
    cross-doc links, 88–89
    general preferences, 85–89
    Greeked text, 86
    images, large, 87
    images, smooth, 86
    link information display, 92–93
    Open dialog box at startup, 88
    page, display to edge, 87
    Page Cache, 88–89
    page layout, 85–86
    page numbering, 89
    page units, 86
    smooth text, 86
    splash screen at startup, 88
    substitution fonts, 86
    Web browser, selecting, 94
    Web browser progress dialog, 93
    Web browser toolbar button, 93
    WebLink preferences, 91–95
    WebLink Preferences dialog box, 92
    zoom, default, 87–88
    zoom, fit visible, 88
  Reader Online Guide, 105
  registering, 107–108

text, selecting
    Column Select tool, 96–98
    introduction to, 94–95
    Text Select tool, 95–96
  using, 77–112
  word processors, copying to, 98–100
Acrobat Scan plug-in dialog box, 464
Acrobat Search
  Acrobat Search dialog box
    Author, 61
    With Date Info, 62
    With Document Info, 60
    Find Results Containing Text, 60
    Indexes Searched, 63
    Keywords, 61
    Match Case, 63
    Proximity, 63
    Sounds Like, 62
    Subject, 61
    Thesaurus, 62
    Title, 61
    using, 59–60
    Word Stemming, 62
  introduction to, 11–12
  using, 55–73
Acrobat viewers, 11. *See also* Acrobat;
    Acrobat Reader
Acrobat.ini file, 434–436
AcroForm plug-in, 596
AcroViewer Xtra plug-in, 654
Add an Action dialog box, 405
Add Font Name dialog box, 165
Adobe Acrobat (suite of applications)
  components, 9–14
  history, 3–5
  usage of the term in this book, 4
  WWW, integration with, 53–54
Adobe FDF Toolkit, 418

Adobe Illustrator
  editing PDF files, limitations, 218–220
  editing QuarkXpress data with, 221–223
  exporting to PDF from
    compression settings, 217
    export options, 216
    introduction to, 214–215
  imaging problems, using to solve, 220–223
  opening PDFs in, 217–218
  opening PostScript files in, 222
Adobe PageMaker
  Export Adobe PDF plug-in
    advanced options, 247
    article options, 247
    bookmarks, 247
    color model, 245
    compression, 244–245
    document information, 245
    features removed from, 249
    fonts, 244
    formats, 244
    general settings, 244
    hyperlinks, 245–246
    installing, 243
    notes on first page, 247
    PDF styles, saving, 247
    PDF styles for cross-platform use,
      248–249
    pre-3.01 versions, 225–227
    using, 243–244
  exporting to PDF
    Distiller, role of, 224–225
    general process of, 224–225
    overriding Distiller job options,
      228–229
    PDF Advanced Job Options dialog box,
      229
    using Export Adobe PDF, 225–227
    watched folders, 227
  PDF control options
    device dependent, 238

(continued)

Adobe PageMaker *(continued)*
    device independent, 238
    Distiller, quitting after use, 238
    EPS screen preview, 238
    file name, confirming, 237
    folder location, confirming, 237
    printer style conflicts, 238
    printing all publications in book, 237
    saving publications before export, 237
  PDF options
    article properties, 236
    bookmarks, 231–232
    creating articles, 234–236
    document information, adding, 236
    Edit Bookmark Names dialog box, 233
    editing names, 233–234
    hyperlinks, 230–231
    index bookmarks, 232
    notes to first page, adding, 236
    stories in current article, 235–236
    stories in publication/book, 235
  pdfmark, 249–263
    annotating EPS files with, 258–263
    annotating PostScript files with,
      250–257
  printer styles
    color settings, 241
    Define Printer Styles dialog box, 239
    document attributes, defining, 240
    paper attributes, defining, 240–241
    print options, 241
    Print Options dialog box, 241
    Print Paper dialog box, 240
    resolution settings, 240
Adobe Photoshop
  Acrobat, using with, 202–212
  color modes
    bitmap, 204
    CMYK, 204
    duotone, 205
    exportable to PDF, 205
    grayscale, 204
    indexed color, 205

    lab, 204
    multichannel, 205
    RGB, 204
  composite color printing to PDF, 206
  exporting to PDF, 203
    compression issues in, 206–207
  importing PDF files
    Generic MPS PDF Parser dialog box,
      208–209
    missing fonts, 210
    multipage documents, 211–212
    Rasterize Generic PDF dialog box,
      209–210
    rasterizing, 208–210
    thumbnail issues in, 208
    using Open command, 208
AdobePS printer driver
  Macintosh, 185–188
  Windows, 188–189
Adobe's Web site
  accessing from Adobe applications,
    106–107
  Acrobat home page, 108–109
  customer experiences pages, 110
  Customer Support pages, 109
  exporting form data help, 419
  Product Feedback page, 109–110
  tips and techniques pages, 111
advancing PDF pages
  Advance Every N Seconds, 34
  Advance On Any Click, 34
Aerial plug-in, 603–604
.aiff files, 297
  importing, 377
Alt key (toggle Select tools), 96
Amiga IFF files, capturing, 474
annotations
  annotation tools, 291–292
  annotations palette
    Navigation Pane, opening with, 294
    as navigation tool, 316–317
    palette hierarchy, 315
    Rescan Document command, 314–315

sorting annotations, 316
using, 313–319
Annotations Preferences dialog box, 268
Annotations window, 314
audio annotations
Audio Annotation tool, 297
Audio Properties window, 298
recording, 297
Sound Comment dialog box, 298
deleting, 318–319
exporting, 318
file annotations
File Annotation Properties window, 306
File Annotation tool, 306
uses of, 306
filtering
Annotations Filter option (note
properties), 294
Filter Manager, 321–322
finding, 317–318
hypertext links, 51
importing, 318
navigating, 316–317
note annotations
attributes, 292
collapsing, 293
deleting, 293
expanding, 293
note icons, 296
Notes tool, 292–293
properties, 294–296
Reset Note Window Location option,
295
resizing, 292
PDF workflow, place in, 291
preferences
in Acrobat Exchange, 267–268
in Acrobat Reader, 89–91
in note properties, 295
printing, 322–323
sorting, 316

stamp annotations
adding images, 300–304
customizing, 299–304
introduction to, 298
properties, 299
summarizing, 319–320
text annotations
annotation properties, 296
background options, 297
borders, 297
color, 297
Text Annotation tool, 296
Text Properties dialog box, 297
working with, 291–307
Annotations Preferences dialog box
(Exchange), 268
Annotations window, 314
Annots/Annots32.api plug-in, 596
Apogee plug-in, 601
Append Web Page command, 528–531
Append Web Page dialog box, 528
AppendPDF plug-in, 614
AppendPDF Pro plug-in, 614
Apple ➪ Control Panels ➪ PDFWriter Shortcut,
119
Apple QuickTime files, 378
ApproveIt for .pdf plug-in, 648
APS PDF AdTool plug-in, 604
APS RIP3 plug-in, 604
Ari's Toolbox plug-in, 616–618
Article Properties dialog box, 337
articles
Article Properties dialog box, 337
article threads, ending, 340
Article tool, 338
Articles palette, 52, 336
combining, 342–343
defining, 339–340
Delete Article dialog box, 341
deleting, 340–342
navigating, 336

(continued)

articles *(continued)*
    in PDFs exported by PageMaker
        creating, 234–236
        options, 247
        properties, 236
        stories in current article, 235–236
    properties, 236, 337
    uses of, 335
    viewing, 336–339
    working with, 335–343
    zoom issues in, 337
Arts AcroBuddies plug-in, 647
Arts Duplex plug-in, 647
Arts Import plug-in, 646
Arts Joust plug-in, 647
Arts ThumbOpt plug-in, 646
Asura plug-in, 635–636
Audio Annotation tool, 297
Audio Properties window, 298
AutoIndx/Autidx32.api plug-in, 596
Automount Servers, 69
.avi files, importing, 378

B

background color, 34
Banner Print plug-in, 610
Base 14 fonts, 164
BatchPrintPDF plug-in, 606
bitmap color mode basics, 204
BMP files, capturing, 474
Bookmark Properties dialog box, 349, 502
bookmarks
    basics of, 49–50, 343
    Bookmark Properties dialog box, 349, 502
    creating, 344, 346–348
    deleting, 344
    in Export Adobe PDF, 247
    navigating in Web browsers, 496
    ordering, 345–348
    in PageMaker

bookmark options, 231–232
    Edit Bookmark Names dialog box, 233
properties, 348–349
renaming, 348
structured bookmarks, 348
working with, 343–349
Bookworm plug-in, 646
Boolean search operators, 72–73
Brisque Digital Front End plug-in, 647–648
Brookhouse Software Web site, 660
buttons
    introduction to, 46–47
    radio button options in forms, 394–395
buttons in a PDF document, 46–47

C

Capture/Capture32.api plug-in, 596
Capture Server dialog box, 471–472
capturing imported images
    Amiga IFF, 474
    BMP, 474
    GIF, 474
    JPEG, 474
    PCX, 475
    PICT, 475
    Pixar, 475
    PNG, 475
    Targa, 475
    TIFF, 475
Catalog Preferences dialog box, 430
CCITT compression in PDFWriter, 131
CD-ROM, publishing on
    artwork issues
        continuous tone images, 587
        Photoshop file transfer functions,
            587–588
        printable area of CD, 587
        templates, 589
Catalog, using to optimize, 580–581
color issues, 582

content design, 578–583
cost, 578
data, supplying to manufacturer, 582
design charting, 580
distribution issues
    registering as distributor, 585–586
    rights, 583–586
file naming, 582
file preparation, 580
folder design, 582–583
font issues, 581
jackets, 577–578
mastering, 577
replication, 577–578
welcome files, 579–580
CGI application for exporting form data,
    418–420
check box options in forms, 394–395
CheckUp plug-in, 619–620
Clipboard contents, viewing, 101
CloneLink plug-in, 636–637
Cmd+. (exit Full Screen view), 34
Cmd+- (zoom out), 32
Cmd++ (zoom in), 32
Cmd+0 (fit in Window), 32
Cmd+2 (fit width), 32
Cmd+3 (fit visible), 32
Cmd+A (select all), 99
Cmd+B (create bookmark), 344
Cmd+G (find again), 55
Cmd+L (exit Full Screen view), 34
Cmd+L (full screen mode), 32, 34
Cmd+M (zoom to), 32
Cmd+Shift+4 (capture screen), 370
Cmd+Shift+F (search), 59
Cmd+Tab (find next), 472
CMYK color mode, 204
Collect Pro plug-in, 620–622
color modes, 204–205
    bitmap, 204
    CMYK, 204

duotone, 205
exportable to PDF, 205
grayscale, 204
indexed color, 205
lab, 204
multichannel, 205
RGB, 204
color separation
    introduction to, 557–558
    process color separation
        correcting problems, 558–559
        printing spot color, 561–565
        steps in, 560–561
combo box options in forms, 396–398
Command Bar navigation tools, 40
Compose plug-in, 602
compression
    CCITT, 131
    Distiller options, 160–162
        automatic compression, 162
        Average Downsampling at [__], 160
        Bicubic Downsampling at [__], 161–162
        Compress Text and Line Art, 162
        Quality, 162
        Subsampling at [__], 161
    in Illustrator, 217
    JPEG, 130–131
    LZW, 131
    in PDFWriter, 130–132
        fonts, 124
        PDFWriter Compression dialog box, 128
    in Photoshop, 206–207
    Run Length (RLE), 131
    ZIP, 131, 207
Conversion Settings dialog box, 523
converting scanned pages to text
    Capture Suspects, 472–474
    capturing a page, 471–474
    dictionaries, 468, 470
    editing with TouchUp Text tool, 472
    font limitations, 467
    font requirements, 468
    OCR language, selecting, 468

(continued)

converting scanned pages to text *(continued)*
  PDF output style, 469
  unrecognized words, 472–474
CorelDraw, using with Acrobat, 214
cpAnnCollector plug-in, 609
Crackerjack Pilot plug-in, 631
Crackerjack plug-in, 555–557, 630–631
Crackerjack printing plug-in, 555–557
Create Link window, 362–363
Create Web Links dialog box, 520
CRF Publisher plug-in, 613
CRFScan & Trade plug-in, 626–627
Ctrl+- (zoom out), 32
Ctrl++ (zoom in), 32
Ctrl+0 (fit in Window), 32
Ctrl+1 (actual size), 32
Ctrl+2 (fit width), 32
Ctrl+3 (fit visible), 32
Ctrl+A (select all), 99
Ctrl+B (create bookmark), 344
Ctrl+click (move to beginning of article), 338
Ctrl+click (open navigation pop-up), 42
Ctrl+G (find again), 55
Ctrl+L (exit Full Screen view), 34
Ctrl+L (full screen mode), 32
Ctrl+M (zoom to), 32
Ctrl+Shift+click
  (ignore link), 338
  (move to end of article), 338
Ctrl+Shift+F (search), 59

D
D Soft plug-in, 613
Date Stamp plug-in, 634
DateD Author plug-in, 615
DateD Viewer plug-in, 615
Define Printer Styles dialog box (PageMaker), 239
Delete Article dialog box, 341

destinations
  basics of, 52–53, 355–356
  creating, 356
  sorting, 356–357
dialog box (the term), 56
dialog boxes
  Acrobat
    Acrobat Search, 59–63
    Add an Action, 405
    Append Web Page, 528
    Article Properties, 337
    Bookmark Properties, 349, 502
    Conversion Settings, 523
    Create Web Links, 520
    Delete Article, 341
    Field Selection, 407
    Find tool, 54–55
    Full Screen Preferences, 33–35
    HTML Conversion Settings, 505
    Icon Placement, 401
    Index Information, 59
    Index Selection, 57
    Open Web Page, 522
    Page Layout, 524
    Purge Warning, 445
    Query, 59–60
    Refresh Pages, 519
    Scan, 450
    Search Preferences, 66–67
    Search Results, 63–64
    Self-Sign Signatures - Sign Document, 414
    Sound Comment, 298
    Text Properties, 297
    Web Capture Preferences, 513
    Weblink Preferences, 510
    Zoom To, 31
  Acrobat Scan Pug-In, 464
  Capture
    Capture Server, 471–472
    Import Image, 476
    Preferences, 468

Catalog
    Catalog Preferences, 430
    New Index Definition, 437
    Schedule Builds, 442, 447
Distiller
    Add Font Name, 165
    Job Options (Distiller), 159, 165, 170
    Watched Folders, 174, 446
Exchange
    Annotations Preferences, 268
    General Info, 273
    General Preferences, 267
    Grid Settings, 269
    Prepress Options, 278
    Security, 282
    TouchUp Preferences, 272
Graphic Markup Tools
    Properties, 309
LaserWriter
    Print Driver, 154
Netscape
    Document Security, 493
    Edit Type, 486–487
    Font Info, 494
PageMaker
    Define Printer Styles, 239
    Edit Bookmark Names, 233
    Export Adobe PDF, 226, 242
    PDF Advanced Job Options, 229
    Print Options, 241
    Print Paper, 240
PDFWriter
    Acrobat PDFWriter Properties, 120
    Document Info, 135–136
    Page Setup, 455
    PDFWriter Compression, 128
    PDFWriter Page Setup, 123
    Save PDF File As, 139
Photoshop
    Generic MPS PDF Parser, 208–209
    Rasterize Generic PDF, 209–210

Reader
    Font Info, 80, 166
    General Info, 79, 136
    Security Info, 84
    WebLink Preferences, 92
    Word Assistant, 74
digital signatures, 413–414
DigSig.api plug-in, 599
Distiller Tools plug-in, 637–638
distribution issues
    registering as distributor, 585–586
    rights, 583–586
DocuCom plug-in, 654
Document ➪ Go To Page, 42
Document Info dialog box, 135–136
document information
    in Adobe PageMaker, 236
    Document Info dialog box, 135–136
    in Exchange, 274–275
    in Export Adobe PDF plug-in, 245
    font, 80–83
    Font Information dialog box, 80, 166
    general, 78–79
    General Info dialog box, 79, 136
    in PDF workflow, 274–275
    security, 83–84
    Security Info dialog box, 84
    viewing in PDFWriter, 135–136
    viewing in search results, 65
    viewing in Web browsers, 491–492
Document menu, 41
Document ➪ Pages, 355
Document ➪ Pages ➪ Insert, 310
document repurposing, 6–8
Document Security dialog box (Netscape),
        493
Document ➪ Set Page Action, 378
Document Structuring Comments (DSC),
        171
DOS file names, 137
dot gain, 565–566

downsampling images
    Acrobat Capture preferences, 469
    Acrobat Distiller compression options,
        160–162
    Average Downsampling at [__], 160
    Bicubic Downsampling at [__], 161–162
    in PDFWriter, 132
DSC (Document Structuring Comments), 171
duotone color mode basics, 205

E

Edit Bookmark Names dialog box
        (PageMaker), 233
Edit ⇨ Clear, 293, 360
Edit ⇨ Edit Story (PageMaker), 231
Edit ⇨ Find Again, 55
Edit ⇨ Properties, 360
Edit ⇨ Search, 59
Edit ⇨ Search ⇨ Query, 59, 60, 66
Edit ⇨ Search ⇨ Select Indexes, 56–57
Edit ⇨ Search ⇨ Word Assistant, 74
Edit ⇨ Select All, 99
Edit Type dialog box (Netscape), 486–487
EFS plug-in, 596
epilogue.ps file, 170
EPS files
    annotating with pdfmark, 258–263
    Distiller job options
        centering artwork for, 171
        preserving EPS info from DSC, 172
        resizing page for, 171
    EPS screen preview (PageMaker), 238
    exporting from Acrobat, 554–555
Esc (exit Full Screen mode), 34
EWH/EWH32.api plug-in, 597
ExecMenu/Excmnu32.api plug-in, 597
Export Adobe PDF dialog box (PageMaker),
        226, 242
Export Adobe PDF plug-in
    advanced options, 247

    article options, 247
    bookmarks, 247
    color model, 245
    compression, 244–245
    document information, 245
    features removed from, 249
    fonts, 244
    formats, 244
    general settings, 244
    hyperlinks, 245–246
    installing, 243
    notes on first page, 247
    PDF styles, saving, 247
    PDF styles for cross-platform use, 248–249
    pre-3.01 versions, 225–227
    using, 243–244
exporting EPS files, 554–555
ExportPS/expps32.api plug-in, 597
EZ-PDF plug-in, 601

F

F5 (show/hide navigation pane), 32
F7 (show/hide Menu Bar), 32
F8 (show/hide Command Bar), 32
F9 (show/hide Tool Bar), 32
Face-It! plug-in, 635
FDF (Form Data File), 418
FDFMerge plug-in, 615
Field Properties window, 390–413
Field Selection dialog box, 407
File ⇨ Adobe Online, 106
File Annotation Properties window, 306
File Annotation tool, 306
File ⇨ Automate ⇨ Multi-page PSD to PDF, 211
File ⇨ Batch Optimize, 280
File ⇨ Batch Process, 349
File ⇨ Document Info ⇨ Fonts, 80
File ⇨ Document Info ⇨ General, 136
File ⇨ Document Info ⇨ index, 278
File ⇨ Document Info ⇨ Open, 275

File ➪ Export ➪ Adobe PDF (PageMaker), 225–226, 242
File ➪ Export ➪ EPS, 554
File ➪ Export ➪ Form Data, 419
File ➪ Export ➪ PostScript, 554
File ➪ Import ➪ Image, 467, 475
file names, DOS, 137
File ➪ Preferences, 266, 427
File ➪ Preferences ➪ Annotations, 89, 268, 292, 295
File ➪ Preferences ➪ Forms Grid, 269
File ➪ Preferences ➪ Full Screen, 33
File ➪ Preferences ➪ General, 47, 48, 266
File ➪ Preferences ➪ Paper Capture, 271, 468
File ➪ Preferences ➪ Search, 66
File ➪ Preferences ➪ Web Capture, 521
File ➪ Preferences ➪ Weblink, 92, 521
File ➪ Printer Styles (PageMaker), 242
File ➪ Printer Styles ➪ Define (PageMaker), 239
FileOpen PDF Publisher plug-in, 623
Find Again command, 55
Find tool dialog box, 54–55
finding. *See also* searching
    compared to searching, 54
    Find Again command, 55
    Find tool dialog box
        tasks of, 54–55
Firebird plug-in, 605
Flightcheck plug-in, 632
font
    embedding
        disabling, 454–455
        in Distiller, 162–167
        in PDFWriter, 124–126
        when scanning, 454–455
    file size, 126
    font information
        Font Information Dialog box, 80–83
        viewing in Web browsers, 493–494
    in form fields, 391–392
    issues in CD-ROM publishing, 581
    licensing, 126

names, 165
in PDFWriter
    compression, 124
    subsetting, 127
substitution fonts (Reader), 86
font embedding, disabling, 454–455
Font Info dialog box (Netscape), 494
Font Information dialog box, 80, 166
Form Data File (FDF), 418
forms
    actions
        Add an Action dialog box, 405
        executing with signature fields, 413–414
        import form data, 405
        mouse behavior items, 404
        resetting form, 406–408
    buttons
        highlighting, 398–399
        Icon Placement dialog box, 401
        icons, 399–400
        options, 398–403
        radio button options, 394–395
        rollover effects, 400–403
    calculation options, 411
    check box options, 394–395
    combo box options, 396–398
    creating, 388–389
    date display options, 409
    definition, 385
    exporting data to Internet, 418–420
    Field Properties window
        Actions tab, 404–408
        Appearance tab, 390–392
        Calculate tab, 411
        Format tab, 408–410
        Options tab, 393–403
        Selected Change tab, 411–413
        tab options for field types table, 490
        Validate tab, 410–411
    fields in
        actions, assigning to, 404–408
        aligning, 416
        appearance of, 390–392

                                    (continued)

forms *(continued)*
    clearing, 407
    color, background, 391
    color, border, 390–391
    color, text, 391
    deleting, 415–416
    duplicating, 415
    editing, 415–418
    Field Properties window, 390, 404
    Field Selection dialog box, 407
    field tab order, setting, 416–418
    font, 391–392
    hidden, 392
    hidden but prints, 392
    introduction to, 385–386
    moving, 415
    naming, 389
    navigating text fields, 387–388
    properties, 389–418
    read only, 392
    required, 392
    resetting, 406–408
    Self-Sign Signatures - Sign Document
        dialog box, 414
    short description field, 390
    signature fields, 413–414
    size, 392
    sizing, 416
    style, 391
    type, 389–390
    visible, 392
    visible but doesn't print, 392
    width, 391
  form contents, 386–387
  Form Data File (FDF), 418
  Form tool, 415
  format options, 408–410
  Forms Grid, 269–271
  hypertext link actions involving
    Import Form Data, 367
    Reset Form, 368
    Submit Form, 369

  importing data, 420–423
  JavaScript in
    using for custom editing, 410
    using for selected change actions,
        411–413
  list box options, 396–398
  mouse behavior items, 404
  numeric display options, 409
  percentage display options, 409
  selected change options, 411–413
  Snap to Forms Grid option, 389
  text options, 393–394
  time display options, 409
  validation options, 410–411
  working with, 385–423
FormView plug-in, 636
full-screen page views
  background color, 34
  exiting, 34
  Full Screen Preferences dialog box, 33–35
  Mouse Cursor pop-up menu, 35
  opening, 33
  transition, default, 34
  usefulness for presentations, 33
Full Screen Preferences dialog box, 33–35

G
Gemini plug-in, 625–626
General Info dialog box, 79, 136, 273
General Preferences dialog box (Exchange),
    267
Generic MPS PDF Parser dialog box
    (Photoshop), 208–209
GIF files, capturing, 474
GraphCopy plug-in, 628
Graphic Markup tools
  Ellipse tool, 309
  introduction to, 308
  Line tool, 309

Pencil tool, 308
Properties dialog box, 309
Rectangle tool, 309
tool properties, 309–310
graphics
editing graphic objects, 329–332
highlighting with Graphic Markup tools
Ellipse tool, 309
introduction to, 308
Line tool, 309
Pencil tool, 308
Properties dialog box, 309
Rectangle tool, 309
tool properties, 309–310
in Reader
copying to other applications, 100–102
Graphics Select tool, 100–101
selecting, 100
TouchUp Object tool, using, 329
working with, 328–332
grayscale color mode basics, 204
Grid Settings dialog box (Exchange), 269

H
HAHT Enterprise Solution Module plug-in, 623
Help ⇨ Adobe on the Web, 106
help on the Web
Adobe's site
Acrobat home page, 108–109
customer experiences pages, 110
Tips and Techniques page, 111
Brookhouse Software, 660
PDFZone, 660
PurePDF, 660
Help ⇨ Reader Online Guide, 105
highlighting
with Graphic Markup tools
Ellipse tool, 309

introduction to, 308
Line tool, 309
Pencil tool, 308
Properties dialog box, 309
Rectangle tool, 309
tool properties, 309–310
with Text Markup tools
columns, selecting, 312
Highlight Text tool, 311–312
properties, 312–313
Strikethrough Text tool, 312
Underline Text tool, 312
HLS/Ahls32.api plug-in, 597
Homer plug-in, 607
HP AccuPage software, 452
HTML
coding, 480–483
combining with PDF, 484–485
compared to PDF
HTML advantages, 484
PDF advantages, 483–484
converting to PDF, 498
editors, 480
embedding PDFs in Web pages, 480–483
programming, 479
HTML Conversion Settings dialog box, 505
HTMLDOC plug-in, 619
HTML2pdf.api plug-in, 599
HyperCard, 45
hypertext links
annotations (*See* annotations)
articles (*See* articles)
bookmarks (*See* bookmarks)
buttons (*See* buttons)
Create Link window, 362–363
creating
basics of, 361–362
steps in, 370–372
destinations (*See* destinations)
historical background, 45
in HyperCard, 45
link actions

(continued)

hypertext links *(continued)*
    execute menu item, 366
    Go to View, 367
    Import Form Data, 367
    introduction to, 360
    Javascript, 367
    Movie, 367
    Open File, 368
    Read Article, 368
    Reset Form, 368
    Select Sound, 369
    Submit Form, 369
  link environment, 361
  link properties, 360, 362–370
  Link Properties window, 362, 495
  link rectangles
    invisible, 363–365
    visible, 365–366
  Link tool, 361–362
  navigating in Web browsers, 495
  page actions
    associating with sound file, 379
    basics of, 373
    creating, 373, 375–377
    editing, 373–374
    nesting, 377
    using transitions with, 374–377
  removing, 360
  thumbnails *(See* thumbnails)

I

Icon Placement dialog box, 401
icons in forms, 399–400
ieweb32.api plug-in, 599
IFF files, capturing, 474
Image Alchemy PS plug-in, 624
imagesetters, 145
imaging devices, 145
Import Image dialog box (Capture), 476
Import/Import32.api plug-in, 597

Impostrip plug-in, 651
IMPress plug-in, 651
Index Fixer plug-in, 634
Index Information dialog box, 59
Index ⇨ Schedule, 442, 446
Index Selection dialog box, 57
indexed color mode basics, 205
indexes
  adding, 56–57
  building, 440–441
  creating, 436–441
  directories, excluding, 439–440
  directories, including, 439
  directories, removing, 440
  hierarchy of, 426
  index description field
    adding IDs to Acrobat 1.0 files, 439
    excluding words, 438
    log file, 430–431
    New Index Definition dialog box, 437
    optimizing for CD-ROM, 439
    word options, 438–439
  index information, 58–59
  Index Information dialog box, 59
  index maintenance, automating
    building indexes, 443
    identifying indexes for Schedule Builds, 442–443
    Purge Warning dialog box, 445
    purging data, 444–445
    Schedule Builds dialog box, 442
    stopping scheduled builds, 443–444
  Index Selection dialog box, 57
  introduction to, 56
  Macintosh defaults, 429–430
  New Index Definition dialog box, 437
  preferences in Macintosh, setting, 427–429
  relocating, 426
  removing from searches, 57–58
  restoring to searches, 57
  structure of, 425–426
  title, 436–437

InfoLink Publishing Enhancement Software plug-in, 629
InfoLinker plug-in, 602
Interpress, 150
Intranets, 19
ISIFile plug-in, 628
ISIS software, 450
ISIToolBox plug-in, 628

J

Jade plug-in, 606
JavaScript
    executing with hypertext links, 367
    forms, custom editing using, 410
    ignored when converting to PDF, 499
    in selected change actions, 411–413
Job Options dialog box (Distiller), 159, 165, 170
JPEG files
    capturing, 474
    compression, 130–131
    exporting from Photoshop, 207

K

Kay, Alan, 6
keyboard shortcuts
    Alt key (toggle Select tools), 96
    Cmd+. (exit Full Screen view), 34
    Cmd+- (zoom out), 32
    Cmd++ (zoom in), 32
    Cmd+0 (fit in Window), 32
    Cmd+1 (actual size), 32
    Cmd+2 (fit width), 32
    Cmd+3 (fit visible), 32
    Cmd+B (create bookmark), 344
    Cmd+G (find again), 55

Cmd+L (full screen mode), 32, 34
Cmd+M (zoom to), 32
Cmd+Shift+4 (capture screen), 370
Cmd+Shift+click (ignore link), 338
Cmd+Shift+F (search), 59
Cmd+Tab (find next), 472
Ctrl+- (zoom out), 32
Ctrl++ (zoom in), 32
Ctrl+0 (fit in Window), 32
Ctrl+1 (actual size), 32
Ctrl+2 (fit width), 32
Ctrl+3 (fit visible), 32
Ctrl+A (select all), 99
Ctrl+B (create bookmark), 344
Ctrl+click (move to beginning of article), 338
Ctrl+click (open navigation pop-up), 42
Ctrl+click+drag (dragging thumbnails), 352
Ctrl+drag Form tool (field selection), 415
Ctrl+G (find again), 55
Ctrl+L exit Full Screen view, 34
Ctrl+L (full screen mode), 32
Ctrl+M (zoom to), 32
Ctrl+Shift+click
    (ignore link), 338
    (move to end of article), 338
Ctrl+Shift+F (search), 59
F5 (show/hide navigation pane), 32
F7 (show/hide Menu Bar), 32
F8 (show/hide Command Bar), 32
F9 (show/hide Tool Bar), 32
Option+click (move to beginning of article), 338
Option+click+drag (dragging thumbnails), 352
Option+Shift+click (move to end of article), 338
Shift+click (move in article column), 338
Shift+drag Form tool (field selection), 415
Shift+Tab (find next), 472
Shift+V (toggle Select tools), 95

L

la32.api plug-in, 599
lab color mode basics, 204
language options, 432–433
large format inkjet printers, 574
LaserWriter 8.5.1 print driver dialog box, 154
Legacy XCHANGE plug-in, 648
Library Manage plug-in, 602
Link Manage plug-in, 602
Link Properties window, 362, 495
list box options in forms, 396–398
local area networks, basics of, 15–17
Local Render plug-in, 610
log file (Catalog), 430
Loop After Last page, 34
LZW compression, 131

M

Macintosh color picker, 270
Macromedia FreeHand, 213
MadeToPrint XT plug-in, 609
Magellan plug-in, 605
magnification button (status bar), 30
MAPublisher Lt plug-in, 605
MarkzScout plug-in, 632–633
Menu Bar commands
    Apple ➪ Control Panels ➪ PDFWriter
        Shortcut, 119
    Document ➪ Go To Page, 42
    Document ➪ Pages, 355
    Document ➪ Pages ➪ Insert, 310
    Document ➪ Set Page Action, 378
    Edit ➪ Clear, 293, 360
    Edit ➪ Edit Story (PageMaker), 231
    Edit ➪ Find Again, 55
    Edit ➪ Properties, 360
    Edit ➪ Search, 59
    Edit ➪ Search ➪ Query, 59, 60, 66

Edit ➪ Search ➪ Select Indexes, 56–57
Edit ➪ Search ➪ Word Assistant, 74
Edit ➪ Select All, 99
File ➪ Adobe Online, 106
File ➪ Automate ➪ Multi-page PSD to PDF,
    211
File ➪ Batch Optimize, 280
File ➪ Batch Process, 349
File ➪ Document Info ➪ Fonts, 80
File ➪ Document Info ➪ General, 136
File ➪ Document Info ➪ index, 278
File ➪ Document Info ➪ Open, 275
File ➪ Export ➪ Adobe PDF (PageMaker),
    225–226, 242
File ➪ Export ➪ EPS, 554
File ➪ Export ➪ Form Data, 419
File ➪ Export ➪ PostScript, 554
File ➪ Import ➪ Image, 467, 475
File ➪ Preferences, 266, 427
File ➪ Preferences ➪ Annotations, 89, 268,
    292, 295
File ➪ Preferences ➪ Forms Grid, 269
File ➪ Preferences ➪ Full Screen, 33
File ➪ Preferences ➪ General, 47, 48, 266
File ➪ Preferences ➪ Paper Capture, 271,
    468
File ➪ Preferences ➪ Search, 66
File ➪ Preferences ➪ Web Capture, 521
File ➪ Preferences ➪ Weblink, 92, 521
File ➪ Printer Styles (PageMaker), 242
File ➪ Printer Styles ➪ Define (PageMaker),
    239
Help ➪ Adobe on the Web, 106
Help ➪ Reader Online Guide, 105
Index ➪ Schedule, 442, 446
Select File ➪ Document Info ➪ Fonts, 165,
    166
Settings ➪ Control Panel ➪ Printers, 120
Settings ➪ Job Options, 158–159
Settings ➪ Watched Folders, 174
Tools ➪ Annotations ➪ Delete All, 319

Tools ⇨ Annotations ⇨ Filter Manager, 294, 321
Tools ⇨ Annotations ⇨ Summarize Annotations, 319
Tools ⇨ Annotations ⇨ Summarize Notes, 320, 372
Tools ⇨ Capture ⇨ Capture Pages, 467
Tools ⇨ Forms ⇨ Align, 416
Tools ⇨ Forms ⇨ Fields ⇨ Distribute, 416
Tools ⇨ Forms ⇨ Fields ⇨ Set Tab Order, 417
Tools ⇨ Forms ⇨ Page Templates, 310
Tools ⇨ Paper Capture ⇨ Capture Pages, 471
Tools ⇨ Paper Capture ⇨ Show Suspects, 472–473
Tools ⇨ Self-Sign Signature ⇨ Log On, 413
Tools ⇨ TouchUp ⇨ Fit Text to Selection, 325
Tools ⇨ Web Capture, 512, 528
Tools ⇨ Web Capture ⇨ Bring Status Dialogs to Foreground, 524
Tools ⇨ Weblinks ⇨ Create, 520
Type ⇨ Paragraph (PageMaker), 231
Utilities ⇨ Book (PageMaker), 237
Utilities ⇨ Create TOC (PageMaker), 231
Utilities ⇨ Index Entry (PageMaker), 232
View ⇨ Continuous, 35–37
View ⇨ Fit in Window, 44
View ⇨ Full Screen, 33
View ⇨ Show Forms Grid, 269
View ⇨ Single Page, 35
View ⇨ Zoom, 31
Web ⇨ Append Web Page, 528
Window ⇨ Show Articles, 52, 336
Window ⇨ Show Clipboard, 99, 101
Window ⇨ Tile ⇨ Horizontally, 38
Window ⇨ Tile ⇨ Vertically, 38
Microsoft Internet Explorer viewing configuration, 486
MIME (Multipurpose Internet Mail Extensions), 486–487
mouse behavior items, 404
Mouse Cursor pop-up menu, 35
mouse shortcuts
    Cmd+Shift+click (ignore link), 338
    Ctrl+click (move to beginning of article), 338
    Ctrl+click (open navigation pop-up), 42
    Ctrl+click+drag (dragging thumbnails), 352
    Ctrl+drag Form tool (field selection), 415
    Ctrl+Shift+click (ignore link), 338
    Ctrl+Shift+click (move to end of article), 338
    Mouse Cursor pop-up menu, 35
    Option+click (move to beginning of article), 338
    Option+click+drag (dragging thumbnails), 352
    Option+Shift+click (move to end of article), 338
    right click (open navigation pop-up), 42
    Shift+click (move in article column), 338
    Shift+drag Form tool (field selection), 415
Movie plug-in, 597
Movie Properties window, 379
movies
    importing, 379–383
    Movie Properties window, 379
    Movie tool, 379
    options
        borders, 383
        Mode, 380–381
        Movie Poster, 381–382
        Player Options, 380
        save preferences, 383
        Use Floating Window, 381
    showing with hypertext links, 367
multichannel color mode basics, 205
multiple documents, viewing, 37–39

Multipurpose Internet Mail Extensions
(MIME), 486–487
Muscat PDF Document Filter plug-in, 635
Muscat plug-in, 635
Myriad plug-in, 630

N

Name It Launcher plug-in, 633
Name It plug-in, 633
navigating PDF documents
    Command Bar, 40
    hypertext links, 45–53
        annotations (*See* annotations)
        articles (*See* articles)
        bookmarks (*See* bookmarks)
        buttons (*See* buttons)
        destinations (*See* destinations)
        thumbnails (*See* thumbnails)
    keyboard shortcuts
        Alt key (toggle Select tools), 96
        Cmd+. (exit Full Screen view), 34
        Cmd+- (zoom out), 32
        Cmd++ (zoom in), 32
        Cmd+0 (fit in Window), 32
        Cmd+1 (actual size), 32
        Cmd+2 (fit width), 32
        Cmd+3 (fit visible), 32
        Cmd+B (create bookmark), 344
        Cmd+G (find again), 55
        Cmd+L (full screen mode), 32, 34
        Cmd+M (zoom to), 32
        Cmd+Shift+4 (capture screen), 370
        Cmd+Shift+click (ignore link), 338
        Cmd+Shift+F (search), 59
        Cmd+Tab (find next), 472
        Ctrl+- (zoom out), 32
        Ctrl++ (zoom in), 32
        Ctrl+0 (fit in Window), 32
        Ctrl+1 (actual size), 32
        Ctrl+2 (fit width), 32
        Ctrl+3 (fit visible), 32

Ctrl+A (select all), 99
Ctrl+B (create bookmark), 344
Ctrl+click (move to beginning of
    article), 338
Ctrl+click (open navigation pop-up), 42
Ctrl+click+drag (dragging thumbnails),
    352
Ctrl+drag Form tool (field selection),
    415
Ctrl+G (find again), 55
Ctrl+L (exit Full Screen view), 34
Ctrl+L (full screen mode), 32
Ctrl+M (zoom to), 32
Ctrl+Shift+click (ignore link), 338
Ctrl+Shift+click (move to end of
    article), 338
Ctrl+Shift+F (search), 59
F5 (show/hide navigation pane), 32
F7 (show/hide Menu Bar), 32
F8 (show/hide Command Bar), 32
F9 (show/hide Tool Bar), 32
Option+click (move to beginning of
    article), 338
Option+click+drag (dragging
    thumbnails), 352
Option+Shift+click (move to end of
    article), 338
Shift+click (move in article column),
    338
Shift+drag Form tool (field selection),
    415
Shift+Tab (find next), 472
Shift+V (toggle Select tools), 95
menus, context sensitive, 42
mouse shortcuts
    Cmd+Shift+click (ignore link), 338
    Ctrl+click (move to beginning of
        article), 338
    Ctrl+click (open navigation pop-up), 42
    Ctrl+click+drag (dragging thumbnails),
        352
    Ctrl+drag Form tool (field selection),
        415
    Ctrl+Shift+click (ignore link), 338

Ctrl+Shift+click (move to end of article), 338

Mouse Cursor pop-up menu, 35

Option+click (move to beginning of article), 338

Option+click+drag (dragging thumbnails), 352

Option+Shift+click (move to end of article), 338

right click (open navigation pop-up), 42

Shift+click (move in article column), 338

Shift+drag Form tool (field selection), 415

scrolling, 43–44

Status Bar, 40

Netscape Navigator

Document Security dialog box, 493

Edit Type dialog box, 486–487

Font Info dialog box, 494

viewing configuration, 485–486

New Index Definition dialog box, 437

Niknak plug-in, 600

O

OCR (Optical Character Recognition)

OCR language, selecting, 271, 468–469

Ole plug-in, 597

Open Web Page dialog box, 522

OpenAll.api plug-in, 599

OPI Doctor plug-in, 631

Optimized/Opt32.api plug-in, 598

Option key (toggle Select tools), 96

Options plug-in, 634

P

P/Comp plug-in, 645

Page Layout dialog box, 524

Page Only view, 28

Page Setup dialog box (PDFWriter), 455

page transitions

creating with pdfmark, 374–375

default, 34

using with page actions, 374–377

page views

cascade view, 38

Command Bar tools

Actual Size, 31

Fit in Window, 31

Fit Width, 31

keyboard shortcuts, 32

continuos views, 35–37

full-screen page views

background color, 34

exiting, 34

Full Screen Preferences dialog box, 33–35

Mouse Cursor pop-up menu, 35

opening, 33

transition, default, 34

usefulness for presentations, 33

multiple document viewing, 37–39

single page view, 35

tiled view, 39

palettes

annotations palette

Navigation Pane, opening with, 294

as navigation tool, 316–317

palette hierarchy, 315

Rescan Document command, 314–315

sorting annotations, 316

using, 313–319

Articles palette, 52, 336

Thumbnails palette, 350

editing pages from, 352

passwords

in Acrobat Distiller, 182–183

adding to PDF files, 281–284

basic parameters of, 284

pcl2pdf plug-in, 652

PCX files, capturing, 475

PDF Advanced Job Options dialog box (PageMaker), 229

PDF Bellhop plug-in, 632
PDF Design XT plug-in, 650
PDF Embedder plug-in, 630
PDF files
    adding IDs to Acrobat 1.0 files, 439
    attaching to e-mail from within Acrobat,
        497
    cataloging on a network, 445–448
    color modes, compared to Photoshop, 205
    combining with HTML, 484–485
    compared to HTML
        HTML advantages, 484
        PDF advantages, 483–484
    creating
        from Web pages, 137–142
    creating by printing to Distiller
        combining by name, 191–193
        combining in folders, 193–194
        drag-and-drop distillation, 190
        launching Distiller, 184–185
        one step distillation, 185–188
        page order, 194–196
        PostScript Files, combining on
            networks, 196–199
        PostScript Files, concatenating, 190
        RunDirEx.txt file, using, 191–196
        RunFilEx.txt file, using, 191–196
        from Windows Run command, 189–190
    document structuring comments (DSC),
        171
    downloading from Internet, 491
    exporting from Illustrator, 214–217
        compression settings, 217
        export options, 216
    exporting from Photoshop, 203–207
    importing into Photoshop, 208–212
    job tickets, 171
    newspaper industry, use in, 565
    opening, 94
    opening in Illustrator, 217–218
    Optimize PDF option in Distiller, 159

passwording
    basic parameters, 284
    in Distiller, 182–183
    in Exchange, 281–284
printing
    to desktop printers, 549
    to high-end devices, 554–557
    to non-PostScript printers, 552–554
    opening Print dialog box, 94
    plug-ins, 555–557
    to PostScript 3 devices, 557
    to PostScript printers, 550–552
Save PDF File As dialog box, 139
small size of, 127
in Web pages
    embedding, 480–483
    viewing embedded PDFs, 488–489
    viewing in a browser, 489–497
writing to, 184–199
PDF Handshake plug-in, 624–625
PDF Import/Export XT plug-in, 641–642
PDF Imposer plug-in, 611
PDF-it plug-in, 618
PDF Librarian plug-in, 632
PDF Measure plug-in, 612
PDF pages
    advancing
        Advance Every N Seconds, 34
        Advance On Any Click, 34
        auto-advancing, 34
        Loop After Last page, 34
    cropping, 305, 353–355
    deleting, 353
    editing, 352–355
    extracting, 353
    highlighting with Graphic Markup tools
        Ellipse tool, 309
        introduction to, 308
        Line tool, 309
        Pencil tool, 308
        Properties dialog box, 309

Rectangle tool, 309
tool properties, 309–310
highlighting with Text Markup tools
columns, selecting, 312
Highlight Text tool, 311–312
properties, 312–313
Strikethrough Text tool, 312
Underline Text tool, 312
inserting, 352
replacing, 353
rotating, 355
transition default, 34
PDF (Portable Document Format)
benefits of
cost-effectiveness, 19
Internet solutions, 25
office workflow solutions, 21–23
publishing solutions, 23–24
introduction to, 5–6
publishing market use of, 20–21, 23–24
relation to PostScript, 8–9
as a standard, 19–21
PDF Protector plug-in, 611
PDF Scantools plug-in, 611
PDF workflow
annotations in, 291
document information in, 274–275
importing form data in, 405
network catalogs, 445–448
in office environment, 14–15
setup issues in, 201–202
taking advantage of Intranets, 18
taking advantage of LANs, 15–17
taking advantage of WANs, 18
watched folders in, 176
PDFaqua plug-in, 610
PDFComposer plug-in, 627
PDFcontrol plug-in, 610
PDFDraftsman Application plug-in, 638–639
PDFfusion plug-in, 610

pdfmark
annotating EPS files, 258–263
annotating PostScript files
creating the annotation, 253–257
note attributes, 251–253
key value pairs, 274
transitions, creating with, 374–375
pdfToolbox plug-in, 607–609
PDFtools plug-in, 610
PDFWorkshop plug-in, 646
PDFWriter
CCITT compression choices, 131
compared with Distiller, 115
document information, viewing, 135–136
font compression, 124
font embedding, disabling when scanning, 454–455
font embedding options, 124–126
Add, 126
Always Embed List, 125
Available Fonts, 125
Embed All Fonts, 125
Never Embed List, 125
Rebuild, 125
Remove, 126
Subset TrueType, 126
Subset Type, 126
font subsetting, 127
image resampling, 127–132
compression, 130–132
downsampling, 132
encoding, 132
file-format compatibility, 127–129
PDFWriter Compression dialog box, 128
introduction to, 12
JPEG compression choices, 130–131
LZW compression choices, 131
Macintosh, accessing in
hot key, 119–120
opening, 118–119

(continued)

PDFWriter *(continued)*
    setting as default printer, 117
    versions to use, 116
  page setup, 122–123
  Page Setup dialog box, 455
  PDF files
    creating from Web pages, 137–142
    creating with, 115–142
  PDFWriter Page Setup dialog box, 123
  Print dialog box, selecting from, 122
  print driver nature of, 117
  print driver notes, 116–117
  printing from, 133–134
  Run Length (RLE) compression choices, 131
  version number, displaying, 116
  viewing PDF files from, 134–135
  Windows, accessing in
    Acrobat PDFWriter Properties dialog box, 120
    adding as new printer, 120–121
    printing test page, 121–122
    selecting as printer, 122
    versions to use with NT, 116
  ZIP compression choices, 131
PDFWriter Compression dialog box, 128
PDFWriter Page Setup dialog box, 123
PDFZone Web site, 660
.pdx files, 431
PICT files, capturing, 475
Picture Extraction plug-in, 626
PitStop plug-in, 620
Pixar files, capturing, 475
plug-ins
  Acrobat Scan
    Acrobat Scan plug-in dialog box, 464
    introduction to, 14, 449
    using, 463–465
  conflicts, diagnosing, 593–594
  contacting suppliers, 654
  disabling, 595
  documentation, 595

Export Adobe PDF plug-in, pre-3.01
  versions, 225–227
Export Adobe PDF plug-in 3.01
  advanced options, 247
  article options, 247
  bookmarks, 247
  color model, 245
  compression, 244–245
  document information, 245
  features removed from, 249
  fonts, 244
  formats, 244
  general settings, 244
  hyperlinks, 245–246
  installing, 243
  notes on first page, 247
  PDF styles, creating for cross-platform use, 248–249
  PDF styles, saving, 247
  using, 243–244
installing, 592–593
introduction to, 10, 591–592
manufacturers/suppliers of plug-ins
  5D, 600, 655
  A Round Table Solution (ARTS), 646, 658
  Acquired Knowledge, Inc., 601, 655
  AGFA, 601
  Aliant Techsystems, 602
  Ambia Software, 602, 655
  Autologic Information International, 604
  Avenza Software, 605, 655
  BCL Computers, 605, 655
  Brook House Limited, 606, 655
  Callas Software GMBH, 607, 655
  Cessna Publishing, 609, 655
  Computerized Document Control, Ltd., 609, 655
  Computerstream Limited, 610, 655
  Consolidated Technical Services, Inc., 612, 656
  Data Technology Group, 613

Datawatch Corporation, 613
Digital Applications, Inc., 614
Dionis, 615, 656
Doculex, 618
Easy Software Products, 618, 656
Enfocus Software, Inc., 619, 656
Extensis Corporation, 620, 656
FileOpen Systems, Inc., 623, 656
HAHT Software, Inc., 623
Handmade Software, 623, 656
Helios Software, 624
Iceni Technology, 625, 656
Image Solutions, 626, 656
Imation, 629
INFOCON AMERICA CORP., 629
Informative Graphics Corporation, 629, 656
Intense Software, 630, 656
Lantana Research, 630, 657
Markzware USA, 632, 657
Merlin Open Systems, 633, 657
Muscat, 635
NetFormation, Inc., 635, 657
One Vision, Inc., 635, 657
Page Technology Marketing, Inc., 636, 657
PDF Solutions Limited, 636, 657
PrePress-Consulting Stephen Jaeggi, 637, 657
PubSTec Corporation, 638, 658
Quark, Inc., 641, 658
Quite Software, 642, 658
Radtke Consulting, 645
Scitex Corporation Ltd., 647
Silanis Technology, Inc., 648
Solimar Systems, Inc., 648
Sys-Print, Inc., 649
Tangent Software, 650, 658
Techno Design, 650
TechPool Software, 650, 658
Ultimate Technographics, 651, 659
Visual Software, 652, 659
xman Software, 652, 659
XtraMedia, 654
Zeon Corporation, 654, 659
printing plug-ins, 555–557
registering plug-ins, 660
standard plug-ins
  AcroForm, 596
  Annots/Annots32.api, 596
  AutoIndx/Autidx32.api, 596
  Capture/Capture32.api, 596
  EFS, 596
  EWH/EWH32.api, 597
  ExecMenu/Excmnu32.api, 597
  ExportPS/exppps.api, 597
  HLS/Ahls32.api, 597
  Import/Import32.api, 597
  Movie, 597
  Ole, 597
  Optimized/Opt32.api, 598
  PrePress/PrePress.api, 598
  Scan/Scan32.api, 598
  Search/Asrch32.api, 598
  Stamps, 598
  TouchUp/TouchUp.api, 598
  WebLink/weblnk.api, 598
standard plug-ins (Windows only)
  DigSig.api, 599
  HTML2pdf.api, 599
  ieweb32.api, 599
  la32.api, 599
  OpenAll.api, 599
  ppklite.api, 599
  SendMail.api, 599
  Taps32.api, 600
  Webpdf32.api, 600
third party plug-ins
  Acrobat CD Installer, 613
  AcroViewer Xtra, 654
  Aerial, 603–604
  Apogee, 601
  AppendPDF, 614
  AppendPDF Pro, 614

(continued)

third party plug-ins *(continued)*
    Approvelt for .pdf, 648
    APS PDF AdTool, 604
    APS RIP3, 604
    Ari's Toolbox, 616–618
    Arts AcroBuddies, 647
    Arts Duplex, 647
    Arts Import, 646
    Arts Joust, 647
    Arts ThumbOpt, 646
    Asura, 635–636
    Banner Print, 610
    BatchPrintPDF, 606
    Bookworm, 646
    Brisque Digital Front End, 647–648
    CheckUp, 619–620
    CloneLink, 636–637
    Collect Pro, 620–622
    Compose, 602
    cpAnnCollector, 609
    Crackerjack, 555–557, 630–631
    Crackerjack Pilot, 631
    CRF Publisher, 613
    CRFScan & Trade, 626–627
    D Soft, 613
    Date Stamp, 634
    DateD Author, 615
    DateD Viewer, 615
    Distiller Tools, 637–638
    DocuCom, 654
    EZ-PDF, 601
    Face-It!, 635
    FDFMerge, 615
    FileOpen PDF Publisher, 623
    Firebird, 605
    Flightcheck, 632
    FormView, 636
    Gemini, 625–626
    GraphCopy, 628
    HAHT Enterprise Solution Module, 623
    Homer, 607
    HTMLDOC, 619
    Image Alchemy PS, 624

Impostrip, 651
IMPress, 651
Index Fixer, 634
InfoLink Publishing Enhancement
    Software, 629
InfoLinker, 602
ISIFile, 628
ISIToolBox, 628
Jade, 606
Legacy XCHANGE, 648
Library Manage, 602
Link Manage, 602
Local Render, 610
MadeToPrint XT, 609
Magellan, 605
MAPublisher Lt, 605
MarkzScout, 632–633
Muscat, 635
Muscat PDF Document Filter, 635
Myriad, 630
Name It, 633
Name It Launcher, 633
Niknak, 600
OPI Doctor, 631
Options, 634
P/Comp, 645
pcl2pdf, 652
PDF Bellhop, 632
PDF Design XT, 650
PDF Embedder, 630
PDF Handshake, 624–625
PDF Import/Export XT, 641–642
PDF Imposer, 611
PDF-it, 618
PDF Librarian, 632
PDF Measure, 612
PDF Protector, 611
PDF Scantools, 611
PDFaqua, 610
PDFComposer, 627
PDFcontrol, 610
PDFDraftsman Application, 638–639
PDFfusion, 610

pdfToolbox, 607–609
PDFtools, 610
PDFWorkshop, 646
Picture Extraction, 626
PitStop, 620
Preflight Pro, 622
PressWise, 629
PubSTec Action Plug-In, 638
PubSTec Floating Text, 639
PubSTec PDFTree, 639
PubSTec PolyLink lite, 639–640
Quite a Box of Tricks, 642–644
Quite Imposing, 644–645
Quite Imposing Plus, 644–645
QX-Tools, 623
RC: Splitter, 645
Redax, 614
Redwing, 614
Remark, 603
Search Results Printer, 634
Simple-PDF, 650
Solvero, 636
Spiffy-Pop, 613
StampPDF, 615
StampPDF Batch, 615
Starter Plug-in, 640
Sys-AFP, 649
Sys-DJDE, 649
Sys-Meta, 649
Sys-PCL, 649
Sys-Print, 649
Sys-TIFF, 650
TableMaster, 628
TimedOut Author, 615
TimedOut Viewer, 615
Transporter Pro, 651
Trapeze, 651–652
UltimateFlow, 652
WordMark, 607
xToolsOne, 652–653
PNG files, capturing, 475
PostScript
    history of, 150–151

introduction to, 145–146
levels, 150–152
relation to PDF, 8–9
PostScript 3 devices
    printing to, 557
PostScript files
    Adobe Illustrator, opening in, 222
    annotating with pdfmark
        creating the annotation, 253–257
        note attributes, 251–253
    combining on networks, 196–199
    concatenating, 190
    creating with Distiller
        color issues, 149–150
        font inclusion issues, 149
        page size issues, 148
        PPD issues, 147–148
        screening issues, 149
        steps, 152–156
    encoding, 150, 152
    overriding Job Options, 171
    preparing for printing
        bleeds, 541
        color conversion, 541
        Distiller color settings, 546–547
        Distiller compression settings, 543–545
        Distiller font selection, 545–546
        Distiller job options, 542–549
        Distiller PressOptimized jobs, 548
        downsampling with Distiller, 541
        duotones, separating, 541
        encoding, 540
        epilogue.ps, enabling in Distiller, 547
        halftone frequency, setting, 540–541
        imaging device format, selecting, 542
        including fonts, 540
        page size, 541
        PostScript level, selecting, 540
        PPD selection, 540
        prologue.ps, enabling in Distiller, 547
    preserving semantics between levels, 171
    printing to, 153
    retaining after distillation, 190

(continued)

PostScript files *(continued)*
    role in exporting to PDF from PageMaker, 224–225
PostScript printers, 550–552
PPD device selection, 147, 540
PPD files, 147–148
ppklite.api plug-in, 599
preferences
    annotations
        in Acrobat Exchange, 267–268
        in Acrobat Reader, 89–91
        in note properties, 295
    Capture
        downsampling images, 272, 469
        location for temporary files, 272, 469
        PDF output style, 272, 469
        Preferences dialog box, 468
        primary OCR language, 271, 468–469
    Catalog (Macintosh)
        Catalog Preferences dialog box, 430
        custom fields, 432–433
        drop folders, 431–432
        index, 427–429
        index defaults, 429
        language, 432–433
        logging, 430–431
        .pdx files, 431
    Catalog (Windows)
        Acrobat.ini file, 434–436
        document word sections, 435
        field settings, 436
        index available group size, 435
        log file size, 436
        memory setting, 435
        purge time, 435
        search engine messages, 435
        Windows-only filenames, 435
    Distiller
        restarting after PostScript fatal error, 156
        startup volume nearly full notification, 157
        watched folders unavailable notification, 156
    Exchange
        annotation, 267–268
        Annotations Preferences dialog box, 268

        color, 270–271, 277
        Forms Grid, 269–271
        full screen, 268
        general, 266–267
        General Preferences dialog box, 267
        Grid Settings dialog box, 269
        initial view options, 275
        paper capture, 271–272
        search, 268
        skip edit warnings, 266
        TouchUp Preferences dialog box, 272
        TouchUp tools, 272–273
        trapping, 277
        user interface options, 276
        Weblink, 268
        window options, 276
    Reader, 84–94
        application language, 86
        background downloading, 88
        color manager, 88
        confirm file open links, 89
        cross-doc links, 88–89
        general preferences, 85–89
        Greeked text, 86
        images, large, 87
        images, smooth, 86
        link information display, 92–93
        Open dialog box at startup, 88
        page, display to edge, 87
        Page Cache, 88–89
        page layout, 85–86
        page numbering, 89
        page units, 86
        smooth text, 86
        splash screen at startup, 88
        substitution fonts, 86
        Web browser progress dialog box, 93
        Web browser toolbar button, 93
        Web browsers, selecting, 94
        zoom, default, 87–88
        zoom, fit visible, 88
    Web Capture
        consolidating menu items, 512
        opening Weblinks, 512
        resetting conversion settings, 515–516
        showing bookmarks, 514
        showing Toolbar buttons, 514
        skipping secured messages, 515

verifying stored images, 512
warning dialog boxes, 514
Web Capture Preferences dialog box,
 513
Weblink
 connection type, 512
 displaying link information, 510–511
 showing download status, 511
 showing Toolbar Button, 511
 Web browser, selecting, 511
 Weblink Preferences dialog box, 510
Preferences dialog box, 468
Preferences dialog box (Capture), 468
Preflight Pro plug-in, 622
Prepress Options dialog box (Exchange), 278
PrePress/PrePress.api plug-in, 598
PressWise plug-in, 629
previous versions
 Acrobat Distiller
  job option compatibility with, 158–159
 using, 128
Print Options dialog box (PageMaker), 241
Print Paper dialog box (PageMaker), 240
printer drivers
 AdobePS printer driver
  Macintosh, 185–188
  Windows, 188–189
printing
 to Acrobat Distiller, 184–199
  drag-and-drop distillation, 190
  files, combining by name, 191–193
  files, combining in folders, 193–194
  launching Distiller, 184–185
  one step distillation, 185–188
  page order, 194–196
  PostScript Files, combining on
   networks, 196–199
  PostScript Files, concatenating, 190
  RunDirEx.txt file, using, 191–196
  RunFilEx.txt file, using, 191–196
  from Windows Run command, 189–190
 annotations, 322–323
 distilling PostScript files
  color settings, 546–547
  compression settings, 543–545
  epilogue.ps, enabling, 547
  font selection, 545–546
  job options, 542–549
  PressOptimized jobs, 548
  prologue.ps, enabling, 547
 to large format inkjet printers, 574
 in PageMaker
  color settings, 241
  creating printer styles, 239–242
  Define Printer Styles dialog box, 239
  document attributes, defining, 240
  paper attributes, defining, 240–241
  print options, 241
  Print Options dialog box, 241
  Print Paper dialog box, 240
  resolution settings, 240
  style conflicts, 238
 in PDFWriter, 133–134
  adding as new printer, 120–121
  printing test page, 121–122
  selecting as printer, 122
 to PostScript files, 153
 preparing files for, 539–542
  layout design, 540
 preparing PostScript files
  bleeds, 541
  color conversion, 541
  downsampling with Distiller, 541
  duotones, separating, 541
  encoding, 540
  halftone frequency, 540–541
  imaging device format, 542
  including fonts, 540
  page size, 541
  PostScript level, selecting, 540
  PPD selection, 540
 Print tool, 94
 variable data printing, 568–573
printing plug-ins, 555–557
prologue.ps file, 170
Properties dialog box (Graphic Markup
 Tools), 309
PubSTec Action Plug-In plug-in, 638
PubSTec Floating Text plug-in, 639
PubSTec PDFTree plug-in, 639
PubSTec PolyLink lite plug-in, 639–640
PurePDF Web site, 660
Purge Warning dialog box, 445

Q

QuarkXpress
editing Quark data with Illustrator, 221–223
PDF export XTension, 223–224
PDF Import/Export XT plug-in, 641–642
PDF integration of, 224
use in variable data printing, 569–570
using in color separation, 562–563
Xdata Xtension, 570–571
Query dialog box, 59–60
query (the term), 59
Quite a Box of Tricks plug-in, 642–644
Quite Imposing plug-in, 644–645
Quite Imposing Plus plug-in, 644–645
QX-Tools plug-in, 623

R

Rasterize Generic PDF dialog box (Photoshop), 209–210
rasterizing PDFs in Photoshop, 208–210
RC: Splitter plug-in, 645
Reader Online Guide, 105
Redax plug-in, 614
Redwing plug-in, 614
Refresh Pages dialog box, 519
Remark plug-in, 603
Rescan Document command, 314–315
RGB color mode basics, 204
RTF (Rich Text File), converting scanned pages to, 471–474
Run Length (RLE) compression (PDFWriter), 131

S

Save PDF File As dialog box, 139
Scan dialog box, 450
Scan/Scan32.api plug-in, 598
scanning
accessing the scanner, 449
Acrobat Scan plug-in
Acrobat Scan plug-in dialog box, 464
introduction to, 14, 449
using, 463–465
Acrobat scan types, 453–455
basics of, 452–455
color scanning, 454
converting scanned pages to text
Capture Suspects, 472–474
capturing a page, 471–474
dictionaries, 468, 470
editing with TouchUp Text tool, 472
font limitations, 467
font requirements, 468
OCR language, selecting, 468
PDF output style, 469
unrecognized words, 472–474
font embedding when, 454–455
grayscale scanning, 453–454
for halftone output, 566
image modes, 453
memory configurations
Macintosh, 457–459
Windows, 459–462
preparing document for, 456–457
Rescan Document command, 314–315
resolution, 453
Scan dialog box, 450
scanning images, 463–465
software
HP AccuPage, 452
ISIS, 450
TWAIN, 451
text recognition, 453
Schedule Builds dialog box, 442
scrolling, 43–44
Search/Asrch32.api plug-in, 598
search operators
* (asterisk) wildcard, 70
<= (back arrow, equal sign) less than or equal to, 70
< (back arrow) less than, 70
= (equal sign) equals, 70
!= (exclamation, equal sign) does not equal, 70
!~ (exclamation, tilde) does not contain, 70
>= (forward arrow, equal sign) greater than or equal to, 70
> (forward arrow) greater than, 70
? (question mark) wildcard, 70
~ (tilde) contains, 70

Boolean, 72–73
definition, 69
Search Preferences dialog box, 66–67
Search Results dialog box, 63–64
Search Results Printer plug-in, 634
search (the term), 59
searching
Acrobat Search, using, 55–73
Acrobat Search dialog box, 59–63
Author, 61
With Date Info, 62
With Document Info, 60
Find Results Containing Text, 60
Indexes Searched, 63
Keywords, 61
Match Case, 63, 72
Proximity, 63, 72
Sounds Like, 62, 71
Subject, 61
Thesaurus, 62, 72
Title, 61
Word Stemming, 62, 71
difference from finding, 54
maximum files returned, 68
Query dialog box, 59–60
query options, 66–67
results
highlighting, 68–69
listing by author, 68
listing by creator, 68
listing by date created, 68
listing by date modified, 68
listing by keywords, 68
listing by producer, 68
listing by subject, 67
listing by title, 67
scoring, 67
sorting, 67
search options identifiers, 71–72
search preferences, 66–69
Search Preferences dialog box, 66–67
search results
found word(s) highlighted, 65
understanding, 63–64
viewing, 64–66
Search Results dialog box, 63–64
document info displayed in, 65
hide while viewing results, 68

Word Assistant dialog box, 74
security
Document Security dialog box (Netscape),
493
general options overview, 83–84
Security dialog box (Exchange), 282
Security Info dialog box, 84
viewing security information, 83–84
in Web browsers, 492–493
Security dialog box (Exchange), 282
Security Info dialog box, 84
Security window, 183
Select File ⇨ Document Info ⇨ Fonts, 165, 166
Self-Sign Signatures - Sign Document dialog
box, 414
SendMail.api plug-in, 599
Settings ⇨ Control Panel ⇨ Printers, 120
Settings ⇨ Job Options, 158–159
Settings ⇨ Watched Folders, 174
Shift+Tab (find next), 472
Shift+V (toggle Select tools), 95
signature fields, 413–414
Simple-PDF plug-in, 650
Skip Edit Warnings option, 266, 293
Snap to Forms Grid, 389
Solvero plug-in, 636
sound
audio annotations
Audio Annotation tool, 297
Audio Properties window, 298
recording, 297
Sound Comment dialog box, 298
importing, 377–379
page actions, associating with, 379
playing with hypertext links, 369
Sound Comment dialog box, 298
Spiffy-Pop plug-in, 613
StampPDF Batch plug-in, 615
StampPDF plug-in, 615
Stamps plug-in, 598
Starter Plug-in plug-in, 640
Status Bar navigation tools, 40
Sys-AFP plug-in, 649
Sys-DJDE plug-in, 649
Sys-Meta plug-in, 649
Sys-PCL plug-in, 649
Sys-Print plug-in, 649
Sys-TIFF plug-in, 650

T

TableMaster plug-in, 628
Taps32.api plug-in, 600
Targa files, capturing, 475
text
    attributes, 326–327
    creating in note windows, 323–324
    editable text, 328
    editing controls, 327–328
    editing with TouchUp Text tool, 324–328
        using with captured pages, 471
    fitting to a selection, 325–326
    font fills and strokes, 326–327
    limitations of Acrobat, 323–324
    moving, 325
    options in forms, 393–394
Text Properties dialog box, 297
thumbnails
    Adobe Photoshop, importing to, 208
    basics of, 50, 349
    creating, 349–351
    deleting, 349–351
    editing PDFs with
        copying pages, 351
        removing pages, 351–352
        reordering pages, 351
    Generate Thumbnails option (Distiller), 160
    navigating in Web browsers, 496
    Thumbnails palette, 350
        editing pages from, 352
TIFF files, capturing, 475
TimedOut Author plug-in, 615
TimedOut Viewer plug-in, 615
tools
    Acrobat tools, 289–290
    annotation tools, 291–292
    Article tool, 338
    Audio Annotation tool, 297
    Column Select tool, 96–98
    File Annotation tool, 306
    Find tool dialog box, 54–55
    Graphic Markup tools
        Ellipse tool, 309
        Line tool, 309
        Pencil tool, 308
        Properties dialog box, 309
        Rectangle tool, 309
    Graphics Select tool, 100–101

Link tool, 361–362
Movie tool, 379
navigation tools, 40–44
    Command Bar, 40
    Status Bar, 40
Print tool, 94
Text Annotation tool, 296
Text Markup tools
    Highlight Text tool, 311–312
    Strikethrough Text tool, 312
    Underline Text tool, 312
Text Select tool, 95–96
TouchUp Object tool, 329
TouchUp Text tool, 324–328
TouchUp tools, 272–273
Tools ➪ Annotations ➪ Delete All, 319
Tools ➪ Annotations ➪ Filter Manager, 294, 321
Tools ➪ Annotations ➪ Summarize Annotations, 319
Tools ➪ Annotations ➪ Summarize Notes, 320, 372
Tools ➪ Capture ➪ Capture Pages, 467
Tools ➪ Forms ➪ Align, 416
Tools ➪ Forms ➪ Fields ➪ Distribute, 416
Tools ➪ Forms ➪ Fields ➪ Set Tab Order, 417
Tools ➪ Forms ➪ Page Templates, 310
Tools ➪ Paper Capture ➪ Capture Pages, 471
Tools ➪ Paper Capture ➪ Show Suspects, 472–473
Tools ➪ Self-Sign Signature ➪ Log On, 413
Tools ➪ TouchUp ➪ Fit Text to Selection, 325
Tools ➪ Web Capture, 512, 528
Tools ➪ Web Capture ➪ Bring Status Dialogs to Foreground, 524
Tools ➪ Weblinks ➪ Create, 520
TouchUp Preferences dialog box (Exchange), 272
TouchUp/TouchUp.api plug-in, 598
transfer functions
    embedding, 565–568
    use in newspaper industry, 565
Transporter Pro plug-in, 651
transversing documents, 241
Trapeze plug-in, 651–652
trapping (prepress option), 277
TWAIN software, 451
Type ➪ Paragraph (PageMaker), 231

U

UltimateFlow plug-in, 652
Undo limitations of Acrobat, 293
URLs, dragging to browser from PDFs, 54
Utilities ➪ Book (PageMaker), 237
Utilities ➪ Create TOC (PageMaker), 231
Utilities ➪ Index Entry (PageMaker), 232

V

variable data printing, 568–573
View ➪ Continuous, 35–37
View ➪ Fit in Window, 44
View ➪ Full Screen, 33
View ➪ Show Forms Grid, 269
View ➪ Single Page, 35
View ➪ Zoom, 31
viewing PDF files
    full-screen views
        background color, 34
        exiting, 34
        Full Screen Preferences dialog box,
            33–35
        Mouse Cursor pop-up menu, 35
        transition, default, 34
    monitor size, effect of, 33
    multiple document viewing, 37–39
    page views
        actual size, 31
        fit in window, 31
        fit width, 31
        keyboard shortcuts, 32
        page only, 28
    zooming, 30–31

W

watched folders
    creating, 177–182
    establishing for network catalogs, 445
    notify when unavailable, 156–157
    options, 174–177
    in PageMaker, 227
    in PDF workflow, 176
    security issues, 184
    Watched Folders dialog box, 174
.wav files, 297
    importing, 377
Web ➪ Append Web Page, 528
Web browsers

file naming conventions, 487
handlers, 488
navigating PDF links in
    bookmarks, 496
    hypertext links, 495
    thumbnails, 496
    Web links, 495
PDFs, viewing in
    browser preferences, 491–494
    document information, 491–492
    embedded PDFs, 488–489
    font information, 493–494
    general preferences, 494
    inline viewing, 489
    opening in browser, 489–491
    security information, 492–493
    security level, 492
progress dialog options, 93
selecting in Reader, 94
suffixes, 487
viewing configurations
    Microsoft Internet Explorer, 486
    MIME types, 486–487
    Netscape Navigator, 485–486
Web browser toolbar button, 93
Web Capture Preferences dialog box, 513
Web pages
    embedding PDFs in, 480–483
    opening with hypertext links, 369
Web pages, converting to PDF
    bookmark issues, 499–502
    conversion preferences, 509–516
    Create Web Links dialog box, 520
    downloading options
        background, 505
        bookmark, 507
        content-type settings, 504
        extent of download, 504
        fonts, 506
        footers, 507
        headers, 507
        image conversion, 506
        landscape autoswitch, 509
        layout attributes, 505
        line wrap, 505
        page orientation, 508
        page size, 508
        PDF structure, 508
        refresh commands, 508
        scaling, 509

(continued)

Web pages, converting to PDF *(continued)*
 text conversion, 506–507
 underlining links, 506
file types, acceptable, 498–499
HTML Conversion Settings dialog box, 505
JavaScript ignored, 499
links, acceptable, 499
non-English characters, 499
with PDFWriter, 137–142
Refresh Pages dialog box, 519
Select Page Links to Download dialog box
 Download tab, 503–504
 General tab, 504–508
 Page Layout tab, 508–509
Web Capture menu commands
 Append All Links on Page, 518
 Append Web Page, 517
 Bring Status Dialogs to Foreground, 516–517
 Create Bookmarks for New and Changed Pages, 520
 Create Web Links dialog box, 520
 Edit Refresh Commands List, 520
 Open Page in Web browser, 516
 Open Web Page, 516
 Page Info, 517
 Re-Submit Form Data, 520
 Refresh, 520
 Refresh Pages, 519
 Remove Weblink, 521
 View Web Links, 518–519
Web Capture preferences
 consolidating menu items, 512
 opening Weblinks, 512
 resetting conversion settings, 515–516
 showing bookmarks, 514
 showing Toolbar buttons, 514
 skipping secured messages, 515
 verifying stored images, 512
 warning dialog boxes, 514
 Web Capture Preferences dialog box, 513
Web sites
 Append Web Page command, 528–531
 Append Web Page dialog box, 528
 appending pages, 510, 528–533
 appending pages by following links, 531–533
 bookmarks, editing with, 534–537
 captured sites, working with, 528–537
 capturing Web sites, 497–527
 comparing captured documents, 526–527

 Conversion Settings dialog box, 523
 converting pages locally, 525
 Open Web Page dialog box, 522
 opening captured site in Macintosh, 510
 Page Layout dialog box, 524
 site structure, 497–498
 steps in, 521–525
 structured bookmarks in appended pages, 531
WebLink preferences
 connection type, 512
 displaying link information, 510–511
 showing download status, 511
 showing Toolbar Button, 511
 Web browser, selecting, 511
 WebLink Preferences dialog box, 92, 510
WebLink/weblnk.api plug-in, 598
Webpdf32.api plug-in, 600
wide area networks, basics of, 183
Window ➪ Show Articles, 52, 336
Window ➪ Show Clipboard, 99, 101
window (the term), 56
Window ➪ Tile ➪ Horizontally, 38
Window ➪ Tile ➪ Vertically, 38
windows
 Annotations window, 314
 Audio Properties window, 298
 Create Link window, 362–363
 Field Properties window, 390
 File Annotation Properties window, 306
 Link Properties window, 362, 495
 Movie Properties window, 379
Windows color picker, 270
Word Assistant dialog box, 74
word processors, copying to from Reader, 98–100
WordMark plug-in, 607

X
Xdata Xtension, 570–571
xToolsOne plug-in, 652–653

Z
Zapf Dingbats, 164, 392
ZIP compression
 in PDFWriter, 131
 when exporting from Photoshop, 207
Zoom To dialog box, 31
zooming, 30–31

IDG BOOKS WORLDWIDE, INC.
END-USER LICENSE AGREEMENT

<u>READ THIS</u>. You should carefully read these terms and conditions before opening the software packet(s) included with this book ("Book"). This is a license agreement ("Agreement") between you and IDG Books Worldwide, Inc. ("IDGB"). By opening the accompanying software packet(s), you acknowledge that you have read and accept the following terms and conditions. If you do not agree and do not want to be bound by such terms and conditions, promptly return the Book and the unopened software packet(s) to the place you obtained them for a full refund.

1. <u>License Grant</u>. IDGB grants to you (either an individual or entity) a nonexclusive license to use one copy of the enclosed software program(s) (collectively, the "Software") solely for your own personal or business purposes on a single computer (whether a standard computer or a workstation component of a multiuser network). The Software is in use on a computer when it is loaded into temporary memory (RAM) or installed into permanent memory (hard disk, CD-ROM, or other storage device). IDGB reserves all rights not expressly granted herein.

2. <u>Ownership</u>. IDGB is the owner of all right, title, and interest, including copyright, in and to the compilation of the Software recorded on the disk(s) or CD-ROM ("Software Media"). Copyright to the individual programs recorded on the Software Media is owned by the author or other authorized copyright owner of each program. Ownership of the Software and all proprietary rights relating thereto remain with IDGB and its licensers.

3. <u>Restrictions On Use and Transfer</u>.

   (a) You may only (i) make one copy of the Software for backup or archival purposes, or (ii) transfer the Software to a single hard disk, provided that you keep the original for backup or archival purposes. You may not (i) rent or lease the Software, (ii) copy or reproduce the Software through a LAN or other network system or through any computer subscriber system or bulletin-board system, or (iii) modify, adapt, or create derivative works based on the Software.

   (b) You may not reverse engineer, decompile, or disassemble the Software. You may transfer the Software and user documentation on a permanent basis, provided that the transferee agrees to accept the terms and conditions of this Agreement and you retain no copies. If the Software is an update or has been updated, any transfer must include the most recent update and all prior versions.

4. **Restrictions On Use of Individual Programs.** You must follow the individual requirements and restrictions detailed for each individual program in the Appendix, "About the CD-ROM," of this Book. These limitations are also contained in the individual license agreements recorded on the Software Media. These limitations may include a requirement that after using the program for a specified period of time, the user must pay a registration fee or discontinue use. By opening the Software packet(s), you will be agreeing to abide by the licenses and restrictions for these individual programs that are detailed in the Appendix, "About the CD-ROM," and on the Software Media. None of the material on this Software Media or listed in this Book may ever be redistributed, in original or modified form, for commercial purposes.

5. **Limited Warranty.**

   (a) IDGB warrants that the Software and Software Media are free from defects in materials and workmanship under normal use for a period of sixty (60) days from the date of purchase of this Book. If IDGB receives notification within the warranty period of defects in materials or workmanship, IDGB will replace the defective Software Media.

   (b) **IDGB AND THE AUTHOR OF THE BOOK DISCLAIM ALL OTHER WARRANTIES, EXPRESS OR IMPLIED, INCLUDING WITHOUT LIMITATION IMPLIED WARRANTIES OF MERCHANTABILITY AND FITNESS FOR A PARTICULAR PURPOSE, WITH RESPECT TO THE SOFTWARE, THE PROGRAMS, THE SOURCE CODE CONTAINED THEREIN, AND/OR THE TECHNIQUES DESCRIBED IN THIS BOOK. IDGB DOES NOT WARRANT THAT THE FUNCTIONS CONTAINED IN THE SOFTWARE WILL MEET YOUR REQUIREMENTS OR THAT THE OPERATION OF THE SOFTWARE WILL BE ERROR FREE.**

   (c) This limited warranty gives you specific legal rights, and you may have other rights that vary from jurisdiction to jurisdiction.

6. **Remedies.**

   (a) IDGB's entire liability and your exclusive remedy for defects in materials and workmanship shall be limited to replacement of the Software Media, which may be returned to IDGB with a copy of your receipt at the following address: Software Media Fulfillment Department, Attn.: *Acrobat PDF Bible,* IDG Books Worldwide, Inc., 7260 Shadeland Station, Ste. 100, Indianapolis, IN 46256, or call 1-800-762-2974. Please allow three to four weeks for delivery. This Limited Warranty is void if failure of the Software Media has resulted from accident, abuse, or misapplication. Any replacement Software Media will be warranted for the remainder of the original warranty period or thirty (30) days, whichever is longer.

   (b) In no event shall IDGB or the author be liable for any damages whatsoever (including without limitation damages for loss of business profits, business interruption, loss of business information, or any other pecuniary loss) arising from the use of or inability to use the Book or the

Software, even if IDGB has been advised of the possibility of such damages.

(c) Because some jurisdictions do not allow the exclusion or limitation of liability for consequential or incidental damages, the above limitation or exclusion may not apply to you.

7. **U.S. Government Restricted Rights.** Use, duplication, or disclosure of the Software by the U.S. Government is subject to restrictions stated in paragraph (c)(1)(ii) of the Rights in Technical Data and Computer Software clause of DFARS 252.227-7013, and in subparagraphs (a) through (d) of the Commercial Computer — Restricted Rights clause at FAR 52.227-19, and in similar clauses in the NASA FAR supplement, when applicable.

8. **General.** This Agreement constitutes the entire understanding of the parties and revokes and supersedes all prior agreements, oral or written, between them and may not be modified or amended except in a writing signed by both parties hereto that specifically refers to this Agreement. This Agreement shall take precedence over any other documents that may be in conflict herewith. If any one or more provisions contained in this Agreement are held by any court or tribunal to be invalid, illegal, or otherwise unenforceable, each and every other provision shall remain in full force and effect.

Every day you face decisions that are critical to the future of your business. Why face them alone?

The International Digital Imaging Association (**idia**) provides the information you need to make sound business and technical decisions.

The **idia** is a trade association dedicated to serving all digital imaging professionals: imaging centers, prepress houses, printers, digital media providers, design studios and others working with digital media.

As an **idia** member, you have an international base of peers and industry experts as resources. You always have somewhere to turn.

As changes like **PDF** continue to sweep through the world of graphic arts services, **idia** will be there to provide the information, networking opportunities and services you'll need for continued success.

INTERNATIONAL DIGITAL IMAGING ASSOCIATION

Simply complete the application below and return it to **idia** headquarters to begin benefitting immediately.

MEMBER BENEFITS:

Valuable, Timely Publications

The Glitch Report

%%timeout

Bulletin

Executive Update

A World of Imaging Resources

Directory of Members

Referrals and Consulting

Meetings and Peer Networking

Annual Conferences

Top Management Weekend Business Roundtables

Technology Seminars

Idea Forum

□ **I want to join the idia immediately.**

□ I'm considering joining. Please send me a free sample of The Bulletin.

Company _____

Address _____

City/State/ Zip _____

Country _____

Phone _____

Fax _____

e-mail _____

Name of applicant _____

Title _____

Signature _____

Date of application _____

How did you first learn of **idia** _____

Please indicate the primary nature of your company

□ Ad Agency   □ Studio   □ Imaging Center

□ Printer   □ Color Separator   □ Consultant

□ Typographer   □ Other

Please indicate your member type

□ **North American**

Annual sales (US$)	Annual dues (US$)
□ 0 – 250,000	325
□ 250,001 – 500,000	425
□ 500,001 – 1,000,000	575
□ 1,000,001 – 2,500,000	775
□ over 2,500,000	975

□ **International**   395

□ **Educational**   150

□ **Retiree**   195

Payment method:

□ Visa/MasterCard   □ American Express   □ Check enclosed

□ Bill Me

Card Number _____

Signature _____ Exp. Date _____

Fax to: (908) 359-7619 or mail to: International Digital Imaging Association • 170 Township Line Rd Ste 5A, Belle Mead NJ 08502
For more information call **idia** (908) 359-3924

LANTANA

PDF TOOLS FOR PROFESSIONALS

OPI Doctor™

PDF Bellhop™

PDF Valet™

PDF LIBRARIAN™

CRACKERJACK PILOT™

CRACKERJACK™

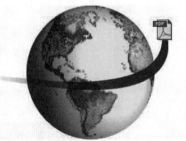

Quite Special Offer

http://www.quite.com/

Exclusive to the Adobe Acrobat PDF Bible! Try our plug-ins and save!

On the CDROM with this book you will find try-out versions of **Quite Imposing**, **Quite Imposing** *Plus*, and **Quite A Box Of Tricks**. You can upgrade these to the full product using our special license-only offer, a 15% discount on our regular prices.

Take advantage of this special offer. The prices we quote are in British pounds, because we're a British company, but drop us a line and we'll tell you what they translate to in dollars or any other currency.

☐ **Quite Imposing** only £169

☐ **Quite Imposing** *Plus* only £329

☐ **Quite A Box Of Tricks** only £106

Photocopy this page and fax it to 011 44 181 522 1726
(outside the USA, call +44 181 522 1726)
Please send me a license to use the product(s) I have ticked above.

Name

Address

Country   Postcode/zip

Phone   Fax

Amex/Mastercard/Visa (choose one)   Credit card number

Expiry date   Name on card

Limit one order per customer. Offers valid until 1 January 2000. Enquiries: **help@quite.com**

Expand Your Horizons
Develop Your Skills

Explore the Computer Graphics, Graphic Design, and

Interactive Multimedia Programs at

UCLA Extension

◎ Offering over 200 courses each year, UCLA Extension provides comprehensive instruction in state-of-the-art visual communications for new, digital, and print media.

◎ Short workshops in digital imaging feature the latest Adobe software, including Photoshop, After Effects, Premier, and Acrobat.

◎ Course offerings are designed to accommodate all types of students—from beginners, to professionals updating their skills, from those making a career transition, to international students.

◎ UCLA Extension also provides full professional certificated programs in computer graphics and graphic design. These cover both the technical and design skills needed to prepare for professional positions in today's growing design-related industries.

◎ If you live in the L.A. area or are planning a visit, attend the free quarterly Visual Arts Open House. Meet instructors, view student work, and learn more about our certificated programs and exciting career horizons.

FOR MORE INFORMATION CONTACT:

**UCLA Extension
Computer Graphics/
Graphic Design Programs
10995 Le Conte Avenue,
Room 414
Los Angeles, CA 90024-2883**

Fax (310) 206-7382

**E-mail
visualar@unex.ucla.edu**

Call (310) 206-1422 and press o

my2cents.idgbooks.com

Register This Book — And Win!

Visit **http://my2cents.idgbooks.com** to register this book and we'll automatically enter you in our fantastic monthly prize giveaway. It's also your opportunity to give us feedback: let us know what you thought of this book and how you would like to see other topics covered.

Discover IDG Books Online!

The IDG Books Online Web site is your online resource for tackling technology — at home and at the office. Frequently updated, the IDG Books Online Web site features exclusive software, insider information, online books, and live events!

10 Productive & Career-Enhancing Things You Can Do at www.idgbooks.com

- Nab source code for your own programming projects.

- Download software.

- Read Web exclusives: special articles and book excerpts by IDG Books Worldwide authors.

- Take advantage of resources to help you advance your career as a Novell or Microsoft professional.

- Buy IDG Books Worldwide titles or find a convenient bookstore that carries them.

- Register your book and win a prize.

- Chat live online with authors.

- Sign up for regular e-mail updates about our latest books.

- Suggest a book you'd like to read or write.

- Give us your 2¢ about our books and about our Web site.

You say you're not on the Web yet? It's easy to get started with IDG Books' *Discover the Internet*, available at local retailers everywhere.

CD-ROM Installation Instructions

To install and run the programs on the CD-ROM, Macintosh users need System 7.5 or above. Windows users need Windows 95, Windows 98, or Windows NT. (The CD-ROM will not function properly with Windows 3.1.)

To gain access to the CD-ROM contents, follow these steps:

Macintosh

1. Insert the CD-ROM in your CD-ROM drive and wait a few moments until the CD-ROM icon appears.

2. Double-click the icon to open the CD-ROM, which will display a window where the contents will appear.

Windows

1. Insert the CD-ROM in your CD-ROM drive.

2. Double-click the CD-ROM icon on the desktop to display a window in which the contents will appear.